Dolcoath Mine

~ A History ~

Allen Buckley

1935-2010 **75** YEARS

The Trevithick Society

Published by The Trevithick Society
for the study of Cornish industrial archaeology and history

ISBN 978-0-904040-86-9 softback
ISBN 978-0-904040-85-2 hardback

Printed and bound by R. Booth Print
The Praze, Penryn, Cornwall TR10 8AA

Typeset, layout and design by Peninsula Projects,
c/o PO Box 62, Camborne TR14 7ZN

DOLCOATH MINE: A HISTORY

Front cover illustration: Late 19th century scene at Engine (New Sump) Shaft by the late Clive Carter. Reproduced by kind permission of Mrs Karen Carter.

Frontispiece: Stained-glass window in Truro museum, dated 1907, depicting various periods of mining at Dolcoath. Photo courtesy of Michael Swift.

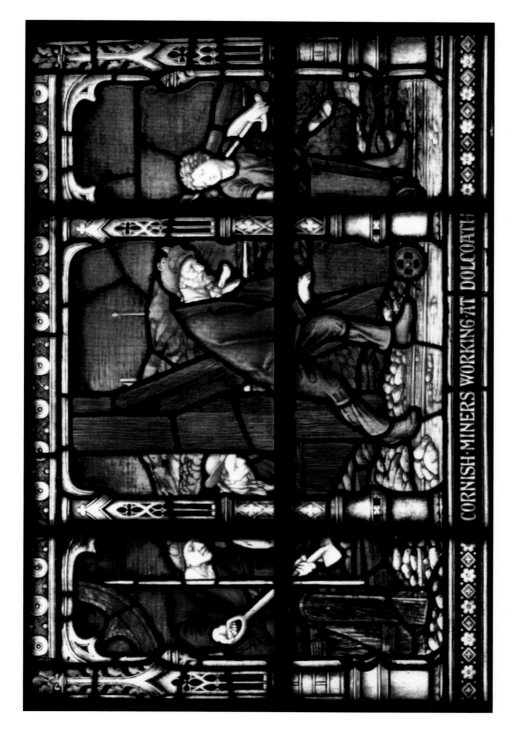

CORNISH·MINERS·WORKING·AT·DOLCOATH

FOREWORD

WHEN as a schoolboy I first became interested in Cornish history, especially anything about Camborne, I was puzzled that in the family library at Lowenac (then my grandfather's home) there was not much about the history of our mines and almost nothing about Dolcoath. Gradually I discovered among old share certificates and reports a four-page *The Dolcoath Mine, Cornwall. Its history* written in 1871. This began as a lecture to the mine's adventurers at a monthly dinner by Mark Guy Pearce senior, one of the Committee, a Camborne chemist, partner of my grandmother's father Robert Hall and of course father of Reverend Mark Guy Pearce. The script was later copied or typed; before 1900 my great-grandfather Josiah Thomas had given this copy to Mr W. Tregoning Hooper of St. Agnes who in 1953 returned it to my father. The story proved fascinating. Mr Pearce believed the mine went back to the 16th century, was worked to 160 fathoms in the 18th, and ceased operating in 1773. The new cost-book venture began in 1799 but by 1835 'ceased making profits as a Copper mine'. Its salvation was due to our great-great-grandfather Charles Thomas (junior), who became managing agent in 1844, sunk to the 210 fathom level by 1849, converted Dolcoath from copper to tin, allowed the first dividend to be paid from tin-working in April 1853, and by his endeavours saved a mine that from 1799 to 1871 had 'given employment to an average of 1000 persons'.

Where was the rest of all this? There were Dolcoath-related pamphlets around; nothing better. I found that dear Joe Odgers (of whom more below) was supposedly compiling a history of Dolcoath that W. Herbert Thomas, whom we often saw at Carbis Bay, had supposedly written much on Dolcoath's past in the (extinct) *Cornish Post Mining News*: and that other appropriate persons were interested - for instance, A. K. (Kenneth) Hamilton Jenkin, a family friend who often dropped by for a proper lunch to escape his wife's vegetarian regime. I later found out that Tom Harris would produce his short *Dolcoath; Queen of Cornish Mines* for the Trevithick Society in 1974. But where was the real, the complete, history? How far back did things go? As I learnt Cornish and studied place-names a doubt emerged that 'Dolcoath' really meant 'The Old Hole, Old Pit' as we were always told. Was it not first 'Dorcoath' (*dor coth* 'old ground') with a chance that, before shaft-mining started, the valley between the railway embankment and Tuckingmill saw late medieval tin-streaming?

What was it like to belong, or to have belonged, to a Dolcoath family, albeit the one that had captained the venture from 1844 to the year of my birth, 1928? Dolcoath was always there, a kind of omnipresent memory. As children we knew where it was, knew where the Dolcoath Halt platform stood on the main railway line. Visits to great-uncle Arthur, Captain R. Arthur Thomas at Porlstrong, meant seeing his exciting photographs and large slides; he was a keen photographer, taught originally by J. C. Burrow. In the 1940s one of the staff at Lowenac was Bill Gerrard from Roskear, who started as a timberman at Dolcoath in the 1890s under Captain Josiah. Bill later became maintenance foreman and in 1923, or 1928, was the very last man to climb out of the last shaft before it closed for ever. He taught us carpentry, and also told us horror stories about young lads being lost underground and coming to grass through a forgotten adit some days later. Then there was Joe, Joseph Frederick, Odgers, historian of Camborne and for me and my brother manager of the Trustee Savings Bank, where he sternly supervised our first small accounts. When in 1961 Joe was present at the Camborne Wesley baptism and Lowenac christening tea (no alcohol) for our first son, Joe reminded me that he now knew five generations of the family; in his youth, he was great-grandfather Josiah's confidential clerk at the Dolcoath count house (and in 1928 saved certain vital documents for us!).

Inseparable from Dolcoath, at any rate in Camborne and Illogan parishes, were the traditions about Cap'n Dick, Richard Trevithick junior, whose statue governed the town at Camborne Cross. We knew how he once stood at the base of Camborne church tower, back and heels against the wall, and threw a heavy weight right over the tower's top. There was no suggestion, despite certain misleading claims, that Richard Trevithick senior (1735-1797) had ever captained the whole of Dolcoath as we knew it; but it was not until 1973 (*Journal of the Trevithick Society* 2. pp 45-53) that I was able to sort this out and show the Trevithicks as a father-and-son partnership of engineers and assay-masters. Again, of course we all knew about Going Up Camborne Hill, and who it was who wore the White Stockings, but not until 1971 did my late cousin Lloyd Woodcock show exactly where the fabulous run took place (*Transactions of the Newcomen Society* 45 (1970-71), pp175-181).

These are not entirely side-lines because along with so much else they emphasise the long-standing need for a proper History of Dolcoath. The most appropriate body to sponsor and publish such a work has to be the Trevithick Society. When, during the last century, what was once called 'industrial archaeology' broke loose from archaeology in general, Cornwall, as so often took the lead. The only possible author has to be Allen Buckley. As a practical miner and established historian, with so many relevant books and papers to his credit already, he represents the answer to a great many prayers. I am indeed sensible of the honour of being asked to supply this Foreword, and can only write it as a Camborne man, local historian and currently head of one particular Dolcoath family.

What else to say? In our family, the first-born in each generation of the direct line has to be named 'Charles' if male, 'Charlotte' or 'Caroline' if female, after Mr Charles Wesley whose brother John stayed with William Thomas at Bolenowe and caused the entire family to become Methodists by the 1780s. The ancestor I most admire is, I think, Charles Thomas (junior) born at Bolenowe in 1794, died at his Killivose home in 1868 - 'junior' because his father, also a mine agent at Dolcoath and elsewhere (1772-1847) was an earlier Charles. They both knew the Trevithicks; C. T. junior was sent to Mrs Pendarves's Endowed School at Penponds in 1801, a school where Richard Trevithick had been a pupil from about 1778. Charles joined his father at the mine in 1806 and in 1814, aged 20, became a junior agent at Dolcoath. His life embraced this and many other mines, including visits to Scandinavia, Prussia and Ireland in the decade after 1852; the Methodism of Camborne (personal conversion 1823, local preacher in 1829); and a fervent desire to promote the education of young miners. His book *Remarks on the geology of Cornwall and Devon*, etc. (Tregaskis, Redruth 1859), together with shorter articles, was part of a wider campaign to establish an eventual Camborne School of Mines - which would be chaired by his son Josiah from 1888, and where in 1922-23 his grandson Arthur would be Principal. What I like most to remember about this veritable saviour of Dolcoath Mine is an inscribed gold watch, presented to him, 7th May 1861, by the 'Shareholders of Cooks Kitchen Mine in Token of their Regard and high appreciation of the Zeal and Ability displayed by him in the successful management of the Mine'. Fine; but on the cover's back is engraved his personal crest, crossed miner's picks above letters C T, in a circlet with STRIVE AND TRUST. The same appears on his own soapstone seal-stamp. I don't know where he got this; it's not apparently Biblical. But it sums up Dolcoath during his period of management, 1844 until his death. The Committee of Management, meeting on 13 April 1868 (and appointing Captain Josiah Thomas, then aged only 34, 'to succeed his Father'), recorded their feelings at this loss, referring to a career 'invariably marked by great soundness of judgement and integrity'. He strove, successfully, to turn an exhausted copper mine into a long-lived tin venture, and others strove with him. He trusted those who worked under him and at all times received the trust of the adventurers or shareholders. Not a bad motto for Dolcoath itself! and now (in our family, seven generations on) we have this tremendous Allen Buckley achievement to provide the world with a proper record.

Charles Thomas

Lambessow, Truro February 2010

INTRODUCTION

The history of the Cornish mining industry goes back to the Early Bronze Age, 4,000 years ago. During that time a variety of metallic minerals has been produced in varying quantities and many mines have achieved prominence sometimes for very long periods. However, the mine which has attained an unrivalled position of pre-eminence in the long history of Cornish mining, is undoubtedly, Dolcoath. From the late eighteenth century onwards, in every mining camp in the world, be it in Africa, America, Australia, New Zealand, India, Canada, Mexico, Peru or any other country, the name Dolcoath was known. Miners in Ballarat and Bendigo had worked there; the copper miners at Moonta and Burra Burra learned their trade there; the men running the mines at Rio Del Monte, the High Atlas or Grass Valley, California, were taught their trade at Dolcoath. No mine on earth had a greater influence on the global metal mining industry than did Dolcoath and the miners who learned their skills there.

In Cornwall Dolcoath has long been seen as the most successful, the most profitable, the deepest and the largest mine in the Duchy. The very name has entered the language of the Cornish: such expressions as 'Deep as Dolcoath!' or 'Mouth on en like Dolcoath Shaft!', referring to people's characteristics, are still heard in west Cornwall. Dolcoath's history continues to fascinate all those interested in Cornwall's past. The great inventors and engineers who have worked at Dolcoath have become almost as famous as the mine itself. Richard Trevithick, William West, Arthur Woolf George John, John Budge and a host of others first carried out their experiments at the great mine. The Fox, Bolitho, Williams, Holman, Harvey, Bickford and Basset families were all involved as adventurers at Dolcoath, some of them for more than two centuries, and they all profited enormously from their association.

The need for a comprehensive history of Dolcoath has long been appreciated, especially as there is so much more material available now than in the past. During the last few decades a great corpus of historical material has been gathered into the archives of the Courtney Library in Truro, the Cornwall Record Office, the

Cornwall Centre, in Redruth, and the Morrab Library, in Penzance. This material has been supplemented by documents in many private collections, and it has been these which have mostly provided material previously unavailable to researchers. Joseph F. Odgers, a former Company Secretary at the mine, spent years gathering information, statistical data and mine reports on Dolcoath, with the intention of eventually publishing it. Professor Charles Thomas, a member of the Thomas family which ran the mine for almost a century, also has made available his large collection of material on the mine and the men who ran it. Others, like Paul Richards and Alastair Neil have searched out obscure facts and figures about the mine, its miners, managers and machinery. During the last 50 years I have listened to hundreds of anecdotes and stories of the men who toiled beneath Camborne generations ago - some of them by the men themselves! All of this vast body of information has been fed into the story of Dolcoath, Cornwall's greatest tin and copper mine.

The book is divided into seven parts: (1) the earliest history until the end of the eighteenth century, (2) the nineteenth century until the limited liability company was formed, in 1895, (3) the period from the formation of the limited company to 1921, when the old workings were abandoned, (4) the 1920s, when the new company was formed, running out of money by 1930, (5) the period from 1936 to 1998 when the setts of Dolcoath were mined by South Crofty, (6) the twenty-first century, when Basresult Holdings, working as Western United Mines, have started to explore the ground of Dolcoath and its adjacent setts and (7) the final chapter deals with the archaeological remains as they are in 2010. The style and layout of these seven sections differ to some extent due to the kind of material available for inclusion. The earliest part is based upon a variety of documents dating from the sixteenth century, and also includes early eighteenth century lease agreements. The middle of the eighteenth century has left detailed financial data from the Tehidy Manor Accounts and lease agreements, together with an eye-witness account by a Swedish industrial spy who visited the local mines. The last part of the eighteenth century is covered by very detailed manuscripts, including the Dolcoath Pay Books for most of the years between 1771 and 1792. These pay books are supplemented by a large body of manuscripts covering every aspect of the Bassets' involvement in mining in the Camborne district.

For the nineteenth century, there is a vast amount of material on all aspects of the mining industry. The engineers, the engines, the managers, the mine captains, the miners and the adventurers have all left extensive records of who they were and what they did. Two monthly and three monthly mine managers' reports cover almost the whole period until the end of the cost book company in 1895. Supplementing these are the reports of the Tehidy Estate mineral agents, James Lanyon and Samuel Davey, covering the years 1848 to 1867. The *Mining Journal, West Briton* and other local newspapers have added to the vast amount of information found in the official reports. Private correspondence, copper and tin sales records, disputes between adventurers, claims and counter-claims about the advantages of one new drilling machine over another, complaints about the way the mine was being run, arguments about the amount of financial support being given to one hospital over another, and reports on tragic accidents, have all found their places in this mass of material.

The twentieth century, divided as noted above into four parts, has also provided a corpus of material which is varied in quality and quantity. Much of the information has come from the six-monthly or annual reports of the companies involved, but as usual other sources, like newspapers, private diaries and official reports by geologists and government agencies have supplemented the managers' reports.

Due to the widely differing types of material available from the several periods of history covered, as well as the quantity and spread of that material, each section of this history has been dealt with as seemed appropriate.

In 1974, the Trevithick Society published the excellent summary of the history of Dolcoath by T. R. Harris. This book, *Dolcoath: Queen of Cornish Mines* was an instant success, but has long been out of print. In 1983, Alison Hodge published T. A. Morrison's *Cornwall's Central Mines: Southern District,* which contained a detailed and informative chapter on Dolcoath for most of the nineteenth century. Since they were printed there has been a massive increase in the quantity of material on Dolcoath, available for research in libraries and record offices. This has been enormously increased by access to a couple of private collections of unique material. It is my sincere hope, that I have made the best use of this historic material, and written a comprehensive history of the greatest and most famous of all the Cornish mines.

ACKNOWLEDGEMENTS

It would be quite impossible to mention everyone who has given me help in locating or understanding the large amount of material used in this book. My interest in the subject was stimulated over 30 years ago by conversations with Dr A. K. Hamilton Jenkin and J. H. Trounson. Dr Jenkin's *The Cornish Miner* and his *Mines & Miners of Cornwall* gave me a life-long fascination with the subject, and with both of these men, Dolcoath would come into almost every discussion. Professor Charles Thomas has given me constant help and has loaned me a vast quantity of unique material for this project. W. L. Watters, of Tuckingmill, has also loaned me many documents and reports on the old mine, together with the notes of Joseph F. Odgers. Dr Fred Harris loaned me a large body of original material, including Tehidy Accounts books, Memorandum and Proposal books and other Tehidy Manor mining documents, for which I am extremely grateful. This is now in the Cornwall Record Office. Dr Paul Mihalop, Managing Director of South Crofty Mine, gave me permission to photocopy all of that material, as well as the large collection held by Tehidy Minerals Ltd, now in the Cornwall Record Office under the TEM category. My particular thanks must also go to Tony Clarke for his lucid descriptions of the dressing machinery and crushing plant developments during the last 150 years. My thanks also to Tony Brooks, for his enthusiastic help, to Clive Carter, whose family were miners at Dolcoath, Bryan Earl, for his wise comments, Paul Richards, for digging out obscure information on the mine, Alastair Neil, for the many pieces of information he has supplied and David Thomas, for his ready assistance. I am grateful to Pete Joseph for giving me access to his lists of mine accidents. I must also thank Kim Cooper and the staff of the Cornwall Centre, Colin Edwards and the staff at the Cornwall Record Office and the staff at all the other libraries who have helped with advice over the last 30 years. I am particularly grateful to Angela Broome, at the Royal Institution of Cornwall Library, Truro, who has shown such patience in assisting me for so many years. Dr Keith Russ and Allan Reynolds at Baseresult have given unstinting help, as have Dale Foster, at Crofty Consultancy, and Karla and Derek Morgan, of Associated Property Solutions.

My special thanks must go to old Mr Collins, of Pengegon, who told me of his days spent mining on the 440-fathom level at Dolcoath, before the Great War, and to Bert Retallack, who described his part in sinking New Dolcoath Shaft at Roskear, in the 1920s. These men, now unfortunately long gone, created for me something of the atmosphere of working in that great mine in a former age.

The photographs of J. C. Burrow, W. J. Bennetts, Michael Swift, Keith Russ, Pete Joseph and Paul Deakin enhance the book, and I am grateful for the use of Tony Clarke's extensive collection of Dolcoath photographs and those held by the Cornwall Centre, Redruth. My thanks also to Karen Carter for the use of Clive Carter's paintings. My thanks must go to the publishers, the Trevithick Society, whose 75th anniversary is being celebrated this year and to Graham Thorne, the publications officer and Pete Joseph, who is responsible for the design and layout of the book as well as drawing all of the maps. Thanks also go to Pete for writing the section on the remaining industrial archaeology.

Last but not least, I once again have to thank my wife, Sonia, for her patience over the many years this volume has taken to complete. I am also grateful for her skilled and diligent reading and re-reading the many versions of the text. Her editing and corrections have vastly improved the final manuscript.

Contents

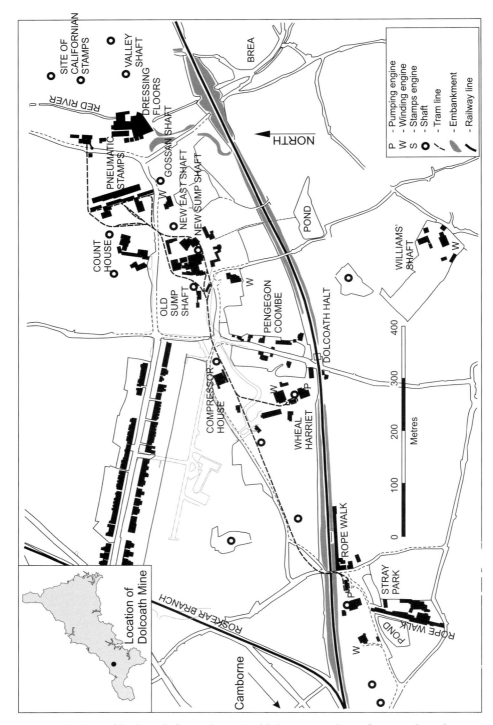

Figure 1. Map of Dolcoath from the early 20th century, later features in pale grey.

Part One
The Early History To 1799

Dolcoath Mine, which was to become for several decades in the eighteenth and early nineteenth centuries the greatest copper mine in the world, and in the nineteenth century the greatest tin mine, had an obscure and unimpressive start. Camborne had long been an important tin-producing parish when Dolcoath began to emerge, and mines such as Tolcarne, in the sixteenth century, and Wheals Gerry, Chance, Hatchet and Weeth in the seventeenth and early eighteenth centuries, were already well-known by the time of Dolcoath's birth.

In the 1730s, when William Doidge was commissioned to prepare his great maps of the Tehidy Estate holdings in Camborne and Illogan parishes, he showed Dolcoath as a tin mine, which stretched from the large field of that name westward into the neighbouring field called Stray Park. Both fields were in the tenement of Pengegon. The maps were completed in 1737 and are a wonderful source of information on the extent of mining in the two parishes at that time. Carnkye Bal is shown in great detail and South Carn Brea, Tolskithy, Brea Adit (Cooks Kitchen), Wheal an Owle (Hoult), Pool Adit and several others are also shown to a larger or lesser extent. But, the workings in the tenements of Pengegon, Entral (North and South) and the southern parts of Roskear, which were to form the mine to become famous as Dolcoath, were also clearly shown.

The original Dolcoath Mine, often referred to in the later eighteenth century as 'Old Dolcoath', was centred in the field called 'Dolcath' and described as 'Dolcooth A Tin Work' by Doidge. Various theories have been put forward as to the meaning of the name, including one that suggests that it originates from the mine's proximity to the dwelling of a woman called Dol Coath, the tenant of a nearby cottage. The real meaning appears to be more prosaic. The first element, Dol, could refer to a piece of ground or field, and the second, Coath, comes from the Cornish word for old (Dol Cornish 'dor' (ground); coath Cornish 'coth' (old). Hence, the field's name could

1

have been 'old field' or 'old ground'. Apparently, Dol or Dole can refer to the field having been divided into shares at some time. T. R. Harris suggests that the name means 'old pit' in Cornish. The Cornish word element 'tol' means a hole (as in Mean an Tol, Tolvaddon and Tolgarrack) or pit (as in Welsh). If Harris was right then the field name might indicate that the locality was worked for tin at a remote time, when Cornish was still spoken locally.[1]

The original field where Old Dolcoath worked has long been obliterated, first by the expanding mine burrows, and then by the main-line railway which was driven across it in the 1830s. Subsequent road and building development have rendered the area almost unrecognisable. We are, however, still able to locate with a fair degree of accuracy the centre of the original mine, for Old Dolcoath Shaft's position is shown on several mine plans and sections. It lies immediately to the north-east of the bridge over the railway at the top of Foundry Road, Camborne. Some years ago, before it had been capped, it was noted for the large amount of mine rubbish, including old stamps heads, in and around its collar.

What we know as Dolcoath Mine stretches from that shaft near Foundry Road, to Eastern Valley Shaft, on the eastern side of the Red River Valley, and embraces Wheal Killas, Wheal Bryant, Wheal Harriet, Bullen Garden, Roskear Broase and South Entral mines. The area now enclosed by Kerrier District Council as a sort of recreational park is really Bullen Garden Mine, which was to form the largest and most productive section of Dolcoath, and eventually contained many of the surface arrangements of offices, workshops and dressing floors of the mine.

The early history of Dolcoath Mine can be conveniently divided into three parts. The first, as we have seen, is a story obscured by insufficient extant records: a few limited and usually imprecise references to tin and copper sales, and the driving of adits into the tenements on which the early mines worked. The name Dolcoath appears in 1731 and even thereafter it is difficult to fix the boundaries of the mine, the adventurers who put their money into it and gained profit from it and the size and extent of the workings. Fortunately, what data there is can furnish evidence for forming opinions on each of these things.

The second period lasted from 1740 until 1770, by which time the mine had expanded to include the larger and deeper workings of Bullen Garden, and became known for several years as 'New Dolcoath', to differentiate it from the old company, which had worked the small, shallower, but extremely rich workings of the original Dolcoath Mine. Records from this period are characterised by a continuous series of copper ore sales figures, together with monthly costs for almost the entire thirty year period. Facts about the personnel employed also increase, as does information on the adventurers. We know considerably more about the machinery used on the mine and some of the ancillary matters with which the mine and its owners were involved.

The third period stretches from 1771 until 1791, during which time the mine worked on a very large scale, produced prodigious tonnages of copper ore and became, perhaps, the principal copper mine in the world. The discovery of a massive deposit of shallow copper ore at Parys Mountain, in 1768, ultimately led to the closure of Dolcoath in 1791. From this period (1771-91) there is an almost unbroken record of wages and other payments for the mine, which furnishes us with a vast amount of information on most aspects of Dolcoath. External evidence from that time also increases so that we know a lot about the people, the machinery, the engines, the extent of the workings and the way the mine operated.

Background to Early Camborne Mining
Tin has been produced in Cornwall since the Early Bronze Age, perhaps for over four thousand years. Until the late-medieval period most tin was produced from alluvial deposits, although it is probable that some lode working took place long before that. By the middle of the fifteenth century shaft and level exploitation of tin ore was well-established. A few miles to the north-east of Camborne, at Cligga Head, a shaft was sunk to a depth of over seventy feet in 1472, and the description, found in a court case over its ownership, indicates that such shaft sinking was not unusual. Stannary records from the 1490s show that in the Camborne, Gwinear and Redruth areas underground mining was long past its infancy.[2]

Early terms of differentiation between tinworks were 'bal' and 'moor'. The latter referred to streaming for alluvial tin along the low moors alongside streams, and the former to lode works or mines. A 'bal' in late Cornish was a group of tin bounds, and most of those identified from the records were on high ground, where the rockhead was at or close to surface. Mineralised structures (lodes/veins) were more easily identified in such ground, and thus cliffs, steep valley sides and high, bare hill sides, where such lodes were seen by farmers and streamers, formed the earliest 'bals'. The lodes were discovered by the presence of 'shode' material on the surface. This was the ore broken by weathering from the outcrop of lodes, and which lay downslope of the lode outcrop. Such finds were worked as eluvial tinworks, and inevitably led to the actual lode working. There were such 'bals' at Breage, Sithney, St Agnes, Trewellard, Hensbarrow, Hingston Down, Beacon, Troon, Carn Marth and Carnkie. All of these were well-established by the time of Henry VII.[3]

Early references to such lode mines appear in the Camborne Churchwardens Accounts. Starting in 1546 these refer to 'tyn soyll' payments from mines at Treslothan, 'Sent Laurence worke yn Karnekye' and 'Gone Antorne' (Woon Antron at Chytodden, Troon). Some seventeen entries between 1546 and 1568 mention fourteen individuals paying dues on yields from half-a-dozen tinworks, most of which were mines on high ground around Camborne.[4]

In 1584 John Norden, in his *Speculi Britanniae Pars*, referred to 'Tolkerne, in Cambourne parishe' as being among the 'chiefe mynes in Kirier hundred'. This mine on the high granite country behind Beacon, exploited tin lodes which were exposed on the hillside. Tolcarne continued to produce tin for its owners and dues for the Vyvyan family of Trelowarren over the centuries. Hanniball Vyvyan, a man well-known in mining circles locally, was involved there at the end of the sixteenth century, and the Focat family, involved in tinworks at Camborne in the first half of the century, were lessees of the mine under Justinian Talkarne (1577) and Sir Francis Vyvyan (1619). Tolcarne Mine continued to be worked for tin sporadically until the final closure of Wheal Pendarves, of which it formed a part, in 1987. It never regained the brief prominence it enjoyed in the late sixteenth century.[5]

The mines at Treslothan and Woon Antron likewise remained small and insignificant. Carnkye Bal, however, grew to great importance in the late seventeenth century, declined in the middle of the eighteenth, and then continued into the late nineteenth century on a relatively small scale. With the formation of the extensive Basset Mines Group, in the 1890s, Carnkye Bal was again at the centre of an important mine, which remained so until the Great War snuffed it out in 1917.

An early mention of tin streaming and mining at Brea and Entral is to be found in a lease dated 1588. Reference is made to 'two stampinge Milles ... water courses letes and buddels' on the moor between the two tenements. It then reserved to the Bassets 'all toll tyn and Tynworks nowe founde or hereafter to be founde in or upon the premises'. Although the source of tin ore to feed the stamps would have been partly alluvial, there is no doubt that lode ore would have formed the bulk of the material stamped, and this came from the lode outcrops on either side of the valley.[6]

These leats and others constructed in the locality to supply water to the mines are mentioned in documents from the reign of Henry VIII onwards. One such, dated 1543 (34 Hen.VIII), refers to a 'new watercourse to Reskeere' which was set to a William Sexton, who paid an annual rent to the Tehidy Estate of 6d. Richard Crane and Henry Brey paid the same amount for another leat in Camborne. In 1613 (9 James I) the leat to Roskear was mentioned again, and this time the document says the water came from 'Entrall Moore and Pengigan' to the land of Alexander Pendarves in 'Reskeere'. Undoubtedly, with the ancient workings on and around Dolcoath being mostly on high ground, the supply of water for powering engines and concentrating the ore necessitated the construction of a network of such man-made watercourses.[7]

Tinworking in the Red River Valley below Entral continued throughout the seventeenth century. On 26 July 1658 John Eudie of Illogan, described as a tinner, took a seven year lease from John Basset, of three pairs of stamps on Entral Bottoms. He paid £16 a year to Basset for the privilege. He had to maintain the stamps and appurtenances in good order, and hand them back in 'good repayre' at the end of the seven years.[8]

The second half of the seventeenth century saw the rise of several important mines around Dolcoath. Wheal Kitty, Wheal Guerry and Wheal Chance were just three mines on the north side of Camborne to achieve fame as tin producers. Wheal an Owle alias Wheal Hoult at the top of Beacon Hill, which became Wheal Harriet in the nineteenth century, was described by Doidge in 1737 as 'an old copper work'. The Pool or Pool Mine was also a significant tin mine in the 1690s, and Tincroft and Penhellick Work, Wheal Dudnance and Parkfriglas Work in Trevenson were all going strong. By the early eighteenth century Longclose Mine, Wheal Vernon, Wheal Knight, Cherry Garden, Wheal Plosh and Copper Tankard were becoming important copper producers, all having started their lives as tin mines. But, it was the discovery of rich tin lodes on the east and west sides of the Red River valley, below Brea Village, which was to lead to the formation of Dolcoath Mine. Brea tenement on Illogan side and Entral on Camborne side of the river were to see developments of major importance to local mining.[9]

The line of Brea Adit is shown on the Doidge map, following the lode eastward toward Tincroft Mine, on the tenement of Penhellick Veor. Almost opposite the portal of the adit can be seen the workings going westward from the valley on Dolcoath Main Lode into Bullen Garden, as well as the workings to the north on North and South Entral lodes. The extensive workings at Dolcoath lay along the lode to the west of Bullen Garden Mine. North and South Entral workings continued westward into Roskear tenement.[10]

With the loss of so much of the old Dolcoath and Basset archive we have little documentary evidence on the earliest development of mining on the Dolcoath side of the valley, although on the eastern side there are some revealing entries in the Radnor records for Penhellick Veor. These records relate to mining at what became Tincroft Mine and also deal with the workings in Brea Mine, later known as Cooks Kitchen and New Cooks Kitchen. As they describe mining between 1663 and 1692 on the same lodes that were worked across the river by Dolcoath Mine, they are of interest in the study of Dolcoath's origins. It seems probable that the missing Tehidy records from the seventeenth century would have contained similar information to that found in the Radnor records.[11]

The second Radnor entry relates to an encroachment by Tincroft miners beneath Dudnance Lane into the mine on Tehidy land operated by John Paull ('Pawle'):

"Some Tinne to be wrought by William Lanyon on the borders of Penhellick in holing against John Pawle in Mr Bassett's ground and incroaching there." In 1666 Lanyon's holing into Brea Mine was referred to again, and in 1678 he sank a shaft on Penhellick Veor side of Dudnance Lane to 'stop men working in Mr Bassett's land'. However, Lanyon had 'digged up some tyn stuff' there and was to give an account of it to the manorial court. During the 29 years covered by the entries the mine operated on and off for much of the time, and worked in several different locations including the 'Gew', 'Tyn Croft', 'Ye Round' and 'Orchard Moor'. 'Horse Park' was used for storing tin stuff prior to crushing and dressing.[12]

The principal workings at Tincroft Mine were centred on the field of that name and stretched along the lode between Brea (bounded by Dudnance Lane) and Tregajorran (bounded by the stream which runs through Pool). The workings at the Gew (Geau) are on what became known as South Tincroft or Dunkins Lode.[13]

Early records for the mines to the north of Tincroft, at Longclose, Dudnance, Trevenson and Penhellick Vean give the same picture for the second half of the seventeenth century and the early part of the eighteenth century. Examination of the detail drawn by Doidge in the 1730s indicates a similar set of circumstances and pattern of development on Camborne side of the Red River.[14]

The Small Mines Which Were To Make Up Dolcoath
Until 1731, when the name 'Doulcath' appears in the extant Tehidy records, the small mines at Pengegon, Roskear and Entral, which were to become parts of Dolcoath, went under various titles. These workings were mostly identified by no other name than the tenement on which they lay. An entry, dated 1716, in a collection of references to tin sold in the early eighteenth century to blowing houses and tin smelters, refers to a tin mine called 'Pengigan' at Camborne. As the other mine in Pengegon, Wheal an Owle (Hoult), was referred to separately, it seems certain that Dolcoath was meant, as it lay in Pengegon, close to the farmhouse. 'Entraile' (Entral) Mine was also mentioned in a reference dated 1713. The Tehidy accounts, which began in 1721, contain a continuous series of entries for tin and copper upon which dues were paid to the Bassets. In February 1721/2 John Priddis, Richard Tellam and William Creed all paid dues on tin from Entral. The context suggests that these payments were probably dues from tin streaming.[15]

On March 9th 1721 (1722) Mr Richard Banbury paid "1/6th part for dues of copper oar weighed from several mines on Entrall nigh the Tucking mill being 10ton 9cwt 2lb att £8 per tun & 3 tun att £4 a tunn = £15 18 8." These mines were at the north-east end of what was to become the Dolcoath Mine Sett; near to Tuckingmill Village. The nearest mines to Tuckingmill on Entral tenement shown on Doidge's map are those on North and South Entral lodes, to the north and north-east of Bullen Garden

Mine, although it is probable that Banbury's mines included Bullen Garden.[16]

1722 saw several payments of dues on tin to the Bassets, from John Dunkyn, Richard Proviss and William Dunkin. These were probably also for tin streamed on Entral Moor. January 2nd 1722 Richard Banbury paid 1/6th dues on 4ton 3cwt of copper from "several mines on the Tenement of Entrall ... £4 9 9." These appear to have been the same mines as those previously referred to, but Banbury's involvement suggests that the mine, which was to become known as Bullen Garden, was also included.[17]

During 1723 there were again several small payments for dues on stream tin at Entral, from William Lethleane, Richard Tellam and Henry Proviss. The half-a-dozen payments amounted to about £11 in dues at a sixth. Capt. Nicholas Tresaderne, the Basset's toller, picked up some of the dues. More dues were received for copper mining on November 9 1723: "John Chapple at the hands of Mr Thom. Stephens for 1/6th dues of 2ton 11cwt of copper oare in Entrall sold att £4 12 6d a tunn - sume of = £1 18 11."[18]

In January 1723/24 a mine called 'Wheale Paull in the Tenement of Entrall' appeared in the records. One of the several scattered mines already referred to had gained a name, although which one it was cannot be stated with certainty. The entry says: "Received of Mr Anthony Cock for 1/6 pte dues of 22tons 6cwt 3lb of Copper Oare weighed this day att a worke called wheale paull in the Tenement of Entrall (viz) 8ton 9cwt 3lb of sd oare being sold att £11 per Tunn & the other third 18cwt being sold for £6 6s per tunn £1 1s over & above upon the whole oare, the whole mony amounting to £181 9 9, the sixth pte whereof is = £30 4 11."[19]

On March 5th 1723/4 dues were paid by Wheal Paull on another 5ton 20cwt of copper ore, and this time the mine company was represented by Mr John Coster, the well-known copper agent, whose father came to Cornwall from Gloucestershire in the last decades of the previous century. Coster worked for the copper smelters in Gloucestershire and was an adventurer in several local copper mines. The entry states, that the ore was raised by John Johns, presumably the manager or mine captain at Wheal Paull. In July Coster and company paid £27 5s 9d on 18ton 4cwt of copper ore, which sold for £9 a ton. In August Captain Nicholas Tresaderne received from Coster 13s 11d dues on £3 worth of copper halvans (low grade copper ore) raised at Wheal Paull.[20]

An entry in the Pool Adit Cost Book for the period June 1st to August 1st 1725, includes Madam Praed as an adventurer in mines at Entral "Nicholas Tresadern for materials from several works in Entral for Madm Praed when she left off adventuring there."[21]

On February 25th 1725/6, John Coster and the Wheal Paull adventurers, paid £10 6s 8d dues on 10ton 7cwt of copper ore, which sold at £6 a ton. In September Mr Banbury, acting for the adventurers, paid £5 19s dues on 5ton 20cwt of copper ore which sold for £6 a ton. This appears to be the last reference to Wheal Paull in the Tehidy account book, and although the payments for Entral tin dues continue throughout the 1720s, the next mention of mining there is from October 25 1734, when the copper ore from the mines in Pengegon and Entral are lumped together: "Recd of Capt Mathew Tellam & ptrs for a parcill of Gosan sold from Entrall and Pencekon about 3 years since £35 expences selling 11s deducted being a bad bargain 4s the ballance due to Mr (?) = £34 5 0." There is compelling evidence that Wheal Paull was Bullen Garden Mine. First, it produced more copper ore than any of the other workings, which is consistent with the evidence of its long section reproduced by William Pryce in 1778. Secondly, the adventurers included Mr John Coster, Mr John Cocke and Mr Richard Banbury, all of them men of substance and position in the community. John Coster had shares in most of the important local copper mines, as he acted for the important Gloucestershire smelters. Bullen Garden Mine would fit the bill for a man with his interests.[22]

Apart from the many references (from 1721) to Wheal an Owle (Wheal Hoult), which lay on the southern edge of the tenement, mining at Pengegon was first mentioned in these accounts on October 24 1729: "Recd of Rich. Jenkins & Co. for 1/6th pte Dues of 11ton 1cwt of Copper Ore weighed this Day in the Tenement of Pengigon & sold at £12 per tun = £22 1 11." This may well have been a reference to Dolcoath. On June

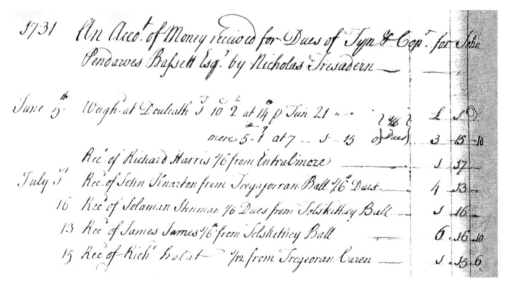

Figure 2. The earliest extant reference to Dolcoath Mine in the Tehidy Manor records.

5 1731 we have the first definite mention of Dolcoath in these accounts: "Weighed at Doulcath 1ton 10cwt 2lb @ £14 per tun 21 more 5cwt 1qt @ £7 15s.(1/6th dues) = £3 15." From December 1735 there is a reference to 'Dollkoth Addit' cost, of which Mr Basset, as an important Dolcoath adventurer, paid an eighth share.[23]

These early and sometimes obscure mentions of Dolcoath and the other mines, which were to be amalgamated, give only a hazy picture of the mine before 1740. However, combined, they do tell us a surprising amount about Dolcoath. The description on the Doidge map of Dolcoath as a tin mine, which traversed the two large fields of Dolcoath and Stray Park, informs us about the origin of the mine. Tin was worked mostly above the water table in the Camborne mines, and the implication is that the shallowest fifteen to twenty fathoms were worked for tin, probably before the end of the seventeenth century. This would agree with the time scale of the rest of the well-documented mines in the Camborne and Illogan mining district. It does not appear that copper was sought in the area much before the 1690s, and by 1710 at the latest, Camborne area was emerging as a copper mining district. Henric Kalmeter, who visited the Camborne mines in the year 1724, makes this point several times: the copper mines grew from older, shallower tin mines. He wrote: "In this parish (Camborne) there are numerous copper mines of value, but by contrast little tin is found. They say, as they went deeper copper took over the ground." Of Carnmough, on the southern side of Dolcoath, near Beacon, he says that an adit was driven below old tin mines, but, "Here, instead of tin they found a considerable quantity of copper ore." Of Wheal an Howl (Wheal Harriet, Condurrow) Kalmeter said that there was a copper lode, but, "Here, too, in olden times, they worked for tin at first." The same was true of the Redruth mines: "Wheal Sparnon was a good copper mine, although it has, as had all the others to begin with, given tin." He says the same of Gwennap, tin mines became copper mines as they went deeper: "like all the others in the country." Chacewater Bal, which became famous as Wheal Busy, was originally: "worked for tin, (although) she is now regarded as a copper mine for when they went deeper the latter ore took over."[24]

Doidge also shows surface workings at Dolcoath. This tells us that the original tin mine was probably partly a coffin or openwork. The map shows the workings at Dolcoath of much greater width than was normal. Recent excavations of Dolcoath Main Lode show it to be up to ten feet wide and almost vertical at surface.[25]

The references to mining at Entral and Pengegon throughout the 1720s were to copper mining, which grew as time went on. There is little doubt that Banbury's and Coster's involvement in these mines suggests that the principal Entral Mine was Bullen Garden, and the main lode being exploited was the same as at Dolcoath. It was not to be long before these mines were joined together as one unit.

Early Mining Methods at Dolcoath

Contrary to received opinion, by the time Dolcoath was being opened up, in the late seventeenth and early eighteenth centuries, mining had become fairly well-organised. Carew's description of late sixteenth century mining, supplemented by the correspondence of the Mines Royal, shows that miners varied their approach to suit local conditions and geological factors. If a lode was vertical, the miners worked it opencast as a trench for as deep as possible. If the lode dipped the miners sank as deep as was convenient, before resorting to shafts and levels. The stability of the ground, richness of the ore, ventilation considerations and need to keep the workings drained all influenced how the mine was opened up. The 1671 description of Cornish mining in *Philosophical Transactions* adds one or two details which show that stoping was carried out according to a design and system. Whilst above adit level, and the earliest tin workings at Dolcoath were certainly that, the account says: "At five fathom we make a drift both wayes, and sinking five fathom more, we make another drift at ten fathom; and so deep as we please." These five fathom (30 foot) blocks of ground were ideal for convenient and efficient stoping, given the tools and technology available. However, once the mine was deeper than adit level the picture became more complicated, as the need to sink winzes to explore the ground, was hindered by water, and sumps from which to pump the water became necessary. The methods described in 1671 would have obtained at Dolcoath, probably until the mine became seriously deep, for by 1754 Dolcoath was 80 fathoms (480 feet) deep.[26]

As will be noted by reference to Doidge, the workings of the various mines in the district follow a pattern. The outcrops of several lodes can be traced by the lines of surface workings along them. Some of these lodes also have adits shown on them, driven in to drain the workings. 'The Tail of Pool Audit' is shown in the valley to the north of Tuckingmill and 'Brea Audit' is shown emerging into the valley side just to the north of Brea Village. Drainage was an important consideration for all lode workings from the beginning. Once the mine was sunk below the water table the problem of keeping the bottoms dry and workable increased. For Brea Mine and Bullen Garden a short adit tunnel was sufficient for their needs, but for mines like Roskear Brause and Dolcoath drainage was more difficult and more expensive. At Penhellick Work and The Pool, which were operating in the seventeenth century, adits were driven in at depths as shallow as thirty feet (9 metres). The blocks of ground made available although small by later standards were sufficient to work on for a generation, but once black powder was used for blasting and the mines moved into copper production, with increased capital and better technology, miners were soon sinking way below the water table and mines could only be kept dry using better machinery and longer adit systems. Thus, the early development of Dolcoath and her neighbours can best be traced by following the progress of their adit development. There is extant a considerable body of documentary evidence concerning the adits driven in and around Dolcoath in the eighteenth century, and this can be supplemented by the huge number of plans, sections and other pieces of information on those mines from the eighteenth and nineteenth centuries.[27]

At both Bullen Garden and Old Dolcoath the lodes were worked from surface, and recent exposure of the shafts along the outcrop of Dolcoath Main Lode has revealed that for long sections it was worked as a coffin or openwork. The outcrop between Bennetts Shaft and Old Sump Shaft was worked downwards from surface for most of its length, and has a gunnis (now filled) some ten feet (3 metres) wide. Stull piece hitches were cut in the wall rock, partly to support the workings and partly to form platforms from which the miners could work. These hitches were clearly evident when the gunnises were opened up in the shaft capping work in 1992. Such hitches could also support the platforms used when deepening on lode by shamelling, or throwing the broken ore up in large steps, one man on each staging. At Dunkins Garden Shaft, at the eastern end of Dolcoath Avenue, the lode was worked away to the west of the shaft from surface. These coffins are probably typical of the way the mines were first opened up for tin.[28]

Early Development of Dolcoath
One of the earliest extant mine leases which grants permission to mine and drive an adit at Entral is dated 1720, and concerns a piece of ground on 'Rachell Moore' and Brea Moor, on either side of the Red River, between Bullen Garden and Cooks Kitchen. The lease grants liberty to Henry John alias Sparnon of Gwinear, to 'carry an Additt or Additts Eastward to the extent of the said Thirty ffathoms of ground.' As the sett lay on both sides of the river the adit tunnel could hardly have been driven far into the hillside. It would, though, be far enough for the miners to evaluate the lode upon which the adit was driven.[29]

An earlier reference to Henry John alias Sparnon occurs in the St Aubyn records, dated 1713, which shows John to have been something of a swashbuckling wheeler-dealer in the copper business. Sir John St Aubyn's toller had tried to stop the miners dividing up and disposing of copper ore raised at Wheal Christo, on North Downs, Redruth, because of a dispute in their agreement with Gabriel Wayne, a copper entrepreneur. However, "Henry Sparnon of Camborne and Henry Carpenter of Illogan went on and carried it off."[30]

Henry John was thus no ordinary mine adventurer. When Henry Kalmeter visited Camborne in December 1724, he specifically mentioned Henry John(s) as a farmer who took a particular interest in local copper production. Kalmeter said: "As this work (Condurrow Mine) gave such rich ore and produced so considerably, one must not omit to mention that while I was there the farmer, Henry Johns, made a contract with Sir William Pendarves, who as lord of the ground made 1/7th of all the ore, and furthermore held 7/16th of the work, as it is divided into 16 parts." Henry John(s)

11

paid Pendarves five shillings for every ton of copper ore raised at Condurrow, as well as paying the costs accruing from his 7/16th share in the mine. John(s) paid out £186 for this ore, a considerable amount in the 1720s. John(s) was the tenant farmer of the tenements of North and South Entral, where Bullen Garden lay. A similar arrangement was made at Bullen Garden, probably between the adventurers and Henry John(s). William Pryce wrote in his *Mineralogia Cornubiensis* (1778): "The manner of setting or leasing a Mine on Tribute, is this; some able Miner takes the Mine of (off) the adventurers for a determined time, that is, half a year, a whole year, nay even seven years, as was the case of Bullen-Garden, and the means of her discoverey." This supports the idea that John(s) was not only the earliest principal adventurer at Bullen Garden, but was the one responsible for the discovery of the rich copper ore beneath the tin.[31]

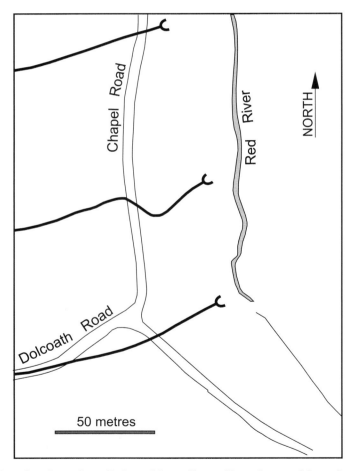

Figure 3. Map showing where Dolcoath's earliest adits exhausted into the Red River.

Camborne parish registers record that Henry John was married on Christmas Eve, 1703. His baptism cannot be found in Camborne or Illogan registers, but as he was described as 'of Gwinear', it is probable that it is there. The Arundell records have a family called John alias 'Spernam' at Coswinsawsen, just over the border from Camborne, in 1549 and 1563. Two of Henry's sons, Henry junior and William appear in the Camborne registers, but another son, George, who also features in the Dolcoath story has not been found in the registers. Henry John's activities must have made him wealthy well before Dolcoath and Bullen Garden began to produce large tonnages of copper ore, for in 1723 he took over the leases of the two substantial farms upon which some of the richest copper ore was to be found. "January 16th 1723. Received of Henry John alias Sparnon in parte of £700 for a lease of ninety nine years of the North & South Tenements of Entrall if the said Henry John and Henry and William his sons shall so long live, the sume of - £200." Bullen Garden, Copper Tankard, North Entrall and South Entrall mines all lay within these two tenements.[32]

In October 1735 an adit was being driven into or extended from Dolcoath Mine, and the record shows that the Bassets held an eighth share in the enterprise: "Dec 9 1735. Paid Mr Bassetts 1/8th of the cost in Dollkoth Addit in full to Oct 1st 1735 = £4 15 10 ½". The following November Basset paid an eighth share in the cost in 'Entrall Addit', which may have been connected to Dolcoath Adit, could have been an entirely separate adit, but may have been just another name for Dolcoath Adit.[33]

On September 2nd 1737 John Pendarves Basset granted to Christopher Hawkins, Samuel Blight, Henry John, Thomas Kniverton, all gentry, and William Churchill, a Redruth innkeeper, liberty to "digg ... and carry on an Addit already begun in the bottom of a certain hill called Entrall Hill and driven from thence into a Garden called Entrall Garden ... and to continue the said Addit through the lands of John Pendarves Basset into a field or park commonly called ... Stray Park (to the) extent of Bassett's land westward with free liberty ... for Hawkins (& Co.) to digg ... for copper & copper ore Tyn & Tyn ore and all other minerals & metals ... upon all loads or veins lying Ten ffathom of land on each side of the said Addit..." Basset was to have 1/6th share as mineral lord, and the mine was to be operated 'according to the custom of the Stannary of Penwith & Kirrier.'[34]

This adit was started some distance south of Tuckingmill and was driven first to 'Entrall Garden', which appears to be the area formerly occupied by South Entral Farm, later the site of Dolcoath Account House and in more recent times the engineering block of Camborne Technical College. It was then driven westward through the field known as Stray Park and on to the western extent of Pengegon tenement at Wheal Gons - now Stray Park Road.

On June 24th 1738 permission was granted to drive an adit into the workings on

North Entral Lode. John Pendarves Basset gave John and William Dunking of Camborne, tinners, and Henry Harvey of Illogan, blacksmith, "liberty to digg delve worke drive and carry on an Addit from the bottom of a field or close of land called Park en Skeba in the tenement of Entrall ... from the River which parts Illogan from Camborne westward to a shaft they are now working & from there further westward for a length of Twenty ffathom more in all Seaventy ffathom with free liberty to ... digg worke & search for Copper Copper Oare Tyn & Tyn Oare & all other minerals & mettalls whatsoever in & upon all Loads or Veins ... to be found or discovered lying Ten ffathom of land on each side of the Addit so to be driven." The agreement also stipulated that the mine must be worked and the adit driven for at least six months in every year with sufficient number of men, unless hindered by extremity of water.[35]

Park en Skeba is shown on the Doidge map as two fields called 'Park Skepper' and 'Great Park Skepper', the latter being alongside the river opposite the tail of Brea Adit. An extant adit portal between the road to Tuckingmill and the river is almost certainly where those miners drove into the hillside in 1738. The adit was eventually extended to the south-eastern side of Camborne Town, along a lode, which runs on the north side of and parallel to Dolcoath Main Lode.[36]

On March 25th 1748 John, Churchill, and Kniverton applied for and were granted an extension to their 1737 lease for Dolcoath Mine, and this time they were given liberty to work a width of forty fathoms; twenty fathoms on each side of the 'Dolcooth Additt'. The lease was for 21 years and again the Bassets were to receive a sixth as the lord's 'pleasure dole'.[37]

On November 16th 1748 permission was given to drive two adits into North Entral and South Entral from the Red River. The one in North Entral was granted to Thomas Moore of Helston, and involved driving the adit through North Entral into the south-east corner of Roskear and then through Pengegon to within five fathoms of the western boundary. The adit had to keep to the south of a mine in North Entral owned by John Sandys and Richard Eudey and another mine in Roskear operated by Walter Husband, and to the north of Old Dolcoath Mine, which was worked by Henry John and William Churchill and their co-adventurers. Moore was also granted liberty to "drive any Addit or drift Addits or drifts either from Dolcoath Addit on the south side or Roskear Brause Addit on the north side thereof into the said Addit intended to be driven ... for the better working thereof."[38]

Thomas Moore's sett apparently comprised South Entral Lode, which was worked as South Entral Mine. It lay to the south of North Entral Mine, owned by Sandys and Eudy, and to the south of Roskear Brause Mine, owned by Walter Husband. His workings lay to the north of Dolcoath Mine, operated by Henry John and William

Churchill.

The lease for the second of these adits, driven into South Entral, was also granted on November 26 1748 to Thomas Moore. This was to be driven through South Entral into Pengegon tenement, and then, after continuing west to the southern side of Dolcoath, it turned south and went on to Croft Nicholas and Wheal an Hoult (Owle) at Beacon. These workings, which were known as Wheal Harriet in the nineteenth century, were spread from Beacon Square past Wheal Harriet Farm and on to the northern flanks of Carn Entral. The depth at which the adit entered Wheal an Hoult gave that ancient mine a large block of drained ground to work. Once again Moore was given permission to "take and drive any Addit or Drift Addits or Drifts from Dolcooth Addit aforesaid into the said Addit driven or to be driven." Moore appears to have been an important adventurer at Wheal an Hoult, which was the principal beneficiary of the new adit.[39]

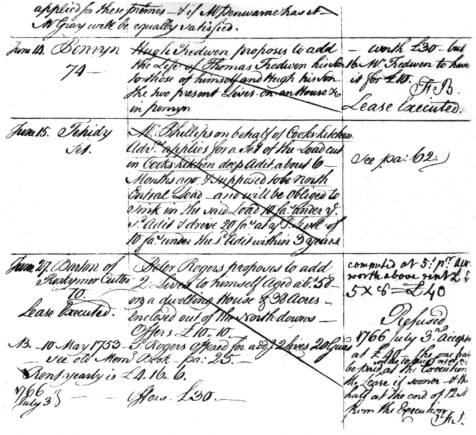

Figure 4. Extract from the Dolcoath memorandum book of 1753 concerning the eastern extension of North Entral Lode into Cooks Kitchen.

15

A List of my Adventures

Poole Adit — expired — — — — — — —	all
Dudnance Old — expired for Copper	all
Gregajotan — expired — — —	1/6
Dolcoath — — — — — — — —	1/8
~~Ballow~~ — — — — — — —	3/20
Polbreen — expired — — —	1/8
~~Wh Pool~~ — — expired — — —	1/8
~~Wh. Longclose~~ — Old — expired —	1/8
Carnhye — — — — — —	7/32
N Wh. Long Close — — — —	4/8
~~S. Wh Longclose~~ — expired	4/8
~~Penhellick~~ — expired — — —	all
~~Cook's Kitchen~~ expired — —	3/4
~~Wh. Rosewarne & y' with~~ expired —	3/32
Roskear & Sengegan al: South Entral	1/8
Tolskithy — — —	1/8
~~South Brea~~ — —	all
~~Giltrick~~	0/8
North Pool — —	1/8
~~New Penhellick al: Tincraft~~	4
New Dudnance — — — —	1/8
Dolcoath Pleasure Dole —	1/8
Eastern Burncose — — —	1/8
Portreath Harbour — — —	9/32
D:to more — — —	9/61

Figure 5. Extract from Francis Bassets's mine adventures list, dating from the 1740s.

In September 1760 Francis Prideaux asked for a mine sett to work Roskear Brause Lode and fifteen fathoms on either side, and also wanted to drive an adit on the lode to the western extent of Roskear at or below the level of the present Roskear Brause Adit. Two years later, the Tehidy Memorandum Book referred to 'the Tail of an old Adit that goes to Roskear Brause', and which lay on Entral tenement 'near Roskear Village'. This appears to refer to the area around Church View Road and Tuckingmill Parish Church, as the 1737 map shows a village there, and Entral tenement comes close to the eastern side of the village. This old adit may well have been the 'present Adit' Prideaux mentioned in 1760.[40]

A short, three year lease was granted in April 1763, for a sett to work an area defined as eighty fathoms east and seventy fathoms west of South Entral Engine Shaft, and five fathoms south and twenty fathoms north of South Entral Main Lode. This was just to the north of Bullen Garden workings. Charles Harvey and Thomas Craze were the principal adventurers, and they agreed to sink at least six fathoms below the current bottoms and to drive at that level at least fifty fathoms on South Entral Lode in that three year period. They were to have the use of all fixed plant on the mine, including whims and dressing gear.[41]

A Snapshot from 1754: The Angerstein Journal

In piecing together the history of an enterprise such as Dolcoath Mine, it is necessary to resort to a host of documents covering many aspects of the story. Rarely, do we find contemporary information laid out in such a way as to answer the type of questions that arouse our curiosity at the present time. For example: we can ascertain production figures for Dolcoath by working backwards from payment of the lord's dues to total mine income through ore sales, and then discovering the average payment per ton of copper ore at the time. We can attempt to identify the mine captains, managers and adventurers by examining the names on lease agreements and the people who paid copper or tin dues to the lord's steward. Occasionally, other pieces of information can be gleaned through the wording of such transactions. Historians are blessed, however, with occasional 'snap shots' of a mine at a particular time, when some visitor came to the mine and left a description of it. Whereas these 'snap shots' can be highly subjective and often influenced by what they or their guide thought was important or interesting, they do help us to put the picture we have built up into focus. When the description is from an experienced observer, or industrial spy, as was probably the case with Henric Kalmeter and Reinold Angerstein, the contribution to our knowledge of the mine at that time is enhanced considerably.

Reinold R. Angerstein was a Swedish visitor, who came to Cornwall as part of his travels around the country to examine and report on the state of industry and society. He visited Camborne whilst staying at Redruth in May 1754. He was particularly interested in the mines of the district, reporting very carefully the important details of ownership, lode structure and ore value, the machinery used and numbers employed. Any other significant fact about the individual mines and how they were related to each other was described and set into context. As well as the mines on the northern side of Camborne, and those at Pool, Carnkie and North Downs, Angerstein visited and described those at Pengegon and Entral; South Entral, Dolcoath and Bullen Garden. The latter was of special interest to him, apparently, because it was becoming the largest and most productive in the district.

On May 20th 1754 Angerstein was taken by a guide to visit the Camborne mines, and such was his interest in Bullen Garden Mine, that he included a description of it before he had actually been there. "Boolongorden is 2½ miles from Redruth. The lode strikes east-west and is 9 feet to 10 feet wide and 40 feet deep. The adit is at the 18 feet level and contains three water wheels. The ore is yellow and grey and sells for £6 to £13 per ton. The mine belongs to Messers Johns and Georgil." Possibly because these details were given him in Redruth before visiting the mine, there are one or two errors. The depth of the mine and the adit level are given in feet when he clearly meant fathoms. The adit he referred to is 108 feet deep, or 18 fathoms. This is the depth given in his fuller account after visiting the mine. The mine depth would have been 40 fathoms not 40 feet. The mine owners were said to be 'Messers Johns and Georgil', or Henry and George John(s). The main lode was nine to ten feet wide and lay east to west. This agrees with recent observations of the lode at and near to surface. The reference to three water wheels at (?above) adit level is interesting and almost certainly refers to the large, overshot water wheel powered pumping engines invented by John Coster and his son and patented in 1714. These engines were improved in the 1720s by Francis Scoble. The illustration in William Pryce's *Mineralogia Cornubiensis* (1778), which shows two such water wheels, one just below surface and the other above the adit level, probably shows two of the wheels mentioned by Angerstein.

Angerstein's description of May 27th is more detailed and although it repeats some of the earlier information, it adds a few more details, and corrects one or two mistakes in the earlier account.

"The 27th May (1754) I visited a copper mine called Boullongordon, located 13 miles from Truro and 3 miles from Redruth, together with Mr Rosen worren (Rosewarne). This mine was missed when I traveled through Redruth on the 20th, due to a mistake by my guide.

The lode strikes east and west and is 10 feet wide. It dips slightly south and lies in a hornstone rock spar, mixed in with a coarse granite veined with spar. The formation runs east and west and cuts through the whole country. The mine is located about 2,000 feet from Carn Brea Hill, and has been worked to a depth of 282 feet. It is provided with two water wheels placed in an adit at the 108 foot level. The adit is 600 feet long, 80 to 100 people work in it, 6 to 700 tons of ore are produced per month and it is estimated that it is worth £6 to £8 per ton. The ore is yellow chalcopyrite interspersed with grey ore."

The 'Mr Rosen worren' or Rosewarne could have been one of several Camborne men of that name, but it may well have referred to John Vivian of Rosewarne, or one of his family, for they were very much involved with Bullen Garden and Dolcoath mines. The lode details are similar to the earlier account, although he adds that the dip is slightly to the south. At Bullen Garden, although the surface outcrop of the lode is almost vertical, by the time it reaches the depths referred to (282 feet), it is dipping to the south. This dip becomes flatter with depth. The statement that the lode 'lies in a hornstone rock spar, mixed with a coarse granite veined spar' is also consistent with the granite-killas contact metamorphism found locally. The depth of 282 feet indicates that the mine had deepened since Angerstein's original guide had obtained the information he supplied him on the 20th. The number of water wheels had reduced to two, also indicating that the informant of the 20th was describing the mine as it had been at an earlier date. The adit depth is correctly given in this account as 108 feet (18 fathoms). Angerstein says the adit was 600 feet long, and he might have meant that that was the measurement from the adit portal to the western side of Bullen Garden workings. It is also possible that he was again using feet for fathoms, for we do know that by 1754 the adit driven along the main lode went as far as the western side of Stray Park at Wheal Gons.

The copper ore was described as 'yellow chalcopyrite interspersed with grey ore', whereas the account of the 20th merely said it was 'yellow and grey'. The yellow chalcopyrite was a primary ore, but the grey ore was possibly from secondary as well as primary mineralisation. The first account said that this ore sold for between £6 and £13 a ton, whereas the account of the 27th narrows the value down to £6 to £8 per ton, which is quite close to the average price received at that period of time. The monthly tonnage given by Angerstein is extremely high, being between 600 and 700 tons a month. The average income from 650 tons at £7 a ton would have been £4,550, a considerable sum at that time.

The number employed at Bullen Garden was given by Angerstein as '80 to 100 people'. This is a remarkably low figure for such a tonnage, and it could be that he was only counting men on production, men underground or some other part of the workforce. However, it seems most likely that he was referring to the number of miners engaged in production.

A surprising amount of what Angerstein tells us in his journal is verifiable by reference to other sources. Nevertheless, the picture he painted is a clear one, and when added to his brief description of Dolcoath Mine, which was to become known as 'Old Dolcoath' some eleven years after his visit, we have a very good picture of those workings in the middle of the eighteenth century.

Angerstein visited Dolcoath Mine on May 20th 1754, on his first trip around Camborne's mining district. He wrote: "Dolcoath copper mine belongs to Mr Johns and partners. It is provided with a large number of shafts, a fire engine and three water wheels. The lode strikes east and west, the same as the aforementioned (Bullen Garden), and dips a few degrees north. It is 480 feet deep in places. It has an adit at the 180 foot level. There is an abundant supply of ore, both yellow and black, which is sold for £6 to £16 per ton."

Henry John(s) was referred to as the principal adventurer as he was at Bullen Garden Mine. The large number of shafts is mentioned, and this ties in with the detail on the 1737 Tehidy Manor map drawn by William Doidge. One of Newcomen's atmospheric engines was on the mine, and was the one mentioned in the Coalbrookdale accounts as having been supplied in September 1746. The engine had a 40-inch cylinder and cost Dolcoath £366, being delivered to John Freeman & Co. as co-adventurers. Other consignments were made to John Jones & Co. of Bristol, engineers, and to William Churchill, who was one of Henry Johns' principal partners. Three water wheel engines were also on the mine, indicating that the great depth of the workings was producing a large volume of water. At that time the mine had reached the depth of 480 feet, making it one of the deepest mines in Cornwall, and probably the deepest in the Camborne-Illogan mining district.

As at Bullen Garden, the lode struck east and west, but somewhat different from there, and emphasising the unpredictable nature of the local tin and copper lodes, at Dolcoath Mine the lode 'dips a few degrees north'. At depth the lode turns over and dips increasingly to the south. The ore was 'both yellow and black', and sold for between £6 and £16 a ton. Apart from appearing somewhat darker than further to the east at Bullen Garden, the ore was similar to theirs. The difference in the value of the ore was, however, considerable.

The depth of the adit level given presents a problem. The deep adit at that time was 108 feet (18 fathoms) as at Bullen Garden Mine. It is probable that the 180 feet of Angerstein was merely a mistake, and 108 feet was intended. This would agree with the depth he gave for the same adit at Bullen Garden and with the known depth of the adit.

On May 27th, when Angerstein visited Bullen Garden, he also looked at South Entral Mine: "The Entrell copper mine is very near to Boulongorden, but it works another parallel lode, that is 2 foot to 3 foot wide and has the same dip and strike as the latter.

The ore is yellow and blue and is sold for £19 per ton and the yearly production is 40 tons."

This small mine eventually formed part of New Dolcoath. Its accounts only begin to register in the Tehidy records in 1748, and by 1754 it was showing a regular, although small profit. The long section for Bullen Garden, drawn in the 1760s and reproduced by Pryce in 1778 (see page 55), shows a crosscut going north from Main Lode to South Entral Mine, over 400 feet below surface. South Entral Mine worked a lode of that name on the southern edge of North Entral tenement. The lode was a narrower structure than that at Bullen Garden, although like its neighbour, it dipped to the south. Its copper ore was described as yellow and blue, and of much higher value than either Dolcoath or Bullen Garden.[42]

Water Power at Dolcoath

Despite the improvements to pumping power in Cornwall's mines through the introduction of the Newcomen atmospheric engine, and its wider use after the legislation of 1741, increased depths and greater volumes of water meant that by the 1760s the deeper mines were again in crisis. Due to this, until the arrival of the Watt engine, water engines remained the dominant pumping machines in all Cornish mining districts. Some historians have argued successfully for the continued

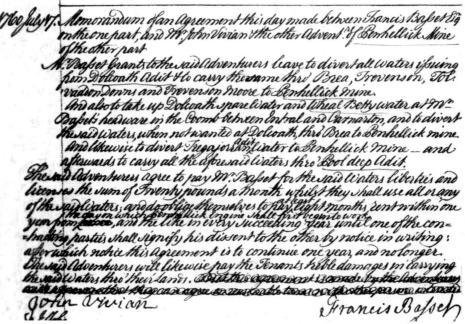

Figure 6. Extract from the memorandum book of 1760 dealing with the extensive use of water-powered machinery at Dolcoath.

21

importance of water power in Britain's industries and mines throughout the eighteenth and nineteenth centuries. In common with other mining parishes Camborne and Illogan were crisscrossed by leats, which gathered and channeled every available fluid ounce of water for use in operating stamping mills, dressing ore and powering the great water wheels which drove tiers of pumps in scores of mine shafts.[43]

The pumping engines in use at the beginning of the eighteenth century were the multi-wheel engines described by Pryce. These engines were located in shafts one above the other, and powered by a stream of water, which drove each wheel in turn as it fell to adit level, through which it was exhausted. The wheels were some twelve to fifteen feet in diameter, and were attended with considerable loss of power and efficiency through friction and poor design. As Pryce says: "If one or two were insufficient, more were often applied to that purpose, all worked by the same stream of water. I have heard of seven in one mine worked over each other. This power must have been attended with a complication of accidents and delays." An illustration of such an engine, which operated at Polgooth in the 1690s, is to be found among the Arundell Papers, where four wheels are shown one above the other in a shaft (see page 210). A similar engine, called a 'Tower Engine', also at Polgooth, worked on the same principle, but this one had all the wheels above the surface in a tower, with an elevated launder supplying the water to power it. Nearer to home, at Carnkye Bal, two of these engines, each with five wheels one above the other, worked from 1699 until 1743. As at Dolcoath, the principal adventurer and mineral lord at Carnkye Bal was Francis Basset.[44]

In May 1714 John Coster and his son patented an 'Engine for drawing water out of deep mines'. Ten years later Francis Scobell patented another such engine for the same purpose. It was the Coster type engine that replaced the multi-wheel engines of 1699 at Carnkye Bal, and the contract for the new engines stated: "To erect and build with ye utmost Expedition two Engines to draw ye Water as deep as ten Wheels did formerly. The Wheels to be thirty-three Feet Diameter." These engines were designed to draw the water to adit from a depth of 24 fathoms below the Deep Adit level. Once again, a Francis Basset was the principal adventurer at Carnkye Bal when these engines were introduced. Doubtless, the two engines illustrated by Pryce, at Bullen Garden in the 1760s, would have been of the type that Basset introduced to Carnkye Bal in the 1740s, with one wheel at surface and another above adit level, and both using the same stream of water, which was exhausted through the adit (see p23). The system of shallow tunnels discovered in recent years at Dolcoath and Bullen Garden undoubtedly served the above purpose. These tunnels, between fifteen and twenty-five feet in depth, and some with the remains of launders still *in situ*, ran between Harrietts Shaft and Dunkins Garden Shaft, and between Bennets Shaft and Old and New Sump shafts. Another tunnel ran south from these two pumping shafts.[45]

Sources of information on Camborne mines' water power are numerous and varied, but the resultant picture is of a complex system of interdependent mines, where water from a single leat served a string of stamps, dressing floors and pumping engines across several square miles. The July 1760 agreement between Francis Basset and the adventurers of Penhellick Mine, at Pool, serves to illustrate the careful and detailed arrangement for the use of all available water. "Mr Basset Grants to the said Adventurers leave to divert all waters issuing from Dolcoath Adit and to carry the same thro' Brea, Trevenson, Tolvaddon Downs and Trevenson Moore to Penhellick Mine … and to take up Dolcoath spare water and Wheal Betty water, at Mr Basset's headware in the Coomb between Entral and Carnarton, and to divert the said waters, when not wanted by Dolcoath, thro' Brea to Penhellick Mine, And likewise to divert Tragajorran Adit water to Penhellick Mine, and afterwards to carry all the aforesaid Waters thro' Pool Deep Adit." John Vivian and the other adventurers agreed to pay £20 per month for this water for at least eight months. They had to give twelve months notice to quit the contract and agree to pay the tenant farmers treble damages for carrying the water through their lands.[47]

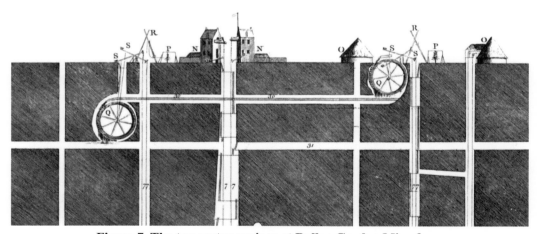

Figure 7. The two water engines at Bullen Garden Mine from William Pryce, drawn in the late 1760s.[46]

Four water sources were involved in this agreement: water from Dolcoath Adit (which lies between Brea Village and Tuckingmill), water already used by Dolcoath stamps, dressing floors and pumping engines (from Dolcoath Leat), water issuing from Wheal Betty Adit (now known as Brea Adit), and water from Tregajorran Adit, which lay to the east of Tincroft Mine and the south of Pool Village. Most of this water had already been used by adjacent mines and went on to supply other mines and streams after going over Penhellick Mine engine at surface and powering another underground engine there, before passing out through Pool Adit to the valley below Tuckingmill. Thereafter it fed the leats which supplied workings along the

Red River to the sea.[48]

The eighteenth century Tehidy records detail water agreements, long-running legal disputes over water rights, water rents and compensation claims involving mines on all sides of Dolcoath. Tregajorran, Pool, Dudnance, Longclose, Penhellick, Tincroft and Trevenson on the eastern side of the valley, Wheal Gons, Camborne Vean and Camborne Veor on the west, Wheal an Owles on the south and Weeth, Pakanbowen, Wheals Gerry, Chance, Kitty and Hatchet on the north, all shared the limited water supplied through the same leat system. When, in July 1767, William John renewed his lease of 'the Foundery', held until the previous year by his father, George John, the main preoccupation of the grantee (Francis Basset) was use of the limited water supply. John was to continue to have use of "Pengigan Moor Water and Dolcoath spare Waters in the same manner as they have been lately used for the benefit of the said Foundery and without doing any prejudice to the Mine of Dolcoath." In September 1756 William's father had been asked to pay the Bassets for diverting water from two ancient stamps near Brea, and in the following July he was granted liberty to erect stamps at Betty Adit, using water from Wheal Betty Adit. At the same time as this agreement was made, there was a dispute over water ownership at Betty Adit and Carnarthen between the Bassets and the Vyvyans. The dispute was not quickly resolved and this water was subsequently fed into Dolcoath Leat.[49]

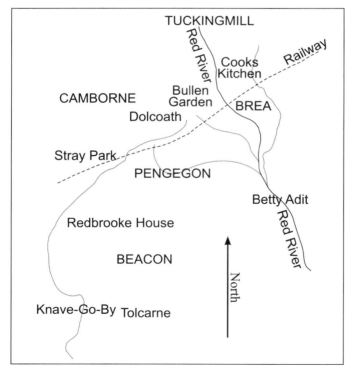

Figure 8. Principal surviving 18th century leats.

To the west of Dolcoath the water being carried by leats from the high ground on the south side of Camborne, together with water issuing from shallow adits, were also being dealt with in the same closely monitored way. In August 1763 an agreement with John Vivian gave liberty to divert the water from these leats, formerly used by Higher Rosewarne and Wheal Gerry mine engines, to Treswithian

Mine. In September 1764 leave was granted to take the water from Wheal Chance engine to serve Weeth Mine engine. In July 1771 it was agreed that water from Camborne Vean Mine could be carried through their adit, between Beacon Lane and Camborne Cross to Roskear, for use at the mine there. In August 1774 Sir Richard Vyvyan granted permission to divert the water which runs to Wheal Chance engine after driving the wheel of Camborne Vean engine, to Wheal Gons engine, and thereafter to ensure that the water returned to Wheal Chance.[50]

These leats were all supplied with water from three fairly modest streams: the Red River, which flows from Bolenow to the sea via Newton Moor, Brea and Tuckingmill; the Connor Stream, which flows from the back of Troon via Barripper to Nancemellin, and the tiny, seasonal stream which rises on Pengegon Moor. These streams were supplemented by several adits, some producing large, regular streams of water, and some small wells and springs to the south of Dolcoath.

As noted above, some of these leats are undoubtedly very ancient, and there are references to them in use in the Camborne district from medieval times, and from the time of Henry VIII around Dolcoath and Bullen Garden. By the end of the seventeenth century they appear to have been in wide use throughout the Camborne-Illogan district. Wheal Jowl Adit fed Filtrick leat, which carried water to Carnkie Bal engines in the 1690s. Subsequently, by the 1740s, another leat carried water from Penventon Shallow Adit, to the south-east of Carnkie Village, to the same engine shafts, where larger water engines had been installed. These leats were to supply one of the longest and most important leats, which was constructed in 1754, and which carried water around the eastern and northern flanks of Carn Brea to Longclose Mine engine, beside Dudnance Lane. A leat which was already in place when Doidge drew his Tehidy Manor Maps in 1737 was the one which carried water from Carnarthen side of the Red River above Betty Adit. This leat runs along the cliff on the south-east side of Brea Village, crosses Tincroft Road behind the public house, and crosses the railway beside the bridge to Cooks Kitchen Mine. Originally it carried water to the water engines at Trevenson and Pool mines. In 1754 it was supplemented by the water from Carnkie leat, which went to Longclose. Another leat carried water from the Reens near Troon, around the western flank of Carn Camborne, past Mount Pleasant, across Trevu Road, alongside Redbrook Road, and through Wheal Gons and Stray Park to Dolcoath. Its metal water channel still crosses the railway to the east of Foundry Road bridge. Dolcoath leat left the western side of the Red River above Brea village, followed the contour of Carn Entral to Pengegon Moor, where it turned north-west across Pengegon Farm to Dolcoath. On route it fed two large ponds on the flanks of Carn Entral, to the south of Bullen Garden Mine. It is not shown on Doidge's 1737 map, but it is mentioned in the Tehidy Proposal Book for September 26 1760: "3 acres of Carn Entral downes above Dolcoath Leat." Presumably, it was constructed in the 1740s or '50s, for by 1754, when Angerstein visited, Dolcoath was using three water-powered engines. This leat is shown on the 1806 James Mills maps of Carn Entral and Pengegon, as are the two ponds it supplied for the Bullen Garden engines.[51]

Early Adventurers & Agents

As noted above, Henry John(s) alias Sparnon, the tenant farmer of North and South Entral tenements, became involved in mining on either side of the Red River between Bullen Garden and Brea Adit, as early as 1720. By 1724 he was purchasing copper ore from Sir William Pendarves, and, in effect, taking over his responsibilities in one of the Pendarves' most important copper mines, at Condurrow. The description by Kalmeter suggests that John was actually working the mine on 'tribute' by paying the adventurers (Pendarves was the principal) so much per ton of ore raised.[52]

In 1720 Henry John had been married for seventeen years, and his son, Henry John junior, was sixteen years old. Which of these two took out the lease of Dolcoath Mine in 1737 we cannot be sure, for it could have been either of them. Certainly, these two, and Henry junior's son, also Henry (born 1733), were to be involved with Dolcoath and its offshoots throughout the eighteenth century. As well as the Dolcoath lease of 1737 the last mining lease in the old Dolcoath Company, dated 1748, was also in Henry John's name. In 1754, when Reinold Angerstein, the Swedish traveller visited the Camborne mines, he described in some detail the mine at Pengegon and Entral. Both Dolcoath and Bullen Garden were described as being owned by 'Mr Johns' and partners. "Boolongorden ... belongs to Messers Johns and Georgil ... Dolcoath copper mine belongs to Mr Johns and partners." The obscure reference to the Bullen Garden proprietors, as 'Messers Johns and Georgil' could refer to Mr Henry Johns, the principal adventurer, and his brother George, who was also Henry's partner (with others) in the Cornish Copper Company, which was formed at about that time. The local practice of calling important members of a company by their first name, to differentiate them from other members of the same family, persists to the present time. At Holman Brothers, for example, one of the brothers, Mr John Holman, was often referred to by the workers as 'Mr John', and other brothers were accorded similar respectful acknowledgment. Angerstein's reference to Henry and George John(s) suggests that the mine owners in 1754 were the second generation of the family. He subsequently mentions that Henry's 'brother and partner' (George) travelled to Norway in 1753 to buy timber, and that he also traded in iron. George John(s) owned a brass foundry at Tuckingmill, known as Dolcoath Foundry, and dealt in iron as well as brasswork. He was probably also principal of an iron foundry known as Dolcoath Iron Foundry, which was located on the edge of South Entrall, facing the end of what is now Dolcoath Avenue. Through his Tuckingmill Foundry George supplied mines throughout the district, and in the 1750s and '60s he is recorded as supplying brass work to Great Work in Breage. He was chief engineer at Dolcoath, responsible for all machinery, especially the water engines and horse whims. The Pool Adit cost book for 1731-36 describes him as their engineer, and details his payments of 2s 6d a day and extra for installing a new engine. He would only have been in his twenties at that time, and so his later reputation as a highly respected engineer appears to have been justified. The Henry John(s) referred to in the 1720s would probably have been too old to have been active in the 1750s. The owner mentioned by Angerstein in 1754 was probably Henry John junior, born in 1704.[53]

Another member of the John(s) family appears to have been a mine captain or manager at Wheal Paull (Bullen Garden) in the 1720s. In March 1723/4 the Tehidy Accounts record that the estate: "Rec'd of Mr John Coster & Company for 1/6th Dues of Copper oare, the whole being 5ton 20cwt, weighed the 26th of ffebruary last att Wheal Paull Worke in the Tenem't of Entrall & sold for £6 per tunn & risen by John Johns = £5 19 0d." It should be noted that a Cornish or long ton was 21cwt not 20cwt as in the rest of the country. A John, son of William John, was christened at Camborne on June 29 1672, and this fifty year old may well have been the mine captain at Wheal Paull in 1723.[54]

Angerstein was shown Bullen Garden Mine by 'Mr Rosen worren', or Rosewarne, and although it is possible that Rosewarne was the guide's name, it is also possible that the guide was Mr John Vivian of Rosewarne, who certainly had an interest in Dolcoath and probably Bullen Garden as well. Mr Richard Banbury appears to have been an important adventurer at Wheal Paull in the 1720s. Given that Wheal Paull almost certainly became Bullen Garden Mine, Banbury was probably involved in the early development of that mine. He was a member of an old Redruth family, being born in March 1683/4 to Richard and Mary Banbury. He is mentioned as paying to the Bassets dues for copper sold by Wheal Paull in 1721, 1722 and 1726. His description as 'Mr Richard Banbury' as opposed to Captain or plain Richard Banbury, suggests that he was an adventurer rather than merely an employee.[55]

Captain Matthew Telam (Tellam) may well have been a mine captain at Dolcoath or Bullen Garden in the 1730s. The Tehidy Accounts quoted above record that he paid dues to the Bassets for a large quantity of copper ore raised in the mines at Pengegon and Entral. The ore was called 'gosan' and appears to have come from Bullen Garden and Dolcoath, which worked the same lode. Although Tellams are referred to in the Dolcoath accounts for the 1770s and '80s, we have no reference to a Captain Matthew Tellam there.[56]

Mr John Coster (or Costar), who paid dues for Wheal Paull throughout the 1720s, was either the man who came to Cornwall as agent for the Gloucestershire copper smelters, in the 1680s, or his son of the same name. John Coster senior, known as the 'father of the Cornish copper industry', had three sons who became prominent adventurers in the Cornish copper mines: John, Thomas and Robert. John Coster senior was certainly an important player in the original development and expansion of the copper industry in Cornwall. Coster was the son of a Forest of Dean ironmaster, and he was involved with attempts to smelt lead ore and other metallic ores in the Forest. He moved to Redbrook on the River Wye in the 1680s and began to smelt copper ores on a fairly modest scale. The small tonnages of copper ore were sent from Cornwall as entrepreneurs began to recognise the potential of the 'poder' or waste being discarded by the tin miners. Very soon larger cargoes of copper ore began arriving at Chepstow from the small ports on the north Cornish coast. As a result, other industrialists became interested, as the need to supply the burgeoning English manufacturing industry grew.[57]

By the end of the seventeenth century John Coster owned shares in a number of old tin mines, which were beginning to produce copper ore. Wall Mine in Gwinear, Pool Adit in Illogan, Chacewater Mine in Kenwyn and Polgooth Mine at St Mewan, were just some of his mining interests. Coster is credited with improving several aspects of the mining industry, including the highly successful overshot water wheel pumping engines, various ore dressing arrangements and even a better method of hoisting ore to surface. Undoubtedly, his major contribution was to help put Cornish copper mining on a business-like footing. He was a link between production of the raw material, transportation by sea to the smelters, smelting and finally, manufacturing. Coster helped organise the capital needed to mine efficiently on the required scale. By the 1720s he and his sons had helped to transform a small, local, inward-looking industry, with its organisation and methods rooted in the medieval Strannary system, into a vigorous, well-organised, highly capitalised and self-confident international industry. Mine records for almost every Cornish mining parish in Cornwall for the decades before 1740 contain the name Coster (Costar). His involvement with mining at Dolcoath and Bullen Garden, is testimony to their importance during that shadowy period before reliable records for those mines exist.[58]

1740-69: Thirty Years of Production & profit
In the Tehidy Manor accounts book entitled 'Adventures & Tinbounds' there is a continuous record of payments made to the Bassets from the sale of copper ore by Dolcoath Mine, as well as their costs at the mine. Basset held a one-eighth share in the adventure and so it is not difficult to calculate the total mine revenue from ore sold and the total monthly costs of the mine. The mine's profits are also given. There are difficulties in calculating the precise monthly or yearly revenue from ore sales, as the parcels of ore were not sold on a regular basis. They could be sold every month, twice a month, every two or three months, or even saved up for six months. Thus, although usually frequent, ore sales followed no regular pattern for those thirty years. On the other hand, costs were usually given for every month.[59]

By arbitrarily deciding the approximate yearly totals (to within a month or so), and taking the monthly costs, we can work out fairly accurately the production figures and mine costs for that period. In 1740 the Bassets received £412 as their one-eighth share of copper ore sold. Multiplied by eight this gives the mine a revenue of £3,296. The Basset costs were £205, making the total mine cost of £1,640. The Bassets made a profit of £207 and Dolcoath Mine total profit was £1,656

During the next two years the quantity of ore sold rose to £4,448 in 1742 and £6,336 in 1743, before gradually declining to £4,344 in 1744, £2,408 in 1745 and £1,408 in 1746. Until 1751 production rose and fell between £2,568 in 1749 and £1,392 in 1750. In 1752 production rose to £4,336, held steady in 1753 and then shot up to £11,832 in 1754. This level of revenue held until 1756, with a slight decline to £9,280, but thereafter the mine's fortunes began to see-saw again. Revenue collapsed to £1,512 in 1757, went up to £9,800 in 1758, held more or less at that

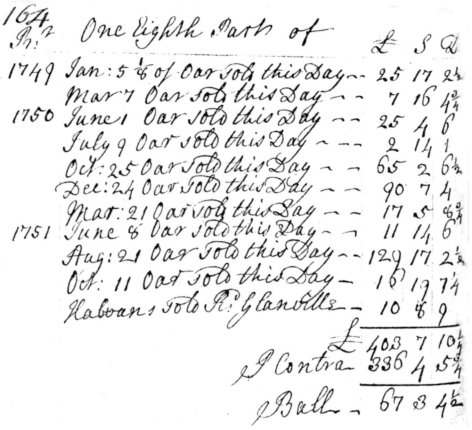

Figure 9. Extract from the list of Francis Basset's mine adventures showing Dolcoath copper production (1740-1769).

29

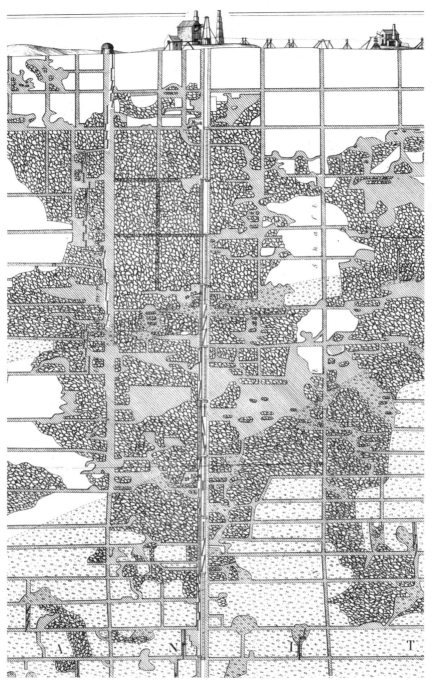

Figure 10. Part of Dolcoath Main Lode, drawn by John Rule junior in the 1820s (from de la Beche).

position until 1761, when it again began to decline, down to £7,424 in 1761, to £2,904 in 1762, up again to £6,704 in 1763 and collapsing again in 1764 to a low of £1,072.[60]

1765 was the year that 'New Dolcoath' came into existence, although the Tehidy accounts continue to give only the revenue from the original 'Old Dolcoath'. In that year £5,328 worth of copper ore was sold, declining to £3,992 the following year and rising again to £7,968 in 1767. In 1768 only £2,944 worth of ore was sold and in 1769, the last year where the figures for 'Old Dolcoath' were given separately from Bullen Garden Mine and the other new sections, revenue was £6,640.[61]

Total revenue from sales of copper ore for that thirty year period (1740-69) by the original Dolcoath Mine amounted to £152,431. The Basset's one-eighth share of this was £19,054. Needless to say, the monthly costs of the mine rose and fell with production, wages being the biggest monthly cost. Total costs for those thirty years were £118,863, which yielded to the mine a profit of £33,569 and to the Bassets a profit of £4,196. Ten of those thirty years saw a loss for the mine. As the Bassets took dues on all ore raised it is probable that they sustained no loss at Dolcoath during that period.

The Basset's 'Adventurers & Tinbounds' book also contains their 'Dolcoath Pleasure Dole' for the years 1756-69. This records the 'One Sixth of Oare sold' at regular intervals over the fourteen year period, which was their share as mineral lords. Costs at a sixth were also given for varying periods throughout those years. Although the total revenue figures do not square with those of the other accounts (at one-eighth), the pattern of income and cost is consistent.[62]

A separate set of accounts called: 'An Account Current of All my Adventurers', lists on opposing pages those adventures which were making a profit and those which were making a loss. These lists begin in 1747 and end in 1765, Dolcoath remaining among the profitable mines throughout the period covered by them. Again, the profits do not agree with the earlier figures, but there were several factors which add to the Basset's profits. Dues on ore raised, water rents and damaged land fines should be added to the calculation.[63]

	Basset's 1/6th Dues	Mine Total
1756 (Ore sold in June, July, August & September)	£721 7s 1d	
1756-57 (Ore sold Oct. Nov. Dec. 1756 & Jan. 1757)	£396 1s 6d	£6,704
1757 (Ore sold Feb. & June)	£421 1s 7d	£2,526
1758 (Ore sold to end of end of July)	£1,082 1s 8d	£6,492

31

1758 (Ore sold Aug. Sept & Oct.)	£877 9s 10d	
1759 (Ore sold to 6th July)	£1,968 19s 9d	£17,079
1760 (Ore sold to end of June)	£2,167 7s 10d	£13,004
1761 (Ore sold to end of June)	£1,484 19s 8d	£8,910
1762 (Ore sold to end of June)	£580 9s 7d	£3,483
1763 (Ore sold to end of June)	£1,340 19s 0d	£8,046
1764 (Ore sold to end of June)	£215 2s 2d	£1,291
1765 (Ore sold to end of March)	£1,066 0s 0d	£6,396
1766 (Ore sold to end of September)	£798 4s 3d	£4,789
1767 (Ore sold to end of June)	£1,594 5s 7d	£9,566
1768 (Ore sold to end of June)	£588 14s 0d	£3,532
1769 (Ore sold to end of June)	£1,327 10s 9d	£7,965

Mine Total (1756-69) £99,784

Mine average for 14 years = £7,127

South Entral Mine eventually became part of Dolcoath Mine, but until at least 1765 it was operated as a separate mine. Angerstein visited it in 1754 and dealt with it as a distinct mine from Bullen Garden and Dolcoath. The Basset entries put the mine under several headings: 'Roskear & Pengegan' (1748), 'Roskear & Pengegon alias Entral' (1749), 'Roskear, Entral & Pengegan' (1750), and 'South Entral Roskear & Pengegan', in 1751, when it moved from loss to profit. Thereafter, the mine was always referred to as 'S. Entral' or 'South Entral' until 1765.[64]

Production figures and costs for Bullen Garden Mine, prior to its uniting with Dolcoath as part of 'New Dolcoath', are not extant. It does not appear to have been included among the Basset adventures, although as the mine leases were issued by them, the Bullen Garden adventurers would have paid dues to them on the ore raised there. One source, which might indicate the possible output and income during the last decades of Bullen Garden operating as an independent mine, is the Angerstein Diary. When Angerstein visited Bullen Garden Mine in May 1754 he estimated the monthly tonnage of ore produced as 6-700, and the average price paid per ton of ore as between £6 and £8 per ton. If we take the average of these figures we have 650 tons of ore sold monthly at £7 a ton, which gives £4,550 per month, or £54,600 a year. We know that the 1750s and '60s were extremely productive because of the evidence of the Bullen Garden section in Pryce's *Mineralogia Cornubiensis*. In 1754 the workings were down to 47 fathoms from surface, and from then until the section was drawn in the late 1760s, the depth was nearly doubled and a vast section of lode removed. If the figures given by Angerstein were a fair reflection of production and income for the years 1750-70 at Bullen Garden, the total revenue would have been well over £1,000,000.[65]

The Cornish Copper Company

The energy and entrepreneurial skills of the John brothers were not just evident in their involvement at Dolcoath and Bullen Garden mines. These far-sighted men saw potential in many directions, and took advantage of all the opportunities that the fast-growing copper mining industry threw up. The possibility of smelting Cornish copper in the Duchy, rather than shipping it to Wales or Gloucester had been explored by several Cornish and up-country industrialists and capitalists, but it was the group of adventurers at Dolcoath, led by Henry and George John who were to make a success of the idea. In the reigns of Edward VI, Mary 1 and Elizabeth 1 the government had encouraged foreign miners and mineral technicians to the country to help find and produce silver, lead and copper. Burchard Cranach in the 1550s and Ulriche Frosse in the 1580s, the latter as part of the Mines Royal set-up, had sought metals including copper and during the time of Frosse there appears to have been a furnace at St Ives, which at least part smelted copper ore, before sending the regulus to Wales for refining. Cranach's operation thirty years earlier had involved setting up a smelting furnace at St Cadix, on a creek on the east side of the Fowey River, near to Lerryn. This had primarily been to smelt lead and extract silver from it. It was not a success, any more than Frosse's copper furnace was in the 1580s.[66]

For the next hundred years copper was not a priority for Cornish miners and mine owners. Technology and capital had enabled tin miners to sink deeper more effectively and more economically, and the result was that lode mining had proved a profitable business. The last decades of the seventeenth century found the Cornish mining industry in crisis, for not only were costs climbing, but as they sank beneath the water tables the miners found the tin ore getting poorer. Fortunately, the tin lodes were found to contain 'poder' or waste, which was discovered to be copper ore. Entrepreneurs from up-country quickly realized the significance of this to the burgeoning English manufacturing industry, for foreign supplies of copper were diminishing rapidly as English copper demand grew. By the time of the Mines Royal Act and the establishment of the Bank of England, coinciding with the growth in joint stock companies and the availability of surplus cash from improved farming methods and the growth of Navigation Act protected world trade, agents from interested parties in London and Bristol were sniffing out supplies of copper ore. Men like Gabriel Wayne and John Costar from Gloucestershire were not only buying up discarded copper ore already at surface, but were buying into mining adventures and even taking over whole mines.[67]

In 1693 the first of several attempts to smelt copper in Cornwall was made. Sir Clement Clarke and his son Sir Talbot associated with several Cornish gentlemen, including Francis Scobell, MP for Mitchell, Henry Vincent, MP for Truro, and the Carlyons of Tregrehan, to establish a copper smelter at Polrudden, near St Austell. This London based company only lasted for four years before closing for a number of reasons, including poor management, dishonesty and lack of easily available ore. The location of the furnaces so far from the tin-producing areas of Camborne, Kenwyn and Gwennap was also a major factor in the company's failure. Sir Clement moved to the Bristol area with his smelting operation, and soon employed Gabriel Wayne and John Costar to manage the works there and also to act as purchasing agents for the copper ore in Cornwall. As noted above Costar was involved at the early mines at Entral and Pengegon.[68]

The next attempt was made by John Pollard of Redruth (Lord of the Manor of Treleigh), who with his partner, Thomas Worth, a St Ives merchant, set up a smelter at St Ives in the mid-1690s. Celia Fiennes travelled through the district in 1696, and commented: "I came by the copper mines … they do not melt (smelt) it here but ship it off to Bristol … at St Ives they do melt (smelt) a little but nothing that is considerable." Presumably it was Pollard's copper furnaces she referred to. Pollard's first attempt did not last long, but in 1712 he had another try and this time he was more successful, continuing to smelt copper at St Ives until 1722, when Pollard left Cornwall for Swansea. Meanwhile, in 1710, Gideon Cosier of Perranzabuloe had established a smelter at Penpol, Phillack, and although he died shortly thereafter, his work was carried on by Sir William Pendarves of Camborne, a large-scale mine adventurer, and his partner Robert Corker, Receiver General of the Duchy of Cornwall from 1709-12. Robert Costar, son of John Costar senior, joined the firm in 1727, the year before Pendarves died. Built close to the coal quays at Hayle this copper smelting operation was the first truly successful Cornish-based copper smelting works, continuing for 25 years until, for a variety of reasons, including the death of its two principal partners, it closed in 1735. Its success in attracting copper ore from many of the local mines, which were not owned or part-owned by the agents of Welsh or Gloucestershire smelting companies, was responsible for the closure of Pollard's St Ives works in 1722.[69]

It is possible that Gideon Cosier's brother, Thomas, carried out copper smelting at Perranarworthal between 1721-24, where he also had four reverberatory tin smelting furnaces. It may have closed due to distance from a reliable coal supply and remoteness from significant copper ore sources. Competition from the successful Penpol smelter at Hayle probably also contributed to Cosier's short-lived attempt. Apparently, there was an experimental furnace erected at Trewinnard House, St Erth, the home of John Hawkins. It appears to have been built before 1700, and it is mentioned in 1716, when it was discovered behind a wall in the mansion.[70]

The story of the Dolcoath involvement may have started in 1721 at Lenobrey, St Agnes, on the border with Illogan. John Costar leased the property from Thomas Tonkin of St Agnes. During the 1740s one Sampson Swaine of St Agnes set up a copper smelting furnace on Rosewarne Downs, Camborne. The furnace was designed by Swaine, possibly using knowledge gained at Lenobrey, for it is probable that he gained his first experience of copper smelting there in the 1720s. A reference in a Tehidy Proposal book, dated June 22 1759, helps to locate the 'copper house' on the junction of Roskear and Rosewarne Downs. "Joseph Boaden, who works at ye Copper house on Roskear, is desirous to enclose about 3 acres of Rosewarne downs, next adjoining Roskear (which tenement is partly ye lands of Mr Basset and p'tly of Mr Percival) as already marked by a gurgy hedge – he will erect a dwelling house therein within 12 months. Nothing done" The smelter appears to have been sited beside Prince William Henry Shaft, close to the border of Roskear and Rosewarne, and its site was rediscovered during excavations prior to the building of a new Kingdom Hall in 1999. A six-foot wide, eighteen-inch thick layer of copper scoria (slag), as hard as glass, was discovered by the geologist investigating the site. The 1806 James Mills map of Rosewarne, shows a field a short distance to the north of this site as 'Copperhouse Field'. Unfortunately, we do not have an equivalent map for the actual area occupied by Prince William Henry Shaft. Two fields on the 1840 Camborne Tithe Apportionment Map are also called 'Copperhouse Field', and these lie some 1200 feet (366m) to the north-north-west of the Prince William Henry site, on Rosewarne tenement, precisely where it is shown on the 1806 map. Prince William Henry Shaft is on Roskear Downs, close to the boundary with Rosewarne and the Boaden reference puts the smelter on Roskear.[71]

Henry John and his partners quickly noted the efficiency and significance of Swaine's furnaces and by 1754 had persuaded him to establish furnaces at Entral, on Bullen Garden Mine. Pryce writing in about 1770 says: "about the year 1754, when one Sampson Swaine, in conjunction with some gentlemen of Camborne, erected furnaces at Entral in that parish; but this situation being too remote from coal, they removed their works to Hayle. The author well remembers the combinations which were formed to overthrow this laudable effort …(etc)" The resultant material was not pure, refined copper metal, but a regulus or matte. Pryce further stated: "the adventurers of Bullen-Garden Mine, some few years past, not only calcined their poor Copper Ore, but smelted it likewise into a regulus, and that at an expence which was easy to be borne for the improvement of the Ore in its value: but the attempt was of no long duration, the Copper Ore buyers very honestly confirming the suspicions of the adventurers, that they did not, neither would they offer at so high a standard for Copper Regule as they would for Copper Ore …(etc)" Some believe that it was these works at Entral that Angerstein referred to in 1754, when he toured the mines of Camborne, rather than to the original works on Rosewarne Downs. It has often been assumed that when Swaine erected furnaces at Entral he removed them from Rosewarne, but it seems certain he built new furnaces and kept his original ones where they were. Angerstein wrote: "In the Parish of Camborne 3½ miles from Redruth, there is a copper smelting mill belonging to Robert Sverin (Swaine) who here smelts the ore to raw matte and then sends it to his copper works in Wales, 20 miles from Bristol, called Redbrook" He then described the furnace and adds that it was, "fired by Welsh mineral coal, and some of this is also placed with the ore." The whole purpose of the smelters at Entral was to by-pass the Welsh works, but it is clear from this that Swaine had an interest in the Welsh operations and supplied them with part-refined matte or regulus from his Rosewarne Downs furnace. As noted above, Joseph Boaden was working at this copperhouse in June 1759, and there is a reference to six tons of galena being sold to Sampson Swaine for his smelting house at Rosewarne in the same year, suggesting that it was equipped to reduce lead as well as copper ore. The lead ore came from Wheal Tobban, on Nancekuke.[72]

When Henry and George John, together with John Vivian of Rosewarne, an adventurer and agent at Dolcoath, and the Reverend John Trevenen, of Lower Rosewarne, decided to move their smelting operation to Hayle, it was very much a Dolcoath exercise. The move took place in 1756, and the three original partners were George John, John Trevenen and John Vivian, with Vivian providing the managerial expertise, John the engineering skill and Trevenen added financial backing. When the first twenty-one year agreement for the newly formed Cornish Copper Company was drawn up, in 1758, a total of £22,000 was raised by the partners, with the lion's share being held by the John brothers (£5,000), John Vivian (£4,000), the Rev. Trevenen (£3,000), and Sir John St Aubyn (Clowance), James Heywood (Devon) and Christopher Hawkins (Trewinnard) each contributing £2,000. The other partners were James Vivian (Camborne), Richard Maddock (London) and William Wayne (London) with £1,000 worth of shares each. John Nicholl (Phillack) and John Edwards (St Erth) both put in £500. Camborne men, mostly involved at Dolcoath, put in £13,000 of the £22,000.[73]

These men were a mixture of merchants, mine adventurers and financiers, with George John being also an engineer and inventor, having a small brass and iron foundry at Tuckingmill, William Wayne described as a metallurgist, and John Edwards, who was to manage the company for over forty years, being technically able and something of a scientist. There was no mention in the Partnership Agreement of Sampson Swaine, who presumably continued his smelting business on Rosewarne Downs, whilst working on inventions to make better use of fuel in the steam engines of the time.

The Cornish Copper Company traded under a variety of names throughout its long history. In the 1770s the Tehidy Accounts dealt with the Company as 'Vivian, Heywood & Hawkins', and in the 1780s as 'Michell, Trevenen & Edwards', the 'Cornish Copper Company' and 'Hayle Copper Company'. In 1783 Cooks Kitchen Cost Book refers to them as 'Basset, Vivian & Michell'. The Company supplied Tehidy Manor and Cooks Kitchen with timber, imported through Hayle, stamps, made at its foundry, coal, imported from Wales, charcoal, bottles, brooms and a host of

Whereas some doubts have been made by the present Adventurers under a sett some time since granted by the Trustees of of John Prideaux Bassett Esq.ᵗ to Jnᵒ Sandys Rich.ᵈ Eeady & partners to dig & search for Tyn & Copper in & within part of the tenem.ᵗ of North Entral in the Parish of Camborn (the Lands of the said Jnᵒ Prideaux Bassett) touching the limits & extent of the said Sett Northward from the run or course of the Addit by them driven in & through the said tenement

Wherefore to prevent any difference or disputes which may for the future arise or be made concerning the same

It is now Proposed and Agreed that the said Adventurers shall have thirty ffathoms (& no more) to the North of the Shafts already sunk & made on the Run of the said Addit and all Veins & courses within the same They paying such share out of & for the same to the Lord of the Soil and at such times & in such manner & form as is mentioned expressed and reserved in the Original Sett And for the more certain fixing the Limits of the Sett as before mentioned It is proposed that boundaries be forthwith Sett up at the distance of the said thirty ffathoms Witness our hands —
21.ˢᵗ February 1752 —

Witness hereto —
Walter Reed

Grace Sims
Noye
Vivian

Figure 11. Agreement for part of the northern sett of Dolcoath (North Entral), 1752.

37

other merchandise. The close association with Dolcoath, meant, not surprisingly, that the CCC was the most regular and significant supplier of gear to be found in the New Dolcoath Pay Books for the years 1771 to 1788. Until 1779 they are always referred to as 'Vivian Heywood & Hawkins', but thereafter the name changes several times. In November 1779 it was 'Sir Francis Basset, Vivian & Co.', in December it was 'Sir Francis Basset & Co.', and in March 1780 'Basset, Vivian & Michell', reverting to 'Basset & Co.' until November 1781, when the company was again known by the names of the principal partners or agents. The 1779 Partnership Agreement included Sir Francis Basset (£2,000), John Edwards, the manager (£3,000), three members of the Hawkins family (£9,000), Thomas and Elizabeth Michell (£6,000) and Thomas Kevill, Basset agent (£1,000). The Vivians remained prominent, with two new partners swelling the family investment to £11,400. Most importantly, Dolcoath's connection was concerned with the original purpose in setting up the Company, copper smelting, and appears that, at least to start with, most of her copper ore was sent to Copperhouse for refining.[74]

Meanwhile, back at the mine, the old furnaces, rather than having been moved or abandoned, remained active, or at least intact, for in the January 1772 entry in the New Dolcoath Pay Book, it is recorded that they were active once again. A total of fourteen workers, eleven men and three women, were employed at the furnaces. The highest paid was Thomas Mill at £2 9s 10d for the month and the lowest was Sarah Harrise who was paid 6d. The wage bill totaled £15 14s 4d. This became a regular entry until October 1773, with the furnace wage bill varying between £8 17s 6d and £23 7s 10d. Whether these furnaces continued to produce regulus, perhaps working on low grade ore, we cannot be certain, but it does seem likely that this short-lived revival of copper smelting at Entral used the existing furnaces left by the attempt begun in the 1750s under the direction of Sampson Swaine and George John. The August 1992 *Newsletter* of the *Trevithick Society* contained a short article by Bryan Earl on the possible remains of those furnaces, entitled 'Unidentified Structure on the Bullen Garden Section of Dolcoath Mine'. He wrote: "The remains of a building which appears to have the base of a chimney built into one wall has been uncovered by the excavation of dump material (at Dolcoath). Several features suggest that it is connected with a furnace: there are some points that lead one to consider the remains as associated with either "burning" or smelting of ore. There is a channel that gives every appearance of having been a flue, lined with hand made grit faced bricks. In one section there is an indication that the bricks have been subjected to considerable heat, although this was insufficient to cause vitrification. The base of the flue is some 2m above what appears to be the floor line of the structure: this would be consistent with a flue leading from a reverberatory furnace. The hand made bricks could show that the flue had been built sometime before the middle of the 19th century." Earl then discusses the fact that the existence of copper slag, both loose and in block form around the site, together with significant metal artifacts, indicates that the structure may have been the ruins of the furnace erected by Swaine and John in the middle of the eighteenth century. Although he states that there is no certainty of the origins of the building, he concludes: "The discovery of the Dolcoath copper smelting furnace would have considerable historical significance." The story of Dolcoath's involvement in copper smelting, leading to the longest-lasting and most successful operation of its kind in Cornwall, is evidence of that enterprising spirit which Henry and George John shared with those other energetic and entrepreneurial Camborne and Illogan families, the Vivians, Trevithicks, Bassets and Holmans.[75]

"1769 Sept'r 5 Mr Basset this day came to a determination
    to reduce his Dues in Dolcoath from 1/6 to 1/8
    on all Ores sold subsequent to this date,
    until farther directions, having considered
    that the present expences are so great, that the
    Adventurers have little or no prospect of
    Profit."
    "Same day Mr B. wrote to Mr Tippet"

Ticketing records for the years 1769-1778 show that although Dolcoath sold a considerable quantity of copper ore to the Cornish Copper Company, they were only one among several buyers. In 1769 the CCC was the fourth highest purchaser of Dolcoath copper ore out of eight, in 1770 they were fifth out of nine, and by 1771 they were down to sixth out of ten. In 1769 (last six months) they purchased £1869 worth of copper ore from the mine, in 1771 (12 months) it was £1822 worth and in 1771 (12 months) they were up to £2881. The largest purchasers were the Mines Royal and Freeman & Co., both of whom dwarfed the CCC's tonnage purchased. During the 1770s the picture varied from the CCC being the third biggest buyer of Dolcoath copper ore out of ten in 1776 and 1777 to the sixth out of eleven in 1778.[76]

Tuckingmill Foundry
In the middle years of the eighteenth century George John established a small brass foundry at Tuckingmill. It was on the site of an ancient tucking mill, which is a west country term for a fulling mill. The water to power these mills came from the Red

River, via leats, which came along the western side of the valley from above Brea Village, as well as from the stream which came down through Pengegon Moor and Coombe. The ancient network of leats supplied from the Red River is accurately shown on William Doidge's Tehidy Manor Map of 1737. This power source for the foundry was referred to in the Tehidy Memorandum book for July 10 1767, the year after George's death, when his son renewed the lease on the foundry. "It is hereby agreed between Francis Basset Esq. and Mr William John that the said William John should continue to hold and occupy the works in Entral in Camborne called the Foundery and Plots etc thereunto belonging together with Pengigan Moor water and Dolcoath spare Waters in the same manner as they have been lately used for the benefit of the said Foundery and without doing any prejudice to the Mine of Dolcoath, at the yearly rent of Twenty pounds from the first of June 1767 to the first of June 1768, which said rent the said William John does hereby agree to pay to the said Francis Basset."[77]

As early as 1731/2 George John, son of Henry John senior, was resident engineer at Pool Adit, the most productive and profitable copper mine of the first half of the eighteenth century. Born in the first decade of the eighteenth century (although the record of his baptism has not been found in any of the local parishes), by his late twenties he was described as 'George John. Engineer' at Pool Adit Mine from February 1731/2, and remained there until November 1736. He was paid the impressive sum of 2/6 a day to supervise the engines there, and was given extra when new machinery was installed. In May 1736 he was paid £3 for directing the erection of a new water engine. By this time he was also, undoubtedly, engineer at the burgeoning Dolcoath Mine, where his father and brother, Henry, were among the principal adventurers.[78]

George John ran Tuckingmill Foundry until his death in November 1766, when his son William (aged 30) took it over. William managed the foundry until he quit through incapacity of some sort in October 1773, and he died in January 1774. His young widow Mary (aged 34) then took over the foundry, operating it as Mary John & Co. until sometime after September 1787, at which time she supplied brasswork for Illogan parsonage. John Budge had taken over the foundry by April 1793, when he supplied brasswork to Tehidy Manor under the name John Budge & Co. Budge offered a partnership in the foundry to William Murdoch, but he declined, and remained with Boulton and Watt.[79]

When Angerstein described the ownership of Dolcoath and Bullen Garden, in 1754, he says that 'Boolongorden belongs to Messers Johns and Georgil', which is taken to mean Henry and George John (see above). He adds, 'Dolcoath mine belongs to Mr Johns and partners'. He further stated that "Mr John's brother and partner traveled to Arendhal last year with a Norwegian ship and is now expected back with the

Figure 12. Group of Dolcoath bal maidens, circa 1900. They are wearing their traditional 'gooks' (head-dress).

Figure 13. Engine (New Sump) Shaft, last quarter of the 19th century.

41

Figure 14. A later photograph of the Engine (New Sump) Shaft engine house with an iron headgear, pentagonal timber extension to fit the larger engine and inclined ramp.

Dolcoath Mine   Camborne

**Figure 15. Looking at Bullen Garden from near Dunkin's Garden Shaft.
The Old Sump Shaft winder can be seen on the right.**

Figure 16. View north over Dolcoath lower dressing floors in the Tuckingmill Valley.

**Figure 17. Looking west towards the two old steam stamps. Note the line
of Brunton calciners in the middle of the picture.**

Figure 18. Engine (New Sump) Shaft circa 1890. Notice the new compressor house behind.

Figure 19. Central Dolcoath seen looking west. New Sump headgear on the left and Old Sump on the right, behind the compressor house.

Figure 20. Group of miners carrying candles and fuzes to Harrietts Shaft.

Figure 21. Looking east across the Red River Valley towards Eastern (Valley) Shaft.

Figure 22. Bal maidens and other surface workers near New East Shaft, circa 1900.

Figure 23. Group of Dolcoath adventurers outside the compressor house, circa 1900.

Figure 24. Looking east across the Red River Valley towards the new Californian stamps. Eastern (Valley) Shaft shown on right.

Figure 25. Stray Park engine house before being rebuilt at the turn of the 20th century.

Figure 26. Another group of Dolcoath bal maidens, circa 1900.

Figure 27. Looking east towards Old Sump Shaft and winder; the timber structure on the left is a launder. Note the rails in the foreground.

load of timber that he has purchased. Mr John also trades in iron, but his entire yearly turnover does not exceed 40 to 50 tons." George John not only travelled to Scandinavia to buy timber for the mine, but he also dealt in iron, which suggests that his establishment of the foundry at Tuckingmill probably dates from this period, although it is possible that he ran the foundry shown on the 1806 Tehidy map as Dolcoath Iron Foundry at that time. He was receiving, on behalf of Dolcoath, parts for their engines from Coalbrookdale, from 1753 to 1756, and carrying out brass casting for Great Work's 47-inch engine at his foundry between 1759 and 1764. The material for Great Work was described in the Cost Book as by 'George John, Camborne, engineer' and included 'casting Brass work for the engine, £30', 'for a Brass cylinder, 10cwt (odd) at 1s per lb, £59' and 'for a Brass working Barrell, £70', as well as other work. Harris says that George John obtained a lease of the old Tuckingmill for use as a foundry in 1761 and was permitted to use 'Dolcoath spare water' to power the works. The above references suggest that George was already established with his works well before 1761, and that he was dealing in iron and brass, as well as producing foundry work for local mines. If work was done as far afield as Godolphin in 1759, he must have been doing work for Dolcoath and other Camborne-Illogan mines for some time. It was as early as 1755 that he obtained a patent for a new method of raising water out of mines.[80]

By 1806, when John Budge was the proprietor of Tuckingmill Foundry, another iron foundry, called on James Mills' map of 'Reskeare', 'Dolcoath Foundery', was shown on the edge of Entral, opposite the end of what is now Dolcoath Avenue. This foundry sat right on Dolcoath Main Lode, close to the workings of Dunkins Garden and Bennets Shaft. The same Mills maps show that John Budge held the land and buildings immediately to the north of Bullen Garden, at and around Dry Stile, on the south-eastern side of Roskear Village. The water from Pengegon Moor ran past the foundry, clearly supplying it with power. No mention is made of Tuckingmill Foundry on these maps, although they do show that the water went from Dolcoath Foundry to the site of Tuckingmill Foundry, beside the main road to Redruth. On the 'Carn Entral' map the same foundry is marked as 'Iron Foundery'. This is of interest because most descriptions and references to Tuckingmill Foundry in the eighteenth century call it a brass foundry, and as with supplies to Great Work, so the principal work done for Cooks Kitchen and Dolcoath by Tuckingmill Foundry was brasswork. Whether George John and his family and John Budge ran the Dolcoath Iron Foundry also, is not known, but it certainly seems likely that they were involved there.[81]

New Dolcoath Mine (1765-1791)
On September 21st and 28th 1766 Sir Francis Basset granted to a group of adventurers in what was described as 'New Dolcoath', liberty to work 'Dolcoath Old Load' and twenty fathoms on each side, between the Red River at North Entral and Wheal Gons in Pengegon. John Collins of Redruth was the agent for the other adventurers.

Dolcoath sett was granted for twenty-one years to Collins and company who were to pay Basset one sixth dues. Such was the potential of the new mine that Basset continued his interest in the mine by taking a large part of the adventure himself. The cost book company was divided into sixteen shares, of which Basset took six and the other adventurers one sixth each. The names of the adventurers reveal an interesting and typical range of people, from local gentry and landowners, like Basset, Sir John Molesworth and John Ennys, to farmers and entrepreneurs such as Henry John, merchants like Philip Richards and clergymen like the Reverend Collins and Reverend Trevenen. The other adventurers, Swete Nicholas Archer, Robert Lovell and Thomas Edwards, were also men of means.[82]

During the next few years there was some movement in New Dolcoath's share ownership, mainly due to the death of adventurers. The *Sherborne Mercury* details the sale of some of their shares. The 7th and 14th of November 1768 issues refer to a one-sixteenth share being available: 'property of gentleman lately deceased', although no name is given. In August 1775 the one-sixteenth share of John Collins ('deceased') was up for auction, in January 1776 the one-sixteenth share of Sir John Molesworth ('deceased') was for sale, in July 1776 the one-sixteenth share of 'the late' Samuel Enys was available and in August 1776 Thomas Edwards sixteenth share became available upon his death.[83]

List of New Dolcoath Adventurers 1767-68[84]

Sir Francis Basset	6/16
Sir John Molesworth	1/16
John Enys	1/16
Swete Nicholas Archer	1/16
Robert Lovell	1/16
The Rev. Mr Collins	1/16
The Rev. Mr Trevenen	1/16
Thomas Edwards	1/16
Henry John	1/16
Philip Richards	1/16
Another	1/16

This New Dolcoath adventure included all the mines between the Red River and the western side of Pengegon along the strike of Dolcoath Main Lode. Bullen Garden, Dunkins Garden, Wheal Bryant, Wheal Killas, Old Dolcoath, Stray Park and Wheal Gons were all part of that enormous mine sett. Parallel to these workings on the north side were South Entral Mine and Roskear Broase Mine, which also were included in New Dolcoath.

The expansion of Old Dolcoath into the larger new adventure is confirmed by a suggestion by Francis Basset on September 3rd 1765: "Mr Basset thinks it will be expedient on behalf of and at the expence of the future Adventurers in Dolcoath to drive the end from Bullen Garden Eastward on the coarse of the Load at the level of Cooks Kitchen deep Adit, and to sink a Shaft at a convenient distance between the said End and the Eastern extent of Dolcoath set to the said level and at that level to drive two ends East and West on the course of the Load for bringing the said Cooks Kitchen deep Adit with due levels more speedily into Bullen Garden." Basset was clearly anticipating the formation of New Dolcoath Mine under new leases of the setts to be granted the following September. Presumably, as this adit drive was carried out initially by the old adventurers, it was assumed that some of the same men were to be involved in the new adventure.[85]

The earliest extant pay book for 'New Dolcoath' begins in April 1771. Whether this was in fact the first pay book we can only surmise, but it is certain that Old Dolcoath and Bullen Garden continued to operate separately for some years after they were joined as a single adventure and known as 'New Dolcoath Company'.[86]

Until the formation of 'New Dolcoath' the deepest adit to drain the larger mines in the district was known as Cooks Kitchen Deep Adit, and had been driven from the western side of the Red River at Tolvaddon Bridge, up the length of the Great Crosscourse and into Cooks Kitchen Mine opposite Bullen Garden. In about January 1765 this adit had cut a lode as it was driven south, which was believed to be North Entral Lode, and in June a Mr Phillips, on behalf of the adventurers of Cooks Kitchen, applied for a sett to work the lode within Brea tenement. In July Tehidy agreed to this, provided the mine completed the adit to the eastern boundary with Tincroft Mine within five years and to the western boundary at the Red River within three years. Within a month Capt. Richard Trevithick, on behalf of Dolcoath adventurers, applied for a sett to work North Entral Lode by driving a branch from Cooks Kitchen Deep Adit right through Entral. This was suspended until Cooks adventurers had completed the adit on lode through their property. On March 22nd 1776 Trevithick re-applied for the North Entral sett and this time it was granted. The adit branch was to be driven through Entral to the western boundary of Roskear.[87]

Within a short time even this deep adit was superseded. In September 1765 Captain Richard Trevithick began a major project to bring lasting benefit to Dolcoath and the whole district. An ancient adit had been driven from the side of the Red River at Roscroggan, into some old, shallow mine workings on Roskear Croft. Trevithick obtained permission to drive this adit south to Dolcoath Mine over a mile away. A comment in Tehidy Proposal Book, dated July 27th 1774, shows that this Dolcoath

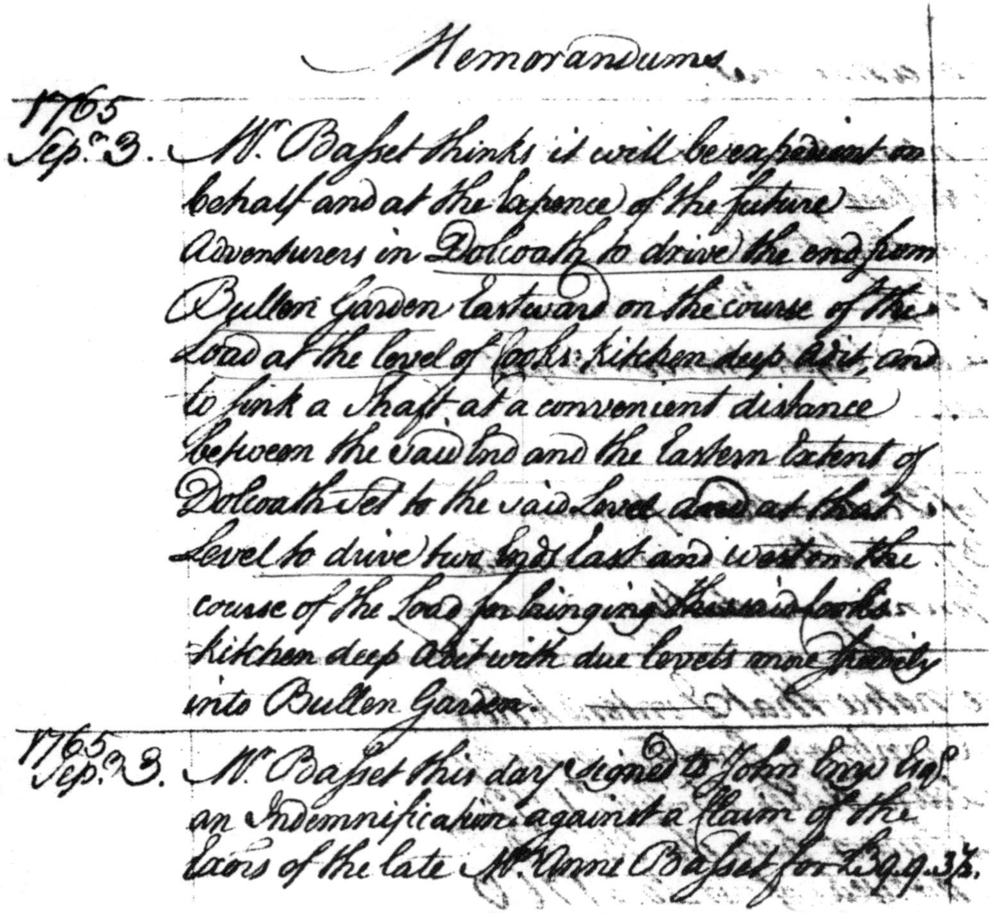
Memorandums.

1765 Sepr. 3. Mr. Basset thinks it will be expedient on behalf and at the Expence of the future Adventurers in Dolcoath to drive the end from Bullen Garden Eastward on the course of the Load at the level of Cooks Kitchen deep Adit, and to sink a Shaft at a convenient distance between the said End and the Eastern Extent of Dolcoath Set to the said Level; and at that Level to drive two Ends East and West on the course of the Load for bringing the said Cooks Kitchen deep Adit with due levels more directly into Bullen Garden.

1765 Sepr. 3. Mr. Basset this day signed to John Enys Esqr an Indemnification against a Claim of the Exors of the late Mrs. Anne Basset for £39.9.3½.

Figure 28. Agreement to link up Cooks Kitchen deep adit to New Dolcoath at Bullen Garden.

New Deep Adit was already past Wheal Gerry and heading toward the western end of Dolcoath Mine. Unfortunately, the two account books of Captain Trevithick, covering the years 1765-68, disappeared from the shelves of Tehidy Mineral Office in November 1978, just before South Crofty took possession of the company, and cannot now be consulted. This adit system, maintained until 1998 by South Crofty Mine, became the most important mine drainage system in the entire district.[88]

What becomes apparent when examining the many lease agreement documents from the eighteenth century on driving and extending adits is the crucial role they played in the development of mining in the district. Most of these adits were driven into mines on lode, whereas the later, deeper adits were frequently driven across country, often along crosscourses to the mines. These agreements almost all detail the restrictions imposed upon the miners and the basic requirements of the mineral lords. The application usually requested liberty to work ten, fifteen or thirty fathoms on either side of the lode along which the adit was to be driven. The lords normally demanded that the adit be extended to the limits of the sett within a set time. They also required that sufficient men be employed for so many months each year in extending the adit, and often stipulated that a minimum of 25 or 50 fathoms a year be driven. This obviously meant that the fixed plant on the property was enhanced, so that when the lease was up the property was a more attractive proposition to new adventurers.

We are fortunate in having at our disposal a very detailed long-section of the principal part of New Dolcoath, drawn at about the time of its formation. Pryce's *Mineralogia Cornubiensis* contains a 'Parallel Section of Bullen Garden Mine in the Parish of Camborne', which was presented to the principal adventurer of Dolcoath, Francis Basset. Bullen Garden section of Dolcoath became the largest producer of copper ore on the mine and its workings were the deepest and most extensive. The section shows the mine at a depth of some 90 fathoms, between the 70 fathom and 80 fathom levels. There were ten shafts shown, from Bennetts on the west to what appears to be Gossan Shaft on the east. One of these shafts was merely an access shaft for the western water engine, between Bennetts and Old Sump Shaft. Five shafts extend to the bottom of the mine, and Bennetts reaches the stopes above the 'western bottoms'. The section does not illustrate the shallow tin workings above Deep Adit level, but confines itself to the vast copper workings below adit. Although only three horse whims are shown, there would undoubtedly have been more, as all the ore needed to be drawn to surface and that at the western end could not easily be drawn from the central and eastern whims shown.[89]

The mine was being deepened by stoping the bottoms, using underhand stoping methods. This involved working downwards in large steps or benches and hoisting the broken attle and ore to the deep haulage level by means of windlass and kibble. These are shown on the section opposite. On the haulage level the stuff was separated into attle (waste) and ore. The attle was 'thrown to stull' and the ore wheelbarrowed to the whim shafts for drawing to surface.

Lode drive and crosscut connections to the other mines included in New Dolcoath are shown on the section, with a crosscut to South Entral Mine shown running north from Main (Great) Lode. This crosscut lay at a depth of some 60 fathoms (360ft) and was driven from just east of New East Shaft. There were also lode drives to Old Dolcoath and Wheal Bryant at depths of 31 fathoms (186ft) and 48 fathoms (288ft).

Like a modern mine Dolcoath was shown blocked out by means of shafts and horizontal levels, running right through the mine or between shafts. Some fourteen levels can be identified on the section, although some were very short, and some had localized, specific use, like carrying water from one water engine to another at a lower elevation. The shallowest level is described by Pryce as: "A shallow level or aqueduct, that conveys the water, after it is discharged from the eastern water engine wheel, to the top of the western water engine wheel, to work that also" (see illustration). Shallow Adit is described as 'The old level or adit', and the Deep Adit as 'The new level or deeper adit'. The old Shallow Adit is shown at a depth of some 12 fathoms or 72 feet below surface, which indicated that the plan was not precisely to scale, as that adit is known to have been at a depth of some 18 fathoms, or 108 feet. The Deep Adit was shown at 25 fathoms or 150 feet deep, which is closer to the actual depth of the deepest adit level at that time. This was the Deep Adit brought into Bullen Garden from Cooks Kitchen Mine in the middle to late 1760s.[90]

Below adit, at a depth of some 31 fathoms, there was a level connecting 'Dolcoth fire engine shaft' and Bullen Garden engine shafts. This level carried water westward to be pumped to adit by the 40-inch Newcomen engine at Old Dolcoath. The western end of the next level Pryce called: "Huel-Bryant drift, or a deeper level driving to Dolcoth." The eastern end of the level, where it connects to the western water engine shaft cistern, Pryce describes as: "An aqueduct or level from Dolcoth Mine." Pryce also says that the water coming from Dolcoath runs into this cistern and is pumped to adit by the western water engine. This level lies at a depth of 48 fathoms. It was still being driven westward and had not yet reached Dolcoath Engine Shaft; when it did, the western water would report to Bullen Garden pumps. At a depth of 44 fathoms a level had been driven between the eastern water engine and the western water engine. At Old Sump Shaft there was a cistern (the 'rose cistern'), which gathered water to be sent east to the eastern water engine, and west to the western water engine (see illustration). A short level ran from Bennetts Shaft to Old Sump Shaft at a depth of some 66 fathoms. At the eastern end of the mine a short level had been extended some 11 fathoms from Magor Shaft, at a depth of 63 fathoms. It was stoped above and below the level. Some 72 fathoms below surface a drive west from Bennetts Shaft went 9 fathoms to 'Kemps end', and east to Old Sump Shaft, and another at a slightly higher elevation went on through New Sump to New East Shaft. At the same horizon a drive went eastward from Magor Shaft for a distance of 22 fathoms. A deep level ran between the western water engine shaft and Magor Shaft at a depth of 76 fathoms. Pryce described it as: "A stull and way to the top eastern end", so it presumably was protected from attle above the level by a continuous stull and lay on a board sollar across stulled attle beneath. Below it, running from the "deep western end, or stool" was "the long sallor (sollar)", which ran along a timber-boarded floor. This level stretched westward from Old Sump Shaft for 40 fathoms and lay at a depth of 83 fathoms. Between Old Sump and Magor shafts was the deep haulage level, at a depth of some 86 fathoms, to which the ore and attle was drawn from the bottom stopes for initial separation. The ore

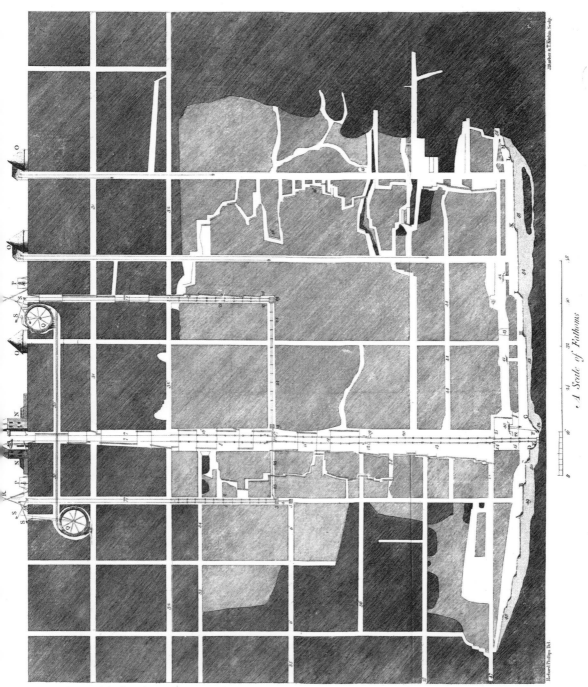

Figure 29. Section of Bullen Garden Mine, reproduced from William Pryce, 1778. Drawn in the late 1760s.

was wheelbarrowed to the whim shafts and the attle or waste was 'thrown to stull'. The bottom stopes lay at a depth of 90 fathoms from surface, which was some 65 fathoms below Deep Adit.[91]

The picture of the actual workings is very revealing. Clearly, the mine was being deepened by stoping downward. However, examination also shows that raises ('rises') were being mined, exploration winzes below levels were being sunk and back stoping had occurred (see illustrations). It is true that most stoping appears to have been underhand stoping the bottoms, or at least stoping downwards between levels, but much of what can be seen was clearly back stoped. This emphasizes that stoping the lode in the bottoms was for economic rather than practical or technical reasons. Stoping the exposed lode at the bottom of the mine although inefficient in the medium and long-term, had the advantage of giving 'instant dirt'. The ore could be raised as soon as exposed and broken. Even in modern mines underhand stoping was sometimes resorted to because it gave quick dirt. Shrinkage stoping was more efficient and economical, but the mill had to wait for the stope to be finished before the bulk of the ore could be drawn out. This could take several months.[92]

The Bullen Garden section is of the workings, levels and shafts on Main ('Great') Lode, and at the deeper level particularly, the lode was divided into North and South branches. Two crosscuts or 'drifts' are shown at and above the deep haulage level, from South Branch to North Branch of Main Lode.

Access to the workings was by means of scores of ladders of varying lengths and set at a variety of angles. The tributers stoping the bottoms had a climb of 90 fathoms or 540 feet to their work places. Although ladder roads are only shown at Old Sump Shaft (surface to the bottom), Eastern Water Engine Shaft (surface to 44 fathoms deep) and two routes through worked-out stopes on the eastern and western sides of the mine, there would, undoubtedly, have been several other ladder roads in all parts of the mine.[93]

The three horse whims ('whyms') shown on the section all appeared to draw from the bottom haulage level, 86 fathoms from surface. Whim kibbles were larger than winze kibbles, but their capacity was still measured in hundred-weights rather than tons, so hoisting ore from the deeper workings was a long and slow process, attended by many mishaps and accidents. Pryce wrote that the larger kibbles would hold 120 gallons of water, so ore kibbles of a similar size could probably hold about 15cwt of ore. John Budge, one of Dolcoath's engineers, was to patent a new whim with a 'spiral cage', which was far more efficient than the whims in use when the Bullen Garden section was drawn.[94]

Pryce's section contained considerable detail on the pumping arrangements. Two

Newcomen engines were sited on Old Sump Shaft, one shown on the west side ('Old fire engine') and the other on the east side ('New fire engine'). As noted above, excavation preparatory to capping Old Sump Shaft in 1992 showed the engine house foundations on the north and south sides of the shaft, so their positions on the section are for clarity rather than accuracy. It is possible that the 'Old fire engine' was the 54-inch supplied by Coalbrookdale in 1753, and the 'New fire engine' could have been the 63-inch engine erected in 1768. Both engines pumped from the sump at the bottom of Old Sump Shaft, to Deep Adit level, and to the level 44 fathoms deep, from where the two water engines pumped some of the water to Deep Adit. The level below Deep Adit carried water to Old Dolcoath fire engine and the level below that carried water back to the Bullen Garden western water engine from Dolcoath. This level was still being driven.[95]

The 'Old fire engine' arrangement consisted of 'tye' pumps or lifts ('adit lift') at the highest elevation, up to Deep Adit, below them was the 'rose' lift, then the 'crown' lift, and at the bottom of the shaft above the sump was the 'lilly' lift. Each tier of pumps lifted the water to a cistern, from which it was lifted to the next cistern and so on up the shaft to Deep Adit. Half way up the shaft some of the water was carried along a level east and west to the water engines, which took it up to adit. There was a small pump to move the water from the rose cistern to the tye pumps. The newer engine's pump arrangement was the same as the old one. Two clack valves are shown for the old pumps and three for the newer pumps. The iron pump bore or diameter for the older pumps was 12½ inches, and for the new brass pumps, 11¼ inches.[96]

The water engines' various parts are shown on the section: the wheels (over 30 feet diameter), the bobs and cranks as well as the pump rods and the tye pumps, which carried the water from 44 fathoms to Deep Adit through eleven inch bore brass pumps, were all clearly illustrated and explained.

Like written descriptions of the mine which give us snapshots of how it worked and who was involved, Pryce's section, with his explanations, give a surprisingly clear and vivid picture of the mine at the time of New Dolcoath's creation. A tremendous amount can be learned about how the mine developed, how it operated and the sophisticated mining systems used at the time. Even the existence of such a detailed and well-drawn mine section tells us something of the mining skills and technical abilities of the management of New Dolcoath. The amalgamation of these Camborne mines in the middle of the 1760s brought about the largest copper mine in Cornwall, and probably the world. Nearly twenty years later, when Gwennap's United and Consolidated mines were formed, to be followed by the Great North Downs amalgamation, Dolcoath was rivalled for size, but for the first two decades of its life, New Dolcoath ruled supreme in Cornish copper mining.

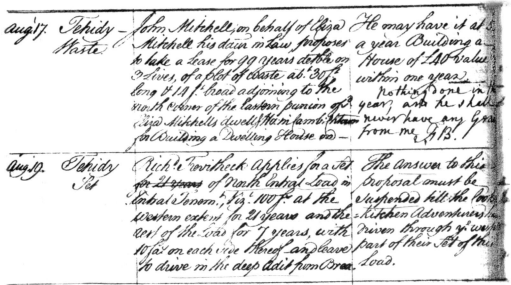

**Figure 30. Richard Trevithick senior's application to drive an adit
into North Entral, 1765.**

New Dolcoath Management (1771-1791)

There has been considerable speculation about the management of Dolcoath Mine during the last decades of the eighteenth century. Much of this has centred on the position of Richard Trevithick senior, the father of the great inventor of that name. Tom Harris, in his book *Dolcoath: Queen of Cornish Mines,* used six pay books for New Dolcoath, covering a large part of the period between April 1771 and August 1782, although there is a gap between November 1773 and June 1775. Professor Charles Thomas, in his excellent article in the Trevithick Society's *Journal*, used the pay book which covers the period October 1786 to February 1790. For obvious reasons different conclusions were reached.[97]

There is no certainty about the status of the most senior mine captain at Dolcoath, due to the common eighteenth century arrangement, where the purser was the senior man at Cornish cost book companies, and the captains were junior to him. However, Pryce indicates that sometimes the senior mine captain held the position of what became known as the mine manager, and this may have been the position at Dolcoath and the other large Basset dominated mines of the eighteenth century. Another difficulty is that men referred to in particular positions in contemporary accounts often shared the same name. For example in the Basset mine adjacent to Dolcoath, Cooks Kitchen, the three names which signed off the monthly accounts in the 1780s were all called John Vivian, and on some pages of the Dolcoath pay books for those years there were several Vivians and sometimes two or three John Vivians. Nicknames sometimes sorted out the differences for contemporaries, but they are not always of use to us. The simple rule applied by Harris and Thomas to sort this problem out has been to assign preeminence according to the order the names appear in the pay books.[98]

Using this reasonable rule the order of precedence in the management of Dolcoath during the twenty years between 1771 and 1791 can be fairly accurately worked out. Roger Vivian tops the list of mine captains in April 1771, with a monthly salary of £2 10s. He was assisted by three junior mine captains, Richard Vivian, John Vivian and Edmund Prideaux, each with a salary of £2 per month. In May the team was joined by William Thomas and this remained the position until October 1773, when there is a gap in the pay books. When they resume, in July 1775, the management team has changed somewhat. Roger Vivian remains at the helm, but Richard Vivian has been replaced by John Trevithick, older brother of Richard Trevithick senior, and John Vivian's monthly wage was reduced to £1. These men continued as named mine captains until May 1776, when Richard Trevithick senior joined them on a monthly salary of £2 5s. In June Richard Trevithick was still there but was paid 15s per month, as he was until July 1777. In August 1777 Richard Trevithick moved to the head of the list of mine captains, although his monthly wage was the same as the other captains, at £2. Roger Vivian was the only missing name, being replaced at the head of the list by Richard Trevithick, and John Vivian was paid £2 as were the other captains. Trevithick remained as the first name until April 1779, although in May John Vivian moved above him, before Trevithick resumed his preeminence in June. In December 1779 Charles Vivian appears to have been paid as a mine captain, although his name is recorded separately from the management team. This monthly wage of £2 became a regular payment to Charles Vivian, although it remained separate from the other captains in the pay books until May 1780, when he was included in the captain's list at the beginning of the month's accounts. Richard Trevithick remained at the head of the list of mine captains until the end of Pay Book DDX 475/4, in August 1782. This evidence indicates that Richard Trevithick senior indeed occupied the position of senior mine captain at Dolcoath for at least five years, although we cannot be certain that that position was exactly equivalent to the nineteenth century position of mine manager.[99]

The New Dolcoath pay book evidence is supplemented by other records, which show Richard Trevithick Senior as a principal negotiating agent for Dolcoath from at least the year 1765, when New Dolcoath came into existence. In August 1765, on behalf of New Dolcoath adventurers, he applied for a sett to drive on North Entral Lode from Cooks Kitchen Deep Adit, westward through Entral and Roskear. This application was turned down by the Basset agent until such time as Cooks Kitchen miners had driven on the lode at adit level to Tincroft in the east and Bullen Garden on the west. It was granted to New Dolcoath in Trevithick's name in March 1776. According to the two volumes of Richard Trevithick's accounts books (now missing) and dated September 1765 to September 1767 (Vol.1) and 1767-68 (vol.2), Trevithick directed the driving of Dolcoath New Deep Adit from old workings on Roskear Croft, to which an adit had been driven by an earlier generation, to Dolcoath Mine, well over a mile to the south. The second volume names the adventurers involved, who appear to be the same as at New Dolcoath. Basset held six-sixteenths, and the other ten adventurers held one-sixteenth each. They included Henry John junior, son of the founder of Dolcoath Mine, and an impressive list of local gentry and businessmen.[100]

The four-year gap in the Dolcoath pay books between August 1782 and October 1786 means we can only speculate on the management structure at that time, for when the pay books resume the team had changed considerably. In October 1786 the entries are headed by Edmund Prideaux followed by John Trevithick. Elsewhere, Richard Trevithick, Charles Vivian and John Vivian are included and paid at the captain's rate of £2 and all three are given the title 'Captain'. Prideaux remained in that position until July 1788, when he left the failing Dolcoath Mine, arriving in October at East Stray Park Mine, another Basset property. John Trevithick followed Prideaux to East Stray Park in February of the following year, and Richard Trevithick left Dolcoath in July 1788 and arrived at East Stray Park Mine in the October. All these moves have the appearance of transfers within one organization, rather than moves between different mines. It appears that by the late 1780s they were largely managed as a single group of Basset mines rather than as separate entities. Captains Charles and John Vivian remained at Dolcoath until September 1789, when they were mostly supervising the dressing and sale of copper from halvans off old burrows.[101]

Perhaps the last word on the position of Captain Richard Trevithick Senior should be left to Davies Gilbert. On 29 April 1839, he wrote to J. S. Ennys, to give an account of Richard Trevithick the inventor, whom he had first met in 1796, and with whom he formed a long and fruitful association and friendship. He wrote: "His father was the chief manager in Dolcoath Mine, and he bore the reputation of being the best informed and most skillful captain in all western mines … I knew the father very well." Gilbert's testimony cannot be ignored, for he was there at the time and knew the people involved well.[102]

Company Account Men
As well as the mine captains Dolcoath employed a large number of men with specialized skills on the 'company account'. These were men who were paid at a fixed rate, and this meant for the skilled supervisors a monthly salary, as with the captains, and for the rest an hourly or day rate, depending upon their skill and level of responsibility. Binders, pitmen, smiths, carpenters, enginemen and others were identified groups with special responsibilities and rates of pay. Without doubt one of the most important men on a mine was the chief or senior 'binder'. The binder

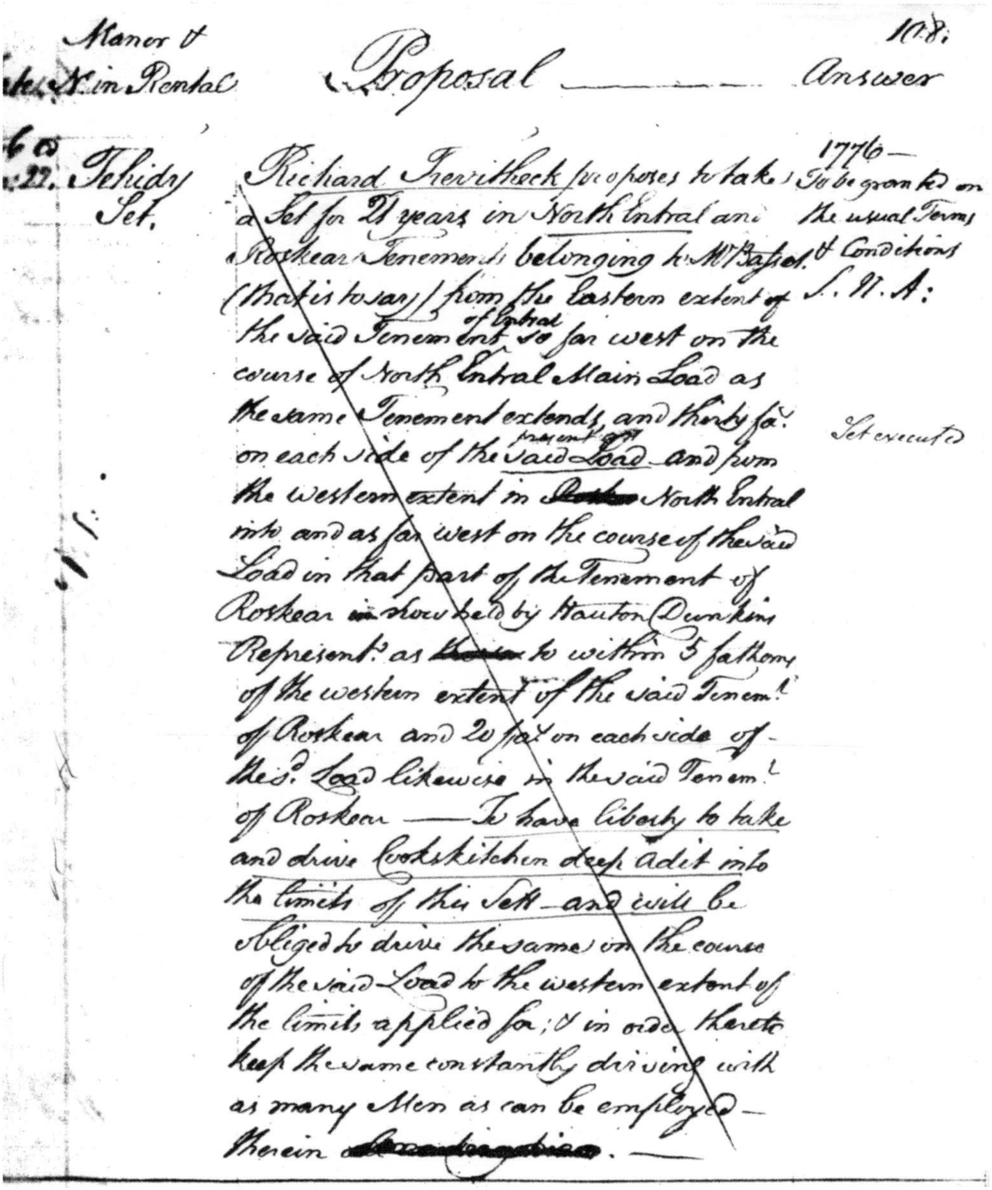

Figure 31. Basset's acceptance of Richard Trevithick senior's proposal to drive an adit on North Entral Lode, 1776.

was what became known in the nineteenth and twentieth centuries as the leading timberman. Timbermen were responsible for all support work in a mine, as well as fixing rearings, timber sets in shafts and making ladderways. Carew mentions this task in his admirably succinct description of the responsibilities of mine captains and others in sixteenth century Cornish tin mines. "The captain's office bindeth him to sort each workman his task, to see them apply their labour, to make timely provision for binding the work with frames of timber if need exact it." For most of the period covered by the New Dolcoath pay books the binders were paid more than the mine captains, although analysis of their pay over the period they feature in the records (April 1771 - October 1788) reveals an inconsistent picture. Very frequently these senior timbermen received pay suggestive of a regular monthly amount, but it appears clear that they also were paid overtime, as the figures at times fluctuate. The first entry, for April 1771, names Christopher Vivian and James Vivian immediately after the captains, and both have a salary of £2 6s 4d, whereas Robert Reed was paid £2 3s 4d and Richard Bennatts £2 1s 10d. It appears that the two senior men's monthly pay was £2 6s 4d, and the other two had a normal wage of £2 1s 10d, because the next month Christopher Vivian received £2 6s 4d, James was paid 3s more and the other two were paid £2 1s 10d. If this was the normal monthly pay for these named binders we can appreciate their relative importance to the mine. Christopher Vivian remained the timberboss until at least October 1773, but when the pay books resume in July 1775, after a gap, James Vivian heads the list of binders, as he does until the mine ceased underground work in (or about) July 1788. Other named binders in the team were John Vivian, who joined in July 1775, and remained for a couple of years, William Thomas, Nicholas Mean, Richard Prideaux, Joseph Knight and Henry Rabling. James Vivian, Richard Prideaux and Joseph Knight remained until work stopped underground at Dolcoath, and some moved to East Stray Park Mine. There were no binders employed at New Dolcoath Mine after July 1788.[103]

A slight mystery surrounds the small army of men needed to assist these timbermen in shifting the often enormous timbers between the shafts and areas to be supported. There was no track in Dolcoath until well into the nineteenth century, and so the great stull pieces and other timbers needed to be manhandled to their destinations by groups of strong men. These groups of men do not appear as separate gangs in the pay books, and the wages received by the timbermen were sufficient for them, not for any assistants. It may be that men were taken from their normal jobs to assist when large tasks needed extra hands, and that these were paid by 'stem'. This would account for the fact that no separate group of underground workers appear in the pay books. Tutworkers and tributers were often paid 'stems' for time spent outside their contracts or normal work, as were other workers, and as with South Crofty and Geevor in the twentieth century, miners of all sorts would be called upon at such times to give a hand and be paid by 'stem'. A stem was a day's work outside ones usual occupation, and which was paid separately. One stem was a shift and a double stem or 'doubler' was a shift plus six hours.[104]

When we reflect upon the great width of Dolcoath Main Lode and the enormous timber stulls needed to support the hanging wall, we can appreciate the skills needed by a binder. Recent exploration of parts of Dolcoath and Bullen Garden has revealed timbers which have remained in position, still supporting, to some extent, those ancient excavations.

The second group of 'company account' men listed were the pitmen, who were responsible for all work on the pumps beneath the collar. They had to ensure that the pitwork of the pumps, whether it be for suction pumps, with all of the complications attendant, or the heavy and cumbersome, but relatively simple, plunger pump pitwork was working efficiently, with as little friction as possible. During the 1770s and '80s the pumps at Dolcoath were suction pumps, with water engines still operating alongside Newcomen engines and then Watt engines. As mines became deeper and engine shafts or sump shafts were sunk to the bottom of the deepest parts of the mine, so the task became technically and logistically more difficult. Operating from the many hundreds of feet of ladderway from which the pitmen worked made the tasks of installing, checking and maintaining the rising mains, and the pump working pieces a nightmare. By the end of the century plunger pumps with rods extending down the length of the shaft came into use. Norwegian pine, sometimes twenty-inches square, in twenty-foot lengths and more, had to be moved through the shafts without damage. Most of the shafts followed the dip of the lode after the first hundred or two hundred feet and so the difficulties multiplied. Dolly wheels, fend-off angles and other ingenious pieces of equipment were invented, modified and installed to keep the whole cumbersome arrangement working with as little friction and as much efficiency as possible. Sometimes the shaft turned over and followed another dip, perhaps going from north to south, and then the whole business became very complicated. Palmers Shaft, at South Wheal Crofty, had, according to Jack Trounson, no less than fourteen changes in angle or direction between Deep Adit and 272 fathom level. This extreme nineteenth century example illustrates the skills required by those Dolcoath pitmen of the 1770s and '80s.[105]

The New Dolcoath pitmen of April 1771 included a famous name. Arthur Woolf's name appears first, being paid £2 9s 10d, followed by Francis Vivian at £2 4s 10d and the third was John Woolf who was paid £2 4s 10d. Arthur Woolf may have been the father of the great engineer of that name, who rose to fame in the early nineteenth century as the most prominent steam engineer in Cornwall, working as chief engineer at John Taylor's mines in Gwennap, although another Arthur Woolf, described on the same page of the pay book as 'Engineman', appears to have a better claim to have fathered the famous engineer.[106]

Until the mine ceased underground operations in the summer of 1788 pitmen continued to be employed maintaining the pumps. Arthur Woolf disappeared from the pitmen list after a while, but Francis Vivian remained till almost the end, and appears to have been senior pitman by 1780. The number of pitmen listed varies, with four employed in April 1776 and five early in 1777. This remained the number for most of the 1770s and 1780s, with occasional decreases to four or increases when installation of new pitwork was needed: for example, in October 1786, seven pitmen were listed, at a total cost to the mine in wages of £13 15s 10d. One of their number, Henry Knight, was killed in an accident in January 1787. We know nothing of the circumstances of the fatal accident, other than that his widow was paid £2 3s as compensation by the mine adventurers, and that the Bassets, as mineral lords, also contributed to a 'Subscription' or collection for the widow, Jane, and her family, starting the ball rolling with £2 2s. It is of slight interest that the normal fatal accident payment by the adventurers to widows was £2 2s. Why Knight's widow was given an extra shilling is a mystery, as is the reason for the Bassets organizing a collection. The pitmen and timbermen were paid a bonus every midsummer for a drink on the mine. These payments could vary from 7s to 8s and were paid in June, July or August.[107]

A group of 'company account' men who assisted the pitmen, not only with installation of pitwork and maintenance, but also in occasionally sinking the engine shafts, were the sumpmen. In the April 1771 pay book ten sumpmen are listed, earning varying amounts of money. Richard Wilkin headed the list on £1 1s 10d, followed by William Saunders and William Warrin on £1 3s 10d, William Dunstone on £1 4s 10d and William Hodge and Henry Vivian on £1 3s 10d. The next three named, Charles Vivian, William Jewell and Samuel Williams all earned a few shillings as casual assistants. The last sumpman named, Nicholas Hocking, earned £1 5s 10d. Charles Vivian appears to have been the man killed in June 1778 in an underground accident. It appears from the above that a sumpman's monthly wage was £1 3s 10d, and that those a shilling above or two-shillings below were either spaled for absenteeism or paid for an extra shift. The average month's work was, apparently, 24 days, so if 23s 10d was the normal monthly pay, after the deduction of the doctor's 2d, which every underground worker paid, a sumpman was paid 1s a day.[108]

Engines, Engineers & Enginemen
New Dolcoath pay books begin in April 1771 with references to Messers Wise & Budge, engineers who jointly received £12 12s for the month, John Budge being paid an extra 15s for added services. During 1771 it appears that Wise and Budge erected a 70-inch engine at Dolcoath, for in June Coalbrookdale were paid £201 10s for engine parts, in July Wheal Weeth adventurers were paid £80 for engine parts, probably including the moorstone boiler (see below), and in December North Downs Mine was paid £139 18s 4d, also apparently for engine parts. These could have been parts for the 70-inch engine referred to by Watt in 1780, as one of the three engines on Dolcoath. There were eight enginemen (engine drivers) on the books, each of whom received £2 4s 10d for the month. Whether these enginemen were concerned with

operating the water engines as well as the steam engines cannot be determined, but it seems likely, for John Budge certainly supervised the erection of a water engine at Cooks Kitchen Mine, in October 1786. There were at least three Newcomen engines on the mine at the time, two being on Old Sump Shaft, Bullen Garden section. The long section reproduced in Pryce in 1778, which appears to show the workings as they were in about 1770 shows, for clarity, these two engines on the east and west sides of Old Sump Shaft, but when the shaft was capped in the early 1990s, the foundations of these Newcomen engines were clearly seen on the north and south sides of the shaft. These were probably the 54-inch supplied by Coalbrookdale in 1753 and 63-inch supplied by the same firm in 1767-68. It is possible that the old 40-inch Newcomen was still operating at Old Dolcoath in 1771. There were also the water engines pumping from shafts to the east and west of Old Sump Shaft. At the head of the enginemen on the pay book list were William George and Arthur Woolf, followed by Robert Vial, Nicholas Mean, George Paull, Henry Hocking, Matthew George and Peter Budge. They were served by eight coalmen or stokers, who earned varying amounts between £2 2s 10d and 17s 2d. As these were not underground workers it seems that they had no need to contribute 2d to the doctor, but it does seem that with the enginemen's monthly rate for 24 days at £2 4s 10d, that they were in fact paid 1s 10½d a day and had the doctor's 2d deducted. The coalmen also appear to have had the doctor's 2d deducted, as their normal rate was £1 9s 10d for 24 days, suggesting that £1 10s was their months pay before the deduction, which would give them 1s 3d a day.[109]

The number of engine drivers and stokers rose and fell during the next seventeen years, but there were rarely less than eight drivers and a similar number of coalmen. In December 1777 there were ten enginemen, and these went up to twelve in April 1778, before settling down to a more normal eight or nine thereafter. In October 1786 the number again rose to twelve, but by the summer of 1788 all pumps had stopped. Arthur Woolf, father of the great engineer, was listed as an engineman throughout that period.[110]

John Budge was paid throughout those years from 1771 to 1788 as an engineer, although until December 1771 he worked with John Wise in that position. Between September 1772 and September 1773 Dolcoath paid John Budge a total of £78 15s, which made him a very highly paid employee. Between January 1776 and August 1780 he received a regular £5 5s a month, with extra for extra work. Between October 1786 and October 1787, with the mine in serious decline due to the attack from cheap Anglesey copper ore, Budge's monthly rate was cut to £4 4s. He had trained as an engineer at Dolcoath under the tutelage of George John, and a letter dated 14 December 1766 tells us something of his background and training. It concerns his appointment to erect a new fire engine at Dolcoath, and although it appears to come from Francis Basset, it is unsigned: Budge was to erect "a New fire-engine not less than 40-inches at Bullengarden. 'Tis computed that the engine so as resolved on will cost £2200 and the engineer which they have agreed to employ proposes that she shall be at work by Midsummer next. This engineer is Mr John Budge who acquired his experience under Mr George John and he is thought a very capable person, but … I told them that I thought if you acquiesced in the erecting the engine, he ought to give security for the effectual performance and more especially as he never finished an engine but under the direction of Mr George John." Budge thereafter became the principal engineer at Dolcoath and went on to acquire a distinguished reputation as a steam engineer.[111]

John Budge was born at Camborne in 1733 and first appears in the mine records in December 1766, in the above letter concerning the contract to erect an engine at Dolcoath. He was then 33 years old and was an engineer in his own right, despite Basset's reservations about his competence. Whether he had served a formal apprenticeship with George John, we do not know, but his training must have been thorough because he became the foremost engine erector and steam engineer in the principal mining district of Cornwall by the 1770s. He was chief engineer at New Dolcoath throughout the period of its existence, and was responsible for erecting and maintaining the mine engines over the period from 1767 to 1788 when underground operations had ceased. After his period with George John, Budge partnered John Wise at Dolcoath, and together they were responsible for the engines until the end of 1771, when Wise disappears from the pay book record. During 1771 they supervised the erection of the 63-inch Newcomen engine at Dolcoath, and in the same year Budge showed that he was not merely a skilled artisan, when he patented a 'spiral cage', which made the horse whim far more efficient, and was only superseded in mine hoisting by the introduction of Trevithick's steam winder, the puffer engine. By the following year Budge's new 'machine for drawing the Work from the Mine to surface' was being advertised in the *Sherborne Mercury*. The advertisement stated: "The advantage gained from this Machine when put in competition with others now in use for the same purpose, is very considerable, as is proved from one now at work in Dolcoath Mine (which is one of the deepest mines in England) one third of the expense in horses being taken off, it dispatches the work from the Mine much quicker and is attended with less danger to the horses and drivers in case of accidents happening by the ropes breaking; several more of these Machines are erecting in the same Mine." Budge also redesigned the pitwork in the shafts, introducing better clack valves, bucket and joints and his brasswork was of a high quality. Watt wrote that he was keen to learn of Budge's 'inventions and whether he had made any experiments lately'. Watt believed that Budge's new haystack boiler was of better design than Hornblowers.[112]

According to Tom Harris, some of the most efficient atmospheric engines in Cornwall were erected by John Budge. Wheal Chance engine, erected by Budge, was considered one of the best of its type in Cornwall, and was used as the standard against which the performance of Watt's engines were compared. Skeptical about the efficiency of the Watt engine, Budge visited the Birmingham Soho Works to inspect it, but remained unconvinced about the superiority of the engines for some time. When Watt visited Cornwall he examined a number of engines erected by Budge, including a 60-inch, 63-inch and a 70-inch, the performances of which he reported to Boulton. Harris mentions two Newcomen engines erected over the same shaft and lifting the water by 'shammelling', *i.e.* one lifting it to a cistern and the other bringing to adit level. Pryce's illustration of Bullen Garden section of Dolcoath shows two Newcomen engines on Old Sump Shaft, and the 'old' and 'new' pumps shammelling the water to the level which carried it to the water engines, on the east and west. They also carried water up to adit level. By 1779 Budge was collaborating with Boulton and Watt by erecting Watt engines at Pool Adit, Wheal Chance and Dolcoath. One of his boilers was used with the engine at Pool.[113]

After the death of George and William John, the latter's widow, Mary, took over Tuckingmill (Dolcoath) Foundry, but thereafter Budge became proprietor. Budge was visiting engineer to several mines in west Cornwall, and although his interest was mostly in steam, as chief engineer at Dolcoath, he also was responsible for the water engines and horse whims, which he improved and modified.[114]

John Budge was a highly respected Camborne man, friend of Richard Trevithick senior and a great influence on Richard junior, who appears to have spent much of his youth in Budge's company, not only as his assistant, but also as his enthusiastic disciple. His position as chief engineer at Dolcoath, consultant engineer, engine erector, and visiting engineer at several mines, as well as his foundry business at Tuckingmill, made him a wealthy man. When he died at the age of 90, in July 1823, he left a legacy of affection among his Camborne neighbours, who regarded him as a generous and charitable Christian, a devoted Wesleyan Methodist.[115]

When the pay books resume in October 1786, after a gap of over four years, Richard Trevithick junior's name appears. He seems to have been working as an assistant engineer under the tutelage of Budge, and although only fifteen years old, he was paid £1 4s a month, or 1s a day. In the following June, after his sixteenth birthday, his rate rose to £1 6s a month, or 1s 1d a day. Young Trevithick remained at Dolcoath until May 1789, by which time his father and most of the captains had gone to East Stray Park Mine.[116]

John Wise worked as an engineer at Dolcoath from at least 1755, when he took possession of some Newcomen engine parts on behalf of the mine. Subsequently, Wise worked jointly with Budge until the end of 1771, when he disappeared from the Dolcoath accounts.[117]

There is no breakdown of engineering expenses beyond the individual wages, but Vivian, Heyward & Hawkins, the Cornish Copper Company, who were suppliers of all sorts of merchandise including engineering gear, were paid £125 14s 8d for two months' supplies. It seems likely that much or most of this was for coal for the engines, although there was usually timber supplied by them also. Tuckingmill Foundry, under William John, son of George John, was paid £6 1s 8d for engineering supplies or services. William appears to have been running Tuckingmill (Dolcoath) Foundry from 1766 until September 1773, by which time he had apparently become incapacitated, for in the October accounts (Dolcoath pay book) there is a reference to the 'Administrators of William John' being paid £21 5s 7d, which followed reference to another £30 being paid to him. William died in January 1774. Between October 1773 and July 1775 there is a gap in the pay books, but when they resume, payments to Tuckingmill Foundry were to Mary John, widow of William. Thereafter payments were to 'Mrs Mary John', 'Mary John' or 'Mary John & Co.'. There were regular payments also to the administrators of William John. William died in January 1774.[118]

Payments made by New Dolcoath for items which appear to be related to engines and engineering are found throughout the 1771-88 pay books. Apart from payments to the Cornish Copper Company, under a variety of names (Vivian, Heyward & Hawkins; Basset, Vivian & Co.; Basset & Co.; Basset, Vivian & Michell; Warwick, Jenkin & Vivian) and those to Tuckingmill Foundry there were also regular payments to John Vivian of Hayle, Thomas Daniell (boiler parts, etc) and Fox, Philips & Fox, merchants of Falmouth and Penryn. There were some large quantities of iron purchased at various times by the mine, with £218 spent at Falmouth in November 1780, and another £52 paid for iron and deal at Penryn in the same month. Some of this may have been for engineering, but undoubtedly most would have been for smiths' work.[119]

The large number of mines which sold items (often expensive) to New Dolcoath also indicates a mine with a growing demand for gear of all sorts. In the years between 1771 and 1782 no less than sixteen mines sold gear and machinery to New Dolcoath, the sums ranging from £210 to Wheal Maiden (June 1780) and £140 to North Downs (December 1771) down to £5 11s to Kestel Adit adventurers (October 1773) and £10 to the adventurers of West Wheal Virgin (June 1780). The mine paid £130 7s 3d in three payments to Carloose Mine for a 45-inch cylinder pumping engine between July 1775 and March 1776. There may have been earlier payments, but there is almost a two-year gap in the pay books before July 1775. Other payments were made to Weeth Mine (£80), Wheal Fortune (£82), Treleigh Wood (£65), Wheal Rosewarne & Gerry (£78), Wheal Virgin (£25), Higher Rosewarne (£33), Wheal Prosper (£44), Pool Adit (£46), North Entral (£20) and Chacewater Mine (£95). These payments amounted to well over £1000, and all for second-hand gear.[120]

The payment to Wheal Weeth of £80 included the purchase of a 'moorstone' boiler. Sampson Swaine, the man who introduced copper smelting to Rosewarne Downs and Dolcoath in the 1740s and '50s, invented apparatus for conserving and re-using waste heat from an engine boiler. Part of his Wheal Weeth construction included a 'moorstone' boiler, which was moved to Dolcoath and re-used in July 1771. It appears to have been used at the Entral furnace, which produced copper regulus in the early 1770s. This moorstone boiler is often referred to as 'Arthur Woolf's Moorstone Boiler' and researches by Maurice Gregory and others point to the Dolcoath engineman, father of the famous engineer of the same name, being responsible for its erection at Entral. The boiler, parts of which can still be seen at Taylors Shaft, Pool, is believed to have supplied steam for a Newcomen engine at Dolcoath.[121]

Supplies of new machinery also accounted for large sums of money. Coalbrookdale, the original nursery of the English industrial revolution, provided a large part of the essential machinery for Dolcoath. During the years of New Dolcoath, covered by the extant pay books (which included bills paid), four payments are recorded to Coalbrookdale for engine parts, totaling £340 2s 7d. Two of these payments were to John Jones & Co. of Bristol, who supplied Coalbrookdale machinery. The four payments were made in June 1771 (£201 10s), September 1771 (£44 19s 7d), January 1772 (£21 16s 1d) and January 1778 (£69 16s 11d).[122]

In 1779 John Smeaton carried out a study of Newcomen engines then at work in Cornwall, and among those he described were three atmospheric engines at Dolcoath. Smeaton produced a table, which reviewed the performance of fifteen engines, giving various details on each one, by which to judge their relative performances. The Dolcoath engines were a 60-inch, pumping from a depth of 42 fathoms below adit; a 63-inch, drawing from 63 fathoms below adit, and a 70-inch which pumped from 71 fathoms below Deep Adit. This put Dolcoath's sump at a depth of some 100 fathoms from surface, some ten fathoms below the sump shown on the section drawn some ten years before.[123]

Eleven payments to Messers Boulton and Watt for coal savings and engine parts were recorded between September 1780 and July 1782, and totaled £867 6s 9d. The highest recorded figure was for £161 18s, and was the first payment, in September 1780, and appears to have been for engine parts, as was the £45 19s 7d in April 1781. The nine months between November 1781 and July 1782 all recorded payments for coal savings, which averaged just over £73 a month. There are no references to Boulton and Watt thereafter, as there is a four year gap in the pay books until October 1786. There was a payment of £10 10s to William Murdoch in January 1781, presumably for engineering work done on the 63-inch Watt engine then being erected at Dolcoath.[124]

James Watt's involvement with Dolcoath was an inevitable consequence of the increasing cost of keeping the mine dry. By 1780 the mine was already 140 fathoms (some 840 feet) deep, nearly twice the depth of old Dolcoath just twenty-six years before. The interested and observant Watt had written to Boulton in 1778: "Nothing can save the mines but our engines … even the infidels of Dolcoath are now obliquely inquiring after our terms! Cooks Kitchen, which communicates with it, has been drowned out some time." The calculating Watt had even worked out the size of the engine Dolcoath needed to replace her existing Newcomen engines and cope with her own and Cooks Kitchen's water. The mine's coal costs had increased dramatically between 1777 and 1779, probably doubling, and as a consequence the need for more efficient and economical engines was urgent. In 1777, recognizing the impending crisis, the executors of Francis Basset's estate had agreed to pay £500 toward the cost of a new 'fire engine' at Dolcoath. Cooks Kitchen adventurers had also agreed to pay the same sum to Dolcoath. "1777. By Dolcoath Advrs towards the Charges of Erecting the last Fire Engine & which was agreed on to be paid them in Consideration of, and as an inducement to Erect the same without which and the like sum contributed by Cooks Kitchen Advrs the Mine must have been stopt as must likewise the West part of Cooks Kitchen Mine." It was to be the 63-inch Watt engine erected during 1780 and 1781 that saved the mine. The June 1781 cost book for Cooks Kitchen refers to this 1777 agreement: "Dolcoath Advrs the proportion fixed by Sir Francis Basset to be paid by this Advr towards the Expence of the Fire Engine men erecting at the Mine - £500." In March 1782 Cooks cost book refers to the monthly expense of this engine as £200, and thereafter there were several payments made for the engine expense (coal, maintenance, etc). The amount Cooks Kitchen contributed was related to income from ore sold, with Dolcoath's and Cooks' income being taken into account. For example, in September 1782 account for the three months of April, May and June, Dolcoath sold £7,093 worth of copper ore, and Cooks Kitchen sold £2,526 worth. This meant that Cooks paid £157 11s 9d toward the cost of Dolcoath's engine.[125]

Cooks Kitchen Payments for Dolcoath's Watt Engine[126]

June 1781: Toward cost of erection of engine	=	£500
March 1782: June 30-Dec 31 (6 months)	=	£1,266 13s 4d
Sept 1782: Mar 31-June 30 (3 months)	=	£157 11s 9d
Dec 1782: June 30-Sept 30 (3 months)	=	£99 14s 1d
Feb 1783: Sept 30-Feb 28 (5 months)	=	£134 12s 3d
Sept 1783: Feb 28-June 30 (4 months)	=	£74 15s 8d
June 1784: June 30-Mar 31 (9 months)	=	£215 7s 3d
Jan 1785: Mar 31-Sept 30 (6 months)	=	£107 4s 7d

It had been in May 1780 that Watt had written to John Wilkinson that Dolcoath would soon order an engine, and suggested that he proceed with the manufacture of an appropriate cylinder. There was slight concern that Dolcoath might buy a second-hand engine from Wheal Union, but Watt remained confident. Later in May John Turner of Bersham was instructed by Watt to "put in hand withall diligence a 63-inch cylinder for Dolcoath Mine, owner Sir Francis Basset & Co., and correspondents Mr Thomas Kevill, Camborne, near Redruth, or Mr John Vivian cashier to the mine." Watt warned against shoddy or careless workmanship, as it was important that the engine was perfect, as it was going "into the heart of the enemies country, into a perfect nest of unbelievers and traducers." He reminded the founders of the criticism the engines received after imperfections were found in the Wheal Chance cylinder. Before the end of May Dolcoath's adventurers had ordered the engine and Watt had promised to deliver within two months – Watt even diverted parts from other orders to Dolcoath. Two drawings of the engine house were then sent to Thomas Kevill, and in June he received drawings of the "general section of Dolcoath Engine", followed by instructions to John Budge to arrange the layout and position of the boiler house. The June 1780 Pay Book records that John Wilkinson was paid £470 19 5d for the cylinder and in July another £6 15 6d was paid for 'bringing home the cylinder'. The full payments to Boulton and Watt based upon a third of the savings on coal are given in the following table.[127]

Table of Payments to Boulton and Watt[128]

Year	Paid	Rebated	Bushels Saved
1781	£176		16,994
1782	£876		72,800
1783	£751		66,673
1784	£680		63,152
1785	£646		60,728
1786	£743		45,478
1787	£702	£110	47,868
1788	nil	£315	29,638

During 1781 James Watt introduced into Dolcoath apparatus for stopping an engine if there was an accidental breakage at high speed. The new gear took away the power and held the beam fast. He also made various significant modifications to his engine at Dolcoath. In 1783 Watt designed a new steam whim for the mine. It had an 18-inch cylinder, was single-acting and had a fifteen foot diameter cage, which incorporated Budge's newly invented spiral drum. This whim could draw efficiently from a depth of 160 fathoms. The whim was not erected at Dolcoath however, as the mine was experiencing problems due to the price of copper, and in July 1784 it was erected at Wheal Maid. It did eventually go to Dolcoath, after the mine reopened in 1799. In

May 1783 Watt wrote about the economic problems that Dolcoath faced, including the difficulties of drawing ore from such great depths: "In Dolcoath £500 per month is spent in timber. A new kibble rope of a ton weight is worn out in a fortnight, and it takes fully 15 minutes to draw a kibble of ore (3cwt), owing to the great depth of the mine." He then adds the inevitable comment: "Had we not furnished them with the means of drawing water, almost all the deep mines would have been abandoned."[129]

Steam Engines at Dolcoath

1. July-September 1746.
   Newcomen 40-inch. Engine cost £366. 1748 parts supplied to John Freeman & Co (Smelters & Adventurers); 1750 parts via John Jones & C. Bristol engineers; 1752 parts supplied to Wm Churchill & Co.(adventurers) Sited at Old Dolcoath. This engine was referred to by Angerstein in 1754.

2. February 1753.
   Newcomen 54-inch. Coalbrookdale supplied new engine to Wm Churchill. £194; July 1753- October 1755 engine parts via John Jones of Bristol. John Wise Dolcoath engineer.

3. March-June 1768.
   Newcomen 63-inch. Coalbrookdale supplied new engine to Francis Bassett & Co. of Tehidy (principal adventurer) for £858 including some pitwork

4. Summer 1771.
   Newcomen 70-inch. Erected by Wise and Budge, probably at Bullen Garden.

5. July 1775-March 1776. Mentioned by Smeaton in 1779.
   Newcomen 45-inch. Second-hand engine bought from Carloose Mine for £414, total cost estimated at £2,000.

6. 1779
   60-inch Newcomen. Mentioned by Smeaton in 1779 and Watt in 1780.
   7 June 1780-August 1781.
   Watt 63-inch engine erected at Dolcoath by John Budge. Supplied to Sir Francis Basset & Co., Thomas Kevill & John Vivian, cashier.

Smeaton's list of 1779 gives a 60-inch, 63-inch and a 70-inch engine at Dolcoath.[130]

Coal Boats & Carriers

As steam engine use in Cornish mines increased, the cost and regular, reliable supply of coal became major problems. The original Newcomen engines at Dolcoath were extremely heavy on coal, and the introduction of the far more efficient Watt engine became an economic necessity. It has been estimated that in 1760, coal, which cost about 4s a ton at the Welsh pithead, cost something like 15s a ton at Portreath and Hayle. Two entries in the New Dolcoath Pay Books for the months July 1781 and

June 1782, recorded the inflated prices paid by the mine at that time. The 1781 entry has 322 tons at £2 12s a ton and the 1782 entry gives 281 tons at £3 3s a ton. Perhaps threats to coastal shipping from French and Spanish warships and privateers were to blame, for they were fraught times, with Britain up against half of Europe as well as the rebelling American colonies. Clive Carter has said that French privateers would not try to capture coal boats, but would just sink them. A typical Newcomen engine of 47-inch cylinder could use between 1,500 and 2,000 tons of Welsh coal a year, and a 70-inch engine as much as 3,000 tons. Watt offered to reduce the tonnage of coal used by Cornish mines and hence solve at least one of the above problems; the cost of fuel. The problem of regular, reliable supply, both by sea to Portreath and Hayle, and by land, from port to mine, was not to be so easily overcome.[131]

Most of Dolcoath's coal came via Portreath, which lies just three-and-a-half miles from the mine, with Hayle, at a distance of some six miles, being an important alternative route. In April 1771 ten coal boats of the so-called 'Welsh fleet' brought in a total of £641 worth of coal to Portreath for Dolcoath. Five of these boats made just one round trip in April, four made two trips, and one, the *John*, captained by Chauncey Howell (twice) and John Lake (once) brought in three loads of coal. The average value per coal cargo was £40, with the *John* averaging £47 per trip and the *Prince George* just £30. The *Dispatch* carried the smallest cargo with a value of just £25 12s 10d. Although known as the 'Welsh fleet' most of these boats were based at Portreath and Hayle and locally owned.[132]

Analysis of the cargos between April 1771 and July 1782 show that in the months of December to March there was an average of 1.4 cargos, with many winter months having no sailings at all, whereas in the months April to July the average number of coal boats making deliveries to Portreath was 11.8, and the highest total was 32 cargos in May 1773. Weather was of course the reason for such seasonal variation in coal supply, Portreath being difficult to enter safely in bad weather and an on-shore wind. Even in summer the narrow entrance to the harbour could be treacherous. Wind and tide permitting, Hayle could be an alternative landfall to weatherbound Portreath. Hence, much of Dolcoath's coal supply came via the relatively distant coal yards at Copperhouse and Hayle.[133]

Dolcoath Pay Books (including merchants' bills) do not differentiate between what was supplied to the mine by the Cornish Copper Company, so what proportion of a bill was for coal we cannot tell. The CCC supplied Dolcoath with tools, machinery, timber, iron, brass as well as coal. For nine complete years, between 1771 and 1782 (there is a gap in the record) CCC's bills came to £11,745, an average of £1,305 a year, or £109 a month, which was a substantial amount. The occasional references in the pay books to the cost of 'Carriage of coal from Hayle' (*i.e.* March 1773 £65 2s 1d; May 1773 £71 9s 10d) does suggest that significant coal supplies went to

Dolcoath from that port.[134]

Dolcoath Coal Boats to Portreath (April 1771)[135]

Prosperous John Fosse	£45 6 7
Dispatch Thomas Williams	£25 12 10
William David Pearce	£34 3 9
Industry William John	£39 10 0
Peggy Thomas Jones	£30 6 9
Mary John Brown	£50 19 9
John Chauncey Howell	£45 7 10
Prince George William Beddoe	£28 19 11
William William Courtney	£38 10 2
John John Lake	£47 15 7
Venus Benjamin Berryman	£43 19 9
Johns Adventurer Robert Landerson	£48 8 4
John Chauncey Howell	£47 5 9
Mary John Brown	£47 18 9
Industry William John	£36 3 9
Prince George William Beddoe	£30 10 2
Total	**£640 19 8**

As with the coal boats so with the coal carriers the pay books are informative. Taking the records between August 1771 and August 1782, we find that an average of twenty carriers a month were employed. The highest number was 31 and the lowest thirteen. Most of the carrier contractors were men, but an average of ten percent were women, with up to three mule trains owned and operated by female carriers. A typical record of coal supply is illustrated by the three months June, July and August 1772; 46 cargos were unloaded at Portreath for Dolcoath, worth a total of £1,643 14s 6d. The cost of carriage of this coal to Dolcoath was £410 2s 4d, or a fifth (20 percent) of the total cost to the mine of £2,053 16s 10d.[136]

The difficulty of driving strings of heavily laden mules up the hill from Portreath and across open country with only deeply rutted and churned up tracks, which were almost impassible in winter, cannot be exaggerated. Each mule carried about three hundredweight of coal, in two panniers, one on each side of its back. It is estimated that up to a thousand mules worked out of Portreath by the end of the eighteenth century. Although the route was undoubtedly easier, the distance from Copperhouse was considerably longer than from Portreath, and so the mule trains bringing coal during bad weather, when Portreath was closed, was an extra financial burden on the mine's adventurers.

Coal Carriers from Portreath to Dolcoath (May-August 1771)[137]

Arthur Fox	£58 4 4
Wm Williams	£23 9 6
John Smith	£17 5 8
Catherine Paull	£8 10 8
Wm Mill	£10 15 0
John Rosewarne	£38 2 4
Andrew Paull	£12 19 2
Richard Lanyon	£8 11 8
Henry Clark	£9 0 0
John Eva	£19 1 8
Wm Murley	£12 0 8
Ambrose Blackwell	£34 17 0
Robert Stickland	£12 9 6
John James	£5 3 6
Chris. Hendra Jun	£27 17 4
John Hall	£29 12 0
Roger Cock	£3 19 8
Thom. Huthnance	£6 6 0
Wm Skewis	£16 7 4
Paul Michell	£3 16 2
Chris. Hendra	£22 18 0
Total	**£381 7 2**

Tributers & Tutworkers

Among the areas of confusion with writers on Cornish mining history concerns the roles of tributers and tutworkers. The single-sentence glossary definitions have done little to help and a couple of generations of writers and researchers have failed to understand an irregular and sometimes complicated series of arrangements between mine management and miner. Obscure and usually inaccurate attempts to find the origins of such words as 'tut' in tutwork, even attributed to the German word 'tod', have not helped the cause of clarity. The simple definition is that tutworker was paid by the 'piece'. 'Tut' is an old West of England dialect word for 'piece', as in a 'pieceworker'. A tutworker, and contract sheets at South Crofty until the 1970s still used the term, was paid by how much ground he had broken during the period of his contract. Usually, but certainly not always, a tutworker or pieceworker carried out development work: either sinking a shaft or winze ('wins'/'winds'), driving a lode or crosscutting. He was also employed to raise ('rise') between levels, and, in more recent times, to drive sub-levels or intermediate levels ('inters'). He would also carry out such work as mining out shaft stations, mining ore passes or excavating for a score of other reasons to do with mining. Very frequently at Dolcoath and other eighteenth century Cornish mines, tutworkers also carried out stoping of either the bottom or the back of the lode. Sometimes the mine captain would contract for the tutworker to drive on lode for a certain distance at a set price per fathom, and when that distance was achieved the price might be altered, usually downward, for the rest of the contract period. Tutwork contracts at Dolcoath were invariably for one month. Sometimes, especially where development was urgent, as with bringing home an adit, the miners would be encouraged to make all speed and break as much ground as possible during the contract period. The price per fathom would then remain fixed for the month's contract. The tutwork contractor would pay for all smith work (such as sharpening his drill steels ('borers') and poll picks), candles and black powder for blasting. Pryce commented that a good labouring man should be able to clear 30s a month on tutwork. Presumably, he did not mean the tutwork contractor, but the miners who worked under him.[138]

Analysis of the tutworkers contracts for the period at Cooks Kitchen, where the mine was similarly owned and managed, and the ground conditions were much the same, helps us to understand the probable situation at New Dolcoath. The tutwork contracts for 1781 reveal that on average tutworkers driving an end received £6 12s per fathom and had an average of 4.2 men in an end. Presumably, three men did the drilling and one wheelbarrowed the broken ore back to the shaft or hoisting platt. Most of these tutworkers also did other work, such as stoping. They were charged for smith's work as well as candles and powder.[139]

It is difficult to ascertain the earnings of individual miners, because the tutwork contractor would earn more than his men, and the skilled adult miner would earn more than the 'boy', who might be no more than eleven or twelve years old. However, it is helpful to look at some of the earnings of tutwork contractors, even if it is only to appreciate their wide variation of earnings. Examples from Cooks Kitchen in 1781 illustrate this, Charles Chaple and partners were sinking and stoping the Western Bottoms on Brea Lode (the eastern extension of Dolcoath Main Lode). They broke 16 fathoms of ground at £2 2s a fathom, and also spent 89 stems at 1s a stem dropping pumps. The total earnings from these tasks was £34 17s, which meant the 24 miners averaged £1 9s each for a month's work. William Corthen and sixteen partners sank Old Water Whim Shaft and carried out work on the engine for a total of £21 4s, which meant the seventeen men averaged £1 4s 10d each for a month's work. Daniel Repper and his fifteen men averaged £2 11s 10d for sinking and stoping 14 fathoms below the 60 fathom level on Brea Lode at £2 5s a fathom. Edward Bone and five men sank West North Whim Shaft below the 90 fathom level at £9 9s a fathom and averaged £2 15s a man for the month. Nicholas Rogers drove the 100 fathom level on Brea Lode for a distance of 2 fathom 2ft 3in at £5 5s a fathom for £12 9s 4d, giving him and his five men an average of £2 1s 2d each. These were probably typical earnings for tutworkers in the Basset mines of the late eighteenth century.[140]

The tributer was paid a proportion of the value of the ore he mined. Clearly, most of the tribute pitches were in ground 'opened up' for mining, i.e., between levels, which the tributer would stope or mine away. The mine captain negotiated on setting day the amount he would pay in the pound for a particular pitch (a stope or part of a stope). A Dutch auction was held, where the tributers would bid against each for a particular piece of ground. The man who bid the lowest would normally get the pitch, but the captain could exercise discretion if he thought the miner was not up to the task or not the best man for that particular job. Pryce wrote that the normal period for a tribute contract was four months, but analysis of the length of time for tributers to work a set pitch at New Dolcoath was slightly different. During the period August 1775 to July 1776 there were three one month contracts, seven two month contracts, eleven three month contracts and one four month contract. Several were of indeterminate length. This suggests that most tribute contracts were two or three months in length. In the Stannary Court case referred to by Harris, where two tributers disputed an agreement of sharing their profits, their contracts were for three months. The single month tribute contracts are harder to identify, so there may have been more of them than is apparent. In very poor ground, where the captain thought there was little prospect of much good ore, as much as 19s 6d in the pound might be paid, but where it was very rich ground the miner might be lucky to get 3s 6d in the pound. The normal high payment was 13s 4d (the equivalent of the obsolete mark) in the pound, with 5s being a normal low payment.[141]

Although there are no extant cost books for New Dolcoath, we can tell from the extant contemporary cost books of such mines as Cooks Kitchen (run by the same purser and with much of the same executive management team and the same mineral lord) how Dolcoath operated its tutworker and tributer systems. The principal lode structures were the same, being the eastward extensions of the Dolcoath lodes, and so working conditions and lode characteristics were also similar.

Tributers and tutworkers are often referred to, by those unacquainted with the realities of mining, as representing the more skilled miners (tributers) and the less skilled miners (tutworkers). This is far from the truth. The fact is they represented two quite different skills. The skill of the tributer was in identifying the best ore and breaking the largest tonnage possible with as little dilution of grade as could be achieved. The contract tributer also needed special skill in the management of large groups of men. A stope could have anywhere from six to sixty miners working in it. All had to be organized, supplied with sharp tools, and rods and powder for blasting. Safety in a stope, especially when most stopes were underhand, was a major consideration, and risk assessment and safety work would have been the responsibility of the contract tributer. There was a relatively small number of fatal accidents in the seventeen years recorded of New Dolcoath's operation, when only fourteen men and boys were killed, and some of them were not involved in actual mining work. This demonstrates the success of the risk assessment and protective timbering strategy of most tributers. The actual mining skill involved in breaking ground in a stope, using benches breaking to a free face, was, in mining terms, minimal.[142]

On the other hand the tutworker needed different skills. Breaking hard rock, without an easily available free face to break to, needed greater skill than stoping off benches. In the days of hand-labour and black powder, especially before William Bickford invented safety fuze in 1831/32, advancing an end was a task which required great skill and expertise on the part, not only of the contract tutworker, but also of each man holding or beating the borer or drill. Advancing an end, whether in a drive on lode, or a crosscut through country rock, in a raise (rise) or sinking a shaft or winze (wins/winds), meant the tutworker had to create a free face, as with the 'cut' of the last hundred years, or drill a pattern of holes to 'drag' the rock away from the face. A normal hand-drilled round in a drive might begin with a couple of holes drilled no more than fifteen degrees off the vertical, followed by two more at perhaps thirty degrees, two at 45 degrees and so on to the top of the face, where the holes would go in horizontally. The strength of the ground and the type of rock would vary the pattern considerably. Given the restricted room in an end, and the hardness of most of the rock at Dolcoath, the end might be advanced with half a round drilled and blasted each shift or core. The above technique was called the 'drag' cut or round, or the stoping cut or round. The fuze in eighteenth century New Dolcoath consisted of an appropriate number of goose quills cut and inserted into each other to form a hollow rod of the required length, probably no longer than eighteen inches to twenty inches. The gunpowder or black powder used in these primitive and unreliable 'rods' was bruised to a fine powder and poured into the rods to form a continuous, thin line of black powder from end to end. The idea was that the flame would travel through the quills at a slow and measured rate, enabling the miners to light it and make their escape. Regrettably, all too often, the miner was caught by a premature blast before he could get away. One-eyed miners, with blackened scars on their faces were a common sight in mining districts, and miners with fingers and parts of their hands missing were also not unusual. Fatal blasting accidents were rarer, but unfortunately at Dolcoath, as at other Cornish mines, there was loss of life and wives were sometimes robbed of their husbands and children of their fathers.[143]

The most important fact to remember when we talk of tributers and tutworkers is that they were frequently the same men. Not only do we find men listed as tributers at Dolcoath one month and tutworkers the next, and back again as tributers a month or two later, but some of the best miners held tutwork contracts at the same time as holding tribute contracts. For example out of 24 men with tutwork contracts in August

1775, seven held tribute contracts during the next twelve months and three held tribute and tutwork contracts at the same time. Richard Rabling was a tutworker between August 1775 and April 1776, when he became a tributer for the next two months. James Martin was a tutworker in August and September 1775. He disappeared from Dolcoath for seven months before re-appearing as a tributer in May 1776, before going again. Sumer Carter was a tutworker between August 1775 and March 1776, when he took a tribute contract as well, after which he reverted to just tutwork for two months before again holding both tutwork and tribute contracts. Stephen Truman was a tutworker in August and September 1775, disappeared for six months, and returned in April as a tributer. Richard Clifton was a tutworker on and off between August 1775 and April 1776, before taking both a tutwork and a tribute contract in May, after which he returned to merely tutwork. These men effectively ran whole sections of Dolcoath Mine, and were responsible to the mine captains for all aspects of development (tutwork), stoping (tribute), 'rolling' or barrowing the ore back to the shaft platt, and ensuring the miners had all necessary gear and worked safely. To some extent this makes nonsense of attempts to analyse the relative wages earned by tutworkers and tributers, certainly for the latter part of the eighteenth century.[144]

Some men worked on the 'company (or owners') account' for long periods, but took tutwork or tribute contracts briefly in between. Others moved up from kibble boys, sumpmen or landers to working under tutworkers or tributers as they matured in years. Arthur Woolf, pitman for most of his New Dolcoath career, briefly held a tutwork contract in May 1776, before returning to more regular work. John Buckley was a coalman (stoker) from April 1771 to April 1772 when he disappears from the pay book to return as a tutwork contractor in March 1773, for one month. He resumed work as a coalman in September 1773. Probably he worked on another's contract in the interim. William Dunstone worked in the sump in April 1771, but by September 1775 he held his own tribute contract, undoubtedly having gained experience under other miners before this. James Eva was employed drawing (hoisting) in April 1771, but held a tribute contract in August to October 1775. Nathaniel Faull and Joseph Knight were both kibble boys in April 1771, but both held tutwork contracts in August 1775.[145]

Analysis of pay book records between August 1775 and February 1789, shows that out of 48 months examined, in no less than 38 months there were miners who held both tutwork and tribute contracts. The highest number in a month was five, in February 1780 and February 1782, and for the most part it was just one or two. Closer examination of the twelve months between August 1775 and July 1776 reveals some interesting facts about these miners. Out of the 89 named contractors, 40 held just tutwork contracts in that period, 33 held just tribute contracts and sixteen held both types of contract in that twelve-month period. There were nine men who held tut and tribute contracts at the same time during the period. The tributers held contracts for one, two, three or four months, with almost half being three month contracts, nearly a third two months and the rest divided between one and four months. Tutworkers often remained at Dolcoath for several months at a time, with some staying there for the whole twelve months and, indeed, remaining at the mine for several years.[146]

In the absence of cost books for New Dolcoath we cannot always cross-reference miners, but it is possible to gain an idea on movements between Dolcoath and Cooks Kitchen by analysing the Cooks Kitchen tutworkers and tributers during the twelve months between July 1781 and June 1782. There was a total of 43 men who took tutwork or tribute contracts there in that period, and no less than seventeen of them worked at Dolcoath as tutworkers or tributers during the sixteen years from 1771 to 1787. John Andrew was a Dolcoath tutworker at times between January 1773 and July 1781, after which he appeared at Cooks Kitchen as a tutworker in October 1781. John Carthew was a Dolcoath tutworker in August 1771, a tributer there in 1773 and 1776, and a tutworker at Cooks Kitchen in 1781. Richard Eudey was a tutworker at Dolcoath in 1776 and a tributer at Cooks Kitchen in 1781. John Hocking worked as both a tutworker and tributer at Dolcoath between 1775 and 1786, and as a tutworker at Cooks Kitchen 1781. John Luke was a tributer at Dolcoath in November 1779, held both tutwork and tribute contracts in February 1780, a tutworker at Cooks Kitchen in July 1781 and a tutworker at Dolcoath in June 1787. John Nettle, a tributer at Dolcoath in 1780 and '81 went to Cooks Kitchen as a tutworker in 1782. Edward Jeffery, William Harris, George Eva, William Carthew, Nicholas Pascoe, Daniel Ripper (Repper), Richard Temby, William Thomas, John Trythel, John Trevillion and Edward Williams all moved between the two mines during that period, and for the most part they worked as a tributer in one mine and a tutworker in the other. This pattern of movement between types of contract and neighbouring mines was a feature of most contract miners at the time.[147]

Figure 32. Monthly costs at Dolcoath, 1771-1788.

	1771	1772	1773	1775	1776	1777	1778	1779
J		1416	1412		763		1320	1352
F		1607	1459		1149		1541	1657
M		1982	1981		1745	1893	1638	1938
A	2245	1984	2325		1640		1605	2359
M	2394	2675	2774		1942	2837	1975	2333
J	2164	2700	1223		1312	2058	2203	2458
J	2200	2094	1433	2485	2127	2286	2745	1869
A	2421	2426		1951	1403	2271	2501	1982
S	2875	2008	1442	1911	1400	1102	2033	1510
O	2025	1737	1694	1373	1954	1326	1526	1348
N	2070	1775		1436		1570	1290	1591
D	2230	1566		1363		1464	1696	1825

	1780	1781	1782	1786	1787	1788	1789
J	1216	1597	1281		950	812	12
F	1652	2127	1561		1174	742	269
M	2261	1457	1992		932	633	106
A	1890	2363	2860		1013	723	6
M	3769	2500	2090		888	811	426
J	4137	2647	2636		1072	720	53
J	3335	2483	2521		900	310	5
A	2545	1568	1560		1002	574	
S	2662	1836			894	160	
O	1436	1336		1091	913	111	
N	2398	1934		862	695	207	
D	2957	1743		1215	859		

Mining Methods Used at New Dolcoath

The development of efficient ground-breaking techniques and the whole organization of metal mining in the eighteenth century have exercised historians and commentators for nearly two-hundred years. Correspondents and contributors to such learned journals as the Transactions of the Royal Geological Society of Cornwall, the Journal of the Royal Institution of Cornwall and the Cornwall Polytechnic Society sought to discover and explain how this or that technique developed and who introduced various methods or systems into Cornish mines. This led distinguished and extremely able men like John Hawkins, Joseph Carne, R. N. Worth and W. J. Henwood to speculate on how the methods employed in Cornish mines in their day developed and who was responsible for their introduction. They sought the answers in many places, culling ancient texts and interviewing old miners, but despite their best efforts there is telling evidence that they reached their conclusions prematurely, usually with insufficient evidence to hand, and their misunderstandings have been printed and subsequently repeated by generations of scholars and researchers as gospel.[148]

More recent research has shown that the conclusions reached by these nineteenth century authors are in serious need of revision. W. J. Henwood, writing in the 1871 RGSC Journal, made some startling claims about the introduction of back stoping into Dolcoath and other Cornish mines. He stated that neither Borlase (*Natural History of Cornwall* 1758) nor Pryce (*Mineralogia Cornubiensis 1778*) mentioned back stoping in Cornish mines: "Back-stopes are not even mentioned by either of the great authorities on Cornish mining in the last (18th) century." Of course, this is simply not true, for had Henwood checked Pryce's glossary ('Cornu-Technical Terms & Idioms of Tinners') on page 328, he would have found the following: "Stopeing … hewing away the lode overhead, is stopeing the back." Based upon his examination of the long-sections of Pool Adit Mine (published by Borlase in 1758, but showing the workings in 1746) and Bullen Garden Mine (published by Pryce in 1778, but showing the workings in the late 1760s), Henwood further asserts that they show no evidence of back stoping and very little of exploration by winzes.

With respect to the limited mention of back stopes by Borlase and Pryce, it should be noted that both texts were primarily describing opening up the ground by exploration, not production mining, although in this context it should be noted that Pryce does refer to the miners often following "these branches of Ore both upwards and downwards" when opening up the ground. Had Henwood and others examined the sections of Pool Adit (1746) and Bullen Garden (1760s) more closely they would have come to different conclusions. Had they examined them in the light of the evidence to be found in the extant eighteenth century cost books, they would certainly have done so. The 1746 section of Pool Adit Mine shows the back (that is the lode above the level) being stoped by means of underhand benches. The broken ore was removed to the level below for transporting to the shaft for hoisting. The bottoms were being opened up by stoping the bottom, also by underhand working by benches, as described by Borlase in the text.[149]

If the Pool Adit cost book is used to supplement the information on the section, we find that back stoping was in regular use in the 1730s. In June 1736 Alexander Coath was 'rising over the adit in Penhellick' he put the raise up 24 feet in 24 working days, which was quite impressive. In December 1736 tutworkers were 'raising six foot against the borrier (barrier)', and 'rising 4 foot under the New Shaft', and in March 1736/7 tutworkers were stoping 'Penhellick Backs'. In June 1737 tutworkers were stoping the backs in both Trevenson and Penhellick Vean. In July 1737 two pares of tutworkers were stoping 'over Penhellick Adit End'. Although these examples are few in number, we must remember that most stoping was carried out by tributers at Pool Adit Mine at that time, and we have no information on the locality of their tribute pitches. The stopes illustrated in 1746 clearly show some of the tribute stopes. It is worth noting that Pool Adit was not only largely owned by the same adventurers as at Dolcoath, but its engineer (George John) was also employed by Dolcoath and its mineral lords were also shared.[150]

More pertinent to the situation at Dolcoath was that at Cooks Kitchen, and here we find that even among tutworkers, back stoping was not at all unusual in the early 1780s. In March 1782 "Nicholas Rogers & ptrs was Stopeing the Back over the sixty fathom level: 10 fathom @ £1 10s per fathom = £15 0s 0d." The twelve men on the contract each paid 2d to the doctor. Rogers and his men continued stoping the back of the 60 fathom level for the next three months, and in June 1782 John Trythal and ten partners took over the back stope there, with Rogers giving up tutwork to become a tribute stoper. Trythal continued back stoping over the 60 fathom level until November 1782, when he was 'Stopeing the Western Backs over the 60 fa. Level'. In

December he also took a tribute contract, presumably in the same stope. In January 1783 Henry Arthur was stoping the back of the 'Bottom Level on South Load' with four men. They earned £11 7s after deductions. Also in January Edward Jeffery was stoping the back of the bottom level and Isaac Walters was stoping the 'Third Level from the Bottom, South Load'. In March 1783 Charles Chapple was stoping the back of the 100 fathom level, in April and May Richard Carpenter was stoping the back of the 100 fathom level on Brea Lode, and in June Henry Rogers was stoping the back over the 10 fathom level on Engine Lode and Joseph Roberts was stoping the back over the 100 fathom level. In July 1783 Richard Crase was stoping the back over the 10 fathom level. Thereafter stoping appears to have been given over entirely to tributers. Between March 1782 and July 1783 there were eighteen tutwork contracts for back stoping, involving ten different 'takers', two of whom worked as tutwork contractors at Dolcoath during the period. How many or what proportion of stopes worked by tributers at Cooks Kitchen were back stopes and how many worked the bottom, we cannot say, but these few examples underline the fact that back stoping was common at Cooks Kitchen by the early 1780s, as it was a generation earlier at Pool Adit, half-a-mile to the north.[151]

All of which makes the assertion that back stoping was unknown at Dolcoath (and other Cornish mines) until the mid-1780s, quite extraordinary. Based upon a misinterpretation of the Bullen Garden long-section from the 1760s, Henwood stated that there was no evidence of back stoping there. This is certainly not the case, for large sections appear to have been stoped above the levels, and in some places the stoped-out areas could only have been back stoped. Henwood then compounds his error by quoting John Rule's words, that before 1788, although the great mass of copper ore had been extracted by 'bottom-stopes', the lode had also been explored and exploited "in levels, winzes, and back-stopes", and deduces that Dolcoath captains must have been taught about back-stoping by Rudolph Raspe, a German scientist, who worked briefly in Dolcoath assay office as a storekeeper, between 1783-84. (See below) There is no doubt that Raspe was briefly employed at Dolcoath in a fairly lowly capacity, and that he impressed some of the young men with his experiments. He also is believed to have written the *Travels of Baron Munchhausen* whilst employed at the mine. The idea that Raspe, even though a distinguished German scientist, could influence the way Cornish mine captains organized their mine, during his brief sojourn there, as a lowly storekeeper, is preposterous. It had more to do with the desire of nineteenth century intellectuals to attribute every advance and improvement to the influence of foreigners, especially distinguished ones, than anything else. Henwood and the others were, for the most part, well-educated intellectuals, not practical miners or mine captains, and so their comments must be seen in context. Given the financial difficulties being faced by Dolcoath in the mid-1780s and the mine's imminent demise, it is hardly likely that the captains would have initiated a major shift in mining technique. The truth is that for the whole of the eighteenth century, and probably from before the 1671 description in *Philosophical Transactions*, stoping the back of the lode, that is working above the level, was a normal means of ore extraction. It is important here to emphasise that stoping the bottom is not necessarily the same as underhand stoping, for one refers to the *location* of the stope, below the level, and the other to the *technique* being used, working the benches one is standing on. Underhand stoping, whether above or below the level, was, until the introduction of machinery, by far the most efficient and productive method of stoping.[152]

	1771	1772	1773	1775	1776	1777	1778	1779	1780	1781	1782	average
J		499	451		238	257	363	402	367			368
F		475	324		324	297	459		385			377
M		484	354		352	317		409	558	566		434
A	306	508	480		387			399	415		447	420
M	668	548	327		335	372		416	405	476		443
J	510	551	346		303		446	433	605	552	550	477
J	524	553	449	362	306	267	342	386	426		371	399
A	530	521		411	239	435	346	370	393	444	427	412
S	561	519	317	350	294			468	579			441
O	516	518	478	402	315			331	388			421
N	545	483		343				421	405			439
D	510	493		343		334	426	556	648	529		480

Figure 33. Numbers of underground workers at Dolcoath, based on 'doctor's pence'.

Employment Figures
There are difficulties in calculating the number of men employed on an eighteenth century mine, because the figures extracted from such sources as pay books and cost books can be misleading. For example, a simple total of the underground workers can sometimes be arrived at from the payments to the doctor. If we know that a particular mine's underground workers each paid 2d a month to the doctor, then we merely need to divide the total paid by 2d to arrive at the total. However, this fails to take into account several variables. First, some company account men normally employed on surface also paid their monthly 2d. As noted above, enginemen and stokers ('coalmen') sometimes paid their 2d for the doctor. Second, evidence from contemporary cost books for other local mines shows that many underground workers failed to pay their doctor's 2d. At Cooks Kitchen in the 1780s it was common for tributers to avoid paying for the doctor, although it was less so for tutworkers. At Poldice, in the 1790s, something like 45% of tributers did not pay the doctors' 2d and even the occasional pare of tutworkers failed to pay into the doctor's column. However, based upon the doctor's pence

at 2d per man, the following list gives some indication of the numbers employed underground at New Dolcoath for most of the months between April 1771 and August 1782. The pay book from October 1786 to the mine's closure, in March 1790, does not have the doctor's column. There are figures for 91 months (7 years 7 months).[153]

There are a number of difficulties in determining the total number of workers at New Dolcoath. It is possible to estimate the number for April 1771 as 562, made up of 306 underground workers, 176 ore dressers, 28 other surface workers and 52 operating the stamps. But, this is only an estimate, as undoubtedly there are some missing from these totals and some have been counted twice. Tom Harris gives a total Dolcoath workforce for 1787 as 595, and he breaks it down into married men, 265, unmarried men, 95, and women and children, 235. He does not give the month for these figures.[154]

Fatal Accidents

There is no complete accident record for New Dolcoath, just as there is none for most mines, but the pay books of the mine do allow us to estimate quite accurately the number of fatal accidents to miners in the years 1771 to 1788. During that seventeen year period we find some fourteen deaths at the mine recorded. These are detected by the references to payments to, for example, 'The widow of Thomas Terrill = £2 2s.' which was a typical entry recording a fatal accident underground. The amount paid, £2 2s was the normal payout to widows, although there were exceptions. The first fatality mentioned was to Richard Williams, whose widow received £1 1s in March 1773. Williams was buried at Crowan churchyard on March 5th 1773. Why the widow received only half the normal payment cannot be said, but it is likely that she had the rest separately. It is probable that he was a miner working under a tributer or tutworker, as his name is not on the record and the only miner whose name appeared on the pay book account was the contractor, the rest, perhaps as many as fifty men on a tribute contract, were paid by the contractor.

Robert Skewes was killed in June 1776 and was buried at Camborne on June 27th, his widow being paid £2 2s in July 1776. Again we have no information from the pay book on his job underground, but like Williams he probably worked for a tutworker or tributer.

John Dunston was killed in February 1777, was buried at Camborne on February 14th, and his widow was given £2 2s. The pay book shows that Dunston was a tributer at the mine, and so the accident probably took place in a stope.

John Rowe was killed in late January 1778 and was buried at Camborne on January 30th, his widow receiving prompt payment of £2 2s in the January account. What job he was doing when killed we do not know, but seven years earlier he had been a 'kibble boy', a lad who filled the kibbles at the shaft platt before they were hoisted to surface. He had probably advanced to being a full miner by the time of his accident, working for a tributer or tutworker. In the same month John Clymo was killed, perhaps in the same accident which claimed John Rowe. His widow was given the usual £2 2s compensation, but we have no other information on him.

Charles Vivian's widow was given £2 2s in June 1778 after he was killed, probably in the same month. In 1771 he was listed as a 'sumpman', one who worked with pitmen in maintaining the pitwork and doing other work at the bottom of the engine shaft. His burial record has not been found, but he is likely to have been a Camborne man, for most miners with the same name at Dolcoath and Cooks Kitchen were. The December 1778 pay book records two deaths together. The parents of two youngsters, referred to only as 'Johns' and 'Bennets', received £2 2s for each of them. It seems that they were involved in the same accident, probably working for a contractor. Without Christian names we cannot trace the boys.

In July 1779 a lad called Samuel Jewell was killed at Dolcoath and his mother was paid £2 2s by the mine. We have no other information about him. In October 1779 Stephen Carbis, a tutworker, was killed. He was buried at Redruth October 27th, and his widow was given £2 2s in the October account. He was named as a tutworker in July 1778 account.

Thomas Terrill, a tutwork contractor, was killed in September 1780, was buried in Redruth churchyard on September 21st, with his widow being given £2 2s compensation. The Redruth Parish Burial Register briefly notes: 'Killed at Dolcoath'.

William Bellman was killed underground at Dolcoath in May 1782 and his widow had her £2 2s compensation paid the same month, although he was not buried at Camborne churchyard until June 13th. As his name is not listed in the pay books he was probably working under a tributer or tutwork contractor. Also killed in May 1782 was William Angove, who was buried at Redruth on May 19th, and his widow received her £2 2s payment at the end of the month. He may have been involved in the same accident as Bellman, although as their burials were over a month apart, it is unlikely. We have no other information on him, so he probably was also working under a named contractor.

The last fatal accident referred to in the New Dolcoath pay books was to Henry Knight, a pitman, in January 1787. He was buried at Redruth on January 20th. In the October 1786 pay book he was paid £2 9s 10d, with 2d deducted for the doctor. His widow, Jane, who had a young family, was paid £2 3s compensation by Dolcoath, which was a shilling more than normal, and, interestingly, the Bassets paid into a 'subscription' or collection for Jane and her family, with a donation of £2 2s. What was special about Henry Knight, or about his accident, we do not know, but it certainly appears unusual for the Bassets to take such exceptional measures as to contribute to a fund for a miner's widow. The Tehidy Accounts say: "Jane Knight (whose husband was accidentally killed in Dolcoath) towards a subscription opened by the Adventurers for his Family – £2 2s 0d."

Of these men four came from Camborne, four from Redruth and one from Crowan. No burial records for five of them have been found. Two of the dead had been tutworkers, one was a sumpman, one formerly a kibble boy and one a pitman. At least eight were probably working under tributers or tutworkers on contract.

When we consider the number working underground during the years covered and the large number working in stopes, many of them underhand stopes, the safety record is quite good. New Dolcoath was clearly a 'safe' mine to work in, and it certainly does not warrant the reputation given mines of the period by some commentators and historians. If we compare their record with, for example, Wheal Jane in the 1970s and '80s, when ten were killed in ten years, we can appreciate that the contract miners, mine captains and others involved in miners' supervision at New Dolcoath maintained a high standard of professionalism.[155]

Dolcoath Costs & Copper Ore Sales 1740-69

Year	Ore Sold	Basset's 1/8th	Total Cost	Basset's 1/8th of Cost	Total Profit	Basset's Profit
1740	£3,296	£412	£1,642	£205	£1,656	£207
1741	£3,375	£422	£2,072	£259	£1,303	£163
1742	£4,448	£556	£2,269	£284	£2,179	£272
1743	£6,336	£792	£3,434	£428	£2,912	£364
1744	£4,344	£543	£2,240	£286	£2,104	£263
1745	£2,408	£305	£824	£109	£1,584	£198
1746	£1,408	£176	£1,640	£205	Loss £232	Loss £29
1747	£1,744	£220	£2,248	£281	Loss £504	Loss £63
1748	£1,592	£199	£1,744	£218	Loss £152	Loss £19
1749	£2,568	£321	£1,376	£172	£1,192	£149
1750	£1,392	£174	£1,568	£196	Loss £176	Loss £22
1751	£1,480	£185	£1,920	£240	Loss £440	Loss £55
1752	£4,336	£542	£3,592	£449	£744	£93
1753	£4,568	£571	£3,224	£403	£1,344	£168
1754	£11,832	£1,479	£4,856	£607	£6,976	£872

1755	£11,048	£1,381	£6,416	£802	£4,632	£579
1756	£9,280	£1,160	£8,216	£1,027	£1,064	£133
1757	£1,512	£189	£1,320	£165	£192	£24
1758	£9,800	£1,225	£10,128	£1,266	Loss £328	Loss £41
1759	£9,848	£1,231	£8,560	£1,070	£1,288	£161
1760	£10,840	£1,355	£8,344	£1,043	£2,496	£312
1761	£7,424	£928	£7,616	£952	Loss £192	Loss £24
1762	£2,904	£363	£3,272	£409	Loss £368	Loss £46
1763	£6,704	£838	£6,424	£803	£280	£35
1764	£1,072	£134	£1,928	£241	Loss £856	Loss £107
1765	£5,328	£666	£4,712	£589	£616	£77
1766	£3,992	£499	£4,952	£619	Loss £960	Loss £120
1767	£7,968	£996	£5,048	£631	£2,920	£365
1768	£2,944	£368	£2,376	£297	£568	£71
1769	£6,640	£830	£4,912	£614	£1,728	£216
Totals	**£152,431**	**£19,054**	**£118,863**	**£14,858**	**£33,569**	**£4,196**

The Bassets also took 1/6th dues on all ore sold (£152,431 = £25,405)

None of the above totals include Bullen Garden Mine, although the two amalgamated in 1765

'An Account of all my Adventures' (Basset Manor Records) Dolcoath

Profit	July 5th 1747	£1,332 2s 7d
Profit	July 23rd 1748	£1,308 12s 10d
Profit	July 22nd 1749	£1,340 13s 4d
Profit	July 13th 1750	£1,472 19s 6d
Profit	June 13th 1751	£1,483 4s 5d
Profit	June 29th 1752	£1,410 0s 8d
Profit	June 29th 1753	£1,576 10s 9d
Profit	June 29th 1754	£1,874 18s 7d
Profit	July 22nd 1755	£2,710 15s 4d
Profit	July 22nd 1756	£3,715 0s 0d

'Roskear & Pengegon alias Entral'

Loss July 1748	£18 9s 7d	
Loss July 1749	£33 5s 10d	
Loss July 1750	£21 18s 2d	(Roskear, Entral & Pengegon)
Profit June 1751	£66 18s 7d	(Roskear, Entral & Pengegon)
Profit June 1752	£67 3s 4d	(South Entral)
Profit June 1753	£106 11s 8d	(South Entral)
Profit June 1754	£170 14s 1d	(South Entral)
Profit June 1755	£286 15s 10d	(South Entral)
Profit June 1756	£243 0s 0d	(South Entral)
Profit June 1765	£243 0s 0d	(South Entral)

New Dolcoath Production & Profit

There is no continuous record of production and profit for the years of New Dolcoath. There are, however, several sources for information on these things, and these enable us to gain some figures for eleven-and-a-quarter of those years. Thomas Wilson, agent of Boulton and Watt provides production figures for five years, the Cooks Kitchen cost books provide Dolcoath production figures for fifteen months, Tehidy Accounts give information on production and profit for two-and-a-half years, and copper ticketing records for several Basset mines provide figures for another two-and-a-half years.[156]

In July 1769 Basset agreed to reduce the dues on copper ore from one-sixth to one-eighth. This was granted due to the high costs incurred in reorganizing and re-equipping the mine when New Dolcoath was formed and Bullen Garden Mine was included in the sett. "1769 Sept. 5. Mr Basset this day came to a determination to reduce his Dues in Dolcoath from 1/6th to 1/8th on all ores sold subsequent to this date, until further directions, having considered that the present expences are so great, that the Adventurers have little or no prospect of profit."[157]

In December 1772, at a time of continuing difficulty, the Bassets again reduced their dues, this time to one-twelfth. "1772 December 23. The Trustees this day came to a resolution to abate the Dish at Dolcoath to one twelfth part, and the following is a copy of the Instrument signed on that occasion – viz. Tehidy Decem'r 23rd 1772. A petition being delivered (dated in Oct. last) from the Adventurers of Dolcoath Mine to the Trustees of Mr Basset for an abatement of the dish of that mine to one twelfth part for the reasons therein given – the said reasons being thought sufficiently strong, I do hereby give my consent thereto till the Cost therein shall be all reimbursed to the said Adventurers the time of the said twelfth dish to commence from the first of this month. John Collins." As the production figures have mostly been calculated upon the basis of the dues paid to the Bassets on the payments made to the copper companies, it is important to take into account the exact percentage of the copper revenue owed in dues.[158]

The total recorded revenue from copper ore sales during the period of New Dolcoath was £297,445. This was for eleven-and-a-half years of the period 1769 to 1790. Clearly the years for which we have no revenue figures were among the most productive of the eighteenth century at Dolcoath, and so we must assume that at least as much income came from the missing ten years as from the recorded periods. This would give total copper ore sales for the years 1769-90 as at least £600,000. Add to this the £152,480 for the years 1740 to 1769 and we have a total copper ore revenue between 1740 and 1790 of over £750,000. As noted above, (page 19) Angerstein and the Bullen Garden section in Pryce, indicate that income from copper ore sold at Bullen Garden Mine for the years 1750-70 might have been as high as £1,000,000. We have no reliable way of estimating revenue for the twenty years before 1740 for Dolcoath and before 1750 for Bullen Garden. Information on tin sales during the greater part of the eighteenth century is also sparse.[159]

Calculation of mine profits for New Dolcoath is based upon the Basset's records. These give their profits as adventurers in the mine, where they held a six-sixteenth share. Information is scattered in their account books, but we do have figures for the twelve months between August 1775 and August 1776, the seven months between August 1776 and March 1777, the six month between March 1777 and September 1777, and the six months between September 1777 and March 1778. This is a mere total of two years and seven months, during which time the Bassets made £9,423.96 profit, and the mine made £24,331.91 profit.[160]

The final years of the eighteenth century New Dolcoath are best illustrated by the production and income figures for the years 1785-1790: [161]

August 1785-September 1786:	5,466 tons sold for	£30,742
August 1786-September 1787:	4,149 tons sold for	£18,812
August 1787-September 1788:	3,745 tons sold for	£13,431
August 1788-September 1789:	1,008 tons sold for	£2,636
August 1789-September 1790:	890 tons sold for	£2,150

Rudolph Eric Raspe (1737-94)

Much has been made by those examining the history of Dolcoath Mine of the employment there of the author of *Baron Munchhausen's Travels*, Rudolph Eric Raspe. Raspe was an extremely learned scholar, who distinguished himself as a man of letters, philosophy and science. In Germany he rose, during his 20s and 30s, to a position of preeminence in academic circles, gaining a European reputation and even writing an article for Philosophical Transactions of the Royal Society, due to which he was made an honorary member in 1769. Sometime after 1775 he began to systematically steal valuable coins from one of his patrons at Cassel. Eventually, he fled the city and after several adventures he reached England. Within a couple of years he had translated a learned work on mineralogy, and, presumably, become an 'expert' on mines and minerals, an impression he was not slow to exploit. However, his notoriety eventually caught up with him in London, and he was struck off membership of the Royal Society. Forced to find employment, he decided to use his newly acquired expertise in mining and mineralogy, and went to Cornwall, where he obtained a position as storekeeper in the assay office of Dolcoath Mine.[162]

His short sojourn at Dolcoath has left few records, and so precisely what he did there is uncertain. The Cash Book of Cornish & Co. (W. G. Wilton), ironmongers of Redruth, for the years 1783-84, which records supplies of assay implements and other metal work to mines and other businesses in west Cornwall, includes three references to Dolcoath Mine, all of which mention Raspe as assay office storekeeper. Raspe purchased several items for the Dolcoath assay office, including 'portable furnaces' to be taken to Truro, a water pot, and a long list of copper, tin and iron implements including iron pans, a blower, tin measures, lamps, a copper still and funnels. He is variously called 'R. Raspe', 'R. Rasp' and 'Ralph Rasp'. His lowly position of assay office storekeeper is confirmed by Henwood in the *Gentleman's Magazine*, where he says: "Perhaps thirty years ago (c.1827) the late Capt William Petherick, manager of Dolcoath, informed me that *Baron Munchhausen's Travels* had been written by a German whilst he performed the duties of Storekeeper at the mine." Henwood added that Captain Charles Thomas, manager of Dolcoath, "tells me that one of the oldest Mining Captains used to speak of the wonderful chemical experiments made in the office by Mr Raspe." Undoubtedly, Raspe impressed the young men with these clever experiments, and was remembered over seven decades later for them. It is of interest that none of them mentioned any contribution he might have made to the underground operation of the mine, or even any improvements to the system of analysis used at the time. In the light of these facts, and in what was not said, it is quite amazing that W. J. Henwood should have suggested that Raspe influenced the way that mining was carried out at Dolcoath.[163]

Subsequent to his short stay at Dolcoath Raspe moved about and by 1786 was seen as something of a mineralogist. He is said to have discovered or identified a previously unidentified ore as 'sulphurated tin' (tin sulphide, the mineral stannite), at Wheal Rock in St Agnes. In 1791 he was in the north of Scotland, claiming to have discovered copper, iron, lead and manganese. Subsequent claims about the mineral wealth of the area were founded upon 'imported' ores from Cornwall, and Raspe again disappeared, only to surface once again as a mining 'expert', this time in County Donegal, Ireland. The arch-deceiver finally died at Muckross in 1794. He would have been astonished that seventy years after his death, well-educated and intelligent men, like Henwood, should still be giving credence to his claims.[164]

Dolcoath Miners to Plymouth to face the Combined Franco-Spanish Fleet
The 1770s and '80s saw England threatened by the combined naval powers of France, Spain and Holland, as they sought to take advantage of her difficulties with the American colonies. In 1779 a Franco-Spanish fleet threatened the south-west and young Francis Basset, principal adventurer at Dolcoath and also mineral lord, raised a militia troop of miners to go to the defence of Plymouth. John Vivian, a Dolcoath mine captain appears to have been appointed by Basset to lead these miners, for the Tehidy accounts, dated July 12 1780, has the following: "John Vivian his bill of disbursements for liquor and for the Tinners at Dolcoath on their going from thence to Plymouth in August last (1779)". Eleven years later another entry in the accounts indicates Vivian's continuing involvement with the miners' militia: "April 28 1791. Jane Dunkin for the hire of a horse for Capt John Vivian in his troop." Basset also organized a battery above Portreath, where the present Battery House now stands.[165]

Education and Schooling
The standard of literacy among Dolcoath miners at the end of the eighteenth century is not easy to evaluate. It is apparent that throughout history observers have meant different things by the term literate, with some meaning merely the ability to read and write and some meaning being skillful in their use. The ability to read is a quite different skill from the ability to write. Reading is, of course, word recognition, whereas the ability to write requires the skill of forming letters and words into sentences in a tidy and recognizable fashion. One way to determine whether a person can write has been to discover if he or she signed their name on documents, or merely made a mark. Although this is not a foolproof method it can act as a rule-of-thumb guide. Analysis of the pay books of New Dolcoath produces some interesting facts.

For the month of April 1771 the number who signed for their pay was 55 out of 138, or 40 percent. This did not include ore dressers and stamps workers. In July 1771 34 out of 153 ore dressers signed, which is 22 percent, and six out of 39 working at the stamps signed for their pay, which is 15 percent. For the twelve months between August 1775 and July 1776 the pay book shows that 25 out of 54 named tutworkers signed for their pay, and nine out of 49 tribute contractors, which is 48 percent and nineteen percent, respectively. These figures are typical, although it must be stressed that every month they varied and some months quite considerably. What they do indicate is that a fair proportion of the skilled miners at New Dolcoath had received some rudimentary education, and could at the very least read and write. The complicated methods of calculating their earnings, suggests that they also possessed a basic understanding of arithmetic. The number of ore dressers and stamps operators who could write appears to be much smaller than for the skilled miners, but here also a surprising number were at least semi-literate.[166]

Provision of education in and around Camborne is hard to quantify for the late eighteenth century, for although there is regular and reliable data on established and endowed schools for the period, the informal 'dames schools' are less well-documented. The Basset family endowed schools for poor pupils in Camborne, Illogan and Redruth parishes, in February 1722, and throughout the period covered by their accounts payments to the schoolmasters of those three schools are recorded. They each received £5 per annum, paid at £2 10s every six-months. We know a fair amount about Penponds endowed school, because the records are detailed and continuous. Mrs Grace Percival, a member of the Pendarves family, endowed a school for twenty poor children in July 1761, nearly forty years after the Bassets had started theirs in the three parishes. Penponds, part of Camborne Parish, lay within the territory of the Pendarveses, and no doubt it was felt that whatever the Bassets could do, they could also. The school was to give free education to twelve boys and eight girls, and the master was to accept no extra payment for these children, nor could he accept payment from prospective parents, seeking to get their child in ahead of others. However, there was provision for another ten fee-paying pupils, so that the master could earn extra income to supplement his £21 per year salary. There was also land provided to help with his income. If we assume that the other three endowed schools for poor children were of a similar size, then at any one time there could be up to 120 children being taught the basics of 'reading, writing and arithmetic'. Some of these children would stay for a few months before being called to become wage earners, and others might stay longer. We know that Richard Trevithick's stay at Penponds School was short and his formal education rudimentary, but he certainly mastered the basics of the above rather restricted curriculum before leaving to earn his living. Trevithick's friend and business partner, Andrew Vivian, who ran several businesses and managed several mines, also was a product of Penponds School. He was co-patentee with Trevithick of the Camborne road loco and was responsible, in 1799, for organizing the re-opening of Dolcoath Mine.[167]

We can learn much from the story of John Harris, fifty years after Trevithick, whose schooling, entirely in 'dames schools', has been described in some detail. He attended four such schools before leaving at the age of nine to work on a local farm. At his first school, run by Dame Trezone, he learned the alphabet and was taught to read. He then attended a more advanced school at Troon Chapel run by Dame Penpraze, after which he went to a school run by the hard Master Reed, a strict disciplinarian, before completing his schooling with one-legged ex-miner called Mr Roberts. He was thoroughly grounded by Roberts in the three 'Rs'. A few months after leaving school he left the farm to work with a tin streamer, before starting at Dolcoath as an assistant ore dresser at the age of ten. When he was twelve he followed his father underground as a copper miner at Dolcoath. John Harris' story illustrates the varying quality of the education on offer in such primitive establishments, but all of those amateur teachers probably accomplished something in 'reading, writing and summing', and it certainly was sufficient to enable their pupils to earn a living in the mines, farms and other forms of employment available. It is interesting to speculate on the number of youngsters who eventually became miners, and who attended these very basic centres of 'learning'.[168]

Tin Mining at New Dolcoath
After the 1730s there is hardly a mention of tin production at Dolcoath, and there is surprisingly little reference to it after the creation of New Dolcoath, despite its very detailed record of expenses. We know that tin continued to be encountered, especially at the higher levels, but we know nothing about quantities, grades or income from it. However, there is one very informative record, which Tom Harris discovered among the Stannary Records at the County Record Office. It has to do with a dispute brought to the Stannary Court in January 1788, between tributers working pitches on the 80 fathom level at Dolcoath. The tributers involved, Richard Luke, John Luke and John Gilbert of Illogan, on the one part, and Henry Sampson, John Richards of Illogan, and William and Arthur Gribble of Camborne, on the other part, were working pitches for copper ore quite close to each other in a stope at the 80 fathom level. The pitches were set for three months. Sampson and partners worked what was called 'Riddlers' pitch, which was a pitch formerly worked by a tributer of that name. The 80 fathom level was well inside the copper zone, and it is apparent that it was copper the tributers were principally concerned with. Because of the existence of payable tin ore at their two pitches, it was decided that they would share the tin ore returns. The tribute for their tin was set at 10s, or fifty percent of its value. When the tin was separated and assayed Sampson and partners had done very well and Luke and company had fared badly. Sampson refused to share the proceeds equally, and Luke demanded his share of over £21. A very large amount in 1788! We are not informed of the outcome.[169]

How typical the above situation was we cannot ascertain, but it is of interest and is also relevant, that thirty years later, working the same levels, copper miners were constantly encountering tin ore in their pitches. In the 'Day & Night Book' of captains James Thomas and William Petherick, for the period December 1822 to October 1823 there are constant references to tributers finding tin ore amongst the copper ore. Tom Roberts and partners worked two pitches, one rich in copper and the other in tin ore. Davy Thomas had tin in his copper pitch on 'Roarer Lode', at the 118 fathom level near North Valley Shaft. Jan Trezona, a tutworker, driving an end on the 145 level, near North Valley Shaft, encountered a lode with a mixture of tin and copper ore. There are references to special payments of 10s in the pound tribute for tin found in copper pitches. All of these pitches were well inside the copper zone. The tin ore mined by Sampson and Luke on the 80 fathom level in 1787/8 was typical rather than rare. The only things missing are the quantities mined and the extent of tin distribution in the workings of Dolcoath in the eighteenth century.[170]

Decline and Closure
The story of New Dolcoath contains high points, as the mine became the most productive and famous mine in Cornwall, and low points, as she struggled to pay her way in the face of mounting costs and diminishing returns. In 1765, when New Dolcoath was formed from the large and successful mines of Bullen Garden and Old Dolcoath, as well as several smaller mines, there was tremendous justified optimism. Old Dolcoath had been extremely rich for both tin and copper, and was the deepest mine in the parish, whereas Bullen Garden was producing vast quantities of good quality copper ore, and had, by the 1750s, become a place of pilgrimage for foreign travellers fascinated by the expanding Cornish copper industry. Dolcoath's fame was justified, and its place in the ranks of the world's great copper producers assured. The 1760s was a period of unprecedented optimism; the 1770s a decade of tremendous expansion and increasing production, but the 1780s went from triumph to disaster in a few short years. Discovery of an enormous body of shallow, easily available copper ore on Anglesey in 1768, led, inevitably, to a decline in the metal price, and with increasing depths at Dolcoath, the mine was becoming uneconomic.

With the supply of British copper far higher than demand and with the Welsh smelters paying ever-lower prices for Cornish copper, schemes were put in hand to combat the smelters' monopoly and secure an economic price for Cornish copper. Thomas Williams, who controlled the Anglesey mines, had set up his own smelters, and with coal close and cheaply available and a deep harbour nearby, he was in a strong position to take on the South Wales smelters. In cooperation with Williams the Cornish, headed by Matthew Boulton, John Vivian and Sir Francis Basset (through his agent Thomas Kevill), set up the Cornish Metal Company, in September 1785. They had capital of £130,000 and intended to keep the price at a reasonable level by buying Cornish produce for eleven years, long enough to see out the crisis. The Company would then sell it to the smelters without use of ticketing. By 1788 it was failing to deliver, and alternative and last-resort remedies were sought, including paying compensation to mine adventurers who agreed to stop production. Dolcoath and North Downs mines agreed to close on this basis. On February 29 1788, John Vivian wrote to Matthew Boulton: "It must not be considered a reduction of interest, but as a bribe to the mines, not to insist upon the Company's doing that which they have engaged to do – purchase all the ores which they can raise. Sir F(rancis) Basset assured me that he would not take a farthing less than he had demanded, for stopping Dolcoath - £1200 per annum - & as the compensation at 40/- per ton would but little exceed to that mine half that sum, there does not appear to me the least probability, that it will be accepted by any other mine, than North Downs." North Downs stated that they would not remain closed for longer than two years, and by the early 1790s they were back in full production.[171]

Thus, in the summer of 1788, with the copper standard down to a disastrous £57 a ton and Dolcoath losing money at an alarming rate, the agreement with the Cornish Metal Company was finally enacted. The 63-inch Watt engine was stopped. According to Charles Hatchett, who visited Camborne in 1796, Dolcoath was 174 fathoms deep when it closed. In July 1788 the senior captain, Edmund Prideaux, and Captain Richard Trevithick, left the mine and moved to East Stray Park Mine, formerly part of New Dolcoath. They were followed by Captain John Trevithick in February 1789, and captains Charles and John Vivian in September. With the management moving to other Basset mines, which were still operating, and all pumping stopped at Dolcoath, the miners confined their activities to the upper levels, before either leaving the mine or resorting to picking over the burrows at surface for low grade 'halvans'. By 1791 even this limited activity was at a standstill, and the mine had every appearance of being abandoned. The 63-inch Watt engine had been sold to Wheal Gons, another Basset mine, which lay on the western side of East Stray Park Mine. It was from these mines that the re-opening of Dolcoath was launched in 1799, by the two old Dolcoath families of Vivian and Trevithick.[172]

References, Part One.

Abbreviations used throughout the references:
CPMN: Cornish Post & Mining News; CRO: Cornwall Record Office; CT: Cornish Telegraph; DMMR: Dolcoath Mine Manager's Reports; MJ: Mining Journal; RCG: Royal Cornwall Gazette; RCPS: Royal Cornwall Polytechnic Society; TRGSC: Transactions of the Royal Geological Society of Cornwall; WB: West Briton

1. O. J. Padel Cornish Place-Name Elements (1985) pp.68,86,261; T. R. Harris Dolcoath: Queen of Cornish Mines (1974) p.9
2. A. L. Rowse 'History' Journal of the Historical Association. New Series. Vol.XXIX (March 1944) pp.17-26; British Library Additional Manuscript 24746;
3. Ibidem
4. Camborne Churchwarden's Accounts transcribed by Mrs Brenda Hull
5. John Norden Speculi Britanniae 'Historical Description of Cornwall' (1966 edition) p.38; 22/M/EB/42 No.15; 22/M/T/1/ 10,13,14,15,17 CRO, Truro
6. HB/5/11 RIC, Truro
7. HB/19/110a pp.44,47 RIC, Truro; HB/5/111 (1538,1539) RIC, Truro
8. Now part of DD TEM collection, CRO, Truro
9. X 101/5/1 CRO, Truro
10. Ibidem
11. Radnor Court Roll. Treloweth Manor. HU 13 (1625-1763) CRO, Truro
12. Ibidem

13. Ibidem
14. X 101/5/1 CRO
15. A. K. Hamilton Jenkin Tin Bounds Lists. Cornwall Centre, Redruth; AD 894/7/1,45 CRO
16. AD 894/7/1 CRO
17. Ibidem
18. AD 894/7/1 CRO
19. Ibidem
20. Ibidem
21. DDJ 1784 CRO; AD 894/7/1 CRO
22. Ibidem; William Pryce Mineralogia Cornubiensis (1972) pp.170,172
23. AD 894/7/1 CRO
24. Henric Kalmeter's Journal (1724) Justin Brooke's Unpublished MPhil Thesis pp.290-292
25. X 101/5/1 CRO
26. Philosophical Transactions of the Royal Society (1671) pp.2106,2107; Reinold R Angerstein's Journal (1753-55) Typed manuscript, translated by T & P Berg (1994) pp.111-113
27. X 101/5/1 CRO
28. Ibidem
29. Basset Mining Lease in Private Collection
30. A. K. Hamilton Jenkin Mines & Miners of Cornwall vol.3 p.31; St Aubyn Family Records, CRO
31. Pryce (1972) p.187; AD 894/7/1 CRO
32. Camborne Parish Registers (1703); AD 894/7/1 CRO; H. S. A. Fox & O. J. Padel The Cornish Lands of the Arundells of Lanherne (14th to 16th centuries) (2000) p.169
33. AD 894/7/1 CRO
34. Tehidy Lease to Drive Adit (1737) Private Collection
35. Mining Lease (June 24 1738) Private Collection
36. Ibidem
37. Mining Lease (March 25 1748) Private Collection
38. Mining Lease (Nov. 16 1748) Private Collection
39. Mining Lease (Nov. 26 1748) Private Collection
40. Mining Lease (Sept. 1760) Private Collection; AD 894/7/4 CRO
41. Mining Lease (April 1763) Private Collection
42. R. R. Angerstein's Journal (1753-55) Berg Translation (1994) pp. 112,113,122,123; Pryce (1972) pp.170-172; Alphabetical Index of Patentees of Inventions (1969) p.55, K. H. Rogers The Newcomen Engine in the West of England (1976)
43. John Kanefski's Unpublished PhD Thesis, Exeter University
44. AR 18/8 CRO; Pryce (1972) p.307; A. K. Hamilton Jenkin Vol.10 pp.5,6
45. Alphabetical Index (1969) pp.127,505; A. K. Hamilton Jenkin vol.10 pp.6-8; Articles of Agreement (May 27 1743) DD TEM, CRO
46. Allen Buckley & Adam Sharpe Journal of the Trevithick Society (1993) No.20 pp.35-38; Pryce (1972) p.170-172
47. AD 894/7/4,5 CRO
48. Journal of the Trevithick Society No.20 (1993) pp.35-38; AD894/7/4,5 CRO

49. AD 894/7/1,4,5 CRO
50. AD 894/7/4,5 CRO
51. HB/19/110a pp.44,47; HB/15/111 RIC; AD 894/7/1 CRO; William Doidge Map (1737) X 101/5/1 CRO; AD 894/7/4,5; AD 894/7/8-13 CRO; Camborne Tithe Apportionment Map (1840) CRO
52. Kalmeter (1724) Justin Brooke Thesis
53. Camborne Parish Registers CRO; Mining Leases. Private Collection; Angerstein (1753-55) Berg (1994); AD 894/7/8-13; AD 894/7/3-5 CRO; DDJ 1784 CRO
54. AD 894/7/1 CRO; Camborne Parish Registers CRO
55. Angerstein (1753-55) Berg. (1994); AD 894/7/1 CRO
56. AD 894/7/1 CRO
57. Pryce (1972) pp.277,278,286,287,307
58. D. B. Barton Copper Mining in Cornwall (1978) pp.12-15; W. H. Pascoe History of the Cornish Copper Company (1981) pp.20-27; J. A. Buckley The Story of Mining in Cornwall ((2005) p.90; Kalmeter (1723-25) Brooke thesis (1997) pp.289-300; J. A. Buckley South Crofty Mine (1997) p.15
59. AD 894/7 CRO
60. Ibid.
61. Ibid.
62. Ibid.
63. Ibid.
64. Ibid.
65. Angerstein (1994); Pryce (1972) pp.170-172
66. Pascoe (1981) pp.17-30; M. B. Donald Elizabethan Copper (1994) pp.300-368; Pryce (1972) pp.277-280
67. Ibid.
68. Ibid.
69. Ibidem; Celia Fiennes The Journeys of Celia Fiennes (1947) Edited by Christopher Morris pp.260-261
70. Pascoe (1981) pp.17-30
71. Ibidem; AD 894/7/5; AD 894/7/8-13 CRO; Camborne Tithe Apportionment Map (1840) CRO
72. Pascoe (1981) pp.17-30; Pryce (1972) p.279; Angerstein (1994); A. K. Hamilton Jenkin Mines & Miners of Cornwall vol.10 p.28; AD 894/7/5 CRO
73. Pascoe (1981) p.31
74. AD 894/7/7,48,49; DD TEM 55 CRO; DDX 475/2-7 CRO; Dolcoath Pay Book (1786-90) Private Collection
75. DDX 475/2,3; Bryan Earl Trevithick Society Newsletter (1992); Pascoe (1981) pp.17-30
76. AD 894/7/7,48,49 CRO
77. William Doidge Tehidy Manor Map (1737) X 101/5/1 CRO; AD 894/7/4 CRO
78. DDX 475/3 CRO
79. AD 894/7/3,7 CRO; John Griffiths The Third Man (1992) p.104; D. B. Barton The Cornish Beam Engine (1969) p.137
80. A. K. Hamilton Jenkin The Cornish Miner (1947) p.200; Harris (1974) p.10; K. H. Rogers The Newcomen Engine in the South West of England (1976) p.24; HJ/7/15 RIC; AD 894/7/8-13 CRO; Angerstein (1994)

81. AS 894/7/8-13 CRO
82. AD 894/7/4,5 CRO; Dolcoath Mining Leases (Sept. 21 & 28 1766) Private Collection
83. Sherborne Mercury (Nov. 7 & 14 1768)
84. A. K. Hamilton Jenkin Vol.10 p.17; Richard Trevithick Senior's Account Books for driving Dolcoath New Deep Adit (1765-68) Stolen from Tehidy Mineral Ltd Office, Basset St., Camborne in 1978
85. AD 894/7/4 CRO
86. DDX 475/2 CRO
87. AD 894/7/4,5 CRO
88. Richard Trevithick Senior's Account Book (1765-68); AD 894/7/5 CRO
89. Pryce (1972) pp.170-172
90. Ibid.
91. Ibid.
92. Ibid.
93. Ibid.
94. Pryce (1972) p.323; Harris (1974) p.21
95. Pryce (1972) pp.170-172
96. Ibid.
97. Charles Thomas, Journal Trevithick Society No.2 (1974) pp.45-53; DDX 475/2-7 CRO; Dolcoath Pay Book (1786-90) Private Collection; Harris (1974) pp.10-24
98. Pryce (1972) pp.173, 325; DD TEM 55 CRO
99. DDX 475/2-7 CRO
100. Richard Trevithick Senior's Account Book (1765-68)
101. DDX 475/2-7
102. Francis Trevithick Life of Richard Trevithick (1872) pp.62,63
103. DDX 475/2-7 CRO
104. Ibid.
105. DDX 475/2-7; J. H. Trounson personal communication
106. DDX 475/2-7 CRO
107. Ibid.
108. Ibid.
109. DDX 475/2-7; DDX 344 CRO
110. DDX 475/2-7 CRO
111. Barton (1969) p.137; DDX 475/2-7 CRO; Rogers (1976) p.25
112. Barton (1969) p.137; DDX 475/2-7 CRO; Rogers (1976) p.25; Harris (1974) p.21; Boulton & Watt Collections Birmingham & CRO Truro; Sherborne Mercury (Nov.23 1772)
113. T. R. Harris, Journal of the Trevithick Society No.5 (1977) p.33; DDX 475/2-7 CRO; Boulton & Watt Collections
114. AD 894/7/2-7 CRO
115. Griffiths (1992) pp.90,91,104
116. Dolcoath Pay Book (1786-90) Private Collection
117. Barton (1969) pp.18,137; AD 894/7/2 CRO; Rogers (1976) p.24
118. AD 894/7/1-7; DDX 475/3 CRO
119. DDX 475/2-7 CRO; Dolcoath Pay Book (1786-90) Private Collection
120. Ibid.

121. Ibidem; Clive Carter 'Early Engineers Around Camborne' Journal Trevithick Society No.25 (1998) pp.55-64
122. Rogers (1976) pp.24,25
123. Bridget Howard, Mr Lean & the Engine Reporters (2002) pp. 9-11,81
124. DDX 475/7 CRO
125. Harris (1974) p.15; Boulton & Watt Collection, Birmingham; AD 894/7/2,4,5,7 CRO; DDX 475/5,6 CRO; DD TEM 55 CRO
126. DD TEM 55 CRO
127. Boulton & Watt Collections Birmingham & Truro; AD 894/7/7 CRO; Harris (1974) pp.15,16
128. Boulton & Watt Collections
129. Harris (1974) p.21; Alphabetical Index of Patentees of Inventions (1969) p.599
130. DDX 475/2-7 CRO; Harris (1974) pp.13,14; Howard (2002) p.10; Rogers (1976) pp.16-27
131. DDX 475/2-7 CRO; Barton (1969) p.20
132. DDX 475/2-7 CRO
133. Ibid.
134. Ibid.
135. Ibid.
136. Ibid.
137. Ibid.
138. Ibid.
139. DDX 475/2-7; DD TEM 55 CRO
140. Ibid.
141. Pryce (1972) p.189; DDX 475/2-7 CRO; Harris (1974) p.24; STA 353 CRO
142. DDX 475/2-7 CRO; Dolcoath Pay Book (1786-90)
143. DDX 475/2-7 CRO; J. A. Buckley 'Introduction of Blasting into Cornish Mines' Wheals Magazine No.12 (1982) p.4
144. DDX 475/2-7 CRO
145. Ibid.
146. Ibid.
147. DDX 475/2-7; DD TEM 55 CRO
148. J Carne 'On Improvements which have been made in Mining' TRGSC vol.3 (1828) pp.35-86; W. J. Henwood, TRGSC (1871) pp.644-7; J. Hawkins 'On Tin Miners' TRGSC (1832) pp.83-94; R. N. Worth Historical Notes on the Progress of Mining Skill in Devon & Cornwall (1872) pp.12-15
149. Pryce (1972) pp.161,170-172; William Borlase Natural History of Cornwall (1970) pp.168-170; DDJ 1784 CRO
150. DDJ 1784; DDJ 1788 CRO
151. DD TEM 55 CRO
152. Henwood TRGSC (1871) pp.644-7; Philosophical Transactions of the Royal Society (1671) pp.2106,2107
153. DDX 475/2-7 CRO; Dolcoath Pay Book (1786-90); DD TEM 55 CRO; Poldice Cost Book (1789-99) Private Collection
154. Harris (1974) p.24; DDX 475/2 CRO
155. DDX 475/2-7 CRO; Dolcoath Pay Book (1786-90); Camborne, Illogan, Redruth and

Crowan Burial Registers CRO; AD 894/7/7 CRO

156. Boulton & Watt Collection CRO; AD 894/7/3,4,5,7,48,49 CRO

157. AD 894/7/4,5 CRO

158. AD 894/7/2-5 CRO

159. Angerstein (1994); Pryce (1972) pp.170-172; AD 894/7/2-7; DDX 475/2-7 CRO

160. AD 894/7/1-7,48,49 CRO

161. Boulton & Watt Collections, Birmingham & Truro; Harris (1974) p.23

162. Philosophical Transactions of the Royal Society (1769)

163. DDX 460/2 CRO; Gentleman's Magazine No.202 (1857) p.2; Henwood TRGSC (1871) p.647

164. Henwood TRGSC (1871) p.645

165. Tehidy Accts (1779,1780); AD 894/7/7 CRO

166. DDX 475/2-7 CRO

167. AD 894/7/1,7 CRO; Charles Thomas Mrs Percival's Endowed School 1761-1876. Institute of Cornish Studies (1982)

168. John Harris My Autobiography (1882)

169. STA 353 CRO

170. Allen Buckley Princes of the Working Valley (2007) pp.7-11; Francis Trevithick Life of Richard Trevithick (1872) p.53; Sketch of the Life of William West CE. Institute of Cornish Studies (1973) pp.9.10

171. Allen Buckley The Story of Mining in Cornwall (2007) pp.82-84; P Watts-Russell 'The Cornish Metal Company 1785-92' Journal Trevithick Society No.32 (2005) pp.10-27; Boulton & Watt Collections, Birmingham & Truro; Report on the Copper Trade to Parliament (1792-98); Barton (1978) pp.36,37

172. Dolcoath Pay Book (1786-90) Private Collection; Harris (1974) p.24; Arthur Raistrick (Editor) The Hatchett Diary (1967) pp.37,38; AD 894/7/7 CRO; Mining Journal (Oct.2 1858) p.646; MJ (Nov.27 1858) p.782

Part Two
The Nineteenth Century (1799-1895)

The Management of Andrew Vivian (1799-1806)

In 1799 the copper standard had risen to £120 a ton, which was double the figure in 1790. When Captain Andrew Vivian approached Lord de Dunstanville for the lease of Dolcoath Mine, in 1799, he was well aware of the enormity of the task which faced him. The mine was over 174 fathoms (1,044 feet) deep, and the largest part of the vast copper stopes were filled with attle – mine waste. Pumping the workings dry was only part of the problem, and despite it presenting the biggest immediate financial and technical challenge in 1799, Vivian, as an experienced mine captain knew that for the short and medium term at least, the big headache would be the hundreds of thousands of tons of saturated rubble that filled almost every void for a depth of over a thousand feet. Added to that was the enormous forest of timber stull pieces and lagging boards, which would be water logged, heavy and weakened. Reclaiming shafts, ladder roads, haulage ways and access levels would be a time consuming, expensive and dangerous job. Clearing the engine shafts and refurbishing the pumps and engines was to prove only a part of the reopening process. A glance at Pryce's long-section of Bullen Garden, drawn thirty earlier, indicates the extent of the problem which faced Vivian, Richard Trevithick and the rest of the new management team.[1]

Captain Andrew Vivian was well equipped to oversee the rebirth of Dolcoath Mine. He was born at Vellynsaundry, Camborne, in 1759, and as a boy attended Penponds village school, which his friend Richard Trevithick was to attend over ten years later. He was an intelligent boy born into a well-to-do family of mine managers and captains. By his early thirties he was involved in various businesses, some of which were connected to mining. He was a banker, tallow chandler, maltster and general merchant, but he was also a mine agent, and by the early 1790s he was managing Wheal Gons & Stray Park Mine, to the west of Dolcoath.[2]

Under Vivian's management Wheal Gons & Stray Park did far better than its more famous neighbours to the east. Between 1792 and 1798, despite appalling trading conditions (commodities and wages increased by fifty-percent and the price of copper remained low), the mine made profits for three of those seven years, of an impressive £8,293. Unfortunately, in the prevailing economic climate, even Vivian could not prevent severe loss in the other four years, which amounted to £15,723, making an overall loss of £7,430. At Wheal Gons and Stray Park Lord de Dunstanville held 1/16th share, with the Vivian family between them holding nearly a third of the adventure. Trevithick held a 1/64th and Vivian a 1/28th share. These two men held shares in other local mines also, with Trevithick tending to hold a 1/64th share where he was engineer.[3]

Dolcoath was not the only enterprise these two men were involved in together: they jointly worked on and patented the first successful road loco, and it was Vivian, on Christmas Eve 1801, who first drove Trevithick's prototype steam car 'up Camborne hill'. George Henwood, many years later, was fulsome in his praise of Vivian, speaking of how he became an able mechanic by associating and working with such men as Trevithick, Woolf and Hornblower.[4]

Vivian intended to operate Dolcoath in conjunction with Wheal Gons and Stray Park. The two mines exploited the same main lode, shared the same mineral and landlord (de Dunstanville) and many former Dolcoath men were employed at Wheal Gons & Stray Park. The new management team included Captain Vivian as manager or chief captain, Captain John Rule as Vivian's right-hand man, and Richard Trevithick as chief engineer. Others, such as the young Captain James Thomas, were probably also included.[5]

The adventurers were an interesting and varied group. Lord de Dunstanville held 1/8th share, and the rest of the adventure was divided between local Camborne men such as Andrew Vivian and Richard Trevithick, John Vivian of Pencalenick, and Solomon Burral, a merchant of Tuckingmill, and outsiders like George and Robert Fox of Falmouth and Perran Wharf, merchants and mine owners, John Williams of Scorrier, the king of Gwennap copper mining, C. B. Agar, landowner, Gilbert Chilcott of Truro, the Richards family, merchants, Joseph Banfield and de Dunstanville's agent and steward, Charles Rashleigh. It was fortunate for them that they all had deep pockets, for the reopening and bringing into production of this great mine was to prove exceedingly expensive and it tried the patience and bank balances of the richest of them. They were not to be disappointed, however, and their joint investment was to be richly repaid.[6]

Andrew Vivian's organisational skills were more than matched by the inventiveness and engineering know-how of the chief engineer. Before any dewatering could take place the pumps had to be put in order and Trevithick was typically inventive and innovative in his approach. Wheal Gons and Stray Park were drained by means of the old 63-inch Watt engine bought from Dolcoath in 1789, and as those workings were, in 1794, 140 fathoms deep, it follows that, some, at least, of the western workings of Dolcoath, would have been drained by the Wheal Gons 63-inch engine. Trevithick got to work immediately on the principal pumping engines sited on Bullen Garden. First, he introduced a plunger pole system to replace the less efficient and difficult to maintain bucket or suction pumps. At the same time he worked on the ancient 45-inch atmospheric engine, purchased from Carloose Mine by Dolcoath in 1775, modifying it and giving it a new cylinder and separate condenser. Three new high-pressure boilers were introduced, with pressure up to 20lbs per square inch. An old 63-inch Newcomen engine was also renovated and put to work with the 45-inch, both of which pumped through New Sump Shaft. The 63-inch pumped from the bottom of the mine, below the 170 fathom level, to the 40 fathom level, and the 45-inch engine pumped to the Deep Adit level. This method was known as 'shamelling'. It is possible that the elderly water engines were also pressed into service during this dewatering phase, for Dr Paris, who visited the mine in about 1815, referred to a fifty foot diameter water wheel powering a pump 150 feet below the surface. The water engines illustrated in Pryce's *Mineralogia Cornubiensis* had also been used in conjunction with two 'fire engines' in a 'shamelling' operation thirty years before Dolcoath's reopening. By 1802 Dolcoath was drained to the 170 fathom level and full production could recommence.[7]

An article in the 1871 *Mining Journal,* which appears to have been based upon financial records of Dolcoath from the beginning of the nineteenth century, gives an interesting and detailed account of the initial financial outlay of the mine, together with the high and low points of the reopening process. "In 1799 a company was formed for re-working the mine; they were but few in number, but clearly enough were men of the right sort. The calls upon their purses must have been very heavy. The outlay from July 1799 to August 1802 appears to have been £37,446 19 5d; from February 1800, to January 1801 inclusive, they were called on to pay £22,675 16 3d. Presuming they were not more than 20 in number, the call on each for one year was £1,130. The mine, however, soon began not only to pay its way, but to make profits. The first dividend that was declared was in July 1803, which was £2,000; in the following year £3,000 was paid; and in 1805, £35,935 0s 7d was divided among the fortunate shareholders. In November of that year (1805) it was £2,157 11s 9d; in the next month, December (1805) £7,058 10s 10d was declared as one month's profit; a larger dividend than this was paid in June 1809, being £7,632 14s 1d; but this was two months profit. The largest amount realised for copper ore sold in one month was £14,119 13s 9d, and in one year £117,515 0s 9d."[8]

According to William Jenkin, Dolcoath was also helped in its fight to move from loss to profit by the liberality of Lord de Dunstanville, who, when the mine reopened, reduced his dues until such time as the initial expense was covered. In May 1806 he wrote to C. B. Agar: "In my judgement Lord de Dunstanville acted wisely when he abated the dues in Dolcoath from one-twelfth to one-eighteenth for seven years (as I understand it and before that time was expired one-eighteenth to one-thirtieth during pleasure) when the adventurers had got back their loss of nearly £40,000. He then resumed the one-eighteenth dues where it now stands." Only a month earlier Jenkin had told Agar that Dolcoath was only just paying its costs, and again in July he wrote that the mine was barely covering its costs.[9]

With rising commodity prices and inflated wages the problem of getting the mine into production before the adventurers' patience ran out was crucial: the labour bill alone in 1801 was £12,277. Fortunately, the copper standard continued its gradual rise and during the first five years of the century it averaged £131 per ton. By 1802 the bottom levels were drained and production could recommence. An impressive 400 to 500 tons of copper ore a month was raised, this notwithstanding the need to clear and make safe all access levels, haulage ways, ventilation raises, footways and stopes. By 1802 the adventurers were feeling the pinch, despite the sympathetic reduction of dues by Basset, and it was commented: "Although the conduct of the lord towards the mine had been of the liberal kind, in reducing dues; yet who is there among the adventurers who do not feel the immense pressure of the expense?" In June 1802 William Jenkin sounded out Fox & Co. to see if they were interested in taking a share of Tincroft Mine, but they had recently taken a share in Dolcoath and were "out a full £34,000 to the end of last month, in getting it into a course of working." 1802 saw an income of £21,149 realised from copper ore sales, a small enough total alongside the enormous cash outlay, but it was a start and despite the pessimism, far more was shortly to follow. In the next two years over £150,000 worth of copper ore was raised, dressed and sold by Dolcoath. In the first three years of productive mining (1802-4) 27,591 tons of copper ore were sold by the mine for £178,416, which still amounted to an overall loss of £30,271 for the first five years since operations began to reopen Dolcoath. Undoubtedly, there were small tonnages of ore raised and sold between 1799 and 1802, but these were insignificant alongside the tonnage raised once the 170 fathom level was reached and proper, systematic ore production began. From 1803 onward production rose rapidly, and £114,121 worth of copper ore was sold in 1805, for a profit of £35,769. Average income from ore sales between 1805 and 1810 was an impressive £89,755, and this despite the copper standard slipping to an average of £127 per ton in the five years till 1810.[10]

Dolcoath Production 1800-1910

1800-1804	£178,416 (average £35,683)
1805-1810	£538,529 (average £89,755)[11]

Once Dolcoath was re-established as a large and important copper mine, she quickly assumed the moral leadership of the Cornish industry, and led by her philanthropic principal adventurer and mineral lord, Sir Francis Basset, Lord de Dunstanville, the mine took the lead in bringing about and financially supporting the county's new infirmary. Basset and Sir William Lemon, two of the wealthiest men in Cornwall, had been at the forefront of the moves to establish a hospital at Truro for the whole county. On May 20th 1799 the *Sherborne Mercury* announced that the hospital building was complete and staff were about to be recruited. However, it was not just the rich and powerful who shared the burden of this new and expensive enterprise, for the proud and independent Cornish miners, despite their often extreme poverty, also took a significant part of the expense upon their own shoulders. *The Royal Cornwall Gazette* of 22nd December 1804 lists the donations to the Cornwall Infirmary: the Dolcoath mine captains gave £3 15s and the miners contributed £18 5s 6d. Several Illogan mines gave cash as did Tuckingmill Methodist meeting house and Crowan and St Michael Penkivel parishes. The parish of Camborne gave £3 17s 11d. The total contribution was £44 18s 11d, of which Dolcoath miners and mine captains handed over almost half. The newspaper commented: "The liberal contributions to the Cornwall Infirmary, which appeared in our paper last week, from the Illogan mines, is highly creditable to the miners of that parish; and no class of people are likely to receive more benefit from the institution than miners, we have no doubt that the laudable example given at Dolcoath, Cooks Kitchen, Wheal Fanny, Wheal Druid, and Tregajorran, will be followed at all the great mines throughout the county." Regrettably, these words were to prove only too accurate, and over the next two centuries miners were to be a significantly large proportion of those treated by the hospital staff at the Cornwall Infirmary, Truro, and the several other hospitals established around the county. Sometime after the establishment of the Cornwall Infirmary, the practice began of miners having to pay their fines or 'spales' into the hospital, usually to the matron. The practice lasted until the second half of the twentieth century, when South Crofty miners, 'spaled' for some offence had to go into the Redruth Miners Hospital and pay the fine to the matron and bring back a signed receipt to the mine captain who had punished them.[12]

Early in 1806, despite increasing production and income, the volatile copper standard and continuing high commodity and wage bills meant that ways must be found to reduce overheads. Trevithick, ostensibly still chief engineer, but more frequently away from the mine pursuing his many other projects, was called upon to help solve the problem. An area of great concern was the cost of drawing ore to surface. Watt and Trevithick had both given the need for efficient winding engines some thought, and whereas the former had continued to rely on old solutions, Trevithick, typically, had sought to innovate. His high-pressure, non-condensing 'puffer' engine seemed to answer the problem. At a trial between his engine and that of Watt, which was situated on Dolcoath's Wheal Bryant Shaft, Trevithick's engine initially came off worst. However, with a few modifications and adjustments his engine soon proved far more efficient than that of his Scottish rival. Benjamin Glanville represented Boulton and Watt and Trevithick turned up to defend his own engine, placing a £50 wager on its success. He was not pleased to find that the piston in his engine was half an inch short, resulting in significant power loss. An eye-witness commented: "A new brass piston was put in, and she beat Boulton and Watt all to nothing. I was landing the kibbals for the puffer, because we tried Captain Trevithick's new kibbal and pincers made in our shop; we unloaded the kibbals, and sent them down again, almost without stopping the engine. The adventurers fixed upon a trial for three or four days; coals were weighed to each engine, and persons appointed to take account of the kibbals raised and coals burnt. Captain Trevithick's engine did the best; and after the trial, a little pit was found with coal buried in it, that Glanville meant to use in the Boulton and Watt engine." Drawing economies affected by Trevithick's 'puffer' made an important contribution to Dolcoath's continuing success.[13]

Trevithick wanted to introduce high pressure-steam into the 63-inch pumping engine, but although the agents were sanguine the adventurers, especially the outsiders led by John Williams, were less enthusiastic. They had heard of an explosion with a high-pressure boiler in South Wales and were understandably cautious. Williams wanted to know if the old boilers could stand high-pressure, and in May 1806 Vivian wrote to Trevithick, once again away from Camborne, to get reassurance. Since 1803 Trevithick had been absent from Camborne almost as much he had been present. Promoting his inventions in London and Wales, sometimes accompanied by Vivian, his business partner and joint patentee, Trevithick had left the day-to-day supervision of Dolcoath's engines to his assistant Richard Jeffery (Jeffree). Jeffery, who was born in 1773, had been employed at the Basset mines since he was a youngster, and he had worked with Vivian and Trevithick on the first road loco from as early as November 1800. From 1807, with Trevithick's almost permanent absence in London, especially whilst directing the driving of the Thames tunnel, Jeffery became Dolcoath's resident engineer. It was a position he was to hold for many years.[14]

Meanwhile Vivian's problems continued, and with money still being tight on the mine, he wrote to Trevithick about 'an old gent' who was supposed to want a large share in Dolcoath. It appears that the prospective investor was found and he put his much-needed cash into Dolcoath. This new cash infusion seems to have secured the future of the mine, and with the business concluded, Captain Andrew Vivian stood down as manager of Dolcoath, handing over to his senior mine captain, John Rule. Vivian was presented with a service of plate by the grateful adventurers of the mine, and given the enormous task he had overseen during the previous six years, it was a fitting gesture.[15]

The Management of John Rule (1806-34)

Captain John Rule was older than Andrew Vivian, being born in 1751, and so he was 55 years old when he assumed responsibility for Dolcoath. All the evidence suggests that although he might not have been the colourful and charismatic man that his predecessor was, he was, nevertheless, an experienced and very capable mine manager. Rule's management covered a period of expansion, turbulence and continuing problems. The mine was sunk deeper than many thought possible and engine and machinery innovations were being introduced throughout the industry. Added to that, nine years into his term, the continuous warfare, which had characterised the previous half century, came to an end, and brought unforeseen problems, both social and economic. Perhaps a bigger headache for a mine manager was the heightened expectation of investors, as new sources of information became available to them.[16]

A long-term problem the mine had faced as the workings deepened and extended along parallel and sub-parallel lodes, was ventilation. Early eighteenth century remedies no longer applied to mines of Dolcoath's size, depth and complexity. It had long been known that water flow helped air movement, but Rule studied the problem and put into practice a system of improved ventilation by water fall. This method supplemented the raises, winzes and floor sollars which were the widely used methods for improving air flow.[17]

The principal problem which faced the new manager was the volatile copper metal price, accompanied by the economic conditions brought about by the resumed war with the French and their allies. The 1802 Peace of Amiens had been broken by the 1803 resumption of hostilities, and given the numerical weakness and cash wealth of the British, it was expedient to subsidise the more populous enemies of France to encourage them to fight in Britain's anti-French coalition. The Austrians, Russians, Swedes and Prussians all benefited from English economic assistance of one kind or another during those years, and following the disastrous European battles of 1805 the British government offered to further assist the Russians. One way, favoured by the Admiralty, was to purchase 1,000 tons of Siberian copper from them at £150 a ton. This, understandably, caused dismay among the copper proprietors in Cornwall. A meeting of the principal copper mine owners took place in Redruth early in January 1807, at which a large number of Dolcoath adventurers attended, including the Foxes, Williams, Rashleigh, Banfield and Basset. It was decided to try to negotiate a deal with the government. On the 4th February 1807 Lord de Dunstanville attended a meeting in London of the Lords Committee for Trade, and before the meeting he canvassed the support of an influential member of the Committee. Basset sent him a copy of the Cornish proposals for him to 'peruse and consider it previous to our Meeting tomorrow'. De Dunstanville wrote that the Committee member would find in it a 'short statement of the recent distressed state of Cornwall occasioned by the Rapid fall in the price of Copper'. *The Royal Cornwall Gazette* of February 21st 1807 gloomily stated that the Cornish petitions had been unsuccessful, and that Dolcoath and the other mines "continue to drag on heavily and at great loss, in the hope of a favourable change; and if this does not happen soon they must inevitably stop." The newspaper spoke with foreboding about the preparations the mines were making which would lead to final closure. On the 11th March de Dunstanville wrote again to the committee member, and said: "We expected to have been able to forward to the Lord's Committee for Trade the Memorial on the Copper Trade … as the subject is of great importance to all those who are concerned in the Cornish Copper Mines … we hope in the course of a few days to be able to present it to the Board." Lord de Dunstanville's efforts were not successful, for despite the Cornish offer to supply the required 1,000 tons of copper for £140 per ton, on May 23rd 1807 he wrote again: "Though in some measure prepared for it, I am much concerned to see the intelligence conveyed by you of yesterday respecting the Contract for Russian Copper." Basset added that he would inform the Committee in Cornwall of the position, but that he would continue to press for another "interview with the Lords of the Committee, as the resolution of the Board of the Admiralty must be highly detrimental to the Proprietors of the British Copper Mines."[18]

In 1806 Dolcoath had paid four dividends to the adventurers, a total of £11,000, but during 1807, Rule's first full year in charge, only one dividend of £1,500 was paid out, and in October 1807 William Jenkin wrote to Agar that he believed Dolcoath would fail shortly, surprisingly adding just over a month later that 'no ores in the county are more desirable to the Smelter than those of Dolcoath'. The following year nothing went back to the adventurers at all, and things looked even bleaker at the mine. In June 1808 it was reported that Dolcoath was over 200 fathoms deep and had lost over £10,000 in the previous two years, and not just in costs, but also in the depreciation of 'the stock of ore and materials on the mine'. However, notwithstanding the relentless gloom that tended to pervade all of William Jenkin's comments about Dolcoath, 1809 saw the mine bounce back, with an impressive £40,000 profit, paid out in six dividends, although 1810 saw a more modest profit of £5,377.[19]

In February 1808 a one-hundred and twentieth share of Dolcoath was up for auction, and the advertisement stated that the adventurers had been paid £40,000 in dividends during the previous four years, and that there were materials and ore to the value of £40-50,000 on the surface. In the autumn Dolcoath was visited by the Reverend Richard Warner, who wrote a book called *A Tour Through Cornwall in Autumn 1808*. Like some of the eighteenth century industrial spies who visited and described the mines of Cornwall, Warner was a keen observer and careful recorder of facts. His account is most informative and deserves quoting, for it gives the clearest description of Dolcoath at a time of great change.[20]

"I have before observed that of all the Cornish copper works, Dolcoath is the largest; though many of them employ 600 men, besides a large tribe of women and children." (p.290)

"Dolcoath Mine lies about three miles to the westward of Carn-bre… here everything is upon a great scale. The works of the mine stretch upwards of a mile in length from east to west; an extent of ground penetrated by innumerable shafts, and honeycombed by as many subterraneous passes. Its depth is 1200 feet. Five engines are occupied in bringing up ore and rubbish; and three in freeing the mine from water. The largest of these, made by Boulton and Watt, is upon a stupendous scale … executing the work of 200 horses, and bringing up at every stroke (seven of which it makes in a minute) upwards of fifty gallons of water. … The persons employed at Dolcoath Mine, including men, women, and children, those who are above and those who are under the earth, amount to about 1600. Its produce is from 60 to 70 tons of copper per month, and about £30 worth of tin. The copper is worth, when dressed, £90 per ton."

Monthly charges: (1808) [21]

Coal	£700
Timber	£300
Cordage	£300
Gunpowder	£150
Candles	£200
Iron	£150
Sundries	£2,500
Total	£4,300 (p.133)

Warner wrote that Dolcoath was supervised by a purser or book keeper who was paid £8 8s a month, a chief captain, who was paid £13 13s a month, eight 'inferior' captains, who were each paid £6 6s a month and an engineer. He said that the miners paid for their own tools, candles and gunpowder, and that the tributers were not paid a wage but gained a proportion of the profits, that is, they were given an agreed percentage of the value of the ore they raised. There were five lodes being currently worked at the mine, and Warner commented that the mine had seen its best days. It had previously employed 2,000 workmen and cleared £6,000 a month, but that at that time copper had been £180 a ton and in 1808 it was only £90. Warner was informed that the "The largest sum ever cleared by her monthly produce, in the term of forty-five years, during which she worked, was £7,040." Warner had been given a tour of the underground workings by Captain Rule's son, Captain John Rule junior, who had impressed the clergyman by his knowledge and explanations. Warner was also impressed by the plans and sections of the mine, drawn by the young man who showed and explained them to him. He described them as: "These scientific delineations, the productions of an untaught youth." As with so many mine captains of the time, Capt Rule's education had been of the village or dame's school variety.[22]

As with a modern mine these 'inferior' mine captains, including the manager's son, were responsible for particular sections of the mine. At surface were the 'grass' captains, either responsible for preparation and delivery of all supplies to the underground workings, or for the landing and dressing of the copper and tin ore. The horse whims, water whims, stamps, crushers, bucking sheds, cobbing houses, spalling floors, picking tables and supervision of ore separation for assaying and ticketing, were the responsibility of these surface captains. Underground captains each had their own section or district, based upon particular shafts or groups of shafts. The eastern section was known as the Valley Section, and included the workings on Great (Main) Lode, between Gossan Shaft and Water Whim (Eastern Valley) Shaft, and the workings in Roskear Broaze, Wheal Susan and North and South Entral. The Middle District was the old Bullen Garden Mine between Gossan and Bennetts shafts. To the west lay Wheal Bryant and Old Dolcoath sections, with Wheal Gons & Stray Park, when they were operating as part of Dolcoath, and to the south of Wheal Bryant was Harriet Section, including workings on Caunter Lode. Sections were run by two mine captains working the day and night shift alternately. As we know that by the 1820s Valley Section was run by two mine captains, and their section was an extremely large one, it may be assumed that Dolcoath was divided into three districts in the early nineteenth century, each with two captains. This would have left two 'grass' captains to supervise the surface activity.[23]

Despite Warner's comment that Dolcoath's best days were past, the years that followed his visit were to be among the most productive and profitable in the long history of copper mining there. 1809 saw a vast improvement, and this increase in profitability was to last throughout the next two and a half decades. Dolcoath became the premier mine at the copper ticketing and her position of pre-eminence only began to slip in 1816, when she moved from top mine to second, and by 1822 to third, remaining among the top three for most years until the 1830s.

During 1810 a substantial quantity of silver ore was discovered at the 60 fathom level, on South Entral Lode. The silver ore was associated with cobalt and some native silver. Subsequently, a larger quantity of native silver, with galena, blende and red silver ore was found, possibly where a small crosscourse intersected South Entral Lode. According to Watson, the silver was worth some £2,000, but Harris said it was worth upward of £1,740, of which £1,300 worth was smelted on the mine. Charles Thomas stated that the Bassets had some silver plate made from it.[24]

Concern continued among the Cornish copper adventurers about the ongoing import of foreign copper into the country, and in November 1810 a meeting was called to try to find means to advance the copper standard. It was feared that without a price increase there could be a general collapse of the local mining industry, and stopping import of foreign copper seemed to be part of the answer, together with more freedom to export British copper. Another suggestion was that Cornish copper be used in the base metal coinage in circulation. The meeting felt that Lord de Dunstanville's efforts with the government were bearing fruit, and helping the gradually increasing copper standard. By December the increasing copper standard prompted the *West Briton* to comment: "The advance last week on the price of Copper Ore, will produce a difference of nearly a pound to each labourer in Dolcoath Mine, at their next pay day." This has been taken to mean that the mine was going to pay a pound bonus to the miners due to the improved copper price, but what it actually appears to have meant was that with the increased copper standard the tributers would gain 'nearly one pound' extra; that is, their ore would be worth that much more to them.[25]

1810 saw Dolcoath's production at 7,893 tons of copper ore, which sold for £76,964 15s 6d. This was down from the 1809 totals, which stood at 9,203 and sold for £102,258.[26]

In December 1810 Trevithick again appeared on the scene at Dolcoath, this time with the suggestion that by "borrowing Fox's and Neath Abbey blast furnace in which they used to Smelt Iron ore" Dolcoath and other mines' poor halvans could be smelted effectively. With his usual confidence Trevithick wrote to Davies Giddy in January 1811: "Tomorrow Dolcoath accounts will be held, when I expect to have orders to begin to erect a furnace on the spot." There is no certainty that this blast furnace was ever erected at Dolcoath, the scoria blocks scattered about the site appear to have been left from the eighteenth century smelting operation set up by Swaine, or by the furnace's operation in the 1770s.[27]

From the beginning of the century there had been wild fluctuations in the copper standard, creating an atmosphere of uncertainty and lack of confidence. In 1805 and again 1808 the standard had jumped to £200. It became profitable to melt copper coins down, as their value in weight was higher than their face value. A shortage of copper coins resulted, to the great inconvenience of the mine owners, local tradesmen and the miners. In 1806 the government sought to remedy the situation with a limited issue of new coins, but it was too little, so the Cornish copper proprietors found their own solution to the problem. They issued their own copper tokens with a face value of a penny. The Dolcoath Penny, which was designed and made by Halliday of Birmingham, had de Dunstanville's arms on one side and on the other side the words. 'Payable in Cash Notes at Dolcoath Mine. Cornish Penny'. The Williams family of Scorrier House had a similar one made for the Gwennap miners. The tokens were issued in 1811 and 1812. By 1817 the government were ready to mint sufficient copper coins to satisfy demand, and in July they passed a bill making the circulation of the Cornish penny tokens illegal from January 1818.[28]

The efficiency of the great steam engines was becoming an issue in the second decade of the eighteenth century, and with engineers and mine proprietors competing, various influential men, like Arthur Woolf and captains William and John Davey, encouraged Captain Joel Lean to begin the publication of his regular *Engine Reporters*. 1811 saw the first issue, and among the first engines to be reported on were those at Dolcoath Mine. The *Reporters* measured 'duty', that is the pounds of water lifted one foot by a bushel of coal. A bushel was originally 84lb, but was subsequently given as 94lb. Three of the first eight engines reported were at Dolcoath: the 63-inch or Great Engine at Bullen Garden, described as double-acting, with a 7 feet 6 inch stroke, and having a duty of 14.2 million, the 45-inch Shammal Engine, double-acting, also at Bullen Garden, which had a 7 foot stroke and a duty of 10.7 million, and the 36-inch single-acting Watt engine at Stray Park, with 5 feet 4 inch stroke and a duty of 12 million. There were also six steam whims on Dolcoath in 1811, and with the pumping engines they consumed a total of £11,180 worth of coal. When Lean inspected Dolcoath's engines he was not impressed. "The loss sustained by the mine was incalculable, for such a wretched state were things reduced by the inattention and carelessness of engineers and engine men, that not a winter passed by without leaving a very considerable portion of the mine deluged." These comments could hardly have pleased the adventurers, the agents or the chief engineer, Richard Jeffery. In the months that followed the old-fashioned wagon boilers were replaced by Trevithick's cylindrical ones, and the improved generation of steam increased duty to 21 million for the Great Engine. These new boilers were 30 feet long and had a diameter of 6 feet. The internal tube measured 3 feet 6 inches. In 1811 coal consumption at the mine had been 6,912 bushels, but in 1812 it had dropped to 4,752. Another consequence of the need for greater efficiency on the engineering side, was the promotion, in June 1812, of James Gribble to the position of joint chief engineer with Richard Jeffery. Gribble had been engineman at Wheal Gons & Stray Park, looking after the old Watt 63-inch there. He was a brilliant engineer, and although very much the younger partner, he is believed to have taken the lead in revitalising the engineering side of the mine. Arthur Woolf believed that Gribble was one of the most promising young engineers in Cornwall. The two men became friends and when improvements were needed to Dolcoath's plant it was to Woolf that Jeffery's young partner turned for advice. Just as the young Trevithick had surpassed John Budge, who had tutored him, so Gribble was to overtake the older Jeffery.[29]

In May 1811 the *West Briton* advertised a one-thirtieth share in Dolcoath, and mentioned that the mine was now united with Roskear Adit. When Richard Trevithick senior had supervised the extension of this adit into Dolcoath in the 1760s and '70s, a separate company had been formed to finance and maintain it, although the adventurers were the same as at New Dolcoath. Clearly, by 1811, it was decided to bring Roskear Adit, which was by then in 75 shares, into the fold. For most of its existence this adit system was known as Dolcoath New Deep Adit.[30]

With the copper standard continuing to swing up and down optimism was replaced by gloom, especially for observers such as William Jenkin, who wrote to A. M. Agar, in August 1811: "Not a mine in the parishes of Camborne and Illogan is gaining 1s to the adventurers although Dolcoath, Cooks Kitchen and Wheal Fanny are some of them." Tonnage was up for the year, but revenue was down by some £8,000, making life difficult once again for the adventurers. The copper standard dropped from £140 in 1811 to £130 in 1812, and although the mine's tonnage was up by 1,546, revenue was down some £4,804.[31]

Cobalt continued to be found on South Entral Lode and in November 1813 the *West Briton* advertised the sale of three tons of cobalt ore, together with ten tons of 'old junk', indicating that this particular ore had no ready, local market. The price of copper swung upwards again in 1813, with the mine selling over 1,000 tons less than the previous year, for over £4,000 more. Although this ore was hoisted from numerous shafts spread across the mine, the largest tonnages came via the five steam whims lying along the Main ('Great') Lode. On the western side of the mine was Stray Park 14-inch whim, which hoisted ore from a depth of 1,020ft, and Wheal Bryant 16-inch, which drew from the same depth. Teague's 24-inch and Middle 20-inch whims drew from the deeper central section of the mine, hoisting from 1,320ft and 1,260, respectively. East 10-inch whim drew from a mere 810ft. In April-May of 1813 these five whims hoisted a total of 13,132 kibbles. We have no indication of what the tonnage was, nor can we determine the quantity hoisted by the numerous horse and water whims on the mine, for the tonnage of ore sold does not include the significant tonnage hoisted, separated and thrown onto the vast burrows on and around the mine.[32]

1814 saw the copper price increase again, with the tonnage sold once again down, by 340 tons, and the income from ore up by £5,828. The pumping engines performed well in 1814, and following disappointing duty figures for 1813, the three engines increased efficiency impressively, with the old 63-inch Watt engine at Stray Park being top performer in Cornwall. In November Lean's description of the three engines gave the 63-inch Great Engine as double-acting, 'Drawing perpendicular 138 fathoms, on the underlay 19 fathoms, with cylinder over the Shaft, and Bob over the cylinder, and three Balance Bobs in the shaft.' The 45-inch Shammal engine was described as single-acting, and 'Drawing perpendicular with bob under the cylinder'. Stray Park 63-inch was single-acting, 'Drawing perpendicular 123 fathoms, underlay 12 fathoms, with bob over the cylinder.' R. Jeffery and J. 'Gribbel' (Gribble) were the engineers. Duty performed by the engines was 21.45 million, 26.76 million and 32.03 million, respectively. The three engines delivered an average of 348 gallons per minute to the Deep Adit level. The Bullen Garden shammal system brought up an average of 198 gallons per minute in two stages from a depth of 210 fathoms below Deep Adit, and the Stray Park engine lifted an average of 150 gallons per minute from the 140 fathom level.[33]

In November 1814 an enormous cavern or 'vugh' was discovered in killas at the 170 fathom level on Main Lode. This cavity, measuring some 18 to 20 fathoms long, by 3 fathoms high and 4-9 feet wide, was the largest of its kind ever found in Cornwall. It contained very bad air, and the miners' candles would not burn in it.[34]

In 1815 Dolcoath was visited by Dr J. A. Paris, who wrote a book entitled: *A Guide to the Mount's Bay & the Land's End.* This was probably the first of many guide books on Cornwall. Paris was extremely impressed by Dolcoath Mine, and after repeating a local 'old wives tale' about the origin of the mine's name (the 'Dorothy Koath' story), he describes the mine in the most glowing terms. He wrote that Dolcoath was "a copper mine every intelligent traveller ought to visit." The many steam engines, water wheels, horse whims and stamping mills, which could be observed across the mine, Paris found most impressive. "The same stream of water pouring down the hill turns successively numerous overshot wheels, and serves various purposes in its course; … it is conducted into the bowels of the earth, where, at a hundred and fifty feet beneath the surface, it again turns an overshot wheel of fifty feet diameter, and becomes again subservient to the skilful exertions of the miner. … The works stretch upwards of a mile in length from east to west; an extent of ground penetrated by innumerable shafts, and honey-combed by subterranean galleries." The underground water engine Paris referred to, was probably one of those illustrated by Pryce or a replacement wheel for one of them.[35]

It was in about 1815 that Charles Thomas (1794-1868), the future manager of Dolcoath, became a mine captain. The young man had started work at the mine, where his father, James, was a mine captain, in 1806, when he was just twelve years old. Like his father, he walked down the valley from Bolenow to the mine and home again each day.

The New 76-inch Pumping Engine
In 1815 Dolcoath's engineers realised that with the mine's increasing depth the aging and limited engines needed replacing. It appears that James Gribble took the lead in designing a replacement, and together with Jefferys, he consulted with Arthur Woolf on what was needed and how best to go about it. Woolf examined Gribble's drawings before they were submitted to the factories, and the 76-inch diameter cylinder engine, which was of traditional Watt type, incorporated several design features based on

Woolf's patent of 1804. It was single-acting with a 9-foot stroke, and was steamed by Trevithick's new cylindrical boilers. The cylinder was made at Neath Abbey Iron Works, Wales, and the beam was cast at Perran Foundry. It was referred to in 1824 by Hitchens and Drew: "In 1815, a very large engine beam was cast, the two parts of which weighed twenty-five tons." Part of the beam has been preserved and lies at Taylors Shaft, East Pool & Agar Mine, Pool. The engine was put on New Sump Shaft, Bullen Garden section, and replaced the old 63-inch and even older 45-inch engines. By 1816 this new engine was erected and becoming the best performer in the county, outstripping even the Woolf engine at Wheal Abraham. It was to pump from a depth of 200 fathoms below Deep Adit, and give a duty of 42 million.[36]

There was a total of 9,838 tons of copper ore raised and sold in 1816, which up by 912 tons of the previous year. However, the £54,087 income from ore was down an enormous £12,307, indicative of the continuing extreme fluctuations in the copper price.[37]

Dr Paris, who had visited Dolcoath and the other western mines in 1815, extended his interest in the mining industry by researching the causes of accidents and bringing forward a solution to one of the commonest types of underground accident, premature explosion. In 1817 he wrote a paper advertising his new 'Safety Bar'. This non-ferrous tamping rod was intended to replace the iron rods then commonly in use, and the cause of so many accidents. Paris researched some 98 cases of such accidents in west Cornwall, and came to the unavoidable conclusion that sparks produced by iron scraping or striking rock, whilst tamping the gunpowder of the charge, killed and maimed far too many Cornish miners. Eight of the accidents investigated occurred at Dolcoath. Four of the men: William Vincent, aged 55, John Tenby, aged 39, Thomas Wallis, aged 23, and John Bowden, aged 65, lost an eye, as well as sustaining other injuries. Four others: Stephen Freeman, aged 52, James Thomas, aged 66, Solomon Cundy, aged 30, and Walter Hosking, aged 51, had injuries ranging from fractured skull and broken leg, through to broken jaw. Only two of the eight were able to return to mining after recovery. It is of interest that these men between them had 37 children, many of the younger ones still in need of support. Of the 98 cases eleven were fatal accidents, none of them at Dolcoath. The ages of these men are also of interest, in that the old myth about 'all miners being dead by forty' is set to rest. Among the rest of the cases reviewed by Paris were several miners in their 60s and 70s, the oldest being 75 years of age, and working at Wheal Kitty, Camborne. These were all men at the cutting edge of mining, not relegated to softer jobs underground or at surface.[38]

Subsequent to Paris' report, an accident of exactly the kind he hoped to eliminate occurred at Dolcoath. On Saturday June 20th 1817: "Two men named John Allen and Francis Harris, having been employed in the dangerous experiment of tamping a hole with a common (iron) bar, the charge prematurely exploded; when Allen was killed on the spot, and his companion was so shockingly mutilated that but little hopes are entertained of his recovery."[39]

In April 1817 Dolcoath's two engineers offered their skills to the wider mining world, when they placed an advertisement in Cornish newspapers. "Improvements in Steam Engines. James Gribble and Richard Jeffree, of Camborne, have recently made improvements on the engine of Messrs. Boulton & Watt, and can now undertake to erect an Engine which shall perform greater duty than others with two cylinders. The grounds of these improvements are to obviate the necessity of two cylinders with their appendages and expense. An engine, erected originally with these improvements will cost no more than one on Boulton & Watt's Plan, and to apply these improvements to a 63-inch cylinder of Boulton & Watt's single cylinder will not cost above £150 and the improvements will be completed in forty eight hours. April 11 1817." No doubt this extra-mural activity was approved by the adventurers at Dolcoath, who were to continue to demonstrate their support for these engineers.[40]

Production at Dolcoath was down in 1817 to 9,321 tons, a fall of 517 tons. Income from ore sales was also down by £5,503, to £48,584. In 1818 this trend was reversed dramatically, with tonnage increasing by 1,894 to 11,215 tons, and income from ore up an impressive £34,220 to £82,804. Despite these vastly improved figures Dolcoath had lost her pre-eminence at the ticketing, and although she maintained her position among the top copper producers for several more years, the mine was never to regain its former position among Cornish copper mines.[41]

In 1818, Richard Thomas, a surveyor and civil engineer, carried out a massive survey of the mines between Camborne and Chacewater. He reported on each individual mine in the district, including many which were long abandoned. His report on Dolcoath covers all important geological and mining aspects of the working, and gives a clear picture of the mine at the time. The mine was 230 fathoms deep, and its sump was 170 fathoms below sea level. Dolcoath was the deepest mine in the district. The workings were drained by two steam engines, the 76-inch erected in 1815/16, and the older 63-inch, at Stray Park. The adit to which these engines pumped came into the western end of the mine as far as New Sump Shaft, but the shallower, Cooks Kitchen Deep Adit, carried away the infiltrating surface water in the Valley Section of the mine. Thomas referred to seven steam whims, ranging from 14 inches to 24 inches in cylinder diameter, and a 20-inch stamps engine. The number working at Dolcoath was 1,600, making it by far the largest employer in the district. The two ports used by Dolcoath for shipping ore out and bringing coal in were Hayle and Portreath, the former being 6¼ miles and the latter some 4 miles away.[42]

The lodes being exploited in 1818 were North Entral Lode, which was the most northerly worked, a small unnamed copper lode, Entral (South Entral) Lode, Great (Main) Lode, and three small branches or lodes south of Great Lode. North Entral Lode, which contained copper and tin, was worked right through Entral and Roskear Broase tenements, and had a northern underlay. The unnamed lode to the south of North Entral Lode was worked for copper, and also dipped to the north. Entral Lode worked for copper and tin, dipped slightly to the south in the east but flattened out as it went west, before steepening again. The lode split into two branches a short distance west of the Great Crosscourse, the south branch being the wider, entering the footwall of Great Lode some 150 fathoms west of the crosscourse. This branch was almost perpendicular. Great Lode, known for generations as Main Lode, is the principal copper and tin carrying mineralised structure in the district. It dips to the south, although at surface it is almost vertical. On the east side of the Great Crosscourse, which faults it, Thomas believed it was called Duncan's Lode of Cooks Kitchen. More generally it has been known as Highburrow Lode in the mines to the east of the Great Crosscourse. The three branches to the south of Great Lode were described as copper lodes, and they dipped to the south.[43]

There was an unusual move in 1818 to cause tributers who were earning well to save some of their wages. The *West Briton* reported on 10 July 1818 that Dolcoath adopted a system by which a tributer who earned more than £3 in a month, would deposit thirty percent in the Redruth Savings Bank. Whether this was entirely due to altruism on the part of the agents and adventurers, or a subtle way of bringing cash into a bank owned by the same men, we do not know, but the newspaper stated that £250 was deposited due to this policy in June 1818.[44]

On 29 August 1818 William Jenkin wrote to P. Grenfell about an interesting system at Dolcoath and the other Basset mines in Camborne and Illogan: "The principal agents of Lord de Dunstanville's mines in Camborne and Illogan are allowed to supply the mines with a small share of the materials consumed therein – such as gunpowder, etc, which makes a very considerable addition to their salaries – but they are men much above the rank of common captains, and are much esteemed and respected for their superior skill and intelligence in mining affairs." No doubt, by allowing some of the senior agents, like Captain John Rule, to benefit from their involvement in the mine in the same way that in-adventurers did, their loyalty to Dolcoath would be cemented.[45]

An interesting example of loyalty among the higher echelons of the mine occurred in 1818, when an anonymous writer to the *West Briton* accused the senior engineer at Dolcoath of acting dishonestly to the detriment of the mine and the adventurers. Richard Jeffery was accused of appropriating some old iron, owned by the mine, for his own use. The adventurers vigorously defended Jeffery, writing a letter to the newspaper, explaining that he had in fact purchased the old iron from the mine to make fire grates at his own expense. Not only was Jeffery not guilty of dishonesty or fraud, but the adventurers wished "to bear witness to the great professional services, as well as the general integrity, of Richard Jeffree's conduct." Jeffery was to remain engineer at Dolcoath, and other local mines, for several decades, until his death.[46]

Dr Forbes' Experiments

Dr Forbes, writing in the *Transactions of the Royal Geological Society of Cornwall*, stated that in 1819 Dolcoath was 1,386 feet deep and the country rock was killas. Forbes was interested in air, rock and water temperatures underground, and in cooperation with Captain John Rule the manager, and Captain Rule's son, also a mine captain, experiments were carried out to monitor temperatures on different levels in a variety of locations. In one location, 230 fathoms from surface, a 4 feet long thermometer was inserted into a 3 feet deep hole in an end on a copper lode. This was at the time the deepest level at the mine. There was little air movement in the end and no workmen were currently employed there. The temperature recorded in the hole was 75 degrees Fahrenheit. Subsequently, a table of temperatures was created from this monitoring, which showed the increase in heat as the mine went deeper. At the 40-50 fathom levels it was 58 degrees, and the same at the 90-100 fathom levels, but at 120-130 fathoms it rose to 63 degrees, at the 190-200 fathom levels, 64 degrees and at 220-230 fathom levels it was 78 degrees Fahrenheit. Below the 230 fathom level the temperature went up to 82 degrees. Clearly, these temperatures would vary considerably according to such factors as the heat of water issuing from lode or granite, and according to the ventilation.[47]

Production in 1819 was down 1,116 to 10,099 tons, with revenue from copper ore down £15,049 to £67,755. Although tonnage increased by 169 in 1820 to 10,268 tons, income was down £6,615 to £61,140. This trend continued in 1821, with tonnage up 834 tons to 11,102 tons and with the price falling income from ore sales was down £5,277 to £55,863.[48]

After the initial work with Forbes, in 1819, Captain Rule junior, continued with this monitoring in the years that followed, tieing it into the work of his father a decade earlier when he sought to improve ventilation by such things as water fall. In 1822 Rule, described as 'one of the superintendents' at Dolcoath wrote: "I have made some experiments to ascertain the direction of the currents of air in this mine, and find that in 25 of our principal shafts (the whole of those on the main lode) 13 have a strong current of air downwards, and 12 about the same degree of current upwards." Rule commented that this varied with the wind strength and direction, and added: "We find no want of air underground, even in the deepest parts, where communication is made from one level to another by means of a shaft or winds (winze), or from one shaft to another by a level … the current of air is frequently so strong even toward the bottom of the mine as sometimes to blow out a candle."

Rule also was concerned with air movement in stopes, a potentially more difficult problem to monitor, especially where so much broken ground was thrown to stull and attle movement was a constant problem.[49]

It was in May 1822 that William Petherick, a nephew of Captain Rule senior, became a mine captain at Dolcoath, and he proved himself a very intelligent and able miner. He was to work with his cousin in trying to solve some of the problems that this deep and extremely complex mine was beginning to face. Petherick, who was in his mid-twenties, worked alongside the much older and very experienced Captain James Thomas, in the eastern Valley Section of the mine, and their friendship and mutual respect was to serve him well during his time as agent, joint manager and then sole manager of Dolcoath. Captain Thomas, who was 44 years old in 1822, lived at Bolenow, where he had a small-holding or small farm, and he walked each day the two miles down the valley to the mine. He carried out all the tasks on the farm, planting and lifting potatoes, harvesting the furze and hay, and looking after his stock. Thomas also managed the small South Bolenow Mine, which was being re-opened, and on which he spent some time. His son, Captain Charles Thomas, was to become manager at Dolcoath, and became the most respected mine captain of his generation. Captain Petherick lived with his mother, and at the time, does not appear to have been married. He was part of a large extended family, including the mine manager, his cousin and senior agent, John, and other members of the Rule family involved at Dolcoath. The two men were devoted family men, whose affection for their kin can be clearly seen in their numerous references to them.[50]

We are fortunate, that these two mine captains, Thomas and Petherick, who worked alternate day and night shifts in the Valley Section of the mine, kept a daily journal of their activity. Undoubtedly, this was normal practice throughout the better-organised mines of west Cornwall, but this one survived. It gives an unequalled picture of how Dolcoath operated at the time, what the daily tasks and responsibilities of the captains were, where their jurisdiction ended and where the manager and purser became decision makers. Discipline, assignment of work, negotiating with tributers and tutworkers, safety, payments for special tasks, which varied according to difficulty or danger, checking the ore's value in the lode and at surface, determining where stulls should be erected or strengthened, maintaining shafts, ladderways and levels, settling disputes between miners over the extents of their pitches or about private agreements between miners, all were the daily tasks of these two remarkable mine captains. They were also concerned, with the 'grass' captains, about the maintenance of the machinery at surface, such as horse and water whims, whim ropes, pulleys and kibbles. By night, security was also partly their responsibility. They were involved with such tasks as helping to divide and prepare the ore for ticketing, and ensuring that each tributer's ore was not mixed with others prior to its assay or valuation. Adit maintenance was another area of concern for these two men, as their section extended in an arc covering the workings and shafts on Main Lode between Gossan Shaft and Water Whim Shaft (Eastern/Valley), the two Entral lodes, including Roskear Broase, and the shallow workings at Wheal Susan, below Tuckingmill Village. There were at least two adits they monitored, part of Cooks Kitchen Deep Adit, and a shallower adit on the western side of the valley. Dolcoath New Deep Adit (Roskear Adit) was not their responsibility.[51]

The Mine Management

The management of the mine can be ascertained by searching through the journal. At the top was the purser, 'Mr Reynolds', who was almost certainly Mr William Reynolds of Trevenson House, Pool. He was also the Basset family agent, and was purser at other important mines like East Wheal Crofty. Captain John Rule senior was the mine manager. His son, John Rule, was his right hand man, as he remained until taking a contract with John Taylor, in Real del Monte, Mexico, and becoming even more famous than his father. Other captains were James Thomas and William Petherick, captains Christopher ('Kit') Robin and Jilbert, both 'grass captains', Captain Tregoning, one of the Middle Section mine captains, possibly Charles Thomas, brother of James, Captain John Lean and 'Cousin William' Rule. Another Charles Thomas, although not mentioned in the journal, was probably already a mine captain at Dolcoath in 1822-23. Other mine captains mentioned, who may have been employed at Dolcoath, were captains Harry, Skinner and Tucker. James Gribble and Richard Jeffree, Dolcoath's two senior engineers, were referred to several times. John Phillips was assayer and probably surveyor. He appears to have been the same man who drew survey plans at East Wheal Crofty, and also ran a 'Mining School' at Tuckingmill.[52]

The journal mentions at least 63 tributers by name, and these held pitches on many different levels. Over a dozen tutwork crews were mentioned, mostly being directed on a daily basis by the captains. Like the tributers, who sometimes did work by the stem, these tutworkers often had tribute contracts, especially where they were driving on lode or driving a crosscut through a lode. Nineteen levels are referred to, from Shallow Adit 'east of Roskear Broase', down to the 200 fathom level. Most of the mining in Valley Section between December 1822 and October 1823 took place between the 40 fathom level and the 145 fathom level, and work elsewhere was frequently to do with improving ventilation, safety or access. A considerable number of shafts were in use in the eastern section: Gossan Shaft, South Valley Shaft, Water Whim Shaft, North Valley Shaft, often merely called 'Valley Shaft', Roskear Broase Shaft and Machine Shaft.[53]

The *West Briton* of 27 September 1822 carried a very optimistic report on the mine. "We understand, that there has lately been cut in Dolcoath Mine, a rich copper lode, which is said to be worth one hundred pounds a fathom. This discovery is the more valuable from its being what the miners term, all in whole, that is, all in dry ground. – We have also heard, that there has been discovered in the same mine, a rich lode of tin, about two hundred fathoms from surface." The newspaper was particularly glad of these discoveries because of the generally depressed state of local copper mining, upon which so many poor people depended for their subsistence. The rich copper lode was what interested the *West Briton* most, but it was the other lode that was to prove the most valuable in the long run. Just over three months after this report Captain James Thomas wrote to Captain Petherick: "I went down this morning with Capt Tregoning in the Middle District, to the 200 fathom level & 190 saw some good tin etc ..." Richard Thomas had mentioned in his 1819 Report on the 'Chacewater to Camborne' mining district, that Dolcoath was selling some £200 worth of tin a month, that tin was found in all the principal lodes and that the mine had a 20-inch engine for its tin stamps. There are over twenty references to tin being discovered, mined, stamped, dressed or sold in the Thomas-Petherick journal, indicating that knowledge of the increasing frequency of tin as the mine went deeper, was not a new discovery of the 1840s, but was a recognised fact among the miners and mine captains at Dolcoath from an early date.[54]

Health and safety were important responsibilities for Thomas and Petherick, and there are nearly fifty references to accidents or dangerous situations in the ten months of the journal. Several funerals were also mentioned, but whether the deaths occurred at the mine or elsewhere cannot always be determined. Henry Vincent, aged 59, of Helegan Carne, was buried at Camborne 30 December 1822. In the January 6 1823 entry in the journal James Thomas said: "I saw H'y Vincent Jun'r – His father's Coffin Cost 45/- and say for all other expenses on the occasion 15/- or 20/- more. I don't think it wou'd be out of the way – mind to put it in the Book." It seems likely that either Vincent was killed in the mine, or he was a long-serving employee. Petherick reported late on the evening of 9 January 1823, owing to going to Henry ('F') Bartle's funeral at Camborne. He described the funeral as being attended by an 'Immense Concourse of people'. Henry Bartle, aged 32, of Gwinear, would seem to have been employed at Dolcoath, by the large number of the mine's employees who attended. There is no information on how he died. On 4 June 1823 Matthew Harris, uncle of the miner poet, was buried at Camborne. He appears to have been the victim of a mining accident at Dolcoath, for there are several references to his brother John Harris awaiting his Club Money for the accident. Captain James Thomas, Harris' neighbour, attended the funeral. In John Harris' autobiography, he speaks of his Uncle Matthew blowing out a wall of the family cottage at Bolenow, when the poet was a child. He would have been less than three years old when his uncle died. The Burial Register merely records him as 'Matthew Harris of Bolenno, aged 36'. In the entry for the night of 2 July 1823, James Thomas wrote: "I shall if I am pretty well go to the Funeral of H'y Eva." Camborne Burial Register records the funeral of 'Henry Eva, aged 21, of Condurrow – 3 July 1823." Again, we have insufficient information to determine if Henry Eva died as a result of an accident at the mine, but the context certainly suggests a connection between the mine and Eva.[55]

The many potentially dangerous situations noted by Petherick and Thomas in their daily (and nightly) inspections of the working places underline the serious hazards of mining. Bad ground falling on careless or unsuspecting miners in stopes; damaged or worn-out ladders; moving attle due to settlement or rotting stull pieces; timber rearings (casings) giving under pressure of loose ground or attle thrown to stull; premature explosions due to primitive fuze rods or ferrous charging bars; falls due to poor lighting or sheer exhaustion, and many other hazards were present, and all were noted by the two mine captains. Typical of the mine captain's daily routine was that described by William Petherick for January 13th 1823:

> Captain James,
> I've been down to day. Trezona's End is not looking so well for ore or tin, but the Ground is far better. If it holds until Survey day as it is now We must lower their price Considerably. The hard stones appear to be nearly all gone. Saw Tom Oppy & ptrs. There is very bad ground about the shaft at the 134. Saw Pascoe & ptrs throwing deads like sons of bitches at 118. Went to examine the state of the stulls up over them west of Valley Shaft at 110 on N Part & found all the attle from 8 or 10 f'ms west of the shaft in a sinking State. We quickly decamped from there & came back through Iveys pitch on South pitch. Crawl'd in through a small Hole & found the attle in the same state all Sinking. Retreated as quick as possible from these scenes of danger & arrived in Tom Rogers's pitch, which is as dangerous as any of them – arrived up at ½ past 2 oclock Hungry & tired. Will eat all the day Bread.
> Wm Petherick[56]

These regular inspections carried out by the mine captains, were followed by the senior timber men, Abraham and Crase, examining the unsafe areas to remedy dangerous situations. The day after Petherick's report on the state of the stulls over Pascoe and partners, he reported: "Abraham & Crase have been down to day examining the stulls over Pascoe & ptrs again, & the place where we were yesterday is all sunk away 2 or 3 f'ms. Still they believe there is no danger."[57]

On 3 March 1823 Captain James Thomas carried out an inspection and gave orders for necessary safety work. "I have been down thro' Valley to day measuring Trezona's End. There is some good bits of ore in it with a large quantity of mundick – I was also in the Gossan Shaft at the 40. There is a very dangerous piece of ground and a great deal of attle just ready to come away in the shaft. I order'd Abraham & Sampy Roberts & Wm Thomas to repair it. I have got the ladders put in their old place in the Valley Shaft near 40."[58]

On 12 March 1823 Petherick wrote that two men were working in the shaft when four men should have been assigned to the task. Petherick was concerned that saving money should not compromise safety. Petherick also commented on a dangerous occurrence in a shaft a fortnight later: "Abraham has been bravely frightened to day. A piece of ground came away on him while he was in the couch, but no harm came of it. I have sent Crase & him to take a drop of something to comfort their hearts." The 'couch' appears to have been a cradle of some sort that was hung in a shaft from which the timber men could carry out safety work. Two months later, 23 March, Abraham and his fellows had another bad experience whilst working in the shaft on the couch. "Abraham & pare was frighten'd to day down in the couch. Some attle fell from under."[59]

Another ever-present danger was the state of the ladders. Climbing to and from a working place many hundred feet from surface, on old, worn, slippery and often insecurely fixed ladders, was always dangerous, but doing so with only a candle by which to see, was doubly so. On February 26th 1823, Richard Rule was climbing up the ladderway to surface at Dolcoath, and had almost reached the surface, when a rung on the ladder broke, pitching him backwards down the shaft to his death. Whilst going underground, on the night shift of June 9th 1823, James Bennetts, known to his mates as 'Patience', had a potentially dangerous accident. "James Bennetts (Patience) in going underground to night sprained his side & was oblig'd to come up again, it was owing to three staves being gone in the second ladder above the 80." The poor man had already climbed over 600 feet down, and was then obliged to climb the same distance up, with a sprained side. With out a doubt, Bennetts would have been able to claim from the Club whilst off work injured. A miner in danger of unsuccessful claiming was a tutworker called Kit. On 20 June 1823 Petherick visited an end on the 70 fathom level west of Entral Shaft, and commented: "Sollars choaked no air in the end." Floor sollars were a system for ventilating a dead end. A false wooden floor was laid, leaving a space beneath, so that air could circulate by moving along the tunnel and back through the floor space. Twelve days after his first visit Petherick checked the end again, and he was not pleased: "I've been down to Entrall to day. Kit & pare are in the old core again. They have driven only 3½ feet. They have left the good ground standing to the north & are got away to the south in very hard ground. Sollars all choaked & end full of stuff, which according to custom Kit promised to clear against I came again. I told him he should not work there any more if he did not be cleaner in his work, and if he was hurted by means of the bad air he should not be paid for it from the Club." It is an interesting example of how discipline and safety were seen at Dolcoath in the early nineteenth century, and what responsibility the captains had toward entitlement to payment from the miners' Club. These few examples serve to illustrate the breadth of a captain's work, and type of accidents typical of Cornish mining at the time.[60]

Nearly five months after 'Patience' Bennetts slipped and injured himself on a ladder above the 80 fathom level, there was another more serious accident of the same sort. The *West Briton* reported on the 32 October 1823: "On Tuesday last, as a young man was ascending a ladder, in Dolcoath Mine, he fell into the shaft, and was killed on the spot." Quite possibly, exhaustion played its part in the accident. There was another fatal accident at the mine in the same week.[61]

Dr Forbes made various observations about the mine in 1822, and noted that Dolcoath had been deepened to 1,428 feet, forty-two feet sunk since 1819, and that there were some 800 miners working underground. He also said that 6,000lbs of candles a month were being consumed by the miners, and 2,600lbs of gunpowder. The two pumping engines were delivering 535,173 gallons of water an hour to the Deep Adit. The temperature of this water was 72 degrees Fahrenheit at the western end of the mine and 64 degrees at the eastern, shallower end.[62]

Petherick and Thomas made constant mention in their journal of the gradually subsiding ground. Although their experience was at the eastern end of the mine, it was a problem throughout the workings as waste rock, thrown to stull, as far back as the middle of the previous century, began to settle, and ancient timber stull pieces, wet and rotten with age, gave way beneath the thousands of tons of attle resting on them. In October 1823 a cannon was referred to, which was used to bring down loose and hanging ground. William Petherick, supervising night shift on 16 October, apologised to Captain Thomas, for "I quite forgot to have the mouth of the Culverin cleaned up on Tuesday." This long-barrelled cannon was still being used to bring down rock hang-ups in the late 1820s.[63]

In 1823 Lean commented that the cost of coal consumption at Dolcoath had dropped since 1811 from less than £11,180 to £6,587 in 1823. This, despite an increase from six to eight steam whim engines on the mine, and the addition of a 20-inch stamps engine. Production was down 1,631 tons to 9,471 in 1822, and revenue from ore sales was also down by £7,846 to £48,017. 1823 saw a further significant fall in tonnage and revenue, with the former down to 7,696 and the latter down to a depressing £39,851, a fraction of what it had been only ten years before.[64]

Captain John Rule Goes to Mexico
It was in about 1823-24 that the manager's son, John Rule junior, began his association with John Taylor at Gwennap Consolidated and United mines. Perhaps it was Arthur Woolf who made the contact, for he had had a long association with Dolcoath, had a house at Camborne and was familiar with all the important mining men of the parish, including Captain Rule, manager of Dolcoath, and at that time one of the most important men in Cornish copper mining. The following year Captain John Rule junior, aged 42, was off to Real del Monte in Mexico, to manage the mines

there on behalf of Taylor. Rule became something of a legend in Mexico, dominating metal mining there for a generation, and establishing a miners' migration route that remained strong long after his death. Even after Rule returned to Camborne, where he died in 1866, Camborne and Gwennap miners continued to follow the trail blazed by him in the 1820s. William Petherick, John's cousin, was to benefit from his departure, for he replaced him as the manager's right-hand man, and took over his work of investigating how best to improve efficiency and safety underground at Dolcoath.[65]

Wheal Gons, which with Stray Park, had formed the original western section of the newly re-opened mine in 1799, became separated shortly thereafter, and in the early years of the nineteenth century it produced only tiny tonnages of copper ore. Stray Park was also eventually worked separately, before becoming idle. It appears that in 1825 Stray Park was reorganised and re-opened, taking in the Wheal Gons and Camborne Vean setts in 1828. Stray Park had an adventurous history thereafter, taking in and relinquishing adjacent setts for several decades until 1870, when the mine was again abandoned. Thereafter Dolcoath found it necessary to acquire the sett to avoid the threat of flooding, and it was to remain part of Dolcoath for much of the time until the final demise of the old mine in 1920.

A Fatal Accident

There was another tragic accident at the mine in November 1824, and once again it was caused by falling from a ladder underground. "On Wednesday last, a young man named Oliver Rule, who was employed in a shaft at Dolcoath Mine, slipped his foot and was precipitated to the bottom, a depth of fifty fathoms, and was killed on the spot." Rule was twenty years old and lived at Condurrow, over a mile south of the mine. Another accident also was reported in the same issue of the *West Briton*: "Two young men fell into a shaft at Wheal Bryant Mine, last week; but the depth was not great, though severely bruised, they are likely to recover." Wheal Bryant was part of Dolcoath. No information on what the two men were doing was given in the report, and so we do not know if they were employed on the mine, were miners walking to or from work, or just a couple of youngsters acting dangerously.[66]

In 1824 copper ore production was down 192 tons on the previous year to a total of 7,504 tons. Revenue from ore sales was also down by £2,713 to £37,138. On March 5 1824 the *West Briton* reported a dispute at the ticketing. Dolcoath had long held the place at the head of the list, but in March of that year Gwennap Consolidated insisted that as it had taken over as the largest copper ore producer, she should take the chair. Dolcoath's agent disagreed, stating the 'long usage gives the first place in the sale to Dolcoath', but to no avail. Copper wise, Consols was now top dog! Dolcoath's decline in tonnage continued in 1825 to 7,191, but there was an upswing in revenue to £43,093. This reflected the national situation, where economic and industrial expansion, started in the early 1820s, boomed in 1824, and led to great optimism in the metal mining industry as copper and other raw materials became more valuable. On February 4th 1825 there was an advertisement in the *West Briton* for the sale of ten tons of cast iron and seven tons of scrap iron, together with a complete steam whim engine with a 26-inch cylinder. Lean lists no such whim engine at Dolcoath at the time. In October a 1/96th share in Dolcoath was also advertised for sale.[67]

The Death of the Engineer James Gribble
In April 1825 James Gribble, one of Dolcoath's engineers, died at the age of only 39, thirteen years after joining Richard Jeffery as joint engineer at the mine. Gribble had been regarded by many, including Arthur Woolf, as being one of the best young steam engineers in Cornwall. In 1815 he had designed the 76-inch engine at Bullen Garden and was credited with great inventiveness, improving the efficiency of Boulton and Watt engines and work on a 'trunk engine' of some sort. He was to be sorely missed at the mine.[68]

The economic expansion and confidence of the early part of the 1820s was reversed as suddenly as it occurred, and in 1826 there was despair among Cornish copper proprietors as once again the price of copper dropped. This depressing situation continued until the end of the '20s, when things began again to improve. In 1826 production was up by 784 to 7,975 tons, but income from ore sales dropped by £8,816 to a disastrous £34,277, the lowest it had been for twenty-three years.[69]

At the end of the year there was another fatal accident at the mine. The *West Briton* reported on 15 December 1826: "Accidents – Last week a young man, a miner, whilst walking on a plank placed over the mouth of a deep shaft, at Dolcoath Mine, struck his head against a piece of timber placed across, and was precipitated to the bottom, where he was found quite dead." A short distance to the north of Dolcoath, at North Roskear, there was another dreadful accident mentioned in the same report, where two young miners had been maimed by a premature blast, one losing both eyes and the other having both arms broken, one of them later being amputated.[70]

In March 1827 Alfred Jenkin wrote to P. Grenfell and mentioned that Dolcoath ore was showing considerable quantities of tin. Dolcoath was not unique in this respect and Jenkin commented that "the Wheal Vor and Cooks Kitchen ore also contain much of this objectionable metal." Jenkin, concerned with copper mines all his professional life, could not be expected to understand the long-term significance of the increasing existence of tin ore as the mines deepened.[71]

1827 saw income stabilise at the mine, as tonnage rose by 775 tons to 8,750 and income returned to a relatively healthy total of £47,923, a rise of £13,646. The following year tonnage was down 187 to 8,563 tons and income from ore sales was up £991 to £48,914.[72]

In February 1828 the *Royal Cornwall Gazette* carried an article entitled: 'Mineral History of Cornwall', and among other things it gave some interesting facts about Dolcoath. The mine was 240 fathoms deep, employed 800 workers, used 6,000lbs of candles a month and 2,600lbs of gunpowder. It pumped half-a-million gallons of water a day to Deep Adit, and was 85 degrees Fahrenheit at the 240 level and 61 degrees at surface.[73]

Scientific Visit
Following on from the experimental work on ventilation and ground and water temperature of Dr Forbes and John Rule junior, in the early 1820s, a group of scientists visited Dolcoath in 1828 to carry out research into the density of the earth. They centred their experiments on the 171 fathom level and appear to have been well satisfied with the results. The scientists, the Reverend Sedgwick, Professor of Geology, the Reverend Whewell, Professor of Mineralogy, and Professor J. B. Airy, Professor of Astronomy and Mathematics, together with several others, had spent two summer months at Dolcoath carrying out their work. These Cambridge dons were fulsome in their praise for the assistance and cooperation given by the mine captains and adventurers. In August, when their work was concluded, Lord de Dunstanville invited them to dinner at Tehidy, where they were among some twenty guests present at the presentation to his lordship of a magnificent candelabrum made from silver mined at Dolcoath. The beautifully finished carved silver object stood three feet high and weighed some forty pounds. Basset said that delighted as he was with this highly valuable gift, he was even more pleased with the words on it. "This candelabrum of silver, Raised from Dolcoath Mine, is respectfully presented to Lord de Dunstanville, Proprietor of the Mine and Zealous Advocate of the Mining interests, By the Adventurers, as an acknowledgement of the liberal protection which they have invariably received and of their admiration of His Lordship's Many public and private virtues. 9 June 1828." Obsequious as these words now seem in a different age with different attitudes, it cannot be denied that Basset was extremely generous in his support for miners and fellow adventurers during the often difficult years from 1799 to his death in 1835. Compared to many of his contemporaries, Basset appeared to the Camborne and Redruth miners who were employed in his mines, as a good master and one they were grateful to work for.[74]

Other adventurers also had objects made from Dolcoath silver during those years. John Harris, the Bolenow miner poet, recorded that he had taken tea at Penjerrick, the home of R. W. Fox, and the silver tea pot used had been made from Dolcoath silver. Another artefact bore the crest of a Henry Shilson, the Cornwall arms, and the words: "This silver was raised from Dolcoath Mine in the County of Cornwall, 1828."[75]

Captain John Rule, the mine manager, reported in the 1828 *Transactions of the Royal Geological Society of Cornwall*, on a major subsidence incident in the mine. This subsidence or series of subsidences had been going on for some years. As noted above, the 1822/23 'Day & Night' book of captains Petherick and Thomas had made several references to these movements of attle. In 1828 the movement became more general and so widespread was it, that miners in the deeper parts of the eastern workings had to carefully work their way upwards by moving in a westerly direction before emerging at surface half-a-mile to the west of where they started. Rule commented that the movement did not extend far from the lodes and did not reach the surface. Overall, the subsiding rock only moved a few inches, but it did close many small gaps the miners were wont to move through, and its slow creep downwards meant that miners trying to escape could wait until it stopped moving, before slipping through the narrowing gaps. The general subsidence lasted several weeks. Large tonnages of waste material was taken back underground to fill dangerous hollows, and once it was safe, and dangerous hang-ups brought down by use of the culverin or cannon, huge timber stull pieces were taken underground to support the ground against future movements. Rule said, "some thousand loads of timber were used in keeping open the requisite communication." Pumping shafts, whim shafts, ventilation shafts and winzes, as well as the essential access ladder roads, all had to be protected against future movement.[76]

In 1828, when Stray Park acquired Wheal Gons sett, she also took over Camborne Vean Mine, to the west of Gons, and in October a 1/50th share in the venture was offered for sale in the *West Briton*. These three mines all shared Dolcoath's adit system, and they also worked the Main Lode, and were extensively connected to a considerable depth.[77]

In June 1829 Alfred Jenkin wrote to Grenfell about Dolcoath's use of Portreath harbour instead of Hayle, for shipping out its ore. "Three parcels of the Dolcoath ores for sale next week are at Portreath, having been carried there by the miners previous to sampling – a majority of the adventurers in Dolcoath are interested in Portreath and the object of the measure is to ensure the shipments of a larger proportion of the Dolcoath ores at Portreath than has usually been sent there even in summer, most of the companies having of late particularly preferred sending their ores from the Camborne mines to Hayle, where at almost all seasons of the year the facility for shipping is greater than at Portreath – and the sending the ores to the former place not being attended with an extra expense … but let the Dolcoath adventurers beware of sending their ores to Portreath for sale in the winter, unless Fox & Co will engage to keep them harmless – the Williams' being largely interested in both the mine and the shipping place."[78]

This fascinating letter tells us much about the interconnected interests of these merchant and mining families. A majority of Dolcoath's adventurers had an interest in Portreath harbour, and the Fox and Williams families, especially so. Jenkin says that Hayle was the preferred port for the export of Camborne ores, and that only in the summer can Portreath seriously compete. He hoped that Fox & Co. would protect their fellow adventurers against loss, when ore at Portreath was weather bound. In 1823 Captain William Petherick had referred to mules trains carrying ore up Gwinear Hill to Hayle, but in the 1770s the record shows that Portreath was the preferred option.[79]

Shares in Dolcoath Mine were being progressively divided and sub-divided into ever smaller units, so that in the *West Briton* of May 1st 1829, there was advertised for sale 4/279th shares in the mine. Adventurers with such relatively small investments in the mine probably had little say as to which port the mine used to export its ore.[80]

In 1829 the mine's tonnage jumped 2,710 to 11,273 tons, and income from ore sales rose £19,523 to £68,437, the highest since 1818. The following year production dropped by 1,194 tons to 10,079 and income went down £11,477 to £56,960.[81]

Death from a Rockfall
Toward the end of April 1830 another miner was killed at Dolcoath. *The Royal Cornwall Gazette* reported: "On Thursday last a poor man, named John Bennatts, was unfortunately killed in Dolcoath mine, by some ground falling on him while at his labour. He has left a wife and six children to lament his untimely fate." Bennatts (Bennetts), who was aged 44, lived at Pelutes, on the south side of Troon, a couple of miles south of Dolcoath. Rock fall, one of the ever-present dangers of mining, had claimed another victim.[82]

During 1830, Captain William Petherick, nephew to John Rule the manager, became joint manager of Dolcoath. He was about 33 years old and had been a mine captain since 1822, having served alongside the older and far more experienced Captain James Thomas in running the large Valley Section of the mine. In about 1824 he had replaced Captain John Rule junior as the manager's right-hand man, and in 1830 he was being groomed to take over the management. Captain Rule was 79 years old, in 1830, and he had been manager since Andrew Vivian quit in 1806. Captain Petherick was to have a new approach to the management of the mine, and like his cousin, John, then making his name in Mexico, Petherick was to be innovative in his approach. He was described by observers during his time as manager as 'the intelligent manager of Dolcoath', and his frequent reports on the lode structures, faulting of crosscourses and other geological facts about the mine, in learned journals, showed he was no ordinary nineteenth century mine captain.[83]

A significant series of events took place in 1830, which were to change the lives of thousands of miners. William Bickford, a Devon man, who had moved to Tuckingmill from Liskeard made a brilliant discovery. Bickford was a leather merchant and devout Methodist, and after Bible Class one evening, he walked with a group of friends along the valley at Tuckingmill and noted a man plaiting rope as he walked backwards along a ropewalk. His Methodist friends, a miner, a rope maker, and another practical man, like Bickford, were preoccupied with the high incidence of premature explosions in the local mines. Dr Paris' safety bar had no doubt improved things, where it was used, but the problem of getting the flame to the gunpowder charge in a shothole, without premature explosion, concerned all these sincere Christians. Every day they saw miners in the village with one eye, no eyes, fingers missing and other horrible results of premature explosions. Bickford had the idea of pouring finely ground gunpowder into the centre of the rope or cord as it was being spun, by means of a cone-shaped feed. This, he reasoned, would produce a slow, even burn, so that the miner could make his escape having lit the fuze. This group of practical men experimented with the idea, sealing the rope or thick cord with water-proofing tar, and then within a short time they perfected the 'safety fuze'. On January 7 1831 the *West Briton* carried an advertisement for this 'Improved Safety Rod', by then being offered to mine owners for use, and on September 6th 1831 Bickford registered his patent (No.6159). The patent was described as: "Instrument for igniting gunpowder when used in blasting rocks, and in mining. Miner's safety fuze." Use of this invention spread rapidly, and Dolcoath Mine was, within a short time, the largest user of this life-saving fuze.[84]

In 1830, at the age of ten, John Harris, the future poet, followed his father to Dolcoath. For a little over two years he worked on the copper dressing floors carrying out a number of tasks. His description of that time is graphic. In his *Autobiography* Harris tells how he worked at the kieve (barrel, half filled with water to wash ore), the hutch (where fine copper ore was sifted in water) and the slide (place where ore was stored at surface), helped on the copper floors, and worked with the bal maids on the picking table and in the cobbing house. In all weathers the young lad wheel-barrowed ore between the various parts of the dressing floors, scorched by the sun, drenched by the rain, his arms almost pulled out by the weight of the barrows and the skin worn off his hands. Typical of the other youngsters working with the bal maids, Harris left home at six o'clock in the morning and returned home, three miles away, at six in the evening. His comment that he never complained about his lot, because he knew it was right, tells us much of the stoical attitude to work of our ancestors.[85]

At about the time that young Harris went to work on the surface at Dolcoath, Thomas Allom did his famous engraving of the mine. Much of what Harris tells us of the tasks he performed is illustrated by Allom. Bal maidens are seen spalling the ore with their 5-7lb spalling hammers, and cobbing the lumps of ore off waste. Others sit at tables either bucking or picking the ore. A boy is seen tipping his wheel barrow,

131

and in the background a lander is pulling the kibble from the shaft whilst operating the crash doors with his other hand. The capstan and enormous rope, the 76-inch pumping engine with all its appurtenances, and another engine in the background, were all there as signs of a large and busy copper mine.[86]

Between January and April 1831 the *West Briton* and *Royal Cornwall Gazette* carried a series of advertisements for Dolcoath. In January and April there were sales of a 1/279th share in the mine and in February there was an advertisement for 12 tons of 'old junk', 30 tons of scrap and 'bushel' iron and 10 tons of cast iron. The *Gazette* also carried news of the marriage of 'Captain John Lean of Dolcoath' to Mrs Ann Vincent. Was this John Lean a member of the engine-reporting family of engineers? Perhaps he was the same man who had split with his brother, Thomas, over the questionable accuracy of the engine reporters, in 1827, and had produced his version between 1827 and 31. Or was this the Captain John Lean who left Dolcoath in 1834, as mine captains were being laid off, and joined East Wheal Crofty, the up-and-coming mine to the north-east of Dolcoath?[87]

In 1831 10,838 tons of copper ore were sold, which was an increase over the previous month of 759 tons. Income from ore sales was down by £280 to £56,680, due to a drop of about 8s a ton for ore sold. In 1832 tonnage was down 1,644 to 9,194 tons, and income was up £962 to £57,642, due to ore selling for an average of £1 a ton more than the previous year.[88]

In 1832 or '33 the young John Harris left Dolcoath dressing floors and joined his father underground. He was about thirteen years old. He remained a Dolcoath miner for more than twenty years. In his *Autobiography* he describes how he descended some sixty to seventy ladders to a depth of nearly 200 fathoms. His father tied a rope around his waist to ensure that he did not fall. Harris spoke of the precarious ladders lying in several different directions, and indicated how frightening that first underground experience was. His first job, as with most lads of his age, was wheel barrowing ore from the workplace to the shaft 'plot'. With a candle stuck to the front of the barrow, the youngster had to thread his way to the shaft along narrow, twisting levels, skinning his knuckles constantly. In the early 1820s his father and uncle Matthew had worked in the Valley Section of Dolcoath, under Captain James Thomas, and Harris' references to Captain 'Jemmy' (James) Thomas helping him with his reading by throwing open his library to him, suggests that it was in the Valley where John had his first mining experiences.[89]

Harris spoke of the constant dangers of mining, in his *Autobiography*. He narrowly escaped injury when a kibble chain broke, sending the kibble and its contents hurtling to the bottom of the shaft. On one occasion a falling stone cut open his forehead, and on another a stone broke his teeth and cut his mouth open. A hole exploded beneath him as he crossed a winze on a plank, nearly precipitating him to his death. He attributed his survival on another occasion to his religious faith. He and a group of devout Methodists, five in all, and all Sunday School teachers, were sinking a winze. The five missed their core to attend the Sunday School Tea Treat, and whilst they were absent, providentially, the winze collapsed, filling the sump, where they should have been working, with rock. One of the most frightening incidents related in his book, was of light failure. Whilst working with 'Old Uncle Will' he accidentally knocked out his candle, after warning his workmate that they had to be careful as they had no other light. Will, however, also let his light go out, and their nightmare began. The two men were working in a remote part of the mine at some depth. They had to find their way through the tortuous workings and up through the shafts and winzes in total darkness. There were no safety matches or 'Lucifers' to strike when their lights went out. Such a journey was fraught with danger and difficulty with light, without it the whole thing must have been terrifying. With typical stoical determination they made it to surface, and went back for more the next shift. Not long before his mining days ended Harris experienced another frightening accident. The rod on the newly installed man-engine, erected in autumn 1853, broke. Harris and about twenty other miners were thrown off the engine, and miraculously, escaped serious injury. All they suffered were a few cuts and bruises.[90]

Notwithstanding the efforts of the management to improve ventilation and working conditions, as much for improved productivity as for the good of the miners, Harris said that for much of his life as a miner he had to endure working in sulphurous, choking dust, which almost suffocated him and his fellow miners. He often stood up to his knees in water whilst working, and at other times he drilled holes for the gunpowder charges from timber stages hung by ropes in the vast open stopes. Some of the tunnels he worked in were too low to stand upright in, and the combination, heat, bad air, restricted conditions, water-logged levels, extreme danger, almost constant half-darkness and frequent pay days with hardly anything to show for his efforts, failed to totally disillusion him. Modern Cornish miners, surprisingly, will recognise many aspects of Harris' experience, for such conditions remained features of hard rock mining until the final decades of the twentieth century. As a tributer he sometimes 'had wages to receive at the end of the month, and sometimes I had none', but at another time he found he had earned £200, and was, for a short time at least, a rich man.[91]

The Main Lode in the Valley Section was extremely wide, and by the 1830s some of the stopes, where all payable copper ore had been removed, were so wide that no timbers could be found to support the hanging wall. A bad practice had sprung up at Dolcoath, of removing all payable ore and leaving either no pillars or insufficient to support the hanging wall. As the mine deepened and the Main Lode flattened, this problem became worse, and during the later nineteenth century the results were sometimes disastrous. It is possible that the practice was encouraged by the diminishing copper returns. In the eastern end of the mine tin was increasingly encountered at a higher level, but as the workings went westward the level at which tin was encountered was deeper. This mostly related to the depth of the killas-granite contact, which is around the 130 fathom level in Bullen Garden Section. Near Valley (Eastern/Water Whim) Shaft the contact is actually quite close to surface, but at Old Dolcoath it lies at the 220 fathom level. Copper ore persisted well into the granite, before giving way to mostly tin, but little tin was found above the contact, apart from the tin mined over a century earlier above the water table. The 1830s witnessed a difficult time for the mine, as tin became more prevalent with diminishing copper ore, but the former was not a viable alternative until at about the 200 fathom level. One of the difficulties, which had to be overcome, was the mind-set of the adventurers and agents. They were copper men; brought up since youth to see their mines as copper mines. Many, like Captain William Petherick, in 1823, knew so little about tin that he went out of his way to learn about it. On January 16th 1823 he wrote: "The tin samplers have been here & sampled the tin. I staid up from underground to see how they managed it, but 'twas nothing very particular to see or do." His curiosity and determination to find out about this unfamiliar skill tells us much about how tin was viewed by copper captains in a long-established copper mine. Captain James Thomas had shown similar curiosity when he had been taken by Captain Tregoning to see 'some good tin' at the 190 and 200 fathom levels, in Bullen Garden, the previous week.[92]

As the 1830s continued, the search for good grade copper was proving increasingly difficult and unsuccessful. Times were becoming harder and miners were being laid off. There was a small diversion, not untypical of the times, when in June 1833, a John Richards was sent to prison with hard labour, for stealing old brass from the mine. If production was diminishing the accident rate showed no sign of slowing down, and 1833 saw the deaths of two more Dolcoath miners. In July the *Illogan Parish Burial Register* recorded the death of Samuel Richards of Red River, aged 37, who was 'killed at Dalcoath'. In November the *West Briton* reported: "Fatal Accident – On Monday se'night, whilst a miner called William Warren was filling a kibble in a shaft at Dolcoath mine, a stone fell from the top, and rebounding from the side of the shaft, struck him on the head, inflicting a severe fracture. The unfortunate man, however, was able to ascend the ladders and return to his home – which is about a mile from the mine – without assistance; he lingered until Friday last, when he expired, leaving a widow and two children. – The deceased was a truly pious Christian, and was respected as an upright and conscientious man by all who knew him." Warren was 58 years old and lived in Camborne town.[93]

Over thirty years after Richard Trevithick, then chief engineer at Dolcoath, had demonstrated the world's first steam-powered locomotive, an Act of Parliament was being considered to bring a railway line through Dolcoath. In November 1833 application was made for this line, which was to run from Hayle to Portreath and Tresavean Mine, with another terminus at West End, Redruth. The line was to run sub-parallel to Dolcoath Main Lode, cutting through the mine where Dolcoath met Stray Park, at the top of Foundry Road, Camborne. This proposed new railway had enormous financial implications for Dolcoath and the entire mining district. The Redruth and Chacewater railway, which ran from Devoran to Redruth, through the great copper mining district of Gwennap, had already transformed the economies of some of the most important copper mines in the world, as had the earlier Portreath-Poldice tramway, started in 1809.[94]

Production in 1833 was down 1,032 tons to 8,162, and revenue from ore sales was down £5,895 to £51,747. In 1834 it dropped even further, with tonnage down 1,116 to 7,046 tons, the lowest for over a quarter of a century, and revenue down by £11,139 to £40,608. Once again, in January 1834, the local paper was advertising the sale of Dolcoath shares, as out-adventurers, sought to offload unprofitable assets. Small investors were not the only ones affected by the falling off of profits at the mine, and a much larger shareholder, William Hambly, was declared bankrupt in June 1834, and his shares of over four percent of the mine's value were also up for sale. With such a large investment in a huge, struggling enterprise like Dolcoath, it is no wonder that this adventurer was at the limit of his resources. The claim in the advert that Dolcoath had made £60,000 profit over the previous ten years might have been true, but it hardly reflected the real state of the mine in June 1834.[95]

Lean's *Engine Reporter* for 1834 lists Dolcoath's 76-inch Great Engine and six whim engines: two 16-inch, an 18-inch and three 20-inch cylinder engines. In 1835 the Great Engine consumed 25,686 bushels of coal, and lifted an average of 211 gallons of water a minute 190 fathoms to Deep Adit. Its average duty for the year was 45,020,374. Richard Jeffery (Jeffree) was still the mine engineer.[96]

A Fatal Accident
In February 1834 there was another fatality at Dolcoath, when a miner named James Kemp fell down a shaft whilst working underground. Kemp was 21 years old and lived at Forest, between Four Lanes and Bolenow. He was buried at Illogan Church on February 21 1834.[97]

On 7th June 1834 the *Royal Cornwall Gazette* carried a doleful piece of news. Captain John Rule, the ailing 'Managing captain' of Dolcoath Mine, died. The report stated that Rule, who was 83 years old, had been manager of the mine for 30 years, and a Wesleyan Methodist for 27 years. In fact he had been manager for 28 years, since 1806. The *Bibliotheca Cornubiensis*, of 1878, tells us that he had been a mine captain for 60 years. John Rule was a miner of exceptional ability and had steered Dolcoath through some of the most difficult years of its history. Those 28 years had seen world wide warfare, periods of unstable peace, national financial crises, the price of copper collapse and rise rapidly, British industrial demand boom and bust, social unrest and rioting, technical improvements and innovation on an unprecedented scale, and massive geological problems as the mine deepened and values in the lodes fluctuated wildly. In all these changing conditions Rule had kept the respect of the miners and the adventurers, and had maintained his sense of humour. Perusal of the Day and Night book of 1822-23 informs us of his sense of fun and light touch with respect to his captains and miners. One story well illustrates this. Two of the older mine captains, Captains Jilbert and Robin, had to go to Truro to meet the mine debenture holders. They were given an allowance for their lunch and drinks. Captains Harry and Thomas were also to be there, and Rule asked his nephew William Petherick, to wind up the two older men. Petherick wrote to Thomas: "Capt Rule wishes you & Capt Harry to get Capts Jilbert & Robin to spend more money than they will receive, go to dinner with them if possible & order 2 or 3 bottles of wine & make them pay their part, & if Capt Harry can find any old coal woman with her corval to dog them around the streets 'twould be glorious fun." An N. B. was added to the entry: "Capt Rule is enjoying the thought of your swigging Capts Jilbert & Robin, he says, he hopes you'll do for them." The idea of these two working class mine captains, in their Sunday best, displaying the dignity their position afforded them, being embarrassed by an old coal woman, with sack upon her back, following them around the streets of Truro, gave Captain Rule and the younger captains enormous amusement. Until his powers began to fail him, Rule was at the centre of all decision-making, although his ability to delegate and trust his captains was also evident. The Day and Night book shows a manager with his finger firmly on the mine's pulse. In the 1820s he began to use his son, John Rule junior, as his right-hand man, and after he had gone to Mexico, he leant more on his nephew, William Petherick, who joined him as joint manager in 1830. On Captain Rule's death, Captain William Petherick was immediately appointed sole manager of Dolcoath Mine. Like John Rule, Petherick, as manager, was paid the fairly advanced salary of 14½ guineas (£15 4s 6d) a month.[98]

Management of William Petherick (1834-44)

With rapidly diminishing tonnages of copper ore and seriously declining revenue, William Petherick was faced with running an ancient mine, which many experts thought was reaching the end of its productive life. What copper ore remained was of a lower grade than the average for Cornish mines, and the price received by Dolcoath was commensurately less than for other mines, and less than she had gained a few years before. Within a short time of taking over the management, Dolcoath was inspected by outside mining 'experts' and pronounced worthless. What they perceived as a problem, the increasing presence of tin in the ore, was to prove the salvation of the mine. In the mean time, Petherick's task was to hold the mine together whilst the crisis was faced and a different future planned for Dolcoath.[99]

Petherick's first full year in charge could not have been worse. In 1835 tonnage dropped by 1,521 to 5,525 tons, and income from ore sales went down £6,777 to £33,831, possibly the lowest total since the mine re-opened in 1799. 1835 was to be the last year that Dolcoath paid out a dividend on copper. The following year saw production fall even further to 3,373 tons and income from ore was a depressing £17,763, almost half of the previous year. The reality of the situation was brought home to Petherick when it was announced that no dividend was to be paid. The ten years of his sole management of the once great mine were to be a severe test of Petherick's courage and character. That he had the support and loyalty of his senior mine captain, Charles Thomas, was of immense encouragement to Petherick. Since 1834 agents had been laid-off, with Captain John Lean going to East Wheal Crofty and possibly Captain Tregonning joining him there, and as 1835 progressed Petherick and Thomas cast about for an answer to the problem. Petherick had known since the discovery of the rich tin in the lode at the 190 and 200 fathom levels, in 1822, that the white metal was a possible significant future source of income for the mine, and Charles Thomas was an early advocate of its value, but the adventurers were sceptical, and unconvinced that Dolcoath had a future in tin. Charles Thomas spent long hours working out the economics of working the deeper levels profitably, aware of the growing pressure from some of the adventurers to pull up the bottom lifts of the pumps and let the water into the deeper workings. The constant toil and worry made Thomas ill, and so sick was he, that his friends feared for his life. In the autumn of 1835 he began his recovery and was soon restored to his usual robust health.[100]

As production and income continued to fall in 1836, pressure upon Petherick grew to draw up the bottom pumps. It was at this time, probably at the instigation of the Gwennap adventurers, that it was agreed to have the lower levels inspected by outside experts. "About the year 1836 the bottom of the mine was inspected by the 'knowing ones' of that day (from a district that was rich, not seven miles off), and pronounced to be worthless, although the present mass of tin ground had actually been cut at two points. The adventurers, placing more confidence in those wise men than their own agents, stopped the mine." These geological 'experts' were the copper men of Gwennap, who had spent their lives working in copper mines, and whose knowledge of tin ore was extremely limited. Backed by their report it was proposed to draw up the pumps to the 125 fathom level, and concentrate the search for copper, rather than tin, at an horizon Petherick and Thomas knew had long since been thoroughly searched. Petherick and Thomas, backed by knowledgeable outsiders like Captain Joseph Vivian of North Roskear Mine, argued vehemently against the plan, talking to Lady Basset's agent and the mine purser, William Reynolds, and eventually obtained a small but significant concession – 30 fathoms! Instead of the 125 fathom level the pumps would be drawn up to the 155 fathom level. Interestingly, the *West Briton* newspaper carried a surprisingly perceptive comment in January 1836: "We believe several of the copper lodes in our deepest mines, as Wheal Abraham , Dolcoath, etc, went out in tin and the workings were subsequently discontinued … We doubt not (that) these workings may be profitably resumed." This comment, notwithstanding, the decision was taken in December 1836, and in the first issue of the *West Briton* of 1837, it was duly and dolefully reported: "We are sorry to learn that the adventurers in Dolcoath Mine, in consequence of its poverty, have resolved in drawing up about forty fathoms of the pumps, and on lessening the number of agents … we cannot look at this step without foreboding that it is a preliminary to stopping the mine … the step has been recommended by parties of great practical knowledge and experience." In fact, it was 55 fathoms of pumps to be drawn up, not 40 fathoms, and notwithstanding the depressing, loss-making situation of the mine, due to the care and diligence of Petherick, backed by Thomas, not only did Dolcoath weather the storm, but the situation stabilised.[101]

Captain Petherick's Geological Interest

Despite Dolcoath's unremitting problems, Captain Petherick continued his scientific work, examining the lode structures and crosscourses, and reporting to learned journals and interested parties on the peculiarities of the geology of Dolcoath. In 1836 a report from the Royal Cornwall Polytechnic Society said: "Captain Petherick, the intelligent manager of Dolcoath, informs Mr R. W. Fox, that in that mine, 'in one of the lodes (the Caunter) the hanging wall is evidently lower than the foot wall'." Petherick also reported on characteristics of Harriets Lode, at the 197 fathom level, and on the heaving of Wheal Bryant Crosscourse by North Entral Lode, some nine feet to the right. At the same time Petherick carried on his work to improve the lot of his men. He continued to improve the underground ventilation, by introducing more effective wooden air pipes to poorly ventilated ends and striving to provide better facilities for the miners' return to surface.[102]

In May 1837 the *Mining Journal* reported a serious accident at the mine, and in describing the circumstances of the incident, it gave a fascinating pen-picture of the eastern workings, in what was known as The Valley: "On Thursday, 11th inst. a pair of miners, working in that part of Dolcoath Mine commonly called 'The Valley', had a very narrow escape for their lives. A large portion of rock above them gave way, threatening them with instant destruction." No lives were lost, although both miners were seriously injured, one with a badly fractured thigh. The account goes on: "In this part of the mine the workings are carried to a most unusual extent, being so wide that no timber can possibly reach from side to side, and still the lode is found to extend to a greater width. In order to come to work on the sides of these immense chasms, or gunnies as they are commonly called, the miners commence their operations at a level where timber will fetch, to which timber they fasten to what they denominate a 'swing stage', this they contrive to drop against such part of the side as they intend to take away, and then letting themselves down by means of a 'swing-chain ladder', they continue to blast down immense quantities of rock." Some of the enormous rocks that were blasted down from the walls of these immense stopes had to be blasted again and again until small enough to remove by tram or wheel barrow to the shaft plot. Sometimes these rocks yielded so much ore as to give a couple of tributers good wages for two months. "In operations of this sort the casualties are numerous, and frequently of a very serious character." Death and maiming were not uncommon as a result of working in such dangerous places. Not infrequently, the gunnis sides, most commonly the hanging-wall, collapsed due to lack of support or to being weakened by blasting. There can be few more hazardous places to work in a mine. John Harris and Thomas Oliver also describe these enormously wide and dangerous workings.[103]

As the mine soldiered on, with some adventurers giving up their shares and others threatening to, Petherick steadied the ship. In 1837 tonnage dropped again to 3,251 and income from ore also was down some £3,665 to £14,098, but in 1838, despite a drop in tonnage, income rose by £778 to £14,876, which at least gave some adventurers a slight hope for the future. Underground, the search for tin and copper continued, with just enough being discovered to very slightly increase the flow of ore and revenue. An increase in the sale of copper ore was welcome news in December 1837, as good ground was being successfully opened up in Wheal Bryant section of the mine. Rich ore in lodes parallel and sub-parallel to Main Lode at Wheal Bryant, although extremely hard, making development slow and expensive, gave the captains further reason for optimism. Figures from the time give the total Dolcoath workforce as 590, with 300 of them men, 220 women and 70 children. Despite concerns for the long-term future of the mine she continued to be a major employer in West Cornwall, and a vital part of the Cornish economy.[104]

1838 was a bad year for the country as a whole, with an economic depression making life difficult for industrialists and raw material suppliers. The great social and constitutional reforms of the 1830s, which had followed the Catholic Emancipation Act of 1829 and the Reform Act of 1832, transformed many aspects of the country, changing fundamentally the attitude of government and the governing classes to the national workforce. The owners and management of Dolcoath, together with many other 'enlightened' mine and factory owners, had quietly sought the improvement of working conditions since the early nineteenth century, but now the country's legislators were taking a hand, and particularly after the Whigs had set up commissions to investigate working conditions for youngsters, in 1840, wide-ranging changes were bound to follow. Peel and his Tory government, which was in power when the Commissioners' reports were made, were to see through many recommended changes in the law.[105]

Production rose in 1839 to 3,535 tons of copper ore, and income also went up to £17,039. In 1840 tonnage went up again, to 3,638, but, due to an extremely low price for her ore, Dolcoath's income from sales dropped to £13,892, by far the lowest total for forty years.[106]

The Royal Polytechnic Society's Questionnaire

In 1840 the Royal Cornwall Polytechnic Society sent out a questionnaire to mine agents in Cornwall, and the answers provide an interesting picture of Dolcoath in that year. The mine was described as a copper and tin mine, its depth was 210 fathoms below adit, which was 30 fathoms deep. The depth of water below the current workings was 55 fathoms, so the water was still held at the 155 fathom level. There were thirteen ends being driven by tutworkers, varying from 50 to 240 fathoms from the nearest access shaft. The levels were described as dry, which was not the impression given by John Harris, who worked there at the time, and stated that he sometimes worked up to his knees in water. There was no stoping carried out between an end and the nearest winze, due to poor ventilation. Two places were ventilated by means of rectangular wooden air pipes, measuring 7 inches by 5 inches. The hardness of the ground varied, as might be expected in a mine which was nearly a mile long and working several lodes. The men's tools were raised and lowered by the company, which made a difference when climbing hundreds of feet of ladders. Despite Dr Paris's Safety Bar, used since 1817 in Cornwall, the normal tamping rod was still of iron, presumably being thought less dangerous in killas than granite. Bickford's 'safety fuze' was in general use at Dolcoath, and the holes were drilled generally by one man holding and another striking the drill steel. It was noted that the men were not normally careful about re-entering an end after blasting, which was harmful to their health. There were 200 miners employed, working on some ten tribute and eight tutwork contracts. The average monthly wage for these miners was 55s for a man and 25s for a boy. Not surprisingly, the report comments that there were no 'cold ends'. Some of Captain William Petherick's improvements were also mentioned: upon arriving at surface the miners walked through a shallow tunnel to the dry, where warm water, dry clothes and half a pint of hot soup were provided. These measures reduced the incidence of consumption and colds. It was also said that two-thirds of all men employed lived within a mile of the mine, and nobody came further than three miles.[107]

Parliamentary Commission on Child Employment

Early in 1841 the Parliamentary Commission on the Employment of Children began to interview miners, former miners, mine managers and captains, and others involved in the local mining scene. Local magistrates were also interviewed on their experience and observations of the treatment of youngsters in the mines and their general health and habits. Dr Charles Barham was to conduct the interviews and report on his findings. The investigation was wide-ranging and, at times, very detailed. Barham did not merely collect a series of answers to a questionnaire, as had the Polytechnic Society, but went into some detail on how things worked and the precise results of various conditions or improvements. One of the most important aims was to quantify the problem of child labour, and in line with the true Benthamite utilitarian doctrine of the time, gathering accurate statistics was all important. Tables were created that listed the numbers of each age group and sex working at surface and underground. For example at age 8-9 years there were 4 males and 2 females working on the surface at Dolcoath. The youngest male working underground was in the 10-11 age group. In all there were two males underground under the age of 13, together with 58 males and 34 females at surface under the age of 13. Between 13 and 18 years there were 45 males working underground and 27 at surface. There were 74 females between the ages of 13 and 18, all on the surface. There were 451 underground workers at the mine. In total there were 534 males employed by the mine and 198 females, making a grand total of 732 workers at Dolcoath in 1841.[108]

The Commission looked closely at the provision of soup at Dolcoath. Captain William Petherick had introduced it in January 1837. Dolcoath was not only the first to give the miners hot soup on their arrival at surface, but they appeared to be the only mine which made it available to boys as well as men. Lady Basset was an early supporter of the scheme and she apparently paid for its provision. Statistics were provided by Petherick to Barham, to show the extent of the soup provision and how it all worked. Figures for the three previous years showed that for the three months of January to March 1839, 8,186 servings of half a pint of soup were handed out. In 1840 for the same three months there were 7,121 servings and in January to March 1841 there were 10,927 servings. The average monthly expenditure on soup was £5 10s, with the soup costing £1 15s and its delivery £3 15s. Elizabeth Davey delivered the soup by day and James Trezona by night. The soup was provided close to the footway shafts, near the blacksmith shops, and one point was at the western end of the mine and the other at the eastern or Valley end. Petherick commented that consumption was reduced by this provision, and the morale of the men was also improved by it. The mine gave £2 a month toward the soup cost and assigned four men to distribute it, as men were coming to surface at several different times day and night. Petherick said that Club payments were reduced by the improved health of the miners, and although the Club officially did not pay out for consumption cases, they generally did.[109]

The Miners' Club interested the Commission as it supported those in need. Petherick said that the Club was comparatively rich, with £1,500 in it, and this was partly due to the Dolcoath men giving more than most miners into it. The miners paid 6d in the pound into the Club, and 1d in the pound was added to merchants and tradesmen's accounts for the Club. A percentage of the lord's dues was also paid into the Club. Attempts were made to get the bal maids to contribute, but there was general resistance to this and they did not pay. The Club was set up to assist injured, wounded or distressed miners, but the Dolcoath practice was also to relieve illness, especially where the victim was very poor and had worked at the mine for some time. Where a miner could not afford decent food, his mates would approach the captains who would ensure there was financial help for him and his family. Widows of miners and mothers of unmarried miners, killed at the mine, were assisted well beyond the strict Club rules. Some widows had received over £100 spread over several years, from the Club.[110]

The miners' dry, or changing house, was also described by Petherick. A large iron tube, 18 inches in diameter, ran the length of the dry, enabling the miners to dry their underground 'rags'. Upon reaching the surface the miners could change into dry clothes, in a warm building and drink hot soup.[111]

Petherick referred to the ladders, a major cause of complaint by the miners, who attributed their poor health and exhaustion more to climbing ladders than anything else. He said they were now a standard 15 feet long, with iron staves 12 inches apart. Wooden staves were found to break suddenly and without warning, causing many accidents. The ventilation was described as better than most mines, and air was moved by means of shafts, winds and wooden air pipes. The air pipes were carefully constructed using whole boards, not odd off-cuts. Ventilation winzes ('winds') were put down every 20 fathoms, and no pitches were set between a winds and the end. Universal use of safety fuze was also a major factor in reducing serious accidents. However, a serious problem remained, which was a long-term health hazard, that of miners returning too quickly to their work place after blasting. The smoke and dust was extremely injurious to the miners' lungs. Of the 75 fatal accidents in Cornish mines over the previous twelve months, only one occurred at Dolcoath. This was due to a rock fall, and the report showed that ground falling onto miners was the commonest cause of fatal accidents in the mines. Twenty-six Cornish miners were killed by rock fall, 25 due to falling (mostly off ladders) and eight were blasting accidents.[112]

Petherick told of the many miners who had cleared croft ground and built their own cottages, which they held of the local estates on three lives and a small rent. Captain James Thomas and John Harris' father were Dolcoath miners who had done this half a century before, and throughout the eighteenth and nineteenth centuries the miners of Dolcoath and its neighbours had done the same. These cottages Barham's report described as clean and healthy.[113]

Referring to the problems the mine had overcome in the recent past, Petherick told the Commission of the serious subsidences experienced in the 1820s, when some one-and-a-half million tons of attle had fallen or subsided, reaching almost to the surface. The mine had taken half-a-million tons back underground to support the workings, and this had cost £10,000. Elsewhere it was stated that a thousand loads of timber support was also put in during 1828.[114]

John Phillips of Tuckingmill was also interviewed by Barham. Phillips was assayer at Dolcoath, and he was also employed as surveyor at some of the other local mines. He advertised various technical mining instruments of his own devising, and ran the Camborne Mining School at Tuckingmill. Phillips also ran a day and evening school for the sons of the mining community, and he specialised in teaching the use of 'mechanical contrivances' for mining operations. Assaying and surveying appear also to have been on his curriculum, as were physics, chemistry, and mensuration, although the usual reading, writing and arithmetic were probably the stock-in-trade. It cost the miners £2 to £3 per year for their sons to attend day school, and 5s a quarter for the evening classes. The evening classes were four evenings a week, and ran from 7 to 10 o'clock. Phillips had an impressive forty pupils in his day school, and bodies like the Royal Cornwall Polytechnic Society recognised his school. The report suggested that Camborne was particularly well served by schools for its youngsters, although it was lamented generally that children tended to leave for work at about 10 or 11 years of age.[115]

Two examples of pay slips were given to the Commissioners, one for a tributer and the other for a tutworker. The first was for William Rule, who held a tribute pitch and employed two men and two boys. His tribute was 13s 4d in the pound, and he raised £60 3s worth of ore in January and February 1841, which gave him £40 2s. Costs deducted, for 'mixing & dividing' and grinding his ore, boxing and drawing it to surface, smiths' cost, candles, sundries and gunpowder, came to £8 8s 1d. Subsist, probably taken out after the first month of the contract, came to £10 6s and the doctor's pence was 1s 6d. Total deductions were £18 15s 7d, which left £21 6s 5d. The Club was 13s 2d. With the subsist payment, the total earnings for three men and two boys for two months was £30 19s 3d. The tutwork pay slip was for James Richards & ptrs, six men. Their contract was for one month, to drive two fathoms at £10 a fathom, and thereafter to be paid £8 10s for every fathom over that. Richards and company drove 3 fathoms, and thus earned £28 10s. Their deductions for 'box & drawing', smith, candles, sundries and powder, came to £8 8s 2d. They drew no subsist payment, probably because they were on a monthly contract, and paid 1s 9d doctor's pence. Their total was £20 0s 11d, with a 10s deducted for the Club. If these two examples were typical, Dolcoath miners were relatively well-off, especially as we are looking at the beginning of the aptly named 'hungry forties'.[116]

The testimony of ordinary miners to Barham is enlightening. Henry Warren, who was 60 years old, first went underground at Dolcoath when he was fifteen, and he worked above the adit level, 'rolling' (wheel barrowing) the ore to the shaft.

Forty-five years before 1841 was in the mid-1790s, when Dolcoath was officially closed. Warren's testimony that he worked 'above adit' shows that despite the mine's closure, unofficial mining continued above adit, or above the water level, in the old tin ground. George Bailey, who was 40 years old, had worked at Dolcoath for 21 years, with one four month break. He complained that work he was paid a pound for in 1841, he had previously been paid £1 10s for. He also had started underground at Dolcoath at 15 years of age, after working on the surface there. He found that climbing ladders too fast had the biggest adverse affect on his health. As a 15 year old he had been employed 'rolling' and said that the bigger, stronger lads would overfill the barrows, making the smaller boys complain. Bailey had looked forward to going to evening school after work and felt it benefited him. He could not recall any cases of sudden illness or accident to boys when he was a youngster. Richard Trezona, aged 52, who worked at North Roskear, testified that when he worked at Cooks Kitchen he had heard about Dolcoath's provision of soup, but it had not caused him to go there for a job. Another North Roskear miner, William Richards, aged 46, said that he had gone underground at Dolcoath when he was ten years old, and he had worked fifteen fathoms below the adit level. He had also later worked on the 201 fathom level at Dolcoath for some three years. Dr Barham's report to parliament was to bring fundamental changes to employment practice in Britain, and Dolcoath in common with other Cornish mines was forced to make changes.[117]

Provision of Education for Camborne Youngsters in 1841.

"In Camborne parish there were, in 1841, two classical schools, one British and Foreign school, and two ladies schools – all in the town; one endowed school at Penponds; a mining and commercial school at Tuckingmill; and twenty minor schools (total 27), with several church and dissenting schools."

In 1841 the tonnage of copper ore increased slightly by 201 to 3,839 tons, and income from it jumped £6,163 to £20,055, the best figures for six years. A statistic that was a harbinger of better things to come was the income from black tin, for the year ending June 1841, some £1,078 worth was sold. Unfortunately, the improvement in copper ore sold was short-lived, and the following year saw tonnage drop by 219 tons to 3,620 and income from ore sales go down by £3,064 to £16,991. The situation was so bad at Dolcoath that, notwithstanding the large workforce and vast area of working machinery, the mine could not pay its parish rate.[118]

In 1842 J. Y. Watson prepared his book, entitled: *Compendium of British Mining,* etc, which was published the following year. He discussed all the principal mining districts of Cornwall, and includes a small description of the individual mines. Some of what he says is interesting, some manifestly inaccurate, and much was repeated

Figure 34. Group of miners outside the Harriets section dry.

Figure 35. View east over the enclosed dressing sheds, new
Californian stamps centre left.

Figure 36. View north at the Cornish steam stamps engine houses.

Figure 37. The count house before the fire in 1895.

Figure 38. The Great Stull, looking east on the 412-fathom level.

Figure 39. The Great Stull, looking west on the 412-fathom level. Photograph taken a few days before it collapsed, causing the deaths of seven miners in 1893.

Figure 40. Looking east towards New Sump from the Dolcoath Avenue compressor. Note the miner carrying a water barrel. The right-hand track goes to Harriets Shaft and the main line goes towards Stray Park.

Figure 41. Locomotive transporting full wagons to the stamps.

Figure 42. The first photrograph of a 'Cousin Jack' chute 1893, 412 fathom level.

Figure 43. Southern end of the old dressing floors in the Red River valley. Valley Shaft and and new Californian stamps to the right.

Figure 44. Shaking (Wilfley or Buss) table, circa 1905.

Figure 45. Frue vanners, circa 1905.

Figure 46. Round frames in operation on slime tin recovery, circa 1900.

Figure 47. Old stamps on the left, 50-foot dippa wheel, launder and array of slime pits and rag frames on the lower dressing floor.

**Figure 48. Locomotive pulling full wagons from Stray Park
past the Dolcoath Avenue compressor.**

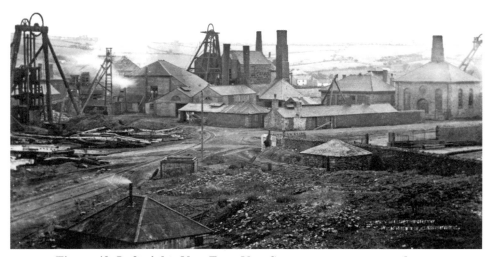

**Figure 49. Left-right: New East, New Sump, new compressor house
and Old Sump headgear.**

from other previously published accounts. He estimated that Dolcoath had 'left a profit of £600,000', during the previous century of operating. He also stated that, "In four years, ending June 1842, the mine returned 14,829 tons of ore yielding £68,638 16s., which left a small profit." In 1842 he said about 200 persons were employed at the mine. It is of interest that Watson refers to the opinion among many that the mine had seen its best days, and expresses the view that this was a fallacy. Among other things he mentions the enormous 'vugh' found at the 170 fathom level in 1814, the discovery, in 1810, of rich silver ore worth £2,000, and the great width of the Main Lode in the Valley Section of the mine. It is of interest that in his general description of Cornish mining methods, Watson describes the normal mode of ore transportation underground as by wheel-barrow, pushed by young boys. Eighteen years earlier, in October 1824, Joseph Carne read a paper to the Royal Geological Society of Cornwall in which he spoke of the 'use of railways in the levels of the mines', and believed that their use would shortly supersede, or 'at least greatly lessen, the use of wheelbarrows'. Taylor had adopted them at Consolidated Mines, and they were in use at Poldice, Treskerby, Wheal Damsel and other mines. Captain John Rule junior would have observed their use and the advantages in economy and efficiency they had brought to these Gwennap mines, and there can be no doubt that he had spoken of the use of track and trams underground to his father and his cousin, William Petherick. The reason for a mine like Dolcoath being tardy in introducing them is not far to find, for the tributers and tutworkers were paid, as part of their contract, to deliver the ore to the shaft plat, and the adventurers might, understandably, be reluctant to spend their money on solving what they perceived as someone else's problem. Alongside the Cornish miners' innovative approach to most problems, there existed an innate conservatism, which manifested itself in a stubborn reluctance to change long-standing practices.[119]

In 1843 production went up by 350 tons to 3,970, and income from ore sales also rose by £1,730 to £18,721. The mine continued to lose money and had every appearance of marking time, as the manager, William Petherick and his senior mine captain, Charles Thomas continuously sought authority from the adventurers to pump the deeper workings dry and go for tin.[120]

By the end of 1843 William Petherick's battle to save Dolcoath was over. On January 13th 1844, at the premature age of 47, he died. He had started mining as a youngster and risen to mine captain when he was only 25 years old, in May 1822. He had worked with John Rule junior to improve conditions at the mine, and when Rule left Dolcoath, Petherick became the manager's right-hand man. In 1830 he became joint manager with his aged uncle and in 1834 he took over the ailing mine as sole manager. He presided during the mine's most difficult period in the nineteenth century. Due to the esteem his predecessor, Captain John Rule, was held in, and the undoubted and deserved respect afforded his successor, Charles Thomas, Petherick's managership has been regarded by historians almost as an interlude between the reigns of two great men. Some accounts of Dolcoath have dismissed him in a single sentence. This is far from representing the truth. Captain Petherick was an exceptional man, an outstanding miner and a highly original and innovative mine manager.[121]

The Day and Night book of 1822-23 shows Petherick as a man of great wit and humour. It shows that although he did not suffer fools gladly, he had unusual compassion for his men, especially when they were in difficulty. He could be stern and sarcastic when faced with miners' deviousness and dishonesty, and humbly contrite when he was proved wrong. He was outspoken when necessary and not slow to apologise if or when he went too far. He showed loyalty and deference to the manager, Captain Rule, and respect to men like James Thomas, his older colleague at the Valley section. He was conscientious in the discharge of his duty and unflagging in his demand that others also did theirs. When he caught the North Roskear bal maids stealing anvils, he demanded their dismissal, and when other bal maids stole a whim rope he demanded the culprits own up or all be fired. His language was colourful, crude and sometimes downright outrageous, but he was a miner of his generation, with limited schooling and a background among the hard and basic Camborne mining community. He had an exceptional ability to learn from his own experiences and those with whom he worked. He was religious, but debated difficult philosophical questions. He scorned those like Captain Thomas, who believed in dreams as a guide to rich copper or tin lodes, but he did so on the basis of argument and reason. He participated in elaborate jokes, as with the 'winding up' of captains Jilbert and Robin with the coal woman in Truro. Petherick's management was marked by his enlightened approach to the miners. He was genuinely concerned with having better ventilation, safer working conditions and improved working practices. He was the man who introduced the issuing of hot soup for the miners, who ensured that the miners' dry was warm and well organised, and that the state of the ladders was improved. His researches into the geology of the mine and association with the Cornish intelligentsia gained for him the reputation of being an unusually intelligent mine manager, and his innovative and determined leadership of the mine raised him above his fellows at a time when outstanding mine managers were the rule rather than the exception. Without William Petherick's energy, courage and resilience it is doubtful whether the mine would have survived those most difficult years until the management of Charles Thomas and the pursuit of the deep tin ore.[122]

The Management of Charles Thomas (1844-68)
With the death of Captain Petherick, the adventurers were placed in a quandary: should they cut their losses and accept the end of Dolcoath, or listen to the enthusiastic voice of Captain Charles Thomas? Lady Basset, who had taken over her late husband, Lord de Dunstanville's, share in the mine, which was 32/186th, making her, as mineral lord, the most significant individual adventurer, decided to

look closely at Thomas' ideas for the mine's survival. She appointed Captain Joseph Vivian, manager of North Roskear Mine, to inspect the mine and advise her on the best route forward. Vivian backed Thomas, and supported by Lady Basset, who offered financial incentives to those more timid adventurers who wanted to close the mine, he was given the go ahead to pump the lower levels and search for tin. The amount of dues given up by Lady Basset in support of the mine, between 1836-52, was £17,000. In 1846, when the Fox family decided to pull out of Dolcoath, the Williams family of Scorrier stepped in and took a large part of their share, which was to prove one of their shrewdest investments. The mine at the time was valued at only £4,000, and even in 1852 it was only worth an estimated £5,000. According to Professor Charles Thomas, Captain Thomas' salary remained the same as his predecessors, Petherick and Rule, at £15 4s a month.[123]

Sixteen years after taking over the management of Dolcoath, Charles Thomas wrote to the *Mining Journal* to set the record straight on the series of events which led to the de-watering of the deeper levels of Dolcoath and the pursuit of tin ore. The letter represents Thomas' version of the great crisis, which he and Captain Petherick faced, and his part in solving it. "In the year 1836 the adventurers resolved to abandon the deep part of the mine from 210, the bottom level, to the 155 fathom level. I was then underground captain, and, as such, made an estimate of the cost and produce by working below the 155, which showed, to the satisfaction of the worthy manager, the late Capt W. Petherick, that the deep part could be worked without loss. I then put the question – Why abandon the part that will pay cost, and forego the chance of improvement or discovery? The answer was, as the adventurers had resolved to do so he had no power to prevent it. It was accordingly done. In January 1844, in consequence of the death of Capt Petherick, I was appointed manager of the mine, and soon turned my attention to drawing out the water, for the purpose of working for tin, as the copper had nearly been exhausted. On the 12th May 1845, when some preparatory work in the engine-shaft had been done, I succeeded in getting the adventurers to resolve to commence drawing out the water, which was done forthwith. At the time of Capt Vivian's inspection, in December following, it was drawn out from 155 to 180, and that level was partly cleared. In March 1846, a steam-engine was ordered for stamping tin, which was set to work in October following. The remainder of the water was drawn out fast enough to lay open tin ground, to keep the stamps in full work. Capt J. Vivian's report had nothing to do with drawing out the water, 25 fathoms of the 55 having been drained before he inspected the mine. A new steward having been appointed by Lady Basset in 1845, an inspection of all her mines, as proprietor, was requested, which was done by Capt J. Vivian and myself in equal portions. The adventurers of the mines were no parties to any of these inspections. I am glad of the opportunity, however, of publicly stating that Capt J. Vivian, as well as other good practical miners, approved of my objecting to abandon the deep workings in 1836, and of the course taken to draw out the water in 1845. Dolcoath Mine. Jan 16 1860."[124]

Charles Thomas' success in persuading the adventurers to let him draw out the water from the bottom levels did not meet with everyone's approval, however, and some of the adventurers "still persisting in the old impression that the mine was worthless, they sold or gave away their shares, and the firm lost by that act something like £25,000." Fifteen years later, the *Mining Journal* commented that "the mine is now making a profit of about £24,000 a year, with a reserve of a quarter of a million sterling."[125]

Although de-watering the deeper levels and pursuing tin ore at the bottom of the mine were Thomas' principal preoccupations, he still had to run the mine with as little loss as possible until those longer-term aims could be realised. Soon after taking over from Captain Petherick, Thomas' tutworkers, opening up ground at the western end of the mine, discovered good copper ore, and for the moment revenue held up. According to one account, Thomas then gathered "together some good miners from the neighbouring Tin mines, and they examined the 145 fathoms level and they stated their willingness to work some parts on tribute." The account makes the point that such a system represented no risk of loss to the mine proprietors, and hence they raised no objection to Thomas' scheme. These tin miners were successful, and soon were paying their way at the same time as opening the adventurers' eyes to new possibilities. Thomas had undoubtedly learned from his old uncle, Captain James Thomas and William Petherick, of the tin discovered and worked in the Valley on and above the 145 level, in the 1820s. New tin discoveries at Carn Brea and Tincroft mines, a short distance to the east of Dolcoath, also weighed in favour of Thomas' arguments.[126]

The years 1844 to 1848 saw revenue from copper ore drop continuously, from 3,970 tons in 1843, to 3,860 in 1844, 3,504 in 1845, 2,156 in 1846, 2,057 in 1847 and 1,254 tons in 1848. Income from copper ore sales also dropped dramatically, from £18,721 in 1843 to £5,588 in 1848. With operating costs at £2,050 a month in 1846, and the mine losing an estimated £100 a month, Thomas was hard put to keep the support of the adventurers. However, this gloomy picture was to be changed by the increasingly successful search for tin. The steam stamps engine, ordered in March 1846, was up and running by October, and the increasing supply of tin ore was soon keeping it busy. At first tin revenue was modest, but it gradually increased, and in the years 1845-46 it is said to have represented some 42 percent of the mine's total income. If we take the 42 percent as an indication of the average tin revenue for the years 1844 to 1848, when the tin ground was opened up at the bottom of the mine, its significance can be appreciated. Sales of black tin for the five years 1844-48 would have been over £43,500, and greatly boosted the overall income of the mine.[127]

In 1846 there was a crisis over the financial management of the mine, when P. V. Robinson, the purser, was caught acting dishonestly, and was declared bankrupt. A Committee of Management, including Charles Thomas, was set up and assumed the pursership. Due partly to his increased responsibility and workload, in 1856 Captain Thomas' salary was raised to 18 guineas a month, and in 1859 it was increased again to 21 guineas.[128]

Average Monthly Miners' Wages in Camborne in 1847

Wheal Seton £3 1s 6d; North Roskear £3 1s 0d; East Wheal Crofty £3 0s 8d; Carn Brea £3 18s 4d; Stray Park £2 17s 10d; Tincroft £2 17s 10d; South Roskear £2 16s 6d; Dolcoath £2 14s 6d.[129]

As a rough estimate, based on tin being 42 percent of ore revenue, income from black tin sales between 1844-48 would have been:

1844:	£13,463
1845:	£12,308
1846:	£6,913
1847:	£6,813
1848:	£4,046

In October 1848 James Lanyon inspected the mine for E. C. Marriott, the Basset steward, and reported that the 190 fathom level was drained and being opened up for renewed production. Below the level, as the water went down, samples showed excellent tin ground, and Lanyon expressed confidence in the 200 fathom level, when it was drained and explored. But, it was not just below the 190 that new tin ground was being opened up, for in January he had reported the 180 fathom level on Main Lode, west of Engine Shaft, was also being driven, and more tin ore was being made ready for stoping. The whole block between 180 and 190 levels, west of Engine Shaft was standing ready and tributers were already starting to work it. On North Valley Lode work to open up tin ground below the 145 level progressed as did tutwork to develop tin ground on the 170 level. Twenty-four tributers were working for tin between the 110 and 145 levels, with values from £15 to £20 a fathom. Development took place on New South Lode, with mixed results, and on South Entral Lode development on the 27 and 42 fathom levels met with varying values, north of Freemans Shaft, in Roskear Broase. A lode seen at Adit Level was sought by crosscutting at the 42 fathom level. There were 48 tutworkers, 28 men stoping tin ground on the company account, 106 tributing for tin and 52 tributing for copper, making a total of 234 men on development and production underground. Lanyon supported Thomas' general ideas for the mine, and he stated: "The Tin ground below

157

the 190 at Engine Shaft has rather improved during the last quarter & there can be no doubt if the water was drained to the bottom (210) that Tin enough would be raised to pay the extra Cost." He was also sanguine about the higher levels of the mine, and concluded: "The present state of the Mine is rather improved, & great economy is observed in carrying on the various operations."[130]

By January 1849 the 200 fathom level was in process of draining, ready for cleaning up and development. The extreme width of Main Lode was causing problems, as discovering the best part of the lode to drive on was constantly uncertain. Lanyon remarked that the bottom levels needed dialling, so that the plans could be brought up to date before the next account day. Work to open up more ground on North Valley Lode, New South Lode and South Entral Lode continued, with encouraging results. The number of men carrying out tutwork increased to 60, company account stopers were 26, tin tributers rose to 111, and tributers for copper numbered 54, making a total of 251 on development and production. The price of tin was improving and Lanyon expected the mine costs to be met.[131]

On March 2nd 1849 Captain Charles Thomas wrote to Marriott to explain the mine's current position. The statement showed Thomas' careful analysis of the position of the mine, and what was needed for its efficient and economic working. The average tin grade was two percent (4cwt black tin from 100 2cwt sacks). With another twelve heads the steam stamps could stamp 1,750 tons of tin stuff a month, for a produce of 35 tons of black tin. There were 13 water stamps on the mine, with 46 heads, and there was usually enough water to work them for 4 or 5 months in winter. This was enough power to stamp all accumulated rough tin halvans for the year, with a produce of some 24 tons of black tin. The three steam whims in the central and eastern part of the mine drew from four shafts, and working from 2am Monday till 10pm Saturday they could draw some 9,000 kibbles a month, producing (excluding halvans) up to 1,800 tons of tin stuff. This was the amount the steam stamps could cope with, when the extra twelve heads were added. Thomas noted the problem with Dolcoath's shafts – they ought to be larger, for a bigger hoist, and many were underlie, with a lot of timber to support them. Two important shafts went through attle for long distances, and these were in constant need of repair. There was another steam whim on the western end of the mine, but this worked only a third of the time, and hoisted mostly copper ore. This whim shaft could be brought into more use, and the 190 was being cleared to connect to it and the 180 was also being driven to it. It could increase the ore at surface by up to 400 tons a month. Thomas reckoned it could be ready within a month. However, he pointed out that the extra distance of tramming underground and carriage on surface would be expensive. This is possibly the first reference to tramming underground at Dolcoath, but when it was first used to replace wheel barrows for haulage, it is impossible to say. Thomas spoke of the rationalisation of labour which he had worked out two months earlier, and believed he had the tributer-tutworker ratio about right, with tutworkers working flat out to keep ahead of the tributers. He had carried out a similar exercise with the monthly whim hoist and stamping capability. Unfortunately, despite the manager's best efforts, there was a growing tonnage of ore awaiting hoisting from underground – some 3,000 tons, increasing at a rate of 500 tons a month. It is interesting that the average tin grade was similar for both tutwork development ends and tribute pitches. He commented that the mine had lessened the average number of tutworkers driving an end from six to four men. This, he believed, gave a saving of some ten percent to the mine. Thomas gave examples of costs and profits/losses on ends driven. The 180 end on Main Lode being driven west, was worth £14 a fathom, cost £6 6s a fathom to drive and dressing cost for the ore raised was £1 14s. This gave a profit of 11s 6d in the pound. He then showed how changed mining practice had led to more economical development. Twelve years before, when the 200 level, west, on Main Lode was last driven, the drive measured six feet high by three foot six inches wide, and lost about £2 10s a fathom to the company, but now, the drive was carried eight feet high by seven feet wide and gave a profit of £9 a fathom to the company. Thomas pointed out that the levels above the 180 were not looking good, but the deepest workings were. They needed to get into the granite, for none of their lodes or those of their neighbours produced much tin in the killas. "Until discoveries shall be made at the bottom of the Mine at the 210 or by sinking deeper, or at the deepest levels of the Valley, we think that our present returns of 35 Tons a month at the present price of Tin is as much as the continued welfare of the Mine will warrant us in raising." The manager had not neglected his main aim in life – to persuade the adventurers to support his drive to sink deeper![132]

In May 1849 Lanyon reported that the 200 level was being developed east and west of Engine Shaft on Main Lode, that the water was forked three fathoms below the 200 and it was expected that the 210 fathom level would be drained within a month. Tin values were improving as the deeper levels were explored, and work continued on the higher levels on North Valley, New South and South Entral lodes, with mixed results. There were 76 men on tutwork, 20 stoping on the company account, 130 tin tributers and 66 copper tributers, making a total of 292 development and production miners. Lanyon was concerned at the low price of tin.[133]

By August Lanyon was reporting that the 210 fathom level was being opened up west of Engine Shaft, and the values were encouraging. He commented that the tin values were on the north part of Main Lode. When the level was first opened up, several years before, it was, apparently, the south part of the lode which was developed, for its copper ore. As soon as the 210 level was reached, stoping had started close to Engine Shaft on the north part of Main Lode. Work continued to explore and stope on North Valley, South Entral and New South lodes. In August 1849 there were 70 men on tutwork, 16 stoping on the company account, 128 tin tributers and

58 copper tributers, making a total of 272 on development and production. Lanyon commented that the tutworkers had accomplished less development recently, due to their being employed on 'other work'. With so much reorganisation going on it is hardly surprising that men were constantly being taken off their normal jobs.[134]

Sinking The Engine Shaft Resumed
On December 14th 1849 Lanyon reported that sinking below the 210 level had been resumed, with six men being paid £30 a fathom. They were one fathom below the 210, and the values were given as £12 a fathom. Main Lode on the 170, 200 and 210 levels was being developed, with varying results. On the 200 level east of Engine Shaft, the south part of Main Lode was giving tin and copper ore. Work continued on North Valley, New South and South Entral lodes, and North Entral Lode was also being driven at the 42 fathom level. There were 76 tutworkers, 8 stopers, 122 tin tributers and 66 copper tributers, totalling 272 development and production miners. Lanyon was hopeful of finding payable tin on North Valley Lode, and commented that it had produced good quantities of tin above the 155 fathom level, during the previous two years. The monthly black tin output was 31 tons, but Lanyon expected this to increase in the first half of 1850, helping to pay off the '£650 now charged on account of Tin in stock'.[135]

Production of copper ore in 1849 fell 226 tons to 1,028, and income from it went down by £391 to £5,197. If Lanyon's estimate of 31 tons of black tin being produced a month in 1849 was accurate, it would give a total of 372 tons for the year. At an average of £40 per ton at the mine, the income from tin in 1849 would have been £14,880, and with the copper ore sales the mine would have gained over £20,000 for the year. 1850 saw copper production rise slightly by 87 tons to 1,115, and income from copper ore drop again by £288 to £4,909. Increasing tonnages of black tin improved the revenue position. At an average of 26 tons a month at the low price of £41 a ton the mine would have gained an extra £12,792.[136]

The early part of 1850 saw the price of tin fall away, making some lower grade pitches uneconomic to work. Despite this, and the suggestion from James Lanyon that the tutworkers be reduced further – they had already gone down to 60 by May 1850 – Thomas continued to sink toward the 220 fathom level at Engine Shaft. On Main Lode development continued on the 170, 200 and 210 fathom levels. The other three lodes were also developed, although not with as much vigour as hitherto. The number of men on tribute dropped to 162, and the overall number of miners on production to 250. In August 1850 the *Mining Journal* reported that Dolcoath had a loss, in May-June, of some £210, which increased the mine's debit to £2,756. Overall monthly costs stood at £1,745.[137]

In June 1850 Captain Thomas wrote to E. C. Marriott to explain his proposals for the short-term working of the mine, in the light of recent heavy expense and the continuing low tin price. He suggested that Marriott ask Captain James Lanyon to explain anything he failed to understand. Once again Thomas was able to demonstrate his meticulous attention to detail and careful analysis of the mine's problems, and his ideas on the remedies. Thomas wrote: "I beg to add the following list of costs in new work during the last five years:

Clearing Valley Shaft & levels	
Forking water from 155 to 210	£1,000
& additional materials for that depth	£1,800
Improvements in surface machinery	£250
Working on South Lode & materials	£3,700
Steam stamps & floors with additions	
Since the erection	£3,000
Total	**£9,750**

"4 years ago our calculations were all made on the price of Tin at £50 per ton, but the great fall in the price has occasioned a loss on the quantity of (tin) sold during that time of nearly £8,000, or I should rather say that at £50 a ton the Tin sold in the last 4 years would have brought nearly £8,000 more than it has done." Thomas then offered his calculation of the 'cost and credits for May & June 1850', and offered various possible solutions to the problems facing the mine.

Tutwork labour cost 2 months		£1,420
Tribute labour cost 2 months		£980
Merchants Bills	ditto	£1,000
Bank Charges	ditto	£60
		£3,460
Tin 56 tons @ £41		£2,296
Copper		£845
Arsenic		£120
		£3,261
Estimated loss without dues		**£200**

"Note 1 – Present cost might be met at £45 per ton for Tin, or suspend all the unproductive tutwork as below." The proposal was to suspend for the time being nine tutwork tasks, which were developing Main Lode at 200 level east of Engine Shaft, driving a crosscut to South Lode and opening up tin ground in the Valley, carrying out exploration developments near Stray Park boundary, and work on North and South Entral lodes. This would save the cost of 22 tutworkers. The tutwork which was deemed economic with tin at £41 a ton, employed 54 men, and their work included sinking Engine Shaft below the 210 fathom level, developing the 210 east and west on Main Lode, stoping the back of the 210 near to Engine Shaft, on the company account, and sinking a winds under the 200 level. Thomas noted in June 1850 there were 168 men on tribute at an average of 12s in the pound, and 52 tutworkers, making a total of 220 on development and production. There had been, he said, for some years about the year 1840, between 180 and 200 tutworkers and tributers. Thomas gave the cost per month of working below the 200 fathom level as £170, but income, at £41 a ton, (6 tons) was, after dressing costs, £196, giving a profit of £26, which after engine charges, etc, would just about break even. He believed that there was every indication that the 220 fathom level would prove very valuable, and was optimistic about the mine at depth.[138]

By August 1850 Engine Shaft had been sunk 8 fathoms below the 210 fathom level, and Old Engine Shaft (Old Sump) was sunk 7 fathoms below the 200. Lode development was significantly reduced, with all tutwork on North Valley Lode stopped and North Entral tutwork confined to a north crosscut. Two ends were being driven on New North and South Entral lodes. Tutworkers were down to 52, company account stopers to 10, tin tributers to 88 and copper tributers 61, making a total of 211 men on development and production. Lanyon gave the monthly black tin average as 25 tons.[139]

Lanyon's December report announced that the 220 fathom level had been reached at Engine shaft, and preparations were in hand to drive east and west on Main Lode. Although the lode at 220 was seen over a width of seven feet, neither wall could be seen, and as well as its great width the lode continued to be exceedingly hard. Some development continued on New South Lode, but otherwise most tutwork was restricted to the deeper levels on Main Lode. The crosscut to North Entral Lode at the 20 fathom level was 14 fathoms from it. There were 52 men on tutwork, 12 stoping on the company account, 92 tin tributers and 59 copper tributers, totalling 215 men on development and production. Lanyon reckoned that production of black tin had risen since the summer to about 28 or 29 tons a month, and not only would the mine costs be met, but some of the debt might also be cleared.[140]

The Mine Returns to Profit
In 1851 copper ore production dropped to a record low, going down 314 tons to 801, and income from it dropped £1,280 to £3,629. It was fortunate that black tin production continued to improve, with some 25 tons being produced monthly. The mine averaged perhaps as much as £50 a ton for its black tin, and this would give an income from it of £15,000. The *Mining Journal* reported that Dolcoath made a small profit in the years 1850 and '51, and although it might have been optimistic, it certainly recognised growing confidence in the future of the mine. In September-

October 1850 tin revenue was over 76 percent of the mine's income, with copper 19 percent and arsenic 4 percent, which totalled £3,148, leaving a profit of £30 after all expenses.[141]

James Lanyon was more objective in his comments on the progress of the mine toward profitability, but even he did not fail to identify the straws in the wind. In May 1851 he noted that Engine Shaft was six feet below the 220 fathom level and by October it had been sunk a further three fathoms. The 220 was opened up during the year, lode drives going east and west from Engine Shaft, and the north part of Main Lode, where the best tin was, was being explored. In May there were 14 stopers working the back of the 210 on Main Lode, west of Engine Shaft, but by October they were reduced to just four. Tin values below 220 were £35 a fathom, and 8 tutworkers were sinking at £30 a fathom. Old Sump Shaft was also being sunk below the 210 level, improving ventilation in the central part of the deepest levels of the mine. Development and stoping continued throughout the mine, and North and South Entral, South (Brea) and New South lodes were all explored and exploited, with crosscuts going north and south to pick up new mineral ground. At Deep Adit level the drive south from Tuckingmill hoped to intersect South Roskear Lode and at the 20 fathom level a crosscut was being driven south to intersect North Entral Lode.[142]

The use of development and production miners changed during the year, with tutworkers increasing from 52 in May to 72 in October, company account stopers dropping from 14 to 4, tin tributers going down from 112 to 104 and copper tributers being reduced from 30 to 20. Overall the total number on development and production went down from 208 to just 200 men. Clearly, Thomas' drive to open up new tin ground was being given priority.[143]

Sinking continued in 1852, with Engine Shaft 8 fathoms below 220 fathom level by April, and a fathom below the 230 by October. With depth, the price paid per fathom for sinking went up from £30 to £35. In April, concentration on exploration of the deeper levels continued, with a winze being sunk below the 220, west of Engine Shaft, on Main Lode, and a rise and winze intended to meet between the 210 and 220 levels progressing well. The 190, 210 and 220 levels were driven on Main Lode, and tribute pitches were set between the 180 and 190 fathom levels. North Entral was explored by crosscut at 20 level, on a crosscourse, and the 42 level, north of Freemans Shaft was driven east of the crosscourse there. South Entral Lode was also driven on 42 level, but the values were poor. On New South Lode the 150 was driven east and the 180 driven west, with some tributing there. South or Brea Lode, despite little to encourage the miners, was still being worked. The Deep Adit, being driven south from Tuckingmill, was expected to intersect a 'Caunter lode', but it appeared to be still further south of the end. In April tutworkers dropped slightly to 68, stopers

163

rose to 18, tin tributers went down to 80 and copper tributers went up to 31, giving a total of 197 men on development and production.[144]

The *Mining Journal* reported that during the summer of 1852 the mine was doing very well. New ore ground to the value of £20,000 had been discovered, and profits were said to be running at between £130 and £175 per month. By the end of the year Dolcoath's black tin was fetching £57 a ton. Black tin sales amounted to 86 percent of the mine's revenue, with copper 13 percent and arsenic a mere one percent. An adverse balance of over £1,000 was wiped out in October, as a call of £5 15s per share was made. The accounts for September-October showed over 59 tons of black tin were sold, creating a profit of £261. Production of copper ore in 1852 amounted to 832 tons, a rise of 31 tons over the previous year. Revenue from it was down £284 to £3,345.[145]

By October 1852, with the 230 fathom level reached and the levels from 190 to 220 looking good, concentration on the extreme western parts of the mine was given priority. The ground above the 180 level along the western boundary with Stray Park Mine was attracting interest, and it was posited whether Stray Park adventurers would be interested in their ground at those levels, as they had done nothing there for years. Work to the east of Wheal Killas Shaft was carried out in the second half of 1852. Harriets Lode was worked at the 100 level west of Old Sump, as was North Entral Lode on the 20 level, and on the 42 near Freemans Shaft. The Deep Adit south of Tuckingmill was extended. Above the adit, miners explored to within four fathoms of the surface. Lanyon expressed the hope that the 230 level would start to be opened up in November. South or Brea Lode was abandoned, with the pitwork there removed. There were 66 tutworkers, 16 contract stopers, 52 tin tributers and 73 copper tributers in October, making a total of 207 miners on development and production. This dramatic rise in copper tributers was probably due to the unexpectedly large increase in ore, discovered in the summer – it was clearly copper ore! Lanyon reported that the mine was producing 30 tons of black tin a month in October, and that two-thirds of it came from below 180 fathom level. He estimated there would be a profit of £100 a month in the next quarter, if the tin price held. The *Mining Journal* reported that in November-December 1852 there was a profit of £351. It also stated that Charles Thomas claimed that Dolcoath had returned £3,000,000 over the previous half century, and paid out £130,000 in profits.[146]

As revenue flowed into Dolcoath's coffers from increasing tin production, the adventurers were more sanguine about Captain Thomas' plans for the future of the mine. In the winter of 1852-53 the new twelve head battery of steam stamps, advocated by the manager in his June 1850 plan, was erected. They cost £4,000. This increased the capacity of the mine considerably. In April the *Mining Journal* announced that, due to Dolcoath's recent heavy expenditure on steam stamps of 'superior power', and other plant, Lady Basset had given permission for the mine to take the 'Barrier' into its sett. This was a piece of ground on the western boundary of Dolcoath, and was previously unworked. April also saw Dolcoath pay out it first tin dividend of £3 10s a share. The amount paid out for the whole year amounted to £2,595, and was surprisingly high, considering the large expenditure on shaft sinking, the new stamps battery, preparation for a 'man engine', and other development work. Thomas told the *Journal* that it was the first dividend for 14 years. It was also stated that there was an ore reserve worth some £30,000, and that the mine plant was valued at £10,000. Full credit was given to the manager and to John Hocking and Michael Loam the engineers who looked after the engines of Dolcoath and several other mines. At the Falmouth Polytechnic Exhibition Dolcoath won first prize for having the 'best laid out tin floors' in Cornwall. The discovery of 'North Tincroft Lode' in its sett caused the adventurers to believe they had a whole 'new mine' on the property.[147]

Lanyon's report, dated June 10th 1853, described continuing progress throughout the mine, but particularly on the deeper levels. Engine Shaft had begun sinking below the 230 fathom level which was being driven west on the south part of Main Lode. The shaft-sinking cost had risen again, from £35 to £50 a fathom. Presumably, poor ventilation was one of the reasons. Tutworkers were employed between the 180 and 230 level on Main Lode, opening up what was proving to be rich tin ground. Harrietts Lode was developed on 29 and 100 fathom levels, North Entral was developed on the 42 level, near to Freemans Shaft, and on the 20 fathom level. A new shaft was started to ventilate the end on the 20 level. The adit drive south from Tuckingmill had still not found anything worthwhile. There were 88 tutworkers, 66 copper tributers and 56 tin tributers, making a total of 210 on development and production. Lanyon complained that the tin price had fallen 'considerably since the last account', and any dividend should be no more than £2 per share.[148]

Construction of a Man Engine
By the autumn work had begun to construct a 'man engine' on the mine. As early as 1829 Michael Loam, engineer at Consols Mine, Gwennap, had been working on ideas for such a machine, and some believe that in 1829 he offered to erect one at Dolcoath, using the pump rod. Encouraged by Dr Paul, a mine surgeon, he had toyed with a variety of designs, and in 1833, at about the same time that a *fahrkunst* was introduced into a German mine, the Royal Cornwall Polytechnic Society began to encourage the introduction of such a machine into Cornwall, where depths of over 1,200 feet were becoming commoner. The first man engine erected in a Cornish mine, by Loam, was at Tresavean, in January 1842. Loam's engine was powered by a water wheel, as were the German machines, and like those machines his had a double-rod, so that as one went up the other went down. Steps on the rod and small platforms in the shaft corresponded to the height of the rise and fall of the rods. Thereafter, man engines were erected on several deep Cornish mines, with United

Mines following in 1845, also with a double-rod, and a 32-inch steam engine to power it, and in 1851 Fowey Consols introduced a single rod version, with a 30-foot waterwheel. Dolcoath, Levant and Wheal Vor all erected man engines in the 1850s. Dolcoath's man engine was powered by a 19-inch cylinder engine, with a 5-foot stroke, running at 42 spm, reduced by gearing to a more sedate 3½ spm in the shaft, which meant that miners were lifted at a speed of 42 feet a minute. From the surface the first 300 feet was vertical, thereafter the shaft inclined at between 72 and 76 degrees from the horizontal. Dolcoath's man engine, in common with most others erected in Cornwall, was worked by cog-wheels and crank, with 27 fathoms of flat rod between the crank and top of Wheal Bryant Shaft. There was an emergency ladder road alongside the engine rod, and a knocker line was there should communication with the driver be necessary. Sixteen inch square steps were fixed to the rod, and the sollars in Wheal Bryant were mostly spacious, with the gaps through which the rod moved also being wide. A two-foot long handle at about chest height gave the miner something to hold onto whilst travelling. Initially it was intended to carry the rod down to the 190 fathom level, but as the mine deepened, so the length was extended. In December 1853 Lanyon commented that, "18 men are engaged cutting down Wheal Bryant Shaft, etc, & preparing for the new engine." He went on, "To erect the 'New Engine', prepare the shaft & bring down the rod to the 190 fathom level, is estimated to cost about £1200. This will probably be completed in eight months, the cost would then be £150 per month."[149]

In September-October 1853 tin, copper, arsenic and sundry sales brought in £5,898, and despite costs of £4,618, and expense of the new man engine of £150 a month, there was a dividend paid of £3 a share.[150]

By early December Engine Shaft was sunk 6 fathoms below the 230 level on the south part of Main Lode. Old Sump Shaft was sunk 4 fathoms below the 220 fathom level, by 4 men who were paid £3 a fathom, plus 5s in the pound tribute for tin. From 180 down to 230 level driving and stoping were going on apace, with excellent results. North Entral Lode at the 42 and 20 fathom levels was being developed between Freemans Shaft and the eastern boundary. The new shaft, being sunk to improve ventilation of the 20 fathom level on North Entral Lode, progressed well. Lanyon made some interesting observations on the mine's progress: "The north part of the lode (Main Lode) … discovered on the 210 and 220 fathom levels, appears likely to be of very great importance. When the lode was very productive for copper, several 'droppers' of this kind were discovered at the upper levels from which considerable returns were made – but at this depth, this is a new feature in the mining of this locality – in the ensuing quarter some important information will be obtained respecting it." These 'droppers' appear to be branches falling from the foot wall of the Main Lode.[151]

There were 96 tutworkers, 22 stopers and 138 copper and tin tributers, totalling 256 men on development and production. Lanyon reckoned that the mine would soon be producing 30 tons of black tin a month, and he expected a payout of about £3 per share. Production for 1853 was 1,040 ton of copper ore, which sold for £4,920, and 360 tons of black tin, which sold for £22,680, at an average of £63 a ton.[152]

By June 1854 Lanyon was reporting that Engine Shaft was sunk 8 fathoms below the 230 fathom level and New East Shaft was sunk 2 fathoms below the 190. Engine Shaft was by then costing £60 a fathom compared to £10 for New East Shaft. There was considerable activity at the deeper levels of the mine and the tin ground being opened up was very valuable. Fourteen men were stoping the back of 220 level, where the south part of Main Lode was 18 feet wide and worth £40 a fathom. Twelve men stoped the north part between 220-230 levels, where it was 6-8 feet wide and worth £40-£50 a fathom. In places these two branches of Main Lode were 30 feet apart, and had an underlay of some 15 degrees from the vertical. Work continued on North Entral Lode at the 42 level near to Freemans Shaft and at the 20 fathom level, where the rise to meet the new shaft continued.[153]

Lanyon was excited by the sheer width and value of the north and south parts of Main Lode at the bottom of the mine, and was confident that raising 30 tons of black tin a month was well within their sights, due to 'the great size of both lodes (from 20 to 30 ft wide) these returns appear likely to be increased'. Copper was still being returned as tributers were being paid at a high rate for what they could find. There were 68 tutworkers, 26 stopers and 117 tributers, making a total of 211 on development and production. The big project was still the man engine, and Lanyon said: "20 men are engaged preparing the shaft & other work connected with the 'Man Engine' which is expected to be in course of working within the next 3 months. ... The completing of the 'Man Engine' with all possible dispatch is therefore very important as the men have to descend about 230 fathoms or more to their work." He concluded by adding that £150 a month was being spent on the man engine, and because of this, and the fact that the tin price had gone down by more than £10 a ton, 'no Dividend can be made for the present'.[154]

A Serious Accident on the Man Engine
By October 9 Engine Shaft had only a fathom to go to the 240 fathom level, and New East Shaft was 5 fathoms below the 190. Development and stoping continued to good effect on all the deeper levels on the north and south parts of Main Lode, which were wide and rich. The new shaft sinking on North Entral was sunk below Deep Adit and the rise toward it was within 15 fathoms. There were 72 tutworkers, 20 stoping on so much a ton, and 110 tributers, totalling 202 miners. The man engine was expected to be working 'in a few days – about £600 is charged in July & August cost towards this object', and due to this heavy expense, and despite the expected

production of 30 tons of black tin a month, Lanyon did not expect a dividend for the rest of the year. The *West Briton* reported that in its first month of operation there was a serious accident on the man engine, when the cog-wheel broke in two, causing the rod to fall and injuring some 14 miners, four of them very seriously. It is just possible that this accident was the one referred to by John Harris, when he said 20 miners were thrown off the machine and injured. However, apart from the number of men involved, which Harris' memory might have exaggerated, he said there were no serious injuries, and it is unlikely that he would have forgotten the four seriously injured in an accident in which he was involved. Thus, it seems, that there were two major accidents on the man engine during its teething troubles.[155]

Copper ore produce went down by 48 to 992 tons in 1854, and revenue from it dropped by £606 to £4,314. Black tin went up 4 tons to 364, and it sold for £25,621, an average of £69 8s a ton. In 1855 copper ore dropped 281 tons to 711, and copper revenue went down £1,680 to £2,634. Black tin also dropped slightly by 12 tons to 352, and it sold for £23,170, a fall of £2,451.[156]

On April 6th 1855 Lanyon reported that Engine Shaft had reached the 242 fathom level, and after opening a plat at the station the tutworkers would begin a crosscut to the north part of Main Lode. Main Lode was being developed and stoped between Valley Shaft at the 155 level at the eastern end of the mine, and to 60 fathoms west of Wheal Bryant Shaft, at the 190 level, at the western end. New East Shaft was sunk 15 fathoms below the 190 level, and the new shaft on North Entral Lode was making progress to the 20 fathom level. Generally, values in new ground were not as good as previously, but there was two years worth of good tin ground opened up and ready for stoping. The end on South Lode was suspended for the moment. Lanyon was optimistic about the 242 level, and once again the mine was attaining 30 tons of black tin a month, which should give a small profit for the next six months. There were 75 tutworkers, 28 stoping tin ground and 131 tributers on tin and copper ore, giving a total of 234 on development and production. Finally, Lanyon commented: "The 'Man Engine' is now in a most efficient state of working affording important facility in laying open the bottom of the Mine, from whence the greater part of the Tin is now obtained."[157]

Thomas Oliver, who wrote his autobiography in the early years of the twentieth century, spoke of an interesting conversation between himself and his mine captain, Captain John Tonkin in 1855. Oliver was working as a tutworker driving a north crosscut to intersect North Lode on the 220 fathom level. It is very revealing about the education and intelligence of the mining community at the time. Oliver himself had been to evening classes run by the mine manager's brother, and he had attended covered with dirt from underground because he had no time to clean himself up before the class started. He had worked at Condurrow Mine at the time, and that small mine had no dry or washing facilities. Tonkin had commented on some beautiful crystals in a vugh or natural cavity, and when Oliver had asked him what he thought, Tonkin had replied: "They were made when the earth and the heavens were created, about six thousand years ago." Oliver replied, "more than six million years ago." Tonkin was a local preacher, as was Oliver, and before becoming a mine captain he had been a schoolmaster. Oliver then related, how shortly after their conversation, Captain Tonkin visited London and the British Museum, where he saw animal fossils "that had lived many million of years ago." When Tonkin returned he said to Oliver "I am converted to your belief. The old book says, in the beginning God created the heavens and the earth, and no one knows when the beginning was."[158]

Leon Moissenet at Dolcoath

In 1855 Moissenet investigated the current methods of hoisting ore at Dolcoath and reported his findings in the *Mining & Smelting Magazine* of 1863. Despite the introduction of skip hoisting in Cornish mines as early as 1840, Dolcoath continued to use the old-fashioned kibbles until 1878. These essentially iron plated buckets, narrow at the base (15-inch diameter), wide in the belly (24-inch diameter) and 22-inch at the top, had a capacity of only 7cwt. The plates were 1¼ inches thick, with the base over 3 inches thick. Due to friction in the inclined shafts at Dolcoath, these kibbles quickly wore out and just two hoisting shafts wore out 62 kibbles in 1855. A kibble lasted up to twelve 24-hour days, including time for repairs, before being totally worn out. In 1855 Dolcoath drew 20,000 tons of ore through two of its shafts from an average depth of 250 fathoms. Hoisting from such depths the mine used tapered chains, with the lower links being ½ inch and the higher ones 11/16th. Dolcoath used 12¾ tons of chain for its kibbles in 1855 at a cost of £339, and after the sale of scrap chain the cost was £275 for the year. Chains frequently broke in the shafts, and apart from the danger to men working in the shafts, the cost to the mine was great. Notwithstanding the daunting cost of kibble replacement and repair, and the cost of chains, the greatest burden in hoisting was the cost of coal. In 1855 Leon Moissenet estimated that nearly 65 percent of the cost of hoisting went on coal, 32 percent on whim drivers' wages and less than 4 percent on tallow, grease and sundries.[159]

1856 saw the mine's value gradually increase and in October a dividend of £5 a share for the months July-August was announced, which totalled £895. For those two months ore sold, after the 1/24th dues were paid, amounted to £5,968 9s 10d. Labour and merchants costs were £5,002, and there was an overall profit of £971 6s 4d. Assisting Captain Charles Thomas were captains William Provis, John Tonkin and Charles' son, Josiah Thomas. From 1856 Charles Thomas had managed Dolcoath and several other mines in partnership with Josiah, as 'Charles Thomas & Son'. There were 104 miners on development, 43 stoping at so much a ton, and 122 on tribute, totalling 269 men. Seventy-five tons of black tin were produced in July-

August and the managers were confident that it would rise to 80 tons within a couple of months.[160]

The September-October 1856 ore sales rose to £6,143 3s 4d and costs were £3,646 18s 9d. With a two month profit (after dues and rents) of £973 1s 8d a dividend of £1,074 was declared, giving the adventurers £6 a share. There were 273 miners working on production and development. The *Mining Journal* commented on the heavy expense Dolcoath had on erecting additional ore dressing machinery in 1856. The November-December accounts show £7,767 4s 10d worth of black tin sold, against costs of £5,777 8s. A dividend of £1,074 was paid out at £6 a share.[161]

Production and income from black tin sales increased in 1856 to 417 tons, which sold for £30,727. Copper ore sales dropped to 617 tons, worth £1,998. The price fetched for Dolcoath's black tin went up to nearly £74 a ton, but she received less for her copper ore than hitherto. With an income of £32,725 the mine paid out a total dividend for 1856 of £5,101.[162]

In February 1857 two events were reported which showed that Dolcoath had moved back into its former position as 'mother of the parish' and as a self-confident company, optimistic about its future. The Reverend C. Jenkin, of Tuckingmill Church, requested a donation to support the parish church school. The adventurers obliged with a gift of £10. The same report mentioned a Testimonial Plate, worth 50 guineas, presented to Captain Charles Thomas, manager of Dolcoath, for his sterling work in bringing the mine through an extremely trying time to profitability. The agents were given a bonus of an extra month's pay.[163]

The January-February 1857 accounts showed continuing improvement. The deepest level, the 242, was being developed with values averaging £80 a fathom, and the western end worth £100 a fathom. Throughout the deeper levels the tutworkers were opening good tin ground, and some 45 tons of black tin a month were being sold at an average price of £84 a ton. The adventurers were confident that the mine would achieve 50 tons within two or three months, when the new drawing whim and stamps engine should be up and running. The dividend paid out was £1,074, at £6 a share. A mere 74 tons of copper ore was sold for the previous three months.[164]

In the spring, production and income were maintained, and £600 on new dressing floors and machinery was spent. The 242 fathom level remained good and the high values inspired the adventurers to support a dividend of £7 a share, for March-April. For those two months there was a working profit of £1,254. The July 11th *Mining Journal* reported the visit to Dolcoath of Prince Napoleon and some French scientists. This group of eight or nine distinguished men, including the organiser, Alfred Fox of Falmouth, toured the surface arrangements, but, given the dirty, dark and dangerous conditions underground, declined the invitation to descend to the workings. The prince spoke briefly to a poor little orphan boy of nine years, who tended the stamps, and gave him a half sovereign, which he was urged to take home to his mother. The summer of 1857 saw Engine Shaft some 11½ fathoms (69 feet) below the 242 level, and the manager stated that he hoped to be opening up Main Lode on the 254 fathom level within two months. The south part of Main Lode was looking good, but the really high values were on the north part, with values on 242 west of Engine Shaft of £120 a fathom. Little development was taking place on the other lodes, and the 20 fathom level on North Entral Lode was 'unproductive'. Total production for July-August of tin, copper, arsenic, mundic and black jack (zinc ore) was £8,498 0s 11d, and the two months profit was £1,201 4s 4d. A dividend of £1,432 was paid out at £8 for each 1/179th share. That account shows that £800 was paid to Great Beam Mine for steam engine and stamps.[165]

Child Labour

In 1857 it was reported, that there were 148 boys 14 years old or younger working at the mine, and 119 girls.

Boys	Girls
6 seven year olds	4 seven year olds
16 eight year olds	6 eight year olds
24 nine year olds	15 nine year olds
33 ten year olds	17 ten year olds
33 eleven year olds	18 eleven year olds
10 twelve year olds	26 twelve year olds
14 thirteen year olds	13 thirteen year olds
12 fourteen year olds	20 fourteen year olds

In the October 17th 1857 *The Mining Journal,* it was stated that: "Dolcoath continues to stand at the head of the western mines for profit." Shortly afterwards it announced that Dolcoath shares were almost impossible to obtain and were worth some £320 each. All the deeper levels were producing high grade tin ore and the mine was selling between £40,000 and £50,000 of black tin a year. The *Journal* also commented that since 1815 the mine had sold 241,522 tons of copper ore for £1,364,554. By the end of 1857 the tin price had dropped dramatically from its high of £84 a ton for black tin in February. The average for the year was less than £79 a ton. With the drop in the tin price the adventurers agreed to hold back a third of the mine's September-October production until the price went up again. Consequently, costs for those two months were £6,845 and income from black tin and copper ore was only £4,964. It was estimated that the drop in price cost the adventurers £1,540. As this gave the mine a temporary cash-flow problem it was decided the next year to sell off the black tin held back, which eventually it did for over £10,000.[166]

The report to Tehidy dated April 9th 1858 continued the note of optimistic expansion of the previous year. James Lanyon had been replaced by 'Charles Thomas & Son', as Tehidy mine agents, so that they were effectively reporting on the state of the mine they managed. Thomas laid greater emphasis in his reports on detailing the many points of exploration and development. From its boundary with Cooks Kitchen in the east to Stray Park and the Barrier in the west, and between the 160 and the 254 fathom levels, tutworkers were opening up good tin ground and stopers were producing increasing tonnages of tin ore. On South and Harriett lodes, west of Wheal Bryant Shaft, toward the Barrier, tin and good copper ore was also being mined. Some of the tutworkers were paid by fathoms advanced and also at so much in the pound for the tin ore they raised. North of Machine Shaft the drive to North Entral Lode, on the 'Silver course' was proving poor. The number of miners driving, crosscutting, and sinking shafts and winzes was 96. Stopers numbered 95 and tributers 93, on tributes averaging 10s in the pound. This totalled 284, and showed men on development and production were gradually increasing. Black tin production was 50 tons a month, and this figure was predicted to continue for some time. Thomas believed that the ground already opened up would keep up a steady supply of tin ore 'for many years'. He commented that Valley (Eastern) Shaft had recently been sunk from the 155 to the 170 fathom level.[167]

Thomas summed up his April report with some interesting comments: "The machinery on the Mine is just equal to the present requirements for returning 50 tons of tin a month. The pumping Engine is of sufficient power to sink the Mine 30 or 40 fathoms deeper. If however a new perpendicular Shaft be sunk, & a new 90-inch cylinder Engine erected, the saving in drawing water & ore will be full £1000 per year, with power at command to drain the Mine in case water should flow into it from any neighbouring Mine, & also power to draw & return an additional quantity of tin if the Mine could fairly supply it." The need for a vertical shaft was seen by Thomas well over thirty years before Dolcoath was to start one. His vision of a 90-inch engine, regrettably, never came to fruition. The mine was to soldier on for many years before its problems of crooked shafts and inadequate hoisting system were remedied.[168]

During the year Leon Moissenet was taken underground to see the impressive stopes, which were up to 26 feet wide and 60 feet high. The walls of these immense excavations were not supported by timbers, being too far apart, and where Main Lode junctioned with Harrietts Lode the wall rock was extremely strong and almost vertical. The workings in the Valley section, at the eastern end of the mine were even wider. Thomas Oliver worked as a miner in such workings at Dolcoath at that time, and he wrote: "At one time I worked in a place as wide as an ordinary road, on a swing stage and many a time while working there I have felt my hair rise through fear when a stone fell from above…. Perhaps some will say I was a fool to work in such a dangerous place, perhaps I was, but it is not so easy to give up work when you are getting good wages as some may think." At that time Oliver was working as a tributer on 12s 6d in the pound and earning about £7 a month, which was a lot of money in the 1850s.[169]

The accounts for May-June 1858 showed the mine doing well. Ore sold amounted to £7,331 2s 8d and costs were £5,780 4s 5d, which meant that a dividend of £1,253 could be paid out at £7 a share. Main Lode was proving as rich as hitherto, with the drive west of Engine Shaft worth £60 a fathom in the end. July-August also showed a healthy condition, with ore sold being £7,859 12s 8d, and costs £5,932 9s 3d, giving a profit of £1,596 12s 3d. There was a dividend of £1,432 at £8 for each of the 179 shares. The Bassets received a handsome £330 15s 10d in dues. By August the average tin grade had improved further, with values up to £80 a fathom on 254 fathom level. The contrast between the north and south branches of Main Lode, which were up to 30 feet apart, could be seen in the tin grade, with the former being twice as rich as the latter. At the western end of the mine New South Lode was being driven toward the Barrier with varying results.[170]

Captain Pearce's Silver Medal

The October 9 1858 *Mining Journal* carried a report of an exhibition of mining inventions and innovations at Falmouth, held under the auspices of the Royal Cornwall Polytechnic Society. "Capt Pearce, of Dolcoath Mine, exhibited a model of an improved machine for the purpose, which, it appears, saves a considerable amount of labour; it is in use at Dolcoath, and has affected a saving to the adventurers of £250 a year." The judges awarded Captain Pearce a silver medal and £1 prize. The *Journal* commented that: "The object of the invention is to concentrate the dressing within very narrow limits, so that the operation may be more fully under the eye of the captain, and economise labour."[171]

As a result of the vastly improving situation at the mine it was announced that demand for shares was soaring, and it was decided to re-divide the adventure from 179 shares to 358. The *Mining Journal* stated that the original shares were worth between £160 and £170 each. A dividend for July-August was declared of £8 a share. The September-October account showed that mineral sales were £7,954 0s 5d, costs were £6,085 19s 10d, water and rents were £179 0s 2d, which gave a profit (after dues) of £1,878 2s 1d. A dividend of £1,790 was paid at £5 a share. A dividend of £6 a share was forecast for the next account, but in fact it was better than expected, at £7 for each of the new 358 shares. The last two months of 1858 saw tin and copper sales go up to £9,313 0s 7d, with costs up to £6,354 12s. There was a profit after poor rates, dues and rents of £2,513 19s 2d.[172]

Underground, things continued to improve, with Engine Shaft sinking below the 254 fathom level, and on the north part of Main Lode at the 242 and 254 levels the end values were averaging £100 a fathom. On New South Lode the drives west on the 160 and 190 levels were approaching the Barrier, with the lode in the 190 disordered by a crosscourse and the end on the 160 containing some tin.[173]

On November 5th 1858 Samuel Davey inspected the mine for the Tehidy Estate and gave it a clean bill of health. He described the many development points and gave the costs and values. There were 84 men on tutwork, opening up ground between the 20 fathom level on North Lode and the 254 fathom level on Main Lode. Davey said that there were "101 men Stoping on North & South parts of Main Lode (were being paid) at from 6s to 11s per ton", and "106 Tributers working at from 5s 6d to 15s in the £ Tribute." There were thus 291 miners on development and production. Davey spoke of the high returns and higher expectations from the deeper levels, and believed that the mine's future was secure.[174]

1859 was a year of continuous progress, with the value of ore rising for every two month period, from £9,317 in January-February to £11,331 in November-December. There was a total of £62,072 worth of black tin and copper ore sold, and with costs of £40,596, even after the lord's dues, rents and poor rates were paid there was a profit of £18,832. The dividend was £18,616, which was £52 a share. The Bassets not only earned a considerable amount from their not inconsiderable shareholding, but were paid £2,600 in mineral dues. In April the *Mining Journal* reported that Dolcoath was determined to acquire a new whim engine and use the one presently used for both winding and stamping just for stamping. The same report said that Captain Charles Thomas' salary was to be increased to £21 a month. In the May-June account £200 was paid toward the cost of the new steam whim, and between September and December a further £650 was paid out for the new engine, and a further £300 for the associated buildings. The whim was ready for use early in October. Engine Shaft was slowly sunk below the 254 fathom level, and by the end of the year it was 7 fathoms below that level. New East and Old Sump shafts were also being sunk, the former being holed to the 242 level by August and Old Sump was 6 fathoms below the 230 at the same time. Main Lode was opened up at the 242 and 254 levels, and in places the results were spectacular. The south part of Main Lode saw fairly average returns, but the north part had increasing values of £80-£90 per fathom in the early part of the year, rising to £120-£160 a fathom by April and peaking at £200 a fathom in October. This was ten times the value of most payable ends at Dolcoath and neighbouring mines. Meanwhile, work continued to open up New South Lode and Silver Lode (or Silver Course), where Rules Shaft was being sunk below Deep Adit level. By the end of the year Rules Shaft was 18 fathoms below Deep Adit, although no values were found.

On July 2nd 1859 Captain Samuel Davey reported to the Tehidy Estate on the mine. After detailing all the development points, together with the tin values and costs per fathom, he lists the tutworkers, of whom there were 125, driving, crosscutting, rising, and sinking winzes and shafts, at between £12 and £48 per fathom. This highest rate was for the eight men sinking Engine Shaft below the 254 fathom level. There were also 99 miners stoping for between 5s 6d and 9s a ton, and 110 tributers on tributes between 5s 6d and 12s 6d in the pound. Davey commented that Dolcoath was making a profit of £1,320 a month. The July-August Manager's Report (issued October 10 1858) gave the number of miners on development and production as 359, made up of 108 miners stoping at so much a ton, 135 men on tutwork, driving and sinking, and 116 tributers, at between 6s 8d and 13s 4d in the pound.[175]

Progress was maintained in 1860, with £68,020 worth of black tin and copper ore being sold. Copper ore fetched only £2,365, falling from £690 at the beginning of the year to £254 by the end. There was also £55 worth of arsenic and 18s worth of bismuth, which was sold in July-August. Costs rose to £44,399, lord's dues to £2,839 and profits went up to £20,901. The mine paid out £21,122 in dividends at £59 per share. The average price paid to Dolcoath for her black tin in 1860 was £80 4s.[176]

Engine Shaft was sunk 8 fathoms below the 254 in January 1860 and was down to the 266 fathom level by July, and in August the level was being driven east from the shaft to form an ore plat. Sinking had cost £60 a fathom by the time the 266 fathom level was reached. During September-October a crosscut was going north to intersect the north part of Main Lode, but by year's end it was still five fathoms short of it. The south part of Main Lode remained only average for values, but the richer north part continued to give high grades for most of the ends on the deeper levels, with values on the 254 and 242 up to £120 a fathom. Unexpectedly, in the autumn, values on the north part dropped to between £12 and £60 a fathom. This short-lived dip in values was more than offset in November-December by the sudden rise to £130 a fathom east of Engine Shaft on 254 level and values of £200 a fathom in a winze below that level. On North Lode, Rules Shaft was sunk to the 20 fathom level, and a crosscut north to cut North Entral Lode went on apace. By autumn the crosscut had intersected some copper-bearing branches north of Rules Shaft, but by the end of the year the drive was suspended.[177]

Captain Davey's report for April 5 1860 stated that there were 113 tutworkers on the deeper levels, 6 driving the 20 fathom crosscut from Rules Shaft, 46 cutting down Harrietts Shaft, 123 stoping on Main Lode between 200 and 240 fathom levels, and 90 tributers working at 5s to 13s 4d in the pound. This totalled 378 miners on development and production. By September the numbers were down slightly to 376 with 25 more men on stoping and tributing and less on tutwork.[178]

The August 1860 report refers to the ventilation needs of the stopes and pitches, and reports on a ventilation winze being sunk under the 170 level to improve the air on the 190, so that tribute pitches could be set and a proposed north crosscut to Valley Tin Lode properly ventilated.[179]

New 60-inch Engine for Harrietts Shaft

A major project was undertaken in 1860 in line with Captain Thomas' desire for more pumping power. Captain Davey commented: "As there is only one Pumping Engine on this Mine which is heavily laden it is thought advisable to erect a 60-inch Engine on Harrietts Shaft." The mine ordered the new engine from Perran Foundry. In January 1860 preparations began to place this pumping engine on Harrietts Shaft, and by February some 55 men were cutting down the shaft to prepare it for pitwork. In March the *Mining Journal* referred to Dolcoath's plans for a new engine to drain the western end of the mine, especially South Lode near to Stray Park Mine's boundary. It was stated that it was to cost £5,000. In the spring the number employed in the shaft had risen to 60, and the two month cost for the project was £400. By early summer the shaft was well on the way to receive the pitwork and the engine house was nearing completion, and during May-June £800 was spent on the project, with another £700 in July-August. The report for September-October showed another £1,050 spent and the engine was erected and the shaft almost complete to the 190 fathom level. The lode the shaft was sunk on was worth £40 a fathom. The Mine Manager's Report, dated February 11 1861, for the months November-December 1860, announced triumphantly: "The New Pumping Engine is working satisfactorily!" The report gave the two month's expense on the task as £600 "for labor and materials, for the Erection of the New Engine." During the year £3,550 had been spent on the engine and the necessary shaft preparation work.[180]

Captain Thomas used that February 1861 report to explain the current costs for hoisting, carting, stamping and dressing the ore. "The cost of drawing in this Mine for the year 1860 – from an average depth of 260 fathoms – including filling, landing and repairing Shafts, is 1s 6½d per ton. This is done by large Kibbles, and with Chains tapered from ¾ inch to ½ inch, in Shafts underlying about 2 feet in a fathom (or 72 degrees from the horizontal) for three-quarters of the depth. The cost of drawing by the New Whim – which was erected 1½ years ago – is 1s 3d a ton only. The cost of Carting the Tin Stuff to the Stamps – including filling – is 3¾d per ton. The cost of dressing per ton of Black Tin for labor, is £5 14s; and for Stamping – including coal for Engines and Burning Houses, Engine Men, and wear and tear of Machinery – is £3 19s. The total cost – including Carriage of Stuff to Stamps, and of Tin to Smelting House – is £10 7s per ton of Black Tin."[181]

By 1861 Josiah Thomas was running many aspects of the mine as 'assistant mine manager', for his father was 67 years old and unable to carry out underground inspections as he had. In that year Dolcoath sold £1,589 worth of copper ore and £63,862 worth of black tin, for a combined ore income of £65,451. After costs of some £48,000 a dividend of £16,826 was paid at £47 a share. In the January-February account £320 was paid toward the cost of the new engine, in March-April another £300 and in July-August a further £600 was paid, with the balance of £950 19s being paid in October. The final cost came to £6,000, which was about £1,000 more than the original estimate.[182]

Engine Shaft remained at the 266 fathom level until the summer, when sinking again got under way and by August it had been sunk 2 fathoms below the 266. At the year's end Engine Shaft was 5 fathoms below the level. Meanwhile, the 266 was driven north from Engine Shaft toward the north part of Main Lode, and by August as it opened up the north part of Main Lode, values of £100 a fathom were encountered. In September-October the east and west drives on the north part were both averaging £50 a fathom. A winze under the 254 fathom level north of Engine Shaft showed values of £200 a fathom in February, and by March-April massive values over great widths were encountered in the winze. "The Winds under the 254 North of Engine Shaft, is worth £300 per fm. for 6 feet long, or for the length of the Winds (10 feet), £500 per fm. This lode is reached in the cross-cut at the 266, about 8 feet below the bottom of the Winds. It contains very rich tin … for the last 7 fms. sinking, it has been worth, on an average, £200 per fm." South part of Main Lode had average tin values throughout the year of between £10 and £35 a fathom. At the beginning of the year the north crosscut from Rules Shaft on the 20 fathom level intersected North Entral Lode and found a little copper ore. In the early spring, New South Lode west of Wheal Bryant Shaft, on the 190 level, was also found to have a small amount of tin and copper ore. During the summer and autumn New East Shaft was being sunk below the 242 fathom level, and by August it was 6 fathoms below the level and expected to be at the 254 by early 1862. By the end of 1861 the mine was breaking, raising and selling 80 tons of black tin a month.[183]

Captain Samuel Davey's report to Tehidy Estate, dated April 4 1861, details some 20 development points which employed 110 tutworkers and 13 boys in driving and sinking winzes and shafts. Nine of them were sinking Harrietts Shaft below the 190 fathom level. They were down 5 fathoms and paid £30 a fathom. There were 144 stopers being paid at so much a ton of broken ore, 22 men cutting down Harrietts Shaft, and 124 tributers on 5s 6d to 13s 4d in the pound tribute. Davey's report dated 13th November 1861 showed development proceeding on the south part of Main Lode between the 190 and 242 fathom levels, with values between £8 and £20 a fathom. On north part development was between the 190 and 266 fathom levels, and values were between £12 and £100 a fathom. Sinking of shafts and winzes occupied a large proportion of the tutworkers, with Engine Shaft sunk 3 fathoms below the 266, New East Shaft 9 fathoms below the 242 and Harrietts Shaft 5 fathoms below the 190 fathom level. There were also two winzes being sunk. North Entral Lode west of the north crosscut from Rules Shaft was 1 foot wide and looked hopeful. There were 126 tutworkers, 129 stopers (working values of between £20 and £60 a cubic fathom) and 155 tributers on 8s to 13s 4d in the pound, a total of 410 on development and production. Davey noted the high values on Main Lode and then recommended that a closer look at Valley Lode should be made.[184]

In the last report for the year Captain Charles Thomas reported: "The average price of Tin Sold in these two months (November-December), is £2 per ton less than for the preceding two months, and £7 6s per ton less than the average of the five years from 1856 to 1860 inclusive. We have ascertained from the Cost Book that the Cost of drawing Ores, etc, for 1861, including Coals, Grease, Oil, Chains, Kibbles, Engine-men's Wages and Repairing Shafts – every Cost excepting filling and landing – is £180 per month on an average. The quantity of stuff drawn per month is 3,600 tons, shewing a cost of 1s per ton for an average depth of 260 fathoms. The cost of drawing the water for the same year is £176 per month, inclusive of wear and tear."[185]

During 1862 production continued to improve, with a steadily increasing tonnage of black tin sold, although copper sales continued to decline. Revenue from ore sales amounted to £69,663, costs totalled £49,783 and profits after payment of £2,861 dues to the Bassets and £222 for poor and highway rates, were £16,278. A dividend of £15,752 was paid out at £44 a share.[186]

Engine Shaft was sunk throughout the year, starting at 6½ fathoms below the 266 fathom level in January and reaching the 278 level by the end of the year. During the year Old Sump Shaft was sunk to the 254 level, Valley Shaft was sunk 7 fathoms below the 170 and a rise was being mined to meet it, Harrietts Shaft was sunk 10 fathoms below the 200 and Dunkins Garden Shaft was being deepened below the 220 fathom level. The south part of Main Lode had varying values during 1862, from between £15 and £60 a fathom at the beginning of the year to between £10 and £30 by December. North part of Main Lode maintained its extraordinarily high values, especially on the 266 to the east of Engine Shaft, where ends were frequently well over £100 a fathom and for a third of the year they averaged £150. On North Entral, the lode on 20 fathom level, west of the crosscut north from Rules Shaft, showed poor values, apart from a little copper ore. A winze below the 20, started in the summer, showed reasonable copper values. Values on New South Lode at the western end of the mine were good. A winze was sunk some 150 fathoms west of Harrietts Shaft below the 190 fathom level, and the tin grade was up to £80 a fathom over a width of 12 feet. So hopeful was this piece of ground, that flat rods were fixed to the bottom of Harrietts pump rod and were carried the 150 fathoms to the winze, where a pump lift was installed. This enabled the winze to be sunk and the ground there opened up. Harrietts Shaft was referred to in the October 13th Manager's Report as 'New

Engine Shaft'.[187]

In June 1862 Thomas had reported that there were 452 men and boys on development and production, and in August Davey reported that there were 445, made up of 154 tutworkers (at £7 10s a fathom), 113 stopers (working values of £30-£180) and 178 tributers (at tributes between 10s and 13s 4d). He observed that 39 tutworkers were engaged in sinking Engine, Old Sump, Dunkins Garden and Harrietts shafts, and preparing to sink Valley Shaft.[188]

The January-February manager's report observed: "In this Report, as usual, we have only valued the lode for 6 feet in width; but for several years past we have found by stoping, that the lode has been fully 50 percent more than the value given in our Reports. The average width of the stopes is about 15 feet." Thomas also commented on the extra expense occasioned by the installation of additional stamps heads, and although no figure is given for the first two months of the year, the next ten months saw £967 spent on increasing the stamping capacity, including an extra boiler for the engine. Thomas also commented on the continuing low tin price. The November-December report, dated February 6th 1863, introduced a new underground agent, when Captain John Bawden's name appeared among the captains.[189]

On May 20th 1862 Captain Charles Thomas wrote to the *Mining & Smelting Magazine* in answer to a missive from Captain Joseph Vivian, in which the latter had commented on the best way to work hard ground. Thomas said: "The object ever kept in view is in hard ground, to open the mine as fast as possible." He remarked that at Dolcoath the levels on Main Lode were usually 8 feet wide by 6 feet high and sometimes anywhere between 7 and 9 feet wide and as high as 9 feet. For the period, these dimensions were enormous, but given the great width of the Main Lode and the high values, it was clearly thought best to take away as much ore as possible in the initial development. Thomas also mentioned that these large tunnels helped ventilation, and added, not too unkindly, that it was some years since Captain Vivian had ventured underground.[190]

The statistics for 1863 show a general increase in ore production, costs and profits. Some £73,422 worth of minerals were sold, costs were £53,221 and profits amounted to £17,459, which allowed a dividend of £18,826 at £47 a share. Lord's dues amounted to £3,058 and poor and highway rates to £342. Revenue came from 1,026 tons of black tin, worth £70,283, £2,998 worth of copper ore and £130 worth of arsenic. In January the mine paid nine months fees of £53 15s 5d to the Vice Warden's Court, and £235 4s 1d income tax on profit for the previous six months. Extra expense on additional stamping power and winding machinery increased the overall costs, with £200 in March-April, £400 in May-June, £200 in July-August and the balance for the new equipment of £390 in October. Added to this, a new steam whim cage cost

£167 10s in December.[191]

Captain Thomas' April report showed the mine being deepened at several points, with Engine Shaft at the 278 fathom level and Dunkins Garden Shaft holed to the 230 level, Harrietts sunk 11 fathoms below the 200 level, Wheal Bryant Shaft being sunk below the 190 and Valley Shaft sunk below the 170, as a rise from the 190 was mined toward it. By June Valley Shaft was holed to the 190 fathom level, and Wheal Bryant was almost down to the 200 level by August. Plantation Shaft, in the south part of the sett, was being cleared and secured during the summer, and by the end of the year the adit from it was being cleared by 4 men and 2 boys. South part of Main Lode had mixed results throughout the year, with values varying from £10 up to £100 a fathom. North part continued to give high values up to £200 a fathom. Main Lode on 266 level was 12 feet wide east of Engine Shaft, and worth £120 a fathom. At the 242 level the lode was 18 feet wide and worth £70 a fathom. Good ground was being opened up on New South Lode at the 180 and 190 fathom levels, west of Harrietts Shaft. On North Entral Lode, west of the north crosscut from Rules Shaft the ground was being developed with indifferent results, although some copper ore had been found.[192]

Captain Davey's report to Tehidy, dated March 19th 1863, also spoke of the large amount of development going on in the mine; on south part of Main Lode between 170 and 278 levels and on the north part between the 230 and 266 fathom levels, with three crosscuts, two winzes and a rise being mined. Harrietts Shaft (9 fathoms below 200 level), Wheal Bryant Shaft (one fathom below the 190), and Valley Shaft (16 fathoms below the 170), were also being sunk. In March there were 128 tutworkers, 137 stopers and 159 tributers, totalling 424 on development and production. Davey's November report showed that the total had increased to 469 miners, with the stopers having increased to 176, working values between £20 and £70 a cubic fathom of tin ore. By November Harrietts Shaft was sunk 4 fathoms below the 212 fathom level. Thomas reported that in December there were 142 tutworkers, 184 stopers and 144 tributers, making a total of 470 miners.[193]

In April it was reported that Wheal Harriett, the small working at Beacon, asked Dolcoath for its southern sett, including Plantation Lode, but Dolcoath intended working it themselves, and refused.[194]

Tragic Accident
Early in March 1863, a miner called Thomas Kessel fell down a shaft at the mine and was killed. He was working with two other miners, Nicholas Bate and Samuel Jewell. Kessel was working at Harriett Shaft station, filling kibbles with ore for hoisting to surface. Bate was tramming the ore to him at the shaft plat. The chain on the kibble broke, causing it to fall into the north part of the shaft. The three men set

about repairing the damage, but when they disturbed the chain it released some rock from the side of the shaft and it fell toward them. Kessel jumped back to avoid being struck, and fell into a gunnis on the north side of the shaft. He fell 13 fathoms and was found unconscious by his mates, 4 fathoms below the 220 fathom level. Kessel died five minutes after being taken to surface.[195]

The Kinnaird Report for the Royal Commission

At the end of December 1863 the Royal Mines Commission, under the chairmanship of Lord Kinnaird, visited Dolcoath to inspect it and report on its condition. His observations on the surface arrangements for the convenience of the workforce was most interesting. He was impressed with the 'accommodation for the comfort of the people', and after describing Dolcoath as the largest tin mine in Cornwall, he gave the measurements for the changing houses ('drys'), dining houses and dressing floors. The main dry was located 25 fathoms from the Man Engine Shaft, and was 80 feet long, by 22 feet wide and 20 feet high. The building had eleven windows, all of which opened, and a permanently open ventilator in the roof. The dry had a wooden floor and a fire tube, which was 41 feet long. All around the walls were the men's lockers, which were quite spacious. Some 350 miners used the dry, although never more than 80 used it at any one time. Day shift started at between 6 and 7 o'clock in the morning, and finished at 2 in the afternoon, and night shift started at 10 o'clock. The 20 sumpmen and three boys used two roomy drys, both of which had fire tubes, and the timbermen and pitmen also had their own heated houses where they changed. There were 570 workers on the dressing floors, of whom 260 were girls. These floors were large roofed and enclosed yards. The ore dressers had four dining sheds, all of which were roomy and had fire places and 'slabs' (ovens) for heating the workers' pasties. Women kept them clean and heated the pasties and water for the tea, coffee and cocoa, which the workers brought to work. These sheds were spacious, well-windowed and had tables and chairs. The largest of these sheds measured 64 feet by 17½ feet, and the smallest was 44½ feet by 12½ feet. Kinnaird was impressed with the facilities provided for Dolcoath's large workforce.[196]

Quite a number of Dolcoath's miners were interviewed by Kinnaird and his assistants and examination of some of the results is very revealing. Analysis of one group of fifteen of these miners reveals some interesting facts. The oldest of this group was 80 and the youngest 21 years old. The average age at which they started work was 13. Seven of the fifteen described themselves as having been tutworkers and tributers, four were tutworkers and one said he had been a tributer for 30 years at Dolcoath, had left for a short time to work in other local mines, before returning as a timberman for the last 14 years. Despite suffering from chronic bronchitis he said the air he worked in at the mine was generally good. Another 45 year old, who had worked at Dolcoath on both tutwork and tribute, described working in an end on the 230 fathom level, some 300 feet (90m) from any draught of air, and said it was hot and airless, and he worked stripped to the waist. He said the dry was good, but it often got cold walking from the shaft to it. He suffered from bronchitis. A 51 year old miner who had started underground at 13 and had worked as both a tutworker and tributer, suffered from chronic pneumonia, due apparently to working in bad air. Another 51 year old who worked as a tutworker and tributer at Dolcoath for 15 years, commented that the air at the mine was generally good, although occasionally it was poor. He had a heart condition and emphysema. A 27 year old tutworker, who started underground at 13, spent twelve years at Dolcoath, working for a year on 170 fathom level, where the air was good, 42 level, where the air was colder, the 210 level where the air was good. Once the Man Engine was up and running he went down to the 250 fathom level to work, and found it warm, but the air was good. Nine of the fifteen, who worked on the 42, 155, 160, 170, 210, 220, 230 and 250 fathom levels, testified that the air was generally good in their workplaces. Some complained about bad air and heat, especially if they were too far from a winze or shaft. One 41 year old emphysema sufferer, who spent nine years underground at Dolcoath, said, there was 'no bad air in the mine'. However, a 42 year old miner with bronchitis, who had worked underground at the mine for 32 years testified: "I was working (on the 190-fathom level) with my son, and whilst he was turning the borer for me he would faint, and I was obliged to carry him out of the level and pour cold water over him. We were 40 fathoms from any draught." He said he worked for three years in very bad air on the 190 fathom level. One quite amazing miner, who was 80 years old, said he had worked underground at Dolcoath for about 65 years. He was deaf, had lost an eye in an accident, but still felt healthy. He had retired a few weeks before the interview. Another 61 year old, who had started underground when he was 17, had worked underground at Dolcoath for 42 years, and was still 'quite healthy for his age'. As we can see, these interviews gave a very mixed picture.[197]

An interesting aspect of Dolcoath (in common with other Camborne mines) was revealed. When a miner was too ill, weak or old to continue underground, they were given lighter jobs on the surface, usually in the ore dressing department. Another fact seen in these interviews is that many miners moved from mine to mine and job to job, with men working as a tributer or tutworker as opportunity or advantage presented themselves. Tutworkers suffered most from hot ends and poor ventilation, whereas most stopes, where the tributers worked, had a winze close by. By and large Lord Kinnaird's report was complimentary about how Dolcoath was run and the condition of most of its miners.[198]

In 1864 the mine sold 621 tons of copper ore for £3,289, at an average price of £5 6s per ton, and 1,030 tons of black tin for £66,959, which averaged £65 per ton, and showed a continuing decline in the tin price. There was a drop in cash received for black tin of £6 6s per ton over the previous eleven years average. £110 worth of arsenic was sold, with £60 worth in March. With a total income from ore of £70,308 a dividend was paid out over the year of £14,678, at £41 a share.[199]

During 1864 Captain Thomas reported that work was going ahead to sink Engine Shaft below the 278 fathom level, and in August it was two fathoms below the level, thereafter progress was slow. Wheal Bryant Shaft was also sunk during the year and it was down 9 feet below the 200 level by June, when New East Shaft was 2 fathoms below the 254 fathom level. The south part of Main Lode continued to give fairly average results, with work going on between the 160 and 278 fathom levels, and the grades being between £10 and £75 a fathom, although that high value was unusual. On the north part of the lode values were between £10 and £100, with the norm being relatively high. Little was found on North Entral Lode, west of the crosscut north from Rules Shaft, and a rise was started above the 20 fathom level to connect to the Deep Adit level. Work continued to explore Plantation Lode at the adit level, but little of value was found.[200]

Captain Davey's report to Tehidy Estate, dated 12 May 1864, gave some interesting facts and figures. There were 27 development points; 20 lode drives, one crosscut, four winzes and two shafts, Engine and Harrietts, being sunk. The former cost £50 a fathom with 12 men, and the latter £38 and 9 men. Davey does not mention Wheal Bryant and New East shafts, although both were being sunk the following month. There were 154 tutworkers being paid between £8 and £50 a fathom, 162 stopers were working values of between £15 and £40 a cubic fathom of tin ore, and 176 tributers, at 9s to 13s 4d in the pound, making 492 miners on development and production. Davey reckoned the six months average monthly returns as £6,110 for ore, £4,683 costs and an estimated profit of £1,427. He believed the mine was in a very sound condition, and notwithstanding the lower tin price, he thought the future looked good.[201]

In October the mine announced one or two changes that were quite significant, including the intention to sell its black tin to a variety of smelters instead of exclusively to Messrs Williams. Dolcoath would sell half its produce to Williams, and the rest to Daubuz, Calenick (Bolitho) and the Redruth Company. It was also announced that Dr Percival had been replaced as joint mine surgeon by the Reverend W. W. Butlin. The *Mining Journal* said that there were 1,300 employees at the mine, with no less than 4,000 people dependant upon their wages. The average earnings for men was between £3 5s and £3 7s 6d a month, which probably referred to the miners rather than surface workers. The *Journal* added that there was a block of tin ground measuring 60 fathoms from top to bottom waiting to be exploited, and it was worth on average £25 a fathom.[202]

Thomas Spargo's Account
In 1865 Thomas Spargo published his series of books *The Mines of Cornwall*, based

upon statistics gathered in 1864. His entry for Dolcoath is interesting. After repeating the tradition that Dolcoath had worked 'from time immemorial', he said that the manager, Captain Charles Thomas, 'had been connected with the mine, in some way or other, all the period between that date (1800) and the present time'. He said that the present company had made profits of £279,777, and that the year 1864 saw profits of £14,678. Spargo said that there were sufficient ore reserves to last more than a generation, but that of late, with the decline in the price of tin, the mine's value had also declined. There was no purser at Dolcoath, but a 'committee of management', which discharged the duty of purser. The geology of the mine was characterised by granite and clay-slate, traversed by elvan dykes. The number employed in 1864 was 1,204, made up of 691 men, 352 women and 161 boys. J. F. Basset was the landowner and mineral lord, and his dues were 1/24th. The Deep Adit was at 30 fathoms and the depth under adit was 280 fathoms. There were two pumping engines on the mine, a 76-inch and a 60-inch, two steam stamping engines, a 26-inch and a 38-inch and five winding engines, a 30-inch, a 26-inch, two 20-inch and a 19-inch. There was also a 40-foot diameter water-wheel for crushing, and six water-wheels powering stamping mills, a 26 foot, two 14 foot, and three 16-foot wheels.[203]

1865 was another difficult year, with the tin price remaining lower than it had been, and rendering large areas of previously payable tin ground, unworkable. During the year £53,247 worth of black tin was sold, £3,412 worth of copper ore and £140 worth of arsenic, giving total mineral sales of £56,799. Costs were £46,023, making an average of £3,835 per month, a considerable improvement on the previous year. In the July-August of 1864 monthly costs had been £5,560, which, with a declining tin metal price, was potentially disastrous. Profits for the year were £8,715, making possible a dividend of £8,592 at £24 a share. The Bassets were paid £2,367 in dues at a 1/24th and local poor and highway rates were £187. In the March-April account there was a payment of £233 toward additional stamping power. Three payments were paid to the Vice Warden of the Stannary Court, totalling £41.[204]

Despite the depressing news on the tin price front, Captain Thomas was determined to continue deepening and opening up the mine. Engine Shaft was sunk 7 fathoms below the 278 level by April, and by December it was 11 fathoms beneath the level. It reached the 290 fathom level at the beginning of 1866. Old Sump Shaft was prepared for sinking below the 254 level in April, and by December it was 10 fathoms below the level. Harrietts Shaft was sunk 4 fathoms below the 224 level between August and the end of the year. New East Shaft was sunk to the 266 fathom level during the year. Due to the low tin price the values in the development ends were significantly down, but the ore on the south part of Main Lode was improving, with values up to £60 a fathom. The north part was disappointing, and the wide bodies of tin ground being opened up were not economical at the low tin price, although they would still be there when the price improved. The manager was pleased with improving values at the 190 level west of Harrietts Shaft, close to the Stray Park boundary.[205]

Captain Samuel Davey's report to Tehidy, dated 13 January 1865, gives a clear account of the state of the mine. There were 21 development points, made up of 11 lode drives, 2 crosscuts, 4 winzes, 3 rises and Wheal Bryant Shaft was sunk 9 fathoms under the 200 fathom level. Payments per fathom varied from £3 10s for men driving an adit, to £26 for the miners driving the 220 crosscut. There were 98 tutworkers, 107 stopers working on values of between £20 and £80 a cubic fathom of tin, 28 men putting in a large stull at the 242 level, and 200 miners on tributes of between 6s 8d and 13s 4d in the pound, making a total of 433 miners on development and production. The development ends on south part of Main Lode gave values up to £55 a fathom over an average width of 5 feet, whilst the north part gave values up to £50 over a width of 6 feet. Exploration continued on Valley Lode at the 190 and North Entral Lode on the 20 fathom level.[206]

Davey's report of 5th September 1865 showed things had not much altered since January, although the tin price was still not improving. There were 18 development points, made up of 11 lode drives, 2 crosscuts, 3 winzes and 2 shafts were being sunk, Engine Shaft under the 278 and Old Sump under the 254 fathom level. There were 98 men on tutwork, at between £10 and £72 a fathom, the latter sinking Engine Shaft, 155 stoping ground worth between £10 and £40 a cubic fathom, and 170 tributers on between 3s 6d and 13s 4d in the pound, making a total of 423 men on development and production.[207]

In his report of 9th October 1865, Captain Thomas described an interesting piece of cooperation between Dolcoath and its western neighbour, to their mutual benefit: "In accordance with the views expressed by the Adventurers at their last Meeting, we have allowed Stray Park miners to use our Man Engine; and the Stray Park Agents have re-commenced driving their 215 fathom level to reach our boundary as quickly as possible. That level will then be taken up by this Mine, to be driven under very promising ground in the bottom of the 190, by which mode of working the western part of this Mine can be brought into working order some two or three years sooner than could be done by driving the several levels westward from our western Engine Shaft." Davey's 24 August report on Stray Park Mine adds somewhat to Thomas' comment: "Since my last inspection a communication has been made from this mine into Dolcoath at the 190 level and Dolcoath Adventurers have consented for the men employed in Stray Park to descend and ascend to and from their work by the Dolcoath Man Engine for which the Advrs of Stray Park are to pay Dolcoath Advrs a fair renumeration and the Stray Park Advrs have granted permission to Dolcoath Advrs to take up any level in their mine and drive such levels into Dolcoath." The report also stated that the Stray Park miners had driven the 215 level some 40 fathoms east from their Engine Shaft toward the Dolcoath boundary, thus when the drive was restarted, by early October, it should not have taken long to get to Dolcoath. However, in January 1866 the distance from Stray Park Engine Shaft given by Davey, shows the 215 end had not yet moved. In February Thomas reported that his miners were driving east from Stray Park, presumably taking over from Stray Park men when the boundary was reached, or when Dolcoath took up the offer to drive into their mine themselves.[208]

A Series of Underground Accidents
During 1865 an enormous 'horse of ground', through which several levels had been driven, fell away, leading to a panicky rumour that 'Dolcoath mine has runned together'. Undoubtedly, memories of the terrifying subsidences of the 1820s would have been fresh in the minds of the older men in Camborne. Fortunately, production was undisturbed and nobody was hurt by the accident.[209]

In March 1865 there was fatal accident at the mine. A miner called Robert Vial fell through a trapdoor in the mine and was killed. Also in March, a 24 year old Dolcoath miner called Phillip Dawe was hit by falling rocks and was killed. The rocks fell some 12 fathoms from the footwall of the stope in which he was working with four other men.[210]

In the summer of 1865 there was another tragic accident at Dolcoath, involving a thirteen-year old lad. At Dolcoath it was normal practice to store gunpowder in barrels in the magazine ('powder house'). It was issued to the miners every Monday morning, and they put their powder into their individual lockers or chests, in a room which contained dozens of them. On August 30 a miner called William Bryant gave his thirteen-year son, John, his key, and asked him to collect 15lbs of gunpowder from the powder house and put it into his chest. Unfortunately, the boy did what many others had done, and thought he would have a bit of fun. He invited his friend, Ben Rogers, to join him in setting a small explosion. Wisely, Rogers refused, but half-an-hour later heard the explosion which killed his mate. Loose gunpowder, spilled by careless miners filling their powder cans, was ignited by John's explosion, and the locker house was destroyed by the explosion and the resultant fire. Some twenty chests had blown up and the lad was blown to pieces. At the inquest his father refused to believe his son had deliberately set off the charge, choosing to believe that his hob-nailed boots had struck a spark and caused the explosion. An open verdict was returned.[211]

During 1866 the mine continued to struggle, and although copper revenue was very slightly up on the previous year, at £3,512, income from tin, at £46,121, was well down. There was also £85 worth of arsenic sold, giving total revenue from ore of £49,178. Costs were just over £41,300, and the monthly working cost average was down to a creditable £3,445. A dividend of £3,938 was paid out at £11 a share.

186

The tonnage of copper sold, at 688, was the highest for six years, but with only 919 tons of black tin sent to the smelter, the lowest for five years, the manager was forced to make stringent economies. Most of these appear to have been at surface, for although there was a certain movement between numbers of tributers, tutworkers and stopers, by and large the overall numbers remained similar. In April the *Mining Journal* referred to the new dressing-floor machinery and stamps installed at the mine, and commented on the great savings made due to it, however, it still thought that: "This valuable old mine is suffering deeply from the present depressed state of the price of tin."[212]

On 12th January 1866 Captain Davey reported to Francis Trevithick, the Tehidy Agent, that there were 22 development points, made up of 15 lode drives, 2 winzes, 1 rise, 1 crosscut and 3 shafts being sunk. Engine Shaft was below the 276 fathom level, with 12 men on £72 a fathom. Old Sump Shaft was below the 254 level, being sunk by 6 men at £19 a fathom, and Harrietts Shaft was sinking below the 224 level by 6 men at £30 a fathom. There were 121 tutworkers, 150 stopers and 180 tributers, totalling 451 miners on development and production. He commented on the proposed lease renewal for Dolcoath and said that with an estimated monthly return of £4,583, costs of £3,992, a monthly profit of £591, and an ore reserve of £58,000, Dolcoath was not in as healthy a position as he would have liked. He was principally worried by the rate at which the ore reserve was being diminished, whilst new discoveries were not keeping ahead of production. His opinion was that if a new lease was granted, the dues should remain at 1/24th, Engine and Harrietts shafts should be continuously sunk, and more attention should be paid to South (Plantation) Lode and North Entral Lode.[213]

The manager's report of February 1866 showed four shafts being sunk, with Engine at the 290, Old Sump almost to the 266, Harrietts 5 fathoms below the 224 and Wheal Bryant sinking below the 212 fathom level. Tin values varied throughout the lower levels, and lower grade ore was being left till the tin price improved. The 215 fathom level drive to connect Stray Park with Dolcoath continued, with a little tin and copper being found. Davey's report of 9th March showed an increase overall of 10 miners, with stopers down by 12 and tributers up by 15 men. There were also 6 men securing bad ground at Engine Shaft. By April the miners' numbers had again dropped, to 433, with tutworkers holding steady but stopers and tributers reduced by 20 men. Harrietts Shaft was sunk 6 fathoms below the 224 fathom level and the miners were preparing to drive from Engine Shaft at the 290. On May 4th Davey reported little change, with 426 men and 8 boys. Development ends remained the same at 21, with 16 lode drives, 1 crosscut, 2 winzes and 2 shafts being sunk. Old Sump was 1 fathom below the 266 and Harrietts was 7 fathoms below 224. Main Lode was being developed between the 200 and 290 levels throughout the length of the mine, and Plantation Lode was driven at adit level 94 fathoms west of the

Plantation Shaft. In June the numbers on development and production dropped to 410 men a 4 boys, mostly due to a reduction in the number of tributers, but Davey was able to report that once again development was ahead of production, although in July he said that tributers were reduced to 158 because the tin grade was too low to work economically at the prevailing tin price. Harrietts was 10 fathoms below the 224 fathom level in July and Old Sump was 6 fathoms below the 266 in October. Plantation adit was still being driven west of the shaft and Main Lode was being opened up between the 190 and 290 fathom levels.[214]

1866 had proved one of the most trying years since Thomas had taken over as manager, with the price per ton of black tin at its lowest point since Dolcoath had been reconstituted as a tin mine. The average price received during the year was just over £50 a ton, a far cry from the giddy heights reached just six years earlier, when the price was over £80 a ton, and the dividend paid out over £21,000. Thomas, however, held his nerve, and he continued to deepen the mine from Harrietts and Wheal Bryant shafts in the west to Engine and Old Sump in the east. He maintained a high number of development points and was careful in his use of stopers, at so much a cubic fathom (or ton) and tributers, at so much in the pound. Despite so much hitherto good ground being left untouched, due to the prevailing tin price, he resolutely continued his search for new, higher grades sources. The uneconomic, lower grade ore was in the bank for when things improved.[215]

Dolcoath received on average over £4 a ton more for her black tin in 1867, and although tonnage was down to 848, revenue from it was up slightly to £46,170. Copper ore sales dropped to their lowest point since the mine re-opened in 1799, with a mere 267 tons selling for £1,068. With the £164 worth of arsenic sold total ore revenue was £47,402. There was a profit of over £7,000, which enabled them to pay out a dividend of £6,802 at £19 a share. Over 118 tons of black tin was held back by the mine in the hope of a better price. It was valued at £6,511. Over £2,100 was paid to the Bassets in dues and £100 was contributed to parish poor and highway rates.[216]

Old Sump Shaft was sunk 10 fathoms below the 266 by February, and Thomas reckoned it would hole the 278 within a month. New East Shaft was also sinking below the 266, and Wheal Bryant Shaft was 6 fathoms below the 212 fathom level. The connection to Stray Park at the 215 was progressing well, it was 10 fathoms east of the boundary and being driven by 6 men at £21 a fathom. The lode was 6 feet wide and worth £10 a fathom. Dolcoath miners were sinking a winze under the 190 inside Stray Park mine to ventilate the 215 end. Main Lode was developed between the 190 and 290 fathom levels, and Plantation Lode at adit level was driven over 100 fathoms west of the shaft. Davey reported that there were 144 tutworkers at 26 development points, including 17 lode drives, 2 crosscuts, 5 winzes and 2 shafts. There were 117 stopers working ore valued at between £20 and £45 a cubic fathom, and 157 tributers working for between 8s and 13s 4d in the pound. Davey estimated the previous six months monthly averages as £4,152 revenue, £3,623 costs and a monthly profit of £529. He thought the mine was being well-managed and things looked good.[217]

Two Serious Accidents
In February 1866 a miner called John Marks was seriously injured by a misfire. Such accidents had become far less common following the introduction of the safety fuze, during the 1830s. In October two miners were killed whilst riding the man engine. Samuel Davies and James Williams slipped from the engine at the 100 fathom level and fell a considerable distance to their deaths. What caused the mishap cannot be stated, but it was unusual for two men to fall from it in one incident. Davies left a widow and four children and Williams a widow and seven children.[218]

During the spring and summer of 1867 the mine was opened up to good effect, and the 266 fathom level was proving extremely valuable. In April Thomas reported that a crosscut through the north part of Main Lode on 266, west of Old Sump Shaft, had gone 12 feet without reaching the north wall (foot wall), and in August he said that values of £60 a fathom were found there and high values on 266 east of New East Shaft were also encountered. It was eventually mined over a width of 20 feet. By October Main Lode on 266 was worth £100 a fathom. The north part of Main Lode at the 278 was also found to be extremely wide. Generally, throughout the mine, tin grades improved in 1867. Sinking New East Shaft under the 266 continued throughout the year, and was 8 fathoms below the level by October, when Thomas reported that preparations were being made to sink Engine Shaft below the 290 fathom level. There was a slight delay whilst a winze was sunk below the 278 to meet a rise being mined from the 290. This would improve ventilation on 290 and make sinking below the level considerably easier. Wheal Bryant Shaft was holed to the 224 level in June.[219]

Captain Davey's report to Tehidy, dated 17th October 1867, spoke of general improvement in all aspects of the mine. There were 24 development points being advanced by 131 tutworkers who were paid between £11 and £36 a fathom: 18 lode drives, 4 winzes, 1 rise being mined, and New East Shaft was being sunk below the 266 fathom level. There were 114 stopers working on values of between £15 and £40 a cubic fathom, and 137 tributers at between 8s and 13s 4d in the pound. This represented a drop in development and production miners of 36 since February, despite the fact that production had actually increased in that time. Davey gave the monthly averages for the previous six months as: £4,239 in ore sales, £3,699 costs and a monthly profit, averaging £540. Davey was undoubtedly pleased with the announcement in the agent's October report to the adventurers: "During the past few months we have been expending considerable sums in enlarging the dressing floors, putting in railroads, etc, for more economical working." The *Mining Journal* spoke of these new surface tramways, and added that a Blake's rock-breaker was also erected on the mine. The Blake's stone-crusher was manufactured by H. R. Marsden of Soho Foundry, Leeds. It was reported that: "Blake's stone-breaker has been successfully introduced as a substitute for hand-spalling." It represented a major economy at the mine, although undoubtedly, men were laid off as a result of its introduction.[220]

It is significant, that when the October report was sent to the *Mining Journal* only one of the Thomases names were on it. It seems that Captain Charles Thomas, the manager, was absent, perhaps already feeling his age, for he was 73 years old, and had been working at Dolcoath since he was a boy.[221]

The December manager's report spoke of various difficulties, which had to be overcome to continue the deepening and extending of the workings. Large volumes of water were encountered in the winze below the 278 and progress to improve ventilation at the bottom of the mine had been held up. The drive to connect the 215 to Stray Park workings was also in need of better ventilation, and a winze below the 190 fathom level was re-started to improve air-flow to the end. That end had improved and tin values of £30 a fathom were found there.[222]

Management of Captain Josiah Thomas (1868-1901)
On 23 February 1868 Captain Charles Thomas died, and was replaced as manager by his son, Josiah. Born on 6th August 1794, Charles was 73 years old, and he had been relying on his son, Josiah, for underground supervision for some time. He had started on the surface at Dolcoath as a boy, then went underground, and by the time he was 21 years of age he had been appointed mine captain by Captain John Rule, then manager of Dolcoath. He served alongside his father, Charles, and his uncle, Captain James Thomas, and during the turbulent and almost disastrous period when Captain William Petherick had struggled to keep the great mine afloat, as copper ore diminished and economically viable tin reserves seemed only a remote possibility, Thomas had worked tirelessly to prove to adventurers and mineral lord's agents, that Dolcoath had a future as a tin mine. His approach was always well-organised and based upon good mining practice. He was the first truly 'modern' Cornish mine manager, for he created a mine where the long-term ore reserve was studied, the distribution of labour organised and thoughtfully manipulated, the control of grade carefully managed, and the latest machinery, where possible, introduced. His period of management, from 1844 to 1868 was one of constant change and continuous introduction of new ideas and new machinery. His achievement in controlling the quantity and grade of ore being hoisted, stamped and dressed was quite new in Cornish mining. Ensuring that the pitches and ends supplied sufficient good grade ore, that the whims could cope with the tonnage to be hoisted, that the stamping power was sufficient to ensure a regular flow of stamped material to the mill, and that the end result in black tin at 'ten-for-twenty' was ensured for the smelter, was

a major achievement. His supervision of development ends was masterful, with an almost constant number of tutworkers he kept the exploration lode drives moving, saw that crosscutting discovered new lodes and branches, ensured that winzes were sunk to give ventilation where needed and indicated ore ground opened up, and kept the principal engine and hoisting shafts sinking at a regular rate. Most important, Thomas kept development ahead of production and the mine ahead of the mill. When the price of black tin dropped from £80 to £50, he made economies throughout the mine, which ensured that revenue and costs remained in balance. Charles Thomas understood modern mining as no mine manager had done before him, and he laid the basis for his son to complete the modernisation of the greatest tin mine in the world. His frustration at being unable to sink a vertical shaft to the bottom of the mine and hoist the ore with wire ropes and skips, can be imagined. Years before his death he had advocated such improvements, but to no avail. His son, Josiah, was to see these improvements brought in, and despite the mine being sunk to depths that were unimaginable to his father's generation, continued to make a profit and pay out dividends.[223]

During 1868, notwithstanding the death of the vastly experienced mine manager, things generally continued to improve at Dolcoath. Production of black tin rose to 984 tons and revenue from it increased to £55,848, partly because the price received for it went up by over £2 a ton. Copper ore sales went down again to 153 tons, which sold for £864. Sales of arsenic went up, with 149 tons selling for £400. Total revenue from ore sales was £57,112, which made possible a dividend of £8,734, at £24 a share.[224]

Captain Josiah Thomas continued where his father left off, and during his first year in charge the five deepest shafts at Dolcoath were sunk below the bottom of the mine. Engine Shaft was sunk below the 290, and by the end of 1868 it was nearly 6 fathoms below the level. It was also enlarged and made ready for bigger kibbles and wire ropes. Harrietts Shaft was sunk below the 236 fathom level, New East Shaft, which was also enlarged and prepared for larger kibbles and wire ropes, was sunk beneath the 278 level, Valley Shaft was 7 fathoms below the 190 by the end of the year, and Old Sump was sunk below the 278 fathom level. No less than 12 levels saw exploration development during the year, with activity proceeding well across the entire mile long workings between the 190 and 290 fathom levels. Tin values continued to improve, with grades up to £120 a fathom. During the summer some £150 a month was being spent on modifying Engine and New East shafts and acquiring wire ropes for more efficient hoisting of ore. By the end of the year Captain Josiah Thomas had supervised the smooth transition to a new regime and had brought to fruition one of the long-standing features of his father's intended modernisation of the ancient mine.[225]

Tragic Death of Three Children

The year 1868 was marred by another tragedy, which in the light of the terrible accident to John Bryant, in 1865, ought to have been avoided. The wooden building, destroyed by the explosion of 1865, does not appear to have been replaced, and rather, the miners' lockers were along a wall in an open courtyard, beside which ran a busy thoroughfare, opposite the mine account house. Children routinely walked through the area, and the sixty lockers containing the gunpowder were in easy access to them. As with the 1865 case, there was plenty of loose gunpowder on the floor by the lockers, spilled by miners filling their cans for taking underground. Tragically, a group of local children, passing through, picked up a small quantity of gunpowder, placed it in a pile, and set light to it. Three of them were killed. A memorial stone in Camborne Churchyard states: "Erected in sad remembrance of three children, sons of William and Ann Walter, late of Devonshire, whose deaths were caused by an explosion of gunpowder whilst at play at Dolcoath on June 20th 1868." Unlike the inquest of 1865, the jury on this occasion made definite recommendations: "For future prevention of such accidents the walls on three sides of the court should be raised and the front protected by an iron or wooden gate."[226]

1869 was another year of progress, with several shafts being sunk and new machinery added to the mine. In April Engine Shaft ('New Sump') was 7½ fathoms below the 290 level and by December the 302 fathom level had been reached. Throughout the year Old Sump Shaft was being sunk below the 278 fathom level, and New East Shaft was also gradually deepened until by December it was over 8 fathoms below the 278 level. Sinking had been held up at New East in August, due to an excess of water. Valley Shaft was sunk 14 fathoms below the 190 level in April, and a raise was started from the 210 level to meet it. By June, the 210 was holed, and by the end of the year sinking below the 210 had started. Tin values held up very well during 1869, with the 290 level east of Engine Shaft increasing from £80 a fathom in April to £160 in October. Values remained high in the winds being sunk below the 254 and 212 levels, and values in New East Shaft improved with sinking, so that the grade improved from £50 a fathom in August to £100 by December.[227]

Eight Year Old Lad Killed

In April 1869, a young boy called James Eva, from Gwinear, was employed in the tin yard as a kieve packer. It was his practice, along with other boys, to climb onto the shed roofs to eat his food at break-time. Whilst up there, James got too close to the moving rod of some machinery, and his clothes caught and dragged him into the moving gear. He was dreadfully injured and died.[228]

The March-April accounts reported that a new calciner had been built. "The increase in the quantity of tin sold in these two months is partly caused by the erection of the New Calciner, which has enabled us to reduce the stock of tin on the floors." This may have been one of the new Oxland and Hocking rotary calciners, which were replacing the older Brunton calciners on some mines, and being increasingly used at the time. However, there is a record of three Brunton machines on the mine in 1869, so it was probably a new Brunton that was referred to. Both were very efficient machines for removing arsenical soot and sulphides from the ore. William Brunton invented his calciner in 1828, and his design soon spread throughout Cornwall, some being still in use in the 1950s.[229]

In the mine accounts for July-August 1869 there is reference to the payment, on account, of £500 toward a 'New Engine'. The October 11th report states: "Since the last Account we have taken out the old 76-in. Pumping Engine and put in the new 85-inch, and the Mine was again drained to bottom on Saturday morning last." A further £500 was paid out for the engine in the September-October account. Despite the reference to the 'new' engine, it is believed that it was essentially, a rebuild of the old 76-inch engine. The light-weight beam of the original 1815 Perran Foundry engine was probably recast, for although the date '1815' remained on it, the use of the title 'Williams Perran Foundry Co' suggests that it was not the original, for the foundry was not known by that name until 1858. The mine was only about 200 fathoms deep in 1816 and when the 85-inch cylinder was put in it had reached a depth of over 330 fathoms. Whilst the engine was being rebuilt and new, heavier pitwork installed, the bottom of the mine was flooded.[230]

The Doering Rock Drill
Another interesting development at Dolcoath in 1869 was the installation of a newly invented rock drill or boring machine. The *Mining Journal* of 24 April 1869 expressed enthusiastic support for this trial: "Boring Machine in Cornwall – We are glad to hear they have at last agreed to use Doering's boring-machine at Dolcoath, on the recommendation of the Committee." The machine was to be installed entirely at the expense of Mr Doering himself, who would seek to prove to the managers that it was efficient and economical. The Committee was confident that it would open up the ground twice as fast as with hand labour. They also believed that it would improve the health of the miners, who, they reckoned, were only able to work for around forty years. The compressed air in the ends would vastly improve ventilation and reduce the temperature. Doering agreed that any dispute with the mine would be settled by arbitration, not through the courts. Mr M. G. Pearce, the company chairman, was an enthusiastic supporter of the machine's use. Eight months after this announcement, on December 13th, Captain Josiah Thomas reported that, "Mr Doering has erected a Steam Engine at surface for compressing air, and has also fixed pipes in the Shaft. He expects to get one of his Boring Machines to work in the 278 end in the course of a few days." The trial lasted for eighteen months and appears to have been only partially successful.[231]

Figure 50. Doering rock drill on carriage.

The introduction of compressed-air powered rock drills, or boring machines, into Cornish mines was tortuous and protracted, with some mine managers showing more willingness to innovate and experiment than others. Dolcoath appears to have been fairly average in its response to the new-fangled machines, being an old and tradition bound mine. Two years before Dolcoath, encouraged by their Committee and go-ahead chairman, decided to take one on trial, East Gunnislake Mine, on the Tamar, tried one out. This was a Crease machine, and it had been used for a decade before that, in Wales and elsewhere. In 1868 Tincroft Mine tried out a Doering machine, and it had proved initially successful. This was probably why the Doering was tried at Dolcoath. To start with Frederick Doering's machine drilled twice as fast as the hand labour miners, but after a time design faults manifested themselves and efficiency fell away.[232]

In June the mine announced various changes to its structure and salary scale. The number of shares was increased from 358 to 1,432, reflecting the increased value of the company, and the desire of new investors to sign up. Captain Josiah Thomas had his salary increased from 15 guineas a month to £21, and the other mine captains had theirs increased by a guinea a month. The mine contributed £50 to the Royal Cornwall Hospital, Truro, and 5 guineas to the 'Redruth Miners Convalescent Hospital'. Another sign of the adventurers' expansive mood, based upon great confidence in the future of the mine, was the commissioning of a life size portrait of the late Captain Charles Thomas, to be hung in the dining room of the account house.[233]

During August there was a joint visit to Dolcoath of members of the *Royal Institution of Cornwall* and the *Royal Cornwall Polytechnic Society*. The visitors were shown around the surface at the mine, and expressed wonder at the vast array of machinery displayed there. The man engine, the new 85-inch pumping engine on New Sump Shaft and the dressing floors were inspected, together with the Doering boring machine, being assembled. The tin concentrating plant impressed them particularly, and the knowledge that with the miners who were underground, over 1,000 workers were employed. They were also shown, and undoubtedly deafened by, the 200 heads of stamps in constant work. The average grade of ore was some two-percent. Captain Thomas informed the visitors that the rock at depth was extremely hard, and that the average level (tunnel) was eight feet high by six feet wide and cost over £20 a fathom. There were two steam pumping engines (New Sump and Harrietts), three steam whims and two steam stamps engines. There was one whim for two shafts, so that as one kibble descended empty another ascended with a ton of ore in it, so that each whim engine hoisted six tons of ore an hour. There was also a steam engine for the man engine at Wheal Bryant. The Blake's Patent Stone Crusher, introduced in the summer of 1867, was still working well. Men were used to break the larger rocks and women used smaller spalling hammers to further reduce the ore for stamping. The bal maids could break down between two and three tons a day. Round buddles and kieves were replacing the older trunks and frames and as arsenic was an ever-present contaminant, three Brunton calciners were also in use.[234]

There is some confusion over the production figures for 1869, as the *Mineral Statistics of the United Kingdom* do not agree with the mine's own figures. The *Mineral Statistics* give the black tin tonnage as 813 and the income from tin as £59,694, whereas the mine's own reports indicate over 1,000 tons of black tin were sold for over £78,000. There was also nearly £650 worth of copper ore sold and £126 worth of arsenic. The mine made a profit of over £27,000 and paid out dividends of £24,000. In his end-of-year address the chairman, M. G. Pearce, was sanguine over the mine's achievements and prospects. He stated that Dolcoath had sold ore to the value of £5 million, and had made twice the profit of any other Cornish mine. The values underground were extremely high and he was very confident about the future.[235]

In March 1870 the adventurers expressed their sadness at the death of Major Bickford, of the safety fuze family, a prominent adventurer in the mine. This was followed in April by the announcement of the demise of Sir William Williams Bart., who had been so prominent in the management of the mine for many years. The Williams family of Gwennap and Scorrier was to continue its involvement in running Dolcoath for the rest of the nineteenth century, having become involved at the re-opening of the mine in 1799.[236]

In 1870 the mine consolidated the progress of the previous year, and although shaft sinking continued, it was at a slower rate than hitherto. New East Shaft was holed to the 290 by April and by the end of the year it had been sunk 5 fathoms below it. Harrietts Shaft was down to the 248 by April and Old Sump Shaft was down to the 290 fathom level by the summer. Wheal Bryant Shaft was sinking throughout the year and was 10 fathoms below the 224 level by October. On North Entral Lode a winze was sunk below the adit to the 20 fathom level. Some very good tin values were encountered during 1870, with the best being on Main Lode east of New East Shaft at the 290 fathom level, where the lode was worth £140 a fathom. As the year progressed the average values improved, so that grades with values between £40 and £90 became common, and by the end of the year, in the sump of New East Shaft, below the 290, the lode was worth £150 a fathom.[237]

With the increased number of shares and shareholders, a new problem appeared. At the June two-monthly 'count house dinner', seventy adventurers turned up, making space a slight problem. The meeting was presided over by Mr M. G. Pearce, the chairman, who again spoke eloquently about the fine job the management and Committee were doing, and how well the mine was doing. He spoke of the depth of the mine, which he exaggerated slightly, and then said that the Main Lode was 14 to15 feet wide, and very rich. He pointed out that Dolcoath was the deepest mine in the district, was 'almost inexhaustible', and that they were then dividing the biggest dividend for ten years. This, he said, was not due to improved grade but to good management and economy.[238]

By late January six Doering machines were at work in the mine, and in the summer of 1870 three Doering boring machines, on the 266, 278 and 290 fathom levels, were monitored for their performance. The machines averaged 14 feet 9 inches in a month, costing £22 a fathom, whereas the hand labour miners cost £25 a fathom. After several months the performance of the machines was compared to that of the hand labour tutworkers and overall it was impressive. The tutworkers were paid at so much a fathom and the machinemen a daily rate. On 266 fathom level the tutworkers averaged 9 feet 3 inches and the machinemen 10 feet 1½ inches. On the 278 level the tutworkers managed 7 foot 10 inches and the machinemen 12 foot 7 inches. On the 290 level the tutworkers did 7 feet 2 inches and the machinemen 16 feet. This meant that on average the machinemen were over fifty percent faster. To start with there were no problems of maintenance with the machines, but later there were cases of hoses bursting, problems with the quality of the water for clearing the grit and some of the machinemen lacked experience. Despite the hopeful results, when the eighteen-month trial period was up, at the end of June 1871, F. B. Doering took his machines away and no contract was given him.[239]

In August the *Mining Journal* announced that Dolcoath had taken over Stray Park

Sett, as a going concern, with all the tin leavings still on the floors. Stray Park Mine was 320 fathoms deep the report said, and its water could be a problem for Dolcoath, as its machinery and pitwork was in a 'sorry plight'. The cost was stated to be £1,920. In the October 10 Manager's Report the above facts were modified somewhat: "Since the last account we have purchased the Machinery and Materials at Stray Park Mine for £1,720. We have 40 men working on Tribute in that part of the Mine at about 13s 4d in the £, which we hope will nearly enable us to pay the cost of working the Engine for pumping water. We are preparing to drive the 238 fathom level eastward into Dolcoath Sett." The October 15th the *Mining Journal* repeated its earlier point about Stray Park water being a potential problem for Dolcoath, and if their 64-inch engine stopped pumping this would certainly be true. The first £700 instalment of the payment to Stray Park adventurers was paid in the November-December account of 1870, and the second £700 was paid in March-April 1871. The remaining £595 16s was paid later in 1871. The total paid for Stray Park was £1,995 16s. It will be remembered that since 1865 Stray Park and Dolcoath had been cooperating over access to Dolcoath's western workings, and Stray Park miners had been using the man engine at Wheal Bryant. From February 1866 Dolcoath miners had been working inside the Stray Park Sett to drive the 215 eastern end into Dolcoath.[240]

At the end of the year the manager gave a summary of the work done in 1870, and it was impressive. Sixty-five fathoms of shafts and winzes were sunk, and over 297 fathoms of levels driven. Ore raised totalled 53,000 tons, which produced 1,055½ tons of black tin. Income from black tin was £82,204, from copper ore, £118, and from arsenic, £246. The average price for Dolcoath's tin was £77.77. There was a profit of £27,369 and a dividend paid of £26,492. The summary also stated that £951,611 worth of black tin had been sold in the previous eighteen years, £44,558 worth of copper ore and £3,682 worth of arsenic. Dolcoath had paid out £43,045 in dues to the Bassets, since January 1853, and there had been a profit of £214,126.[241]

The *Mining Journal* supplemented the above management summary with a few extra facts about the mine. Not only had the shares been re-divided, but the number of adventurers had risen commensurately, from 98, 'a few years ago', to 271. There were 500 men employed underground and some 600 workers at surface, made up men, women and children. Dolcoath had some 232 heads of stamps in permanent use and another 24 to be called on if necessary. The mine used 600 tons of coal a month. The average underground workers wage was £3 8s a month, which contributed to the annual wages bill of £30,000. Added to the £15-18,000 spent at local suppliers, this meant that Dolcoath made a significant contribution to the local economy. The agents responsible for running Dolcoath remained unchanged, with Captain Josiah Thomas at the helm, assisted by captains William Provis, John Tonkin and John Bawden.[242]

1871 was another good year for Dolcoath, with tonnage and profit increasing impressively. The deepening of the mine slowed down somewhat during the year, but production and tin values in the stopes rose considerably. Engine Shaft resumed sinking in the summer, and the June report tells us it was a fathom below the 302 fathom level, and although progress was slow it continued for the rest of the year. New East Shaft, which was 8 fathoms below 290 in April, had reached the 302 level by October and was already opening up the level. The values on the deeper parts of the mine, especially on Main Lode, held up throughout the year. The south part of Main Lode, east of Engine Shaft at 302 level, was eighteen feet wide, and carried values of £60 in April, rising to £120 a fathom by October. The richer north part was six feet wide. New East Shaft, eight fathoms below the 290 level, had values of £180, and these high grades only slightly moderated below that depth. Ends and winzes at the 212, 254, 278 and 290 levels all carried high grade tin, and the ground being opened up for stoping looked very good.[243]

New Railroad

The June 12th 1871 Manager's Report told of various changes and improvements: "We have been putting in a new Railroad from Stray Park to this Mine, and adding to the dressing floors at the New Stamps. We have also prepared Valley Shaft for drawing with wire rope instead of chains, which has considerably increased the current cost." The Report also commented on the drives between Stray Park and Dolcoath at the 238 and 215 fathom level, which carried quite modest tin values. The second £700 instalment for the purchase of Stray Park Mine was also made.[244]

As stated above, at the end of June the eighteen-month trial of Frederick Doering's boring machines came to an end. The *Mining Journal* commented: "The Boring Machine at Dolcoath has ceased to work. Mr Doering closed the engagement at the end of June. We regret this termination of another attempt to apply mechanical power to aid the miner in deep and hard ground mines. The machine is said to be worked with success in many of the foreign mines, and we fully expect to see the time when the principle will be successfully applied in Cornwall." Their optimism for the future was not misplaced, but with so many machines on offer, so many trials and reports of trials having taken place at the time, it is not surprising that there was confusion over the most appropriate machine for deep, hard rock Cornish mines. Captain William Teague's zeal for the introduction of new technology at Tincroft, made him a leading advocate, but although Squire Basset was convinced, others, like Josiah Thomas, were taking a more cautious line, before deciding on the best option for Dolcoath.[245]

In the November-December 1871 accounts it was announced that there was to be another re-division of the shares, from 1,432 up to 4,296, trebling the number of shares. It was the best ever two-monthly return, with profits of £7,514 and a dividend paid of £7,518. Over 207 tons of black tin was sold for £17,984. The two-monthly mine cost, including merchant's bills, was £9,581. Squire Basset's dues were £899 and his dividend was some £294. Due to the large number or adventurers who wanted to attend the 'count house dinners', this institution was suspended, as too big and too expensive. Each of the mine's workers was given a Christmas bonus of one day's pay.[246]

Factory & Education Acts
During 1871 a government inspector visited Dolcoath to enforce the recent Factory Act legislation, which laid down that no person under the age of 14 could be employed. Dolcoath had to dismiss over 60 youngsters who had been employed on the dressing floors. The mine officials believed that as the young workers had satisfied the provisions of the Education Act, which stated that before a pupil could leave school and go to work at the age of 13 years, they had to reach the required standard, it was alright to employ them on the mine. This apparent inconsistency caused confusion, as well as considerable hardship to families who relied on the wages of the young to help feed them.[247]

Tin Dressers' Strikes
During the 1870s, there was widespread dissatisfaction among the Camborne bal maids over their pay. They felt that not only were they poorly paid, but they were usually paid less than the men who were doing the same jobs. The ore dressers, including the women and girls, went on strike for more money in several local mines, including West Wheal Seton (1877), Wheal Basset (1872) and Dolcoath, in September 1871. Few of these strikes were successful, and sometimes, as at West Wheal Seton, the wages were actually reduced. However, some Dolcoath adventurers, like M. G. Pearce, among the most prominent at the mine, sought an improvement in their pay rates. Pearce even went so far as to give 1s each to 100 bal maidens out of his own pocket. In 1880, a series of strikes, which started at Dolcoath, led to improved pay and better conditions for the bal maids.[248]

The manager's 'Summary of Work Done in 1871' contained some impressive figures. Some 78 fathoms of winzes and shafts were sunk, and over 257 fathoms of drives and crosscuts mined. There was 64,000 tons of ore raised producing 1,181½ tons of black tin, which sold for £97,288, and £304 worth of copper ore. £80 worth of arsenic was sold. Profits were £34,662 and the dividend paid out was £33,294. The average price received for Dolcoath's black tin was £80.23. Thomas pointed out that over the previous nineteen years £1,048,889 worth of black tin had been sold by Dolcoath, together with £44,862 worth of copper ore and £3,762 worth of arsenic. The Bassets had received £47,928 worth of dues from the mine, which had made a profit of £248,788. Dolcoath Mine appeared to be at the zenith of its highly profitable history.[249]

1872 saw mining development and production continue to increase. By early February Engine Shaft was 21 feet below the 302 fathom level and Old Sump Shaft was still being sunk under the 290 level. Winzes ('winds') were being sunk on lodes beneath the 290, 278, 266, 224 and 212 fathom levels. Tin values varied throughout the mine, with little tin found in the shafts being sunk, but better results in the winzes, especially the one under the 290, where values of £60 a fathom for a width of nine feet were encountered. Also on the 290, west of Old Sump Shaft, the end on Main Lode was worth £120 per fathom. The most consistent values were found between Wheal Bryant and Old Sump shafts. Stray Park section varied between £10 and £25 a fathom. Development on North Entral Lode east of Freemans Shaft, on the 42 fathom level, was disappointing.[250]

The accounts for January and February 1872 showed an increase in costs and productivity. Tutworkers and surface workers wages were £5,033, merchant's bills were £3,356, the tribute bill was £2,306 and the total cost was £10,696. These two months gave a profit of £7,520 and the dividend paid was £7,518. Black tin sold amounted to 212 tons, which brought in £18,962. Arsenic was sold for £87 and copper ore for £116, making revenue worth £19,165. G. L. Basset's dues of 1/20th came to £958.[251]

The Manager's Report of April 8th 1872 showed continuing progress, with both Engine and Old Sump shafts being slowly deepened and the winzes also opening up ground of varying value. The winze under the 266 fathom level was suspended due to increased water. Values generally remained constant, with the only excitement coming from a drive on 236 level, west of Harriets Shaft, where a "good lode for the past 6 fms driving was worth £70 fm." Stray Park and North Entral continued as before.[252]

The figures for March and April showed an increase in costs as well as production. The tutworkers and surface workers wages dropped slightly to £4,813 as did the tributers' bill, which went down to £2,241, but the merchants cost rose to £4,229 and the Vice Warden of the Stannary Court also made a small charge of £26 17s 6d. Total costs came to £11,311, which after calculating the income of £21,121 from tin sales, and the payment of £1,056 dues to the mineral lord, left a profit of £8,765. A dividend of £8,592 was paid to the happy adventurers. Black tin production rose from 212 tons for the previous period to an impressive 226 tons.[253]

Camborne Gas Company
In the *Mining Journal* of May 25th 1872 there was an interesting report on a modernising innovation at Dolcoath. "The Camborne Gas Company are now laying mains from their works to Dolcoath Mine, with a view to lighting the dressing-floors, in order that dressing operations may be carried on by night as well as by day." The

report commented that it was thought that the outlay would be amply repaid by the improved efficiency. It also said that gas had been used at a St Just mine several years before, to light the underground levels, and was a success. It was speculated that Dolcoath might also use gas lighting underground.[254]

The Manager's Report for June 10th 1872 said that Engine Shaft was sunk 8 fathoms under the 302 level and that Old Sump Shaft was still being deepened beneath the 290 fathom level. The winze under the 290 level was suspended due to increased water, but it was hoped it would resume shortly. The winze west of Harriets Shaft under the 224 level had holed to the 236 level and the ground was set to tributers for stoping. Values in new ground being opened up improved impressively, with drives on the 302 level being worth £80 and £100 a fathom for considerable distances. Values of £70 a fathom on and below the 290 in Bullen Garden Section were also opened up. In Harrietts area tin values were more modest, being between £15 and £30 a fathom, as they were in Stray Park. Five crosscuts were being driven to cut side lodes and branches for development.[255]

The accounts for May and June 1872 continued to impress the adventurers. Tutworkers and surface workers wages were £4,691, tribute money came to £2,281 and merchants' bills were £3,826, making a total cost for the two months of £10,873. Black tin production was 226 tons, which sold for £20,512. The Basset dues came to £1,026 and the Vice Wardens assessment to £24, which left a profit of £8,619 and a dividend paid of £8,055. Captain Josiah Thomas pointed out to the shareholders that the money received for tin during May and June was on average £3 a ton less than the previous period – making a difference in income of some £600![256]

Progress in sinking Engine Shaft remained very slow during the summer, with only one fathom sunk in June and July. Old Sump Shaft also continued to slowly deepen. The water problem in the winze under the 266 level remained and a small lift was fixed, worked by the engine, to pump the winze dry. Winzes under the 278 level and the 215 level in Stray Park also continued to be deepened, the latter on a crosscourse. South part of Main Lode, west of Old Sump Shaft on 290 level, was opened up for a width of 24 feet, and all in good tin ground. North part of the lode was six foot wide and worth £70 a fathom. Very high values of £120 a fathom were found in the winze below the 278 level, and in Harrietts section values of between £10 and £70 a fathom were encountered. The tin grade in Stray Park section, on 215 and 238 levels, was modest.[257]

In July and August 1872 costs, income and profits were steady. Tutworkers and surface workers' wages were £4,861, tribute money was £2,478, merchants bills came to £3,660, Stannary Court charges were £27 and the total cost was £11,026. Tin production was 221 tons, which sold for £19,559 and £9 worth of arsenic was sold.

The mineral lord's dues came to £978, the profit was £7,567 and the dividend paid to shareholders was £7,518.[258]

The Manager's Report of October 14th 1872 showed steady progress, despite tin production and profits falling slightly. Engine Shaft was sunk another nine feet, a slight improvement on the previous period, and winze development improved somewhat, with sinking below the 302, 290 and 278 fathom levels. Good values of up to £120 a fathom were found in these places. On the 266 level a crosscut was being driven along a crosscourse to intersect the South Lode. Near Harrietts Shaft work progressed on the 121, 220, 224, 236 and 248 fathom levels, with tin values of between £14 and £70 a fathom. Work also continued in Stray Park on the 238 level and in the winze between the 215 and 238 fathom levels, which was close to being holed.[259]

The September and October 1872 accounts give tutworkers and surface workers wages as £4,669, tribute paid £2,016, merchants' bills £3,682, water rent for the year £196 and the total costs of £10,564. Black tin produce was 207 tons, which sold for £17,771. A small quantity of copper ore sold for £117. Basset's dues were £895, the profit was £6,467 and the dividend paid was £6,444. Dolcoath Mine was paid £27 10s by Carn Camborne Mine, for the rent of a burning house, presumably one situated in the Red River valley. Dolcoath continued to use Brunton calciners for removing arsenic, which was still being sold in fairly modest quantities.[260]

Two Serious Accidents

In August 1872 there occurred what was probably the first fatal accident in Cornwall from a dynamite explosion. Joseph Trythall, a tutworker, was driving an end on the 278 fathom level with his mates Samuel Roberts and William Henry Eustice. They were drilling a hole in the face, when the drill steel struck some dynamite residue left there from a previous blast. Eustice was holding the drill and Trythall and Roberts were beating it. The hole was 8 inches deep when it went off. With his light blown out, Eustice made his way to a nearby stope, where Trythall's brother, John, was working. After re-lighting his candle, William and John went back to the end to see what had happened to Joseph Trythall, and found him covered in blood. His skull was fractured and he died 2 days later. At the inquest, it was said that Eustice, Roberts and Trythall had been using dynamite for 4 or 5 months, but they had never been given any instructions on its safe use.[261]

On November 23rd 1872 the *Mining Journal* reported another serious accident at Dolcoath. Five men and boys employed on the 212 fathom level, west of Wheal Bryant Shaft, had left work and were at the end of the level "on their way to grass", when a "slip occurred of a most serious character, and two of the lads, Simon Baston, aged 15, and William Henry Moffat, aged 16, were carried away, with something like

400 tons of stuff and debris, which smashed the timbering like pipe-stems." A miner called Oxnam on the level below was also carried away. Apparently, upon hearing the crash, he ran to the shaft plat and failed to escape the falling rock. There were several narrow escapes, the report said. A week later the *Journal* said that Oxnam's body had been found three or four fathoms below the 224 level. His head was smashed in. The report explained in some detail what had happened. The accident, it said, occurred 1,470 feet from surface on the 212 fathom level, where five men were blasting rock. The blast loosened ground, which fell away. Fifty feet below, a miner called Borlase was standing on a stull, when he heard the crack and shouted a warning before running to safety. The two boys, however, sheltered beneath a stull, which was smashed like 'pipe-stems' and carried away with the unfortunate boys to the 224 fathom level. The stull pieces were timbers some 20-inches square and extremely strong! On the 224 level the miners heard the crash and roar and as Oxnam was caught and carried away, his older son grabbed Oxnam's younger son and ran to safety with him. The two boys and two other miners survived the accident. The report described Dolcoath as a 'pattern' or 'model' mine, and stated that the accident could not have been foreseen. The enormously wide gunnises at Dolcoath, left after the ore had been removed, had been causing safety problems for over a century. For the previous half-century there had been constant references to and complaints about the dangers of working in and beneath these wide, open stopes. The weight of attle on timber stulls, the great pressure on timber stulls from the weight of the hanging walls, and the difficulty of 'baring down' the hanging walls, due to the sheer width of the workings, all contributed to these dangers. Accidents were inevitable, and as the century progressed things were to get worse.[262]

The December 9th manager's report stated that Engine Shaft was only two feet from the 314 fathom level, and that driving there would begin within a month. Old Sump Shaft was still being slowly deepened and Wheal Bryant Shaft was to start sinking under the 236 level. The several development ends and winzes were giving good results, with the winze under the 302 level, east of Engine Shaft, being worth £100 a fathom and the winze under the 278 level being worth £120 a fathom. Harrietts and Stray Park sections progressed steadily with more modest tin grades.[263]

The costs and returns for November and December 1872 were much the same as before, with costs up very slightly and income a little down. Tutworkers and surface workers wages were £4,617, tribute payments £2,586 and merchants bills £3,560, giving a total cost for the two months of £10,763. Income from 205 tons of black tin was £17,492, with another £103 from arsenic and £72 from copper ore sales. G. L. Basset's 1/20th dues were £883, which meant that profit was £6,030 and the dividend paid was £4,296 – at a pound a share.[264]

At the Meeting held on December 14th 1872, Captain Thomas announced to the shareholders that Dolcoath, in company with most other Cornish mines, was to move to the 'four week system' for labour costs. This followed agitation throughout Cornish mines, where miners, other than tributers, believed they were losing out to a system which paid them four week's wages for a month's work, which they called the 'five week system'. The miners were effectively losing a week's money every twelve weeks. Most mines paid 'company account' and other day wage men for four, six day weeks, or 24 days, even though they averaged more working days in a working month than this. Thomas explained that from then on they would have 'twelve week accounts', like the other Cornish mines. He also reported that Dolcoath had recently held back 92 tons of black tin from sale, and then sold it when the price rose, which made the mine an extra £150. The Meeting was also told that Captain R. Pearce had asked for a salary increase. Pearce was the only agent to live on the mine, and so the Meeting agreed that he should have £24 a year house rent allowed and a pay increase of one guinea a month.[265]

The *Mining Journal* of December 14th 1872 carried some comments on the history of Dolcoath, and threw light upon the change from copper mining to tin. The comments are surprising, given the then current belief that it was almost entirely down to the foresight and wisdom of Captain Charles Thomas, the father of the present manager, that tin was seen as the future of Dolcoath as copper reserves dwindled. It stated that in 1840, the Dolcoath and Cooks Kitchen adventurers viewed the two copper mines as exhausted, and that even as late as 1850 Captain Thomas took little note of the tin in the mine. "In fact, the discovery of the immense deposit in Dolcoath, 'so valuable in depth', was made by a pare of tributers, who drove a cross-cut at their own risks, upon an agreement to have a high tribute for six months." The crosscut discovered a large and extremely rich tin lode, resulting, said the report, in the adventurers gaining a mine worth £285,000 and dividends of £46,645 a year.[266]

The figures for 1872 were impressive. Total costs were £65,233. Income from black tin was £115,417, from copper ore £233 and from arsenic £199. There was a profit of £44,968 and a dividend paid to adventurers of £42,423. Captain Thomas remarked that not many years before the 179 shares the mine was divided into were worth £15 each, which meant the mine was worth £3,000, but now it was worth £45,000. Thomas also advocated the replacement of the present, 18 year old man engine, with a new one. The old engine managed only three strokes a minute, whereas a new one could work at five strokes a minute. He estimated that each miner, on average, lost half-an-hour productive time each day through this – which meant that with 400 miners underground, 200 hours work a day was lost! Thomas reckoned the cost of a new man engine, together with a new steam engine and house, would be between £500 and £600. By the end of the year Engine Shaft had, at long last, reached the 314 fathom level – which meant it had taken twelve months to sink 8½ fathoms. Old Sump Shaft continued to sink below the 290 level and Wheal Bryant Shaft (Man

Engine Shaft) was about to be sunk below the 236 fathom level.[267]

Deep Adit Blocked

1873 started badly for Dolcoath, with news that the Deep Adit had been blocked by a serious fall of ground. The February 8th *Mining Journal* said that the choke had caused water to pour into the mine, flooding it, and the neighbouring Cooks Kitchen Mine, up to the 278 fathom level. Captain Thomas stated that the blockage had been cleared and the water was being pumped as quickly as possible to clear the bottom levels. There was also concern for Tincroft and Carn Brea mines, which shared the same adit system. Apparently, the rock fall, caused by old, rotten timbers collapsing, was in the section of adit to the east of Dolcoath, in Cooks Kitchen Mine. The February 22nd 1873 *Journal* reported that the water was being lowered at the rate of about six feet a day, due to them having in place the new 85-inch pumping engine. Thomas said that the old 76-inch engine would not have coped. So far, he said, the loss of the levels below 278 level had cost between 15 and 20 tons of black tin production. Within a month the mine would be back to full production.[268]

The Manager's Report for February 17th 1873, which was clearly written before the flooding of the lower levels, said that the 314 fathom level was being opened up to the east of the shaft, and that the end was worth £40 a fathom for tin. Winzes were being sunk below the 302, 290, 278 and 266 fathom levels and in Harrietts section a winze was being sunk under the 224 level. The winze below the 302 was worth £150 a fathom and the one under the 278 level was worth £100 a fathom. The ends in Harrietts were worth between £15 and £50 and in Stray Park they were between £12 and £15 a fathom. Stray Park Mine had been drained to the 278 level and the sump would be forked 'in less than a month'. All this changed with the adit chokage and the flooding of the lower levels. By March 15th the *Mining Journal* was able to report that Dolcoath was again in fork and all the miners were fully employed at the deeper levels. It stated that one lucky tributer called Barker, had a 'sturt' worth £200, since they restarted the bottom levels, and commented that "This is a notch on the other side to 'Johnny Fortnight!'" A 'sturt' was when a miner discovered an extremely valuable body of ore, which made him a lot of money. A 'Johnny Fortnight' was a pack-man or door-to-door salesman.

The accounts for the twelve weeks prior to April 19th 1873 showed a general decline in the mine's financial position. This was not due to the recent flooding, as the next accounting showed an increase in black tin sold. However, it was sold at a lower price, and this was probably the cause of the decline. Tutworkers and surface workers wages came to £7,059, tributers' bills were £3,272, merchants bills came to £4,126 and the mineral lord's dues to £981. Costs before dues were £14,457, and income from mineral sales after deduction of dues amounted to £18,633, from 231 tons of black tin. The profit dropped to £4,182 and the dividend paid was £4,296 at

£1 a share.[270]

By early May 1873 the 314-fathom level was progressing well with reasonable grades of tin ore, Old Sump Shaft had reached the 302 level and development continued with mixed success in Harrietts and Stray Park sections. The best prospects were in the winze below the 302 level, where values of £180 a fathom were encountered, and on 290 level west of Old Sump, which was worth £100 a fathom. On May 17th the *Mining Journal* reported that Captain Thomas had bought 'an almost new' man engine, which was to be erected during the summer. This new engine would do five strokes a minute and would go down to the 248 fathom level, whereas the present older engine only went to the 212 level. The miners would be able to travel well over 200 feet deeper on the new machine. Also the *Journal* said that the management rewarded the sumpmen, pitmen and enginemen with a grand dinner in gratitude for their sterling work in forking the water.[271]

Captain Thomas also commented on the migration of so many miners to America and the colonies. He said that although they earned good money in America, they also had to work much longer hours for it, and added, that if they worked longer hours at Dolcoath their wages would match those in American mines. Dolcoath tutworkers were earning £6 a month, which, he reckoned, was pretty good![272]

The accounts for the twelve weeks ending July 12th 1873 showed a further decline in the financial position of Dolcoath. Tutworkers and surface workers wages were £7,244, tributers cost £3,133, merchants bills were £5,046, making a total cost of £15,423. The mine produced 258 tons of black tin, which raised £18,617 after the Basset dues of £980. This left a profit of £3,246 and a dividend paid of £3,222.[273]

Visit of Institute of Mechanical Engineers
On July 31st 1873 the Institute of Mechanical Engineers visited Dolcoath and were very impressed by what they saw. Their report described the pumps and the hoisting system used. The kibbles, which were 2½ feet in diameter and 4½ feet high, contained one ton of ore. Wire ropes were used to hoist them. These kibbles came up 350 fathoms in 8 minutes. At the principle shafts about 10 tons an hour were lifted. The average grade was as high as 200lb of black tin per ton – 8 percent. Some shafts were equipped with guides and skips. There were 232 heads of stamps operated by 3 steam engines. There were 30 convex buddles in the tin mill, which was lit by gas so that dressing could continue by night. Some 1,200 were employed, 500 of them underground.

The August 4th Manager's Report was encouraging, despite the reduction of income from a greater tonnage of tin. The miners on 314 fathom level and in the winze under the 302 level were opening up good tin ground, much of it worth £150 a fathom.

Harrietts and Stray Park areas continued as before, with the latter now paying its way. The winze under the 290 was holed to the 302 level and the east winze under the 302 was suspended because of water. On August 9th the *Mining Journal* reported that the adventurers were happy with the way things were going at the mine and had confidence in the management. In the same *Journal* a rumour was reported, that Dolcoath owed some £10,000 for coal, a story which was denied by the manager. A list of Cornish beam engines with their respective performances was also given, and it was stated that the Dolcoath 85-inch gave a duty of 60,300,000 – not the best performance, by any means![274]

The figures for the twelve weeks to October 4th 1873 were reported and once again income and profit was down. The tutworkers and surface workers wages were £7,401, tributers cost £3,150, merchants bills were £4,682 and the total cost was £15,395. Income from the 248 tons of black tin sold was, after dues, £17,570. Profit was down to £2,187 and the dividend paid was £2,148, or 10s a share. A 'New Engine House' cost £160 19s 4d. This may have been for the new man engine, at Wheal Bryant.[275]

The October 27th Manager's Report said that no shaft sinking was taking place, but preparations were in hand to begin sinking below the 314 fathom level. The winze under the 302 level, which was holed to the 314, was worth £200 a fathom. Values throughout the mine varied from £12 to £200 a fathom, with Harrietts section modest and Stray Park poor. In Stray Park a crosscut was being driven toward the Main Lode close to the eastern boundary.[276]

The mine accounts for the twelve weeks ending December 27th 1873 showed costs (merchants, wages, etc) at £15,882, black tin sales at £18,581, unstamped ore at £803 and arsenic at £162. The mine paid G. L. Basset £977 in dues, and there was a profit of £2,712 on an income from sales of £18,594. A dividend of 12s 6d per share was paid, totalling £2,685.[277]

By January 1874 Engine Shaft had begun sinking under the 314 level, by April the sinkers had progressed 3 fathoms and by September they were 7½ fathoms below the 314. The December 21st report stated that the Engine Shaft was 10½ fathoms under the 314 fathom level, which meant that in eleven months they had sunk an impressive 63 feet. Meanwhile, Wheal Bryant (Man Engine) Shaft also began to sink below the 236 fathom level and, despite a hold-up in April due to excess water in the shaft, by December it was 7 fathoms below the 236 level. For much of the year Harrietts Shaft was also being sunk and by the end of December it was 8 fathoms below the 248 fathom level.[278]

Winzes to open up new ground for stoping and to improve ventilation were being sunk below the 314, 302, 290 and 236 levels. In Harrietts section winzes were being sunk below the 224 fathom level, west of the shaft, and under the 212 level. In Stray Park section a winze was sunk below the 215 level, west of the shaft, and a rise was being mined to meet it from the 224 fathom level. By the end of the year the winze below 314 was down 7 fathoms and those under the 302, 290 and 236 fathom levels had holed the levels below. In the eastern end of Stray Park a crosscut was driven north toward Dolcoath Main Lode.[279]

Some very encouraging tin grades were met in the shafts, drives and winzes, with Engine Shaft particularly giving good results. In January the values were £50 a ton, by April £150, September back to £50 and in December up to £100 a ton. The 314 level was no less encouraging, with grades on the North Part of Main Lode, east of Engine Shaft, up to £200 a ton, and on the west drive, £120. In Harrietts section the values varied between £18 and £50 a ton, and in Stray Park, between £15 and £60 a ton. All of the optimism produced by these impressive grades was somewhat moderated by the tin price, which was about £20 a ton lower than at the end of the previous year.[280]

The current low tin price was causing some panic among a few adventurers and others, but Captain Josiah Thomas' attitude was: 'Don't panic!' The tin price fall caused some agitation for the Bassets to lower their dues from one-twentieth to one-thirtieth, but this did not happen, and the mine decided to hold black tin back until the price improved. With some 1,100 employed Thomas was determined to 'soldier on' and see the crisis through. Thomas did comment that the situation was caused by the discovery of rich tin deposits in Australia by Cornishmen. In July the value of Dolcoath shares had dropped so much that the *Mining Journal* reported a 'cute' Camborne man had purchased a share for 2s 6d and with a (totally unexpected) dividend declared of 10s, made an immediate profit of 7s 6d. By December the price was £60 a ton for the best black tin and £57 10s for inferior stuff – but, it was remarked in the *Mining Journal* that Dolcoath generally received about £2 a ton more than the 'standard'.[281]

In July the *Journal* reported that Dolcoath had spent another £375 on the new man engine, which it was predicted, would save the mine a fortune in lost time and injury to miners' health. It also reported on a Dolcoath miner, who worked at the deepest levels for some forty years, and who walked from Connor Downs every day. His round trip of ten miles a day totalled some 12,000 miles during those four decades.[282]

On October 3rd 1874, the *Mining Journal,* reported that at a recent count house dinner, a speaker said that Dolcoath 'was one of the richest tin mines in the world', and between 1853 and 1871 had sold over £1,000,000 worth of tin, £44,862 worth of copper, had paid out some £48,000 in dues and made a profit of £248,788. In the years 1872 and 1873 they had sold another £55,000 worth of tin.[283]

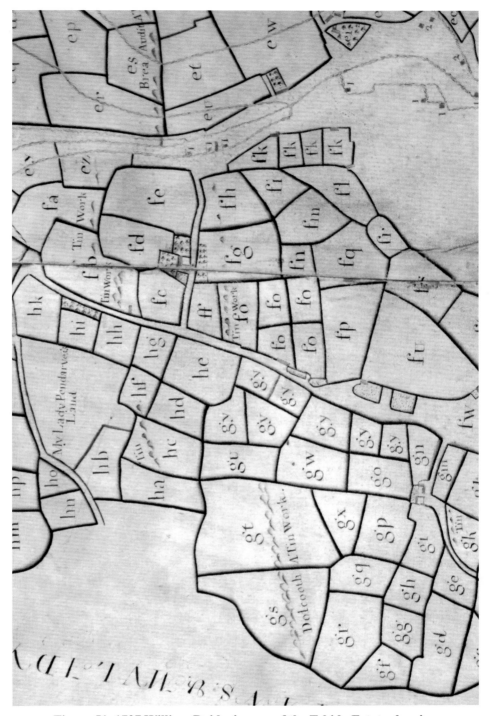

Figure 51. 1737 William Doidge's map of the Tehidy Estate showing Stray Park (gs) and Dolcoath (gt) fields. Bullen Garden is fo.

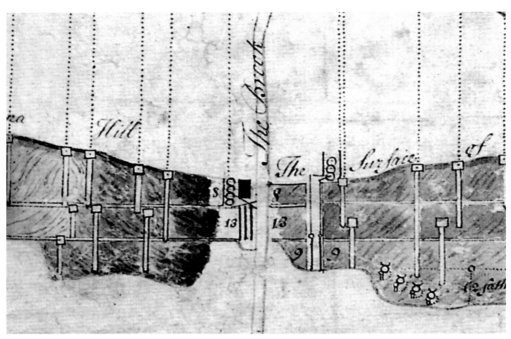

Figure 52. Polgooth Mine pumping engines in the 1690s. Tower engine on right and multi-wheeled engine in shaft left of centre. This was the technology used at Dolcoath in the beginning of the 18th century.

Figure 53. Loading wagons at Dolcoath from ore bins, early 20th century.

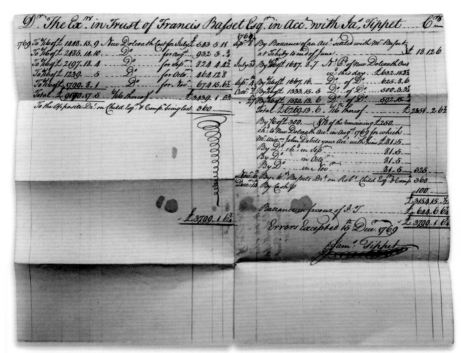

Figure 54. Extract from 1769 accounts of Francis Basset. Costs paid by Basset to New Dolcoath for his 6/16th share.

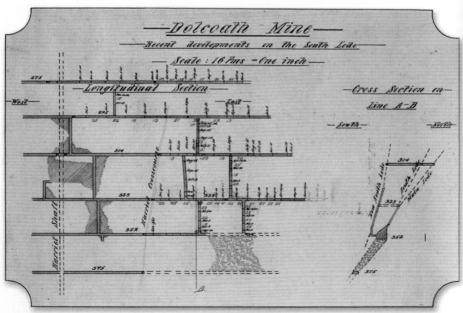

Figure 55. Long section and transverse section of Dolcoath South Lode (working plan, late 19th century).

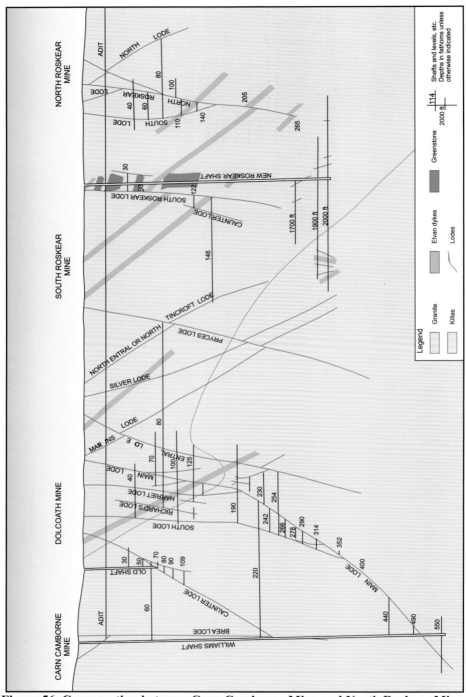

Figure 56. Cross-section between Carn Camborne Mine and North Roskear Mine.

212

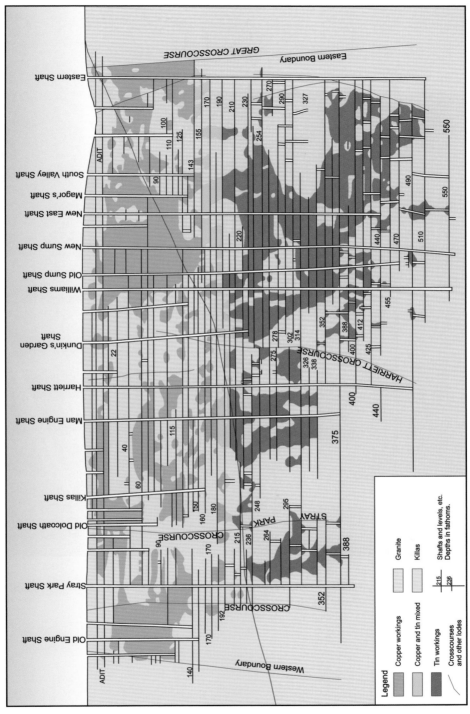

Figure 57. Long section showing the workings on Dolcoath Main Lode.

213

Figure 58. Cyril Penrose and Nigel Durant long-hole drilling on the Roskear A Lode, 420 fathom level. The drilling rig is the Tamrock L500.

Figure 59. Geoff Tonkin long-hole drilling on the Roskear B Lode at the 410-fathom sub-level. Note, Jet-Anol 300 ANFO pressure loader in foreground.

Figure 60. Billy Devlin shrinkage stoping on Roskear D Lode above the 420-fathom level.

Figure 61. Timmy Hocking blowing out long holes before charging with ANFO, 400-fathom level, Roskear B Lode.

Figure 62. Bernie Harradine and Timmy Evans connecting detonators in a long-hole stope on Roskear B Lode, 400 fathom level. The detonators are NONEL (non-electric).

Figure 63. Robin Boon, chief surveyor, on Roskear D Lode, 410 fathom sub-level. He is directly beneath the sump of New Dolcoath (South Roskear) Shaft. He is using a Zeiss 080A instrument.

Figure 64. Mervyn Randlesome and Micky Roberts on a rearing at the end of shrinkage stope above 315-fathom level on Dolcoath South Lode.

Figure 65. Adrian Mugford mucking drawpoint using LM56 Atlas Copco air shovel, 340-fathom level, Dolcoath South Lode.

Figure 66. Kevin Mutton driving LM56 Atlas Copco air shovel, in drawpoint on Roskear B Lode, 420-fathom level.

Figure 67. Alan Brown and Tommy Adams mining the footwall drive on Roskear B Lode at the 420 fathom level. They are using SIG drilling machines.

Figure 68. The author examining the pump on the 2000-foot level station, New Dolcoath Shaft, 1979.

Figure 69. The author carrying out ore recovery on Dolcoath South Lode, 50 feet below the 290 fathom level, 1994. This spot is beneath Dolcoath Road.

Figure 70. Carnon Consolidated preparing to plug the two shafts at Dunkin's Garden. A shallow tunnel can be seen leaving the shaft at the right.

Figure 71. Drive on copper lode at deep adit level, south of Old Valley Shaft. Driven in 1908. June 2010.

Figure 72. Stope on copper lode (5 fathoms north of Main Lode) north of Water
Engine Shaft. Note, ladder and timber stulls. June 2010.

Figure 73. Stope on copper lode above deep adit level, just north of Main Lode, north of Water Engine Shaft. Note, stull timbers and ladderway. June 2010.

Figure 74. Drive on copper lode at deep adit level, south of Old Valley Shaft. June 2010.

Figure 75. North crosscut from Old Valley Shaft at deep adit level. June 2010.

Figure 76. Stoping above adit level, north of Water Engine Shaft, Dolcoath. June 2010.

Figure 77. Remains of windlass over winze at old deep adit level, south of Old Valley Shaft. Windlass dates from 1908. June 2010.

Figure 78. Remaining gable end wall of Williams Shaft winding house. July 2010.

Figure 79. Compressor loadings on the north side of Williams Shaft winding house. July 2010.

Figure 80. Interior of Williams Shaft winding house, looking at supported remaining gable end. July 2010.

Figure 81. Harrietts engine house and winding engine with miners' dry in background, seen from Williams Shaft. July 2010.

Figure 82. Harrietts engine house with winding engine on loadings and boiler to left. July 2010.

Figure 83. Stray Park engine house showing gabled end wall, cylinder arch and stack. Landscape context destroyed by recent work. July 2010.

Figure 84. Bob wall of Stray Park engine house and site of shaft. July 2010.

Figure 85. Compressor house seen from Williams Shaft. July 2010.

Figure 86. Concrete loadings for high-speed horizontal winding engine acquired from Botallack Mine in 1896. Compressor house stack in background. June 2010.

Figure 87. Desolate surface scene at Dolcoath, looking towards the New East engine house. June 2010.

Figure 88. New East engine house with New Cooks Kitchen headgear in the background. June 2010.

Figure 89. Engine house loadings for Old Sump whim. June 2010.

Figure 90. The 1888 compressor house in Dolcoath Road. June 2010.

Figure 91. Landscaped area showing shaft markers and wall to Old Sump Shaft (right)

**Figure 92. Part of former Bennetts' fuze factory, used by New Dolcoath.
January 2005.**

**Figure 93. Base of the stack at the end of the boiler house, New Dolcoath.
January 2005.**

Figure 94. New Dolcoath (South Roskear) Shaft headgear erected by South Crofty in the 1990s. January 2005.

Figure 95. Harrietts Shaft winder in the winder house at New Dolcoath. This has since been taken back to Harrietts Shaft. January 2005.

The mine accounts for 1874 showed a problem at the beginning of the year, with a profit on the first twelve weeks a mere £29. Costs were £14,661 and the value of the ore (sold and held in stock) was £15,450 – presumably the reason for the low profit was the tonnage held back. Basset received £772 in dues and there was an overall income of £14,804. No dividend was paid. Things picked up thereafter, and by September profits were again over the £2,000 mark and they had risen by the end of November to £2,726 for the previous three months. Costs had remained constant, at from £13,110 to £13,763 between April and December.[284]

During 1874, the *Mining Journal* reported that Dolcoath discharged a million gallons of water into the Red River a day, carrying about 200lbs of 'metallic' arsenic, equivalent to 264lbs of white arsenic. It also sent a large tonnage of black tin down the river, giving the tin streamers below Tuckingmill some 375 tons, worth £30,000 per annum. One stream employed 210 workers, mostly youths, who averaged £1 a week.[285]

Dolcoath 1875

1875 saw Captain Thomas continuing to sink the mine deeper and keep exploration ahead of production. In March Harrietts Shaft was being sunk below the 248 fathom level and Old Sump Shaft was almost down to that level. By June Harrietts was 13 fathoms below the 248 and Engine Shaft was about to go below the 326 fathom level. The August Report said that Engine Shaft was 6 feet below the 326, and sinking then continued throughout the rest of the year. By late summer Harrietts Shaft was sunk to the 264 fathom level and work could begin to open up the level there. Of vital importance also, was the progress in sinking Man Engine Shaft, which, by August, was about to be holed to the 248 fathom level.[286]

The value of the tin ore varied throughout the early part of 1875, with grades worth £70 a fathom on the 326 level west of Engine Shaft and £60 east of the shaft. Grades for most of the ends on the levels above were fairly modest by Dolcoath's standards, and results in Stray Park were poor. By the summer the values had fallen slightly on the 326 but had picked up on the levels above, with the winze under the 314 level worth £80 a fathom, and the winze under the 290 worth £100 a fathom. Other points had picked up somewhat and the drive east of Stray Park was worth £15 a fathom. By the end of August the 326 level was looking very good, with the east drive worth £100 a fathom and the shaft itself finding values of £120 a fathom. Elsewhere values varied from between £90 in the winze under the 290 to £10 on the 290 east of New East Shaft. November saw the grades hold up well in Engine Shaft and on the 326 level and throughout the development ends at all the deeper levels the mine looked to be in a healthy state. Unfortunately, the tin price remained low, being a mere £50 a ton in the late summer.[287]

The March 20th *Mining Journal* reported that Mr Rule, one of the adventurers, questioned the price Dolcoath paid for its coal, and several other adventurers joined in, suggesting that they were paying too much for poor quality coal. It was thought that the Portreath Company was making more from the coal than the mine was. It was not covered, they said, and hence because it was wet, they were paying for the water in it. Captain Thomas was to look into the claims. Mention was made of stone breaker being installed, and also that there was no compressor on the mine to operate any boring machines they might acquire. It was vaguely suggested that perhaps a compressor might 'work by water or some appliance underground'. Thomas remarked to the adventurers that a boring machine could work three times faster than hand-labour, at two-thirds the costs, and so it was clear the management had not given up on the introduction of rock drills. Mention was made of Captain John Bawden's forty year service at Dolcoath.[288]

The April 24th 1875 *Mining Journal* reported: "The Dolcoath management have purchased an engine of Pendarves United to work their man-engine … money will have to expended on the new purchase to place it in proper working order."[289]

In the June meeting of the adventurers, at which Sir Frederick M. Williams, Bart MP presided, the disputed subject of the cost and quality of Dolcoath's coal was again raised by Mr Rule and his supporters. Thomas defended both the cost and the quality, but his antagonists were not to be placated, and Rule told the meeting that he had spoken to Mr Basset, who had assured him that the mine would not be penalised if it purchased its coal direct from the collieries. The argument became heated, bitter and personal, as Rule ranted about 'monopolists' and others who used advantage to make larger profits. At the same meeting it was remarked that £375 was being paid out for the steam engine to power the man engine and that £570 was being spent on various pieces of machinery.[290]

The Barrow Rock Drill

By June despite distractions that continued over the coal argument, it was clear the management was to press ahead with the move to powered rock drills. This time the drill to be tried was the Barrow rock drill, invented and built by two Cornishmen, Hosken and Blackwell, based in Barrow-in-Furness, Lancashire. The machine had early teething problems, due to the extremely hard granite it was drilling, and the distance the compressed air was being carried. Despite the Cornishmen's prejudice against the 'new-fangled' machinery, Thomas knew the future lay with such machines, and was determined to press on. The September 11th 1875 *Mining Journal* reported on the progress of the Barrow machine at Dolcoath. The old compressor, left on the mine some years before by Doering, and used for the Barrow, was not man enough for the new machine, and Messrs Tangye of Birmingham was asked to supply a new one. In October various mechanical engineers examined a new, improved Barrow machine and pronounced themselves happy with it. It was constructed of the strongest available metal, gun metal; it was light in weight (about 120 lb), could be easily carried by one man, and despite problems with the pipes bringing the compressed air to it, they thought it was fit for the purpose. This improved drill was to be given a proper, monitored trial underground immediately.[291]

THE BARROW ROCK DRILL

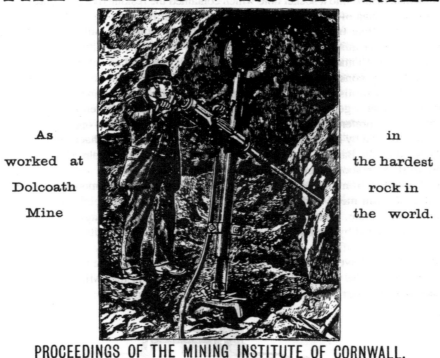

As worked at Dolcoath Mine

in the hardest rock in the world.

PROCEEDINGS OF THE MINING INSTITUTE OF CORNWALL.

Figure 96. The first successful rock drill to be tried at Dolcoath.

Despite the low tin price the mine accounts show that Dolcoath remained in a financially healthy condition. The twelve weeks ending February 20th 1875 saw a profit of £2,051, and a dividend of 10s a share paid out £2,148. Costs (wages, merchants bills, tax, etc) were £13,763, and tin sales were £16,634. The dues paid to G. L. Basset were £832, which left an income of £15,814. The next period, ending on May 15th saw a profit of £2,349 and a dividend of 10s again. Costs were £13,093 and the value of the black tin sold was £15,846: for 294 tons. £396 worth of arsenic was sold. The costs included £145 for the 'stone breaker', but whether this was the total cost or a part payment the accounts do not say. Dues were £812. The August 7th accounts show costs down to £12,071, tin sales down slightly to £14,912 (for 499 tons) and profit down to £2,106. The dividend remained at 10s a share – there were 4,296 shares. Basset dues were £746. The October 30th accounts show costs down still further, to £11,999, income from black tin sold up slightly to £14,998 (288 tons) and the dividend at 10s a share. Dues were 1/20th and £746 was paid to the Bassets. There was a profit for the twelve week period of £2,198. The January 22nd 1876 accounts for the previous twelve weeks showed everything remaining steady. Costs were £11,377, tin sales were £13,943, copper ore sold was £97, arsenic was £163, profit was £2,127 and the dividend remained at 10s a share. The Basset dues were £710.[292]

1876 saw the mine continuing to sink deeper as the grade of tin ore remained high and greater depths were attained. By May Engine Shaft was sunk 7 fathoms under the 326 level, by July it was nearly 10 fathoms below and in October it was announced that the 338 fathom level had been reached, which meant that by the end of the year the shaft was cased and divided down to that level and the sump drained for work to begin there. Meanwhile, New East Shaft, a short distance east of Engine Shaft, was also being sunk, and by the end of the year it was down to the 326 fathom level and its timber work could be installed. Old Sump Shaft, immediately to the west of Engine Shaft, was also being sunk below the 314 fathom level, and by the end of the year it was 8 fathoms below that level. By October Harrietts Shaft was being sunk below the 264 level, and by the end of the year it was 3 fathoms down.[293]

The tin ore values held up very well in 1876, although as usual with Cornish mines, they were patchy. In February, the values in Engine Shaft below the 326 were £80 a fathom, and on the 326 the drives east and west both showed values of £60 a fathom. The levels above produced values of between £10 and £45, modest by Dolcoath standards, and some places, on the 266 west of Old Sump and the 278 west of Old Sump there was very little tin. West of Harrietts and in Stray Park also values varied widely, from £45 a fathom to £10. In May the ore in Engine Shaft had improved to £120 a fathom, but the results elsewhere remained modest. July saw some improvement, but it was below the deepest level where the grades appeared to be highest. In October the grades continued much as before, with a winze under the 326 level, east of Engine Shaft, showing the best results with a value of £60 a fathom. By the end of the year exploration had opened up another large area for stoping, and although the overall results had been unspectacular, the mine continued to produce tin ore at an impressive and profitable rate. The many ends and winzes being driven and sunk to open up tin ground, together with the determination to continue sinking all the principal shafts to ever greater depths, demonstrated Captain Josiah Thomas' desire to keep exploration and development way 'ahead of the mill', ensuring the mine's future.[294]

At the adventurers meeting of May 8th it was resolved: 'That a vote of condolence … be given to the Widow and Family of the late Capt. Tonkin, who for 30 years has been an Agent of this Mine.' John Tonkin had been a mine captain at Dolcoath since the mid-1840s, when the crisis of diminishing copper reserves and increasing costs had almost brought the mine to a close. He was a devout Wesleyan and before becoming a mine captain had been a school teacher. At the same meeting it was agreed to take on Captain James Johns to replace him. Johns had been mine captain at South Wheal Crofty, and had been lured to Dolcoath by Captain Josiah Thomas, who was officially manager of South Crofty. In reality Thomas was 'external agent' at Crofty, with the day-to-day running of the mine left to the on-site mine captains.[295]

During 1876 discussion about the cost and quality of Dolcoath's coal continued. In February it was reported that good quality coal had been obtained for 18s 3d a ton, and the colliery company had given a two-and-half percent discount. Portreath Company had quoted 18s 6d a ton. The report that the mine's dressing costs were 8s a ton was refuted by Captain Thomas, who insisted that they were in fact only 4s. Optimism was expressed about the future of the Barrow rock drill and also about the savings to be expected from the new man engine. In May Hosken and Blackwell offered to operate the Barrow drill, using their own skilled men. They felt, reasonably, that this would be a better proof of its ability. Matthew Loam, their Cornish engineer, was to arrange it, and it was suggested that the Lancashire machinemen should be paid at the same rate as the Dolcoath tutworkers. The *Mining Journal* further reported that Cornishmen working in Cumberland had used the machine to open up several mines successfully. Mr Rule once again saw the need to be controversial and stated at the Adventurers Meeting that the Doering machine had operated better than the Barrow in hard granite. He added that although Doering still owed Dolcoath £200, he hoped the mine would write it off, as he had spent so much in promoting his machine at the mine. This statement was at odds with the accounts which showed Dolcoath owing Doering £90, a debt which was eventually paid off after some ten years in 1882. It was also stated at the adventurers meeting, that since 1799 Dolcoath had sold ore worth £5,000,000. By July Hosken and Blackwell's six month contract to drive two level themselves, using their own men got under way. The new Barrow machine was on the mine, and by August it was at last proving very successful. The patentees contracted to drive the 302 and 314 fathom levels, using their own Cornishmen, who had gained experience using the machine in Lancashire and Cumberland. The men were experienced, the new machine was stronger and more resilient than its predecessor, and the adventurers expressed themselves delighted at the prospects. Thomas was asked about the pay rates for the skilled machinemen, and he admitted that they were paid twice as much as the locals, but pointed out that they were only at the mine for a short time while they trained Dolcoath men in the machine's use. The Barrow company paid all its own expenses, which included the cost of compressed air.[296]

The August 19th 1876 *Mining Journal* gave some interesting comparative figures on the Barrow rock drill and hand labour.[297]

Manual Labour	=	9 feet a month
Machinemen	=	32 feet a month
Manual Labour	=	9 feet costs £37 10s
Machinemen	=	32 feet costs £100

Three skilled machinemen paid £8 each	=	£24
Three 2nd class machinemen paid £4 10s each	=	£13 10s
Three labourers paid £3 each	=	£9
Total =		£46 10s

In October Dolcoath's Chairman, Sir Frederick Williams, was fulsome in his praise of the Barrow machine. Its success at Dolcoath, he believed, could not be questioned, despite the many Cornish doubters. He reckoned that although the hand labour tutworkers had averaged 9 feet 10 inches during the year, the Barrow machinemen had averaged 34 feet 7 inches, drilling the same hard ground. Another bonus was mentioned – the compressed air reduced the temperature in the hot ends by between 10 and 15 degrees. There was a vote of thanks to Josiah Thomas and Matthew Loam, Dolcoath's engineer. Matthew was the son of Michael Loam, the well-known Cornish engineer, and he was trained in his father's firm of Hosking and Loam. Eventually he had his own company, Loam & Son. It was also mentioned at the same meeting, that dynamite was being used by the machinemen, but not by the hand drillers. Mr Cunnack, the agent for 'Tonite' explosives argued in favour of his product, stating that it was not only superior in efficiency to dynamite, but, despite its higher cost, it was more economical than its rival. Fumes were not a problem, he argued, if the safety rules were followed. Captain Rich pointed out that seven years use of dynamite had proved it safe, and there was little smell and smoke from it.[298]

The whole debate about the use of drilling machines, and which of the several available was best for use in deep Cornish mines continued for a considerable time. In December 1876 the *Mining Journal* reported the interest of Squire Basset in the issue, and stated that through his agent, Mr Bolden, he had given £300 toward the £1,000 needed to properly trial Major Beaumont's boring machine. The *Journal* also reported the figures for the five months trial of the Barrow machine at Dolcoath.[299]

1st month	= 4 fathoms 6 inches
2nd month	= 5 fathoms 8 inches

3rd month	= 5 fathoms 4 feet 7 inches		
4th month	= 5 fathoms 2 feet		
5th month	= 6 fathoms		
	Total	= 26 fathoms 1 foot 9 inches
	Average	= 5 fathoms 1 foot 6 inches
Hand labour average	= 1 fathom 3 feet per month	

Cost of coal for compressor about	= £14
2 enginemen	= £6
1 engineer	= £5 5s
1 smith and 1 boy	= £6
3 machine @ £8	= £24
3 men @ £4 10s	= £13 10s
3 men @ £3	= £9

Costs: Dynamite, candles, etc	= £34 15s (22s per foot @ 5fms 1ft 6inches)
	Total = £113 10s
	Profit over hand labour = £18 15s

The management pointed out, that with more machines being used, the relative costs would reduce, making them even more economical. As Tom Morrison has pointed out, using a machine efficiently took a long time to learn. The ability to set it up and operate it in drilling a straight hole into a face is one thing, but the whole process of positioning the machine to avoid unnecessary movements, and to drill the maximum number of holes accurately is quite different from a pare of miners using a hand held drill. The setting up of the drill, including the firm positioning of the metal bar to which it was attached took time and a certain amount of skill. The machineman needed to plan his pattern of holes carefully, to avoid time-consuming movement, and a lot of extra hard work. The ground varied also, and not just its relative hardness, but also drilling on lode or in crosscourse material meant the miner had to vary his hole pattern. Cornish miners fortunately 'knew their ground', but it took an intelligent miner to use this knowledge to the best advantage when using these new machines. Unlike hand labour, machines break down, or are adversely affected by such things as poor air supply or grit in the water supply. Moving the machine and its stabilising gear into the end at the start of the shift and out again before blasting was also time-consuming and heavy work, which needed to be planned efficiently.[300]

The August 5th *Mining Journal* reported that the new engine for the man engine was successful, and miners were being raised in 20 minutes instead of the previous 50 minutes. Thomas said than each man at the deeper levels saved an hour a day due to the new man engine. He also commented that the mine employed some 400 underground and 500 at surface. At the count house dinner there was a mood of optimism as the manager outlined recent progress and spoke of future prospects. He told the adventurers that he had visited Great Wheal Vor to view the new Husband pneumatic stamps, and had been impressed by them. They were fast, efficient and very economic. Captain Craze, who had recently visited the German metal mines, commented that Cornishmen worked twice as fast as the German miners, and that their much acclaimed abilities were more 'theoretical than practical' Another adventurer, Captain Nancarrow, thought that the dues paid the mineral lord, Mr Basset were too high. The meeting decided not to pursue it.[301]

The mine accounts for 1876 show a falling off of income from tin sales and a consequent drop in profits. In the twelve weeks ending April 15th 1876, costs, including wages, merchants bills, water rates and tax, were £10,793, profit was £1,553, the dividend paid was 7s 6d a share (4296 shares), which came to £1,611, and the lord's dues were £649. Tin ore (296 tons) sold for £12,981 and the income after dues and expenses was £12,347. The twelve weeks ending July 8th had costs of £11,205, Profit of £1,598, a dividend of 7s 6s a share, at £1,611, dues paid the Bassets of £673, black tin sales of £13,464, for 296 tons, and an income of £12,803. The twelve weeks ending September 30th had costs of £10,735, profit of £1,596, dividend of 7s 6d, copper ore sales of £60, tin sales of £12,839 (297 tons), 1/20th dues paid of £648 and income after expenses of £12,331. The final three month period, ending December 23rd 1876, saw costs of £11,004, profit of £1,616, dividend of 7s, 6d, copper ore sales of £47, tin sales of £13,225 (290 tons), dues of £664 and an income after all expenses of £12,619.[302]

By April 1877 Engine Shaft was prepared to sink below the 338 fathom level. Old Sump Shaft had been holed to the 326 level and Harrietts Shaft was being sunk in granite under the 264 level. Shaft sinkers had commenced to sink Man Engine Shaft below the 248 fathom level. July saw Engine Shaft 15 feet below the 338 level, Harrietts Shaft was 9 fathoms under the 264 level, and Man Engine Shaft was sunk 6 fathoms below the 248 fathom level. The September 24th Mine Report said Engine Shaft was sunk 5 fathoms under the 338, and a new plunger lift had been fixed at the 338. Harrietts Shaft was sunk 12 fathoms below the 264 level, but it was stated that they intended to sink a further 3 fathoms before opening up a level there. Man Engine Shaft had holed to the 264 fathom level. The December Report stated that Engine Shaft was sunk over 7 fathoms below the 338 fathom level and Harrietts Shaft was at the 275 level. Thomas was maintaining his drive to keep deepening the mine into what he believed were ever better values.[303]

The tin ore values throughout 1877 once again were patchy. In Engine Shaft the lode was worth £80 a fathom at the 338 level, when sampled in April, but as the lode was some 20 feet wide it was reported that its real value was about £300 a fathom. The drives east and west of the shaft on the 338 level gave values of £50 and £60 a fathom, but elsewhere the ends and winzes gave results of £10 to £30 a fathom. East of Stray Park the end was showing only a little tin. The July Report showed some improvement, with Engine Shaft having values of £120 a fathom, the drives east and west of the shaft at the 338 level having grades of £60 and £40, and the drive west of Harrietts Shaft, on the 264 level, being worth £70 a fathom. Again, the results for other levels was mostly disappointing. South Lode was being opened by a cross-cut from near New East Shaft at the 290 level, and at the 302 level it was already looking promising. It was intended to open up this lode from several levels higher up the mine, where it was anticipated a large body of ground remained to be exploited. In September, the lode in Engine Shaft five fathoms below the 338 level, maintained its high value, being sampled at £120 a fathom. The drives east and west of the shaft at the 338 level also kept up well, with values of £50 and £80 a fathom. The 264 west of Man Engine Shaft was worth £70 a fathom. Elsewhere the values were moderate. South Lode continued to be opened up, with a cross-cut on the 278 being driven toward it. A winze was being sunk below the 290 level, and tributers were working below the 302 level at 8s 6d in the pound. Values in the December Report were again mixed, with Engine Shaft still at £120 a fathom, the drive west on 338 worth £70 and the east drive worth only £20 a fathom. However, a winze under the 338 level, west of the shaft had values of £75 a fathom over an impressive width, indicating that the deeper the mine went, the better the tin grades. The rest of the ends on Main Lode were fairly modest, although the work on South Lode continued to look promising.[304]

The April 6th 1877 Mine Report only contained the names of Captains Josiah Thomas, John Bawden and James Johns. For the first time in over twenty years William Provis' name did not appear among the agents. The April Adventurers Meeting was told that Captain Provis, 'a very old servant' of the mine, had had 'an accident in the discharge of his duties'. The adventurers voted him £5 a month until he could resume work. At the same meeting it was reported that the price of tin was down £2 4s a ton over just three months – a difference of £650 in the mine's income. Once again, Mr Rule, that arch-demander of answers, wanted to know how much tin the mine was holding in stock. When Captain Thomas replied 'Not Much!' Rule asked, '100 tons?' and Thomas confirmed the figure. He then demanded to know what Thomas was getting for Dolcoath's tin, and Thomas replied '£43 2s 6d'.[305]

Early in 1877 the contract for Hosken and Blackwell to operate their machine at Dolcoath ended, and the mine acquired the machines. The drive by the Barrow on the 314 fathom level was 6 feet wide by 7 feet high, which was not dissimilar from levels at Geevor a century later. The machine had a 2-inch diameter piston rod, a 3¼-inch cylinder, was 3 feet 4 inches in length and worked at 300 strokes a minute.

Theoretically, the machine operated best at an air pressure of between 55 and 60 pounds per square inch. It used three sizes of drill steel, with the first bit measuring 1¼ inch diameter, the next 1⅛ inch and the third an inch in diameter. The diminishing size meant the bits would not jam as the hole was deepened. The drill round consisted of 20 to 24 holes, drilled, ideally, to a depth of about 20 inches. Interestingly, hole barrels from South Crofty's Barrow rock drill, measured in 1979 on the 205 fathom level north of Bickfords Shaft, have an average depth of 13 inches. Compressed air came through the shaft in 2-inch pipes, reducing to 1½ inch on the levels and then down to one inch hose to the machine. In September there was discussion about the high cost of equipping the mine with new machines and compressors, and again the idea of approaching the mineral lord for a reduction in dues, which stood at 1/20th, was mentioned.[306]

There was a report by the mine engineer, Matthew Loam, on Dolcoath's needs with respect to new rock drills and compressors. He said that the mine needed two compressors, one at Engine Shaft and the other at Harrietts Shaft, and that both should be capable of supplying six machines. He also suggested that there should be six Barrow drills working through Engine Shaft and another three at Harrietts. He estimated that two steam condensing engines and air compressors would cost £900; 720 fathoms of main pipes would cost £450; loadings, buildings and other necessaries another £250, totalling, exclusive of drilling machines, some £1,600. He added that drilling capacity could be doubled, as and when required, for a mere £800 extra. Basset's steward, Mr Bolden, tried to persuade the adventurers to try out the machine of Colonel Beaumont, which he insisted had done brilliantly at Carn Brea Mines and was far superior to the Barrow. This led to a fierce debate between Matthew Loam and Bolden on the merits of the machines they championed, in which Loam demanded to know why, as lord of Dolcoath, Squire Basset had not given Dolcoath the financial assistance he had given Carn Brea in their trial of the Beaumont drill.[307]

The argument resumed at the December Adventurers Meeting, when the engineer of the Ingersoll Rock Drill Company challenged Loam to try his machine against the Barrow for one, two or three months. Winner take all! Loam declined the challenge. In a letter the Ingersoll engineer lamented the fact that although it was a local man, Richard Trevithick, who had invented and built perhaps the first mechanical rock drill, the Cornish mine managers half-a-century later appeared to lag behind other mining districts in their use. Perhaps, he asked sarcastically, Cornish miners were so good that they did not need machines! He did mention that his machine worked well on 40 to 50 p.s.i. Other challenges to the Barrow came from the makers of the Delta rock drill and the Dunn machine, all insisting that their drills were superior to the Barrow.[308]

Accident on the Man Engine

On June 24th 1877 there was a serious accident on the man engine. There was a rule that prohibited men riding up on the engine whilst others travelled down. When it was ignored there was the danger of men obstructing each other and causing accidents. On this occasion a 55 year old miner called Walter Williams was ascending the shaft at about seven o'clock in the morning, when he met a boy coming down. He tried to step onto the rod as the boy stepped off, causing him to strike the rod with his right leg. The result was a compound fracture of his leg. Despite this accident the miners for the most part continued to view the machine as a 'God send', which saved them a long and exhausting climb.[309]

The mine accounts for 1877 showed a fall in profits, despite an impressive increase in tin tonnage and a small rise in income; undoubtedly this was due to the lower tin price. The twelve weeks ending March 11th 1877 had costs of £10,992, profit of £1,079, a dividend paid of 5s a share, totalling £1,074, lord's dues of £635 (1/20th), tin sales of £12,696 (294 tons) and an income of £12,072. The three months ending June 9th were little better, with costs at £11,455, profit of £1,081, dividend of 5s a share, totalling £1,074, G. L. Basset's dues of £658, arsenic sales of £125, tinstone (12 tons) £378, black tin sales of £12,662 (302 tons) and an income of £12,536. There was also £18 worth of 'Old Materials' sold. The twelve weeks ending September 7th 1877 had costs of £11,503, profit of £986, dividend of 5s a share, making £1,074, dues of £654, copper ore sales of £65, tin ore sales of £13,015 (332 tons), and an overall income of £12,489, which included renting a burning house, presumably to a neighbouring mine. The twelve weeks ending November 24th 1877 had costs of £12,001, a profit of £1,072, dividend of 5s a share, for £1,074, 1/20th dues of £688, black tin sales of £13,750 (330 tons), and an income of £13,073.[310]

During 1878 Thomas' sinking programme continued, and Engine Shaft was sunk over 9 fathoms below the 338 fathom level by March, and by November 18th it was at the 352 fathom level. Old Sump Shaft was also being sunk and by November it was 7 fathoms under the 326 level. Man Engine Shaft was sunk fairly quickly, being just below the 264 level at the beginning of the year, and down to the 275 fathom level by November 18th. Stray Park Engine Shaft, after having the sump forked at the 282 fathom level early in the year, was sunk 6 fathoms below the level by November. New East Shaft, which resumed sinking in the early summer, was holed to the 338 fathom level by mid-November. This shaft had a new skip road installed by November, which ran from surface down to the 338 fathom level. The mine took only three weeks to install this skip road, and used over 100 men for the task. It could hoist three 35 cwt skips an hour – 5¼ tons! The manager reported that it was working well, and they would soon install a skip road in Engine Shaft and two other shafts.[311] Tin ore values were much the same as the previous year, with the usual fluctuations in grade. In March it was reported that Engine Shaft under the 338 level was seeing values of £100 a fathom, and the winzes being sunk to the east and west of the shaft under the 338 gave values of £60 and £70 fathom respectively. The other ends and winzes varied between £10 and £40 a fathom. In June Engine Shaft had ore worth £80 a fathom, and the two winzes below the 338 fathom level were worth £70 and £55 a fathom. The other levels had fairly moderate values. On South Lode the 290 fathom level was being opened up and an end there was worth £25 a fathom. In August, Engine Shaft was down 14 fathoms below the 338 level, and the ore there was worth £100 a fathom. The two winzes were worth £70 and £45, and the drive east on the 338 was worth £40 a fathom. New East Shaft had values of £60 a fathom just above the 338 fathom level. The rest of the mine had values between £10 and £40 a fathom. Stray Park eastern end was showing 'a little tin', but not worth much. South Lode was showing £16 a fathom on the 290 level end and £18 a fathom in the 276 end. The November report gave similar results at these points to the rest of the year. South Lode was being opened up at the 266 level by means of a crosscut, and it was intended to exploit the lode on several levels above 290 fathom level.[312]

The mine reports for 1878 showed changes in the agents. On March 11th there was added the name 'J. Thomas', who joined Josiah Thomas and James Johns. He replaced John Bawden, who had left his position at the beginning of the year. J. Thomas was on the June 3rd Report, but the August 26th report showed J. Thomas replaced by Jos. Chynoweth. There was also a change at the very top, with the death of Sir Frederick M. Williams, whose death was announced at the adventurers meeting of November 18th 1878. In August Captain Thomas responded to an accusation that Dolcoath miners were generally lazy, by saying that a few indeed were lazy, and liked to wander round the mine and explore, but the overwhelming majority were very hard-working. One wonders how those critics would have managed a shift or two 'beating the borer' in the heat of the mine.[313]

A Variety of Rock Drills Tried
During 1878 the miners really began to appreciate the Barrow rock drill, and as their confidence and skill improved they advanced the levels at a faster rate. In August the machine on the 314 fathom level drove 10 fathoms, nearly twice as fast as in 1876. In autumn the machinemen advanced 29 fathoms in twelve weeks – which was four times faster than the hand labour tutworkers. In the Autumn Ullathorne's agreed to trial their Champion rock drill on the 352 fathom level. Major Beaumont offered to trial his machine at Dolcoath for £28 a fathom, but as this was £3 a fathom more than the tutworkers were getting the committee refused. Beaumont then offered to drive for £16 5s a fathom, provided that Dolcoath supplied the air, but again this was refused. Beaumont gave figures for the performance of his machine at Carn Brea Mines, which were very impressive. In twenty weeks he claimed a Beaumont advanced a level in Carn Brea 92½ fathoms, and average of 18½ fathoms a month. The committee also approached the Eclipse Company to see how their

machine operated at Dolcoath, but they merely offered to sell machines to the mine, and the approach was aborted. In March 1878 Dolcoath ordered 4-inch, cast iron, compressed air pipes from a Glasgow firm, at a cost of £5 15 a ton. They hoped to install these at the bottom of the mine.[314]

In August a Mr S. F. Cox offered to trial his new stamps at Dolcoath, but his offer was turned down, possibly because his claim to stamp tin ore at 1s a ton was no improvement on the current position. In November 1878 it was reported that a Tangye 'Special' compressed air pump was being used to drain a very wet winze under the 302 fathom level. It removed 300 gallons in four hours, a task which would have taken three shifts baling with bucket and winch.[315]

The mine accounts for 1878 showed a similar picture to the previous year. The twelve weeks ending February 16th 1878 showed costs of £12,149, a profit of £1,058 and a dividend of 5s a share, totalling £1,074, lord's dues of £694, arsenic sales of £58 and black tin sales of £13,832 for 360 tons of black tin. The total income was £13,195. The May 11th account gave costs of £11,803, profit of £1,075, a dividend of 5s a share, at £1,074, Basset's 1/20th dues of £677, arsenic sales of £71 and tin sales of £13,472 for 372 tons. The overall income was £12,877. The twelve weeks ending August 3rd had costs of £11,669, profit of £1,101, a dividend of 5s a share, totalling £1,074, dues of £671, copper ore sales of £27 and tin sales of £13,402 for 372 tons. The total income was £12,770. The twelve weeks ending October 26th 1878 had costs of £11,360, profit of £1,059, a dividend of 5s on the 4,296 shares, totalling £1,074, dues of £653, black tin sales of £13,063 for 372 tons, and a total income of £12,420. The twelve weeks ending January 18th 1879 showed costs of £11,698, profit of £197, no dividend paid, dues of £626, arsenic sales of £69, black tin sales of £12,442 for 356 tons, and a total income of £11,895. This dramatic drop in profit was undoubtedly due to the broken piston of the pumping engine and the unusually wet weather, which allowed the bottom level to flood and stopped production from down there. By mid-January the bottom level, the 352, was clear of water and work recommenced there. With the tin price down to about £40 a ton, Thomas reported in October to the adventurers that he was reducing the standard for tributers from £38 down to £36 – which meant they lost about 5 percent on the tin they mined. The mine received an average of £36 2s a ton in 1878.[316]

The sinking programme continued in 1879, and despite problems with the main pumping engine, once the piston was repaired work could continue. In February Captain Thomas was called on to scotch a rumour that Engine Shaft had 'runned together' – there was no truth in it, he said. It was also reported that the cage on one of the principal whims had broken, causing a severe loss in tonnage hoisted. In July it was reported that 'we have fixed a new skip road in the Engine Shaft from surface to the bottom of the Mine, which is working satisfactorily'. This was done in four weeks by 130 men. In July Thomas remarked that the new skip road could hoist 22 35-cwt skips in an eight hour shift – which was 40 tons! By October Engine Shaft had been sunk 4 fathoms below the 352 fathom level. Old Sump Shaft was holed to the 338 level by early summer, and work immediately began to sink below that level. In February Harrietts Shaft was sunk 10 fathoms under the 275 level, and a raise was put up by a Barrow rock drill from the 314 level to meet it. Clearly, the miners were learning to use the machine effectively by then, not just driving levels, but also raising. By October the boring machine had risen 18 fathoms over the 314 fathom level. The heat was so great in the raise that it is possible the tutworkers could not have worked there, but the machinemen had the benefit of the compressed air and were able to work effectively. The shaft was holed by December 1879. New East Shaft was being sunk below the 338 level, and in Stray Park the Engine Shaft was sinking under the 282 fathom level, although in February it had been suspended due to excess water. Man Engine Shaft was 8 fathoms below the 275 fathom level by October 20th 1879.[317]

Boiler Explosion
In February 1879 a new stamps engine boiler blew up. Fortunately, Downing, the engineman was behind a dividing wall at the time, and was not seriously injured. Apparently, he had just checked its pressure and moved on to the next one when it exploded. Dolcoath had 22 boilers in service at the time, and this was the first accident with one for 13 years.[318]

In 1879 tin ore values remained similar to the previous year. Early on in the year the grades were modest with values of no more than £70 a fathom on the 352 fathom level, and the other levels showing between £10 and £40 a fathom. However, the February 10th Report shows that development was being carried out on nine different levels on Main Lode: the 352, 338, 326, 314, 302, 282 (Stray Park), 275, 264 and 254. There were drives to open up South Lode on the 266, 278 and 290 fathom levels. By May the values on the deepest level had slightly improved, and by July high values of £100 a fathom were being found in Engine Shaft under the 352 level, once again filling the hearts of the adventurers with optimism. Crosscutting toward South Lode continued on the 254, 266 and 290 fathom levels. In October it was reported that 4 fathoms below the 352 level ore worth £140 a fathom had been found, and the east drive from Engine Shaft on the 352 had ore worth £100 a fathom. The rest of the development ends returned ore worth between £10 and £40 a fathom. In October a lode known as 'New Lode' was discovered by a raise over the 314 fathom level, near Harrietts Shaft. The management believed it could be untouched between the point of discovery and the surface – possibly 200 fathoms of exploitable ore![319]

In May 1879 it was reported that Dolcoath had ten steam engines on the mine: three pumping engines, three whim engines, three stamping engines and the engine driving the man engine. Some interesting ancillary costs were also detailed in the *Mining Journal* of May 19th 1879: a ten ton boiler for the whim and compressor engine cost £85; wire rope was bought at £2 14s a cwt, coal was costing 15s a ton; balk timber from Norway was costing nearly 6s a foot and yellow pine nearly 13s a foot. Iron track cost £5 a ton, which was a massive reduction from its price less than ten years before. Steel stamps heads cost £32 a ton, but lasted 3½ times as long as the far cheaper iron heads.[320]

Another Fatal Accident

On Saturday the 9th August 1879, a timberman called Joseph Gilbert fell 220 fathoms down Old Sump Shaft, and was killed. Gilbert and three other timbermen were engaged in an examination of the shaft when the accident happened. Gilbert was being let down from the 100 fathom level, seated on a board attached to a rope. James Rodda, William Jose and Henry Rogers were lowering him as he inspected the shaft timbers. Apparently, Gilbert accidentally struck the rope which supported him, causing it to break. The three men immediately set off down the shaft to rescue him, but, unfortunately, a new ladder, only recently installed in the shaft, collapsed and they fell 20 fathoms to the next level. They were hoisted to surface by the skip, where Dr Hutchinson attended them. Jose had concussion and a badly cut head, but the other 2 escaped with cuts and bruises. Thereafter, the body of Joseph Gilbert was recovered. He left behind a widow and 4 children.[321]

By October 1879 Ullathorne's had decided to give up their contract to drive the 352 level east and west with their Champion rock drills. Tutworkers took over the ends, which lay a short distance from Engine Shaft. In the autumn Dolcoath bought a new 28-inch diameter cylinder engine from Holman Brothers to power its stamps. This was installed by its partial designer, John Dalley, Dolcoath's on-site engineer, who worked under the superintendence of Matthew Loam, who was based in Liskeard. Thomas reckoned that the new engine could run two more batteries of 32 heads each, which would only cost a further £300 to £400. By December the mine had 228 heads of stamps in three batteries of 48, 60 and 120 heads. The stamps engine capacity was severely under-used, for the 36-inch engine, which powered the 48 head battery, was capable of driving 96 heads, and in January 1880 twelve more were added to the 48 heads. The largest stamps battery, with 120 heads, was driven by a 38-inch engine, which had a duty of nearly 41 million, and consumed 25 tons of coal in one month.[322]

New Factory & Education Acts

A major change came to Dolcoath in the summer of 1879, when the provisions of the recently passed Factory Act were put into effect. All youngsters between the ages of ten and fourteen were either dismissed or made to work part-time. This was to enable them to attend school, at least some of their time. The Mines Inspector insisted that the law be observed to the letter, but so long as children went to school at least half of the week, he conceded that they could work at Dolcoath the rest. Captain Thomas observed, probably correctly, that the parents would be bigger losers than the mines. Some would be forced onto the parish rates, which was unfortunate. There was some confusion with respect to child labour. Since 1833 there had been a series of acts of parliament that sought to reform working conditions and improve education. Various Factory Acts and Education Acts had reduced the age children could work and restricted the conditions in which children could work. These acts sought to make working conditions safer, reduce exploitation and improve the health and education of children. Women were also affected by this legislation. The Factory Act of 1875 and the Education Act of 1876 sought to tidy up some of the confusion, but much of it was still left to local officials to interpret. The following year the Mundella Act made schooling compulsory for all children, undoubtedly creating new problems for mine owners and parents struggling to make ends meet.[323]

The accounts for 1879 showed the mine's financial position gradually strengthening. Dolcoath paid £5,000 to the receivers of the failed Cornish Bank. In August the mine arranged to pay off its debt of £1,700 to the new bankers by the end of the year, and by the end of October they had done so. The twelve weeks ending April 12th 1879 showed costs for wages, merchants, rates, etc at £11,610, profit of £2,006, a dividend paid of 5s a share, totalling £1,074, G. L. Basset's 1/20th dues of £716, copper ore sales of £19, and tin sales of £14,301 for 370 tons. Overall income rose to £13,616. The next three months figures gave costs of £11,755, profit of £1,468, dividend of £1,074 at 5s a share, dues of £695, arsenic sales of £130, and black tin sales of £13,776 for 379 tons. Total income was £13,223. The twelve weeks ending September 27th had costs of £12,283, profit of £3,673, a dividend of 10s a share, totalling £2,148, dues of £839, black tin sales of £16,781 for 386 tons. Total income was £15,956. The December 20th accounts for the previous twelve weeks showed costs at £12,996, profit of £6,037, a dividend paid on the 4,296 shares of £1, Basset's dues of £999, tin sales of £19,981 for 376 tons sold and an overall income of £19,033. The dramatic increase in the profits was due to the rapid rise in the price paid to Dolcoath for her black tin. In April it was £38 13s a ton, in July it was £36 9s, in September it rose to £43 9s 6d a ton, and in December it had risen to £53 3s.[324]

Dolcoath's Bank Collapses
There had been a financial crisis involving Dolcoath in February 1879, when the Cornish Bank of Messrs Tweedy, Williams & Company collapsed, with Dolcoath owing them some £15,165. Williams, Williams & Grylls replaced them as the mine's bankers. At the same time George Williams was appointed to the committee, replacing the recently deceased Sir Frederick M. Williams, Bart. By the beginning of the following year, due to the strengthening position of the mine, Dolcoath was able to pay off £11,300 of its debt. The remarkable turnaround in Dolcoath's finances, brought about by continuing high grades in its deeper levels and the rising price of

tin metal, started a protracted period of high profits and generous dividends.[325]

The programme to deepen the mine did not slacken in 1880, and no less than six shafts were being deepened at the beginning of the year. Engine Shaft was sinking under the 352 fathom level, Old Sump Shaft was 8½ fathoms below the 338 level, with a raise about to be put up from the 352 by boring machine to meet it. New East Shaft was sunk 8 fathoms under the 338 level, Harrietts Shaft was holed to the raise over the 314 level Man Engine Shaft was sunk 13 fathoms below the 275 level and Stray Park Engine Shaft was sunk to the 290 fathom level. By April much more had been done, and Engine Shaft was 7 fathoms below the 352 level and New East Shaft was sunk 14 fathoms below the 338. Meanwhile, Man Engine Shaft, which had been sunk 15 fathoms below the 275 level, was suspended due to the large volume of water it was making. A level was being driven by boring machine below the shaft at the 295 level, and this, it was hoped, would drain the sump by seepage. The June 28th mine report shows progress in connecting up those deep workings. Engine Shaft was over 9 fathoms below the 352 level, and a drive east from the shaft at that level had holed New East Shaft. The 352 level west of Engine Shaft had holed Old Sump Shaft, and the 295 level west of Harrietts Shaft had holed Man Engine Shaft. The September report showed a slackening of the shaft sinking programme, and Engine Shaft was the only one being deepened. It was nearly 11½ fathoms below the 352 fathom level. However, at the extreme western end of the mine, plans were afoot to sink Stray Park Engine Shaft below the 290 fathom level. By December it was decided to put a skip road into Harrietts Shaft.[326]

Old Sump Shaft Blocked
The September 20th mine report detailed a serious incident, which proved expensive for the mine. "About a fortnight after our last meeting (in June), an accident occurred in Old Sump Shaft, between the 40 and 60 fathom levels – the timber in the old workings (which was probably put in more than 50 years ago, and which could not be got at to be examined) having given way, and filled the Shaft at that point. We have been engaged from that time to the present in clearing and securing the Shaft, and have consequently not been able to draw any tinstuff through it for the past ten weeks, which has interfered considerably with our returns for this Account. The Shaft is now approaching completion, and we hope to be in full course of working in three or four weeks time."[327]

The December 13th 1880 report has Engine Shaft sunk over 13 fathoms below the 352 fathom level, and the plat had been cut on the 290 level at Stray Park Engine Shaft to start sinking there. It was also announced that the repairs to Old Sump Shaft had taken far longer to complete than anticipated, but that they had been 'drawing stuff therefrom for the past fortnight'.[328]

In January 1880 the ore continued to be patchy in the ends and winzes, but in Engine Shaft below the 352 fathom level it maintained high values, being worth £180 a fathom. The drive east from the shaft on the 352 level was worth £50 a fathom, and the ground, which had been relatively soft, had become as hard as in the rest of the deeper workings. Most ends had values of between £15 and £35 a fathom. South Lode was being opened up for stoping from the 266, 278 and 290 levels, where the tin ore was worth between £10 and £15 a fathom. The April report showed that values held up well, with the ore in Engine Shaft being worth £200 a fathom across the 12 feet width of the shaft. A winze under the 352 level, east of Engine Shaft, was worth £80 a fathom, although the drives on the 352 showed modest values. The six levels being developed above the 352 had values of between £15 and £45 a fathom. South Lode continued to open up for the tributers, and 'New Lode' was being opened up west of Harrietts Shaft on the 248, 265 and 295 levels. In June the 352 lode drives and the Engine Shaft below the 352 looked good, with values of £140, £80 and £75. The rest of the development points varied between £8 a fathom in Stray Park, and £40 in a winze under the 264 west of Man Engine Shaft. South Lode continued moderate and New Lode continued to look promising. In September the values were quite good on and below the 352 fathom level, where the ore was worth £140, £85 and £70 a fathom. Between the 275 and the 338 levels the grades were variable on Main Lode, although on South Lode and New Lode they were between £10 and £18 a fathom. The end of 1880 saw ore worth £120 a fathom 13 fathoms below the 352, and worth £80 and £70 a fathom in the west and east of the shaft. The other ends improved somewhat, so that five ends (between 266 and 352 levels) had values between £30 and £45 a fathom. South Lode and New Lode continued to progress quietly.[329]

January 1880 saw Captain Thomas again seeking to increase the mine's stamping capacity. He proposed that the mine attach 12 more heads to the 'bottom' stamps battery, and reckoned that the 'top' stamps 30-inch engine was capable of powering 96 heads, an increase of 48. The December 18th *Mining Journal* reported that Thomas intended to obtain a new stone-breaker for Dolcoath, and replace two of the axles on one of the stamping engines.[330]

Controversy over Ticketing
In April an important discussion took place at the adventurers meeting, when the question of the method used to sell the mine's black tin was raised. Captain William Teague, of Carn Brea Mines, asked if it was not time to sell Dolcoath's tin by ticketing, rather than by fixed contract to particular smelters. He conceded that it had been tried before and failed, but thought that was because the scheme had not been well supported. Captain Josiah Thomas felt that they should carry on as they had done, as Messrs Willyams, Harvey & Co. and Redruth Smelting Co. had consistently paid the mine above the standard. Captain A. T. James asserted that other Cornish

mines were paid more for their tin than Dolcoath, and he was opposed to monopoly in any form, believing in 'free trade'. Mr Bolden, Squire Basset's agent, joined the argument by referring to the mine's lease agreement, which said Dolcoath tin must be sold by 'public sale', on the open market, 'for the best price that can be obtained'. Bolden asserted that Thomas had refused to sell the mine's tin at 15s a ton more than he was selling it at, but Thomas retorted that two smelters had indeed offered to pay more, but they only wanted small quantities, and his regular smelters took all that he could supply, all the year round, and paid above the standard. Discussions with Bolden over a change in the rate of Basset's dues resulted in an increase from 1/20th to 1/15th.[331]

The mine accounts for 1880 showed a continuing improvement in the finances of the mine. The twelve weeks ending March 13th 1880 showed costs of £13,319, profit of £6,574 and a dividend paid of £1 10s a share, totalling £6,444. G. L. Basset's 1/20th dues were £1,046, mundic sales £44 and black tin sales of £20,880 for 370 tons of black tin, which sold for an average of £56 8s 6d. Total income was £19,893. The three months ending June 5th had costs of £13,255, profit of £4,214 and a dividend of £1 a share, making £4,296, dues of £912, arsenic sales of £36 and tin sales of £18,214 for 376 tons. An old whim engine was sold for £115 and the total income was £17,469. The twelve weeks ending August 28th had costs of £13,415, profit of £3,675, dividend of £1 a share totalling £4,296, dues of £899 and tin sales of £17,975 for 348 tons. Total income was £17,091. The period ending November 20th 1880 gave costs of £13,931, profit of £4,314, dividend of £1 a share, at £4,296, dues of £1,155, mundic sales of £7 and tin sales of £19,380 for 361 tons. Overall income was £18,245. The price paid for Dolcoath's black tin varied during the year between £56 8s 6d early in the year, down to £48 9s in the summer, and up again to £53 13s 6d in November.[332]

A new mine agent, Captain James Rodda, joined the management team at the beginning of 1881. By March Engine Shaft was a little over 12 fathoms below the 352 level, work being held up due to excessive water. The wet season also held up the sinking of a couple of winzes under the 352 level. The only other shaft being sunk in early 1881 was Stray Park Engine Shaft, which was still being deepened below the 290 fathom level. The new skip road in Harrietts Shaft was reported to be 'working very satisfactorily'. In May Engine Shaft was sunk to the 364 fathom level and a drive had been pushed west to link with a winze about 18 feet from Engine Shaft. This opened up some good ground for the tributers. At the same time the 364 was driven east by boring machine, and a winze being sunk toward the 364 fathom level. All over the mine, especially at the deeper levels, winzes were being put down to open ground for stoping. A winze under the 295 level, on the north part of Main Lode, to the north of Harrietts Shaft was holed to a raise from the 314 level. In May it was announced that a skip road was shortly to be extended in Harrietts Shaft, to the

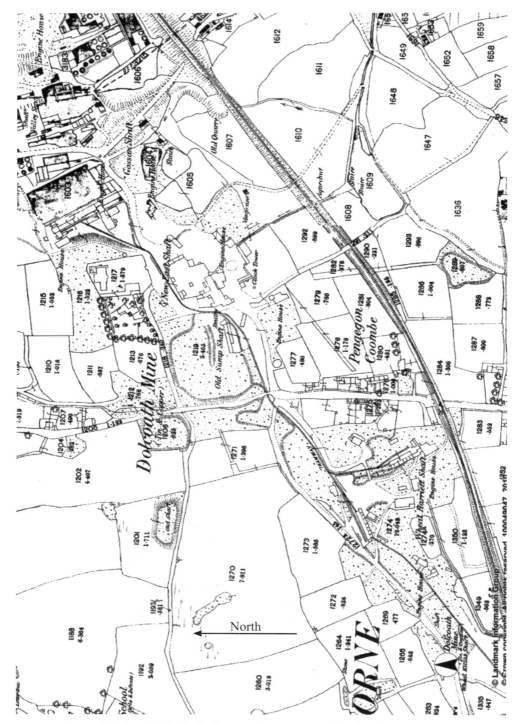

Figure 97. 1880 25-inch Ordnance Survey map showing Dolcoath Mine.

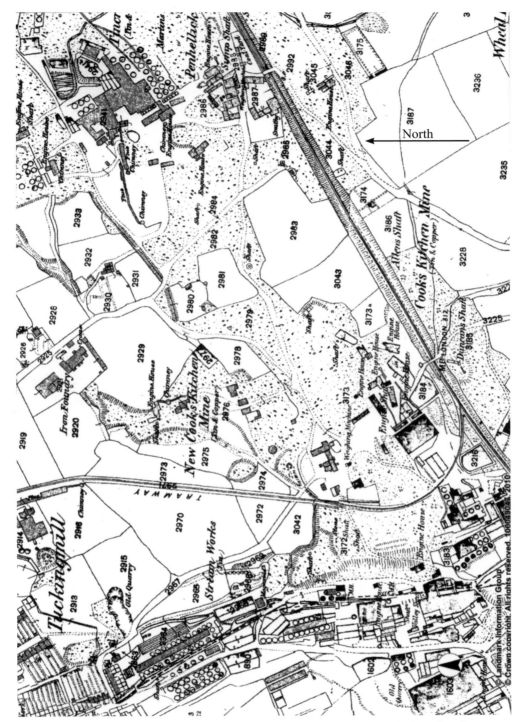

Figure 98. 1880 25-inch Ordnance Survey showing the Dolcoath dressing floors and Cooks Kitchen Mine.

261

314 fathom level. The August report had Engine Shaft being prepared for deepening below the 364 fathom level and Man Engine Shaft in Wheal Bryant also commenced sinking below the 295 level. By November 14th Engine Shaft was sinking below the 364 and Man Engine Shaft was down an impressive 6½ fathoms. The winze to the east of Engine Shaft below the 352 level had been holed to the 364.[333]

In 1881 the tin ore values remained high at the bottom of the mine. In March they were reporting ore worth £120 a fathom in Engine Shaft below the 352 fathom level, and £70 and £80 a fathom in the winzes sunk under the 352 to the east and west of the shaft. Throughout the levels between the 275 and 338 the values were fairly average, most being between £10 and £40 a fathom. On South Lode work progressed moderately with the 266, 278 and 290 levels giving modest returns, whilst the 242 fathom level had a crosscut being driven toward the lode. New Lode also opened up between the 248 and 295 levels. In May the results from the 364 and 352 levels had moderated somewhat, with ore worth £50 a fathom on 364 and £75 a fathom in the winze under the 352 level. Elsewhere, the values were between £10 and £40 a fathom on Main Lode, and between £10 and £20 on South Lode. New Lode ends were worth between £10 and £20, on the 275 and 290 levels. Crosscuts continued to this lode on the 238 and 248 fathom levels, the former in Stray Park section of the mine. The August results were much better, with the ore in the lode on the 364 station plot of Engine Shaft, worth an incredible £250 a fathom. East and west of Engine Shaft on the 364 level the ends were worth £70 and £80 a fathom, with the winze under the 352 level being worth £75 a fathom. Elsewhere the values were higher than hitherto, with several ends worth £40 a fathom. South lode continued as before and New Lode also continued to progress well. The November 14th report said the ore below the 364 in Engine Shaft was worth £200 a fathom, and ends and winzes between the 338 and the 364 all maintaining good values. On South Lode the ore grades had improved and those on New Lode remained steady, with work on the former on 314 fathom level starting to get respectable results.[334]

Dynamite Patent
In the March 12th 1881 *Mining Journal* it was reported that Dolcoath's management were anticipating the ending of the Dynamite Patent, in about two months time. They believed that the cost would reduce from about 2s a pound to 1s, and that would result in a saving by the mine of about £1,000 a year. In June plans were put in place to install a skip road in Harrietts Shaft, down to the 314 fathom level. Captain Thomas stated that the mine employed constantly between 1,100 and 1,200 workers. In September Dolcoath was described as having the most extensive machinery of any mine in Cornwall. There were 240 steam powered stamps heads, with another 32 about to be added, which were working by November. Also eight water powered stamps heads operated in the valley, making a total of 280 heads. There were also 195 buddles and 537 tin dressing frames. This machinery was constantly being added

to as the tonnage hoisted continued to increase. By the end of the year a new skip road was planned for Old Sump Shaft, which was sorely needed, as the mine was hoisting some 200 tons of ore a day. There were 95 women working in the spalling sheds, together with 150 boys and 120 girls employed on the dressing floors. All of this stamping and dressing plant lay between the account house and the Red River Valley bottom.[335]

In November Captain Thomas reported that some 200 to 300 miners were paid an average of £4 5s a month – and this included the top earners as well as the old, tired and lazy. The following summer a tributer and his son earned £60 in one month, demonstrating that the gap between the average earnings and the fortunate and skilful could at times be very wide indeed.[336]

Captain William Teague's Venturi Ventilator
The December 10th 1881 *Mining Journal* carried a report on the Cornish Mining Institute's presentations of new inventions. Captain William Teague of Tincroft Mine showed his 'new patent ventilating apparatus' which was 'in action in Dolcoath'. The device was called a 'Venturi' ventilator. Its object was to clear dynamite smoke and fumes from the ends. The air supply came through a 6-inch pipe, reduced to a 4-inch and finally down to a 1-inch pipe, with five 'proportionate jets opening outward' to blow away the unwanted air contamination toward the shaft. At the same presentation the new McCullock-Holman rock drill was mentioned, although it had already been demonstrated at an earlier meeting.[337]

The accounts for 1881 showed the profits continued at a good level, until by the summer they began a spectacular rise, due to a significant rise in production and in the price of Dolcoath's black tin. The twelve weeks ending February 12th 1881 had costs of £14,373, Profits of £4,510, a dividend of £1 a share (4,296 shares), 1/15th dues to the Bassets of £1,348, arsenic sales of £60 and tin sales of £20,160 for 372 tons. The average price per ton received by the mine was £54 4s and the overall mine income came to £18,883. £872 was paid in income tax on profits and the 'poor and way rates' came to £400. The three months ending May 7th had costs of £14,733, profits of £4,507, a dividend of £1 a share, dues of £1,372, arsenic sales of £16 and tin sales of £20,566 for 391 tons. Total income was £19,240. F. B. Doering was shown to be owed £90 by the mine, the miners' club figure was £245, doctor's pence was £188, copper ore in stock was £19 and H. Waddington was owed £46. The period ending July 30th had costs of £15,707, profits of £7,242, a dividend of £1 12s 6d, totalling £6,981, dues of £1,637, and black tin sales of £24,560 for 447 tons. The average price per ton paid the mine was £54 19s. Total income was £22,949. Club money was £237 and doctor's pence was £192. Doering was still owed £90. The twelve weeks ending October 22 had costs of £16,150, profits of £8,633, a dividend of £2 a share at £8,592, dues of £1,768, arsenic sales of £66 and tin sales of £26,458 for 450 tons, at an average of £58 16s. Total income was £24,784. Club money was £154 and doctor's pence was £197. The mine still held copper ore in stock and Doering and Waddington had still not been paid. The twelve weeks ending January 14th 1882 had costs of £15,954, profits of £10,840, dividend of £2 10s a share at £10,740, dues of £1,911, tin sales of £28,662 for 438 tons, which sold for an average of £65 9s. Overall income was £26,794. Waddington had been paid but Doering was still owed his £90. Both arsenic and copper were being held in stock and the club and doctor's pence varied little.[338]

During 1882 the mine continued to be deepened. The February 6th mine report showed Engine Shaft sinking below the 364 fathom level, Old Sump Shaft 3 fathoms under the 352, Harrietts Shaft below the 314 and Man Engine Shaft sunk 11 fathoms below the 295 level. By May an end was being driven from Engine Shaft at the 364 level toward New East Shaft, and it was intended to put a raise up by boring machine to meet it. Harrietts Shaft continued to be deepened below the 314 level and Man Engine Shaft was still sinking below the 295 fathom level. Old Sump Shaft, which was sinking under the 352 level, had a new skip road installed, and the manager reported that it 'is working very satisfactorily'. In July Engine Shaft was still being sunk below the 364 level and the raise from the 364, by machine, toward the bottom of Old Sump Shaft, 4 fathoms above, continued. As Harrietts Shaft went deeper below the 314 level, a drive west from it had holed Man Engine Shaft. Preparations were immediately put in hand to lengthen the man engine to the 314 to save 65 fathoms of ladder climbing by the miners. The October 16th report said that problems with water were holding up Old Sump Shaft from sinking, but the raise above the 364 was expected to hole the shaft 'in a day or two'. Engine and Harrietts shafts both continued to be deepened. The man engine was completed to the 314 fathom level by October, and was working well. The end of the year saw Engine and Harrietts shafts still being sunk, below the 364 and 314 levels respectively, and a raise being put up from the 364 level toward the bottom of New East Shaft, which was sunk five fathoms below the 352 level. It was expected to hole by mid-January 1883.[339]

From the beginning of 1882 the ore values soared, with tin in Engine Shaft below the 364 level worth £250 a fathom, for the whole 12 feet width of the shaft. The values east and west of Engine Shaft at the 364 were £50 and £100 respectively, and on the 352 there were values of £80 a fathom sampled. The average tin grades throughout the deeper levels showed improvement on Main Lode, and on South and New lodes the tin continued to be worthwhile mining. The May report had ore in Engine Shaft worth £200 a fathom and values on the 364 and 352 remaining high. The rest of the mine also looked good. In July the grade in Engine Shaft was £220 a fathom, and there were values of £80, £75 and £60 on the 364 and 352 levels. Generally Main Lode was good everywhere, and South Lode improved at the 314 level, with tin worth up to £50 a fathom. New Lode continued to be worthwhile. In October it was reported that the ore in the Engine Shaft was £230 a fathom and everywhere else the ends showed good results. Work on New Lode was suspended as the miners there were reassigned to install the bottom section of the man engine down to the 314 fathom level. By the year's end the management were able to report continuing high values throughout the mine.[340]

Employers' Liability Act

The February 6th accounts contained another piece of potentially complicating news for the mine management. The Committee resolved: "That steps be taken effecting an Insurance of the Labourers in the Mine, under the Employer's Liability Act." How this would affect the way the miners' club and doctor's pence was administered, remained to be seen.[341]

Telephone System Underground

Also in February it was announced that the new skip road in Old Sump Shaft was about to be installed, and that a telephone system was put into the mine, connecting the Account House with levels down to the 250 fathom level. Thomas said that at first 'he was doubtful as to whether it would answer underground', but it was 'found to be a great advantage'. The adventurers were each provided with plans of the workings. These long-sections, which showed the extent of the underground workings, between Old Dolcoath and the Valley Section, were up-dated from the ones issued to adventurers in 1874.[342]

To take the weight off the main engine, in July iron pipes were laid along the 190 fathom level, to carry water from the Valley Section, past Engine Shaft to Harrietts Shaft, to be pumped to surface. In October, after several years of carrying the £90 debt owed to F. B. Doering, Thomas agreed that it should be repaid – and even suggested that as Doering had made such a valuable contribution to Cornwall, a public collection should be made for him. It was also announced that the man engine had been extended 66 fathoms, leaving only 300 feet of ladders to climb from the bottom of the mine.[343]

Another Fatal Accident

On October 9th 1882 there was a serious accident in Engine Shaft. Three trammers who had been working on the 352 fathom level, filling ore, decided to ride up in the skip, as they were tired and late. A shaftsman, called William Mitchell, who lived in Beacon, decided he would join them, but as there was not room for him and the boy working with him, he decided to ride up on the top of the skip. He nonchalantly rested his back on one side of the skip and his feet on the other. Unfortunately, as it was night, the engine driver stopped the skip 20 feet short of the surface, thinking there might not be a lander there. Mitchell, fearing detection for his illegal mode of travelling, attempted to jump from the top of the skip to the ladderway, and missed.

265

The other miners heard a 'strange sound' but did not know of Mitchell's intention, and thought nothing of it. His smashed body was found by Captain James Rodda below the 40 fathom level. Tragically, the man engine was working at the time, and the men could have used it, but preferred to use the skip, which was nearby.[344]

The *Mining Journal* of December 30th 1882 carried a letter from F. B. Doering, attacking Mr Loam, the engineer, who worked both for Dolcoath and for the Barrow Rock Drill Company. Doering claimed that Loam had miss-represented him and his machines, accused him of failing to understand how his machines worked, and denied that a conversation between the two men, as reported by Loam, had ever taken place. Doering pointed out that the first six machines supplied to Dolcoath were 'automatic and hand motion', both in turning and advancing the drill. His second batch of six drills were non-automatic.[345]

The mine accounts for 1882 showed continuing high profits. The twelve weeks ending April 8th 1882 had costs of £16,756, profits of £8,842, a dividend paid of £2 a share, at £8,592, dues to the Bassets of £1,827, and tin sales of £27,401 for 437 tons at an average to the mine of £62 14s a ton. There was £19 worth of copper ore and £10 worth of arsenic in stock, with the club account showing £467 and the doctor's pence standing at £216. Total income was £25,598. The three months ending July 24th had costs of £16,912, profits of £7,038, a dividend of £1 12s 6d a share, making £6,981, dues of 1/15th paid of £1,709, arsenic sales of £16 and tin sales of £25,615 for 441 tons. Dolcoath received an average of £58 2s a ton for its black tin. Doering was still owed £90 and there were small amounts of copper and arsenic in stock. The club stood at £461 and the doctor's pence was £220. Overall income came to £23,950. The twelve weeks ending October 16th had costs of £17,824, profit of £8,795, paid dues of £1,897, and sold £28,457 worth of tin (460 tons). The average price paid to Dolcoath for its tin was £61 17s a ton. There was a total income of £26,618. No dividend was paid. The accounts for the twelve weeks ending January 8th 1883 had costs of £17,530, profit of £6,451, a dividend of £1 10s a share, totalling £6,444, lord's dues of £1,708, and tin sales of £25,618 for 451 tons, which sold for an average of £56 16s a ton. Total income was £23,981. At long last, after some ten years, F. B. Doering was paid the £90 the mine owed him.[346]

The January 8th 1883 Mine Report was signed by captains Josiah Thomas, James Johns and Joseph Chynoweth, Captain James Rodda having disappeared without comment from the reports. By September he had been replaced by captains John E. Williams and Edwin Prideaux – although to start with the reports called him Edward Prideaux![347]

1883 saw Captain Thomas continue to open up new ground at an impressive speed, using boring machines whenever possible. Engine Shaft was down 13 fathoms below the 364 fathom level by September and by the end of the year the 375 level had been reached and some 14 fathoms of lode drive driven on it. By April New East Shaft was holed to the 364 level and two winzes had been sunk to that level from a drive on the east side of New East Shaft. Levels were being hastily driven from these winzes to the shaft to open up the ground for stoping, and by September both had holed New East Shaft. The December 10th Mine Report said New East Shaft was being sunk under the 364 level. Harrietts Shaft was being sunk under the 314 fathom level, and by September it was 12 fathoms under the level, reaching the 326 level by December. Winzes were being sunk to the east and west of Engine Shaft under the 364 level, although there was a problem with water in them. South Lode continued to be opened by winzes and crosscuts at the 302, 290, 278, 266 and 242 fathom levels.[348]

The ore grades continued to be high in 1883, with the lode in Engine Shaft below the 364 worth between £240 and £260 a fathom. The values remained high in most of the ends and winzes between the 375 and 352 level, with the rest of the mine continuing to be well worth stoping. South Lode also remained steady, with values between £10 and £35 a fathom, between the 242 and 314 fathom levels. In August it was reported that the average produce from the bottom of the mine was about 2½ percent tin, and that in Engine Shaft the ore was up to 15 percent tin.[349]

A New Lease with Crippling Demands
The 1883 mine accounts show a number of problems which the management had to face and cope with. Gustavus Lambert Basset's steward, Mr Marriott, had demanded £40,000 of Dolcoath, to renew its lease. The *Mining Journal* of February 17th 1883 was scathing about the demand, and in uncharacteristic language, one of its contributors was almost insulting to the Bassets. "The whole attention of the mining interests has this week been concentrated on Dolcoath. Nothing else has been thought of or talked of in mining circles, and with good reason. ... What was at first a mere rumour became a substantial certainty, it was seen that much more depended upon the issues at stake between the Dolcoath adventurers and Mr Basset than the fortunes of Dolcoath itself. Already confidence has been hopelessly destroyed, and a good feeling which it had taken centuries to foster replaced by bitterness. A system which had been regarded as essential a part of the mining system of Cornwall and the Cost-book itself has been assailed from the least likely quarter, and a custom which had almost the force of law abrogated by the will of one mineral lord ... We regard the action taken on behalf of Mr Basset as wholly indefensible from every point of view." In just one week the value of the mine lost three times the amount of Basset's demand. The *Journal* asserted that nobody would ever risk dealing with the Tehidy Estate again, and further said that the demand was not merely unjust, but an evidence of an 'evil system' which benefited the mineral lord at the expense of all others. The Bassets had made between £8,000 and £9,000 every year for decades and suggested

that they were just plain greedy. Marriott was demanding that Dolcoath pay £40,000 for the privilege of giving Basset another £9,000 a year. Marriott's claim that Basset was a 'characteristic liberal' fell on deaf ears, and the mine appointed a committee to negotiate, for not only was Marriott demanding a renewal fine of £40,000, but also the mine was told it had to sink a new, vertical shaft at an estimated cost of another £40,000, and all for a 21 year lease.[350]

Unsurprisingly, this caused panic among the adventurers, and there was a general feeling of gloom in Camborne. However, negotiations brought the figure down to £25,000, which was to be paid in two installments. The demand for a new, vertical shaft was also dropped and the offered lease period was increased by four years to 25 years. The report on the September 17th 1883 meeting of the adventurers, under the chairmanship of William Rabling, contained the following. "The Committee having recommended that no dividend be declared to-day, but that the balance be placed towards the payment of £25,000 to Mr Basset for the new lease, and also, Messrs. John Champion and F. W. Thomas be appointed Clerks of the Mine, and Mr Henry Michell, Auditor." The December 10th report added, that George Williams, William Rabling and Josiah Thomas have 'consented to become Grantees of the New Sett of the Mine'. The success of Dolcoath, despite giving G. L. Basset enormous returns as mineral lord, now had to provide him with a massive bonus of £25,000 to renew the mine lease. The above demand led many to agree with the above article in the *Mining Journal,* and view Basset as a typical greedy landlord, who was willing to grab all he could at whatever cost to others. Many still maintain this view. But, it must be remembered that the Tehidy Estate was a business, and the ore underground was owned by that business. The duty of Basset's stewards was to maximise profit from that mineral commodity.[351]

A Miner's Opinion of Gustavus Lambert Basset
Another and quite widespread, contemporary opinion of Gustavus Basset is shown by the words of Thomas Oliver, a Dolcoath miner of many years standing, who had worked in some of the hardest mining fields of Australia. After describing the hardships endured by mining families with barely enough to money to eat, never mind pay for coal, clothing and schooling for the children, he added: "G. L. Basset, Esq., had not long come to Tehidy, and did not know anything about these hardships until a few miners from Camborne, Illogan, and Redruth formed a committee and interviewed Mr Basset and laid the matter before him, he could scarcely believe it possible for the miners to live on so small earnings. I was appointed to get up a paper and read it to Mr Basset. For this purpose we canvassed the families of the miners to ascertain the average number, which was about five. Then we canvassed the mines to ascertain the average pay, which amounted to about £3 10s. per month. To sum up there was only about three farthings per meal per head for food. Mr Basset said, 'I will use my influence to get this terrible hardship abolished,' which he did. The

committee thought we ought to present Mr Basset with a little testimonial for his kindness, and we collected from the miners in the three parishes named, about £70, but Mr Basset said 'give it to the Miners' Hospital at Redruth,' which we did. Then fortnightly pay was established by Act of Parliament, and this has been a great boon, not only to the men, but also to the agents."[352]

The Mayne Scandal

Unfortunately, the £25,000 lease renewing fine was only one of the shocks for the adventurers in 1883. In that year also a massive fraud was discovered, in which one of Dolcoath's clerks, John Mayne, had forged and sold 203 'shares' in the mine, and pocketed the money. The accounts for December 10th 1883 briefly states: "To Dividend Account overdrawn – Mayne frauds = £173 2s 6d." But, this was only a small part of the loot, for it was estimated that he had robbed the mine of at least £10,000 by his frauds. This news was potentially worse for the mine than the massive cost of the new lease, for it attacked the morale of the management, the adventurers, the miners and the whole town of Camborne. Mayne was a cousin of Josiah Thomas, and a member of that close-knit family which virtually ruled Camborne mining. Even now, over 120 years later, the story causes embarrassment and anger locally. Distant relatives still find it difficult to speak about it. In that close, largely Methodist community, where everyone in the town had a relative or other connection to the great mine, people just could not believe that one of their own could do such a thing. The seven years hard labour Mayne was given, hardly seemed to be sufficient to assuage the anger and confusion his fraud caused.[353]

When it was revealed that Mayne had been stealing from the mine for at least five years, and that he had been virtually 'forgiven' by his cousin, the manager, there was even more anger. The confidence of the adventurers appears to have been totally shaken in the whole management team, and at the August adventurers meeting, the adventurer's anger and outrage over Captain Josiah Thomas' handling of the matter boiled over. He was taunted that the man was his cousin, and that he was noted for appointing relatives to positions at the mine. We trusted you and you had 'implicit confidence in Mayne', they said, so how can we trust any of you? How can you manage Dolcoath, the biggest mine in Cornwall, and still be paid to manage other mines, including Cooks Kitchen, South Wheal Crofty, New Cooks Kitchen, West Frances, West Shepherds and West Seton? Thomas replied that he could not help Mayne's fraud, and he did not routinely appoint relatives to positions of responsibility at the mine. This situation got worse, and by the next adventurers' meeting, in September, a whole gang of adventurers were prepared to join in a general criticism of all aspects of the mine management. Some, like Mr Rule, were the usual suspects, but others also were involved. Rule wanted to comment on the fact that the Committee members were all in-adventurers, they all supplied materials to the mine, and had an interest which compromised them. A figure of £4,000 was mentioned, but Thomas denied this. Rule then asserted that Messrs Williams were paid £3,821 for materials, but Thomas retorted that that was for three months. Rule then said that Mr Rabling supplied £467 worth of gear to the mine, and the argument went on. The attack then switched to Captain Pearce, who was a principal ore dresser at the mine, and he was accused of owning tin streams, which profited from Dolcoath tin tailings, which went down the Red River. This followed a complaint the previous month about the quantity of black tin that Dolcoath lost down the river, when it was asserted that £43,000 worth was lost there. Thomas had reasonably pointed out that that figure included the tailings from eleven mines, not just Dolcoath. He defended Pearce, and said his streams were three miles downstream and could hardly have gained much. Then Captain Pearce's son joined in, pointing out that his father had been a servant of the mine for over 50 years, and for 40 of those years he had been an agent. He was outraged at the attack on his father, and the meeting was eventually called to a halt by the chairman declaring it closed. Another meeting, reported in the December 15th *Mining Journal*, witnessed a row over the amount the mine was charged by Henry Rogers for the prosecution of John Mayne – £1,178 6s 5d. It is apparent that the lease renewal demand and the Mayne frauds had seriously undermined the confidence of several of the adventurers, who a short time before were full of hope as they regularly received their generous dividends.[354]

In August the Committee appointed to sort the financial problems out went to Chyandour, Penzance, to talk to Mr T. S. Bolitho about the fraud, the entry fine, and the other problems facing Dolcoath. It was agreed that the final figure for the forged shares was 203. The number of shares was increased from 4,296 to 4,499, and it was agreed to sell another 201 shares to bring the total up to 4,700. The proceeds were to go toward the £25,000 owed to Basset. It was recommended, despite the misgivings of some of the adventurers, that Josiah Thomas be appointed purser as well as manager, and that in future, all cheques and share certificates be signed by both the purser and a clerk. They also agreed to allow the chief clerk, Mr W. Reynolds, who had not been well for some time, to work part-time for a reduced salary. He had worked at Dolcoath for 40 years, and Thomas said they could not 'just turn him adrift'. It was later agreed to pay him £3 3s a month for part-time. It was also decided to reduce the pension of Captain Provis, who had retired several years before, from 5 guineas to 2½ guineas a month. The Committee was clearly feeling a bit mean with all the financial problems which beset them.[355]

Massive Collapse Underground
Alarm and scandal on the financial front were not the only major cause for concern at the mine, for in August there was a near disastrous collapse deep underground. The accounts for the period ending August 25th 1883 carried this brief comment: "In consequence of an accident we have not drawn any stuff from any of our principal shafts during the past three weeks. But for this we should have sold about 30 tons of

tin more." Back in 1865 there had been a dangerous fall of ground at the 242 fathom level, east of Engine Shaft. It had already been noted that there was risk there, but timely support work had minimised the affect on the mine. This later collapse of August 1883 was potentially far more serious, as it involved a piece of granite 180 feet long by 144 feet high and weighing many thousands of tons. After the ground was supported by a combination of timber stulls and iron pumps, set close together, it was inspected by Mr Frecheville, the Mines Inspector, and Captain Hosking, the Tehidy mineral agent. Frecheville's report, as carried by the *Mining Journal*, painted a frightening picture. Under the heading: 'The Dangerous Method of Mining in Cornwall', Frecheville details the position where the collapse occurred. He said the mine at the time was 375 fathoms below adit, which made it over 400 fathoms deep. The richest and widest part of the workings, on Main Lode, lay between Engine Shaft and New East Shaft, some 43 fathoms apart. The lode between the 290 and 364 fathom levels varied between 18 feet and 42 feet wide, and was underlying at an angle of sixty degrees from the horizontal. Almost all of this lode had been removed, and the hanging wall left with the minimum of timber and pillar support. At the 364 level South Lode joined Main Lode's hanging wall, and this also had been stoped out opposite the massive Main Lode gunnis. South Lode was far steeper than Main Lode, and so between these two shafts and the 290 and 346 fathom levels, an enormous 'horse of granite', forming the hanging wall of Main Lode, was left virtually unsupported and 'hanging'. Frecheville commented that the 'liability of the ground to fall (was) being largely increased'. He referred to 'huge empty spaces or gunnisses with very little timber' being left by the stoping on Main Lode. His description of the collapse was graphic: "On the night of August 24th 1883, a portion of this horse, constituting the hanging-wall of the main lode, and extending from just below the 290 fathom level to the 314 fathom level, with a length of about 30 fathoms came away, thousands of tons of rock falling into the open spaces or gunnisses, smashing the timber, carrying roadways and everything before them to the bottom of the mine." He commented that it was fortunate that the following day was a pay day, and no miners were in the affected area, and so nobody was killed or injured by the collapse. Once the safety work was complete Frecheville and Hosking could inspect it, and although they appeared satisfied with the support work, Frecheville remained of the opinion that such wide workings could never be adequately made safe. He also commented on the speed that timber rotted out at Dolcoath, due to the damp and hot conditions there underground.[356]

The mine accounts for 1883 show a difficult year, due partly to the above problems. The twelve weeks ending April 15th 1883 had costs of £17,955, profits of £5,096, a dividend of £1 a share, totalling £4,296, Basset's 1/15th dues of £1,642, and black tin sales of £24,624 for 442 tons, which sold for an average of £55 14s a ton. Overall income was £23,051. The club account showed £633 and the doctor's pence was given as £233. A small amount of arsenic and copper was held in stock. The next accounts report was for 24 weeks, possibly due to the problems raised by the lease negotiations and the Mayne fraud. The period ended August 25th. Costs were given as £35,062, profits of £8,240, Bassets dues of £3,084, and tin sold of £46,255 for 842 tons, which sold at an average of £54 18s 6d a ton. Total income was £43,392. The accounts also mention the £25,000 lease renewal payment to Basset and the sale of 201 shares for £13,435. The lease payment meant no dividend was paid. The miner's club was given as £483 and doctor's pence as £354. A small quantity of arsenic and copper ore was in stock. The twelve weeks ending November 17th had costs of £18,786, profits of £3,006, dues of £1,552, and tin sales of £23,276 for 445 tons, which sold for an average of £52 6s. Total income was £21,792. The club was given as £384 and doctor's pence as £362. Once again there remained a small amount of arsenic and copper ore in store. In December it was reported that a new boiler, two new drilling machines and the new skip road in Eastern Shaft had cost £500.[357]

The argument at the adventurers meeting in April 1880, about Captain Thomas only selling the mine's black tin to two favoured smelters, appears to have had an effect, for from the end of 1883 to the autumn of 1884, Dolcoath tin was sold to no less than nine different smelting houses. Comparison of the dozens of parcels sold to those smelters, suggests that there was little difference in the price Dolcoath received from them. But, it does seem that much of the mine's tin was being sold on the 'open market', and theoretically, for the best price available, as per their lease agreement. Between December 13th 1883 and August 16th 1884 the tin sales figures are interesting. Williams, Harvey & Co. purchased 55 parcels of tin, at an average of 21¼ tons, and totalling over 1,166 tons. Redruth Smelting Co. bought 12 parcels averaging 13 tons, and totalling 151 tons. The other seven smelters bought 28 parcels with a total tonnage of about 388 tons. Although Dolcoath was clearly opening the door to the principle of 'free trade' it was clear that they were still selling to their preferred customers. The highest figure in that period was £49 15s and the lowest was £47 7s 6d, and no smelter paid more than any other.[358]

This new arrangement did not seem to benefit Dolcoath, however, for the price received for its black tin was less as a result. Captain Thomas, as reported in the *Mining Journal* of March 8th 1884, thought that "doing away with the much-attacked 'smelter's monopoly' in Dolcoath produce and taking the tin to the open market 12s 6d a ton less is realised, and he does not think a return to the old arrangement possible." The *Journal* editor agreed, and said Dolcoath lost out over the new system. Another former cause for concern was referred to in the same Journal, when it was mentioned that the supply of Straits tin was diminishing, hopefully improving the price.[359]

In March 1884 the shaft sinkers were preparing to sink Engine Shaft below the 375 fathom level. By May they were 9 feet down and by November they were 9½ fathoms under the 375 level. The managers reported that they were then sinking on the south part of Main Lode, as the north part was very hard. It meant that they sank Engine Shaft more than twice as fast as hitherto. Early in the year sinking began under the 364 level in Old Sump Shaft and by August it was 7 fathoms below the level. New East Shaft was also being sunk, and by May it was 9½ fathoms below the 364 level. In May preparations were in hand to begin sinking Harrietts Shaft below the 326 fathom level, and three months later it was down 2 fathoms. In August Man Engine Shaft was sunk 7 fathoms under the 314 level. Eastern Shaft, that had been called Water Whim Shaft earlier in the century, and is now known as Valley Shaft, went down to the 145 fathom level. The task of cutting the old, narrow shaft down and enlarging it from surface, so that it would take two skip roads, took over two years to complete. Started in early 1884, it was not complete until early 1886. The shaft was eventually to be sunk to the 510 fathom level, and became the principal hoisting shaft for the eastern end of the mine. It should be mentioned that as these shafts were being sunk ever deeper, winzes were also being put down to open up the ground, so that almost as soon as the shafts reached the next level drives connected them to winzes which were sunk at the same time. Thus, stoping ground was being opened up at the deeper levels right behind the main developers.[360]

In March the values remained high at the 375 level, with the drives east and west of Engine Shaft both being worth £80 a fathom, and the shaft itself worth £85. The 364, 352, 326, 314 and 295 levels all showed good results on both parts of Main Lode. South Lode on all levels between the 242 and 302 fathom levels also was valuable. In May, with Engine Shaft 9 feet below the 375 level, values of £200 a fathom were sampled. The ends and winzes continued to look good, and a winze under the 364 level, east of New East Shaft was worth £90 a fathom. The August report gave the value in Engine Shaft as £200 a fathom and parallel winze under the 375 gave values of £120 a fathom. Another winze under the 364 level east of New East Shaft was worth £90 a fathom, and a second winze close by was worth £75. Everything in both parts of Main Lode looked good, and South Lode was also worth working. The end of the year saw the high grades continue, although Engine Shaft, having switched to the softer, south part of Main Lode, showed more modest values than it had.[361]

A Serious Accident with Miraculous Escapes

In February 1884 there was a very serious accident which could have been disastrous. A pare of miners was descending the ladderway to work the nightshift on the 375 fathom level, in Engine Shaft, when the ladder gave way. They had reached the 326 level on a ladderway between Harrietts and Old Sump shafts, when the ladder, with eight miners on it, gave way. John Richards, aged 60, of St Ives, had his left leg broken in two places and sustained bruising to his foot. William Pope, of Camborne, had both his thighs smashed and had serious head injuries. John Spargo, of Illogan Highway, suffered serious leg injuries. Edward Angove, of Camborne, fell almost the whole distance of 12 fathoms between the 326 and 338 levels, and escaped with minor injuries. Frederick Chinn fell all the way to the 338 fathom level, and apart from being sore and shaken, was not injured at all. Three other miners on the ladder were uninjured. It was an amazing escape for all these miners, although the seriously injured among them might not have thought so.[362]

Tin in Dakota

In August Captain Thomas informed the adventurers that in 1876 he and the mine engineer, Matthew Loam, had travelled to the North of England to inspect boring machines, and that he had, out of his own pocket, hired an agent in that connection. It had cost him between £50 and £60, for which he had never been reimbursed. In November it was reported that the house of the main pumping engine was 70 years old, and the front wall was in a poor state. It had been repaired with iron plates and some granite blocks measuring between 5 feet and 6 feet square. It was further stated that Harrietts engine, which had been 'getting poor', was being replaced with a larger, new engine, which was essential for the increased development and output. A report of tin discovered in Dakota was dismissed as not something to worry about. Earlier claims had been found to be without substance, and so the message was 'Don't panic!' Apparently, there was some alluvial tin discovered in the Black Hills, but some of the ore sampled turned out to have been 'tantalite' (a mineral containing rare earth elements), and not cassiterite. The report added that there was no railway in Dakota, and so even if cassiterite was found there, it would be some time before it could be properly exploited.[363]

The accounts for 1884 showed an improvement in the mine's position. The twelve weeks ending February 9th had costs of £19,437, profit of £5,057, a dividend of 10s a share, giving £2,350, 1/15th dues to G. L. Basset of £1,744, and tin sales of £26,155 for 537 tons, which sold at an average of £48 14s a ton. The accounts showed the mine received £237 13s 2d from the fraudster J. Mayne, and the Committee was disconcerted by a rate assessment from Redruth Union which included the £25,000 paid to Basset for renewing the lease. They resolved to explain what the figure was for, and F. S. Bolitho was to negotiate on their behalf. The club stood at £325 and doctor's pence at £249. Total income was £24,494. The three months ending May 3rd had costs of £18,854, profit of £7,580, a dividend of 10s a share at £2,350, dues of £1,882, and tin sales of £28,227 for 577 tons, which sold for an average of £48 19s 6d. The miners club was £483 and doctor's pence was £259. Total income was £26,434. The twelve weeks ending July 29th had costs of £18,703, profit of £7,699, a dividend of £1 10s a share for 4,700 shares, at £7,050 dues of £1,879, and tin sold was £28,191 for 593 tons at an average of £47 10s 6d a ton. The club was £460 and doctor's pence £256. Total income was £26,401. The period ending October 18th 1884 had costs of £18,828, profit of £5,013, a dividend of £1 10s a share making £7,050, dues paid of £1,697, and tin sales of £25,450 for 572 tons which sold for an average of £44 10s. The miners club stood at £375 and doctor's pence at £257. Total income was £23,842. It was agreed in August to increase Captain Thomas' salary to £500 per annum, and the salaries of captains Chynoweth and Johns by one guinea a month. The twelve weeks ending January 9th 1885 had costs of £18,526, profit of £3,666, a dividend of £1 1s a share, totalling £4,935, 1/15th dues of £1,579, tin sales of £23,690 for 553 tons which sold for an average of £42 16s 6d. The club was £295 and doctor's pence £264. Overall income was £22,192. Throughout the year a small amount of arsenic was kept in stock, worth less than £10.[364]

At the beginning of 1885 Engine Shaft was 11 fathoms below the 375 fathom level, and by the end of the year it was at the 388 level. Down the increasingly flat lode on which the shaft was sunk, the shaft had been deepened 15 fathoms, but allowing for the actual depth the management decided to call the level the 388. Harrietts Shaft was 7½ fathoms below the 326 level in February, and by October it was sunk 13½ fathoms to the 338 fathom level. From Harrietts a drive on the 326 level was beneath Man Engine Shaft, and expected to hole it shortly. Winzes were sinking below the 375 level throughout the year and by the end of the year they were almost deep enough to connect to the drives heading for them at the 388 level. By the end of the year New East Shaft was also being sunk and by January 1886 it was 3½ fathoms below the 375 fathom level. Some of the winzes being sunk were experiencing difficulties with excess water, and the captains believed that in some they would have to put pitwork to solve the problem. The July report says "we have been obliged to fix pitwork in both these winds on account of the large quantity of water, and can now proceed without interruption."[365]

In February 1885, the tin values in Engine Shaft were more modest than they had been, because the south part of Main Lode they were sinking on remained poorer in tin content. Ore grades remained good on and below the 375 level, with ore worth £45, £50, £80 and £90 a fathom. The rest of the ends and winzes on Main Lode remained much as before, but on the 295 east of Harrietts Shaft the values were improved at £40 and £50 a fathom. South Lode ore was worth between £8 and £12 a fathom. Throughout the year the values were maintained, although by the end of the year the captains were again commenting on the amazing width of Main Lode. "At the Engine Shaft we have opened on the lode at the 388 fathoms level for 18 feet in width, but have met with no granite on either side, so that the size of the lode is not yet known." As the report gives the tin ore as worth £100 a fathom – a cubic fathom – we can only guess at the true value of the lode in the deepest part of the mine.[366]

Stray Park Mine for Sale
On February 7th 1885 the *Mining Journal* reported that Captain Thomas commented on the loss of revenue for the mine, of about £1,000, due to the tin price being £2 less than in the previous quarter. The low price caused him to adopt a policy

of concentrating on development rather than production, so that when the price improved the ground opened up could be quickly exploited. The 375 level was being rapidly opened up, and some 130 fathoms had been driven on it. Output had been affected by the need to cut down New East Shaft for pitwork to the 375. Hoisting from New East was reduced to a half-a-week for the fortnight of the Christmas period. Thomas' attention was being drawn to the eastern end of the mine, close to the Great Crosscourse, where the ore tended to be richer. He believed that the valley Section, not exploited below the 145 fathom level, held a large tonnage of good ore. He also believed that the crosscourse heaved the Main Lode some 70 fathoms to the right and was unaware of any connections below Adit Level into Cooks Kitchen Mine. At the western end of the mine Stray Park was still for sale, and some interest had been shown by an entrepreneur from Plymouth, called Elliot J. Squares. He had purchased Long Close section of South Wheal Crofty in the 1860s, which he renamed Wheal Crofty. Three months later the possibility of Squares buying the sett was again raised, and this time it was connected to 'Wheal Camborne', which was described as being 'west of Dolcoath', and may have been Camborne Consols Mine.[367]

In February there was some discussion about the cost of explosives. Dynamite had gone up from £66 a ton to £120, and this caused the management concern. Thomas wanted to persuade the miners to use Tonite, which he thought was often as effective as dynamite, and only cost £100 a ton. He also reckoned that the 'compressed powder' sold by the Kennal Vale Co., which cost £50 a ton, was perfectly effective in ordinary ground.[368]

In May it was announced that Eastern (Valley) Shaft was cut down to the 140 level for a skip road and ladderway. Thomas anticipated using the shaft to open up some 200 fathoms depth of unworked ground below the 145 fathom level in the Valley Section. During the May adventurers' meeting there was lively discussion (and argument) on two sore subjects. Complaints continued about the high bank charges Dolcoath continued to pay, with several adventurers raising their voices in concern. Mines like East Pool, it was pointed out, were better run and paid no such charges. Thomas batted away the protests, although they were to continue and become more strident. In July Thomas defended the mine's practice again, stating that Dolcoath was better off as a cost book company than as a limited liability company, with respect to bank charges.[369]

The Miners' Hospital
A topic which exercised several adventurers concerned the payments Dolcoath made to Redruth Miners' Hospital. The South Devon & East Cornwall Hospital was given £10 10s a year, whereas the Royal Cornwall Infirmary, at Truro, had its contribution reduced from 10 guineas to £5 5s a year. Thomas and others felt the facilities at

the Devon Hospital were better than at Truro, and three Dolcoath miners had been taken there and received better treatment than at Truro: it was 'more modern' than the Royal Cornwall. Some adventurers thought this attitude damaged the Royal Cornwall Infirmary. It was agreed that complaints about inadequate treatment should be looked into further, and Captain Thomas would be invited to give evidence. This was a subject which was not to go away.[370]

The count house dinners had been suspended for some time, due to the large number of adventurers and hangers on who had turned up to eat and drink at the mine's expense. In May 1885 it was decided to resume the custom, but to restrict attendance to ticket holders. Adventurers could obtain these tickets. One example of 'taking advantage' was described in the *Mining Journal,* where an adventurer with a single share had turned up for dinner with his wife and two friends.[371]

In October it was reported that the mine had three pumping engines at work, and Harrietts new 60-inch was working well. Dolcoath had a new air compressor, had rearranged all the mine's pitwork, replacing old rods and strapping plates, and the work to install skip road and ladderway in Eastern (Valley) Shaft was going well. The shaft was being sunk by nine miners. The 375 fathom level had been driven for a distance of 160 fathoms and Main Lode varied from between 18 feet and 24 feet in width on the level.[372]

The accounts for 1885 again show the strength of the mine's financial position. The twelve weeks ending April 4th had costs of £18,502, profits of £4,914, a dividend of 16s a share totalling £3,760, 1/15th dues paid to the Bassets of £1,666, and black tin sales of £24,997 for 557 tons, which sold for an average £44 16s 6d. The miners club was £461 and doctor's pence was £266. The Committee resolved to pay 10 guineas to the South Devon & East Cornwall Hospital, annually. Total income was £23,416. The twelve weeks ending June 27th had costs of £18,735, profit of £8,615, a dividend of 21s totalling £4,935, dues of £1,947, and tin sales of £29,210 for 571 tons, which sold for an average of £51 5s a ton. The club was £450 and doctor's pence £266. Total income came to £27,350. The three months ending September 19th had costs of £18,851, profit of £9,486, a dividend of 30s totalling £7,050, dues of £2,017, and black tin sales of £30,261 for 594 tons, which sold for an average of £50 19s a ton. Miners club was £393 and doctor's pence was £262. Overall income was £28,337. The twelve weeks ending December 12th had costs of £18,742, profit of £8,702, a dividend of 30s a share totalling £7,050, dues paid the Bassets of £1,952, and tin sales of £29,236 for 562 tons, which sold for an average of £52 a ton. The club was £353 and doctor's pence was £258. Total income for the three months was £27,444.[373]

By the end of March 1886, drives on the 388 fathom level had opened up good tin ground and although the extent of the Main Lode had not yet been reached it was at least 18 feet wide. Thomas hoped to resume sinking Engine Shaft 'in the course of a few days'. Old Sump Shaft was sunk two fathoms below the 375 level, New East Shaft was 7½ fathoms below the 375 and a winze was sunk 8 fathoms below the level. At the 375, a crosscut was driven from New East Shaft to intersect the south part of Main Lode, which was found to be 24 feet wide. Exploration by winze continued to open up good ore at the bottom of the mine. On South Lode drives from crosscuts on the 238 (at Stray Park), 242, 290 and 302 fathom levels were all opening up potentially valuable ground. The June 21st report announced that Engine Shaft was 3½ fathoms below the 388 level, on the south part of Main Lode and Old Sump Shaft was sunk 5 fathoms below the 375 level. New East Shaft was 10 fathoms below the 375 and east of the shaft the winze was also making good progress. To cope with increased water there, a small pump was installed in the shaft, powered by the main pump, using flat rods from Engine Shaft. A crosscut west of Harrietts Shaft was being driven south to pick up a lode although a winze near Harrietts, below the 325 level, was suspended due to excess water. By June the 375 level crosscut had reached South Lode and good values encountered. Other development ends on South Lode and in Stray Park continued to show hopeful results. Thomas reported that a contract had been awarded to Mr R. H. Harris, to sink Eastern (Valley) Shaft from the 145 to the 254 fathom levels, at £25 15s a fathom. Harris was also to drive the levels to that depth at £15 per fathom. The contractor was to supply all his own gear, including compressor and boring machines. It was hoped to be on 254 fathom level within 18 months. Thomas believed that Eastern Shaft was on Dunkins Lode of Cooks Kitchen. Harris' boring machines had already proved successful in West Frances and New Cooks Kitchen mines, and it was thought they might also be used to open up South Lode more quickly.[374]

Compressed Air Problems
The September manager's report to the adventurers highlighted the worsening problems of air pressure for the growing number of rock drills underground. At the 375 fathom level an end west of Old Sump was suspended due to insufficient air pressure and there was a need for new and more efficient compressors. Meanwhile, Engine Shaft was sunk 5 fathoms below the 388 level with a new lift for the pump installed, and New East Shaft had reached the 388 level. Harris' men had sunk Eastern Shaft to the 155 level, using his own compressor and drills, and the 170 level had been driven beneath the shaft so that a raise could be put up by boring machine to meet the sinking shaft. On South Lode winzes and crosscuts continued to open up tin ground for stoping. By early December Thomas could report that Engine Shaft was still sinking and that both New East and Old Sump shafts were holed to the 388 fathom level. South Lode was opening up well on the 375 level, and not only was the grade good but the lode was also very wide. Eastern Shaft had

reached the 170 level and was already sunk 9 feet below it. The 190 level was driven by boring machine to within 10 fathoms of the shaft position and the 210 fathom level would shortly be started to make a connection when Eastern Shaft was sunk to that level.[375]

At the beginning of 1886 the tin values at the bottom of the mine remained high, with values of between £50 and £280 a fathom. This latter value was at the 375 level east of New East Shaft, where the lode was 24 feet wide. Throughout the higher levels the ends were worth between £10 and £20 and on South Lode between £15 and £20. In June the grades on the lower levels remained good, with the lode in Engine Shaft below the 388 fathom level worth £60, and other ends and winzes worth between £60 and £160 a fathom. Elsewhere on Main Lode the ore was worth between £15 and £20 a fathom, and on South Lode the ends were worth between £10 and £75, with the higher grades being on the 375 level. The September report shows that 5 fathoms below the 388 level the tin in the shaft was worth £90 a fathom. Most of the ends on the 375 and 388 levels were worth between £45 and £90 a fathom. Elsewhere on Main Lode the values varied and on South Lode the ore was worth between £15 and £75 a fathom. Thomas's December report again showed good values on the 375 and 388 fathom level, of between £40 and £100 a fathom, with the ore in Engine Shaft below the 388 level worth £60 a fathom. Once again the ends on Main Lode at the shallower levels had more modest values. On South Lode the 375 level continued to produce good results.[376]

The Man Engine to be Extended to the 375 fathom level
Early in 1886, it was announced that the Man Engine was to be extended from the 314 to the 375 fathom level. At the same time a new dry was to be built, the current one, which was over forty years old, was in a 'miserable condition'. The new one, as the old one had been in its day, was to be 'the finest in the county'. It would cost an estimated £500. At the adventurers' meeting of January 1886 there was considerable discussion about waste from Dolcoath's tin mill. Mr R. J. Frecheville, the Mines Inspector, had read a paper on the unacceptable waste from Cornish tin mills, and one of the adventurers, Samuel Lanyon of Manchester, said he was 'astonished at the waste asserted to be the case'. Frecheville had said that 11 percent of stamped tin was wasted, but Captain Thomas replied that the Mines Inspector had actually thought this figure 'extremely good', and that anyway this waste was from 16 or 18 mines, not just Dolcoath. Thomas then added that the answer to improved efficiency was more machinery, and said the mine should buy 'shaking tables', a Hungarian invention by a Mr Richter. These had been tried in Japan for dressing gold and had worked well. On the subject of the Red River streamers, who were believed to be 'making a fortune', Thomas said this was not the case. Alfred Lanyon of Redruth, said he was an adventurer and also had interests in Red River tin streams, and was amazed that people thought the streamers were making a fortune. He said over

£100,000 had been spent on machinery in the valley, and he had never gained a penny from his stream. He added that as a tin smelter, he did not make the profits some adventurers thought.[377]

A Fatal Accident & a Family Tragedy
In late April there was a fatal accident at Dolcoath, which was particularly tragic for the family. A young miner, called Walter, was killed by a rock fall. Nearly eighteen years previously, his three young brothers had been killed by an explosion of gunpowder, with which they had been playing.[378]

The need for more efficient and powerful air compressors was becoming acute, and in June Thomas expressed concern over the position, asserting that particularly at the centre of the mine, there was need for far more power. He had ordered a powerful new compressor, which should be with them inside three months, and would work 8 to 10 machines. R. H. Harris placed an advertisement in the October 9th 1886 *Mining Journal,* for his new compressor. He said it was a 12-inch air compressor, lately put to work sinking a new shaft at Dolcoath, and that he had six working in the district and there would soon be another, but much larger, at Dolcoath. This compressor would supply several rock drills with enough air to work efficiently.[379]

In December Thomas reported that with so much activity being centred on Eastern Shaft on the eastern side of the valley, the mine would soon need new stamps there. He also said that the new Harris compressor was on its way, with most of the parts already at Camborne railway station. The new compressor house was built and all it needed was its roof.[380]

The December adventurers meeting saw the revival of old arguments. Bank charges, ticketing and support for local hospitals were again on the agenda. A Mr Heard once again complained that the mine was paying unnecessary charges to the bank and that more of the tin should be sold by ticketing. He further complained that Dolcoath was slow in paying its merchants' bills. Thomas replied to this last point, that if they got a discount from these merchants, which was 'only fair', they would be paid more promptly. The Committee would discuss the ticketing issue again. Mr Thomas Pryor raised the question of contributions to Redruth Miners' Hospital. He asserted that the previous year Dolcoath miners had cost the hospital £138, and the mine had only contributed £12 12s to it. The meeting unanimously agreed to increase their annual contribution to £21. This really only told a part of the story. Dolcoath was contributing 10 guineas yearly to the South Devon & East Cornwall Hospital; it was giving 5 guineas to the Royal Cornwall Hospital, in Truro, and as from December 1886 it was giving £21 to the Miners' Hospital. Over a ten year period Dolcoath gave nearly £400 to these three hospitals.[381]

A New Air Compressor

The *Mining Journal* of January 29th 1887 reported that the new Harris air compressor was installed, and whilst working 'at a slow rate', had kept the air pressure to 70lbs per square inch at the bottom of the mine, which was half-a-mile down, and the ends were a quarter-mile in. It was said that the compressor was the only one like it in Cornwall and could supply 12 drills. Captain Thomas had designed the compressor house himself, and he was proud that concrete had been used for the loadings, instead of the usual granite. There was optimism over the improvements to development that this new equipment would bring.[382]

Two Dolcoath miners, recently returned from America, reported that the tin in the Black Hills of Dakota was not worth much, and reckoned it would never pay to work. Three years before, other returnees had said that some of the supposed cassiterite was in fact 'tantalite'.[383]

The accounts for 1886 continued to show the mine in a strong position. Costs for the twelve weeks ending March 6th were £18,739, there was a profit of £9,462 and a dividend of £1 15s a share, totalling £8,225. Income tax on profit came to £843. The mineral lord's 1/15th dues came to £2,008, and 563 tons of black were tin sold for £30,093. £24 worth of arsenic was sold. The average tin price received was £53 9s. There was £566 in the club and doctor's pence came to £256. Total mine income was £28,201. The twelve weeks ending May 29th had costs of £18,745, profit of £10,595, dividend paid of £8,225 at £1 15s a share, dues of £2,089, and black tin sales of £31,342 for 564 tons and a total income of £29,340. The average tin price paid the mine was £55 11s. The club had £472 and doctor's pence was £255. The twelve weeks ending August 21st had costs of £18,857, profit of £9,946, dividend of £9,400 at £2, lord's dues of £2,051, black tin sales of £30,730 for 543 tons, arsenic sales of £41, and total mine income of £28,802. The average price paid the mine for its tin was £56 12s. In the club was £407 and the doctor's pence was £255. The accounts for the period ending November 13th had costs of £19,413, profit of £11,803, dividend of £9,400 at £2 a share, dues paid of £2,219, black tin sales of £33,290 for 551 tons, and a total mine income of £31,217. The average price received by Dolcoath for its tin was £60 1s. The club had £382 in it and doctor's pence came to £254.[384]

The manager's report dated February 28th 1887, said Engine Shaft was sunk 8½ fathoms below the 388 fathom level, and by October, the 400 level had been reached. The end of the year saw drives to the east and west on the 400 level progressing well. New East Shaft also continued sinking throughout the year, with the November manager's report stating that it was 11 fathoms under the 388 level. Meanwhile, Harris' men were sinking Eastern Shaft very quickly. In February they were 14 fathoms below the 170 level, and by November they were 13 fathoms under the 210 fathom level – averaging a sinking rate of 4 fathoms a month. Within a month they hoped that the 254 fathom south crosscut would be under the shaft. Winzes were being sunk in several places under the 375 level and a couple close to Old Sump and New East shafts had holed the 388 fathom level. A considerable amount of stoping ground was opened up by these winzes.[385]

Tin grades continued to hold up well in 1887, with the ore in Engine Shaft being moderate at between £25 and £40, but the tin in New East Shaft being worth between £120 and £400 a cubic fathom. The lode in Engine Shaft became progressively more disordered and poor in 1887. Elsewhere, the values varied, with the deeper levels being highest at between £80 and £100 a fathom on South Lode and up to £120 on Main Lode. Higher up the values were mostly between £10 and £75 a fathom.[386]

By the May 23rd adventurers meeting, Captain John Williams had gone from the mine, to be replaced in August, by Captain George Davey. The August meeting also announced the death of Mr Thomas Simon Bolitho of Penzance, who had been a good friend to the mine, helping the Dolcoath Committee negotiate the new lease with the lords of the mine, and other delicate matters.[387]

In March, James Wickett, one of the adventurers (whose family was involved with the Redruth Brewery), expressed concern over a letter printed shortly before in the *West Briton* newspaper. It was written by a shaftsman called Josiah Luke, who complained that shaftsmen at Dolcoath were only paid £3 15s a month. Wickett thought that this would be a scandal if it was true, and asked Captain Thomas about it. He replied that it certainly was not true, that shaftsmen in the deeper shafts were paid £5 5s a month, and that Luke, who had worked in Stray Park Shaft, had been paid £4 10s 9d a month. Thomas added, that Luke only worked some 20 hours a week and he had only been kept on out of charity – because he was not really needed there. He then said that Dolcoath did not lay men off when they were invalid, but gave them light jobs at surface. Disabled ex-miners were given £1 a month for life. The adventurers supplemented the miners' club with £100 to £150 a year. They had recently spent £800 on a new dry for the shaftsmen.[388]

The March 5th 1887 *Mining Journal* reported the recent adventurers meeting, and once again it heard arguments over the system used for selling Dolcoath's tin, with the question of ticketing inevitably being raised. Arthur Strauss argued in favour, as he had done for years, whilst Thomas reckoned the mine would lose by it. Dolcoath were receiving about £2 a ton more for their tin than East Pool. Ticketing benefited mines in a 'rising market', but not in a 'falling market'; such a situation would be 'fatal to Dolcoath', said Captain Thomas. In August some of the same adventurers queried the amount Dolcoath paid for its coal, and once again Thomas was forced to defend their practices. In March there was fire in Dolcoath's blacksmith's shop.[389]

The summer of 1887 was a dry one, and the mines around Camborne suffered through lack of water for dressing their tin. Thomas also complained about the loss of work due to such things as Camborne Agricultural Show, and the miners having a paid holiday to celebrate Queen Victoria's Jubilee. These holidays cost the mine an estimated £140. Despite this, Thomas proudly announced that the mine still made £1,000 profit a week. He was very happy with some of the results underground, where tin worth £350 a cubic fathom was found whilst sinking New East Shaft. Some samples were as high as £500 a fathom.[390]

The pitwork in Engine Shaft had experienced severe problems during the autumn, and some of the pump rods had been changed. The pitmen had advised that the 'surface connection of the rods with the main bob' be replaced. It was in a bad condition, and if it broke there would be serious consequences for the mine. This was immediately done. At the same time a new steam capstan was bought to replace the old, worn-out horse driven one. Two second-hand boilers were purchased and also an engine, which cost £150, although it was valued at £500. Work was carried out to improve the stamps engine.[391]

A New Stannary Act
The new Stannary Act had come into law and the mine had to make various adjustments. Surface workers must be paid weekly and underground workers fortnightly. Miners had previously been paid monthly. The adventurers agreed that this was just, good and fair. The Act also said the miners' club belonged to the miners, and not the mine. The miners also had the right to vote to keep the *status quo* with respect to the club, or do away with it. They voted unanimously to keep it as it was. They knew they benefited from the current system, with the old and sick receiving payment when they were not strictly entitled to it. They also benefited from the adventurers' top-up of the club, when it ran short. The miners could also choose their own doctors under the Act, which they had done for the previous 18 years.[392]

In 1887 the mine continued to increase its profits. The twelve weeks ending February 12th had costs of £20,073, including £500 toward Harris' compressor, profit of £11,141, dividend of £11,162 10s, for £2 7s 6d a share, dues paid the Bassets of £2,222 at 1/15th, and black tin sales of £33,333 for 552 tons, which sold for an average of £60.7s a ton. Income tax on profit for the previous year came to £964, which left total income of £31,214. The club held £383, doctor's pence came to £255 and there was a stock of arsenic worth £41. The three months ending April 30th had costs of £20,012, including £765, the balance of Harris' compressor, profit of £11,779, dividend of £10,575 for £2 5s a share, dues of £2,264, tin sales of £33,956 for 557 tons at an average of £60 19s, and a total income of £31,791. The miners' club was worth £652 and doctor's pence was £256. £41 worth of arsenic was held in stock. The period ending July 23rd had costs of £19,706, profit of £12,009, dividend of £11,750 for £2 10s a share, dues of 2,259, tin sales of £33,883 for 555 tons, which sold for an average of £61 1s a ton, and total income was £31,715. There was little change in the club, doctor's pence and arsenic stock. In May Dolcoath paid £360 for a new boiler for a compressor. The twelve weeks ending October 15th showed costs of £20,197, profit of £11,910, dividend of £11,750 at £2 10s a share, G. L. Basset's dues of £2,288 at 1/15th, black tin sales of £34,316 for 535 tons, which averaged £64 3s a ton, and a total income of £32,107. The club, doctor's pence and arsenic stock remained similar to the previous months.[393]

With the 400 fathom level reached and being opened up Captain Thomas continued with his sinking programme, and by April 1888 Engine Shaft it was 6 feet below the level. Sinking continued throughout the year and by December 31st the shaft was 4 fathoms below the 400 level, although sinking was held up due to excess water. In April preparations were underway to sink Old Sump Shaft below the 388 fathom level, but by October, with the shaft sunk 7½ fathoms below the level, work was suspended due to excess water. Meanwhile, Eastern Shaft was going down extremely quickly. In April it was announced that it would reach the 254 fathom level by mid-May, and by the end of the year, the shaft was 31 fathoms below it. Winzes were deepening the mine below the deepest levels almost at the same speed that Engine Shaft was going down. Ground between the 388 and 400 fathom levels was being opened up by these winzes for stoping. The drive east from New East Shaft toward Eastern Shaft on the 375 fathom level was suspended due to unusually high temperature and extreme humidity in the end. It would be restarted when Eastern Shaft reached the 375 level, and ventilation improved.[394]

The tin values in Engine Shaft varied as it sank beneath the 400 level, with 'a little tin' found at one fathom, and the grade only improving by the autumn. It was back up to £30 a fathom by the end of the year, when the shaft was 4 fathoms below the level. Values on the 375, 388 and 400 levels varied generally between £40 and £120 a cubic fathom early in the year, improving up to as high as £150 in the summer, and falling away to highs of £120 in the autumn and winter. Early in 1888, on South Lode on the 254, 266, 278, 302 and 314 fathom levels, the tin was worth between £15 and £40 a fathom. By the autumn it had improved to as high as £120 a fathom, which was maintained till the end of the year.[395]

The adventurers meeting of April 23rd 1888 discussed the possible sale of Stray Park sett as a going concern, and resolved to leave the problem in the hands of the Committee to resolve. In October 1888, Captain William James replaced Joseph Chynoweth as one of the mine captains, who had died suddenly. The adventurers voted that £50 be given to his widow.[396]

A Fatal Accident & Dreadful Discovery

In May 1888, a 15 year old surface worker was killed when he fell down Man Engine Shaft. Thomas Henry Stapleton, of Tolcarne Street, Camborne, was about to start working underground, and naturally nervous of what this would entail, decided to practice using the man engine. When the afternoon core had come to surface, unbeknown to his workmates and supervisors, he went to the engine rod and tried getting on and off the moving timber. Unfortunately, he slipped, and fell to the adit level, 180 feet below. He was terribly battered and died immediately. A couple of weeks after recovering the lad's body, the adit men had another depressing experience. Whilst engaged in clearing the Shallow Adit, they came across the body of a male child, hidden in a culvert. Apparently, it had been placed there during the previous night.[397]

At the adventurers meeting of December 31st, a proposal was adopted which showed the extraordinary position Dolcoath was in. "That at this last Meeting for the year 1888, the Adventurers of Dolcoath Mine desire to recognise the fact, that during the past year a larger amount of profit has been divided than in any previous year in the history of the Mine, and that the reserves opening out are greatly in excess of the tin being at present taken away. They hereby tender their best thanks to the executive, and especially to Capt. Josiah Thomas, for the very able and energetic manner in which the Mine has been and still is being developed under his skilful management." This far-sighted approach to keeping development well ahead of production was one of the reasons for Dolcoath's success in weathering storms, which sank other potentially rich mines. It should be noted, that this was the result of the work not just of the manager, but of the whole team of mine captains, whose skill in identifying potentially good tin ground and supervising its development was crucial to the success of the mine.[398]

During 1888 negotiations to sell the Stray Park sett continued with little signs of progress. Some adventurers licked their lips over the £25,000 offered, but others thought if it was worth that to a purchaser it was worth the same to Dolcoath. As the year progressed it became clear that Mr Basset (or his agent, Edmund Marriott) did not want to sell it, and by insisting that the company that owned it was a cost book company, and that all the terms of the original lease with Dolcoath were adhered to, he virtually killed off the deal. Those who were keen on the sale pointed out the advantages in bringing in a new company with extra capital to invest in the district, and as it was to be worked by a company which was intended to amalgamate Camborne Consols, Camborne Vean, Carn Camborne and Wheal Harriet, it was thought it would also benefit the Tehidy Estate, through increased rents and dues. In the end it was decided to leave the matter in the hands of the Committee, and Captain Thomas said he was happy with the *status quo*, and would work Stray Park profitably. In October Tehidy asked Dolcoath to start to sink Stray Park Shaft below the 282 fathom level, which appears to have decided the fate of the negotiations. At the same time, Dolcoath told Marriott of its intention to sub-divide the shares from 4,700 to 5,000, and then sub-divide again to 20,000 shares. Tehidy was not happy with the suggestion.[399]

During discussions about tin sales it was announced that Williams, Harvey & Co. had sold their smelter to another company, possibly Harvey & Co. of Hayle. George Williams had previously bought the bulk of Dolcoath's black tin. In July, Mr Basset, who insisted he was neutral in the argument, threw his weight behind the adventurers in favour of ticketing, by suggesting that his share of Dolcoath's tin be sold by ticketing as an 'experiment'. This amounted to about 12 tons a month, and Thomas reckoned that the mine lost by the experiment.[400]

On April 21st, the *Mining Journal* reported a major 'run' underground at Dolcoath. Fortunately, nobody was hurt, although two miners had just passed beneath the collapse when several thousand tons of waste rock fell.[401]

Pump Rod Sabotaged
A far more worrying series of occurrences was reported in the summer of 1888. Captain Thomas stated that a lot of essential maintenance work had been carried out on the main pump rod in Engine Shaft. Over the previous three years all the rods had been changed, some of them being replaced by larger oak timbers. Ten inch rods had been replaced by twelve inch rods. He thought that the extra weight of these rods might have caused some to fall onto the footwall of the shaft. Also, some of the replaced timber had signs of dry rot. An extra balance bob was installed to take some of the weight. This work was carried out in the summer so that all would be ready for the wetter winter weather. Thomas also mentioned that when the main rod was idle, no pumping took place from the sump of New East Shaft, which was drained by means of flat rods from the main rod. However, there was another serious matter that Thomas spoke of to the adventurers. He believed that the pump rod had been sabotaged by 'unscrupulous persons', who had bribed miners to unscrew the bolts, which held the rods together. This had led to several breakages in the previous quarter. Missing bolts had been found hidden on levels remote from the shaft. Although a £5 reward for information had been offered, no miner had come forward with evidence as to who was to blame. Thomas pointed out that this 'malicious meddling' could easily have led to death for miners and disaster for the mine.[402]

The Globe Mill Pulveriser
The *Mining Journal* of October 27th 1888 carried a very detailed report and advertisement concerning the experimental use of a Globe Mill for pulverising Dolcoath's tin ore. This machine, which worked at 25 to 30 horse power, could crush 60 to 75 tons of ore a day. Its two 12-inch cylinders worked at up to 350 revolutions

a minute. If the trial was successful, and the Globe accepted, it would add materially to the vast array of machinery on the mine. Earlier in the year, the adventurers had been told that the mine had spent £40,000 on machinery during the previous twenty years: a new 85-inch pumping engine, a new 40-inch stamps engine with 80 head of stamps, a second-hand 60-inch pumping engine for Harrietts Shaft and a considerable amount of new pitwork and skip roads. During those twenty years, £436,784 had been paid out in dividends and some £8,000 paid in tax on profits.[403]

Major Improvements Above & Below Ground

At the Adventurers Meeting of December 31st 1888 Captain Thomas reported that a new calciner had been purchased, a new railroad had been laid on the 314 fathom level, and a 'water engine underground for conveying stuff from the centre of the mine … to Harrietts Shaft', installed. This 'little engine at Harrietts Shaft … worked by water to draw stuff by a railway', and was described as a hydraulic engine, what we would call a pressure engine. It worked by means of a small column of water 1,800 feet high and achieved 800 psi. This water was pumped up by the main engine. Thomas reckoned it cost only 3d a ton. The use of electricity was discussed, but Thomas thought this too expensive. Hauling ore to Harrietts Shaft for hoisting would relieve the pressure on the three central shafts, through which most of the ore was being hoisted. By early December this pressure engine was installed and working. At the same meeting it was suggested that Dolcoath issue monthly progress reports through the press, particularly the *Mining Journal* and the *West Briton*. Thomas had no objection to this. During the discussion about the progress the mine had made over the years, the manager mentioned that he had started at Dolcoath when he was 15 years old, and had been there for 40 years. He also stated, rather proudly: "He had dialled every inch of ground for 30 years."[404]

In 1888 there were wide fluctuations in the price of tin and Dolcoath's profitability. The twelve weeks ending April 7th had costs of £20,101, a leap in profits to £25,880, a dividend of £16,450 for £3 10s a share, dues to the Bassets of £3,278 (at 1/15th), and tin sales of £49,167 for 548 tons, which sold for the impressive average of £89 13s a ton. Total mine income, after tax on profit of £920, was £45,981. The miners' club was worth £874, doctor's pence was £163. The three months ending June 30th had costs of £18,687, profit of £4,747, dividend of £23,500 at £5 a share, dues of £1,665, and black tin sales of £24,982 for 493 tons, which sold for an average of £50 13s a ton. Overall income came to £23,434. The club was similar to the previous month. The period ending September 22nd had costs of £19,062, profit of £7,072, dividend of £4,700 at £1 a share, dues of £1,857 and tin sales of £27,858 for 498 tons, which sold for an average of £55 19s a ton. Total income was £26,134. The club money held dropped slightly to £843. The twelve weeks ending December 15th had costs of £18,982, profit of £7,098, dividend of £7,050 at £1 10s a share, dues to the Bassets of £1,855 and tin sales of £27,835 for 489 tons, which sold for an average of £56 17s. Overall income was £26,080. The club cash dropped further to £753.[405]

The Death of Gustavus Lambert Basset

With the death of Gustavus Lambert Basset, the mineral lord, dues were paid to his successor after September 1888. The adventurers expressed their sympathy to his family, for although relations had been somewhat strained in recent years, the family had been closely associated with the mine as adventurers as well as mineral lords, for two centuries.

In 1889 the sinking of Engine Shaft continued slowly. In March it was 5 fathoms below the 400 fathom level and by the beginning of December the shaft was still only 7 fathoms below the level. In June a new pump lift was being fixed in the shaft and this was complete by September, when it was announced that sinking was to be speeded up by the use of boring machines. By March Old Sump Shaft was holed to the 400 fathom level by means of a rise to its sump and preparations were made to bring a skip road down it to the 400 level. Once the skip road was fixed it was anticipated that developments could proceed to open up the 400 level faster. By the end of the year plans were in place to begin sinking Old Sump Shaft below the 400 level. Meanwhile, work went on during the year to repair the skip road and ladder road in Stray Park Shaft, in preparation to sink it deeper. The pump engine house at Stray Park was in poor condition, with the front wall falling down. This needed urgent repairs, especially as Dolcoath hoped to sell the sett. By March 25th, Eastern Shaft, which was being sunk below the 254 level, was within 2 fathoms of the 302 level, and this level, which was being driven from New East Shaft, was within 4 fathoms of the shaft. By the beginning of December, Eastern Shaft was 44 fathoms below the 302 fathom level, and the drive on the 352 level to it was fast approaching.[406]

Values remained steady during 1889 with most at the deeper levels being worth between £10 and £80 a fathom. However, by the end of the year some of the development points looked a lot better, with the tin in New East Shaft, which was being sunk under the 400 fathom level, showing values of up to £200 a fathom. The ends on the higher levels on Main Lode, varied in value between £10 and £20 a fathom and on South Lode were worth between £10 and £70 a fathom.[407]

In his December 2nd 1889 report the manager made some interesting comments about the ground in the locality of Eastern Shaft: "We have intersected what we believe to be the main lode at the 302 fathom level north of Eastern Shaft. So far as seen, it is about six feet wide, and contains a little tin. The end, however, is close to the little cross-course on which the cross-cut was driven, and we hope for an improvement in driving east toward the great crosscourse, where the main lode in the shallow levels was very productive."[408]

Under pressure to restart sinking Stray Park Shaft Captain Thomas reported in March that things were delayed due to the poor condition of the skip road and ladderway in the shaft. In June he added to the list, the dangerous condition of Stray Park engine house's bob wall, which urgently needed attention. He was harassed by the need to increase the rate that ore was drawn to surface, complaining that with all the available whims working from early Monday morning till late Saturday night, they still could not keep up with the ore being hauled to the shafts – Stray Park was not at the top of his priorities. As usual, when under pressure, the manager indulged himself at the March adventurers meeting, talking about the vast tonnage of tin sold since he had become manager – 21 years earlier – some £2,000,000 worth. He added that £484,959 in dividends had been paid out in that period. With these heady statistics ringing in their ears, an adventurer took advantage to request that the mine contribute to a fund to support a qualified nurse for the town of Camborne. A figure of £5 was suggested and accepted, before a meaner-spirited adventurer suggested that they defer the question to the Committee. Whilst on the subject of paying for health, J. Wickett brought up the thorny problem of subscriptions to hospitals. He thought the 20 guineas paid yearly to the Miners' Hospital derisory, stating that the Dolcoath miners treated there, cost the hospital between £100 and £150 a year. The manager did not accept that these were all Dolcoath men, and said that in future he would sign for Dolcoath men going for treatment. Three local doctors at present sent men to the hospital, but Thomas would check they were from the mine. He added, again rather proudly, that he had only been laid up once in his career, due to an accident on the man engine.[409]

In June Captain Thomas told the adventurers that he intended to have a 'small stamps at the bottom of the mine for pulverising rows (poor, rough, large pieces of ore)'. This would be on a trial basis. These underground stamps were working effectively by early December. He said he was not impressed with most of the pulverisers he had seen, as they were expensive to maintain, and subject to frequent break-down. However, Thomas was impressed by new stamps which were being tried at the mine. They delivered 120 blows a minute, and the 8 heads were lifted 4 inches high instead of 8 inches. These stamps were better and cheaper than the new pulverisers. He intended to erect batteries of stamps on the eastern side of the valley once the expected tonnage of ore was being hoisted from Eastern Shaft. At the September 5th adventurers meeting Thomas announced that Harvey & Co. of Hayle were erecting an 8 head battery of revolving stamps, for pulverising 'rows' (roughs) and sand. If the trial were successful, the mine would have another battery, which would deliver 200 blows a minute. Harvey's would pay for the erection and trial of these stamps.[410]

In September the death of Mark Guy Pearce was announced. He had been involved with the mine, mostly on the Committee, since 1862 – 37 years. At the same meeting the adventurers were told of a serious 'fall of ground' in the 114 fathom level, which had held up production for two days. Large timber stulls were sent down to repair the damage and support the workings. Once again, Mr Heard raised the question of tin lost down the Red River. He thought the mine should buy adjacent land to install extra dressing floors. In December Thomas reported that the Committee had increased the rate Harris was paid for sinking Eastern Shaft from £29 2s 6d to £31 a fathom, and he had agreed to continue sinking to the 375 fathom level.[411]

Once again the adventurers discussed the amount Dolcoath paid in dues or royalties to the Tehidy Estate. A Royal Commission had been set up by parliament to investigate the possibility of regulating the payment by mines of these royalties. Captain Josiah Thomas was one of the Cornish mining men representing the industry in these discussions. Mr Pendarves represented the mineral lords on the Committee.[412]

At the December meeting a question was asked about the miners pay and Thomas replied that on average the miners received £4 a month, with the best of them getting £5 a month. The 138 tributers averaged £4 a month. He remarked that the deep workings were hot and humid and that the miners at Dolcoath were 'steady and industrious' workers. Interestingly, Thomas said that no tributers were used at the bottom of the mine and in the richer stopes, especially where the values were constant. Where they were essential, was where the lodes were 'patchy' and skill in identifying and extracting the good ore was required. They were a godsend in those stopes, and were the saviours of many a mine. The rich stopes were worked at Dolcoath by 'stopers', these were miners who were paid by the cubic fathom of ore they broke – not its value! They were in effect tutworkers or piece workers.[413]

Buried Alive
In October 1889, two boys were engaged in digging away an old mine waste tip beside Dolcoath Road. William Thomas, whose father was mining in Africa, and a lad called Mayne, whose father was mining in Mexico, had undermined a 12 foot high part of the shaft burrow, when it collapsed onto them, burying them. The burrow was from a shaft worked some 50 years before on Silver Lode. Immediately the alarm was raised, miners working nearby rushed to the boys' assistance and managed to dig Mayne out alive. Unfortunately, William Thomas was pronounced dead by Dr Thomas, who attended. Mayne was not badly hurt.[414]

During 1889 profits became more modest. The twelve weeks ending March 9th showed costs of £19,212, profit of £6,640, dividend of £7,050 at £1 10s a share, dues were £1,838, and tin sales of £27,571 for 506 tons, which sold for an average of £54 9s a ton. Mine income, after £876 income tax was paid, was £25,852. The club stood at £779. The three months ending May 25th had costs of £19,282, profit of £5,910, dividend of £5,875 at £1 5s a share, dues of £1,791 and tin sales of £26,864 for

508 tons, which averaged £52 18s a ton. Total income was £25,192 and the miners' club stood at £1,015. The period ending August 24th had costs of £19,434, profit of £4,713, dividend of £5,875 at £1 5s a share, dues of £1,717, and black tin sales of £25,738 for 496 tons, which sold for an average of £51 18s. Some 3½ tons of copper ore was sold, for nearly £11. Overall income was £24,147. The club money dropped to £976. The twelve weeks ending November 16th had costs of £19,894, profit of £5,337, dividend of £4,700 at £1 a share, dues of £1,794, and tin sales of £26,912 for 493 tons, which sold for an average of £54 11s. Total income was £25,230 and the miners' club money stood at £928. The twelve weeks ending February 8th 1890 had costs of £19,628, profit of £3,756, dividend of £5,287 10s at £1 2s 6d a share, 1/15th dues of £1,662, and black tin sales of 24,937 for 450 tons, which averaged £55 8s a ton. After the annual income tax bill of £1,046 the mine income was £23,385. The club money stood at £814. Dolcoath's annual subscription to the Miners Hospital was increased from £21 to £25, but the payment to the Royal Cornwall Hospital remained at £5 5s a year.[415]

Using boring machines Engine Shaft was sunk faster in 1890, and by the end of February it was down more than 10½ fathoms below the 400 fathom level. By early August the 412 level had been reached and the level opened up 11 fathoms to the east of the shaft, and a short distance to the west. By the end of the year preparations were underway to sink below the 412 fathom level. In February Old Sump Shaft was being sunk under the 400 level, although no progress was reported in the succeeding months. Meanwhile, New East Shaft was down 6½ fathoms under the 400 fathom level by late February, and in August it was reported that the 412 level had been reached by it and the levels east and west were about to be driven. The November report said the 412 level was driven 7 fathoms east from New East Shaft. Eastern Shaft was 60 fathoms below the 302 level by February 1890 and the 375 end was only 10 fathoms to the west of it. In August the shaft was 16½ fathoms below the 375 level, and by November drives south to find Main Lode and west to link up with the drives from New East Shaft were going well. The January 1891 manager's report stated that the south drive to pick up Main Lode from Eastern Shaft, had found the ground disordered by a crosscourse. Thomas also said that Harrietts Shaft, previously sunk on the north part of Main Lode, had been holed between 314 and 338 fathom levels on the south part of the lode.[416]

The tin ore values held up quite well in 1890, although there were some wide variations in places. Engine Shaft had ore worth £35 a fathom in February, 10½ fathoms below the 400 fathom level, but by the end of the year, when sinking below the 412 level the sinkers were finding only 'a little tin'. Under the 400 level in New East Shaft ore was worth up to £240 a fathom. Generally, the values were between £20 and £150 a fathom on the deepest levels, and somewhat less in the ends higher up in the mine.[417]

Fire Underground

During January 1890 there was a very dangerous fire underground. Captain Thomas' February report to the adventurers showed the seriousness of the incident: "The fire which occurred last month hindered the working of the mine for about a week, and thus seriously interfered with our returns of tin for this account. It is some consolation however, to remember that no life was lost, and the timber and sollars adjoining the man engine being now repaired the mine is again in full working order. The sum of £81 was contributed by the public to shew their appreciation of the bravery of the men who went to the rescue of their comrades who were in danger, and this sum has been divided between 9 of the men who chiefly distinguished themselves on this occasion." The January 11th 1890 *Mining Journal* carried a graphic account of the fire. A miner had apparently carelessly thrown a lighted candle end into the workings, near to the man engine, at the 265 fathom level. Soon some of the adjacent stull timbers and man engine sollars were on fire, and the smoke quickly affected night-shift miners working on the 300 fathom level. As the man engine was out of use, the miners had to make their way to Eastern Shaft to ascend to surface. Four shaftsmen had gone down Engine Shaft to check the pumps and were reported missing. These men, Trevarthen, Weekes, Sowden and Wake had narrow escapes. Two miners, called Eva and Rule, the latter being related to Trevarthen, volunteered to go down to search for them, suspecting that they would be on the 60 level shaft plot. Trevarthen and Wake were found on the 60 station, locked in each other's arms and quite unconscious. Meanwhile several miners went down to search for other survivors and Sowden and Weekes made their way up through Eastern Shaft. Although relatively unscathed, they were both violently sick. Adit water was turned down Man Engine Shaft to extinguish the flames and compressed air was turned on with the end taps open to blow away the smoke from the workings. The fire took three days to put out. Some stull and sollar timber had to be replaced, but the inconvenience was relatively short-lived.[418]

Campaign to Improve Bal Maidens' Wages

At the February adventurers meeting there were more complaints about tin lost to the mine down the Red River and the need for more dressing floor space. Some moaned again about the profits being made by the tin streamers, and there was general concern about this perceived problem. There were also questions asked by a new adventurer, called Chew, about the female employees at the mine. Thomas replied that they employed some 300 bal maidens on the dressing floors, and their wages were between 4d a day, for the younger ones, and 2s a day for the older, more experienced women. Mr Chew suggested that these wages were far too low and they should be paid more. A bitter discussion then ensued as Mr Alfred Lanyon pointed out that Chew had recently asked the same questions at South Wheal Frances adventurers meeting. Lanyon said that Chew had only become an adventurer at South Frances 24 hours before the meeting, and had sold his share immediately following the meeting. He had recently bought a share at Dolcoath for the same purpose – to raise these questions! His questions were politically motivated, said Lanyon. Although Chew said he remained an adventurer at South Frances, he did not deny his motive was political.[419]

In his May report to the adventurers, Thomas said that he was not entirely happy with 'little stamps' being used underground to pulverise the rough ore. He thought they should persevere for a while to see how things worked out. He intended to increase the stamping capacity at surface, to cope with the anticipated increase in tonnage hoisted. He favoured trying the Husband pneumatic stamps, being used successfully at Tregurtha Downs Mine. Apparently, one head could do the work of 16 traditional Cornish stamps heads. He did not know the costs of maintaining them, but Harvey & Co. were going to examine them and report to him. The Tregurtha Downs manager spoke highly of their effectiveness. The stamped ore would be sent to the present dressing floors. In August Thomas reported that the new calciner which was being used to 'burn slimes', was very effective, and the resultant concentrate increased the amount paid by the smelter by £1 a ton. He also mentioned that Eastern Shaft was being sunk by 18 men, who were using an air winch to draw the dirt from the bottom. They suffered problems due to increasing water in the sump.[420]

At the August adventurers meeting Mr Heard once again raised the perennial question of ticketing, and Thomas replied that some of the mine's black tin was then being sold at the Redruth ticketing, but most was still sold by private treaty. Another regular point was raised at the November meeting – a complaint about the size of the dues paid to the Bassets. This question was to be answered satisfactorily in the near future. Some interesting points were made by Captain Thomas at the November meeting, about the methods employed in working the mine. Most of the stopes on South Lode were worked by tributers at an average of 10s in the pound. Some of the larger stopes were worked by piece workers ('stopers'). As with Main Lode, where skilled 'selection of ground' was needed, tributers were used. Flat rods, powered by the main pump rod, were being more widely used for pumping winzes. In November it was announced that Harris, whose men had been sinking Eastern Shaft, was to take over the sinking of Engine Shaft as well as several other ends, rises and winzes.[421]

The mine continued to show similar profits in 1890 to the previous year. The twelve weeks ending May 3rd 1890 had costs of £19,587, profit of £4,122, dividend of £3,525 at 15s a share, lord's dues of £1,685 at 1/15th and tin sales of £25,271 for 475 tons, which averaged £53 4s a ton. The miners' club had £1,052 in hand and the total mine income was £23,709. The period ending July 26th had costs of £19,546, profit of £4,792, dividend of £4,112 10s at 17s 6d a share, dues of £1,730, black tin sales of £25,946 for 470 tons, which sold for an average of £55 4s. There was £1,035 in the miners' club and the total income was £24,339. The three months ending October

20th had costs of £19,864, profit of £5,479, dividend paid of £4,700 at £1 a share, dues of £1,803, tin sales of £27,050 for 470 tons, which sold for an average of £57 10s. The club stood at £912 and the total income was £25,342. The twelve weeks ending January 10th 1891 had costs of £20,025, profit of £3,291, dividend of £4,700 at £1 a share, dues paid of £1,659 and black tin sales of £24,879 for 467 tons, which averaged £53 5s a ton. This was £4 5s less a ton than the previous quarter, and lost the mine an estimated £2,000. The club had £802 in the bank and the overall income for the mine was £23,316.[422]

The April 20th 1891 manager's report said that Engine Shaft was 4 fathoms below the 412 fathom level, and a new pump lift had been fixed to that level. In October the shaft was down 5 fathoms under the 412, and then the sinkers experienced difficulties, as excess water, due to 'heavy floods', disrupted their work. Despite this, the shaft was sunk another 2½ fathoms by the end of the year. Part of the problem was caused by the main bob on the pumping engine breaking. The two deepest levels were flooded for a month. In October, it was announced that R. H. Harris was contracted to sink Engine Shaft for £75 a fathom. It was hoped he could sink 9 feet a month – he had sunk Eastern Shaft at the rate of 5 fathoms a month, but the ground at Engine Shaft was much harder. In April, Harrietts Shaft commenced sinking below the 338 fathom level, near to the south part of Main Lode, and by the end of the year was 10 fathoms under the level. The 400 fathom level driven east from New East Shaft was holed to Eastern Shaft by October, and preparations were made to put in a skip road to the level. A railroad at the 400 level was to be installed between New East and Eastern shafts. The three winzes to the east of New East Shaft were progressed in 1891, linking the 400 to the 412 fathom levels. These were sunk at 20, 25 and 30 fathom spacings, giving blocks of stoping ground of 72 feet by up to 180 feet. More than one stoping 'pare' would probably work in these stopes. On December 28th, it was reported that Old Sump Shaft would soon resume sinking.[423]

The extremely high tin values of previous years were not immediately found in 1891, with Engine Shaft finding 'little tin' below the 412 fathom level, despite 'rich stones of tin' being also occasionally encountered. The ends and winzes at the bottom of the mine had ore worth between £10 and £100 a fathom. The higher levels had values of between 'a little tin' and £60 a fathom. South Lode's grades were average, apart from ore in a rise over the 314 fathom level, where it was worth £120 a fathom. The Main Lode at 412 level was 24 feet wide, which looked good for the future. In two places near Eastern Shaft Main Lode was worth £80 a fathom.[424]

At the January 1891 adventurers meeting, the death of George Williams, the company chairman, was announced. His brother, Michael Henry Williams replaced him. Captain Thomas commented on the support the Williams family had always given his father when he wanted to sink deeper for tin. At the same meeting, the chairman,

Mr W. Rabling, commented that Dolcoath should pursue their request of the Tehidy Estate to have their 1/15th dues reduced, as they were the highest in Cornwall. He thought that as Mr Marriott had dealt fairly with other mines on the estate, he should be sympathetic to Dolcoath's position, as the deepest mine in the county. By April Mr Justice Sterling of the Court of Chancery, acting for Tehidy (after the death of G. L. Basset in 1888), had appointed Mr R. J. Frecheville, the former Government Inspector of Mines, as 'receiver of the mineral properties of the Tehidy Estate'. He was to meet Marriott to discuss Dolcoath's dues. After correspondence between Frecheville and Thomas the Court of Chancery agreed to 'temporarily' reduce the dues from 1/15th to 1/18th. Unfortunately, the court did not agree to the sale of Stray Park and insisted that the Engine Shaft there be sunk below the 282 fathom level. Because the small mines which it was proposed to amalgamate – Camborne Vean, Carn Camborne, Wheal Frances, Wheal Harriett and Stray Park – were owned by different estates, Tehidy thought it an inadvisable move.[425]

Bad Weather Affected Production

In January and again in April Captain Thomas complained about the snow and frost, which had caused problems to the dressing floors. With leats choked with snow the dressing floors were inactive for over a week. He also moaned about the lower price of tin – the mine had lost about £2,000 in the previous quarter due to it. On the up side, Thomas commented on the vastly improved ventilation at the deeper levels, due mainly to levels being holed to Eastern Shaft. Levels without a connection to the shaft had 'unbearable' heat in the ends. The 400 fathom level was being driven toward that shaft by 9 men using a boring machine. Thomas remarked that they would soon need more stamping capacity, particularly when Eastern Shaft started to produce ore. The mine produce at present, he said, was 60lbs a ton – over 2½ percent! As usual, Mr Heard raised the question of ticketing, commenting that most of the smelters who bought Dolcoath tin were adventurers in the mine. Thomas remained adamant, however, saying he still preferred to sell only part of their tin by ticketing. Captain Bishop, of East Pool, agreed with Captain on this point. The opinions of 'speculators' were voiced in criticism of the way the mine had been run by Thomas. He replied to this by saying he would sooner resign than 'pick the eyes' out of the mine. Of course, he could produce very high profits for a short time by going for the high grade points to the neglect of the average ore, but the mine was there for the benefit of the 1,300 workforce and their families, and the people of Camborne, not just the quick profit of 'speculators'. The adventurers applauded his words.[426]

1891 ended with more weather problems as heavy rain, which had virtually destroyed the harvest in the summer, continued, making ore dressing difficult and flooding the bottom of the mine. Some local mines had been brought to a standstill due to it. The January 2nd 1892 *Mining Journal* reported that the mine was fixing a stronger cage and new loadings for the steam whim. Some ore from the 314 fathom level on South

Lode was of such high quality that it was being stamped and dressed separately from the other ore and was gaining a much better price from the smelters. The loadings of the old stamps were also failing and had to be replaced. This had been carried out by March 1892 when granite blocks replaced the weaker material originally used. The mine currently had 700 tin dressing frames in use.[427]

During 1891 profits remained steady and the mine continued to look financially healthy. The twelve weeks ending April 4th 1891 had costs of £19,879, profit of £3,010, dividend paid of £2,937 at 12s 6d a share, and dues of 1/15th paid to the Bassets came to £1,341. There were black tin sales of £24,138 for 456 tons, which sold for an average of £52 18s. Income tax of the year's profit was £1,031 and the overall income was £22,888. There was £950 in the miners club. Subsist payments to tributers and tutworkers came to £749. The Committee was attempting to negotiate a reduction of the dues from 1/15th to 1/20th, with Mr Frecheville, the Tehidy agent. Some adventurers still wanted to sell the sett of Stray Park section, but were meeting resistance. The period ending June 27th had costs of £20,597, profit of £4,880, dividend of £2,350 at 10s a share and dues paid of £1,492 at 1/18th. Negotiations with Tehidy had clearly been partially successful. Tin sales came to £26,856 for 494 tons, which sold for an average of £54 6s a ton. The club money in the bank was £852 and the total income was £25,478. The three months ending September 12th had costs of £20,365, profit of £4,752, dividend of £4,700 at £1 a share, dues of £1,473 at 1/18th, and black tin sales of £26,520 for 491 tons, which averaged £53 19s a ton. The club money in the bank was £700. Total income came to £25,117. The twelve weeks ending December 5th had costs of £20,186, profit of £5,338, dividend of £4,700 at £1 a share, dues paid of £1,489 at 1/18th and tin sales of £26,802 for 492 tons, which sold for an average of £54 9s. There was £557 in the club account. Total income was £25,524.[428]

By March 21st 1892 Engine Shaft was sunk 10 fathoms below the 412 level, and the September 5th manager's report announced that the 425 level had been reached. The 425 level was driven 8 fathoms west from Engine Shaft by the end of November. Old Sump Shaft was down 4 fathoms under the 400 level in March and had reached the 412 fathom level by early September. It then continued below the level toward the 425 level. Meanwhile, New East Shaft was also being sunk under the 412 level, and by the end of November it was 12 fathoms below the level, and within a fathom of the 425 fathom level. Harrietts Shaft was 13 fathoms under the 338 level in March, and was 22½ fathoms below the level by the end of November. It was intended to put a rise up from the 375 level to meet the shaft as it was sunk. Captain Thomas reported in November, that "Due to great heat and bad ventilation", the end on the 375 fathom level, toward Harrietts Shaft from Old Sump Shaft, had been suspended. In March a double skip road was completed to the 400 fathom level in Eastern Shaft, and by June, it was 'ready for drawing'. Also in June, a winze west of Eastern Shaft,

Figure 99. Man-engine
balance bob at the 236-fathom
level.

Figure 100. Holman Brothers
compressed air winch over a
winze in Dolcoath.

Figure 101. Slime pit at the west side of the Red River Valley.

Figure 102. The 50-foot dippa wheel.

Figure 103. Rag frames and slime pits in the valley.

Figure 104. The man-engine at the 234-fathom level.

Figure 105. Two-man gig. Note, miners in background, preferring to climb the ladder.

Figure 106. Western side of the Red River Valley looking towards Tuckingmill showing the old stamps and Brunton calciners. Probably taken in the 1920s.

Figure 107. Machine men operating a heavy drifter machine at Dolcoath in 1900. These drifters became known as 'bar and arm' machines as they were attached to a vertical steel bar by a horizontal steel arm. Note, water spray.

Figure 108. Williams Shaft from the north-west, early 20th century.

Figure 109. Williams Shaft from the south-west, early 20th century. Old Sump and new compressor house on left.

Figure 110. Williams Shaft from the south-east, early 20th century.

Figure 111. Compressor house near Williams Shaft.

Figure 112. Holman's traversing winder at Williams Shaft.

Figure 113. 550 fm Pump Station at Williams Shaft.

sunk 16½ below the 302 fathom level, had a new air winch fixed. Aided by this the winze was sunk some 31 fathoms by the end of November.[429]

In 1892 the tin ore values remained modest for the most part, although the June Manager's Report did announce spectacular results 50 fathoms east of New East Shaft, on the 412 fathom level. Main Lode was over 36 feet wide and worth £100 a cubic-fathom – £600 over the width of the lode! The higher levels gave results of between £10 and £12 a fathom. South Lode also had wide variations in its grades, with the highest being ore worth £45 a fathom. In the March Adventurers Meeting, Captain Thomas described the unusually rich ore found on the 314 fathom level on South Lode as having large tin crystals, and it also contained a lot of iron. It was still being stamped and dressed separately.[430]

More Support for The Miners' Hospital
At the March Meeting there was a prolonged discussion on the contribution Dolcoath and its miners paid to the Miners Hospital at Redruth. Mr J. Wickett gave some facts and figures about the various local mine's contributions over the previous ten years. East Pool had sent 28 miners to the hospital and the miners had contributed £428; Wheal Basset had sent 169 miners and had contributed £329; Carn Brea had sent 431 miners and contributed nothing, and Dolcoath had sent 323 miners and they had given £20. Thomas pointed out that the mine also contributed £25 a year, which was £250 for the period. The discussion centred on whether the miners should be asked to give to the hospital out of their, often meagre, pay. Thomas did not think it right to ask. Other mine managers had asked and the money was willingly given – in the case of East Pool the miners contributed 3d a month from their wages. It amounted to £40 a year. Twelve months before Dolcoath men had been asked, but to no effect. It was suggested that Wickett talk to the miners at the next setting day and he agreed. Once again, Thomas demanded to know who gave authority for Dolcoath men to go to the hospital. The reply was, Dr Erskine, Dr Hutchinson and Dr Telfer Thomas, the manager's own son. The good captain still refused to believe that all of those 323 patients were from Dolcoath.[431]

An Amazing Escape
The June 4th *Mining Journal* carried a report of a 'Curious accident' at Dolcoath. A cage with four miners in it ran away and fell some 600 feet through Eastern Shaft. Two shaftmen and two miners got in the cage at the 375 fathom level, to go up. When the cage got up to the 254 fathom level it suddenly stopped and then plunged down at terrific speed. The accident was caused by a breakage of the fly-wheel shaft of the whim. Fortunately, the whim men fought desperately with the brake and when the cage hit a sharp turn in the shaft, the downward plunge was halted. The men got out shaken and frightened. They were otherwise unhurt. If it had not actually happened, the *Journal* said, it would have been dismissed as impossible! Had 'safety clutches'

been installed the cage could not have fallen so far. A similar accident at Killifreth had resulted in the almost immediate halting of the cage.[432]

The June 13th 1892 Adventurers Meeting, resolved, "That in accordance with the recommendation of the Manager, a New Steam Stamps consisting of 40 heads of the California type with a Steam Engine capable of working 80 heads be at once erected." Thomas reckoned theses stamps would cost £2,775. He said that Harvey & Co. had erected the same type in South Africa and they were very efficient. One of Josiah Thomas' sons managed a gold mine in the Transvaal and swore by these Californian Stamps. Matthew Loam, Dolcoath's engineer, reckoned these stamps, with a new boiler and extra dressing floors would cost in total about £5,000. Loam believed the whole plant could be ready in less than six months. Two payments were recorded for the new plant, including these new Californian Stamps: £862 13s 2d in November 1892 and £5,043 14s in 1893. The stamps were to be erected on the eastern side of the valley.[433]

In June Captain Thomas announced that he was to go to America to inspect machinery and report on the mineral prospects there. He should be back within the month. Captain James Johns was to take charge in his absence. At the adventurers meeting in June, Mr Conybeare, the Mining Division Member of Parliament and an adventurer, spoke warmly about Dolcoath and its future prospects. He rebutted the accusation that he had slandered Cornish mine owners in a recent speech in Birmingham.[434]

At the September 1892 Adventurers Meeting, a letter was read from a Mr R. Tangye of Newquay, with which he sent a cheque for one guinea, to be paid to the widow and family of a Dolcoath miner, who had recently been killed there. He suggested that the adventurers might like to set up a fund for the family, but it was pointed out that the mine had already sent the widow £50. At the same meeting progress on the new crushing and dressing plant was discussed. Water was to be pumped from the adit to supply the dressing floors, and a new railway was to be laid to bring ore to a new stone-breaker and from there to the Californian stamps. On the subject of stamps, Captain Thomas waxed eloquent about the sheer size of the stamping batteries he had seen working in the USA. One gold mine's stamps pulverised 2,800 tons a day, and these were the same type as the Californian stamps Dolcoath was installing. He would not comment on the Dakota tin prospects, as the report he had been paid to prepare for some London investors, was confidential. Captain Bishop of East Pool had inspected Dolcoath and reported that Main Lode at the 412 fathom level was the finest he had ever seen, indeed, he reckoned there was not another lode like it in the world! He also noted how cool the 400 fathom level was, now that ventilation at the bottom levels had been improved.[435]

A New Chief Engineer

A new problem had arisen by November, when it was pointed out that boilers had to be regularly inspected, and it was the personal responsibility of the chief engineer to do it. The Committee felt that the engineer needed to live close at hand to do this, but as Matthew Loam lived in Liskeard, he needed to move closer to the mine. Loam said moving was impossible and promptly resigned. The adventurers thanked him for his valuable work over the years, and gave him a parting gift of £50. He was immediately replaced by Mr Nicholas Trestrail of Redruth. Trestrail was an experienced engineer, having worked for twenty years as engineer for several local mines. During his career he acted as engineer at South Wheal Crofty, Carn Brea Mines, South Wheal Frances and Wheal Jane. It was also reported in November that the Californian stamps and related plant were up and running inside the six months promised by Harvey and Co. The adventurers voted a bonus payment of £30 to the workers who had done such a good and fast job. As well as the new engines erected, there were also revolving frames for treating slimes. The water from the adit was alright for dressing purposes, but it proved too acidic for the engine boilers. Mr J. J. Beringer, the Principal of the School of Mines, who was an assayer, tested it for them. The boiler water was eventually obtained from Camborne Waterworks via Tuckingmill, the annual cost of which was to be £20. The final cost of all this new work came to £6,000, somewhat more than anticipated, but still well worth it. It was also intended to erect a new fitting shop for routine, on-site maintenance. The tools for this would be supplied by Tangyes of Birmingham, a world-renowned engineering company of Cornish origin. To put the icing on the cake, Captain Thomas suggested that for a mere £100 extra, the stamps and floors could be lit by electricity.[436]

1892 saw the profits leap to over double the previous year, and this was due to increased output, rather than a higher tin price. The twelve weeks ending February 27th 1892 had costs of £20,308, profit of £5,150, dividend of £5,288 at £1 2s 6d a share, dues paid of £1,492 at 1/18th, and black tin sales of £26,852 for 506 tons, which averaged £53 a ton. The club stood at £465 and the mine paid £934 tax on the previous year's profit. The total mine income was £25,458. The twelve weeks ending May 28th had costs of £20,770, profit of £10,783, dividend paid of £4,700 at £1 a share, dues of £1,850, and tin sales of £33,307 for 594 tons, which averaged £56 a ton. The club money was £652 and subsist paid came to £680. Total income was £31,554. The three months ending August 20th had costs of £20,845, profit of £11,008, dividend of £9,400 at £2 a share, dues of £1,867, and tin sales of £33,623 for 600 tons, which sold for £56 a ton. Club money was £594 and subsistence payments came to £652. Overall mine income was £31,854. The twelve weeks ending November 12th had costs of £20,907, profit of £10,746, dividend of £9,400 at £2 a share, dues of £1,855, and tin sales of £33,398 for 603 tons, which averaged £55 8s a ton. Extra bills for the new stamps came to £862 13s 2d. The club was £469 and the subsist payments were £697. Total income was £31,653.[437]

The February 20th 1893 manager's report showed Engine Shaft at the 425 fathom level, which was being quickly opened up to the east and west of the shaft. New East Shaft was sunk 16 fathoms below the 412 level, Old Sump Shaft was down 7 fathoms under the 412 level, and Man Engine Shaft was sunk 18 fathoms below the 314 fathom level. By May New East Shaft was on the 425 level, which was being driven west toward Engine Shaft. Old Sump Shaft was down 10½ fathoms under the 412 fathom level, and Harrietts Shaft was within 7 fathoms of the 375 level. In May, Man Engine Shaft was down 19 fathoms under the 314 fathom level, but sinking was suspended due to problems in the shaft. One of the winzes being sunk below the 412 level had 12 men working in it, using an air winch for hoisting the dirt. They had sunk 48 feet in three months. Main Lode was estimated to be over 30 feet wide in one of the winzes below the 412 fathom level. By August Engine Shaft was being prepared to sink under the 425 level, Eastern Shaft was about to go below the 400 level and Harrietts Shaft was expected to hole to the 375 fathom level shortly. This would vastly improve ventilation in that section. The 425 level had been holed to Old Sump Shaft. R. H. Harris' men were offered bonuses of £5 a month if they could achieve 2 fathoms a month in sinking Engine Shaft, and £10 if they could sink 3 fathoms a month.[438]

The ore values in early 1893 remained fairly moderate for most of the ends, but two of the winzes under the 412 level, east of New East Shaft had ore worth £100 to £150 a fathom. By August these values had risen to £120 and £150 respectively. The higher levels mostly had values of around £10 a fathom. South Lode values varied between £10 and £30 a fathom. Toward the end of the year, the lower grade stopes, were being worked by 130 tributers.[439]

As the new stamping and dressing plant came into operation there were the usual teething problems. In February Captain Thomas reported that only 20 of the new stamps heads were working as the engine only had one working boiler, but this would soon be rectified. The 'grass captains' followed a well-known course with new plant, by stamping and dressing low grade ore first. This would 'fill up the dressing floors so as to lose in future as little tin as possible'. All the cracks and crannies would be full of poor material before the better ore came through, thus avoiding waste. Already, the Californian stamps were proving twice as efficient as the old ones, said Thomas. He also reported the introduction of more 'revolving frames for slimes', making a total of 8 in use – some convex and some concave. Both types worked 'exceedingly well', and he reckoned they needed another 10 or 12 more. He believed that these new buddles would solve the problem of tin going down the Red River. Problems with boilers also affected the underground work, for the capacity of the air compressors was reduced and fewer boring machines and winches could operate. By August Thomas reported that the new stamps and dressing plant had increased production 'from 450 tons to 620 tons' a quarter. Before it was installed, there had been a large tonnage of ore underground and at surface awaiting the new plant.[440]

In May 1893 the adventurers resolved to give Captain Josiah Thomas a piece of silver plate worth 100 guineas, in recognition of his 'successful services as Manager of this Mine during a period of 25 years'. Earlier in the year, Thomas had detailed the progress the mine had made during his period in charge. He said that between 1799 and 1867, some 68 years, the mine had paid dividends of £309,395, which averaged £4,550 a year. Under his 25 year stewardship, the mine had paid dividends of £580,134, which averaged £23,203 a year. This was five times the average of the previous period. In 1868 the mine produced 70 tons of tin a month, but now it was producing 200 tons a month. In the last 25 years, Dolcoath had sold 43,049 tons of black tin, worth £2,460,137, had met costs of £1,708,935 and paid dues to the mineral lords of £180,382. No wonder the principal recipients of these dividends wanted to reward Captain Thomas. In August the *Mining Journal* reported on the presentation, which was a 'set of silver epergnes'. The chairman, Michael Henry Williams, who had himself been associated with Dolcoath for over 50 years, made the presentation and gave a fulsome speech about Thomas' immense contribution to the success of the mine.[441]

The Collapse of the Great Stull
On September 20th 1893 there occurred possibly the worst accident ever to happen at Dolcoath. As Main Lode became wider at the deepest levels it also became flatter, making the hanging-wall in need of very strong support. The eastern workings were extremely wide and the distance between the foot- and hanging-walls at the 412 and 425 fathom levels was over 35 feet in places. The accident happened on the 412 fathom level just east of New East Shaft, at an extremely wide excavation, where the hanging-wall was supported by the 'great stull'. After an inspection of this stull by the mine manager, Captain Thomas, and the senior underground agent, Captain James Johns, it was decided that it needed strengthening, as one of the timbers appeared to be showing stress. The stull consisted of 22 pieces of 18-inch to 20-inch square, pitch-pine timber, the average length of which was 33 feet. These were set at an angle of about 45 degrees, which was at right-angle to the hanging-wall. Under the stull, timbers were set horizontally across the level to support the stull pieces. These were in turn supported by vertical timbers. Above the 'great stull' was a smaller stull, and between these was packed debris. Above this, for a height of some 600 feet, was a huge tonnage of waste rock of varying stability, with levels driven through it at regular intervals, each protected by timber-work.[442]

Following the inspection, Captain Johns told the timbermen to insert into the stull two large pieces of 20-inch square pitch-pine, to strengthen it. One piece was on the 412 level and the other had to be brought from surface. The leading timberman was John Pollard and his right-hand man was Charles White. Both were very experienced timbermen or 'binders'. They were assisted by a gang of at least fourteen others, as they struggled to man-handle the enormous timbers into place. There were eleven timbermen and miners, one boy and four Camborne Mining School students. The gang was split into two groups, one of which was working at the western end of the stull, nearest to the tunnel leading to New East Shaft, and the other group, led by Pollard and White, was engaged in installing the new timbers. The top end of a 23 feet-long timber had been lifted to the hanging-wall by the eight-man, crew using a rope-block. Suddenly, there was a 'God send', a fall of gravel and rock, which can give timely warning at such times. About a ton of debris fell, and although the miners were all used to such things, they all ran for the tunnels at either end of the stull. The men nearest the tunnel to New East Shaft made it to safety, but those beneath the middle of the stull stood no chance, for before they could move far, there was a dreadful and cataclysmic roar as thousands of tons of rock and earth destroyed the entire massive stull and buried the 8 men beneath it.

The violent movement of air caused by this tremendous displacement of ground swept miners off their feet and hurled stones far along the level. Two miners were struck by them as they fled and one young lad, Jimmy Tresawna, was carried through the air for a distance of over 20 feet. A heavy wagon was blown a similar distance along the level, injuring a miner. Miners had their clothes blown off and others suffered a variety of injuries from flying debris. The noise was heard all over the central part of the mine. Those close-by picked themselves up and headed back to the scene of the accident to see what could be done. They were faced by a massive and impenetrable mass of rock, timber and debris. They shouted, but received no reply. One of them climbed to the 400 fathom level, but found the stull there entirely swept away. A mass of rock and debris some 600 feet high had moved down, filling the workings beneath.

Quickly, the news was carried to the surface, and almost immediately a massive rescue attempt was initiated. Gangs of miners worked round the clock, tunnelling from both ends of the blockage, to reach the buried miners. Progress was agonisingly slow, as many of the rocks were very large and the debris had to be supported as they tunnelled. Undeterred the men pushed on tirelessly, determined to find their mates. It was 3 o'clock the following afternoon before the rescuers had any encouragement – from the eastern end they heard a voice shouting: 'Praise the Lord!' The tunnelers, who were about 16 feet into the pile, were delighted and pressed on with renewed vigour. William John Osborne of Camborne, had been lying beneath the debris, his legs pinned by a piece of timber, 'praising the Lord' for over 26 hours. He shouted to the rescuers that he had heard no other voices. A couple of small miners were able to crawl through the pile for over 30 feet toward Osborne, but could not get close enough to pass a tube to him with liquid food. Despite their best efforts they could not get to him before he died. However, his courage, faith and steadfastness inspired them to even greater effort, and just before 8 o'clock that evening they heard another voice from the rock pile. It was from Richard Davies of Troon, and he was able to tell the rescuers that he was unhurt, with no rock or timber on any part of him. He lay about 30 feet from the eastern tunnelers and was able to crawl some distance toward them. One of the rescuers, called Smith, crawled to meet Davies, and when he was close, he reached out with his hand to touch him and comfort him, but upon remarking how cold his hand was, was informed by Davies that both his hands were free. Smith had gripped the hand of a dead miner. Eventually, Smith was able to pass a hatchet through to Davies, so that he could cut away some of the timber blocking his exit. Finally, Davies was able to squeeze through to safety. He tried to stand up, but had to be helped. His mates hauled him to the 400 fathom level, from whence he was taken by gig to the surface.

Richard Davies was the only survivor of those eight entombed men. The hundred or so rescuers, many of them exhausted, worked on to clear the rock and find their mates. These miners soldiered on around the clock, enduring not only tremendous difficulty and danger, but also suffering the appalling stench from the bodies of their dead friends. The last body, that of Charles White, was recovered almost three weeks after the accident, on October 9th. The dead men were John Pollard, chief timberman, Charles White, senior timberman, William John Osborne, John Henry Jennings, Frederick John Harvey, James Adams and Richard James.[443]

The miners, the town of Camborne and the whole of the Cornish community at home and abroad were shocked by the scale of the tragedy. Every mining district in the world had men who had been trained or had worked at Dolcoath. Some of the dead men were known personally to miners throughout North and South America, Australia, New Zealand, South and West Africa and everywhere where hard-rock mining took place. The scale of the accident was particularly shocking because Dolcoath was widely thought of as a 'safe' mine. Dolcoath immediately made claims on behalf of the men to the Employers Liability Assurance Company. The company quickly paid out £50 for each miner. Following the accident there was considerable discussion about a County Relief Fund for assisting miners and their families after accidents. J. C. Williams MP gave £500 toward it and Arthur Strauss promised £100 a year for fifteen years. Polberro Mine adventurers promised £10 a year and Dolcoath offered £50 a year. Mr Heard, ever the rebel, suggested £100 and the adventurers agreed to double their original offer.[444]

The finances of the mine remained good for much of 1893, before plummeting in the autumn, as Dolcoath was faced by its many problems. For the twelve weeks ending February 4th 1893 costs were £20,481, profit was £12,024, the dividend paid was £9,400 at £2 a share, dues of 1/18th totalling £1,904 were paid to Tehidy and £34,272 was received for 625 tons of black tin, which sold for an average of £54

16s. A year's income tax of £827 was paid, and £5,044 was paid toward the new stamps and dressing plant. The miners club stood at £436, and subsistence payments advanced to miners came to £704. Overall income was £32,505. Mr Heard, one of the adventurers, expressed delight at the February adventurers meeting, because for the first time there were no bank charges paid. The twelve weeks ending April 29th had costs of £20,707, profit of £10,771, dividends paid of £9,400 at £2 a share and dues of £1,845 paid to the Basset Estate. A total of 605 tons of black tin was sold for £33,208 at an average price of £54 18s. The club stood at £521 and subsistence payments came to £746. Total income was £31,478. The three months ending July 22nd had costs of £21,012, profit of £9,024, dividends of £8,789 at £1 17s 6d a share, and 1/18th dues paid of £1,760. £31,682 was received for 623 tons of tin, which averaged £50 17s a ton. The quarter ending October 14th had costs of £21,220, profit of £2,700, dues paid of £1,399 and total black tin sales for 516 tons, of £23,787, which averaged a mere £46 a ton. The twin disasters of a massive loss of production due to the horrific accident at the 412 fathom level and the sudden, dramatic drop in the tin metal price, saw financial gloom descend upon the mine's adventurers. The twelve weeks ending January 7th 1894 had costs of £19,997, profit of £533, dues paid of £1,201 and tin sales of £20,426 for 476 tons, which sold for an average of £45 9s a ton, which was down £3 7s on the previous quarter. Thomas reckoned this cost the mine £1,660. There was no dividend. Total income was £20,530.[445]

Despite the many problems the mine had endured in the last half of 1893 its programme of sinking and developing continued without significant pause. By January 1894 Engine Shaft was sunk 5 fathoms under the 425 fathom level, and a new cistern cut with plunger lifts fixed to the bottom level. By April it was 10 fathoms under the 425. In January Eastern Shaft was sunk 4½ fathoms below the 400 fathom level, and the 412 level was being driven toward it: this, despite the appalling problems there. The good news was that the large replacement stull on the 412 seemed unaffected by the flooding. By April Eastern Shaft was 6 fathoms under the 400 level, and preparations were in hand to begin sinking New East Shaft below the 425 fathom level. Once the problems of the second half of the year were solved sinking continued in all three central shafts, with two boring machines used in Old Sump Shaft, where they hoped to sink 2 fathoms a month. There were 8 rock drills in use in the mine in October, mostly sinking shafts and driving the deeper levels.[446]

Work in the stopes above the 412 level, east of New East Shaft, was suspended while the ground was secured. The 425 level east of No.1 winze was worth £100 a fathom. The rest of the mine showed values of between £10 and £60 a fathom. However, Main Lode between the 412 and 425 levels, east of where the accident occurred, was extraordinarily rich, being worth up to £600 a fathom. Main Lode on the 425 level, east of New East Shaft was 30 feet wide and worth £80 a fathom.[447]

An interesting discussion took place at the January 1894 adventurers meeting, in which the state of the world metal markets, and global financial and trade problems were discussed. Captain Thomas put it into the context of widespread protectionism, by the Americans and others, and the frantic armaments race which seemed so dangerous. He commented that all countries were 'armed to the teeth', and were taxing to the hilt to maintain 'great armies'. He believed that a 'great war' was imminent. He thought that this would be potentially disastrous for trade and the tin industry. At the April meeting this discussion continued, with comments about the attachment the price of tin had to the price of silver. Thomas was optimistic about the imminent rise of the tin price due to this, but worried about the reduction in purchases of tin by the Americans. He also commented that half the Welsh tin platers, who were large users of the metal, were idle. To the suggestion that the mine goes for the higher grade ore to keep the dividends up, he replied that it would mean firing 200 workers, which would not only be bad for Camborne, but also it was the wrong policy in the long-term for Dolcoath. He would pursue the policy he always had, of keeping development well ahead of production.[448]

Collapse, Fire & Sabotage Underground

On April 19th 1894, there was another serious and expensive accident, when a large amount of rubble from old copper workings fell into the Engine Shaft at the 125 fathom level, choking the shaft and causing the pumps to stop and the bottom of the mine to fill with water. The water rose to within 3½ fathoms of the 388 fathom level. A dam was placed in the 375 west of Old Sump Shaft, which kept the water back and the water from the upper levels was diverted to Harrietts Shaft, where it was pumped to surface. Pumps operated by compressed air brought the water up to the 314 level, where it ran to Harrietts. Meanwhile, heavy timbers were installed between the 107 and 132 fathom levels, to secure Engine Shaft. The main pump was idle for 9½ weeks – it did not restart till June 24th. During the crisis a large proportion of the ore raised came up Eastern Shaft. As if this was not bad enough, there was another, more sinister problem. Thomas reported that the air pumps had been deliberately sabotaged. Apparently, 'malicious persons' had removed the screws and flanges on the pumps, inserted a length of shovel handle into the pipe and then replaced the screws and flanges to appear normal. Also, old jackets had been pushed into the joint of the lift of the main pump, to stop the clack valve working. Nonplussed, Captain Thomas queried whether the culprit had been paid to do it, as no intelligent miner would want to put his mates out of work. Mr Heard said the same thing was happening in America and France, but Mr Bailey thought this was not the work of anarchists, but of someone who speculated in shares. Mr Vivian suggested the mine offer a reward of £100 for information, but the chairman thought £50 would be enough.[449]

As a result of this crisis, in July, Mr Goddard, the Tehidy agent, negotiated with Mr

Basset a temporary reduction of the dues to half the 1/18th for that quarter. Basset expressed his dismay and disgust over the activities of the saboteurs. "I think it should be made known that your position would have been much better if it had not been for the disloyalty of some of your men. … I, of course, allude to the tampering with the lifts which prevented you forking the water as soon as you otherwise would." Basset was stating the obvious, but the management was well aware that perhaps only one man might have carried out the sabotage and that his motive may well have been money.[450]

Also in April there was a serious fire underground. A discarded candle appears to have been left burning on a stull near New Sump Shaft, at the 375 fathom level, resulting in more damage and loss of production.[451]

It was also at the July adventurers meeting that the question of a new vertical shaft to the south was raised. Mr Wickett asked how much it would cost, and Thomas and Williams answered, between £40,000 and £60,000. This had been discussed among the agents and the Committee for some time, but with the tin price so low and the other problems the mine was facing, it did not seem the appropriate time to consider an expensive, new, vertical shaft.[452]

The accounts for 1894 were even worse than 1893, for the problems which beset the mine were even more expensive than those of the previous year. The twelve weeks ending April 2nd 1894 had costs of £20,994, profit of £4,083, a dividend of £1,384 at 12 6d a share, and tin sales of £24,909 for 617 tons at an average price of £40 7s. The twelve weeks ending June 24th had costs of £19,810, a loss of £1,529, no dividend paid and dues paid of £533 – half the 1/18th due. Tin sales were £19,205 for 451 tons, which averaged £42 11s, and total income after deductions was £18,281. The quarter ending September 14th had costs of £17,604, a loss of £2,529, no dividend was paid and the Bassets were paid £879 for dues. Mundic sales were £2 10s 6d and tin sales were £14,952 for 371 tons at an average of £40 6s a ton. Total income after all deductions was £15,074. The accounts for three months ending December 6th 1894 showed a further decline in the financial position of the mine, with the amount received for the mine's tin below £40 a ton, at an average of £37 14s. Despite a massive jump in production of 123 tons, over the previous quarter, the mine still lost £189. Tin sales realised £18,604 for 494 tons. Dues paid were £1,075. Needless to say, there was no dividend paid.[453]

The Account House Burnt Down
1895 started with another calamity, when the account house burnt down. The fire started at about 10.15 pm, on Tuesday 22nd January, and all the men working nearby rushed to put it out. With the fire out of control they pulled as much furniture and contents out as they could, before Camborne Fire Brigade arrived, three-quarters-

of-an-hour later. The mine plans, lining the walls were destroyed as were a lot of important papers, but the cost books and other essential records were kept in a strong room and were safe. The large plan of the mine, just completed by R. Arthur Thomas, was burnt, but it was fortunate that duplicates of all plans were held by the Tehidy Office, and could easily be copied. The cause of the fire remains a mystery, but it is possible that it was another act of sabotage by person or persons unknown.[454]

With the water forked and essential repairs carried out shaft sinking continued. The March 23rd 1895 *Mining Journal* reported that Engine Shaft was 16 fathoms below the 425 fathom level and that the 440 level had been driven 5½ fathoms east of the shaft. There was a 6 feet deep sump below the level. New East Shaft was down 11½ fathoms under the 425 level, but there had been a serious run of ground in New East Shaft a fortnight before. This new problem underlined the need for a new perpendicular shaft, and discussions were becoming serious about it. It was to be sunk well to the south of the main workings, to intersect Main Lode at great depth. The management was questioning the desirability of spending time and money repairing damaged shafts and sinking so many shafts, when one vertical shaft could be used to pump all the water and hoist most of the ore. It would still be essential to protect Engine Shaft, however, and concrete arches had been put in at the 352 level to protect it. They re-emphasised the value of Eastern Shaft, and saw it as essential for the efficient working of the mine.[455]

The March discussion was led by Captain R. Arthur Thomas, the oldest son of Josiah, who, for the first time since becoming manager, missed a meeting through illness. The chairman said he thought the mine was in good hands as three of Josiah's sons were running things. Josiah had been taken ill the previous month and was convalescing at Carbis Bay, from where he had written some of the above observations. There had been a panic when he was taken ill, because there was a rumour that Captain James Johns, the senior mine captain, was to retire due to his advanced years. Johns was described as 'invaluable' in the *Mining Journal,* and it was widely thought that Dolcoath needed his intelligent skill as much, if not more, than that of Captain Josiah Thomas. A new recruit to the management team at that time was Captain Joseph Tamblyn, who, like Captain Johns 19 years before, had been filched from South Wheal Crofty. He was described by the *Mining Journal* as 'one of the most energetic agents it is possible to find in Cornwall'. He had previously also worked in Italy, Wisconsin and South Africa, before becoming a mine captain at Killifreth Mine. After leaving Dolcoath, in 1903, he worked in Spain, East Pool and Condurrow.[456]

It was at this point that the possibility of the mine changing to a limited liability company was first seriously mooted. Captain Josiah Thomas wrote of 'going to the market' for capital, and hence being quoted on the Stock Exchange as a limited liability company. The *Mining Journal* of May 11th 1895 reported the Adventurers

Meeting which was to discuss the proposal and make one of the most momentous decisions in the mine's long history.[457]

References Part Two (1799-1895)

1. Pryce (1972) pp.170-172; Hatchett Diary (1967) p.38; Harris (1974) pp.27,46; MJ (April 15 1871) p.303
2. G. C. Boase Collectanea Cornubiensia (1890) p.1153; George Henwood MJ (May 30 1857); MJ (April 15 1871) p.303
3. Report on the Copper Trade (1792-98)
4. MJ (May 30 1857); Alphabetical Index of Patentees of Inventions (1969) pp.575,587
5. Harris (1974) pp.27,46; MJ (April 15 1871) p.583
6. Report on the Copper Trade (1792-98)
7. Francis Trevithick Life of Richard Trevithick (1872) pp.67-102; Pryce (1972) pp.170-172; Harris (1974) pp.27-29; Bibliotheca Cornubiensis Vol.2 (1878) p.827; Dr Paris A Guide to the Mounts Bay & the Land's End (1824) p.198
8. MJ (April 15 1871) p.303
9. Observations Addressed to the Adventurers in Tin Croft Mine by a Cornishman (1802) Ms. in Morrab Library, Penzance; HJ/1/5 RIC Library, Truro
10. Observations (1802); A. K. Hamilton Jenkin Mines & Miners of Cornwall vol.10 (1965) pp.30,31; A State of the Account of Cornish Copper Mines (Ms. of A K Hamilton Jenkin in RIC Library, Truro)
11. MJ (April 15 1871) p.303; TRGSC vol.8 p.447
12. Sherborne Mercury (May 20 1799); Royal Cornwall Gazette (Dec.22 1804); Ronnie Opie (South Crofty Shiftboss) Personal Communication
13. Trevithick (1872) pp.90-106; Harris (1974) pp.28,29; Anthony Burton Richard Trevithick: Giant of Steam (2000) pp.60-62; RCG (May 3 1806)
14. Journal Trevithick Society Vol.5 (1977) pp.45,46; Burton (2000) pp.75-100
15. Harris (1974) p.8; *Bibliotheca Cornubiensis* vol.2 (1878) p.827; MJ (May 30 1857)
16. MJ (May 30 1857); Bib. Corn. vol.2 (1878) p.607; *Collectanea Cornubiensia* (1890) p.730
17. Pryce (1972) pp.198-202; TRGSC vol.8 p.220
18. RCG (Feb.21 1807); Letters from Lord DeDunstanville to the House of Lords Committee for Trade (1807)
19. HJ/1/5 RIC Truro; MJ (April 15 1871) p.303; TRGSC vol.8 p.447
20. RCG (Feb.27 1808)
21. Richard Warner A Tour Through Cornwall in Autumn 1808 (1808) pp.133,290
22. Ibid.
23. Warner (1808) pp.133,290; Buckley Princes (2007) pp.15-44
24. TRGSC vol.8 pt.2 pp.112,113; J. Y. Watson Compendium of British Mining (1843) p.36
25. West Briton (Dec.14 1810); HJ/1/5 RIC Truro
26. Statistics provided by Alastair Neil
27. A. K. Hamilton Jenkin News from Cornwall (1951) p.154; Trevithick (1872) vol.2 p.10
28. Harris (1974) pp.31,32
29. Thomas Lean On the Steam Engines of Cornwall (1969); Harris (1974) p.32; Barton

(1969) p.32; Journal Trevithick Society No.29 (2002) pp.123-128; J Trev. Soc. No.5 (1977) pp.37,38,45,46; T. R. Harris Arthur Woolf (1966) pp.62,63

30. West Briton (May 3 1811)
31. HJ/1/5 (Aug.1811) RIC Truro
32. WB (Nov.26 1813); T. Lean Engine Reporter (1813)
33. T. A. Morrison Cornwall's Central Mines: Southern District 1810-95 (1983) p.15; J Trev. Soc. No.5 (1977) pp.37,38,45,46
34. TRGSC vol.1 (1814) p.225
35. Paris (1824) pp.125-127,196-199; Pryce (1972) pp.170-172
36. Harris (1966) pp.57,58; J Trev. Soc. No.5 (1977) pp.37,38,45,46; F Hitchens & S Drew The History of Cornwall (1824) vol.2 p.487
37. TRGSC vol.1 (June 1815 to June 1816) pp.252-261; Morrison (1983) p.53
38. Dr J. A. Paris On Accidents Which Occur in the Mines of Cornwall (1817) p.30
39. Paris (1817) p.30; RCG (June 20 1817); C Noall Cornish Mine Disasters (1989) p.107
40. T. Lean On the Steam Engines of Cornwall (1969) p.32; WB (April 11 1817); T. R. Harris J Trev. Soc. No.5 (1977) p.37
41. TRGSC vol.1 (June 1816 to June 1817) pp.252-261; Morrison (1983) p.53
42. Richard Thomas Survey of the Mining District of Chacewater to Camborne (1819) pp.34-36
43. Ibid.
44. WB (July 10 1818)
45. HJ/1/5 (Aug. 29 1818) RIC
46. T. R. Harris J. Trev. Soc. No.5 (1977) p.45
47. Dr Forbes TRGSC (1819) p.189
48. TRGSC vol.1 pp.252-261; vol.2 pp.428-437 (June 1818 to June 1819 & June 1819 to June 1820 & June 1820 to June 1821); Morrison (1983) p.53
49. Forbes TRGSC (1819) p.189; John Rule Junior TRGSC vol.2 (1822) pp.167,168
50. Buckley Princes of the Working Valley (2007) pp.10-15
51. Buckley Princes (2007) pp.7-44
52. Buckley Princes (2007) pp.17-27
53. Buckley Princes (2007) pp.27-44,96-127
54. WB (Sept.27 1822); Thomas (1819) pp.34-36
55. Buckley Princes (2007) pp.35-43
56. Ibid.
57. Ibid.
58. Ibid.
59. Ibid.
60. Ibid.
61. WB (Oct.23 1823); Buckley Princes (2007) p.38
62. Forbes TRGSC (1822)
63. James Thomas & William Petherick Day & Night Book of Two Dolcoath Mine Captains (1822-23) Thomas Collection, CSM Library, Tremough, Penryn
64. T. Lean Engine Reporter (1823)
65. Bibliotheca Cornubiensis vol.2 (1878) p.607
66. WB (Nov. 12 1824)
67. TRGSC vol.3 p.242; WB (Oct.28 1825)

68. T. R. Harris J Trev. Soc. No.5 (1977) pp.37,38,45
69. TRGSC vol.3 p.242
70. WB (Dec.15 1826)
71. HJ/2/6 RIC
72. TRGSC vol.3 p.242; vol.4 pp.492-496; Morrison (1983) p.53
73. RCG (Feb.9 1828)
74. Harris (1974) pp.41,42,48; TRGSC vol.1 p.122; Life of William Whewell (1881); Life & Letters of Sedgwick (1890)
75. Harris (1882) p.36
76. TRGSC vol.8 pt.1 (1871) p.666; Buckley Princes (2007); Day & Night Book (1822-23)
77. WB (Oct.3 1828)
78. HJ/2/6 RIC
79. DDX 475/2-7; Dolcoath Pay Book (1786-90); Day & Night Book (1822-23)
80. WB (May 1 1829)
81. TRGSC vol.4 pp.492-496; Morrison (1983) p.53
82. RCG (May 1 1830)
83. Collectanea Cornubiensia (1890) p.730; TRGSC vol.5 pp.58,197,327,342; Report from the Royal Cornwall Polytechnic Society (1836) p.92; Buckley Princes (2007) pp.13-15
84. Paris (1817); WB (Jan.7 1831); Alphabetical Index (1969) p.47 (No.6159)
85. Harris (1882) pp.2,36,37
86. Thomas Allom picture (1831) in the Royal Cornwall Museum, Truro
87. WB (Jan.7 1831); WB (April 22 1831); RCG (March 12 1831); J. A. Buckley A History of South Crofty Mine (1980) p.40; Buckley Princes (2007) p.20
88. TRGSC vol.4 pp.492-496; Morrison (1983) p.53
89. Harris (1882) pp.2,36,37,39,46; Buckley Princes (2007) p.102
90. Harris (1882) pp.64,79
91. Ibid.
92. Buckley Princes (2007) pp.44-47
93. Illogan Parish Registers (July 22 1833) Cornwall Centre, Redruth; WB (July 5 1833); WB (Nov.8 1833)
94. Allen Buckley The Story of Mining in Cornwall (2007) pp.98,99
95. WB (Jan.31 1834); RCG ((June 21 1834); Morrison (1983) p.53
96. T. Lean Engine Reporters (1834 & 1835)
97. WB (Feb.28 1834)
98. Biblio. Cornub. (1878) p.607; RCG (June 7 1834); Buckley Princes (2007) pp.20,21; Day & Night Book (1822-23)
99. Buckley Princes (2007) pp.13-15; MJ (Dec 17 1859) p.877
100. Buckley (1980) p.40; Buckley Princes (2007) p.20; Morrison (1983) p.53
101. MJ (Dec.17 1859) p.877; Joseph F Odgers (Dolcoath Mine Secretary) Notes on history of the mine. Prof. Charles Thomas' notes and records of Dolcoath; WB (Jan.8 1836); WB (Jan.6 1837)
102. Trans. Royal Cornwall Polytechnic Society (1836) p.92
103. MJ (May 11 1837); Thomas Oliver Autobiography of a Cornish Miner (1914) p.18
104. Morrison (1983) p.53
105. Anthony Wood Nineteenth Century Britain 1815-1914 (1982) pp.73-77
106. Morrison (1983) p.53

107. Harris (1882) p.64; RCPS 9th Annual Report (1840)
108. Report to the Commissioners on Employment of Children (1842) vols. 7-9 (1839-41)
    p.132. Chairman Dr Charles Barham
109. Ibid.
110. Ibid.
111. Ibid.
112. Ibid.
113. Ibid.
114. Ibid.
115. Ibid.
116. Ibid.
117. Ibid.
118. Morrison (1983) p.53
119. Watson (1843) pp.35,36; J Carne TRGSC vol.3 (1828) pp.35-85
120. Morrison (1983) p.53
121. Collect. Cornub. (1890) p.730; TRGSC vol.5 (1843) pp.58,197,209,327,342
122. Buckley Princes (2007) pp.13-15,60,70,74; Day & Night Book (1822-23)
123. J. F. Odgers & Charles Thomas. Correspondence in Private Collection; MJ (Jan.21
    1860) p.35; MJ (Dec.17 1859) p.877
124. MJ (Jan.21 1860) p.35
125. MJ (Dec.17 1859) p.877
126. Odgers & Thomas Correspondence. Private Collection; RCG (June 15 1838)
127. Morrison (1983) pp.18,54; MJ (Dec.17 1859) p.877; WB (Feb.14 1845); WB (Sept.18
    1846)
128. J. F. Odgers Ms. Notes on history of Dolcoath
129. WB (October 1912)
130. DD TEM 43 CRO
131. Ibid.
132. Ibid.
133. Ibid.
134. Ibid.
135. Ibid.
136. Morrison (1983) p.54; DD TEM 43 CRO
137. MJ (Aug.24 1850) p.403; DD TEM 43 CRO
138. DD TEM 43 CRO
139. Ibid.
140. Ibid.
141. Morrison (1983) p.54; DD TEM 43 CRO; MJ (Dec.14 1850) p.594
142. DD TEM 43 CRO
143. Ibid.
144. Ibid.
145. DD TEM 43 CRO; MJ (Oct.16 1852) pp.503, 610
146. DD TEM 43 CRO; MJ (Mar.19 1853) p.164
147. DD TEM 43 CRO; MJ (April 16 1853) p.228; MJ (April 2 1853) p.196
148. DD TEM 43 CRO
149. Buckley Story of Mining in Cornwall (2007) pp.95-97; Barton (1969) pp.207-218; DD

TEM 43 CRO
150. MJ (Dec.24 1853) p.816
151. DD TEM 43 CRO
152. DD TEM 43 CRO; MJ (Dec.24 1853) P.816
153. DD TEM 43 CRO
154. Ibid.
155. DD TEM 43 CRO; WB (October 1854); Harris (1882) p.79
156. DD TEM 43 CRO; Morrison (1983) p.54
157. DD TEM 43 CRO
158. Oliver (1914) pp.77,78
159. Mining & Smelting Magazine (1863) vol.3 p.225 ff. (Moissenet)
160. DD TEM 43 CRO; MJ (Oct.18 1856) p.704
161. MJ (Feb.14 1857) p.117; DD TEM 274; DD TEM 43 CRO
162. Morrison (1983) p.54
163. MJ (Feb.14 1857) p.117
164. DD TEM 43 CRO
165. MJ (July 11 1857) p.424
166. MJ (Oct.17 1857) p.731; MJ (Oct.24 1857) p.747; DD TEM 43 CRO; Dolcoath Mine
     Manager's Reports (DMMR)
167. DD TEM 43 CRO; DMMR
168. Ibid.
169. L. Moissenet 'Observations of the Rich part of Lodes in Cornwall' p.59; Harris (1882)
     p.52; Oliver (1914) p.18
170. MJ (Aug.14 1858) p.535; DD TEM 43 CRO; DMMR
171. MJ (Oct.9 1858) p.670
172. MJ (Oct.16 1858) p.683; MJ (Dec.18 1858) p.839
173. DMMR; DD TEM 43 CRO
174. DD TEM 43 CRO
175. DD TEM 43 CRO; DMMR; MJ (April 16 1859) p.269; MJ (Aug.13 1859) p.566; MJ
     (June 18 1859) p.433
176. DD TEM 43 CRO; DMMR
177. Ibid.
178. DD TEM 43 CRO
179. DMMR
180. DD TEM 43 CRO; DMMR; MJ (Mar.17 1860) p.179; MJ (Aug.18 1860) p.561
181. DD TEM 43 CRO; DMMR
182. DD TEM 43,44 CRO; MJ (Dec.14 1861) pp.826,829; Morrison (1983) p.54
183. DD TEM 44 CRO; DMMR
184. Ibid.
185. Ibid.
186. Ibid.
187. Ibid.
188. Ibid.
189. Ibid.
190. Mining & Smelting Magazine vol. 1 (May 20 1862) p.404
191. DD TEM 44 CRO; DMMR

192. DD TEM 44 CRO; DMMR; MJ (Oct.17 1863) p.741
193. DD TEM 44 CRO; DMMR
194. MJ (April 18 1863) p.269
195. C. Noall Cornish Mine Disasters (1989) pp.29,30
196. Report to the Commissioners Appointed to Enquire into the Condition of Mines in Great Britain (Lord Kinnaird Chairman of Royal Mines Commission 1863,1864)
197. Ibid.
198. Ibid.
199. DMMR
200. DMMR; DD TEM 44 CRO
201. DD TEM 44 CRO
202. DMMR; MJ (June 25 1864) p.451; MJ (Oct.15 1864) p.733
203. T. Spargo The Mines of Cornwall: The Camborne Area (1865) pp.17,18
204. DMMR; MJ (Oct.15 1864) p.733
205. DD TEM 44 CRO; DMMR
206. DD TEM 44 CRO
207. Ibid.
208. DD TEM 44 CRO; DMMR
209. Harris (1974) p.53
210. Cornish Telegraph (March 15 1865)
211. Noall (1989) pp.115,116
212. MJ (June 17 1865) p.385; MMR; DD TEM 44 CRO
213. DD TEM 44 CRO
214. DMMR; DD TEM 44 CRO
215. Ibid.
216. DMMR
217. DMMR; DD TEM 44 CRO
218. Cornish Telegraph (Feb.14 1866); Cornish Telegraph (Oct.31 1866)
219. DMMR; DD TEM 44 CRO
220. DMMR; DD TEM 44 CRO; MJ (Aug.17 1867) p.545; MJ (Oct.19 1867) p.705
221. MJ (Oct.19 1867) p.705
222. DMMR
223. Bibliotheca Cornubiensis (1874) p.712; DMMR
224. DMMR
225. Ibid.
226. Noall (1989) pp.171,172
227. DMMR
228. Noall (1989) pp.170,171
229. DMMR; MJ (June 19 1869) p.441; Alphabetical Index (1969) p.78 (Feb.21 1828 No.5621)
230. DMMR; Barton (1969) p.127
231. DMMR; MJ (April 24 1869) p.308
232. DMMR
233. DMMR
234. DMMR; Harris (1974) p.55
235. DMMR; R. Burt, P. Waite, R. Burnley Cornish Mines (1987) p.163

236.DMMR
237.Ibid.
238.Ibid.
239.Ibid.
240.DMMR; MJ (Aug.13 1870) pp.674,677; MJ (Oct.15 1870) p.865
241.DMMR
242.MJ (Feb.25 1871) p.160
243.DMMR
244.Ibid.
245.Ibid.
246.Ibid.
247.Harris (1974) p.59; E. C. Midwinter Victorian Social Reform (1968) p.50; D. Thomson England in the 19th Century (1950) p.138; R. J. Evans The Victorian Age (1981) p.186; DMMR
248.Royal Cornwall Gazette (Sept.23 1871); RCG (Jan.6 1872); RCG (June 8 1872); RCG (Jan.30 1880); RCG (Feb.27 1880); MJ (April 9 1877)
249.DMMR
250.Ibid.
251.Ibid.
252.Ibid.
253.Ibid.
254.MJ (May 25 1872) p.483; DMMR
255.DMMR
256.Ibid.
257.Ibid.
258.Ibid.
259.Ibid.
260.Ibid.
261.Noall (1989) pp.116,117
262.Noall (1989) pp.57,58; MJ (Nov.23 1872) p.1119
263.DMMR
264.Ibid.
265.Ibid.
266.DMMR; MJ (Dec.14 1872) p.1207
267.DMMR
268.DMMR; MJ (Feb.8 1873) p.139; MJ (Feb.22 1873) p.214
269.DMMR; MJ (March 15 1873) p.289
270.DMMR
271.DMMR; MJ (May 17 1873) p.546
272.MJ (May 17 1873) p.546
273.DMMR
274.DMMR; MJ (Aug.9 1873) p.876
275.DMMR
276.Ibid.
277.Ibid.
278.Ibid.

279. Ibid.
280. Ibid.
281. DMMR; MJ (April 18 1874) p.430; MJ (July 11 1874) p.755
282. MJ (July 11 1874) p.755
283. MJ (Oct.3 1874) p.1088
284. DMMR
285. MJ (June 13 1874) p.635
286. DMMR
287. Ibid.
288. DMMR; MJ (March 20 1875) p.320
289. MJ (April 24 1875) p.443
290. DMMR; MJ (June 12 1875) p.650
291. DMMR; MJ (Sept.11 1875) p.1003
292. DMMR
293. Ibid.
294. Ibid.
295. DMMR; J. A. Buckley South Crofty Mine: A History (1997) pp.87-92
296. DMMR; MJ (Feb.19 1876) p.209; MJ (May 13 1876) p.539
297. MJ (Aug.19 1876) p.919
298. DMMR; MJ (Oct.28 1876) p.1183
299. MJ (Dec.9 1876) p.1351
300. DMMR; MJ (Dec.9 1876) p.1351; Morrison (1983) pp.34,35
301. MJ (Aug.5 1876) p.864
302. DMMR
303. Ibid.
304. Ibid.
305. DMMR; MJ (April 14 1877) p.408
306. DMMR; Author's own observations
307. DMMR; MJ (Sept. 29 1877) p.1067
308. DMMR; MJ Supplement (Dec. 22 1877) p.1412
309. Noall (1989) pp.35,36
310. DMMR
311. DMMR; MJ (Nov. 23 1878) p.1308
312. DMMR
313. DMMR; MJ (Aug.31 1878) p.971
314. DMMR; MJ (June 8 1878) p.638; MJ (Nov.23 1878) p.1295; Clive Carter J Trev.Soc. No.20 (1993) pp.2-22
315. DMMR; MJ (Aug.31 1878) p.971; MJ (Nov.23 1878) p.1295
316. DMMR
317. DMMR; MJ (Feb.15 1879) p.170
318. Noall (1989) p.151
319. DMMR
320. MJ (May 19 1879)
321. RCG (August 15 1879)
322. DMMR
323. R. J. Evans (1981) p.186; Anthony Wood Nineteenth Century Britain 1815-1914

(1962) pp.118,301,363,364
324.DMMR
325.Ibid.
326.Ibid.
327.Ibid.
328.Ibid.
329.Ibid.
330.DMMR; MJ (Dec. 18 1879) p.1467
331.DMMR
332.Ibid.
333.Ibid.
334.Ibid.
335.DMMR; MJ (March 12 1881) p.318
336.DMMR
337.DMMR; MJ (Dec. 10 1881) p.1541
338.DMMR
339.Ibid.
340.Ibid.
341.Ibid.
342.Ibid.
343.Ibid.
344.Noall (1989) p.47
345.DMMR; MJ (Dec.30 1882) pp.1595,1596
346.DMMR
347.Ibid.
348.Ibid.
349.Ibid.
350.MMR; MJ (Feb.17 1883) p.209
351.DMMR
352.Oliver (1914) pp.65,66
353.DMMR
354.DMMR; MJ (Dec.15 1883) p.1432
355.DMMR
356.DMMR; MJ (Aug.23 1884) p.979
357.DMMR
358.Ibid.
359.DMMR; MJ (March 8 1884) p.296
360.DMMR
361.Ibid.
362.Noall (1989) p.22
363.DMMR
364.Ibid.
365.Ibid.
366.Ibid.
367.DMMR; MJ (Feb.7 1885) p.147
368.Ibid.

369. DMMR
370. DMMR; MJ (May 2 1885) p.504
371. Ibid.
372. DMMR
373. Ibid.
374. Ibid.
375. Ibid.
376. Ibid.
377. DMMR; MJ (Jan.9 1886) p.40
378. DMMR; MJ (May 1 1886) p.508 (Three brothers killed June 1868)
379. DMMR; MJ (Oct.9 1886) p.1174
380. DMMR
381. DMMR; MJ (Dec.11 1886) pp.1437,1438
382. DMMR; MJ (Jan.29 1887) p.142
383. Ibid.
384. DMMR
385. Ibid.
386. Ibid.
387. Ibid.
388. DMMR; MJ (March 5 1887) p.285
389. Ibid.
390. DMMR; MJ (Aug.20 1887) p.1016
391. MJ (Nov.12 1887) p.1354
392. Ibid.
393. DMMR
394. Ibid.
395. Ibid.
396. DMMR; MJ (Oct.13 1888) p.1156
397. RCG (May 3 & 17 1888)
398. DMMR
399. DMMR; MJ (July 21 1888) pp.817,818; MJ (April 28 1888) p.470
400. DMMR; MJ (July 21 1888) pp.817,818
401. MJ (April 21 1888) p.451
402. MJ (July 21 1888) pp.817,818,828
403. DMMR; MJ (Oct.27 1888) p.1210
404. DMMR
405. Ibid.
406. Ibid.
407. Ibid.
408. DMMR; MJ (Jan.5 1889) p.8
409. DMMR; MJ (March 30 1889) p.365
410. DMMR; MJ (June 22 1889) p.711; MJ (Sept.14 1889) p.1045
411. DMMR; MJ (Sept.14 1889) p.1045 MJ (Dec.7 1889) pp.1391,1392
412. DMMR; MJ (Dec.7 1889) pp.1391,1392
413. Ibid.
414. RCG (October 24 1889)

415. DMMR
416. Ibid.
417. Ibid.
418. DMMR; MJ (Jan.11 1890) p.48; MJ (March 1 1890) p.244
419. DMMR; MJ (March 1 1890) p. p.244
420. DMMR; MJ (May 24 1890) pp.590,591; MJ (Aug.16 1890) p.939
421. DMMR; MJ (Aug.16 1890) p.939; MJ (Nov.8 1890) p.1297
422. DMMR
423. DMMR; MJ (April 25 1891) pp.472,473
424. DMMR
425. DMMR; MJ (Jan.31 1891) p.124
426. DMMR; MJ (April 25 1891) pp.472,473
427. DMMR; MJ (Jan.2 1892) p.10
428. DMMR
429. Ibid.
430. Ibid.
431. DMMR; MJ (March 26 1892) p.338
432. MJ (June 4 1892) p.631
433. DMMR
434. DMMR; MJ (June 18 1892) p.690
435. DMMR; MJ (Sept.10 1892) pp.1014,1015
436. DMMR; MJ (Dec.3 1892) p.1359
437. DMMR
438. Ibid.
439. Ibid.
440. DMMR; MJ (Feb.25 1893) p.230
441. DMMR; MJ (May 20 1893) p.551; MJ (Aug.12 1893) pp.886,887
442. DMMR; MJ (Sept.23 1893) p.1067; Noall (1989) pp.58-66; Allen Buckley (Editor) Hazards & Heroes in Cornish Mines (2007) pp.45-48
443. Ibid.
444. DMMR; MJ (Nov.4 1893) p.1223
445. DMMR
446. Ibid.
447. Ibid.
448. DMMR; MJ (Jan.27 1894) pp.88,89
449. DMMR; MJ (April 21 1894) pp.428,429; MJ (July 14 1894) p.760
450. DMMR; MJ (July 14 1894) p.760
451. Evening Tidings (April 4 1894)
452. DMMR; MJ (July 14 1894) p.760
453. DMMR
454. DMMR; MJ (Jan.26 1895) p.105
455. DMMR; MJ (March 23 1895) p.329
456. DMMR; MJ (March 23 1895) p.329; Buckley (1997) p.80; Buckley (1980) pp.99,102,111
457. DMMR; MJ (May 11 1895) p.543; MJ (March 23 1895) 329

Part Three
Dolcoath Mine Ltd, 1895-1921

Dolcoath Mine Ltd.

With the decision no longer to operate Dolcoath as a cost book company and to switch to being a limited liability company, an era ended. From June 1895 onward, control of the mine would not be entirely in the hands of Cornishmen, but capitalists far removed from Camborne would have their say and many of these knew precious little about tin mining. Dolcoath Mine Ltd. was floated with £350,000 of capital, which was guaranteed by the British and Foreign Exploration Co. Ltd, of London. 188,000 £1 shares were credited as fully paid by the end of December 1895. Most of the principal adventurers in the old company became shareholders in the new, and most of the Committee and management team retained their places. Michael Henry Williams remained Chairman and Josiah Thomas became Managing Director. His son, R. Arthur Thomas, became Assistant Manager and Frederick William Thomas remained as Mine Secretary. Daniell & Thomas were still the company solicitors and Walter Pike, who was joined by W. B. Peat, remained as company auditor. The other mine agents were still James Johns, senior mine captain, Joseph Tamblyn, William James, Edwin Prideaux and George Davey. At the mine, continuity was the order of the day.[1]

Williams Shaft

The other major event of 1895 was to start the sinking of the new vertical shaft. For some time there had been discussions about the need for such a shaft and it was universally appreciated that it should be in such a position and of such a design to enable the mine to work efficiently and economically. It was decided that the shaft would be sunk well to the south of the present workings, to intersect Main Lode below the present lowest level, which was the 440 fathom level. The shaft was initially to be sunk to the 500 fathom level, but eventually it was decided to take it down to the 550 fathom level – 3,000 feet deep. The mine plans indicate that its sump was eventually sunk some 90 to 100 feet below the 550 fathom level. It was decided to sink it as an 18 foot 10 inch long rectangular shaft, but subsequently this was changed to a circular, brick-lined shaft, of 17 feet 6 inch diameter.[2]

On Monday October 28th 1895 a vast crowd of miners and their families gathered on the lower, northern slopes of Carn Entral to witness the cutting of the first sod. Michael Henry Williams, the Company Chairman, was handed an appropriately engraved silver shovel, the cost of which was £22, and in the presence of this enormous gathering, which also included dignitaries from far afield, symbolically removed the first turf to start sinking the shaft. All the adult male employees were given 2s and each boy and girl 1s to celebrate the event. Some indication of the significance with which this event was seen at the time can be gauged by the important people who witnessed it. There was Oliver Wethered, chairman of West Australian Share Corporation, Arthur Strauss the local MP, A. F. Basset, the mineral lord, S. D. Stoneham, chairman of Arrow Brownhill, G. H. M. Batten, chairman of Hyderabad Deccan, H. C. Godfray, chairman of San Luis, Francis Oats, director of De Beers and a host of other wealthy company chairmen and directors of some of the most important mining houses in the world. The principal men from nearly all the working mines of Cornwall were also present. It was universally agreed that the name Williams Shaft was most appropriate, not just because the present chairman was of that family, but because the Williams family of Scorrier had been the principal backers of Dolcoath from the time of its reopening, in 1799, till 1895. They had supported captains William Petherick and Charles Thomas as they strove to persuade reluctant adventurers to agree to drain the deeper workings and then sink deeper for the anticipated tin which lay below the copper. It is of interest that, right up until the present day, Carn Entral and Pengegon locals still refer to Williams Shaft as 'New Shaft', reminding us that it was always seen as something special.[3]

With the formation of the new company the old twelve week accounting and reporting system gave way to six monthly reports. The report for the first six months, from June to December 1895 shows that at the mine things continued as they had. R Arthur Thomas headed the list of agents who signed off the mine report, as his father was now managing director, and one remove from the day-to-day mining activity. The ongoing sinking programme continued, although inhibited by questions about the desirability of continuing to sink New East Shaft and the other central shafts, now that Williams Shaft was to replace them in so many ways. Engine Shaft, now normally referred to as 'New Sump Shaft', was being prepared to sink under the 440 fathom level, which had been holed to New East Shaft. Old Sump Shaft was sunk 7 fathoms 4 feet below the 425 level and a level was being driven toward it at the 440 fathom level from New Sump. Eastern Shaft was sinking in granite and had reached the 425 fathom level. Winzes were being sunk to the 440 level in the centre of the mine, and all the ground on Main Lode between Harrietts and Eastern Shaft was being opened up for stoping at the bottom levels.[4]

The values varied on Main Lode in the ends and winzes between £15 and £50 a fathom. On South Lode the tin grade was generally lower. The report stated that during the previous six months 174 fathoms of drives and crosscuts had been mined and 69 fathoms of sinking had taken place. Some 216 fathoms of this development had been on lode and the rest in granite. Stopers on piecework had broken 20,422 tons of ore and tributers 5,593 tons. Tutworkers on development broke 2,702 tons of ore.[5]

In a separate report Captain Josiah Thomas spoke of his plans for Stray Park section. Engine Shaft was to be sunk below the 282 fathom level by rock drill, and the preparation work for this had already been done. The whim engine had been overhauled, an air compressor was to be installed and the new skip road in the shaft was almost complete. Once air pipes were fitted, sinking would begin. He was optimistic about the 'immense reserve of virgin ground' in Stray Park. He also reported on progress with Williams Shaft. By January 23rd 1896, the shaft was sunk 17½ fathoms – 105 feet! The initial intention to sink a rectangular shaft was abandoned due to the soft ground continuing to a greater depth than anticipated and the truly awful weather. The 36 shaft sinkers actually began work in an unseasonal snowstorm. Having started as a rectangular shaft, they quickly changed to a circular one. It was lined with 9-inch thickness of brickwork. Safety was one of the reasons given for the circular design, although some felt that the rectangular shape would have allowed more space for the services which were to use the shaft. A circular shaft was also considered to be stronger. Temporary headgear, winding engine and boiler had been erected to facilitate sinking, and a compressor was about to be installed. The shaft was almost down to the level of an old adit, which had been cleared for a distance of 180 fathoms so that unwanted water could be more easily drained from the shaft. The adit lies some 35 fathoms below Williams Shaft collar.[6]

Michael Williams' report spoke of the erection of new plant. A pair of powerful new whim engines was to be erected at Eastern Shaft. There was to be a new steam engine, stone-breaker and tramway from this shaft to the 40 head Californian Stamps. A new battery of 20 heads of stamps was to be installed, a new air receiver put in and several new tin dressing frames. Messrs T. & W. Morgans were appointed as consulting mining and mechanical engineers, to supervise and inspect the enormous amount of machinery on the mine.[7]

With all the problems, changes and expense, it is hardly surprising that the year was not especially profitable. The twelve weeks ending at the beginning of March 1895 had costs of £18,831, a loss of £5,101, no dividend paid, dues of £798 and tin sales of £14,360 for 391 tons which sold for an average of £36 15s a ton. Total income was £13,730. The last six months of 1895 showed a slight improvement, but was hardly encouraging. Costs were £36,183 at £1 5s 3d a ton, and there was a profit,

329

after £1,326 dues were paid, of £3,230. Income from tin sales was £39,758 for 1,015 tons which were produced from 28,717 tons hoisted and stamped. The average price the mine received for its tin was £39 17s a ton. The average recovery was 79.19lbs a ton or 3½ percent. No dividend was paid. For the whole year £68,389 worth of black tin was sold. This was for 1,766 tons, which sold for an average of £38 14s 4d. 1895 was the first year since 1853 that no dividend was paid.[8]

1896 was Dolcoath's first full year as a limited liability company and despite the many difficulties which attended its birth, it continued to progress satisfactorily. There were several changes in emphasis in the company's reports, so that the continuing deepening of the central shafts no longer dominated the news. Engine Shaft, once the most significant news item, was replaced by Eastern Shaft and 'New' or Williams Shaft. From 1896 onward Engine Shaft was normally referred to as 'New Sump Shaft', and although it continued to be deepened it was progress on Williams and Eastern shafts which took priority. By the end of the year New Sump was sunk some 9 fathoms below the 440 fathom level by miners using two rock drills. There was still a sense of urgency in this shaft's sinking and a winze was also being sunk below the 440 just 120 feet to the east of the shaft. By the beginning of 1897 Williams Shaft was sunk 330 feet from surface and had been connected to the Deep Adit. It had been bricked to that level and most of the infiltrating surface water was being drained through this adit. Captain Josiah Thomas referred to the granite being sunk through as 'hard but jointy'. With the shaft now fairly dry it was anticipated that sinking would go on apace. It was decided by the directors to put the sinking out to tender and at the same time a pair of powerful winding engines had been ordered to facilitate sinking to 3,000 feet. They would be installed and working within six months. The next point of connection to the old workings was the 60 fathom level, which had been driven below the shaft in anticipation of an early intersection.[9]

By the end of 1896 Stray Park Shaft was sunk 7 fathoms below the 294 fathom level by means of two rock drills. The 294 level had been driven 60 fathoms eastward at a rate of 14 fathoms a month and it was hoped that within three months it would connect to the 314 fathom level driven west from Harrietts Shaft. This would not only improve ventilation at Stray Park, but would also mean that all rock could be trammed to Harrietts for hoisting to surface, by the new whim engine being erected there. This new winding engine was also to be used for raising and lowering the miners to and from the surface, eventually replacing the man engine. It was estimated that this ore would cost 4d a ton less in haulage than bringing it up Stray Park Shaft and hauling to the stamps on surface. Tom Harris has pointed out that haulage up Harrietts Shaft at one time was by wire rope from Old Sump Shaft engine, the rope being carried the whole distance between shafts on guide pulleys. Subsequently, a hydraulic engine was used at Harrietts for the purpose.[10]

Toward the end of 1896 the 440 fathom level on Main Lode had been connected to Old Sump Shaft and then driven further west, where good tin grades were anticipated. South Lode continued to be opened up, with work on the 375 suspended whilst the miners carried out more urgent work on the 352 level. North Lode was being developed below the 400 level and at the 375 and 352 levels. The 425 fathom level had been holed to Eastern Shaft, and raises and winzes in that part of the mine were being used to open up the ground there. Captain Arthur Thomas reported that some 386 fathoms of development had taken place since June, which consisted of 218 fathoms of lode drives, 61 fathoms of crosscuts and 106 fathoms of winzes and raises. The stopers had produced 24,150 tons of ore, the tributers 6,048 tons and the tutworkers 3,514 tons.[11]

The values in 1896 were for the most part more modest than hitherto, with many ends and winzes showing ground worth between £25 and £30 a fathom. On North Lode there was tin ore worth £50 a fathom in a raise above the 375 fathom level, and ore worth £45 a fathom in a winze below that level. South Lode and Stray Park workings were worth less than this.[12]

A great loss to Dolcoath Mine was that of Captain James Johns. This venerable old man had been senior mine captain under Josiah Thomas for many years and had been considered among the most knowledgeable and skilled of all the Cornish mine captains. His name does not appear on the list of agents who signed the report for the last six months of 1896.[13]

The directors reported that the 60 heads of Californian Stamps were working well, as were the new frames, and Josiah Thomas added that the present stamping capacity could deal with 300 tons of stuff a day. He felt that there was a need for more stone breakers, and said that six new pulverisers that were ordered to be erected are "working satisfactorily, and their number might advantageously be increased". Some ore had been sent to Krupps Works in Germany for trial, to see if they could improve their dressing costs. Senior ore dressers from the mine went with the samples to witness the experiments. Captain William Mill, the senior 'grass captain', had designed 'revolving tables' for improved concentration of fines, and after several trials and experiments they had worked well. Each table consisted of two round beds, which were inclined toward each other, and sloped at appropriate angles. The top, or outer, deck was concave, and from there the feed was carried to the lower, or inner, deck, which was convex. They were 19 feet in diameter and each revolution took three minutes. They were later manufactured by Holman Brothers as the Acme Concentrating Table. After the German trip it was decided to erect their own trial plant at Dolcoath, and a Frue vanner was tried against a Bilharz table and found to be superior for dressing Dolcoath's ore. Thomas also commented on the production of arsenical mundic in the stone, which he hoped to sell to a new plant being erected in the neighbourhood – possibly referring to the plant at South Crofty. Much of this, together with 'several tons of blende', was being raised from shallow levels. If enough was found, he was keen to erect machinery to crush it and dress it.[14]

A Series of Accidents

On October 15th 1896, *The Cornish Telegraph* reported on the inquest of a miner killed at Dolcoath. The headline read: 'Fatal Accident at Dolcoath – The result of Scruffing'. Henry Poat, of Four Lanes, a stoper, had been given permission to ride to surface in the Eastern Shaft cage, in order to attend a funeral. He normally travelled up on the man engine. When he arrived at the crowded 400 fathom level shaft station, he found a large group of men trying to get into the cage. The cage officially held 8 men, 4 in the top part and 4 in the bottom. Four men were already in the top compartment and they were reluctant to let Poat in, especially as he did not normally use the cage and others were eager to get to surface. There was some argument, with pushing and shoving, or 'scruffing' as the witnesses said. As Poat attempted to enter the top part of the cage, above the level, the order was given to raise it. The man who signalled claimed he was looking at the signal arm and did not see Poat half in and half out of the cage. The cage went up and Poat was struck by the rock at the top of the shaft station and killed instantly. The coroner was extremely concerned over the circumstances of the accident, and recorded a verdict of: "Killed improperly trying to get into the cage after the signal was given to go."[15]

On November 5th 1896, The *Cornish Telegraph* reported a serious accident to an old Dolcoath tributer, called Moses Trezinia. Two pares of men were working close to each other in a stope. Trezinia believed that 7 holes were to be blasted at the end of the shift, but in fact there were 8. When the seventh hole went off he hurried into the stope to see the amount of ground broken and was caught by the last hole going off. He was badly cut about the head, face and upper body, but fortunately, his eyes were not damaged and no bones were broken.[16]

A week later, on November 12th, the *Telegraph* reported another even more serious accident. On November 5th, 2 different miners fell down different shafts at Dolcoath and were badly injured. John Miners, of St Just, who lodged in Camborne, fell 38 fathoms and sustained serious back injuries. Charles Harvey, of Camborne, fell 12 fathoms and was less-seriously hurt. Both men were taken to Redruth Miners' Hospital. A fortnight later (December 3rd), the same newspaper reported an accident to Samuel Lugg, of Connor Downs, who was hit by a falling rock whilst working underground at Dolcoath. He also was taken to the Miners' Hospital for treatment.[17]

On October 15th *The Cornish Telegraph* reported rumours of mass redundancies at Dolcoath, but although the rumours were exaggerated, there was some truth in them. Some surface workers 'on special work' were discharged as their tasks were completed, and others went due to new machinery making them redundant. The mine announced that they needed more, not less, miners, especially as work at Williams Shaft was going well.[18]

The accounts for 1896 show the mine being held steady in changing circumstances. The first six months to the end of June had 30,015 tons crushed for 1,030 tons of black tin. The grade averaged 76.86lbs per ton and the average price was £37 4s a ton. Lord's dues were £1,278 and the net profit was £2,931. The second half of the year had 33,712 tons crushed for 1,009 tons of black tin. The average grade was 67lbs a ton and the average price received was £36 9s 2d. Dues came to £1,230 and the net profit was £1,480. Total costs for the year were £72,427 and tin sales came to £75,104. A dividend of £5,577 was paid. By the end of 1896, £25,248 had been spent by the new company on new buildings, plant and machinery.[19]

The End of the Man Engine
1897 saw more changes at the mine and further outlay on expensive new machinery. By the end of June Engine (New Sump) Shaft was sunk 16 fathoms under the 440 fathom level and preparations were made to drive on the new 455 level, toward a winze which was being sunk from the 440 level, 120 feet to the east. By the end of the year the 455 level was being driven on Main Lode, as 4 winzes were sunk from the 440, to open up stoping ground and ensure ventilation. Williams Shaft was down 500 feet by August and 720 feet by February 1898. The 60 fathom level on Brea Lode was being driven from the new shaft. Stray Park Shaft had been sunk to the 314 fathom level and a new skip road fixed in it, and by the end of the year a connection between Stray Park and Harrietts Shaft had been made at the 314 level. At Harrietts, new pitwork was being installed to the 375 level, and the shaft was being used to hoist and lower the miner so that the man engine could finally be dispensed with. On February 14th 1898 Josiah Thomas reported that 'The man-engine has been idle for some months', and would no longer be required. Thus, the ancient method of raising and lowering miners by means of this machine, came to an end in the last few months of 1897.[20]

Michael H. Williams resigned as Chairman at the August 28th 1897 shareholders meeting, because of differences with some of the other directors. Earlier in the year he had announced his intention to resign, but had been persuaded to carry on for another year, but he found he could not. Mr Frank Harvey then became Chairman. Like Williams, Harvey's family had had a long and profitable connection to Dolcoath.[21]

Old Sump Shaft was holed to the 440 fathom level by August 1897, but serious runs of ground in the shaft caused major problems for hoisting dirt. Later in the year, more runs in the shaft, this time at the 302 level, caused further delays and expense. By February 1898 the blockages had been cleared and hoisting resumed.

In the Valley Section around Eastern Shaft, where Main Lode was divided by a huge granite 'horse of ground', developments continued with mixed results. The northern branch of Main Lode was referred to in the eastern part of the mine as 'North Lode' after 1895 and treated as a separate structure.[22]

The ore values generally were more modest in the ends and winzes than hitherto, but the management remained optimistic that this was merely a temporary position. On Main Lode at the 455 level the ore was worth about £10 a fathom, on the 440 it was worth between £20 and £35, on the 425 it was worth between £14 and £20 and on the levels immediately above, the tin being sampled was worth between £12 and £20 a fathom. On North Lode, beneath the valley, the ore was worth between £10 and £45, the higher values being at the 400 fathom level. On South Lode samples from the ends at the 242, 327, 352 and 375 fathom levels were worth between £10 and £30 a fathom. In Stray Park at the 314 fathom level the ore was worth £15 a fathom, but in the 294 level the lode was 'disordered'. The grade generally was dropping, but the tonnage hoisted and crushed was increasing significantly.[23]

The Shift Boss System
In 1897 there was a total of 735 fathoms of development, with 386 fathoms driven on lode, 108 fathoms of crosscut and 241 fathoms of raising and sinking. The tonnage crushed in 1897 was 73,566 and this was made up of 62,473 tons by stopers and tutwork developers and 11,093 tons by the tributers. As noted earlier, Dolcoath had adopted a policy of using stopers, who were paid by the cubic fathoms they broke, in the larger and more uniform stopes (so far as values were concerned), and tributers where the lodes were patchy and the good ore more difficult to identify. This system had served the mine well, but there had been a tendency for stopers, not unnaturally, to break as much ground as they could, often without too much concern about its value. This prompted those mine captains with experience in America and South Africa, to incline toward more effective supervision of these stopers. In 1897, there was introduced an innovation which was quite new to Cornwall – the shiftboss system! The system had been introduced into other mines where the managers and captains had worked abroad, and one well-documented case was that of Killifreth Mine. In 1896 Herbert Thomas, the journalist, had interviewed Captain R. A. James, the manager of Killifreth, who had spent several years working in the mines of the American west. Thomas wrote: "Captain James thoroughly believes in the American system of constant supervision underground, and has introduced it at Killifreth." Within a decade or so shiftbosses were introduced to most Cornish mines. Another change came with the arrival of Captain James Trevarthen as an underground agent, and he was also to make his name at Dolcoath.[24]

1897 saw a considerable increase in the mine expenses, with 'runs of ground' causing costly delays in Old Sump Shaft and new and expensive machinery bought for the mill. At the eastern end of the mine two new pulverisers were installed, along with six new revolving tin dressing frames. The valley stamps were being improved and it was estimated that two of the new pneumatic heads could do the work of 20 Californian heads. A new stone breaker was installed by the eastern floors and trials of 'modern concentrators' were made. They were to replace the older, less-efficient buddles there. These Bilhartz tables and Frue vanners were installed during 1897, and the latter were to prove of long-term value to the mine. Renewing worn-out boilers also proved expensive.[25]

The new company sold much of its tin concentrate by ticketing, the management giving ground after decades of argument among the old Committee and some of the adventurers. The principal buyers remained the same, however, with Williams, Harvey & Co. and the Consolidated Tin Co. continuing to dominate among the buyers. In the last six months of 1895 these smelters purchased £33,281 worth of black tin from Dolcoath, out of a total of £39,769. The other three smelters, Redruth Tin Company, Cornish Tin Company and Penpoll Tin Company, buying the rest. Penpoll only purchased 9¼ tons in 1895 and by 1897 had dropped out of the picture completely. In 1897 Consolidated bought £36,699 worth of Dolcoath's tin and Williams, Harvey purchased £30,774. Redruth Tin bought £5,278 worth and Cornish Tin £6,646 worth.[26]

Working plans/sections dated between 1897 and 1914 show details of many of the 'owners' account' stopers and tributers working the deeper levels on Main Lode. We do not know how many men were working on each contract.

S. Rule stoping the back above the 388fm level west of Old Sump Shaft
F. Moon stoping the back above the 388fm level west of Old Sump Shaft
W. Bray & J. Rowe stoping the back above the 400fm level west of Old Sump Shaft
C. Mitchell stoping the back above the 400fm level between Old & New Sump shafts
J. Bowden stoping the back above the 388fm level next to New Sump Shaft
J. E. F. Ford stoping the back above the 412fm level west of Old Sump Shaft (1897)
Bawden underhand stoping above the 412fm level west of Old Sump Shaft
James stoping the back above the 412fm level west of Old Sump Shaft (18/7/1896)
R. Willoughby stoping the back above the 440fm level west of Old Sump Shaft
T. Roskilly stoping the back above the 440fm level east of New Sump Shaft
B. Lobb underhand stoping under the 455fm level east of New Sump Shaft
M. Hugo stoping the back above the 470fm level east of New Sump Shaft
P. Thomas stoping the back above the 490fm level east of New Sump Shaft
S. Vivian stoping the back above the 490fm level west of Eastern Shaft
H. Martin underhand stoping under the 490fm level west of Eastern Shaft
Truan stoping the back above the 510fm level west of Eastern Shaft
Wallace stoping the back above the 510fm level east of New Sump Shaft (1913)
Trembath underhand stoping under the 490fm level west of Old Sump Shaft
S. Jeffery stoping the back above the 470fm level east of New Sump Shaft

---

W. J. Stephens stoping above the 412fm level east of Old Sump Shaft @ 8/6 in the pound
J. Ward stoping above the 375fm level east of New Sump @ 12/6 in the pound
Henry Jeffrey stoping the back above the 375fm level @ 13/4 in the pound
T. Hugo stoping above the 375fm level @ 12/- in the pound
Stanley Mitchell stoping above the 400fm level east of New Sump Shaft @ 7/6 in the pound
R. Warren stoping above the 400fm level east of New Sump Shaft @ 12/- in the pound
Ben Lobb stoping above the 400fm level east of New Sump Shaft @ 10/- in the pound
J. Whear stoping under the 400fm level east of New Sump Shaft @ 12/- in the pound
Fred Thomas stoping above the 400fm level east of New Sump Shaft @ 11/- in the pound
Gundry Edwards stoping above the 425fm level east of New Sump Shaft @ 8/6 in the pound
James Moon stoping above the 425fm level east of New Sump Shaft @ 12/- in the pound
Ed.Quentral stoping above the 425fm level east of New Sump Shaft @ 13/4 in the pound
J. Pearce stoping under the the 440fm level east of New Sump Shaft @ 13/4 in the pound
William Bray stoping under the 425fm level east of New Sump Shaft @ 13/4 in the pound
J. D. Heather stoping under the 425fm level east of New Sump Shaft @ 8/- in the pound
J. Henry Williams stoping under the 425fm level east of New Sump Shaft @ 13/4 in the pound
G. Downing stoping above the 375fm level east of New Sump Shaft @ 10/- in the pound
J. Salmon stoping above the 375fm level east of New Sump Shaft @ 13/4 in the pound
Isaiah Uren stoping above the 375fm level east of New Sump Shaft
Stanley Roberts stoping above the 352fm level east of New Sump Shaft @ 10/- in the pound
Telpher Heard stoping above the 400fm level east of New Sump Shaft @ 11/- in the pound
J. R. Jeffrey stoping above the 412fm level east of New Sump Shaft @ 12/- in the pound
E. J. Taylor stoping above the 412fm level east of New Sump Shaft @ 6/8 in the pound
Joseph Hooper stoping above the 400fm level east of New Sump Shaft @ 9/- in the pound
Stoping also took place in 'Moon's Bottoms' under the 375fm level east of New Sump Shaft
Selwood's stope above the 425fm level had ore worth 30lbs a ton – no reference to amount paid him![27]

The accounts for 1897 show that the mine received £79,397 for the 2,095 tons of black tin it sold. The average grade was 63.78lbs per ton, or nearly three percent. The average price received during the year was £37 18s a ton. Dues paid to the mineral lord amounted to £2,653 and there was a net profit of £5,565. Total income, including sundry sales (£263 6s), and arsenic and mundic (£119 9s), came to £81,199.[28]

1898 saw more expenditure on machinery and underground development. The value of the tin ore, which had been relatively disappointing between the 400 and 440 fathom levels, picked up once again on the 455 fathom level, with grades worth around £35 a fathom. Again, there was concentration on the eastern end of the mine, where Main Lode splits into North and South Lodes. Despite his age and failing health, Captain Josiah Thomas visited these eastern workings at the 375 fathom level, and examined the lodes. He commented that the ore there was worth between £30 and £40 a fathom. Some concern was expressed in the March 5th 1898 *Mining Journal* about the 'falling off' of the value of Dolcoath's ore. Some £2,656 was spent on sinking Williams Shaft, its new machinery and in developing Brea Lode on the 60 fathom level, where 'spots of native copper' were found. Harrietts Shaft was straightened and enlarged to accommodate new pitwork, before sinking could be resumed below the 375 fathom level. It was intended also to sink Stray Park Shaft from the 338 to the 375 and to link it with Harrietts Shaft at that level.[29]

Meanwhile, the trials and expansion of the crushing and dressing plant continued at speed. In the March 5th *Mining Journal* it was reported that the mine had installed two Bilharz tables and Fraser & Chalmers were keen for Dolcoath to buy their Frue vanners. Consequently, 27 vanners were ordered and by September 1898, 20 had been installed by Fraser & Chalmers. The pneumatic stamps were also proving efficient and £600 had been spent purchasing them. Thomas reckoned they were already proving twice as economical as the Californian Stamps. A sour note was struck by a correspondent to the *Mining Journal* in February 11th 1899, when he wrote that if the new dressing plant was so efficient, why were the tin streamers below Dolcoath catching more tin and making more money than ever?[30]

The Saturday May 7th 1898 *Cornish Post & Mining News* carried the following report: "Accident at Dolcoath. A rather serious accident occurred at Dolcoath Mine on Thursday by an air-blast, when two men named Maddern, of Brea, and Thomas Huthnance, of Condurrow, had narrow escapes. Maddern has his thigh and leg broken in two places, and Huthnance is severely bruised about the head and body." The unpredictability of such accidents caused the miners to be constantly on the alert.[31]

Concern was expressed at the August 27th meeting about the quality and cost of the coal the mine was purchasing. Due to a strike at the Welsh collieries, the only coal available was of poor quality and expensive. Dolcoath's coal had cost £585 more during the first six months of 1898 than in the previous six months.[32]

Albert Bluett's Underground Visit

In July 1898, a writer called Albert Bluett visited the mine and was given a trip underground, accompanied by the manager, Captain Arthur Thomas. His description of the visit is interesting, in that it tells us something of the new method for conveying miners to and from the surface. He wrote: "You can go down Dolcoath Mine by ladders fixed on one side of the shaft or, as we did, in a gig, which is an iron box thirteen feet long hanging in the shaft to a wire rope worked by a powerful engine. A shelf divides the gig into two equal compartments, and, with an adjustable iron bar across the open front of each, eight men usually ride in it." After Thomas and Bluett left the gig, a signal was sent to the whim driver at surface by means of a hang line or knocker line, so that the six miners still in the gig were conveyed down to the next level. They appeared to have left the gig at the 375 fathom level, after which they climbed on down to the 412 and 455 fathom levels by ladder road. The shaft was probably Harrietts Shaft, as this had had a gig for man-riding in it since late 1897. Bluett said that the gig went down at 200 fathoms a minute, which is pretty fast! Although he said that eight men usually rode in the gig, he later commented that ten men ('half a score') travelled down in it for the 'afternoon core', whilst he was underground. He commented on the several changes of angle as the shaft followed the dip of the lode downwards. Each man was issued with six candles, five of which were hung from a button on his jacket, whilst the other was attached to his hard 'bowler' by 'a lump of clay'. Bluett found the climb down the ladder road frightening, as the mine manager who was leading him quickly left him far behind and his candle gave only limited light. He noted that the air was cool close to the shaft, but extremely hot and humid once into the ends, where the miners worked nearly naked. He mentioned that on Dolcoath's extraordinarily wide Main Lode, the drives were advanced with a height of seven feet and a width of six feet, which were then turned into tram-ways. Thereafter: "By degrees the spaces are increased in height, while the width is regulated by the size of the lode. In Dolcoath they are often more than thirty feet across, and enormous quantities of timber have to be employed to prevent the ground running together. The chief supports are balks of American pitch pine, thirty to forty feet long and eighteen inches to two feet square, which stretch from the foot-wall to the hanging wall and are supported by smaller timbers where necessary, the whole making a framework technically called a 'stull'. When miners have to take away a section of ground between two levels they cut a narrow shaft, termed a 'winze', through the lode from one to the other, and this is gradually widened along the length of the level. Such a place, where men work week after week and month after month hacking away the lode, is a 'stope', and down its rugged length the tin stuff falls to shoots opening on to tram-roads." Whilst on the 412 fathom level they visited the spot where eight miners had been entombed five years before, when the Great Stull had collapsed. Bluett asked Captain Thomas about the miner who came out alive after "being doubled up in that hole, with darkness and death for companions, for a whole week. 'Oh, he went to America some time after, and is now working in South Africa'." Tom Harris commented in his book *Dolcoath: Queen of Cornish Mines*, that Richard Davies, the rescued miner, was trapped for forty hours.[33]

The accounts for 1898 were generally far healthier than the previous year, with net profits soaring to £21,418, due to an increased tonnage crushed and a vastly improved tin price – up from £37 18s a ton, to an average of £46 18s for the second half of 1898. Production costs were £81,058, at just over £1 a ton. Dues paid the Bassets came to £3,993. Tin sales amounted to £99,907 for 2,302 tons, obtained from 78,697 tons of ore hoisted and crushed. The average tin grade was 65½lbs a ton, which was about 3%. The directors were voted £1,000 for their first three years service to the new company.[34]

1899 witnessed increased optimism among mining investors as Dolcoath's profit continued to rise. The net profit for the first half of 1899 was £22,458 – which was more than for the whole of 1898! Once again the management and shareholders looked forward to a return to the halcyon days of yore, when production and profits had given the old adventurers a steady income over many decades. The average price the mine received for its tin rose to over £73 a ton in 1899 and income from tin sales went up by nearly £52,000. Not unnaturally, shares in Dolcoath were quickly at a premium. The *Mining Journal* reported that the AGM was held in London and that it was decided to hold them alternately between Camborne and London in the future. The report by the managing director, Josiah Thomas, was very up-beat, stating that the mine had been worked continually for one-hundred years, since 1799. There was a proposal that a commemorative medal be struck to celebrate the hundred years continual working at Dolcoath, but it is not known whether this was actually done. Thomas said the sett was nearly a mile long, that the deepest level was the 455 and that they were currently making £1,000 a week profit. He also reported that a new stone-breaker was being erected at New Sump Shaft, a new light railway laid between the hoisting shafts and the stamps and crushers and that more round frames and Frue vanners were being erected. He was pleased to announce that the miners' wages were to be increased by ten percent due to the increased tin price, as they had been reduced by ten percent when the tin price fell. The shareholders applauded this announcement.[35]

At this meeting Oliver Wethered proposed that Dolcoath buy the sett known as 'Dolcoath West', and run it as a separate company. There was also a dark cloud on the horizon, as one of the shareholders, Mr Allen Stoneham, argued that all available tin should be raised and sold as quickly as possible, regardless of the price. Captain Josiah Thomas, probably remembering his decades of opposition to Limited Liability, because of the anticipated interference from ignorant 'outsiders', wrote in exasperation to Frank Harvey: "I quite despair of converting Mr Stoneham or altering his opinion, a man who says that the price of tin ought not to affect the profit is beyond the reach of argument." Stoneham was to return to this theme again and again during the following months. The March 3rd 1900 *Mining Journal* reported him as demanding that more tin should be hoisted, regardless of its grade or the tin price, and he still did not think that the tin price affected the mine's profits.[36]

Sinking resumed at New Sump (Engine) Shaft and by August, the 18 men sinking it were 12 fathoms below the 455 fathom level. By the end of the year the 470 station shaft plat had been cut and development had begun there, showing some good tin ore. No.5 winze under the 440 level was down 12 fathoms and the ore was worth £120 a fathom. This was a return to some of the grades experienced above the 412 fathom level and was viewed with delight by the miners. A winze under the 400 fathom level west of Old Sump Shaft was worth £60 a fathom, which was also encouraging, although Stray Park ends were not very good, despite short lengths of rich tin there. Captain Josiah Thomas gave an optimistic report for the second half of 1899, stating that the area to the west of Eastern Shaft was looking good between the 352 and 375 fathom levels, that Main Lode on the 400 level east of New East Shaft was worth £50 to £60 a fathom and west of Old Sump Shaft the lode was worth £60 a fathom. The 412 level was said to be merely 'moderate', as was Harriett's section. He remained hopeful for Stray Park and said they were to sink below the 352 fathom level there.[37]

Meanwhile, the sinking of Williams Shaft was suspended whilst a new contract was negotiated, although it was felt that nothing could be done until permanent headgear and winder were installed. The contract was let by the end of the year but it was to be some time before they could resume sinking. The *Mining Journal* commented that every manufacturer was finding it difficult to obtain delivery of materials. 1899 was a year of consolidation and modernisation as the new century approached and major plans laid for the future of the ancient mine.[38]

At the February 1900 Meeting Captain Josiah Thomas spoke passionately about the charge that the Cornish were slow to adopt new ideas and new machinery. He said that it was 'foolish to adopt every new invention' before its effectiveness was proved. It was always best to be cautious and to trial new ideas, techniques and machines. Every new piece of equipment brought to the mine was offered a trial, but only if the manufacturers were willing to erect and operate them at their own expense would Dolcoath agree to such trials. He cited Fraser & Chalmers' trial of their Frue vanners, 30 purchased and 40 more ordered, and Harvey's trial of their pneumatic stamps, which had subsequently been purchased by the mine. He could also have cited the many rock drill types tried at the mine during the previous few decades.[39]

The accounts for 1899 showed costs of £99,702 and a net profit of £53,524. A dividend of 13½ percent was paid. Dues paid came to £10,126 and tin sales were £151,871 for 2,079 tons, which sold for an average of £73 3s a ton. The average recovery was 56.28lbs a ton, or about 2½ percent. Total ore hoisted and crushed was 82,740 tons. In August Captain Josiah Thomas said that Dolcoath was selling half its ore by ticketing – so the battle over selling it by private treaty was still not finally settled! The cost of wages was up, partly due to increased pay rates, but also because 134 more workers were employed than in the previous six months. The price of coal was down from the previously high figures, as the industrial disputes in Wales appeared to settle down. Walter Pike and W. B. Peat, the mine auditors, were paid 100 guineas for their year's efforts.[40]

The period at the turn of the century, showed some interesting variations in the pattern of labour use underground. In June 1899 there were 8 tutwork contracts carrying out development in various parts of the mine; 22 stoping contracts by men working 'on the owners' account', and 12 tribute contracts. In December 1900, there were 10 tutwork contracts, 19 stoping contracts and 32 tribute contracts. In December 1906, there were 9 tutwork contracts, 21 stoping contracts and 11 tribute contracts. This followed the introduction of the shiftboss system at the mine, and it is likely that closer control of the production points was being exercised. By this time the stopers, who worked on the 'owners' account', were being paid by tonnage rather than cubic fathomage, as previously. It also of interest that none of the 11 tributers named in the 1906 account were listed as tributers in 1899. The tradition of miners moving about from mine to mine and job to job clearly continued.[41]

Owners' Account Stopes.

Jan. 7-June 24 1899. (6 months) James Odgers & pare. 3,139¾ tons tinstuff
Paid £740 5s 6d
Men's costs £269 1s 11d Total £1,009 7s 5d @ 6s 3d a ton.

Jan. 7-June 24 1899 (6 months) Samuel Andrew & pare. 1,648 tons tinstuff
Paid £516 14s
Men's costs £124 13s 9d Total £641 7s 9d @ 7s 6d a ton.

Feb. 4-June 24 1899 (5 months) James Davies & pare. 872½ tons tinstuff
Paid £250
Men's costs £96 Total £345 15s @ 7s 11d a ton.

May 27-June 24 1899 (1 month) David Treverrow & pare. 527 tons tinstuff
Paid £115
Men's costs £28 11s 6d Total £143 14s 5d @ 5s 5d a ton.

May 27-June 24 1899 (1 month) Joseph Lugg & pare. 309½ tons tinstuff
Paid £56 17s 4d
Men's costs £29 11s 7d Total £86 8s 11d @ 5s 5d a ton.

If we assume that these stopers worked 24 days in a 4 week month, then they broke between 7 tons and 22 tons a day. We have no information on the numbers employed in each stope, nor how wide the stopes were.[42]

1900 opened with shareholders noting the 'complete change in the fortunes' of the mine, with the constant tin price fluctuations of 1899, which continued into 1900. The price fell from nearly £81 at the beginning of November 1899 to under £65 at the end of the year, only to rise to £78 by the first week of February 1900. On March 3rd 1900 the *Mining Journal* reported that Dolcoath had received the highest price ever for its tin – £88 a ton and before the summer was over it had reached £92. The committee said the mine was richer than ever. However, there were still clouds on the economic horizon as coal rose in price once again. The August 25th 1900 *Mining Journal* reported that Dolcoath's hoisted tonnage was higher than ever before and that its tin, previously partly sold by 'private contract' for cash, was now entirely sold by ticketing – paid for in '30 day bills'. The death of the mine engineer, Mr Jewell, was reported in August, and he was described as a 'very able man'. His family was voted a grant by the shareholders. At the same time, Allen Stoneham once again voiced his demand to hoist every ton of ore available, regardless of its value and the price of tin.[43]

Captain Josiah Thomas detailed the situation underground and at surface during the first six months of 1900. He said that South Lode east of New East Shaft and particularly above the 302 fathom level had a large area of unexplored ground. On the 302 the lode there was worth 60lbs a ton. The ground at Harrietts Shaft was improving in value and the 352 at Stray Park was worth £40 a fathom. Thomas pointed out that with the tin price at £80 a ton, ground, which had hitherto not been worth working, could now be worked at a profit. A new compressor was needed for Harrietts Shaft, with power to work 20 rock drills. Harriett's old compressor could then be moved to Stray Park Shaft. He said that New East Shaft was currently only used for hoisting ore. By August 10 Frue vanners were already erected below the Cornish stamps, another 12 were working elsewhere on the mine and a further 18 were on site ready to erect. Josiah Thomas was quick to scotch the rumours, gaining credence among some shareholders, that with the closure and flooding of the mines immediately adjacent to Dolcoath, on the eastern side of the Great Crosscourse, Dolcoath itself was in danger of flooding. Cooks Kitchen, New Cooks Kitchen and South Wheal Crofty, he said, were not directly connected to Dolcoath and the lodes were all heaved by the crosscourse some 70 fathoms to the right, making junctions unlikely.[44]

Fire Underground

The reports for the second half of 1900 highlighted several small, but costly problems for the mine. A serious fire underground cost the mine about 80 tons of black tin sales, which was a severe loss. At Stray Park there was a continuing delay in erecting the pumping engine, the average tin price fell by nearly £2 a ton and the cost of coal rose sharply in the middle of the year. On the other hand, things were progressing at Williams Shaft, where the machinery to resume sinking was nearing completion. The company, which won the contract to sink the shaft, Messrs. Isaiah Piggott & Sons, was described as an 'eminent firm of contractors'. The shareholders were told that a new 'traversing drum' was being installed at Williams Shaft by T. & W. Morgans, a highly respected firm of engineers. This piece of innovative machinery had been demonstrated at the Paris Exhibition that year by Holman Brothers, and the scale model had impressed all who saw it. This winding engine was invented and patented by William Morgans in 1896, and it was intended to avoid angularity of the wire rope on the drum, which was 10 feet in diameter and 21 feet between the flanges. The carriage upon which it was mounted had 20 flanged railway wheels and travelled 16 feet whilst winding 1,000 feet of rope. This kept the rope in perfect line with the headgear sheave. Its engine cylinders were 24-inch diameter with 5 feet stroke. Twelve firms had submitted tenders for the manufacture of the machine, but Holman Brothers of Camborne won the contract.[45]

Captain R. Arthur Thomas presented the half-yearly (June-December 1900) report on behalf of the mine managers, stating that he thought it was the first meeting in 33 years his father had missed. In fact, it was the second, but it was still a very rare event. Captain Josiah had become quite ill by the end of the year, and the January 12th 1901 *Mining Journal* had reported that he had been taken to consult the 'eminent physician', Sir Douglas Powell. An 'affection of the lungs' had developed, which was 'a puzzle to his medical advisors'. His health continued to cause concern for several months, but in August 1901 it was reported that he was 'better'. Captain Arthur Thomas went on to say that there was a large block of ground to be developed on North and South lodes, east of New East Shaft and west of Eastern Shaft on the 302 fathom level. Four rock drills were being used there, with another pare using hand labour. West of Old Sump Shaft the ground was patchy, but the average grade was good. North Lode near Harrietts Shaft had been extensively developed for stoping between 264 and 314 fathom levels. Because of its 'bunchy' nature, it was being stoped by tributers. The 375 level at Harrietts Shaft was improving as it was driven westward and further west the 352 (worth £35 a fathom) was suspended to concentrate on sinking Stray Park Shaft. Around New East Shaft at the 470 fathom level the ore was worth £18 a fathom. Captain Thomas said that there was a considerable amount of low-grade tin ore in the mine, which was now worth working, as the price was relatively high. He was pleased to report good progress installing the new Frue vanners – there would soon be 40 working! In the valley below the stamps, there was further improvement to the machinery for dealing with fine slimes.[46]

A letter was read to the shareholders which expressed the fear of flooding from the mines to the east, but Arthur Thomas merely referred them to his father's comments at the previous meeting. On this occasion those present were able to laugh at the 'threat'. The shareholders were told of the resignation of Walter Pike, one of the company auditors, who had already left the county to move up-country. This left W. B. Peat & Co. as the sole auditors. Frank Harvey JP CC, of Harvey & Co. of Hayle, chaired this meeting, as he had most shareholders meetings since August 1897, when he replaced Michael Williams as Company Chairman.[47]

The 1900 accounts showed the tonnage crushed up by 5½ thousand tons to 88,356, but with the average grade down from 56.28lbs a ton to just 50lbs, the tonnage of black tin sold was down to 2,004 tons. This sold for £164,120, up from £151,871, due to the increased tin price, which averaged £81 17s a ton. Dues paid came to £10,941 and production costs were £110,445 at £1 5s a ton. The profit was a healthy £54,958.[48]

The half-yearly report for the period ending June 30th 1901 made sober reading for the shareholders. With the drop in the average tin metal price of nearly £8 a ton the mine's profits were commensurately down. And although the tonnage hoisted and crushed was the highest since the company was formed, income from it was the lowest for two years. The Chairman, Frank Harvey, announced that with the death of William Rabling, a long-serving director and adventurer at the mine, Gilbert Bennett Pearce had been appointed director. Gilbert Pearce was brother to Richard Pearce of Denver, one of the most highly respected mine managers in America. He had inspected Dolcoath's dressing plant and said it was the best he had seen anywhere. It is of interest to note that Gilbert Pearce had started his working life 47 years earlier, as a junior clerk in Dolcoath's office.[49]

The report of Captain R. Arthur Thomas and his five assisting mine captains (Joseph Tamblyn, William James, Edwin Prideaux, George Davey and James Trevarthen) revealed steady progress being made in opening up the bottom of the mine and in re-examining ground higher up in the mine. On Main Lode the 470 fathom level had been driven past the No.1 winze and was heading toward the second winze below the 455 level, thus opening up well-ventilated stoping ground close to the shaft. This second winze was down 13 fathoms and would soon be connected to the 470 level. No.3 winze was even deeper below the 455 and was within a couple of feet of the 470. These three winzes were spaced 32 and 35 fathoms apart, indicating the extent of ventilated stoping blocks. Main Lode had been driven 15 fathoms west of New Sump Shaft at the 470, on the south part of the lode. It was hoped to put up a raise to the bottom of Old Sump Shaft when the level was below it. Old Sump Shaft was 4 fathoms below the 455 fathom level. The section between Old Sump and Harrietts shafts was being opened up between the 314 and 425 levels. The values were between £15 and £25 a fathom, which were similar to those being found at the 470 level. At the eastern end of the mine work progressed well to open the ground west of Eastern Shaft. A short distance from the shaft a raise was being put up from the 400 fathom level. It was 20 fathoms above the level and was about to meet a winze being sunk from the 375 level. Thomas believed this would give the mine a large area of 'moderately productive tin ground' for stoping. Other winzes and raises in the area were progressing well and there was considerable optimism about its contribution to the future of the mine.[50]

Work on North Lode was also progressing well, with some of the development work west of Eastern Shaft ahead of that on Main Lode. Work to open up North Lode for the full length of the property, between Eastern Shaft and Stray Park was in hand, and a crosscut was being driven at the 238 level in Stray Park to connect with a winze below the 224 fathom level. Man Engine Lode was being opened up from the shaft of that name and the ground right down to 400 level was being explored. So far the results had been disappointing, especially west of the shaft. South Lode was being explored between the 242 fathom and the 352 levels, from as far east as Eastern Shaft (327 level) and as far west as Stray Park (352 level). Values varied between £15 a fathom, east of Stray Park to £60 a fathom to the west of Eastern Shaft. Stray Park Shaft was sunk 14 fathoms below the 352 level and the lode in the shaft was worth £30 a fathom.[51]

Captain Thomas reported that there was a total development in the six months ending June 30th 1901 of approximately 459 fathoms, being made up of 310 fathoms on lode, 12 fathoms of crosscut and 137 fathoms sinking and raising. Stoping and tutwork produced 37,432 tons of ore and the tributers 10,183 tons.[52]

On July 18th 1901 Josiah Thomas was sufficiently recovered from his illness to be able to write his report on the first six months of the year. He was keen to emphasise the progress being made in equipping the mine with the latest gear and in the results from the eastern end of the mine, long his great hope for the future. He said that ore worth £35, £45, £50 and £60 a fathom had been encountered there. He enthused about the new machinery being installed 'in the Burning House Yard for dressing the tin after it has passed through the Calciner', and said mining would soon be improved with the completion of the new 20 rock drill capacity compressor at Harrietts Shaft. He remained optimistic about the future of Stray Park section.[53]

The following day Thomas and William Morgans reported on the progress at Williams Shaft. They reckoned that Piggott's could restart sinking in about three weeks, by which time the extensive engineering required would be ready. The ventilator was soon to be fixed, the wire ropes would soon be delivered, balance flaps fitted, mains pipes installed, winding indicator fixed and hand rails for the engine put in. Morgans added that the boilers, flue culvert, stack and connection steam pipes were all complete and working well. The traversing winding engine had been run on July 18th and worked efficiently. It had been run for an hour to test the reversing gear and was easily controlled. The cylinder valve gear needed some adjustments, which were in hand. The buildings were all roofed in and doors and windows completed to a high standard. Morgans regretted that this work had taken longer than predicted in January, by about two months.[54]

The Death of Josiah Thomas
At 4 o'clock in the morning of Tuesday 22nd October 1901, at his summer home in Carbis Bay, Captain Josiah Thomas died. For over thirty years he had dominated Cornish mining as no man had done before or since. During his heyday he was the undisputed 'King of Camborne', and his advice on mining matters was sought

the world over. On his word alone, progress on the incipient tin mining fields of North Dakota was temporarily abandoned and nobody was thought to 'knaw tin' like old Josiah. Since February 1895 he had been severely incapacitated by a lung disease, but he had remained at the helm at Dolcoath and other mines until his final illness. Josiah Thomas was born in 1833 at Killivose, the house his father had built. He was the son of Charles, who had preceded him as Dolcoath manager, and his was the third generation of the family to serve as mine captains and managers at the mine. Unsurprisingly, his son R. Arthur Thomas, replaced him as manager and his other sons also

Figure 114. Holman Brothers sinking machine.

served in various capacities at the mine. Josiah started work underground at 15 years of age, and within 25 years he was the mine manager. With his father, he became 'external agent' and nominal manager of several Cornish mines, including Cooks Kitchen, New Cooks Kitchen, South Wheal Crofty and West Wheal Francis. The Camborne miners wanted to erect a statue to him when he died, but eventually they were satisfied with the building at the old School of Mines, which still bears his name.[55]

The tin ticketing for the first half of 1901 was dominated by the Consolidated Company, who purchased well over half of Dolcoath's black tin (559 tons). Their nearest rival was Williams, Harvey & Co. (277 tons), with the Cornish Co., Redruth Co. and Penpoll Co. only buying about 164 tons between them.[56]

The 1901 accounts showed the mine remained in a healthy condition, but with the average tin price falling from £81 17s a ton the previous year to £70 14s a ton in 1901, profits were inevitably down. Tonnage crushed rose to 96,578 tons, the grade dropped to an average of 47.2 lbs a ton, tin sales dropped to £143,808 for 2,034 tons of black tin and profit was down to £33,176. Dues paid the Bassets were £9,587. Although costs per ton were down on the previous year, to £1 3s 3d, production costs went up to £128,449. In the summer, one of the shareholders, J. Wickett, proposed that the directors be paid £650 for their efforts.[57]

1902 saw serious progress in sinking Williams Shaft, and the report of the directors at the end of the first half of the year stated that nearly 63 fathoms had been sunk by Piggotts since the last report, reaching a depth of almost 186 fathoms from surface. By the end of the year the shaft was down 242 fathoms and by the end of February 1903 it had reached 250 fathoms from its collar. Sinking also resumed in New Sump (Engine) Shaft and by the end of the year it was 5 fathoms below the 470 fathom level. After fixing a new plunger lift at the shaft bottom, sinking was to continue using two rock drills. In the mean time the bottom levels continued to be opened up by driving and sinking winzes between the levels; most of this development was by rock drill. Main Lode generally had fairly average ore grades of between £15 and £40 a fathom. North Lode continued to be developed from Eastern Shaft to Harrietts Shaft with good results and South Lode also saw mining from the valley to Stray Park section.[58]

Preparations were in hand by the end of the year to resume sinking Stray Park Shaft, below the 375 fathom level. The manager was still optimistic about the future of that section of the mine. Great efforts were made to link Harrietts and Stray Park shafts at the 375 level, due to the urgent need for improved ventilation there. Ventilating machinery was installed to improve the situation, where the heat was intense. Arthur Thomas believed that the abnormally high temperatures were partly due to the 'oxidation of the Iron Pyrites in the Lode'. Thomas also reported that the new headgear was erected at Stray Park and that shortly the new winding engine would be put to work. Screening plant and an ore bin were being installed to reduce cost of ore handling at surface. A mile of 22-inch gauge railway track, on steel sleepers, was laid between Stray Park and the stamps at the eastern end of the mine. The railway was eventually extended to some 1½ miles. While awaiting the delivery of the steam locomotive the wagons were hauled by horses.[59]

During 1902 some 895 fathoms were driven, sunk and raised by the developers, including over 200 fathoms of crosscuts and 250 fathoms of sinking and raising. Out of the 100,000 tons of ore broken, tributers accounted for just over 13,000 tons.[60]

Ankylostomiosis or Hook Worm
Captain Thomas drew attention in his report, dated January 21st 1903, to a serious problem the mine had had for many years. What local doctors had put down to 'anaemia' or 'phtisis' was discovered to be a worm, which apparently originated in the tropical countries where Dolcoath's miners had often worked. Dr J. S. Haldane MD FRS was called in to identify the problem and trace its origin. His advice would also be needed to find a cure. The report by the Chairman, Frank Harvey, explained the situation as it was then perceived. "For years past it has been known that men employed in the Mine have suffered from anaemia, for which some were admitted to Hospital, though no one died. It was conjectured by Mr J. S. Martin, HM Inspector of Mines, that the disease might he due to defective ventilation, and this belief was shared by others. Dr J. S. Haldane MD, FRS, was commissioned by the Home Department to enquire into the health of Cornish miners, and visited Dolcoath. He soon arrived at the conclusion that the disease was not due to any defect in the ventilation of the mine, which he declares 'to be on the whole extremely satisfactory' but to a worm in the intestines of the patients named ankylostomiosis, which was amenable to medical treatment. This is a tropical disease which has been introduced by men returning from the tropics. Dr Haldane further declares that 'the spread of the disease may be entirely checked by preventing pollution of the mines'. A system has now been introduced for effecting this, and Dr Haldane hopes that the disease will soon be stamped out here."[61]

Captain Thomas added to this the comment that, "The temperature in certain parts of Dolcoath particularly favours the development of the ova in the faeces but by the proper use of cheap disinfectants and other regulations already put in force the germs of infection will be destroyed and a considerable charge on the Company will consequently cease." Toilet buckets were introduced to all levels of the mine, so that the standard of hygiene was universally improved. In 1912 a Royal Commission investigated the high incidence of the disease in Cornish mines, and found that at its height no less than 69 percent of Dolcoath miners suffered from the condition:

Basset Mines had 51 percent, East Pool 47 percent, Tincroft 25 percent and South Crofty only 11 percent.[62]

Originally, due to the large numbers of Dolcoath miners returning from South Africa at the time of the Boer War, it was thought that that was where Dolcoath's ankylostomiosis had originated, but recent research suggests that it had appeared in Cornish mines by the middle of the 19th century, and probably first came from Chile and the Kola gold fields of India.[63]

The accounts for 1902 showed some interesting fluctuations with the tonnage crushed rising and income from tin sales falling. Net profit dropped to £26,433, dues paid the Bassets were £8,792, tonnage crushed was 100,450, and black tin sales were £131,863 for 1,828 tons. The average tin price received during the year was £72 10s 4d and the average grade was down from 47.21lbs to 40.88lbs per ton. Costs per ton were £1 1s 3½d and production costs were £108,486.[64]

The Chairman's reports for 1903 contain some interesting facts about the way the mine was to operate in the future and the extent to which the mineral lord would cooperate. Frank Harvey's report dated August 29th 1903 for the first six months of the year stated that Williams Shaft had reached the depth of 250 fathoms from surface and it was connected to the rest of the mine by a crosscut at the 220 fathom level. This crosscut had intersected a lode named Caunter Lode 15 fathoms north of Williams Shaft. Drilling machines opened up the lode east and west of the crosscut, but as the lode was only 3 feet wide it was temporarily abandoned in favour of developing Brea Lode, intersected within 4 fathoms of Williams Shaft. Brea Lode proved even narrower than Caunter Lode, although the values on both were quite encouraging. Under instruction from Mr Basset, the mineral lord, Mr R. J. Frecheville, 'a well-known expert', examined the mine and made several suggestions. These supported the view of the Manager, who thought that a sump winze should be sunk at the extreme eastern end of the mine, below the 470 fathom level, to a depth of about 50 fathoms. The ground there should then be opened up by levels to examine the value of the ore at that depth. He also believed that a crosscut should be driven north to intersect South Crofty's lodes, which he thought were untouched in that area. Meanwhile, until the company's funds improved, the sinking of Williams Shaft should be suspended. If the ground opened up from the winze was good, then Williams Shaft sinking could be resumed. With these changes in mind, Mr Basset agreed to Frecheville's recommendation that the dues be reduced by 50 percent for the three years following March 31st 1904. The Committee thanked Basset for remitting £1,000 from the dues of the second half of 1903. Frank Harvey also reported on the success of the 'Light Railway from Stray Park to the Stamps' and the satisfactory performance of the new locomotive, which worked efficiently and improved the economy of surface haulage.[65]

Work continued to deepen the New Sump Shaft below the 470 fathom level and by the summer the 485 level had been reached and work started to prove Main Lode there. The shaft had been sunk underneath the footwall of the lode, and so once a shaft plat or station had been established, a crosscut was driven south to establish the width and value of the lode. By the end of the year the crosscut had been driven 7 fathoms south of the shaft and was through the lode and into granite. Main Lode was worth 25lbs a ton, or just over one percent. Meanwhile, extensive activity was taking place between the 327 and 470 fathom levels to open up the ground for stoping. The values averaged between one and two percent tin. On North Lode there were developments between the 190 and 375 fathom levels and the values were a little better than on Main Lode. South Lode was opened up between 220 and 375 fathom levels for the entire length of the sett, between Eastern Shaft and Stray Park, with mixed results. Once again, the management stated their optimism about the prospects for Stray Park Section, where the shaft had been sunk 5½ fathoms below the 375 fathom level and the values in the lode were about one percent. There was a serious problem at Stray Park Shaft with incoming water being too much for the pitwork, especially in late 1903, when extremely wet weather had flooded the bottom of the mine there.[66]

Another Serious Fire
On the 26th January 1903 there was another disastrous fire underground, this time being caused by a candle end left burning on a stull. It started on the 290 fathom level, near to the eastern side of New East Shaft and rendered the shaft entirely useless. The levels in the vicinity were impossible to work between the 278 and 302 fathom levels due to the fire damage. All development in that area was suspended while the levels were put into order. By using a system of bells and telephones to warn the miners, most of whom were over half-a-mile underground and spread throughout the miles of workings, all of the 400 or so men were on the surface within 2 hours.[67]

During the year the peripatetic Captain Joseph Tamblyn moved on from Dolcoath and was replaced by Captain Ben Nicholas. This appears to have been the man who had spent many years mining in Africa, and in 1908 was to become manager of Levant Mine, near St Just. During the year there was some 881 fathoms of development, with 475 fathoms being lode drives and 226 fathoms of sinking and raising. There were 180 fathoms of crosscutting during the year. Captain Arthur Thomas was pleased to announce the installation of an additional 80 rag frames and 3 revolving frames into the dressing plant, with plans for more revolving frames. The light railway and ore bin also led to improved economy at surface. On the back of the Frecheville report, Thomas wrote a long and detailed plan for the future development of the mine, in which he outlined a general deepening of the western side of the mine between Old Sump and Stray Park, with connections at the 400 and 425 fathom levels. He felt that there was considerable potential on lodes like Brea Lode, which had hitherto been largely untouched.[68]

The accounts for 1903 showed a net profit of £28,118, dues paid of £7,897 and tin sales of £133,492 for 1,740 tons. Tonnage crushed was 98,910 at a cost per ton of £1 1s 6d a ton. Recovery dropped to 39.43lbs a ton and the average price Dolcoath received for her black tin was £76 14s on ton, an improvement over the previous year of over £4 a ton. Production costs dropped slightly to £106,822.[69]

1904 started badly, with the bottom of the mine flooded up to the 440 fathom level, until May. Extremely wet weather had overwhelmed the pumps, and particularly at the western end, at Stray Park, they totally failed to cope. Although some stoping took place as the water went down, no development was carried out there. Ore values continued to fall at the deeper levels and although it averaged between 1 and 3 percent of cassiterite there, wide variations were experienced. Main Lode remained impressively wide at depth, with widths of over 18 feet and values in places of nearly 3 percent. Values on North Lode were somewhat better than on Main lode, with ore on the 352 fathom level being nearly 5 percent tin. The deeper levels in Stray Park remained flooded into the second half of the year. The drive west on South Lode at the 375 level was within 35 fathoms of the drive from Stray Park Shaft by the end of the year, and it was hoped that the holing would vastly improve ventilation in this area.[70]

During the year the developers advanced 817 fathoms, being made up of 127 fathoms of crosscuts, 434 fathoms of lode drives and 256 fathoms of raising and sinking. This represented nearly a mile of developments, and considering the depths and difficulties involved, including the flooding of the levels below the 440 fathom level for several months, it was very impressive.

The manager's reports dealt with various problems the mine was struggling with. New Sump engine had much-needed work done, replacing its 36 year old condensing gear, and it was hoped the engine would better cope with the increased weight of water being lifted. The same problems needed solving at Harrietts engine, where the whole engine was overhauled. The pitwork at Stray Park also needed work, as it was not as efficient as it should have been. Additions were made in the tin mill, where more Acme tables were being introduced to improve efficiency.[71]

Captain Arthur Thomas also dealt with the two ongoing problems concerning the health of the miners. With Dr Haldane and Mr J. S. Martin, the Mines Inspector, he formed a Departmental Committee, to resolve the problems of dust from the drilling machines and hook worm from fouling the workings. Thomas said the "death rate amongst Rock Drill men is high. I have therefore instituted Rules, and equipped the Boring Machine places with watering arrangements to improve the conditions under which these men work, and anticipate that Rock Drill work can be made as healthy an occupation as that of the ordinary miner." The introduction of improved sanitary arrangements, with toilet buckets and disinfectant being made widely available, was also a great improvement in the move toward healthier miners.[72]

The rules introduced by Captain Thomas stated:
1. In every place where rock drills are in use, means shall be provided and used for watering the dry holes in such a manner as to entirely prevent the formation of dust.
2. Every working place where rock drills are in use shall be furnished with a suitable arrangement for laying or removing the smoke and dust after a blast, and no man shall return to an end, rise, or any other close place, until the air is clear from dust caused by blasting.
3. All stone breaking machines shall be furnished with an efficient watering arrangement for the prevention of dust.
4. No person shall relieve his bowels underground except in cases of necessity and on such occasions the sanitary pails which are provided must be exclusively used.
   Signed R. Arthur Thomas, Camborne. June 11th 1904.[73]

The accounts for 1904 showed a slight drop in the mine's profits, but overall the picture was little changed from the previous year. Net profit was £21,730, dues paid the mineral lord were £5,255, income from 1,705 tons of black tin came to £129,495. Tonnage stamped was 110,549, at an average cost per ton of £1 1s 8d. The recovered grade was down from 39.43lbs to 37.98lbs per ton. The average price received by Dolcoath for her tin was £75 19s, down 15s a ton. Production costs were £108,293.[74]

During 1905 Mr Allen Stoneham died and was replaced on the Board of Directors by Hugh Charles Godfray, of London. The new Board of Directors was made up of Frank Harvey, Chairman, Oliver Wethered, Vice-Chairman, G. H. M Batten, James M. Holman, G. B. Pearce and H. C. Godfray. Dolcoath's bankers were Barclays, the auditors were W. B. Peat, the solicitors were Daniell & Thomas and the Secretary was F. W. Thomas. Captain R. Arthur Thomas remained as manager and the mine captains were William James, Ben Nicholas, Edwin Prideaux and James Trevarthen.[75]

1905 saw the ship steady somewhat, with tonnage hoisted down slightly, the grade up very slightly, and the price up by about £10 a ton. Income was also commensurately higher than the previous few years. The January to June report speaks of deepening New Sump Shaft beneath the 485 fathom level, the level having been driven a short distance to the west, but by the second half of the year it was decided to increase the distance between levels from 15 fathoms to 20 fathoms, and so the 485 drive was abandoned and the shaft was to be sunk to the 490 fathom level before opening a new level. A cause of great excitement, given the general falling off of ore grades at the bottom of the mine, was the report that the winze under the 470 level, which was down 21 fathoms, had ore values of 100lbs of tin per ton – 4½ percent! Elsewhere, between the 210 fathom level and the bottom of the mine, values varied from between 30lbs and 56lbs per ton. At the western end of the mine, work continued to improve ventilation, and a drive east from Stray Park on the 388 level, was, by the end of the year, within 3 fathoms of a winze sunk from the 375 fathom level. This was expected to vastly improve ventilation and reduce the heat in that area.[76]

The Manager's reports for the year make interesting reading, for they show that over 40 percent of production came though New and Old Sump shafts, so that the richest part of the mine remained the Bullen Garden Section. Returns from Harriett Section were about 10 percent and from Stray Park only 6 percent of the total. Valley Section continued to be opened up, and a lode called New North Lode was being developed there. About 40 percent of the mine's production was through Eastern Shaft. Thomas also reported another fire on the property, this time at surface, where the sheds housing the eastern stone-breaker and sorting floors were burnt down. Fortunately, the cost of the new, replacement buildings was covered by the insurance money. The modernising of the dressing plant continued, with new screening plant, ore bins and four new Acme shaking tables installed. Early in the year Old Sump Shaft's 30 year old headgear was replaced as it was becoming unsafe. The shaft collar was also renewed.[77]

During the course of 1905 there was a total of 855 fathoms of development at the mine, consisting of 498 fathoms of lode drives, 178 fathoms of crosscuts and 179 fathoms of winzes and raises. This was nearly a mile of development. Added to the 98,446 tons or ore, which was mostly removed from the stopes between the levels, this represented a vast amount of work by the 637 miners. There were also 464 surface workers at Dolcoath in 1905, making a total workforce of 1,101.[78]

An Electrical Ore-Finding System
During the year the mine was approached to try out an innovative method of lode finding. For some years several scientists and inventors had been experimenting with what they called 'An Electrical Ore-Finding System'. Mr Ernest Lidgey MIMM; MAmer.IM; MAust.IME, had been giving lectures since 1903 on the method, and although the system was invented by two 'Americanised Englishmen' called Daft and Williams, it was Lidgey who appeared to have been its principal advocate. Interest in the electrical conductivity of metallic veins was not new. In 1830 Robert Nere Fox had written a paper on the subject, entitled: 'Electro-Magnetic Properties of Metalliferous Veins in the Mines of Cornwall'. In the winter of 1841-42 W. J. Henwood had carried out similar experiments at East Wheal Crofty and in 1849 J. W. Wilkins did likewise. In the 1880s, Sir William Preece did similar work. Experiments had been tried in places as far apart as Western Australia, Wales, Alaska and Cumberland, with varying results. Extravagant claims were made by Lidgey,

whose boasted success in Cwmystwyth Lead Mine, Wales, was dismissed by the manager there as somewhat exaggerated.[79]

The system worked by driving two metal spikes into the ground about 100 yards apart and sending an electric current through the ground – six volts running at 5 amperes to the hour. It was thought by Lidgey and company, that the electric currents would be deflected from their paths by any metallic lode nearby. The experimenters were not sure why it worked, but they all thought that it did. Interestingly, later work showed that although copper lodes caused a measurable deflection in the current, tin lodes did not. Dolcoath was primarily interested in using the method to locate ore bodies in the northern part of the sett, where it was believed lodes worked successfully on the eastern side of the Great Crosscourse, by South Crofty Mine, were relatively untouched. The experiments did not appear to assist Dolcoath in finding new lodes.[80]

The 1905 accounts showed a vastly improved position, mostly due to the much higher tin price. Net profit was £34,726, an increase over the previous year of £13,000. Dues paid were £4,900 and revenue from tin sales was £146,790, for 1,697 tons of black tin. Recovery was up a little to 38.63lbs a ton and the price per ton received was £86 10s, an increase of £10 11s a ton. Costs per ton were £1 3s, giving total production costs of £113,213.[81]

1906 was a good year for Dolcoath, as the price of its black tin rocketed to an average of £109 10s a ton – a rise of £23 a ton on the previous year. Underground, things also looked good, with the 490 fathom level being opened up on Main Lode throughout the length of the mine and the ore showing values of up to 100lbs a ton (4½ percent). By the second half of the year Main Lode was found to be an incredible 35 feet wide in the eastern Valley section, and was worth 80lbs to the ton – 3½ percent. Values on Main Lode on all levels between the 235 and the 375 fathom levels were good and so the widely variant grades on the bottom levels were balanced out somewhat. Work on South Lode east of the 220 fathom crosscut to Williams Shaft was being developed, but the tin there was poor. Captain Arthur Thomas expressed concern about a large 'horse of ground' in the Valley Section. He hoped it would not cause production problems there. By the end of the year Stray Park Shaft was sunk 12½ fathoms under the 388 fathom level. Earlier in the year there had been a hold-up in sinking whilst a new plunger lift was fixed at the 388 level, but by the second half of the year sinking had been resumed.[82]

During 1906 ore production was largely through Eastern Shaft, where over 38 percent of the ore was raised, but although New Sump Section hoisted a little over a quarter of the ore, it did account for 36 percent of the tin produced. Harrietts Section produced about 12 percent of ore hoisted and Stray Park only 5 percent. A winding accident at Eastern Shaft reduced output there for a while, and the management estimated that about 288 tons was lost.[83]

Elmore Vacuum Plant
Dolcoath's management was concerned to exploit the large tonnage of ore left behind on the higher levels. The lodes there contained a complex mixture of ores, including zinc, arsenic, copper and tin. Throughout much of the 19th century mineral dressers had been trying out different methods of separating low-grade mixed ores effectively. It had been noted since the 1820s, that some metallic minerals tended to float and that some adhered to grease or oil. This led to many experiments to remove such metals as silver and copper from gangue material. In the 1890s a new recovery system was developed by the Elmore brothers and was known as the Elmore Vacuum System, or the Elmore Bulk Oil System. William Elmore took over the Glasdir copper mine in North Wales in 1896, and assisted by his two sons, Frank and Stanley, sought to improve recovery from the largely unsuccessful plant then operating. This was a flotation method using oil in solution to extract sulphides and arsenides from the crushed ore. The unwanted material adhered to the bubbles created in the frothy, oily water. The bubbles floated to the top of the water and were floated away with the help of a 'paddle'. It was immensely successful, and after experiments at their own mine, the brothers set up plants in Cornwall to establish its reliability. The plant at Tywarnhayle Mine, near Porthtowan, proved the method and in 1906 it was decided to introduce it at Dolcoath.[84]

The plant was set up in 1907 and was intended to treat mixed ore containing chalcopyrite and cassiterite. The plant was located near Wheal Killas Shaft, which was re-equipped and refurbished to facilitate the hoisting of the ore for processing. By the late summer of 1907 the plant was working satisfactorily, and within a couple of years it was deemed profitable. A skip road was installed in Wheal Killas Shaft to the 140 fathom level, to exploit the large quantity of ore the old mine plans indicated was available there. Eyes were also turned toward Stray Park, where it was anticipated large tonnages of suitable ores had been left. Although improved during the following decades, the basic flotation system introduced by the Elmore brothers remained in use until the end of the century. (I am grateful for much of this information to Tony Clarke)[85]

The accounts for 1906 showed the vast improvement in the mine's financial position. Net profit was £81,923, dues paid were £6,621, and income from tin sales was £198,633, for 1,814 tons of black tin. The average price per ton received for their tin was £109 10s and the average recovery was 40.56lbs per ton. 100,179 tons of ore was hoisted and crushed at an average cost per ton of £1 3s 7d, which gave a production cost of £118,211.[86]

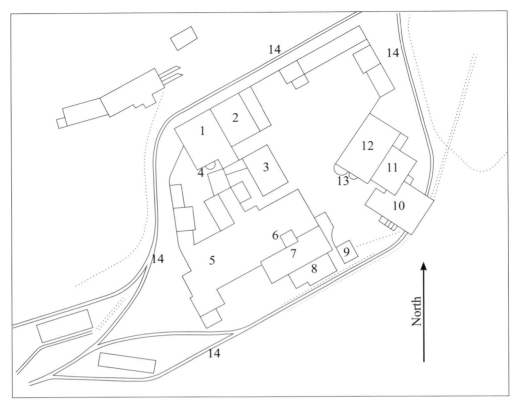

Figure 115. New Sump Shaft in its final layout.
1: boiler house; 2: air compressor; 3: engineers' shop; 4: stack; 5: smithy/stables etc.;
6: square stack; 7: boiler house; 8: New Sump Shaft engine house; 9: New Sump Shaft;
10: rock crusher station; 11: steam hoist; 12: boiler house; 13: boiler plate stacks;
14: Dolcoath light railway.

Early in 1907, Mr Harry Meyerstein of Surrey, tried to buy the mineral rights for Dolcoath from Mr A. F. Basset, but although negotiations were initially successful, they never came to fruition. In 1915 they were sold to Messrs A. H. Bond and Hamilton Edwards, along with the rest of the Basset property in Cornwall, for £250,000. There was also talk at this time, of Dolcoath setting up its own tin smelter, but although the idea was raised on several occasions over the years, it was not deemed worth pursuing. It would probably have contravened their lease, as it stated that at least half of Dolcoath's ore should be sold by 'public competition'. There was a change at this time to selling their black tin by dry weight. The remission of dues to half the contracted amount, ended on April 1st 1907, partly in response to the high tin price and increased profits of the mine. Wheal Killas Shaft was refurbished with new collar, winding engine, boiler, headgear and skip road down to the 90 fathom level during the year. By the end of the year the Elmore plant was treating between

356

30 and 40 tons of mixed ore – zinc, copper, arsenic and tin. This all came up from the shallow workings at Wheal Killas and further west. During the first half of the year the contract to resume sinking Williams Shaft was granted, and by the end of July the sinkers were 30 fathoms under the 220 fathom level, and sinking at the rate of 10 fathoms a month. They were using rock drills and lining the shaft with 9 inches of brickwork. They had attained a depth of 1,680 feet from surface by August, and at the end of the year the manager was predicting that they would be connecting to the main workings at the 490 fathom level by the end of 1908. There were also preparations to sink Eastern Shaft from the 455 to the 490 fathom level and to drive the level west from New Sump Shaft, so that a crosscut could be driven south to meet Williams Shaft when it reached that level. By the summer Stray Park Shaft was 16 fathoms under the 388 fathom level. Between June and December 1907 New Sump Shaft experienced several problems with breakages in the pitwork and the whim. This caused a loss of production for a while.[87]

Although ore values were not that impressive at the 490 level, nevertheless stoping began above the level by 12 men and their results were quite good. Values were generally quite modest throughout the mine, although the raise above the 470 level to the 455 had values of 100lbs a ton. Development was taking place for the whole length of the sett at the 220, 235, 248, 254, 278, 352, 375, 400, 455, 470 and 490 fathom levels.[88]

Captain Arthur Thomas' reports contained analysis of production from each section and they make interesting reading. The Middle Section (Bullen Garden), drawing from New and Old Sump shafts, accounted for 39 percent of the ore raised and 50 percent of the tin produced. Eastern Shaft had 44 percent of ore raised through it and produced 37 percent of the tin. Wheal Harriett section hoisted 16 percent of the ore for 11 percent of the tin, and Stray Park Section hoisted 4 percent of the ore for 2 percent of the mine's tin. By 1907, the mine captains were reduced to just three men; Arthur Thomas (manager), William James and James Trevarthen. They reported that there were 795 fathoms of development that year, consisting of 551 fathoms of drives on lode, 109 fathoms of crosscutting and 135 fathoms of raising and sinking. This was a considerable drop from the 923 fathoms carried out the previous year.[89]

Dolcoath Avenue: Cottages for the Workforce.
Another significant development took place in 1907, when the mine purchased the freehold of a plot of ground on the mine property, for the purpose of erecting 58 'miners cottages'. This was the idea of Frederick William Thomas. Thomas was particularly concerned for a group of miners who walked to the mine each day from Penponds and other more distant places. He felt it would be better for the men and the mine if they lived closer to work. These dwellings are now known as Dolcoath Avenue, although they included a few on Dolcoath Road. It was hoped

that the miners would eventually purchase the houses they tenanted, but although the company sought to help them do this, it was the late 1920s before a significant number took advantage and bought the houses from the mine. By 1934, they had all been sold off, mostly to the tenants, but a few to others. They consisted of 24 four room houses, 28 six room houses and two 8 room houses. These two larger houses were for mine captains or agents. They all had back-kitchens attached.[90]

The accounts for 1907 showed a drop in the financial position of the mine, with profits down, income from tin sales down and production costs up. Net profit was £58,176, dues were up to £10,794, an increase of over £4,000, and tin sales were £184,464, a drop of more than £14,000 over the previous year. Tonnage stamped was 101,038, with 1,708 tons of black tin sold. The average price received for Dolcoath's black tin was £108 a ton and recovery was 37.77lbs per ton, both of which were down on the previous year. Costs were up slightly to £1 5s 8d a ton, giving a total production cost for the year of £129,329, a rise of more than £11,000 over 1906.[91]

1908 saw the search for new bodies of ore in shallower and remoter parts of the mine continue, at the same time as deepening the mine and carrying out considerable development on the newly opened up deeper levels. By the end of the year Williams Shaft was down 2,274 feet below surface and was sinking at a rate of 42 feet a month, which was not quite the anticipated 10 fathoms hoped for in the 1907 report. As the shaft was deepened, the 9 inches of brickwork was installed. The sinkers had encountered more water in the shaft than anticipated and this had slowed them down. In the second half of the year work was resumed to sink New Sump Shaft below the 490, and by the end of the year it was down 12 feet below the level. Meanwhile, the sinking of Eastern Shaft below the 455 fathom level had gone on apace and by the end of the year it was 37 fathoms under the level and was 4 fathoms below the 490 level. It was intended to sink it another 12 fathoms before forming a level, although it eventually opened up a level at the 510 horizon.[92]

Wheal Killas Shaft had its skip road deepened to the 100 fathom level, facilitating the hoisting of copper and zinc ore from the western end of the mine. Developments on the 200 level south of Harrietts Shaft had encountered mixed tin and copper ore, and from this and other sources the Elmore plant produced £843 worth of copper. Exploration at the adit level was also producing some good grade copper ore at the eastern end of the mine, with values of between 5 and 10 percent encountered.[93]

Ore values at the deeper parts of the mine were beginning to look very good, with ore of between 90lbs (4 percent) and 112lbs (5 percent) a ton found. Elsewhere, the ore grades were also looking up, producing a feeling of optimism among the agents and shareholders. The manager's analysis of production from the various sections of the mine showed where the tin was coming from. Despite breakages in both New and

Old Sump shafts, the Middle section produced 37 percent of the tinstuff hoisted and 51 percent of the tin. Eastern section produced 43 percent of the stuff hoisted and 36 percent of the mine's tin. Wheal Harriett section hoisted 18 percent of the ore and produced 12 percent of the tin. Stray Park produced even less than the previous year, which was only 4 percent of the ore and 2 percent of the tin.[94]

There was a further expansion of the slime dressing plant and additions were made to the number of electric motors in use. The current motors were 12 years old and failing to keep up with increasing demand for power. 1908 saw a big increase in development, with a total of 945 fathoms being opened up. Drivage on lode was 472 fathoms, crosscuts were driven 125 fathoms and a total of 348 fathoms were sunk or raised.[95]

During 1908 the Royal Cornwall Polytechnic Society held an exhibition at Camborne, and Dolcoath took part. The mine displayed a magnificent, gilded model of the Carn Brea Monument to Sir Francis Basset, Lord de Dunstanville. It stood one-eighth the size of the original monument, and was used to represent in gold, the value of the dividends paid by Dolcoath during its working life. The following year the model was displayed at the Imperial Exhibition at Shepherds Bush, London. At this exhibition the mine displayed a range of ores, from rough ore, through the dressing process to the finished white tin metal – tin ingots made from Dolcoath's black tin having been obtained from Messrs Harvey, Williams & Company.[96]

The 1908 accounts showed a dramatic drop in the mine's profits, with the average price received for its tin dropping by nearly £30 a ton. Net profit was £12,184, down £46,000, dues paid came to £9,509 and income from tin sales was £141,945, which was nearly £43,000 less than the previous year. Tonnage crushed was 98,718, which produced 1,783 tons of black tin. Recovery improved slightly to an average of 40.45lbs per ton and the average price received was down to £79 12s a ton. Costs were also up by 1s 4d a ton, to £1 7s 1d, giving a total production cost of £133,269. The mine was holding its own, but with profits at the lowest for several years, some of the up-country shareholders were certain to be unhappy.[97]

Another Appalling Accident

1909 started with an appalling accident in Williams Shaft. Two local men were killed instantly by a dynamite explosion. The dead men were Thomas Henry Weeks, who was 37 years old and had a wife and 7 children, and his brother, Arthur Weeks, 29 years old and single. Thomas lived at Park Holly, Treswithian and Arthur lived at Tolcarne, Beacon. At 6 o'clock in the morning the ten man sinking crew descended the shaft to about the 350 fathom level to begin work. At 10 o'clock they had come to surface for their croust and when they resumed work they began digging the broken rock at the bottom of the shaft. At 12.20 pm Thomas Weeks struck a piece of rock with his pick, and some dynamite, left in a hole, exploded, killing the two brothers instantly. Three of the remaining eight men were also seriously injured and Dr Blackwood sent them to the Miners Hospital at Redruth. Several of the crew were Welshmen, bought to the mine by Piggotts to sink the shaft, and the three injured men all appear to have been Welsh. They were named as J. Ellis, who lodged at Wheal Gerry, C. Robinson, who lodged in Camborne, and George Price, who lodged at Pengegon.[98]

It was stated at the inquest that 17 holes had been drilled and fired by the previous shift, and the shift boss claimed he had counted them as they went off. Captain William James and the Camborne Ambulance Brigade attended the injured men and gave them first aid, before the arrival of Dr Blackwood. One of the Cornish miners present, James Mankee of Brea, gave evidence on the sequence of events, and the crew's working methods. He had been employed by Piggotts, sinking the shaft, for about 14 months. A year earlier, another of Piggotts Welshmen had been killed whilst working in the shaft by a falling brick hitting his head. The accident was tragic for another reason also; some 17 years before this accident, Thomas and Arthur Weeks' older brother, John, had been killed by a piece of falling metal, whilst working in a shaft at Dolcoath.[99]

1909 saw a steady improvement in the mine's financial position and the situation underground was also progressing well. By the summer Williams Shaft was sunk 2,541 feet from surface and by the end of the year it was down 2,832 feet. In September the shaft was connected to the main workings at the 440 fathom level and by the end of the year the Manager reported that Williams Shaft was already 59 feet under the 490 level and would hole the 510 fathom level within 10 feet (vertical). Main Lode had been intersected by the new shaft, just above the 510 level horizon, although its value had not been ascertained. A shaft station was mined out at the 440 level and a permanent loading station was being prepared. During this work sinking was suspended for 9 weeks.[100]

Meanwhile New Sump Shaft continued to be deepened and by the end of the year it had been sunk to the 510 fathom level. A shaft station was mined out and preparations made to drive a connection to Williams Shaft. It is of interest that winzes below the deepest levels tended, at this time, to be well ahead of the shafts being sunk. The 510 level was already being driven from winzes to the east of New Sump and to the west of Eastern Shaft by the time those two shafts had reached that level. Eastern Shaft was being equipped for hoisting from the 510 by the end of the year, and a level was driven to connect to the winzes already there. Three winzes east of New Sump, between the 490 and 510 levels, produced grades of 80lbs, 90lbs and 110lbs of tin a ton – between 3½ percent and 5 percent tin! Unfortunately, a worrying feature in Main Lode began to appear: what was described as a 'sparry course' in the lode.

This spar was also found at the same horizon close to Eastern Shaft. Between the 490 and 510 levels Main Lode was becoming very hard and this, combined with the increasing spar, gave the management cause for concern.[101]

Uranium at Dolcoath
The *Mining World* of February 27th 1909 reported on a meeting of Dolcoath's Board in their London office. A Dr Pearce spoke to the gathered mining men on the subject of radium. He said: "More than fifty years ago, I discovered uranium in Dolcoath, and have a specimen in my house, which is labelled 'pitch-blende from Dolcoath'." He then went on to talk about the interesting radium finds near Grampound, at South Terras and other locations in that vicinity. He then said he had recently found uranium in Harrietts section of the mine, and thought that at some point this ore could be exploited by the Company.[102]

Captain Arthur Thomas' analysis of production points shows interesting variations. During 1909 the Middle Section with Old and New Sump shafts produced 30.4 percent of ore and 47.5 percent of tin. The Eastern Section produced 45.35 percent of ore and 35.45 percent of tin. Harrietts section hoisted 24.25 percent of ore and only 17 percent of the tin. Stray Park appears to have ceased all measurable production. It was optimistically stated that Stray Park Section might come into its own when it is connected to Williams Shaft. Almost all the ore hoisted in the Middle Section was through New Sump Shaft, with less than 2 percent through Old Sump Shaft, although much of the ore actually came from east of Old Sump Shaft.[103]

By the end of 1909 preparations were in hand to sink Harrietts Shaft below the 400 fathom level and connect the workings at Old Sump Shaft. Wheal Killas Shaft had been refurbished and equipped with a new skip road to the 155 fathom level, although it was stated that no tin production had so far taken place there. However, the Elmore plant for treating mixed ores was obtaining ore from various points in the mine and during the first six months of 1909 produced £543 worth of saleable copper concentrates, as well as mundic and blende worth £309. Most of the ore treated by the Elmore clearly came from workings around Wheal Killas Shaft.[104]

The agents reported an impressive amount of development in 1909, with 505 fathoms of drives on lode, 169 fathoms of crosscuts and 288 fathoms of winzes, shafts and raises mined. This totalled 962 fathoms – well over a mile![105]

At that time it was noted that previously unconsidered costs were also beginning to rise inexorably. For example, the cost of insuring the miners against accidents went up from under £300 a year in 1901, to nearly £800 a year in 1903 and over £1,200 a year in 1908. This type of cost would eventually become significant to a mine finding it harder by the day to remain profitable.[106]

In the summer of 1909, it was announced that contracts had been granted to two power companies, to supply the mine with electricity. The Cornwall Electric Power Company and the Urban Electric Supply Company were to provide electricity to power the new pumps to be installed at Williams Shaft, the new electric winder there and the 12 heads of pneumatic stamps on the mine. The new electric pumps were to be installed in a pumping station at the 220 fathom level and on the deepest level, the 550 fathom level. Two sets were to be installed in each station and each pair had a lift of some 1,500 feet. They were to be worked by 3 phase 400 volt, 25 period alternating current squirrel cage induction motors, with variable speeds. The pump room measured 75 feet by 20 feet, and as the granite was soft, the whole excavation was arched with 18 inches of brickwork. It is believed that the pump room on the 220 fathom station was of similar dimensions.[107]

The accounts for 1909 show an improvement in almost every aspect of the mine's finances. Net profit was £27,550, dues paid were £10,312, tin sales came to £154,357, the average price of tin received was £81 1s 2d and the average recovery grade rose to 46.26lbs per ton. There was a total tonnage stamped of 92,229 for 1,904 tons of black tin concentrate. Costs per ton were £1 8s 3d, another rise, and the total production costs were £130,043. Worryingly, the tonnage hoisted was the lowest since 1900.[108]

Williams Shaft at the 550 fathom Level

1910 saw the coming to fruition of years of planning and expense, as the Williams Shaft project neared completion. The manager's report of August 27th 1910 announced that the shaft had reached a depth of 3,030 feet. The 550 fathom level was at 3,000 feet and the shaft initially had a 30 feet deep sump. Contracts for the new pumps and motors were set and it was predicted that the shaft would be operational, with steel rail guides for the skips and cages, by March 1911. By the end of the year the 550 station, pump room and engine foundations for the pumps and winders, were nearing completion. The arched brickwork was also finished. Contracts had been granted for supplying the new stone crushers and screening plant, to be erected at the shafthead. By the end of 1910 the overall cost of the Williams Shaft project was £110,820, with more expense to come. This expense meant that no dividend was to be paid that year.[109]

At the same time as this work at Williams Shaft, the mine was replacing its Cornish Stamps by the more modern and far more efficient pneumatic stamps. Sixty heads of the older stamps were dismantled and 12 heads of the new were being erected, but like the shaft project, this took time and caused great disruption to production. New vanner sheds were also erected and new dressing plant installed.[110]

Underground work to open up the deepest parts of the mine continued, as did the exploration of long abandoned districts of the mine. By the summer of 1910, the 490 fathom level had been connected to Williams Shaft from the Middle Section, and by the end of the year the 510 level was only 18 fathoms from it. By then, a crosscut had been driven south from Williams, and had intersected Main Lode at a distance of 35 fathoms. The lode there was at least 24 feet wide, but was making a considerable quantity of water. Thus, the end was temporarily suspended, and a dam was installed to hold back the coming water. This was primarily to keep the station area, with all of its expensive equipment, dry.[111]

Harrietts Shaft was being sunk below the 400 fathom level and by the end of June it was 14 feet below the level. Wheal Killas Shaft continued to be re-equipped for hoisting the complex ores there, and by the summer of 1910 its skip road was extended to the 160 level. Hopes remained high for the quantity and quality of the zinc, copper, arsenic and tin ground to be opened up there, and to the west.[112]

Production from Middle Section (Old and New Sump shafts) remained high, with 31.95 percent of the ore and 38.2 percent of the tin coming from there. Only about 10 percent came through Old Sump Shaft. The Eastern Section was becoming the biggest producer, with 49.05 percent of the ore and 47.35 percent of the tin. Harrietts section fell somewhat, with only 20.2 percent of the ore and 14.5 percent of the tin. Much of this production came from levels higher up the mine, where dirt from several lodes was being trammed to the shafts for hoisting.[113]

There was a drop in the development work done in 1910, with 475 fathoms of lode drives, 102 fathoms of crosscuts and 233 fathoms of winzes, shafts and raises mined. The total was 810 fathoms, down on the 1909 total by 152 fathoms, which was a considerable drop.[114]

The accounts for 1910 show continuing improvement and although the recovery was down the price of tin increased. This period, which really started in 1909, was described by Jack Trounson as a 'little St Luke's summer', because despite appearances, the high profits of the next three years were really the prelude to a coming winter. He believed the 'writing was already on the wall' for the old mine. Net profit for 1910 was £37,534, dues paid were £10,771, and income from tin sales was £161,364. Tonnage stamped was 91,938, black tin sold was 1,731 tons, the recovery was 42.21lbs a ton and the average price received for Dolcoath's tin was £93 4s 1d. Costs per ton were £1 7s 7d a ton and production costs were £126,874.[115]

At the February 22nd 1911 AGM, Frank Harvey made the following statement: "It is with the most sincere regret the Directors have to announce the death of their valued colleague, Mr G. H. M. Batten. They are of the opinion that the vacant seat on the Board need not be filled at present." By the next meeting his place had been taken by Mr F. A. Robinson.[116]

1911 was another year of mixed fortunes for the mine, but with the tin price up and profits rising, despite continuing problems with new equipment and delays in meeting dead-lines, the mine looked set fair for better times. In his July 21st 1911 report, on the first six months of the year, Captain Arthur Thomas wrote:

"Further explorations are being carried on at Killas Shaft and Stray Park in regard to the zinc-copper ores as also the copper tin ores which we hope it will soon be possible to profitably work.[117]

Cage roads in the Williams Shaft together with the keep gear have been completed, and the cages are at work in the shaft. The pumping plant for the Williams Shaft consisting of 4 electrically driven pumping engines have been delivered, and are being erected. The cables have been delivered, as also the whole of the electrical work in connection with the plant. The stone-breaking and screening plant at the Williams Shaft consisting of main and return roads to and from the shaft, creep, tipplers, screens, four 24 x 12 stone-breakers, the necessary bunker accommodation of steel structural work covered with galvanised iron, is nearing completion. This plant will be found quite capable of screening and crushing the expected and entire output from the Williams Shaft, and will be electrically driven by a motor a duplicate of those driving the pneumatic stamps, eight of which are in operation driven by two motors. An electric haulage has been installed at surface at the Williams Shaft, and the switch gear is being erected in the sub-station. The necessary over-head electric transmission lines throughout have been completed, and the various motors in the electrical scheme are gradually replacing the steam engines formerly driving the sundry plant.[118]

Two new cylinders of larger diameter (28-inch diameter) would replace the existing ones of the traversing winding engine at the Williams Shaft; and this work, together with sundry alterations and general overhauling of these engines, will be shortly carried out, so that permanent winding may be commenced in September next, when, it is expected, with the exception of the remaining 4 heads of Pneumatic stamps, the whole of the new machinery will be at work.[119]"

The ore was to be hoisted using two trucks, each with a capacity of 30 cubic feet. Upon reaching the surface these waggons tipped automatically onto screens (grizzleys), which allowed the smaller ore to pass through and sent the larger rocks to the stone-crushers, from whence the ore went to the new pneumatic stamps. During 1911 the rail track on the surface was further extended and another steam locomotive was employed. Intriguingly, Tom Harris wrote, that Dolcoath employed ponies underground for haulage. The author has failed to find any other reference

364

to this and has never spoken to any old miner or employee of Dolcoath who has heard of this. The only three mines which used ponies for haulage underground in Cornwall, appear to have been Levant until the Great War, East Pool, during the Second World War, and Polhigey, between the wars.[120]

By the end of the year the mine was benefiting from Williams Shaft, as men and ore were already being hoisted through it, although it was not yet fully operational. Its increasing use was helping to reduce operating costs. Meanwhile, New Sump Shaft was being sunk under the 510 level, and by the end of the year it was down 5 fathoms. Drives from Eastern Shaft had also been connected to Williams Shaft, and it was in this eastern area that prospects were looking at their best. All levels below the 145 fathom level at Eastern Shaft were being exploited and at the 270 level a new station plat had been cut to facilitate more efficient hoisting. The connections to Williams Shaft were vastly improving ventilation on the deeper levels, which was good for the health of the miners and also improved productivity.[121]

No.1 winze under the 510 fathom level, initially produced some good ore of between 50lbs and 80lbs a ton, but as the winze went deeper, the grade dropped to about 20lbs a ton. Although there were worrying signs in the results from the bottom of the mine, with grades dropping off and the increasing presence of spar in Main Lode, the management showed their continued confidence in the mine by ordering a new 20 drill capacity air compressor, for Williams Shaft.[122]

Analysis of the production figures from the various sections of the mine showed the increasing importance of the Eastern Section to the mine. Middle Section (New and Old Sump) was holding its own, with 34.3 percent of the ore and 42.85 percent of the tin. Harrietts section continued to drop, with ore down to 12.85 percent and tin down to 12 percent. Eastern Section continued to increase its output, with ore at 51.9 percent and tin at 48.65 percent of the mine total. Stray Park Section showed no produce in the first half of the year and only a tiny output in the second half. Very little of Middle Section's ore came through Old Sump Shaft.[123]

Development fell due to the severe dropping off of winze and shaft sinking. There were 465 fathoms of lode drives in 1911, 131 fathoms of crosscuts, but only 91 fathoms of sinking and raising, compared to the previous year's total of 233 fathoms. The total development fathomage was only 687 fathoms compared to 810 fathoms in 1910.[124]

Dolcoath's First Aid Team
Captain William James, who was a keen first-aider, and member of the Camborne Division of St John Ambulance, took the lead in introducing first-aid cover for the mine. Several miners and others employed at Dolcoath were members of St John and

these formed the nucleus of Dolcoath's new team. The Dolcoath Division became very competitive and won several trophies and awards for their efficiency. The team even did a demonstration before the King, at Windsor Castle and Captain James attended a Royal Garden Party at the invitation of Queen Alexandra.[125]

The accounts for 1911 show that despite a drop in the total tonnage crushed, profits were double the previous year. This was due to the vastly increased tin price and slightly improved recovery rate. Net profit was £71,952, dues paid came to £13,246 and income from tin sold was £198,696. The total ore crushed was 86,658 tons, the lowest for over 10 years, and the black tin sold was 1,706 tons. Recovery averaged 44.30lbs a ton and the average price received for the tin sold came to £116 9s 2d. Costs per ton were £1 7s and the total production cost was £116,988.[126]

New Sump Engine Stopped
June 5th 1912 saw the end of pumping by Cornish beam engine at New Sump Shaft, after 113 unbroken years. The old engine had helped cope with flooding on the bottom levels early in the year, when exceptionally wet weather caused serious problems and loss of production. The new electric pumps, in Williams Shaft, coped well with the water at the bottom of the mine, and were assisted by the Harrietts engine, which pumped the water from the levels above the 220 fathom level. This water was conveyed to Harrietts Shaft by pipes. The electrification of the mine's plant continued successfully during 1912. The electric power to the 12 new pneumatic stamps, the new vanners and Williams winding engine and pumps, proved to be economic, efficient and reliable.[127]

A new air compressor was being erected at Williams Shaft, and it was complete by early 1913. Early in 1912, due to a strike by the Welsh coal miners there was a serious shortage of coal, causing the management to stop all the compressors to save coal for the pumps and stamps. This greatly reduced development as the miners concentrated on production, which was mostly by hand-labour. However, sinking continued at New Sump Shaft, and by the end of the year it was 22½ fathoms below the 510 fathom level. Three winzes under the 510 level also continued, although the grades encountered were disappointing as their depths increased. Above the 510 level the ore continued to be good, and new work on the 412 fathom level was proving worthwhile, with values of between 30lbs and 40lbs a ton. On the 550 fathom level Main Lode was driven 6 fathoms to the east, but the ground was not worth much, although the captains thought it looked 'hopeful'.[128]

In July 1912 there was a tragic accident at the surface by Williams Shaft. A workman was killed whilst engaged in adjusting machinery in the compressor and crusher house. The inquest decided it was his own carelessness which had led to the accident.[129]

By the second half of the year most production from the lower levels was being hoisted through Williams Shaft, with the ore raised through New and Old Sump shafts, Harrietts and Eastern Shaft dropping. These older shafts continued to raise most of their dirt from the higher levels. Middle Section (New and Old Sump shafts) hoisted 31.25 percent of the ore and 23.1 percent of the mine's tin. Eastern Section hoisted 40.7 percent of the ore and 37.7 percent of the tin. Both sections saw a drop in their figures in the second half of the year. Harrietts section produced 9.6 percent of the ore and 11.6 percent of the tin in the first half of the year, but no production was recorded for the second half. For the second half of the year, Williams Shaft hoisted 26.3 percent of the ore and 35.6 percent of the mine's tin, but nothing for the first half.[130]

Despite the suspension of much development in the first half of the year, due to the coal shortage, the final figures were only slightly down. Lode drives were 387 fathoms, down 78 fathoms on the previous year. Crosscutting totalled 111 fathoms, which was down 20 fathoms. However, work in winzes, raises and shafts were up 95 fathoms to 186 fathoms. The total development came to 684 fathoms, almost the same as the previous year.[131]

The accounts for 1912 showed a net profit of £79,108, dues paid of £14,481 and total tin sales of £216,666. There were 109,197 tons crushed for 1,665 tons of black tin, which sold for an average of £130 2s 7d. This was up £14 a ton. The grade dropped dramatically to 34.41lbs a ton – down nearly 10lbs! Costs per ton were also down to £1 5s 10d and the production costs were £140,864.[132]

During the first half of 1913 there was some production loss due to the Williams Shaft whim engine having two new cylinders fitted and a general overhaul. The winder was stopped for a fortnight. The manager estimated that this cost the mine 2,327 tons of ore, amounting, he believed, to 81¾ tons of black tin. The new air compressor at Williams Shaft was working well and more new dressing plant was installed.[133]

In the early months of 1913 there was a great effort to search the northern section of the sett for untapped sources of ore, and a crosscut to South Entral Lode at the 210 fathom level led to drives on the lode to prove its value. Although the results were not particularly good, the management decided to crosscut to the lode on the 190 and 230 fathom levels also, in the hope of finding payable ore there. Due to the high tin price, large tonnages of low grade ore were mined, as it was profitable to do so. During those months, a connection was made on the 550 level between New Sump Shaft and the eastern drive on Main Lode, from the crosscut south of Williams Shaft. There were also connections between the 510 and 550 fathom levels by means of winzes, all of which improved ventilation and facilitated developments on those levels. There were problems with water in the No.3 winze, and the ore values were disappointing on and immediately above the 550 level. The ore was patchy, with very little of any value. However, to compensate for this lack of good ore discoveries at the bottom of the mine, exploration on the levels above went on at a fast pace: the 238 (South Lode), 254, 290, 302, 327, 338, 375, 400, 412, 425, 455, 485, 490 and 510 levels were all searched for payable ore. Stray Park Section remained unproductive.[134]

During the second half of the year, with New Sump Shaft 6 fathoms below the 550 level, it was decided to continue to go as deep as possible, to prove whether there was payable ore at those depths. Meanwhile, the south crosscut at the 550 level from Williams Shaft had been driven 20 fathoms south of Main Lode and discovered nothing of value. Despite determined exploration on the 550 level, there was little good ore found there. A large body of unworked ground to the north of New Sump Shaft, between the 302 and 338 fathom levels, was being opened up and was proving profitable. The east drive on South Entral Lode, on the 210 level, found some tin ore of up to 30lbs a ton, but the lode was patchy. It was decided to crosscut from this lode north to North Entral Lode, where it was anticipated they might find better ore.[135]

The way the ore was distributed throughout the sett was revealed by the Manager's analysis of the production figures. Williams Shaft hoisted 25.5 percent of the ore and 31.55 percent of the tin. New Sump Shaft raised 21.15 percent of the ore and 19.5 percent of the tin. Old Sump Shaft had 4.4 percent of the ore and 3.35 percent of the tin. Eastern Shaft produced 38 percent of the ore and 37.15 percent of the tin. Harrietts section produced 9.35 percent of the ore and 9.65 percent of the tin. Stray Park produced less that one percent of the tin.[136]

There was a vast increase in development during 1913, with 441 fathoms of lode drives, 175 fathoms of crosscuts and 247 fathoms of raising and sinking. This totalled 863 fathoms, the highest figure since 1909.

The accounts for 1913 showed a net profit of £42,193, dues paid of £12,376 and income from tin sales of £185,637. Tonnage crushed was 114,713 for 1,525 tons of black tin. The average price received by the mine for its tin was £121 5s 8d and the recovery was 29.77lbs a ton. Costs per ton were £1 5s 4d and the total production costs were £145,685.[137]

The Great War (1914-18)
1914 was a most dramatic year for the old mine. In August the whole world was plunged into warfare on a scale hitherto unimagined. This situation created conditions which affected every aspect of mining, not just in Cornwall, but throughout the world. The mine reports for the first half of the year looked little different from

those of the previous years, with the mine being steadily deepened and development continuing all over the mine sett. Production remained at the same level and the number of fathoms developed was actually higher than the previous six month periods. New Sump Shaft was sunk 63 feet under the 550 fathom level and a winze was down some 77 feet below the level. The shaft sinking was suspended in March and the tin values in the winze under the 550, which started quite well, fell away as it deepened. Meanwhile, the 550 fathom level was being driven on Main Lode some 150 fathoms east of the south crosscut and 13 fathoms to the west. Other crosscuts were also driven north and south of Main Lode there. Nothing of much value was discovered in these ends. A connection between Old Sump Shaft and Harrietts Shaft was holed on the 425 level, and it was intended to resume sinking the latter shaft. The 'subsidiary shaft' to the north of New Sump Shaft was deepened from the 302 to the 375 fathom level and was opening up 'moderately productive' ground for stoping. It was intended to deepen this shaft to the 400 level. The exploration on South Entral Lode at the 210 level, between Middle Section and Eastern Shaft, was proving disappointing. Hopes were still entertained that Stray Park might produce 'some low grade tinstuff'.[138]

This picture of continuing normality and progress changed totally in the second half of the year. With the Declaration of War, in August, the London Metal Exchange closed, causing confusion in the metal mining world. Tin ticketing was also suspended. Even before the outbreak of the Great War, the manager and directors were sufficiently worried about the state of the mine to ask Dr Malcolm Maclaren, the distinguished geologist, to inspect the mine and report on its future working. Maclaren carried out an extremely detailed study of the mine and his report, delivered on the 29th August 1914, looks at every aspect of the workings. He commented on each lode on the sett in each section of the mine, from Stray Park and the adjacent mines to the west, right through to the Valley Section, at Eastern Shaft. Maclaren's conclusions, for the mine below the 550 fathom level, were stark.

> "It will already have been gathered that I am of the opinion that it is unwise and indeed useless to do any further work below the 550 fathom level in the eastern end of the mine. I base my opinion (a) on the great change in the character of the lode (Main Lode) in the bottom levels (510 fathoms and 550 fathoms) and (b) on the shape and disposition of the scattered ore-bodies in the lower levels of the mine, which together with the downward tongues from the main ore shoot impress me as characteristic of the lower margin of profitable ore. I am confident that quite sufficient work has been done in the bottom to prove the lack of persistence in depth of the known ore bodies, and while the lode-channel certainly persists downward, I can yet see no reason, geological or otherwise, to hope for a recurrence of pay-ore below the 550 fathom level. Nevertheless, while this is so, I think that since so much has been already

done on the 550 fathom level, this exploration should be completed by driving the level to the Little Crosscourse, a further distance from the present face of about 34 fathoms." Maclaren believed that there was payable ore to the west, above the 490 fathom level, and that hitherto unexplored lodes in Stray Park should be developed. His final comments were on six points he felt worth exploring. (1) South crosscut at the 400 fathom level off Eastern Shaft (length 50 fathoms). (2) East drive 550 fathom level (34 fathoms). (3) Deepening Harriett Shaft to the 490 fathom level (65 fathoms). (4) West drive off Harriett Shaft at the 490 fathom level (50 fathoms). (5) North crosscut, Stray Park 314 fathom level (50 fathoms). (6) North crosscut, Stray Park 238 fathom level (40 fathoms).[139]"

Unsurprisingly, Captain Thomas was not entirely in agreement with the recommendations of Dr Maclaren. He felt the famous geologist was unnecessarily 'condemnatory' about the prospects in the central and eastern sections at the bottom of the mine. The manager was convinced that the mine should be deepened 50 fathoms below the 550 level, to prove whether it was worth working. He said the deepest winze was already 14 fathoms below the 550 level, and so why not continue to the 600 fathom level and prove the ground once and for all? Despite Thomas's opinion, external world conditions were against him, and as men left for the armed forces – and by the end of the year some 128 had volunteered, there were less able men to carry out the needed exploration. Apart from work on the two crosscuts on the 550 fathom level, little development took place there. Indeed, very little exploration was done anywhere on the mine as it slowly bled its best young men. Harrietts Shaft was sunk 27 fathoms under the 425 level by the end of the year and some work was carried out to deepen the 'subsidiary shaft' to the 400 fathom level, but generally things began to grind to a halt, and concentration was upon production rather than development.[140]

During the year there were 248 fathoms of lode drives, 276 fathoms of crosscuts and 199 fathoms of sinking and raising. This totalled 723 fathoms, which was not too bad, but when the figures for the second half of the year are examined, it is clear that the loss of so many able miners to the armed forces was taking its toll. Only 22½ fathoms of lode drives, 76 fathoms of crosscuts and 77 fathoms of sinking and raising were carried out in the second half of the year – a total of 176 fathoms as opposed to 547 fathoms in the first half of the year! Although concentration was upon production, the loss of so many miners meant that there were 9,000 tons of ore less hoisted in the second half of the year than the first half.[141]

The manager's analysis of the production points showed that the Eastern Section of the mine continued to dominate. Williams Shaft hoisted 23.5 percent of the ore and 21.65 percent of the tin. New Sump Shaft hoisted 21.9 percent of the ore and 22.95

percent of the tin. Old Sump Shaft hoisted 4.3 percent of the ore and 3.35 percent of the tin. Eastern Shaft produced 39.75 percent of the ore and 43.85 percent of the tin. Harrietts Shaft hoisted 9.05 percent of the ore and 7.6 percent of the tin. Hardly anything came through Stray Park Shaft.[142]

The accounts for 1914 reflected the dramatic events affecting the mine. Net profit was down to £3,893, a drop of over £38,000. Dues paid were £8,481 and tin sales amounted to £127,092. Tonnage crushed was 105,312, which produced 1,439 tons of black tin concentrate. Recovery was fractionally up to 30.8lbs a ton and the price received for the tin averaged £88 6s 5d a ton, a drop of about £33 a ton. Costs per ton of ore were £1 4s 2½d and the total production cost was £118,822. In 1914 there were 959 workers on the mine.[143]

Early in the year Mr Gilbert Bennett Pearce, who had served the mine as a Director for 13 years, died. Gilbert Pearce had been connected to the old mine for 60 years, having started there as a junior clerk in 1854. He was replaced on the Board of Directors by F. W. Thomas, who had served as the Company Secretary since the company was formed in 1895. Before that he had been the Dolcoath Mine Secretary. Mr John Champion replaced F. W. Thomas as Company Secretary.[144]

1915 saw the situation at Dolcoath worsen still further, as more men left to fight for the country and essential materials became harder to obtain and more expensive. By June the mine had lost 189 men to the army and navy and by the end of the year the figure had risen to 240, with 203 of them being miners – a third of the normal total! The mine paid £430 6s 2d to the volunteers' dependants.[145]

New Mineral Lords
The crisis caused the directors to approach the mineral lord for a reduction in the dues (royalties), but as Mr Basset had sold his interests in the district, they had to negotiate with the new owners, Messrs A. H. Bond and Hamilton Edwards. The request appeared to have been favourably received, but time was to tell a different tale.[146]

Despite the few men available some development points were pushed on. The drive east on the 550 fathom level was driven some 42 fathoms toward the Eastern Little Crosscourse, which lay a further 20 fathoms beyond the end. Little valuable ore was found. This was the only exploration on the 550 level for the first six months of 1915. Exploration continued close to the 'Subsidiary shaft' on the 254, 338, 352 and 375 fathom levels, where 'small quantities of tinground' were being opened up for stoping. Work also continued to the west of Eastern Shaft on the 270, 352 and 375 fathom levels. In Stray Park, crosscuts at the 238 and 314 fathom levels were pushed north in search of payable ore. Harrietts Shaft was sunk 53½ fathoms below the 425 fathom level, and it was hoped to hole the 490 in early September. This hot part of the mine needed the improved ventilation the connection would bring. Meanwhile, at the surface, new pulverisers and improved concentrating plant were being installed, to replace small, isolated dressing plant and improve efficiency and economy.[147]

The second half of the year saw development on the 550 fathom level suspended. There was a further 35 fathoms driven at the 'Subsidiary shaft' workings, before stoping got under way. Some exploration took place east of New Sump Shaft, at the 338 and 412 fathom levels, and the results were 'hopeful'. Very little new ground was opened up in the Eastern Section and apart from the two north crosscuts at the 238 and 314 fathom levels, little was done at Stray Park. In November, Harrietts Shaft was holed to the 490 fathom level, and this vastly improved the ventilation throughout that district. Problems with water in the shaft had held up the sinking, but by mining beneath the shaft much of this water was released.[148]

Once again the Eastern Section dominated production and the Manager's reports show this clearly. Williams Shaft hoisted 18.65 percent of the ore and 13.85 percent of the tin. New Sump Shaft hoisted 25.4 percent of the ore and 26.75 percent of the tin. Old Sump Shaft drew 6.55 percent of the ore and 4.55 percent of the tin. Eastern Shaft brought up 43.2 percent of the ore and 47.4 percent of the tin. Harrietts Shaft produced 6 percent of the ore and 7.2 percent of the tin.[149]

The loss of miners had a profound effect upon the development figures. There were only 127 fathoms of lode drives, 110 fathoms of crosscuts and 64 fathoms of raising and sinking. This totalled a mere 301 fathoms, which was 422 fathoms less than the previous year's total. Clearly, this was yet another factor which threatened the long-term future of the mine. Development should always be kept well ahead of production – or, as the old saying goes: 'The mine should be kept well ahead of the mill'.[150]

The accounts for 1915 showed a net profit of £646 (there was a loss in the second half of the year of £4,990) dues paid of £7,394 and tin sales of £110,391. There was a total of 83,070 tons hoisted and crushed for the production of 1,187 tons of black tin. Recovery was 31.88lbs a ton and the average price received by the mine was £93 a ton. Costs per ton were £1 6s 6½d and production costs were £102,953.[151]

During 1916 Dolcoath's problems got worse, with men continuing to leave for the armed forces and others leaving for well-paid jobs being created by the wartime conditions. By the end of June, 248 had joined the forces and by the end of the year this had risen to 260. Thirty-five percent of the miners had volunteered and 5 percent had left for other work. Things were becoming desperate underground, with insufficient men to complete drives which had been started or to start other essential exploration work.[152]

To make matters worse, the request to the new mineral lords concerning lessening the dues, which was initially thought to have been greeted favourably, turned out to have been quite different. Frank Harvey reported on August 25th 1916: "The contribution by way of remission of dues which was promised by Mr Hamilton Edwards on behalf of himself and his associate Mr Bond, in his letter dated 16th February, 1916, which was read at the meeting of shareholders held in London on 24th February last, has, the Directors regret to say, not been made. Messrs. Hamilton Edwards and Bond subsequently offered to advance the Company a sum of £4,000 to be expended in the special development contemplated, but as they stipulated that the amount was to be re-paid under certain conditions, and was therefore not a remission of dues, the Directors did not see their way to accept it." This was a bitter blow to the struggling mine, and combined with the many other problems being faced at the time, potentially disastrous.[153]

During the first half of 1916 nothing was done on the 550 fathom level. Elsewhere, some small bits of exploration continued, but at a much-reduced rate. On the 440 fathom level a lode drive east of the crosscut, east of New East Shaft was opening up 'moderately producing tin ground'. The 412 level was being driven east of New East Shaft into low grade tin ground, and on the 338 and 254 fathom levels, similar ore was being opened up in the Middle District, between New East and New Sump shafts. Developments around Old Sump Shaft and in the Eastern District were suspended due to shortage of miners. West of Harrietts Shaft, on the 440 and 490 fathom levels, on Main Lode, exploration was finding little of value. The Stray Park north crosscuts continued, but without finding lodes.[154]

The second half of the year looked similar to the first, but on the 550 level a lode drive had found tin ground with 30lbs a ton. On the 440 level east of New East Shaft the ore was assayed at 50lbs a ton. Throughout the Middle section, at the 254 and 338 fathom levels, the ore being opened up was moderate to low grade. The same situation obtained in the Harrietts section, but in Stray Park, the north crosscut had intersected a tin lode which was 3 feet wide and valued at 40lbs a ton. This discovery raised the hopes of the depressed management, albeit temporarily.[155]

Analysis of the mine's production points showed a continuing decline in hoisting through Williams Shaft and Harrietts Shaft, and Eastern Shaft maintaining its importance. Williams Shaft hoisted 13.45 percent of the ore and 12.7 percent of the tin. New Sump Shaft hoisted 32 percent of the ore and 33.3 percent of the tin. Old Sump Shaft drew 4.7 percent of the ore and 4 percent of the tin. Eastern Shaft produced 43.8 percent of the ore and 42.75 percent of the tin. Harrietts Shaft hoisted

6.05 percent of the ore and 7.45 percent of the tin.[156]

The exploration figures for 1916 were shocking, with only 82½ fathoms developed in the first 6 months. There was no sinking or raising for the whole year, and most of the work was on lode drives. In the whole year there was a total of 209 fathoms driven on lode and 54 fathoms of crosscutting. The year's total development amounted to a mere 263 fathoms. With more and more of the fittest young miners leaving, there seemed little prospect of the much-needed exploration.[157]

Like the previous year the accounts for 1916 were a mixed bag. There was a net profit in the first half of the year of £6,883, but a loss in the second half of £2,910, which produced a new annual net profit of £3,973. Dues paid amounted to £7,480 and the amount received for the black tin was £113,456. Tonnage crushed was 79,347 and black tin sold totalled 1,077 tons. Recovery averaged 30.36lbs a ton and the average price received by the mine was £104 a ton. Costs per ton were £1 7s 6d and the total production costs were £102,003. Notice was sent out for the February 28th 1917 AGM under the hand of R. Arthur Thomas, as Acting Secretary. Thereafter, Thomas was both manager and 'Acting' Company Secretary. In August John Champion, the Company Secretary, had died. He had been ill for some time. He had worked at the mine for over 30 years as an accountant, and latterly as Secretary. His widow was granted £100 in monthly instalments over 12 months. His salary was paid her till the end of the month. In September 1916 Captain William Mill, the superintendent tin dresser, also died. He was replaced by his son, also called William, who had been his right-hand man for a long time. His widow was also given £100 by the Board.[158]

Diamond Drilling
In 1917 the labour situation got worse, with 287 in the armed forces by June and 297 by the end of the year. Dolcoath paid £423 16s 8d to the dependants of these servicemen during the year. The armed forces were not the only drain on Dolcoath's labour force, for during 1917 there was a definite move to other mines by miners who saw the prospects better there. For example, a dozen miners moved from Dolcoath to South Crofty, where things were looking much healthier. These included four machine miners, who left together for Crofty at the beginning of December. With exploration severely curtailed by the reduced labour force, the mine turned to a less labour-intensive and more modern solution to its problems. For some time past East Pool & Agar United Mine had employed a diamond drill for exploration purposes, and in 1916 South Crofty had hired it to search for lodes in its sett. Now Dolcoath took an interest, and in August 1917 Frank Harvey, the Chairman, made the following statement: "In March last it was decided to do some diamond drilling, and arrangements were made with East Pool and Agar, Limited, for the loan of their equipment for the purpose." The initial cost came to £876 7s 10d and in the next few months there was a considerable amount of work

done by it. Initially, the drill was used in Stray Park Section to drill beyond the north crosscuts on the 238 and 314 fathom levels. The 238 hole was drilled for a distance of 248 feet and the 314 hole for 508 feet. They intersected 'numerous branches' of tin lode. The drill was then taken down to the 510 fathom level and used to explore in the Eastern Section. Conventional development continued on the 338, 375, 440 and 490 fathom levels, mostly in the Middle Section and west of Harrietts Shaft.[159]

During the second half of the year the diamond drill was used to explore the ground beneath the 375 fathom level, 30 fathoms to the east of Stray Park Shaft. The miners drilled down to a depth equivalent to the 430 fathom level. Subsequently, it was used to drill on the 510 level, 10 fathoms east of a crosscourse, west of Eastern Shaft, to Main Lode. Then it was used to drill north on the 470 from the Middle Section and the 375 level at Stray Park. This latter hole went 1,108 feet north. The cost of the diamond drilling programme in the second half of the year was £751 8s 10d. Meanwhile, the 490 drive west, which had been advanced 152 fathoms, was abandoned due to excessive heat. Temperatures reached 110°F, with almost total humidity. Even the electric fans there failed to reduce the temperature sufficiently for men to work efficiently in the end. £13,000 was assigned to this western development and it was proving harder to justify such expenditure.[160]

Developments on the 210, 338 and 375 fathom levels had mixed results. On the 375 east of Subsidiary Shaft low grade ore was found. On the 338 level east of New Sump Shaft, on the north part of Main Lode, 'only small quantities of payable ore' were discovered. On the 210 west on South Entral Lode, which had been driven 32½ fathoms west of the crosscut, a 'small and rich branch of tinstuff has been discovered'. Meanwhile, on the upper levels, near to New Sump Shaft, at the 130 and 159 fathom levels, arsenical pyrites and low grade tin were being found. The mine was beginning to struggle in its search for new tin ground.[161]

During 1917 hoisting ore through Williams Shaft increased as that through New Sump Shaft decreased. Williams Shaft hoisted 37.05 percent of the mine's ore and 45.7 percent of the tin. New Sump drew 10.15 percent of the ore and 9.1 percent of the tin. Old Sump hoisted 8.95 percent of the ore and 4.75 percent of the tin. Eastern Shaft hoisted 37.55 percent of the ore and 33.6 percent of the tin. Harrietts Shaft produced 6.35 percent of the ore and 6.85 percent of the tin.[162]

There was 66 fathoms less development during 1917 than the previous year, with 131 fathoms driven on lode and 24 fathoms of crosscutting. The previous year there were no winzes or raises mined, but in 1917 there was a total of 42 fathoms of these. This totalled an unsatisfactory 197 fathoms of exploration for the year.[163]

The Workers Union at Dolcoath

In October 1917, the Company received a letter from Mr J. Harris, organiser of the Workers Union, requesting permission to negotiate on behalf of his members at Dolcoath, for increased wages. He pointed out that other local mines had workers in the union, on behalf of whom he negotiated with the mine owners. A conference was organised between Mr Harris, for the Workers Union, the Chamber of Mines and Dolcoath's management team. An 'amicable settlement was reached'.[164]

The 1917 accounts showed a net profit of £10,412 and dues paid of £8,833. Tin sales amounted to £131,038. There were 69,714 tons of ore crushed for the production of 968 tons of black tin. Recovery was 31.08lbs a ton and the average price received for the mine's tin concentrate was £135 6s 3d. Costs per ton were £1 16s 1d and the total production cost was £125,485. For the first time for years the mine sold some arsenic, which brought in £2,404 5s 7d.[165]

Purchase of Dolcoath's Mineral Rights

On April 25th 1918, Frank Harvey, the Company Chairman, made the following announcement: "The shareholders are aware that since the close of the half-year covered by the accounts (for July-December 1917) the Directors have, in pursuance of the terms of the circular issued to the shareholders on the 30th January last, carried through the purchase of the Lord's rights over the Dolcoath mine and have, in conjunction with East Pool and Agar Limited, acquired certain outside areas in the district for which purpose Debenture Stock to the amount of £75,000 was created. The issue was over subscribed and the full amount has been allotted." The total purchase price for the many thousand acres of mineral rights and other surface areas in Cornwall, was £90,000, of which Dolcoath bought 2/3rds, for £60,000, and East Pool and Agar 1/3rd, for £30,000. On March 26th 1919 Harvey reported: "In pursuance of the policy laid down in the last half-yearly report and at the last General Meeting, and the consent of the Treasury having at last been obtained, a company was registered on February 3rd last under the title of the Tehidy Minerals Limited, to take control over the mineral rights purchased from the late owners, other than those allocated to the Dolcoath and East Pool & Agar Companies. The Tehidy Minerals Limited has been formed with a capital of £100,000 in £1 shares, of which 40,000 have been allotted to Dolcoath and 20,000 to East Pool & Agar the remaining 40,000 shares were offered at par to the shareholders of Dolcoath and East Pool and Agar Ltd." Messrs O. Wethered and F. A. Robinson represented Dolcoath on the new board and C. A. Moreing and H. M. Rogers represented East Pool. Consultant technical advisors were to be Bewick & Moreing from East Pool, Arthur Thomas from Dolcoath and William Hosking, formerly Mineral Agent for Tehidy Estate.[166]

Ultimately, Tehidy Minerals Ltd. also included the mineral rights of Viscount Clifden's estates in its portfolio, and the total mineral ownership amounted to some

36,000 acres in Cornwall. With this came the ownership of the rights in many China Clay works. The Basset and Clifden estates also passed ownership of thousands of acres of land surface, consisting of many abandoned spoil heaps and almost the whole of the Red River Valley, to the new company. In the Camborne area there were many houses and other properties owned by the new company. With the final failure of New Dolcoath, in 1930, ownership of the company's share in Tehidy Minerals was passed to the Treasury to cover part of the debt the mine owed it. In 1936, South Crofty Mine purchased from HM Treasury the whole of Dolcoath's assets, but Tehidy Minerals Ltd, with its office in Basset Street, Camborne, remained a separate company for many more years.[167]

In November 1978, Tehidy Minerals Ltd. was acquired by South Crofty Mine Ltd, and the massive archive held at the company's office in Basset Street, Camborne was moved either to South Crofty or the Cornwall Record Office, Truro. Subsequently, some time after the closure of South Crofty Mine, in 1998, Tehidy Minerals Ltd. was sold to Baseresult, a mining company which began the work of re-opening the western part of South Crofty Mine.[168]

1918 saw changes on the Board of Directors. With the death of H. C. Godfray, E. W. Jenson was appointed to the Board, and Arthur Thomas, who had been Mine Manager for 23 years, joined the Board as Managing Director, as his father had been before him. Thomas also remained as 'Acting Secretary'.[169]

Acting partly on the advice of Dr Maclaren, Captain Thomas decided to crosscut south from the 510 fathom level, to the west of Eastern Shaft, to intersect the faulted Main Lode. It was also intended to carry out exploration in Cooks Kitchen Mine, recently acquired by Dolcoath. In October 1917 there had been a diamond drill hole into Cooks Kitchen from the bottom of the Eastern Section. Most of the exploration in the first half of the year was by diamond drill, although there was a drive on the 352 level into Camborne Vean Mine from Stray Park, to search for new reserves of payable tin.[170]

Although there was no development or stoping near Williams Shaft for the first half of the year, most of the ore produced in the Middle Section of the mine (New Sump, Old Sump and Subsidiary shafts) was hoisted through it. In Stray Park a diamond drill hole was put down from the 375 level for a depth of 484 feet below the level, and elsewhere in that section exploration continued on the 375 and 352 fathom levels. Camborne Vean Mine continued to be of interest to the developers. On the upper levels also a diamond drill was active, with a 991 feet deep hole drilled north at the 190 fathom level, from a point 81 fathoms north of New Sump Shaft. South Entral Lode was also being explored on the 190 fathom level and holes were drilled from the workings for a distance of 1,457 feet. South Entral Lode had already been worked many years before, above the 80 fathom level, but recent exploration there had not been encouraging.[171]

During the second half of the year there were signs of desperation, as miners began working old 'run stuff' from formerly abandoned workings. Some was just payable. Meanwhile, on the 338 level, east of New East Shaft, Main Lode was found to have ore of up to 2 percent tin and other areas of 'old workings' were proving to contain 'moderately productive tin ground'. By the second half of the year, the current diamond drilling programme was completed. The cost for the first half of the year was £1,829 16s.[172]

It was hoped that with a general demobilisation of the armed forces, and the men flocking back to work, many of the mine's problems would be solved. During the first half of the year 315 men were serving and by the end of the year the number in the armed forces had risen to a peak of 319. The mine paid £538 5s 8d to the servicemen's dependants. Apart from those in the forces, men were still leaving for better paid jobs outside the mine, and South Crofty's records show a constant supply from mines, like Dolcoath, which were perceived as 'in trouble'.[173]

With more ore from Middle Section being hoisted through Williams Shaft the picture for production points appeared to have changed. Williams Shaft hoisted 42.55 percent of the mine's ore and 44.4 percent of its tin. New Sump Shaft figures were 7.3 percent of ore and 5.9 percent of the tin. Old Sump Shaft hoisted 7.65 percent ore and 2.9 percent the tin. Eastern Shaft hoisted 35.3 percent ore and 35.75 percent of the tin. Harrietts Shaft produced 6.25 percent of the ore and 10.2 percent of the tin. Stray Park remained unproductive.[174]

Only 67 fathoms of development was carried out at Dolcoath in 1918 – an all-time low! There were 46 fathoms of lode drive and 21 fathoms of crosscutting. Although this was supplemented by the diamond drilling programme, with such tiny amounts of exploration, the mine's future looked dire indeed.[175]

The accounts for 1918 did not make enjoyable reading for the directors. There was a net profit of £29,259, due almost entirely to the extremely high tin metal price. This profit figure was before the commission of the debenture stock was calculated. Dues for the first half of the year were given as £2,830, which included interest on the debenture stock. No dues were paid in the second half of the year. Tonnage crushed was 61,499 for the production of 827 tons of black tin, which sold for £156,021. Recovery averaged 30.21lbs a ton and the average price received for the mine's tin concentrate was £188 12s 8d, a rise of £53 a ton. Cost per ton averaged £2 4s 10s, a huge jump, and the overall production costs were £134,446. Arsenic continued to provide added income, and during the year some £8,032 worth was sold. With increased labour available, it was hoped that arsenic production could soon be increased.[176]

During the first half of 1919 Joseph F. Odgers was appointed the new Company Secretary, replacing Captain Arthur Thomas, who had been 'Acting Secretary' for several years. Thomas was joined by Major George Bargate, who was to become his Assistant Manager. In the March meeting of shareholders it was resolved to concentrate exploration efforts in the northern part of the mine sett, particularly in the newly acquired North and South Roskear mines. Unfortunately, by the end of the year it was conceded by the management to have been an impossible ambition, and the idea to connect Dolcoath to these mines underground was being reconsidered. However, the management continued to plan ahead, and in September, Frank Harvey announced: "A tramway communication is being made with the eastern part of the Mine so that the whole treatment of ore will be concentrated at the western battery until larger crushings are possible. The completion of this work should enable material economies to be effected." Captain Thomas was able to report on January 22nd 1920: "The Incline Tramway together with the electric haulage equipment connecting the eastern and western parts of the Mine have been completed and is in operation. The eastern stamps and dressing floors have in consequence been stopped, and the crushing of the whole output of tinstuff from the Mine is now confined to the western battery of twelve heads of pneumatic stamps erected some years ago. Great economies will result from this centralisation, and more efficient treatment of the tinstuff is anticipated." It should be stated that the western part of the mine referred to was actually the western side of the Red River Valley, not the extreme western side of the mine, at Wheal Harriet and Stray Park.[177]

Much of the development during the first half of 1919 was in the Middle section of the mine, around New East, New Sump and Subsidiary shafts. Exploration took place there at the 190, 210, 230, 254, 338 and 375 fathom levels. Some also was carried out west of Eastern Shaft at the 400 level. Despite poor results in the past, Stray Park continued to be explored at the 338, 352 and 375 fathom levels. On the 352 level, where the drive west was resumed, ore of 60lbs a ton was found, and the lode was 12 feet wide. The 338 level had values of only 16lbs a ton. Many of these ends were continued in the second half of the year, with mixed results. The 338 level was re-timbered east of New Sump Shaft and the lode drive resumed into ground worth 30lbs a ton. On the 375 level, a lode drive east of the south crosscut from New Sump Shaft, into 'old workings', intersected Main Lode. It was 24 feet wide with 40lbs of tin a ton. There was a south crosscut driven on the 412 level, in Middle section, toward a 'new lode'. In Stray Park, a crosscut at the 295 fathom level had found a narrow tin lode (6-9 inches wide) with stringers in the wall rock. The management was desperately struggling to find new sources of tin, but the results were becoming more meagre by the month.[178]

The government set up the Non-Ferrous Mining Trades Committee, to investigate and report on those metal mines in the country which did not produce iron. Dolcoath's Board of Directors awaited the report of this committee, with the same anxiety felt by all commercial organisations, when faced by possible government interference.[179] Analysis of the hoisting points shows the continuing importance of Williams Shaft. Williams Shaft hoisted 38.8 percent of the ore and 39.65 percent of the tin. New Sump Shaft hoisted 7.45 percent of the ore and 8.8 percent of the tin. Old Sump Shaft hoisted 3.65 percent of the ore and 1.45 percent of the tin. Eastern Shaft produced 38.95 percent of the ore and 37.05 percent of the tin. Wheal Harriet Shaft drew 8.85 percent of the ore and 10.85 percent of the tin. Stray Park hoisted 2.3 percent of the ore and 2.3 percent of the tin.[180]

Development in 1919 showed an improvement over the previous two years, with a total of 200 fathoms driven, raised and sunk. This was three times the total for 1918. There were 145 fathoms of lode drive, 33 fathoms of crosscutting and 22 fathoms of raises and winzes. In 1919 there was a total of 639 workers at Dolcoath, which was 320 less than in 1914.[181]

The 1919 accounts were the mine's worst for over three-quarters-of-a-century. The mine lost £37,573, and this despite the price received for the mine's black tin averaging £140 10s a ton. There were 61,703 tons hoisted and crushed for the production of 733 ton of black tin concentrate. Income from tin sales was £102,059. The average recovery was 26.8lbs of tin a ton – the lowest on record! The cost per ton crushed averaged £2 6s 11d and the total production cost was £139,776. Income from arsenic sales was £2,067. The financial position of the mine had never looked more desperate.[182]

By 1920 it was apparent that the old mine had no future. Despite this, the management did not give up, seemingly unable to accept the evidence plainly before them. In June the management "found (it) imperative to abandon the bottom of the Mine and to continue operations on a modified scale, but owing to increasing difficulties and pending the raising of further capital, the Directors have been compelled to give notice to their employees." The 700 workers were thus warned of the impending closure. On July 27th 1920 Captain Thomas wrote: "Having regard to the large increase in the cost of labour, materials, in particular coal, resulting in greatly increased working costs, it was decided on May 28th last to stop all development operations and to work the mine to the best advantage by tributers and a few stopes only. The expenditure at that time was reduced to a minimum and it was found necessary to discharge 134 of the employees." On the 30th June, Joseph Odgers reported, that 'operations at the mine had ceased'. In July the remaining miners were busy installing dams around the shafts, particularly on the 550 and 510 fathom levels at Williams Shaft. Thomas commented on July 27th: "In consideration of the fact of the very unsatisfactory developments in the bottom of the Mine and of practically the depletion of the reserves there, it was decided to stop the bottom electric pumping sets and to allow the water to rise in the Mine, and as stated above, to endeavour to work the Mine to the best advantage, and chiefly by tribute. The valuable pumping sets, together with the electrical apparatus and cables have been dissembled and brought to surface and safely housed. The bottom levels have been stripped of all available loose plant." In November another 200 men were laid off, leaving only 300-350 workers on the mine. Nevertheless, the managers continued to make plans for the future of the mine, and informed the shareholders, that: "The Managing Director submitted to the Board the plan of development of the Northern areas of the Company's working and of the Mines immediately adjoining it to the North as referred to in the Board's circular to you of the 9th September last, and which briefly stated, is a crosscut from our existing workings to the Roskear Mines intersecting the group of lodes which have been successfully worked at Tincroft, South Crofty, East Pool and later the Rogers Lode which has given such remarkable results in East Pool."[183]

As time went on and the pumps at the bottom of the mine were removed, the water began its inexorable rise up the shafts. The intention to drive a crosscut north from the 338 fathom level at Williams Shaft, to the Roskears, began to look unlikely, and once the water was at that level and nothing in the mine's prospects looked optimistic, this plan was changed. Captain Arthur Thomas submitted his detailed analysis of the situation, together with his plans for the future working of the northern part of the sett and the Roskear mines. He hoped his report would help raise the £120,000 needed for the scheme. Bewick and Moreing carried out their own study of the situation, which was no less detailed and closely argued than Thomas', but the only realistic hope appeared to be based upon the total abandonment of the old mine, the sinking of a new shaft at South Roskear and the development of a totally new mine.[184]

During this period of uncertainty, when men were made redundant or were seeking work elsewhere, many left the mine to join South Crofty, one of the few local mines which appeared to have any future prospects. South Crofty's records show that between July 1920 and January 1921, 20 Dolcoath men went there to work – with 15 joining Crofty between November and January! Interestingly, a third of these men were teenagers.[185]

Unions & the Labour Crisis in Cornish Mines
On March 16th 1920, Mr T. Knowles, Secretary of the Employers' Federation, sent out a circular concerning the labour crisis in Cornish mines. He wrote that, for some time negotiations had taken place between the employers and the union leaders for an increase in wages. In July 1920, the union had demanded a general increase in the wages of all men employed in the mining industry. This demand was for a fifty

CORNISH TIN MINES.

The Labour Crisis in Cornish Tin Mines.

For some time past negotiations have been proceeding between the Employers of the Tin Mines and the Union Leaders for an increase of wages.

A demand was made in July last year for an all-round increase in the wages of the men, of about half as much again as they were then receiving, which would have increased the wages paid by the Mines of the County by a sum of £230,000 a year.

The Employers said the Mines could not afford to pay it ; the men replied they could not live on the present wage. The Employers recognised that the increase in the cost of living had made it almost impossible for the low-paid men to exist, and agreed to make them an increase at considerable sacrifice to development. With regard to the other men it was considered that they have been, and will be, able to earn what any fair-minded man must look upon as good wages, having regard to the position of the Industry.

percent increase in the average wage. The Employers' Federation believed this would cost the mines an extra £250,000 a year. There was stalemate, as the mines said they could not afford it and the men said they could not live on less. However, the owners acknowledged that the men could not live on the present wages and agreed to make a considerable increase in the wage rates. This would force them to cut back on development in the mines.[186]

The discussions took place in an atmosphere of mutual respect, in which both sides understood the difficulty of the other. The main problem was caused by the government's control of the tin price, making it impossible for the owners to charge more for their tin. Both sides agreed to talk to the government commission, set up to report on the condition of Cornish mines. After more talks the government lifted their control from the price of tin and it had soon increased. The miners thought the new price high enough, but the owners did not. Not surprisingly, the owners bemoaned the high price of all materials since the Great War, particularly that of coal – which had almost trebled since 1914![187]

Finally, after much toing and froing and argument, the owners offered the following pay increases.

The figures are average earnings.

GRADE OF MEN.		Present wages.			Federation offer.			Rise per week.
Shaftsmen	...	£2	5	9¼	£2	11	3	5/5¼
Timbermen	...	2	4	0	2	9	6	5/6
Trammers	...	2	1	3	2	7	6	6/3
Day Pay Stopers	...	2	3	0	2	9	0	6/-
Engine Drivers	...	1	19	3	2	5	0	5/9
Pump Drivers (surface)		1	12	6 (6 days)	1	18	7	6/1
Surface Workers }	...	1	17	6	2	5	0	7/6
}	...	2	3	0	2	7	6	4/6

Under these terms no efficient man will receive less than £2:5:0 per week.

The Federation stated that no 'efficient man' will take home less than £2 5s a week, and men's wages would be made up to ensure this. Machinemen were dealt with a little differently, as these skilled miners were essential to the survival of the mines. "In the case of men employed on machines running continuously for seven days, an increase of 2s 6d to be granted over and above the rise they receive under the schedule of increases printed above." A machineman failing to earn at least £12 for a minimum of 23 shifts in a month, would be able to negotiate the shortfall. Stopers taken off contract work would also be compensated.[188]

Working Methods & Miners before the Great War

Long after the old mine had closed, Joseph Odgers, the Company Secretary, contacted several former Dolcoath miners, including Henry Stephens, to ascertain how the various tasks were carried out prior to the Great War. He wrote that most tutwork contractors worked with 12 men and 6 boys, with these being divided into three 'pares' of 4 men and 2 boys on each shift. He believed that most tributers worked with 2 men and a boy. He said that tributers rarely worked by night. They paid out the money at a public house, hotel or restaurant. He said that the pitmen in charge of the engine shafts were Elijah Kent, at Wheal Harriett, Joe Rule, at Stray Park, and George Phillips at New Sump Shaft. Until 1912, Phillips was the senior man on overall charge of the pumping engines. The time keeper, who sat in the dry, was Joe Rickard. He recalled that the dry in the early years of the 20th century had 12 baths and 100 wash basins.[189]

Despite the many difficulties, in the first six months of 1920, there were 74 fathoms of lode drives, 44 fathoms of crosscuts and 8 fathoms of winzes and raises, totalling 126 fathoms of development. Even with the water beginning to threaten the bottom of the mine, Williams Shaft hoisted 41.3 percent of the mine's ore and 43.7 percent of its tin. Eastern Shaft hoisted 39.9 percent of the ore and 38.3 percent of the tin. New Sump Shaft drew 3.6 percent of the ore and 2.9 percent of the tin. Old Sump Shaft produced 5.9 percent of the ore and 1.5 percent of the tin. Harrietts Shaft contributed 6.7 percent of the ore and 10.7 percent of the tin. Stray Park produced 2.6 percent of the ore and 2.9 percent of the tin.[190]

The accounts for the first six months of 1920 showed a loss of £11,276. Total income from black tin sales was £70,752 and from arsenic, £1,918. Tonnage crushed was 30,052, with another 16,362 hoisted and crushed in the second half of the year. Total black tin production for the year was 590 tons. The average price received for the mine's tin during the first six months was £208 19s 9d. The average recovery for the first half of the year was 25.2lbs and for the second half, it was 34.5lbs. The cost per ton crushed averaged £2 17s 2½d a ton. The overall cost for the first six months was £86,006.[191]

During 1920 Frank Harvey, who had been Chairman for almost the entire life of the Company, resigned. It was his 80th birthday, and he undoubtedly believed he had had enough. Arthur Thomas took over as Chairman and Messrs Bewick, Moreing & Co. became the Managers. Frederick William Thomas was offered an 'important position' in Liverpool, and quit as a Director. The two new directors were Montague Rogers and C. A. Moreing, of East Pool & Agar Mine.[192]

The final nail in the mine's coffin came when, in November 1921, the Non-Ferrous Mining Trades Committee, having been hailed as a possible saviour of the mine, failed to deliver a loan to secure its future. The Cornish MPs and the Lord Lieutenant for the county led a deputation to the government, to no avail. In March of that year, the Company had raised £17,500 from its shareholders, to preserve the valuable machinery on the mine. Thus, in 1921, for the first time in 120 years, all activity at Dolcoath Mine ceased.[193]

References Part Three (1895-2010)

1. Dolcoath Mine Manager's Reports (DMMR); MJ (May 11 1895) p.543
2. DMMR
3. DMMR; MJ (Nov.2 1895) Supplement
4. DMMR
5. Ibid.
6. Ibid.
7. Ibid.
8. Ibid.
9. Ibid.
10. DMMR; Harris (1974) p.101
11. DMMR
12. Ibid.
13. Ibid.
14. DMMR; Information from Tony Clarke
15. The Cornish Telegraph (Oct.15 1896)
16. The Cornish Telegraph (Nov.5 1896)
17. The Cornish Telegraph (Nov.12 1896); CT (Dec.3 1896)
18. The Cornish Telegraph (Oct.15 1896)
19. DMMR
20. Ibid.
21. Ibid.
22. Ibid.
23. Ibid.
24. DMMR; Herbert Thomas Mining Interviews (1896) pp.193-204
25. DMMR
26. Ibid.
27. Details from plans held by Baseresult in South Crofty Mine Archive
28. DMMR
29. DMMR; MJ (March 5 1898) p.269
30. DMMR; MJ (Feb.11 1899) p.160; MJ (March 5 1898) p.269
31. Cornish Post & Mining News (May 7 1898)
32. DMMR
33. Albert Bluett The Cornish Magazine vol.1 No.3 (Sept.1898) pp.168-181 (Courtesy of Prof. Charles Thomas); Harris (1974) p.68
34. DMMR
35. DMMR; MJ (March 4 1899) p.244
36. DMMR; DMMR;Harris (1974) p.84; MJ (March 3 1900) p.250
37. DMMR
38. DMMR; MJ (March 3 1900) p.249
39. DMMR
40. DMMR; MJ (Aug.26 1899) p.1020
41. DMMR
42. AD 1140 CRO Truro
43. DMMR; MJ (Aug.25 1900) pp.1037,1038

44. DMMR; MJ (Aug.25 1900) p. 1038
45. DMMR; MJ (March 2 1901) pp.252,253
46. DMMR; MJ (Jan.12 1901) p.42
47. DMMR
48. Ibid.
49. Ibid.
50. Ibid.
51. Ibid.
52. Ibid.
53. Ibid.
54. Ibid.
55. DMMR; J. A. Buckley A History of South Crofty Mine (1980) pp.111,112
56. DMMR
57. Ibid.
58. Ibid.
59. Ibid.
60. Ibid.
61. Ibid.
62. DMMR; Buckley (1980) p.137
63. Ibid.
64. Ibid.
65. Ibid.
66. Ibid.
67. Ibid.
68. DMMR; Benjamin Nicholas (Levant Mine Manager) Letter Book. Private Collection
69. Mine Accounts
70. DMMR
71. Ibid.
72. Ibid.
73. Ibid.
74. DMMR/Accts
75. DMMR
76. Ibid.
77. Ibid.
78. Ibid.
79. Philosophical Transactions of the Royal Society (1830); DMMR; MJ (May 2 1903) p.524; MJ (June 20 1903) p.743; July 11 1903) p.44
80. MJ (May 2 1903) p.524; MJ (June 20 1903) p.743; MJ (July 11 1903) p.44; Buckley (1980) pp.48,50
81. DMMR/Accts
82. DMMR
83. Ibid.
84. DMMR; Information from Tony Clarke
85. DMMR
86. DMMR/Accts
87. DMMR

88. Ibid.
89. Ibid.
90. DMMR; Joseph F. Odgers (former Dolcoath Company Secretary) notes; Information from notes of Prof. Charles Thomas; Harris (1974) p.91
91. DMMR/Accts
92. DMMR
93. Ibid.
94. Ibid.
95. Ibid.
96. DMMR; Harris (1974) p.91
97. DMMR/Accts
98. The Cornish Post & Mining News (Jan.9 1909) p.5
99. Ibid.
100. DMMR
101. Ibid.
102. The Mining World (Feb.27 1909)
103. DMMR
104. Ibid.
105. Ibid.
106. Ibid.
107. DMMR; Joseph Blight 'Mine Drainage' Transactions of the Institute of Engineers (Jan.1916)
108. DMMR/Accts
109. DMMR
110. Ibid.
111. Ibid.
112. Ibid.
113. Ibid.
114. Ibid.
115. DMMR/Accts
116. DMMR
117. Ibid.
118. Ibid.
119. Ibid.
120. DMMR; Harris (1974) p.103; D. B. Barton A History of Tin Mining & Smelting in Cornwall (1967) p.277
121. DMMR
122. Ibid.
123. Ibid.
124. Ibid.
125. Harris (1974) p.92; J. F. Odgers notes loaned by Prof. Charles Thomas
126. DMMR/Accts
127. DMMR; The Cornish Post & Mining News (Dec.7 1911); The Cornishman (Dec.7 1911)
128. DMMR
129. Noall (1989) p.184
130. DMMR

131. Ibid.
132. DMMR/Accts
133. DMMR
134. Ibid.
135. Ibid.
136. Ibid.
137. DMMR/Accts
138. DMMR
139. DMMR; Dr Malcolm Maclaren Report on Dolcoath Mine, Camborne (August 29 1914)
140. DMMR
141. Ibid.
142. Ibid.
143. Ibid.
144. Ibid.
145. Ibid.
146. Ibid.
147. Ibid.
148. Ibid.
149. Ibid.
150. Ibid.
151. DMMR/Accts
152. DMMR
153. Ibid.
154. Ibid.
155. Ibid.
156. Ibid.
157. Ibid.
158. DMMR/Accts; J. F. Odgers notes loaned by Prof. Charles Thomas
159. DMMR; Buckley (1980) pp.140,141
160. DMMR
161. Ibid.
162. Ibid.
163. Ibid.
164. Ibid.
165. DMMR/Accts
166. DMMR
167. DMMR; Documents concerning the creation of Tehidy Minerals Ltd (1919) Buckley (1980) pp.159-161,202,203
168. J. A. Buckley South Crofty Mine: A History (1997) p.178
169. DMMR
170. Ibid.
171. Ibid.
172. Ibid.
173. Ibid.
174. Ibid.
175. Ibid.

176. DMMR/Accts
177. DMMR
178. Ibid.
179. Dolcoath Mine Ltd. Evidence Submitted to the Non-Ferrous Mines Commission (Nov. 1919 & Oct.1920)
180. DMMR
181. Ibid.
182. DMMR/Accts
183. DMMR; J. F. Odgers notes loaned by Prof. Charles Thomas
184. DMMR; Odgers notes; Bewick & Moreing Report on Dolcoath & Roskear Exploratory Crosscuts (Oct.19 1920)
185. DMMR; South Crofty Mine Employment Records (1914-24). Private Collection
186. DMMR; T. Knowles (Secretary Employers Federation) The Labour Crisis in Cornish Tin Mines (March 16 1920)
187. Ibid.
188. Ibid.
189. Odgers notes
190. DMMR
191. DMMR/Accts
192. DMMR
193. DMMR; Non-Ferrous Mining Trades Committee Report (Nov.1921); Odgers notes

Part Four
New Dolcoath (1921-1930)

With the old mine clearly finished, and the whole of the Cornish mining industry at a near stand-still, the directors of Dolcoath showed remarkable optimism. Led by Oliver Wethered and Arthur Thomas, they continued to pursue the other shareholders and the government for financial support. All mining and ore-dressing had ceased in April 1921, and the £17,500 raised by the Company was being used for essential maintenance and the preservation of the valuable machinery on the mine. On June 30th 1921, 131,983 priority shares in the Company were offered, applied for and allotted. On January 16th 1922, the government created the Trade Facilities Advisory Committee, and Dolcoath quickly applied to it for £200,000 to pay for a new shaft at South Roskear. That Committee replied to the application by saying, they could apply "as part of a scheme put up by the Cornish Mining Industry." On April 14th 1922, Dolcoath revised their application down to £120,000, and broke the needed money down into three parts: (a) to sink a new shaft, (b) to equip the shaft, (c) to develop the mineralised lodes the Company anticipated they would find there. Subsequently, the directors shifted again, proposing to raise £87,500 through the issue of 5 shilling shares, and ask the Trade Facilities Advisory Committee for only £50,000. This request was changed again in March 1923, when the Company asked for £65,000 – clearly, there was much negotiation going on, most of it, undoubtedly, behind the scenes. With the £55,000 raised by the Company, the needed £120,000 was found and the project looked set fair.[1]

On May 9th 1923, the new company was incorporated and registered with the number 189861. Oliver Wethered was the Chairman, F. A. Robinson was the Vice-Chairman, Arthur Thomas was the Managing Director, Joseph Frederick Odgers was the Company Secretary, Daniell & Thomas were the Company solicitors and W. B. Peat & Co. were the auditors. E. W. Janson and James Miners Holman were Directors. Janson had worked as a miner at Dolcoath in the early 1890s and was a graduate of the School of Metalliferous Mining in Camborne. Holman was the head of Holman Brothers, of Camborne. He put his son, Leonard, forward as his 'alternate director' in the event of his being unavailable. The Company office was to be the old account house at the top of Dolcoath Road, Camborne. Mr F. Merricks was appointed by the Trade Facilities Committee to represent them, and to inspect the Company, its property and its prospects.[2]

Also in May, the Company approached Nobel Industries, which owned the old Bennetts Fuze Factory at the location of the proposed new shaft, to obtain the site. £1,500 was offered, but in June the land was sold to the Company for £1,350 and 500 shares in the venture. In July the bungalow at South Roskear and the adjacent yard were included in the sale.[3]

The Welsh mining company of G. Piggott agreed to sink the new shaft, and after some discussion about its shape – the Cornish tended to favour the traditional close-timbered, rectangular shaft – it was decided to go with the same design as Williams Shaft, circular and brick-lined. The shaft was to be 17 feet 6 inches in diameter and 1,800 feet deep. In the event it was sunk to a sump below the 2,000 feet level. Piggott estimated that the cost would be £30,000 for the sinking, £5,000 for coal, £9,000 for removal of plant, etc, and about £5,000 for sundry tasks and equipment. Piggott reckoned it would take 18 months to sink the shaft to the 1,800 feet level. Captain Thomas subsequently said that the intended depth was originally 1,860 feet. Mr Merricks, representing the Treasury, needed to approve the final figure of £49,000 before the Company could issue the contract to Piggott.[4]

The Workforce
Although Piggotts were a South Wales company, most of the actual work was carried out by local men. Some of these were Cornishmen who had gone to Wales in search of work during the difficult times, which followed the end of the Great War. Typical of these was Bill Jervis. He had joined the Duke of Cornwall's Light Infantry, where he became a sergeant. On the Somme, in 1916, he won the Military Medal for rescuing his wounded company commander. With little work in Camborne after the war, he went to Wales and found a job with Piggotts. He must have been delighted when the company obtained the contract to sink Dolcoath's new shaft. He has related, how he and his wife lived beside the shaft on North Roskear Road, Tuckingmill, and when the shaft-sinkers were about to blast, they would warn the women to take their washing in, out of the smoke and dust. Bill's son, Jack Jervis, remembered his father telling him that the miners put a chain net over the shaft, to inhibit the rocks from flying too far when they blasted close to the surface. Some of the men who worked in and around the shaft were less fortunate than Bill Jervis. The late Bert Retallack, of Carnarthen Street, Camborne, told of how the foremen would take men on and discharge them without notice, merely on a whim. They might work for a week or two, then when they turned up for work, they might be told they were discharged that lunch-time. Times were hard, and local miners often went from mine to mine in

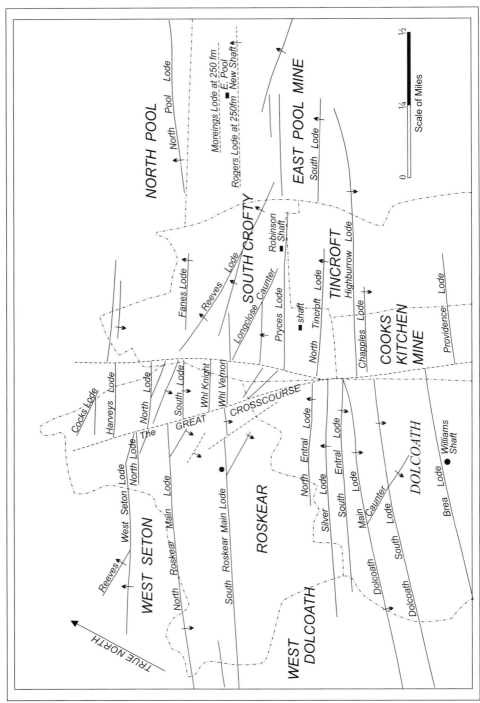

Figure 116. Lodes and sett boundaries, early 20th century.

392

search of work and glad to take anything that was offered.[5]

On July 10th 1923, the Company received the certificate authorising them to commence business. At the Directors meeting, three days later, the question of the pumps for the new mine was discussed. A Cornish beam engine was mooted, but eventually, after considering the relative costs – the beam engine would cost about £20,000, whereas the Williams Shaft electric pumps would only need minor alterations to use effectively – it was decided to go with the more modern option. Removing, modifying and installing the electric pumps would cost about £6,000, a saving of some £14,000. It was also agreed that Piggotts could complete the surface plant, at cost plus 10 percent. Negotiations began with Cornwall Power Company for a temporary electricity supply 'on special terms', and with Camborne Water Company. The Committee also decided to employ a mechanical engineer, but in the meantime they employed a qualified local man to prepare the layout plans for the site.[6]

In the autumn the Managing Director negotiated with Mr Pendarves, of the Pendarves Estate, the mineral owners, over a new lease and the rate at which dues were to be paid. At the same time the Committee agreed that an offer should be made to Mr Rowling for his fields, which were adjacent to the site of the shaft. Although the Company was willing to go up to £350, in November they managed to obtain them for £276.[7]

The Foreman's Log
The daily journal of Mr Jopling, Dolcoath's foreman in charge of the work for the first few months of operation, makes fascinating reading. It begins with the entry for August 8th 1923: "The Cochrane Boiler & Temporary winding engine arrived today with exception of the Chimney stack & Smoke box of the boiler and the Drum of the engine. Putting in the loading for the winding engine." On the 9th he wrote: "The Secretary Complained about an accident happening at the Sinking & which was not reported. To prevent such from happening again I have told Joe Pearce the Timekeeper to report to me any accidents that may happen causing personal injury." On August 10th the men finished taking out the rails and keeps from Williams Shaft, and started to move New Sump Shaft's headgear to Roskear New Shaft. On the 16th the drum, smoke box and 'Donkey Pump' arrived at Roskear from Treveddoe Mine, and work went ahead to install a temporary winding engine. A Mr Sayers, who appears to have been a clerk at the Dolcoath office, was mentioned. During the next two days Messrs Wethered, Janson and Robinson, Directors, visited the site to see the progress. On August 25th the Cochrane boiler was fired up and the mortar mill, for supplying the brick-layers in the shaft, was inspected. The 'Vulcon' boiler was examined on the Monday. These types of detail, typical of a new project getting started, filled the diary for the next few months, with occasional problems, like the

wet weather which stopped the masons laying bricks in the shaft, or machinery or engine failure, which held everything up, being the normal entry material.[8]

On September 11th the foreman received the layout plan for the boilers, winding engine and compressor (from Williams Shaft). At last he could start to organise the site efficiently. Old masonry needed removing and new loadings and foundations needed putting in. The legs and backstays for the temporary headgear had to be fixed before real progress could be made in the shaft. On November 7th there was a setback, when the engine failed to lift the first full bucket of dirt from the shaft. The men removed half the dirt, but it still could not lift it. The engine was overhauled, the valves examined and everything appeared to be alright. The following day they "Sent to Tresavean for two lesser buckets & commence to Sink at 9.30 am." Sinking then proceeded until the miners reached the point at which Piggotts were to take over.[9]

The Shaft Sinking Begins
Thus, the shaft sinking began on November 8th 1923 and continued on three shifts until the 12th, when the diary entry states: "Sinking proceeding favourably. I measured the distance from the pit top to the first ring at the surface as being 15 feet 9 inches. The distance where Mr Piggott commenced to sink by contract was 15 feet 9 inches from the top ring to the bottom ring, therefore all above 31 feet 6 inches from the pit top is to be paid." Piggott's men started sinking in rock on the 13th November, and immediately hit problems, with the appearance of very hard greenstone on one side of the shaft. The following day the whole shaft bottom was in greenstone, and the miners were struggling. Due to the extreme hardness of the greenstone, Piggottt obtained an increase in the rate paid from £50 to £56 a yard, but only when in greenstone. On the 15th there was a 20 minute delay, when the men were taken out of the shaft due to the steam in the boiler failing. More draught was given by raising the height of the stack and the problem was solved. During these first few days, carpenters and smiths were kept busy erecting stages for the brick layers to work from, and the shaft proceeded with sinking stopping for the bricking and only resuming when the stages were removed and the mortar had gone off. Although a greater thickness of brickwork around the shaft was required in places – up to 27 inches – the brickwork was averaging about 20 inches. On November 23rd it was agreed with one W. Jones (foreman bricklayer), that the brickwork should normally be 18 inches thick. Sinking and bricking then continued with few interruptions until the entry for December 17th, when the diarist wrote: "I gave my resignation in to Capt. Arthur Thomas as assistant to him." The rest of the statement has been blacked out, by a later hand. Perhaps this explained his reasons. The rock was variously described as 'greenstone' or 'basalte', and as being very hard to drill, but which was 'good for blasting'.[10]

The Drilling Machines Used

The machines used for sinking the new shaft were made by Holman Brothers of Camborne. They were light-weight sinkers, equipped with a bar through the handle so that the miners could stand on them to add weight to the machines. These machines weighed 50lbs each, and were very efficient. For driving the levels, the miners used heavier Holman bar-and-arm machines, which were also called 'cradle machines', because the machines rested on a cradle fixed onto a stretcher bar, between the floor and roof. When stoping got underway, attempts were made to use these cradle machine in the stopes, without success, and soon light-weight 'Holman Hammer-Jack drills' were used there. They were more efficient and more economical in their use of compressed air than the heavier machines.[11]

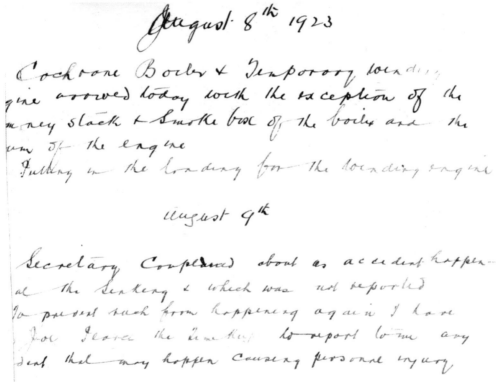

Figure 117. Opening page from the diary of Mr Jopling.

On November 15th 1923, the shareholders were informed that a Mr Harry Laity was to be taken on in a supervisory capacity, with a salary of £260 a year and that Captain Arthur Thomas had spent £1,385 on parts for the winding engine.[12]

On January 3rd 1924, the shaft was 150 feet 4 inches from its collar. The rate paid

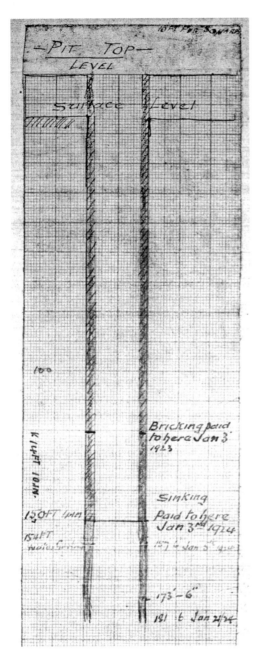

Figure 118. Cross-section of the top of the New Dolcoath (South Roskear) Shaft as recorded by Mr Jopling.

for sinking was reduced from £56 to £50 a yard. On the previous day, a 'slow registering thermometer' was inserted in a 4 foot 6 inch hole drilled into the side of the shaft at a depth of 134 feet. The hole was tamped and after a period of 18 hours the temperature was found to be 52.5°F. The temperature might have been reduced due to the amount of water coming from the hole, despite the tamping.[13]

References were made at this time to putting in 'water garlands 3 ft from the bricking curb'. These garlands were cast iron gutters, which were put in all around the shaft to catch the water. Iron down-pipes were fitted between these garland rings, to carry the water to the pumps at the bottom of the shaft. The garland rings were about 15 feet apart near the surface, but thereafter the distances between varied as the shaft went deeper, sometimes being as wide as 100 feet apart. The garlands were about 9 or 10 inches wide. The brickwork in each section of the shaft was not put in vertically, but sloped slightly inwards. This shamfer gave a drip edge above each garland, allowing the water to be caught by it. The next section of brickwork then began a few inches or so back from the edge. During the 1990s, these garlands and down-pipes were repaired by South Crofty's maintenance men, in preparation for using the shaft as an emergency egress.[14]

Shaft Connected to Dolcoath Deep Adit

On January 12th 1924, the shaft holed the Dolcoath Deep Adit, and just over a month later Mr William James was given the contract to maintain the adits at Roskear and to dismantle and move machinery from Dolcoath to Roskear. He was to be paid £15 a month and provided with a house on Dolcoath Avenue, with rent worth £19 a year.[15]

Meanwhile, the winding engine house was completed and the surface arrangements took on a more permanent appearance. On January 15th one of Piggott's employees, S. Beckett, was sent to Llanbradach, Wales, on behalf of the contractors.[16]

The entry dated January 14th 1924, is the last one by the original diarist, and his final comments reinforce the impression that he and the Company were somewhat at loggerheads. Jopling stated that, he "did not consider you are due these notes, as they are my own and I did not think of them as in any way the property of the Company … However as they are of no further use to me you may have them." After this another person takes up the story, although there is some overlap in their accounts, as the new writer starts his account on November 8th 1923.[17]

On April 17th, the shaft was down 235 feet, having gone through 32 feet of 'hornsfelt with greenstone', between 200 and 232 feet from surface. At 235 feet a caunter lode containing wolfram had been cut by the shaft. In the middle of July the shaft was 433 feet from surface, having gone though a variety of rock types, including 'altered killas', 'slate hornsfelt' and 'greenstone'. Also in July, the Company contracted with the Cornwall County Highways to take the mined stone for the roads, and the slime plant at Dolcoath was let to 'Curnow & Richard Uren'. In August, with the shaft at 478 feet deep, and the rock still mostly greenstone, Piggott negotiated an extra £4 a yard, whilst in this hard rock. A few more feet and the sinkers were probably not delighted to find themselves in an elvan dyke.[18]

On July 25th 1924, The Managing Director described the plant, which was then on the mine at South Roskear. There was 'a pair of 24-inch and 54-inch winding engines, fitted with fast and loose drum with automatic speed control and over-winding appliance'. This had been brought from Dolcoath. It cost £1,500 to move and modify and could wind a full load up 2,000 feet per minute. A Holman compound steam Corliss Valve two stage horizontal air compressor was also brought from Williams Shaft. It had 1,500 feet capacity and an independent condensing plant. The headgear was an 80 feet high steel lattice construction and this also came from Williams Shaft. There were 'four 30ft x 8ft Lancashire boilers of 120lbs per square inch working pressure, with Green's Economiser 192 tubes and induced draft fan'. These came with the necessary steam pumps and water tanks. Thomas added: "It having been decided to utilise the electrically driven pumping plant, removed from the Williams Shaft, the erection of the necessary sub-station, switch-gear, etc., is nearing completion and the supply of electrical energy is to be obtained from the Cornwall Electric Power Co. at a pressure of 3,000 volts."[19]

During September 1924, Captain Thomas was away in Canada, and the Company asked Captain Josiah Paull, Manager of South Crofty Mine, to be available when or if needed. The Camborne mining scene being a close and friendly community, Paull readily agreed. The increasing water in the shaft caused Piggott to recommend that a pump be obtained from John Evans & Co. In October, the Governor of Camborne School of Mines approached the Company about taking over the old Dolcoath offices. Presumably, with such a reduced operation, the new company was not using all the buildings there. A figure of £3,000 was suggested. Captain Thomas, the Principal of the School, was to negotiate on behalf of the Company. Nothing came of the idea. In November, James Miners Holman, of Holman Brothers, resigned as a Director, after a long association with Dolcoath. In December, Mr Merricks, representing the Treasury, enquired about the large number of men employed on the project, and Captain Thomas explained that the number was not excessive, as there was a great variety of tasks which needed doing. By this time the hardness of the rock was beginning to affect the kit for sharpening the drill steels, and Mr Robinson had had conversations with Mr W. J. Anderson, of Anglo-French Exploration Co. Ltd., with regard to using the O'Donovan drill process for sharpening the steels. Thomas agreed to look into it, and in January 1925, Mr Foster, of O'Donovan's, recommended that 'two of their furnaces for the purpose' should be purchased at a cost of £550.[20]

January 1925 found the shaft sinkers at the 800 feet level, and in March, at the 900 feet horizon, they encountered mineralised ground in the south side of the shaft containing quartz, copper and zinc. This structure had disappeared within about 36 feet.[21]

On March 26th the Committee accepted a recommendation from their consultant electrical engineer, Mr W. A. Scott, to purchase a ram pump for £795, with the possibility of a second pump when needed. In April the shaft was 1,038 feet deep and the ground was described as 'mineralised killas'. It was here that a pump chamber was mined out for the new ram pump. A crosscut was driven over 70 feet south from the shaft, with a small station. The pump room was located on the north side and measured 47 feet long (E-W), 16 feet wide and 13½ feet high. The pump room sump was sunk 14 feet 9 inches and measured 10 feet by 9 feet. Captain Thomas commented (in October 1925), that the three-throw electric pumps for this pump room were 'of sturdy design', and would be driven by one of the 130hp motors from Dolcoath. He said the pump room was big enough for two pumps. He also said that the ram pumps from Williams Shaft were to be installed at the bottom of the shaft. Each could pump 300 gallons a minute up 1,000 feet. He still anticipated the final depth of the shaft as 1,860 feet.[22]

In April, the Company received an offer from Mr James Rodda, to work the 'leavings on Dolcoath side of Cooks Kitchen' for three years. He was willing to pay £90 for the privilege.[23]

A New Chairman
On May 21st 1925, the Directors announced the death of Mr Oliver Wethered, the Company Chairman. He had been involved as a Director throughout the life of the old company and had been Chairman of the new company since its creation. Mr F. A. Robinson was elected Chairman in his place. In July the new Chairman announced that a series of lodes had been intersected in the shaft at a depth of about 1,200 feet. The first of these was some three feet wide and contained tin, copper and arsenic. By late October the shaft was down 1,500 feet and by the end of the year it had reached the 1,700 feet level – which was actually 1,693 feet from the surface. Crosscuts were driven north and south from the shaft, and in the south crosscut, a six feet wide lode worth 10lbs to the ton was intersected. Work went on apace during 1926, and on April 29th the 2000 feet level was reached. A 20 feet deep sump was sunk below the 2000 level. By June the 2000 level station was complete and the permanent pump room was being mined out. It measured 26 feet long by 16 feet wide and was 13 feet high. The pump room sump was 15 feet deep and was 8 feet square. The two electric pumps from the bottom of Williams Shaft were to be installed there. It had been mooted that an invitation be sent to Prince Edward, Duke of Cornwall, to officially name the shaft, but it seems, nothing came of it.[24]

The Search for Tin Lodes
The priority from that point on was to develop the levels and open up payable tin lodes. On the 1700 level work progressed to prove the mineralised ground already found and discover more. On the 1900 level, crosscuts were driven north and south to intersect lode structures. As soon as it was reached, the 2000 level was opened up by crosscuts driven north and south of the shaft. All of this work was to be expensive, and with their cash almost gone, the Company again asked the Trade Facilities Committee for help. In September 1926, that Committee approved a scheme for raising £50,000 through debenture stock of £1, with interest at 8 percent payable six monthly. In July, the Board had discussed the need for an assistant to the Managing Director, and in September a cable was sent to Mr A. J. Edwards, who was working in Cyprus, offering him the job of Mine Foreman, responsible for underground operations, at a salary of £400 a year. Captain Edwards became, in effect, the mine captain. At the same time, Mr A. Evans was taken on with a salary of £350. Also in July and September, Mr Frecheville, of Anglo French Exploration, inspected the mine and reported to the Board.[25]

In July 1926, there was some excitement when a wide lode was intersected in the south crosscut on the 2000 foot level. The lode was 14 feet wide and averaged 33lbs of tin to the ton, which was very payable.

In October, the *Mining Magazine* reported that much of the dressing plant of the old mine had been overhauled in preparation for crushing and dressing the anticipated ore from Roskear. A few heads of pneumatic stamps were also put in order and by December the mill was 'run in' on development ore. With wolfram and other potentially valuable materials in the lodes, advice was sought about introducing more sophisticated plant to deal with it. It is likely that the use of magnetic separators to extract the wolfram was discussed, but it was nearly two years before a couple were purchased (I am grateful for this information from Tony Clarke).[26]

Despite the shaft having been completed and a fair amount of exploratory development having taken place, with sound results, the whole enterprise was beginning to look shaky. On January 13th 1927, it was stated that the funds available to the mine were down to £6,247, and development of the crosscuts and lode drives on the 2000 level were suspended, to concentrate on the 1900 level. The lodes cut in the north and south crosscuts on the 2000 level were to be opened up on the 1900 level. In March, a 4 feet wide lode was cut in the south crosscut on the 2000 foot level, which contained 40lbs of tin a ton. Captain Thomas agreed to a request from the Board, to assay the ore monthly, presumably to keep a stricter eye on the ore values. In May, with the monthly costs at £4,802, there were 12 tons of black tin sold, for £2,040. Meanwhile, Captain Thomas suggested that the 1700 level crosscut be suspended, the 1900 level south crosscut be pushed on, the lode drive east be pursued and the west drive suspended. He also wanted the north crosscut on the 2000 level driven another 320 feet.[27]

James Wickett & his Dowsing Rod
The June 17th 1927 Board Meeting was attended by Mr James Wickett of Redruth, who was to become not only a major shareholder in the firm, but an interesting and at times, entertaining member of the Board. Wickett was the owner of Tabbs Hotel, Redruth, and was a wealthy man with a great interest in Cornish mining. He attended the meeting to explain his firm belief in the value of locating mineralised ore bodies through the use of the dowsing rod. This was not a new idea; it was an anciently practised art, much believed in by generations of mining men, both sceptical and gullible. Captain William 'Billy' James, of the old Company, had also been an enthusiastic believer in the use of dowsing rods to locate mineral lodes. Captain Josiah Thomas himself used to talk enthusiastically about an old tributer called John Rule, who 'successfully' practised dowsing to locate lodes.[28]

Mr Wickett was to return to the subject on numerous occasions thereafter, and he managed to convince many of the value of the method. His predictions, based upon his use of the dowsing rod, were sufficiently convincing for one of the lodes to be known as 'Wickett's Lode'. It is ironic, as Tony Clarke has pointed out, that had the mine persisted for a short time longer, the rich lodes worked by South Crofty, 60

Figure 119. The Dolcoath directors at the time of the sinking of Williams Shaft.
Back: Allen Stoneham, Captain Josiah Thomas (Managing Director), Frank Harvey
Front: G. H. M. Batten, Michael Henry Williams (Chairman, with shovel),
Oliver Wethered (Deputy Chairman), William Rabling

Figure 120. Dolcoath miners gathered for the sinking of Williams Shaft.

Figure 121. Temporary sinking headgear at New Dolcoath (South Roskear) Shaft, 1923.

Figure 122. Temporay sinking headgear in working order, 1924.

Figure 123. Construction work at New Dolcoath (South Roskear).

Figure 124. Sinking bucket at the temporary headgear, note wagon for tramming dirt away.

Figure 125. Starting to sink New Dolcoath Shaft, August 1923.

Figure 126. Men digging in the shaft, September 1923.

Figure 127. Shuttering near the top of New Dolcoath Shaft for the first course of bricks.

Figure 128. Sinking bucket at the then bottom of the shaft.

Figure 129. Williams Shaft headgear re-erected at New Dolcoath Shaft.

Figure 130. Williams Shaft headgear re-erected at New Dolcoath Shaft.

Figure 131. Siding for New Dolcoath off the Roskear branch line, late 1920s.

Figure 132. General view of the New Roskear complex looking north-east across Camborne cricket pitch.

Figure 133 . Aerial view of the New Dolcoath complex, train on the Roskear
branch line in the foreground.

years later, and predicted by Wickett, would have been intersected within 100 feet.[29]

A New Six Point Plan

On July 22nd Captain Thomas laid before the Board his plan for the future working of New Dolcoath. There were six main points, which Thomas believed should be concentrated on.

(1) Continue to drive the 2000 foot level north crosscut with one shift a day.

(2) Develop the 15 feet wide complex ore body intersected 250 feet north of the shaft on the 2000 foot level. This should be developed east and west of the crosscut.

(3) Continue developing 'Wickett's Lode' on the 2000 foot level.

(4) Drive crosscut north of the shaft on 1900 foot level.

(5) Continue the 1900 foot level crosscut south of the shaft with one shift a day.

(6) When raise between 2000 and 1900 foot crosscuts, south of the shaft, is holed, stope the ground opened up there – provided ore is payable.

With this scheme in mind, the Board renewed its request to the Treasury for more cash, but despite the encouraging results underground, they did not appear confident about the outcome. In the autumn, it was decided to suspend some of the development work south of the shaft and concentrate on the north drives.

In September, it was announced that the 15 foot wide lode, intersected in the north crosscut on the 2000 foot level, and called 'Complex Lode', contained an average of 49lbs a ton of tin, 30lbs of wolfram and 5 percent of arsenic. However, even with the discovery of rich tin lodes on all three levels, the management continued to fret that they were fast running out of money. By the end of the year, the Manager believed that some 35,000 tons of payable ore had been identified, and stoping was well underway in the blocked out ground. This provided the dressing floors with sufficient ore for continuous working. The optimism these results produced was enhanced when the Treasury finally responded to the good results, and increased its loan by £15,000 to a total of £85,000.[30]

Captain Arthur Thomas Quits: A New Managing Director Appointed

1928 began with the knowledge that the Managing Director, Captain Arthur Thomas, was to quit. His involvement in so many private and public duties, together with his poor health, convinced him it was time to quit this most difficult job. Captain Thomas had been employed as Manager and Managing Director at Old and New Dolcoath for some 27 years. He was given a £300 a year pension by the grateful Committee. There were 22 applications for the job, which eventually was given, in May, to Captain Joseph Chatten Vivian. He was to be paid £800 a year. He was the son of a Camborne mining family of even older lineage than that of Captain Thomas.

The Vivians had been involved in mining in Camborne since the 16th century, and during the 18th century they had been among the principal mining men of west Cornwall. Captain Andrew Vivian had been the first manager, between 1799 and 1806, of the old Dolcoath Company, which had lasted until the limited liability company was formed in 1895.[31]

Meanwhile, in January 1928, Captain A. J. Edwards had his remit extended to cover the surface as well as the underground operation, Mr Norman Rodda was appointed chief tin dresser and Mr James Wickett was appointed to the Board of Directors. Despite the desperate financial situation, work continued to find payable ore, and in February a diamond drill was employed on the 2000 foot level, and it intersected a 12 feet wide lode with tin values of 60lbs a ton. On the 1900 foot level a new lode was found, south of the shaft, and Captain Edwards appeared sanguine about its prospects.[32]

In February, Captain Edwards told Captain Thomas, that the mine had been reported by HM Mines Inspector over what he called the 'poor signalling arrangements'. The Inspector said that the winding 'engine driver can signal underground by tokens only'. He clearly thought this system did not meet the necessary standards of safety, especially when hoisting men. In April 1928 it was reported that the shaft had been divided and a fan was being installed to improve ventilation on the bottom levels of the mine.[33]

The successful introduction of the diamond drill was not the only reason for optimism among the miners at Roskear, for in March the dressing plant was improved and expanded to cope with larger tonnages of ore. In his March 27th 1928 report to Captain Arthur Thomas, Captain Edwards told of the new plant being introduced at Dolcoath. Edwards wrote: "I was not at all satisfied with the various designs for the proposed stone breaking plant at Roskear, as such designs would not fulfil the ultimate requirements if the Mine were to develop so as to provide for say 300 tons upwards per day. … I decided to … put up a temporary plant at Dolcoath North of the existing Mill and assemble therefore the various parts dismantled at the Williams Shaft, and putting in temporary bins at Roskear." Edwards then told Thomas of his negotiations to buy two magnetic separators from the liquidator of Hemerdon Wolfram Mine, near Plymouth. He offered £450, which was turned down, but after taking advice from Mr Belcham, an engineer employed by East Pool, he increased the offer to £550. In the same report, Edwards listed the rest of the plant as four 'Record Vanners', which gave a total of 26 vanners working in the mill, with another ten soon to be purchased. Four pulverisers were erected and another two prepared for, and a new 25hp motor, capable of running the entire plant, was also up and running.[34]

On mining, Edwards expressed concern about the use of underhand stoping where the hanging wall looked 'treacherous'. Stoping north of the shaft on the 2000 level was by this method and the mine captain was not happy about it. They had been taking 50 tons of ore a day from the stope, but Edwards planned to change to back stoping for safety and because he reckoned they could increase output from the stope to 80 tons a day. He also reported that the winze under the 2000 level was down about 100 feet. In April he reported that the stope on the south side of the shaft over the 2000 level was producing 50 tons a day.[35]

Another pointer to expansion was the increased number of employees at the mine. In February 1928 there had been 75 workers, plus the management, but by April 26th, this number had jumped to 153 men and boys. Underground, the number had increased from 43 to 96, with machinemen, stopers and their mates going up from 23 to 47 and trammers increasing from 9 to 26. Edwards gave some of the pay rates for the various types of work at the time. Contractors working back stopes were paid 4s for a ton of ore. Machinemen driving the east lode drive were paid £9 a fathom and those putting up a raise were paid £12 a fathom. Trammers were paid 1s a ton of ore taken to the shaft.[36]

By the end of January 1928 some 51,000 tons of ore had been sent to the mill, and by May they were crushing and dressing 100 tons a day, and hoped soon to double that amount. The May report of the Directors was enthusiastic about the several lodes being opened up and the encouraging tin, arsenic and wolfram grades being found. It was thought that the mine was steadily progressing towards the anticipated 300 tons a day.[37]

In June, Captain Thomas officially handed over the reins to Captain Vivian, and together with Captain Edwards, he formulated a new plan for the future development of the mine.

(1) On the 1900 foot level they were to continue the drive west on the New Lode, south of the shaft.

(2) On the 2000 foot level they were to continue to drive east of the Complex Lode, north of the shaft.

(3) They were to continue to drive the south crosscut on the 2000 foot level.[38]

Fatal Accidents

In 1928 there was tragic accident in a stope above the 2000 foot level. Several men were working in the stope, using compressed air rock drills. The shiftboss, W. H. Hurrell, had visited the stope, inspected the ground and pronounced it safe. Two machinemen were working in the stope with two mates. Herbert Potter, of Harris Mill, Illogan, was working with a youngster called Frank Whitford, who lived in Park

Road, Camborne. Another machineman, Ernest Arthur, of Wheal Buller, Redruth, was also working there, with his mate, Garfield Lee of Camborne. Potter was the 'taker' or contractor. Two other men were also working in the stope: Francis Charles Mitchell, a 50 year old married man from Redruth and Frederick John Morcombe, a 47 year old single man from Vyvyan Street, Camborne.[39]

Herbert Potter, the 'taker', heard a loud crash, and realising the danger, grabbed his young mate and dragged him to safety, saving his life. Mitchell and Morcombe were not so fortunate, and the hanging wall, which collapsed into the stope, buried them, killing them instantly. Whitford, although pulled clear by Potter, was slightly injured and Arthur's mate, Lee, was also injured.[40]

Immediately, the alarm was raised and Captain Edwards hurried from the surface to supervise the rescue of the buried men. A large group of miners worked feverishly to dig their mates out from beneath the debris, but the task was too great, and eventually, despite the obvious dangers and difficulties, it was decided to blast some of the fallen rock, as it was far too large to break or remove by hand. With Dr MacFee standing by to render what assistance he could, the two miners were dug out. It was well into the afternoon before the second body was recovered. MacFee pronounced them both dead, and it was apparent that they had both been killed instantly.[41]

With the deaths of these two miners, the total killed during the work at Roskear Shaft came to four. Early on in the shaft sinking, one of Piggott's shaft sinkers had been killed, and some 18 months before this last tragic accident, a trammer called Boswell had been killed on one of the levels.[42]

The End Game
By October 1928, it was clear that the mine had very little prospect of a long or even medium-term future. Underground operations were almost at a standstill, although the treatment of ore at surface continued. It was determined to carry on as long as there were supplies sufficient to work the plant and cash sufficient to pay the workers. With cash almost gone, Captain Vivian consulted Captain Thomas as to what was best to do, for despite all the evidence to the contrary, the Board still believed they could raise enough cash to continue. At the end of November, Vivian announced to the Board that he was willing to continue on a 'month to month' basis, Captain A. J. Edwards was given three month's notice and the miners were given one week's notice.[43]

During the six years the project had operated, something like £250,000 had been spent on machinery, restoring plant, shaft sinking, development work and stoping. A total of £30,361 worth of black tin had been mined, hoisted, transported to Dolcoath dressing floors, crushed and dressed. Together with the 170 tons of black tin sold, there were about 20 tons of wolfram and 370 tons of arsenic. A large number of local men had been employed: miners, tradesmen, engineers and managers, and a considerable amount of money pumped into the local economy. The Welsh contractors, Piggotts, had also benefited from the job. It appears that only the shareholders and the Treasury – and the tax payers – were losers.[44]

On January 10th 1929, all work on the Dolcoath dressing floors was suspended. There was some talk of keeping the pumps going for a while, but this would cost about £200 a month, and although they could not afford it, the pumps continued working until the summer. On the 27th January Captain Joseph Vivian resigned. In July, Dutch mining engineers from the Billiton company visited the mine and inspected the workings and machinery, but although hopes were raised, nothing came of it. Despite further attempts to raise money, all efforts were in vain, and with all the staff gone and all the plant silent, the mine closed. All that remained of this brave effort to restore Cornish mining to its former glory were 3 or 4 caretakers, who looked after the plant and kept the adits clear.[45]

With the final closure of all operations, in March 1930, the Official Receivers were called in. Some recompense had to be made to HM Treasury, which was still owed a considerable amount of money. In order to reduce this debt burden, the Treasury was offered the Company's considerable share in Tehidy Minerals Ltd., together with the freeholds of the houses the mine owned in Dolcoath Avenue. This would, theoretically, reduce the debt owed the Treasury to £50,000. Even at this point, the Board still hoped to raise sufficient capital to resume working. The Chairman, Mr F. A. Robinson, lamented, that for the first time in the long history of Dolcoath Mine, the 'shareholders failed to support the Board'. With the October 1929 Wall Street Crash still reverberating in the ears of the world's financiers, it is hardly surprising that no more cash was forthcoming to this unproven enterprise.[46]

References Part Four
1. DMMR
2. DMMR; Odgers notes
3. Ibid.
4. Ibid.
5. Personal Communications. Jack Jervis of Illogan & Bert Retallack of Camborne
6. DMMR; Odgers notes
7. Ibid.
8. Notes on Roskear Shaft Working (Aug.8 1923-June 16 1926) Manuscript Book. Private Collection
9. Ibid.
10. Ibid.
11. Letters between Captain R. Arthur Thomas and Captain A. J. Edwards (1927-28); Notes on Roskear Shaft Working; A 50lb Holman sinking machine was found in the sump of

the shaft in 1996.

12. DMMR; Odgers notes
13. Notes of Roskear Shaft Working (1924)
14. Notes on Roskear Shaft Working; Personal communication with Malcolm Batchelor, foreman in charge of refurbishing Roskear Shaft in 1990s.
15. Notes on Roskear Shaft Working
16. Ibid.
17. Ibid.
18. Notes on Roskear Shaft Working; Odgers notes; DMMR
19. Ibid.
20. DMMR; Odgers notes
21. Notes on Roskear Shaft Working (1925)
22. DMMR; Odgers notes; Notes on Roskear Shaft Working (1925)
23. Odgers notes
24. DMMR; Notes on Roskear Shaft Working (1925)
25. DMMR; Odgers notes
26. DMMR; Odgers notes; Mining Magazine (October 1926); Information from Tony Clarke
27. DMMR; Odgers notes
28. Ibid.
29. DMMR; Odgers notes; J. A. Buckley South Crofty Mine: A History (1997) pp.197-99; pers comm Tony Clarke.
30. DMMR
31. DMMR; Odgers notes
32. Ibid.
33. Letter from Captain A. J. Edwards to Captain R. A. Thomas (February 1928)
34. Letter from Captain A. J. Edwards to Captain R. A. Thomas (March 28 1928)
35. Ibid.
36. Letter Edwards to Thomas (Feb.1928); Letter Edwards to Thomas (April 26 1928)
37. DMMR; Odgers notes
38. Ibid.
39. West Briton (1928) Only partial date
40. Ibid.
41. Ibid.
42. Ibid.
43. DMMR; Odgers notes
44. Ibid.
45. Ibid.
46. Ibid.

Part Five
Dolcoath: part of South Crofty Mine (1936-98)

What might have appeared to have been the final closure of the old mine, in 1930, when the Official Receiver and HM Treasury took it over, turned out to be merely the end of just another chapter in its long history. Five years later, another chapter in the story of Dolcoath was opened. In July 1935, the owners of South Crofty Mine, which lies along the eastern boundary of Dolcoath, made a provisional agreement with the Treasury to purchase the whole of Dolcoath Mine's assets. The Managing Director's report to the Board of South Crofty, details what had been acquired.

Mr Josiah Paull's Report re Dolcoath.

We have purchased from HM Treasury the Dolcoath Mine and its assets, the latter comprising, in addition to various substantial buildings and a large quantity of valuable Mine Machinery and Plant, considerable areas of freehold land, the mineral rights of the Old Dolcoath property and the leases of the New Dolcoath Mine.

Both Old and New Dolcoath lie immediately West of our present South Crofty New Cooks Kitchen boundary, and the lodes worked by us extend throughout the area we are taking over for a length of 2,500 to 3,000 feet, and have been explored to a small extent only by the former owners, so that the acquisition of this further large area should, we are confident will, add enormously to our potential ore reserves and consequent life of the Mine as a whole, and should enable us to increase our output of Tin, Wolfram and Arsenic.

At a distance of 1,600 feet from our Western boundary the New Dolcoath Company sunk at great expense a vertical shaft 18 feet in diameter to a depth of 2,000 feet. This shaft is brick-lined throughout and it is our intention eventually to link up our workings with this shaft, as such linking up with our present Robinson's and New Cooks vertical shafts will provide excellent Natural

Ventilation throughout the whole property, but our immediate intention is to extend our South Crofty levels Westwards into the new area, one such level being already practically on the boundary, and to explore and work the lode by this means, and bring the ore to our New Cooks Vertical Shaft, the capacity of which, together with its large winding equipment, is capable of handling some thousands of tons of ore per month beyond what we are now able to supply the shaft with. Our milling capacity also is sufficient for crushing and treating at least 2,000 tons per month more than we are doing at present, so that, beyond the purchase price, by developing the property in the way we propose, we do not contemplate any considerable Capital Expenditure will be necessary and the proceeds of the present issue should be ample for our requirements in these respects.

The New Dolcoath Company had already intersected two or three of our lodes, prior to closing down through insufficient capital, and from the small amount of development and mining operations carried out by them sold some 170 tons of tin, 20 tons of wolfram and 370 tons of arsenic, the aggregate value of which was £29,000, and their reports show the value per ton of ore in development drives as being equal to or in excess of our own at South Crofty."[1]

On February 4th 1936 T. Wallace Evans, South Crofty's Secretary, issued the following statement to the South Crofty shareholders:

"In July last you were informed that my Board had entered into a provisional agreement with the Treasury to acquire the Dolcoath Mine, which adjoins the Company's property, and which will be accessible through our New Cooks Shaft. The formal agreement has now been signed and the sale was approved by the Court on the 29th January, 1936.

The reasons which actuated the Board in agreeing to the purchase from the Treasury are set out in an enclosed report from Mr Josiah Paull, from which you will observe that this acquisition should add largely to this Company's ore reserves and become a valuable asset.

The purchase price is £22,000 payable in cash. In order to carry through the deal and to provide for the development in Dolcoath and for further sinking of shafts on our Crofty properties, without unduly depleting the cash resources of the Company, it has been decided to offer to the shareholders *pro rata,* as rights, 78,000 unissued shares of 5s each, *i.e.,* one new share for every five old shares held on the 14th February 1936, with no fractions, at the price of 7s 6d per share, payable on full application, which will provide £29,250. The share register will be closed on the 14th February, 1936, and the rights must be taken

up by the 28th February, 1936, when the list closes.
This will then make the total issued capital £117,000.

Application and renunciation forms will be posted on the 18th February, 1936.

Your directors consider it necessary to have this issue underwritten. Should shareholders desire to apply for any excess rights in order to round off their holdings, they will be given opportunity to do so. The directors reserve the right to take up the shares (if any) not applied for at the price of 7s 6d per share.

The new shares will rank for dividend after 31st March next. Application to the Stock Exchange for permission to deal in this issue will be applied for in due course."[2]

The managers at South Crofty were well aware of the potential of New Dolcoath. Undoubtedly, when Captain Josiah Paull had kept his eye on the mine, some years before, when Captain Arthur Thomas had visited Canada, he would have noted the presence of valuable lodes containing tin, wolfram and arsenic. Like the rest of the local mining community, Paull also knew that the lodes opened up there had been barely touched before the mine's closure. Despite this, Paull was in no hurry to exploit the lodes on the western side of the Great Crosscourse, for South Crofty was busy opening up its own rich tin lodes, to the north of New Cooks and Robinsons shafts.[3]

The Drive into New Dolcoath (Roskear)
It was to be four years later that Crofty's developers were pointed in the direction of the Great Crosscourse and instructed to start driving through it. In 1940, one of South Crofty's top developers, Bert Rule, using a heavy Climax bar-and-arm machine, drove into the crosscourse from the western end of No.2 North Lode, on the 315 fathom level. The importance of this drive can be gauged from the fact that not only were they using their best men for the job, but the trammers mucking the end were using Crofty's brand-new Eimco Rocker Shovel. This small 4 cylinder automatic loader was the first to be used in a Cornish mine. A Welshman, Bert Shortman, was given a few lessons on its use by the Eimco instructor, and left to get on with it. Once he had the hang of it, the trammers queued up with their 10cwt and 16cwt waggons to be loaded, before pushing them all the way back to New Cooks Shaft ore pass. Unfortunately, the mine did not possess electric locomotives at that time, and so all tramming was by hand. In 1941 Crofty acquired its first electric loco, and as with the Eimco, this was first put to use in the drives into Roskear and Dolcoath. Where Rule penetrated the Great Crosscourse into the Roskear sett, he found that the No.2 North Lode continued as, what Crofty called, Roskear South Lode.[4]

During the next few years the drives into Roskear sett were pursued, and new lodes developed for stoping. In 1947 the mine reports show that these workings were already making a significant contribution to the tonnage of ore being hoisted up New Cooks Shaft. Shortage of skilled labour inhibited development to some extent, as post-war conditions made work in Holmans, Climax and other local factories more attractive to the men returning from the armed forces. In the late 1940s, several Polish workers were taken on by Crofty, and by 1952 there was a determined campaign to recruit Italians, mostly from Sicily. About forty Poles came and went during those years, with a handful remaining at the mine for long periods. Several became skilled machinemen and contributed to the mine's expansion into New Dolcoath and other neighbouring properties. About eighty Italians were taken on in the 1950s, and many of these stayed at the mine for years. Most were trammers, although a few became machinemen also.[5]

Expansion & Improved Ventilation

The 1950s saw a steady expansion of work in Roskear Section. At the 290, 315 and 340 fathom levels the drives through the Great Crosscourse were all from No.2 North Lode into Roskear South Lode. Crosscuts were driven north from this lode to explore other lodes to the south of Roskear Shaft, and access to flooded workings became inevitable. By 1956 the 340 fathom level was directly beneath the workings of the 1900 foot and 2000 foot levels of New Dolcoath and during the next couple of years flooded stopes were penetrated, making it necessary to drain the water from the workings, and rendering Roskear Shaft accessible from South Crofty. Connections to the shaft at the 1900 foot and 2000 foot level quickly improved the ventilation in the western workings of the mine. All of this made serious exploitation of New Dolcoath far easier, and by 1961, with the installation of an electric ventilation fan at the bottom of Roskear Shaft, there was a tremendous improvement in the air quality.[6]

A Dramatic Rescue from Drowning

An amusing story from the late 1950s tells us something about the *ad hoc* arrangements for opening up these workings. A group of miners, including Ronnie Roberts and Howard Mankee, were given the task of bridging a flooded stope in New Dolcoath. They constructed a raft consisting of empty oil drums and 2-inch planks, which they were to float across the stope and use as a drilling platform. They climbed aboard the raft, dragging their drilling machine with them, and after connecting the air and water hoses, turned on the machine to drill a peg-hole in the far side of the stope. This was to carry a chain as the first part of the bridge. Unfortunately, they forgot to anchor the raft, so when the machine's air-leg was turned on, it pushed the raft back at a rate of knots, causing the miners to fall in all directions. Regrettably, Howard Mankee, the only man there who could not swim, was thrown into the flooded depths of the stope. At the same time, all their carbide lamps blew out. Ronnie Roberts, after lying on the raft laughing, suddenly realised that Howard was missing, and without further ado, dived into the water and rescued the terrified man. It is not hard to imagine the total darkness of the water in the stope, which was many fathoms deep, and extremely dirty. It was a story which was retold many times over the years, to the embarrassment of Howard Mankee, especially after he became a mine captain.[7]

Throughout the 1960s the Roskear and Dolcoath setts contributed to the increasing tonnage of ore going up New Cooks Kitchen Vertical Shaft, and it was partly due to the large ore reserves there, that the management decided to increase the crushing and milling capacity of the mine. In 1958, the Californian Stamps had been replaced by a new heavy media separation plant, and by 1969 this was replaced with a much more modern HMS, huge rough ore bins to receive the ore from underground, two large ore bins for the mill feed, and a completely new mill, alongside the old mill.[8]

On 315 and 340 fathom level several lodes were developed during the late 1960s and early 1970s. Crosscuts were driven north from Roskear South Lode and intersected a whole series of lodes. No less than eight mineralised structures were intersected on the 340 fathom level, and all within a relatively short distance. Apart from Roskear South Lode, No.2 North, No.3 North and No.6 North lodes were all worth pursuing. Two less valuable lodes were cut just north of No.6 Lode, thereafter the crosscut entered the killas. On the 315 fathom level there was less success, but the lode drive on Roskear South Lode was found to be one of the lodes developed from the 1900 foot level in New Dolcoath, and a connection was made.[9]

A Valuable New Series of Lodes Discovered
By 1966, the newly opened 360 and 380 fathom levels were also driven into Roskear and it was from these levels that the rich, wide lodes beneath Roskear Shaft were found. As predicted by Captain Arthur Thomas, and for very different reasons by James Wickett in the 1920s, New Dolcoath was within a whisker of intersecting these lodes. In the late 1970s, Roy Stevens and Timothy Hocking drove a crosscut north on the 360 fathom level, and eventually entered the killas. This crosscut and the one below it, on the 380 fathom level, led immediately to the discovery of the series of mineralised structures known as Roskear 'A', 'B' and 'D' lodes. They were all wide and rich in cassiterite, and proved among the most valuable discoveries at South Crofty Mine during its 340 year history.[10]

By the end of the 1980s these lodes were contributing about 20 percent of Crofty's ore and in 1991 some 70 percent of all her tin ore came from these three Roskear lodes. It is true to say, that New Dolcoath at South Roskear was effectively a 'new mine', and was fast becoming the saviour of the old one, as the tin price plummeted and the Company ran into severe trouble.[11]

The Drive into Dolcoath Sett

During the 1970s, south crosscuts were driven from Roskear South Lode into the old Dolcoath sett itself. The first lode opened up was Dolcoath North Lode, which runs from Tuckingmill, beneath the south part of the old Bickford-Smith Fuze Works, and passes just south of Roskear Church, before heading toward the centre of Camborne. This lode proved very valuable and was extensively stoped between the 290 and 380 fathom levels.[12]

As the decade progressed, the south crosscuts were extended, intersecting Dolcoath Middle Lode, which was not particularly rich, and then Dolcoath South Lode, which proved one of the most productive lodes on the western side of the Great Crosscourse. The 290 fathom level drive on this lode entered the killas below Wesley Street, Camborne, and the values stopped. On the 315 fathom level the drive went into killas beneath Albert Street, and the 340 drive hit killas just to the north of Adelaide Street. By 1990 Dolcoath North and South lodes contributed about 20 percent of the mine's tin ore. There were twelve lodes which South Crofty was able to economically exploit on the western side of the Great Crosscourse in the old Roskear and Dolcoath setts.[13]

The drive south into the heart of Dolcoath Mine continued after the discovery of Dolcoath South Lode. This was instigated by Captain Andy Bennie, nicknamed Captain Foo, who was convinced, either by a dream or by some other kind of intuition, that another rich lode lay still further south. Sure enough, after some persuasion, Jimmy Clemence pushed the 340 fathom level south crosscut on, and within a relatively short distance he cut what became known as Dolcoath Second South Lode, or South Branch. The miners dubbed it 'Foo's Folly Lode', and other similar names. Although not as rich as Dolcoath South Lode, this lode was stoped on both sides of the crosscut and produced respectable tonnages of ore on the 290, 315 and 340 fathom levels. Its values did not persist far to the west, however, and the lode drives on it were stopped.[14]

Work continued during the 1990s to remove the pillars left by the shrink stopers and long-hole drillers along Dolcoath South Lode, and until about 1995 Bernie Harradine and Jeff Tonkin were removing them in the central section of the lode and Eric Eckersall and Dave Cunnack were taking them out at the extreme western end of the lode. Karla Riekstins, a planning engineer, and the author, were removing the pillars of ore left in the stope beneath the 290 fathom level, prior to the long-holers taking out the pillars. The ore being blasted down was being trammed out on the 340 fathom level.[15]

Roskear Shaft's New Importance

In March 1995, the task of replacing South Crofty's deteriorating Robinsons

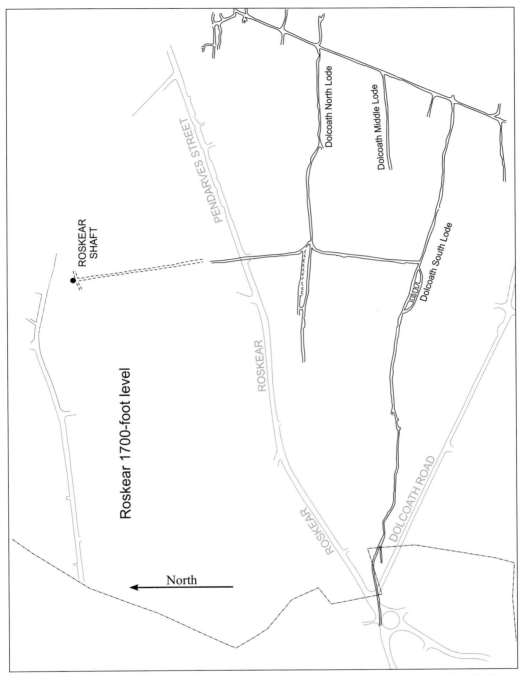

Figure 134. The dotted line from New Roskear Shaft is the 1700-foot level. The Crofty workings are shown at the 290-fathom level.

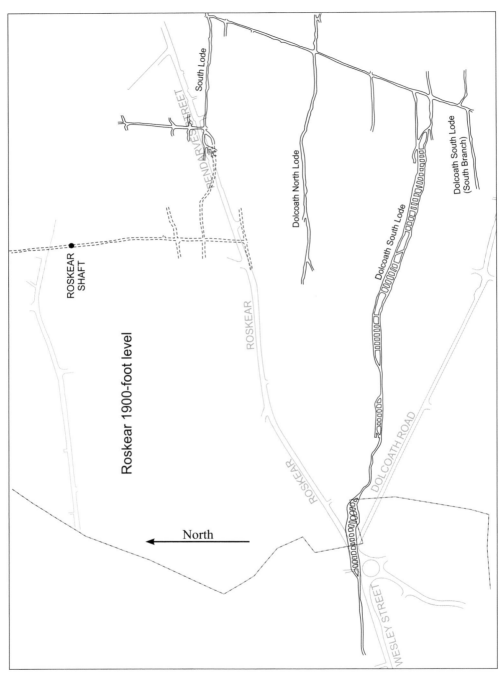

Figure 135. The dotted line from New Roskear Shaft is the 1900-foot level. The Crofty workings are shown at the 315-fathom level.

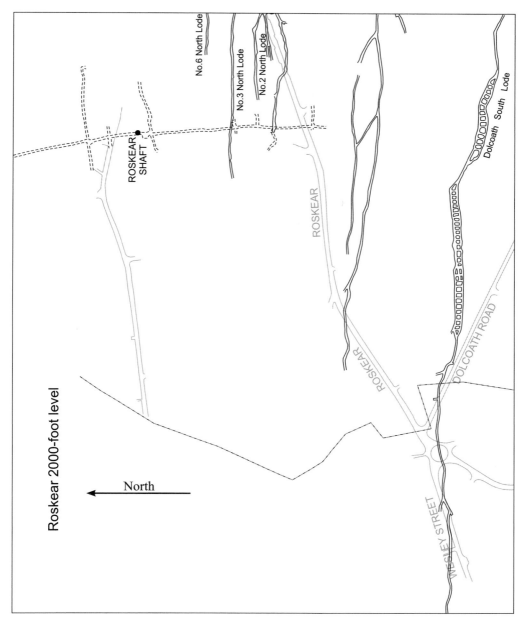

No.6 North Lode

No.3 North Lode

No.2 North Lode

Dolcoath South Lode

ROSKEAR
SHAFT

ROSKEAR

ROSKEAR

DOLCOATH ROAD

WESLEY STREET

Roskear 2000-foot level

← North

Figure 136. The dotted line from New Roskear Shaft is the 2000-foot level. The Crofty workings are shown at the 340-fathom level.

Shaft with a replacement emergency egress shaft began. On June 17th 1996, the changeover was finally complete, when Robinsons Shaft was officially closed. A raise had been mined up from the 400 fathom level to the sump of Roskear Shaft, by Wayne Brown. This sump lay about 20 feet below the 2000 foot level of New

Dolcoath Mine. A new 46 feet (14m) high headframe was erected over the shaft, with a 48-inch (1.2m) diameter winding drum and an 18mm thick wire rope. It had a hoisting speed of about 5 feet a second. The headframe was designed by Crofty's engineers and fabricated locally.[16]

Regrettably, no sooner had this work been done, and the lodes in the Roskear and Dolcoath setts proved rich at the bottom of the mine, on the 400, 420 and 445 fathom levels, than the looming crisis over the ever-lowering tin metal price, threatened the future of mining once again. In June 1997, work was suspended on the newly opened 470 fathom level, and by the end of the year announcements about impending closure were being made. On March 6th 1998, the worst happened, when the pumps were stopped and the old mine, which had operated under a variety of names and many owners for over 300 years, closed down. Once again, this appeared to have been the final chapter in the long history of Camborne mining. The workings of South Crofty at that time stretched from the edge of Redruth in the east, almost to the centre of Camborne, in the west. The Roskear and Dolcoath setts had proved among the great hopes for the future of South Crofty and Cornish mining. But, despite the universal pessimism which prevailed throughout Cornwall, there was to be yet another chapter in the story.

References Part Five
1.   Buckley (1997) pp.133,134
2.   Buckley (1997) pp.134,135
3.   DMMR; Odgers notes
4.   Buckley (1997) pp.143,144
5.   Buckley (1997) pp.145,149,152-154,162
6.   Buckley (1997) pp.161,164
7.   Personal communications from the late Howard Mankee & the late Ronnie Roberts
8.   Buckley (1997) pp.161,172,173
9.   Buckley (1997) pp.175-78
10. Buckley (1997) p.182
11. Buckley (1997) pp.198,199
12. Buckley (1997) pp.182,184,187
13. Buckley (1997) pp.187,193-99
14. Buckley (1997) pp.187,193-99; Personal communications from Jimmy Clemence & Peter Hughes
15. Diary of K. T. Riekstins (South Crofty Mine Planning Engineer) (August 1 & 21 1994); Diary of author (August 1994)
16. Buckley (1997) p.191

Part Six
Baseresult & Great Western Mines

Following a much-publicised but abortive attempt to reopen the mine by a Welsh 'entrepreneur', called Wilf Hughes, the scene settled down to a quieter and more measured attempt to resume mining at South Crofty and Dolcoath. Two mining enthusiasts, Kevin Williams and David Stone, set up an office in Green Lane, Redruth, to plan the reopening of these mines. Kevin Williams had been a shiftboss and manager at Geevor, in the 1980s and had worked as an engineer on the Channel Tunnel. David Stone had worked as an engineer on various mines in Cornwall and abroad. Eventually, after obtaining ownership of South Crofty's New Cooks Kitchen Mine site, they began the slow, laborious process of negotiating with a sceptical and often uncooperative army of officials and councillors.[1]

Exploration & Tourism

The first practical step taken was the exploration of the shallow workings above adit level on the mine. The stoped out areas of New Cooks Kitchen to the south of South Crofty's offices were examined closely through Old Engine Shaft and the Tuckingmill Decline. A visiters' route was quickly established to provide a small income while the many hurdles to reopening were overcome. With the approval of the Mines Inspector, to ensure the public's safety, an area of impressively wide workings was made available. This did not merely provide income, for it also opened the eyes of many people to the importance of Cornish mining and created much-needed sympathy for what Baseresult was trying to achieve. Given the atmosphere of hostility in which the company was operating, these underground trips helped change local minds as to the viability of the mining industry. This hostility was engendered to a large extent by local officials and councillors, who felt a prejudice toward Cornwall's traditional industries. They subscribed to the view that mining was noisy, dirty and bad for the environment. The tourist industry, which has the most powerful voice at most planning enquiries and in the Cornish press, appeared to be a more attractive prospect, despite it providing only part-time, low-paid and seasonal work. Traditionally, Cornish industries like fishing, quarrying, engineering and mining have provided full-time work for good wages. An important boost to the mine was the installation by Baseresult's engineers, led by Paul McDonald, of an Alamack cage and hoist in Old Engine Shaft. This enabled quick and safe access to the main level of the mine for workers, visitors and management.

Preparation for Mining
Having explored the network of tunnels and stopes above adit level, the next step was to drive tunnels to provide emergency egress, improved ventilation and more practicable access for regular working. To these ends a tunnel was driven from the Tuckingmill Decline, at about the 170 foot horizon, to New Cooks Kitchen Vertical Shaft. Access from this tunnel to Old Engine Shaft was also established. This was followed by a drive south-west to Middle Engine Shaft of the old Cooks Kitchen Mine, considerably improving ventilation. As these drives progressed, a programme of diamond drilling was started to locate and evaluate mineralised structures (lodes) on all sides of the workings which were being opened up.

Obtaining Financial Backing
In November 2007 Baseresult was joined by Galena and Trafigura, and these gave enormous financial backing to the project. Trafigura is an international commodity dealer with an annual income of some $50,000,000,000. With this support the mine, under the name Western United Mines, began to drive into the heart of Dolcoath Mine. From the Tuckingmill Decline at the 170 foot horizon a tunnel was driven in a westerly direction almost to the Red River. It then became an incline shaft, going down at a rate of one-in-six. Stub drives were mined for use as diamond drill bays, and a tunnel was started to intersect Dolcoath's North Shaft.

In October 2009 the sinking of the incline shaft was temporarily halted while exploration by diamond drilling took place. At its deepest point, at the western end, the shaft was some 350 feet (108m) below the surface. It extends for well over 1,000 feet (300m) beyond the Red River, to a point just north of Dolcoath's New Sump Shaft.

Diamond Drilling
By October 2009 all main development was suspended to enable the workforce to concentrate on exploration of the ground on the north and south sides of the western drive. Numerous lodes have been intersected, containing a great variety of minerals, including sphalerite (zinc), cassiterite (tin), chalcopyrite (copper), arsenopyrite (arsenic) and several other potentially valuable minerals, including the much sought after, indium. The intention of the owners was to create Europe's first polymetallic mine.

The Workforce

For most of the last ten years the workforce has comprised those involved in technical services. Allan Reynolds and Dr Keith Russ have spent their time examining every old record relevant to South Crofty, Cooks Kitchen, North and South Roskear and Dolcoath mines. Plans, sections and ore grade figures, together with the scores of reports on these workings by mining engineers, mine geologists and mine economists, have been assembled, dissected and evaluated. In 2009, these two were joined by Neil Hitchens, an experienced mining engineer, who has worked all over the world, and Gareth Joseph, a mine geologist. A group of technically able staff were then recruited to assist in the evaluation of the large body of data being produced by technical services.

During the last decade many workers have spent various lengths of time helping Baseresult reopen the old mine, and in October 2009 the company employed a stable workforce of over 50 men and women. There were at that time about a dozen former South Crofty employees, eight from Geevor and three from Wheal Jane. There are also several men who have never worked in a mine before and are being trained from scratch. The underground workforce is led by Michael Sampson, who performs the role of mine captain.

Thus, in 2010, the story of Dolcoath is set to continue hopefully into a long and fruitful future.

References, Part Six

1. Interviews with Kevin Williams (Managing Director of Baseresult), Allan Reynolds (Chief Surveyor), Keith Russ (Planning and Safety Officer), Neil Hitchens (Mine Engineer), Mike Sampson (Mine Captain) John Webster (Chief Operations Officer), Gareth Joseph (Mine Geologist) and Alan Shoesmith (Financial Director). (1998-2010)

Part Seven
Dolcoath's Remaining Industrial Archaeology

Almost fifty years ago, when I was first working at South Crofty, 1 would walk from my cottage on Carn Entral, past Williams Shaft and after crossing the railway, wend my way through the ruins of Dolcoath. Even at 6 o'clock on a winter's morning the remains of buildings, loadings and shaft burrows had a look of mystery about them: a place well-worth exploring. Rabbits, foxes and badgers were my usual companions as I walked past in the half-light. Upon reaching the valley I would be met with a scene some locals called 'Sodom and Gomorrah'. Stretched out between Tuckingmill and the railway embankment was a landscape of amazing interest, including wheel pits, launders, leats, the ruined remains of calciners, water stamps and dressing floors with evidence of ancient buddles and the loadings of shaking tables. The route between the valley and New Cooks Kitchen dry was also littered with the evidences of centuries of mining: an industrial archaeologist's paradise. No wonder visitors from all over the world wandered through this landscape with such delighted fascination.

All of that has now changed. Today there is very little to remind the visitor to Dolcoath that they are walking across the surface of what was once one of the most significant mines in the world. Four engine houses and a couple of other buildings are all that remain of the once great Dolcoath: 'Queen of Cornish Mines'. A series of events have contributed to this situation. There was, in the late 1970s and early 1980s, the massive rise in the tin price, which caused the owners of the site to bulldoze almost everything on the surface for re-treatment in South Crofty's tin mill. This destroyed much of the archaeology of the mine, particularly at the eastern end, on the Bullen Garden section. This was followed by the scandalous destruction of the archaeological remains in the valley, for which Carnon Consolidated received the Queen Mother's Award for land reclamation. The valley was left as a smoothed out place of infinite boredom. Nothing much was left, apart from a signed and framed certificate of congratulations. These acts were followed by demands for the new owners of the land, Kerrier District Council, to make the site safe. An extensive programme of shaft plugging and remediation followed. Bullen Garden became a sort of 'municipal park' for the walking of dogs and other harmless activities. The remaining isolated buildings serve only to remind us of what has gone. The context has been destroyed, the ruins have been mostly removed and the once-distinctive shaft burrows have been flattened.

What Can Now Be Seen?

To inspect what remains it is best to start at the western end of the mine, well away from the pretty 'custom built' car park opposite the bus depot at the top of Dolcoath Road. From the Tesco roundabout, drive south up Foundry Road and across the railway bridge. On Park Lane, which lies on the south side of the railway between Stray Park Road and Foundry Road, is the engine house of Stray Park Mine. Stray Park Mine worked with Dolcoath in the early 18th century, and subsequently was separated and joined with Dolcoath several times in the succeeding two hundred years. The engine house dates from 1864, when Dolcoath installed a second-hand, 60-inch cylinder pumping engine it had acquired from Pentire Glaze Mine, near Padstow. The engine was subsequently recylindered to a 64-inch, and then, in about 1900, the engine house was mostly taken down and rebuilt to accommodate a 65-inch engine. This was the old engine rebuilt by Holman Brothers, of Camborne. Only the stack remained of the original building. Recent work by Kerrier District Council has created a small park area for recreational purposes, but unfortunately, although the place has been made 'attractive', the archaeology of the site has been mostly compromised. There is now little to see of the once extensive mine remains that not too long ago littered the landscape around Stray Park Engine Shaft.

Leave Stray Park Shaft and drive back along Park Lane to Foundry Road. Turn right and take the first on the left. Drive to the end of the road and turn left again until the railway is crossed. Proceed to the end of Dolcoath Avenue and park. From here one can walk across the open ground to Harrietts Shaft. This engine house dates from about 1860, when a 60-inch cylinder pumping engine was installed. The engine was built by Perran Foundry, at Perranarworthal. In 1885 a 65-inch engine replaced the older Perran engine. This engine eventually pumped from the 470-fathom level. In 1912, when the New Sump engine stopped and the electric pumps at Williams Shaft took over the main pumping task, Harrietts engine was used to pump water from the 220-fathom level to surface. Much of this water was conveyed to Harrietts Shaft by means of pipes laid along the 220-fathom level. The shaft was also used for hoisting ore and was the first shaft on Dolcoath to use cages, on any scale, to hoist the men to surface. In late 1897 it replaced the old man engine, which operated a short distance to the north-west of Harrietts Shaft, at Wheal Bryant. Some of the winding gear used at Harrietts Shaft, and removed for use at New Dolcoath (South Roskear) in the 1920s, has recently been returned to the site.

Close to Wheal Harrietts Shaft is the large miners' dry (changing house), which was erected in 1888 close to Wheal Bryant's Man Engine Shaft. This dry was heated by steam pipes from Wheal Harrietts boiler house. The dry was among the most modern to be erected in Cornwall and served the needs of many hundred miners, who used it on a shift basis. The building is presently owned by the local Elim Church and is hired out to local people for various functions. It is of interest to note the many copper scoria blocks used in its construction. These may have come up from Copperhouse, near Hayle, although some probably originated closer to home, as copper smelting took place just to the east of the building at Bullen Garden, in the 18th century.

A short walk from Harrietts Shaft takes one across the road at Pengegon Coombe onto the Bullen Garden section of the mine. This is the area which has mostly been made into a 'municipal park'. Amidst the group of buildings beside Dolcoath Road is the old compressor house. This was built in 1883, and contained two Champion type air compressors. The pipes carrying the compressed air went southward from the building to New Sump (Engine) Shaft. The air was conveyed down the shaft and into the several ends where the rock drills were operating. The principal activity in this group of buildings now appears to be the training of boxers by the Camborne-Redruth Boxing Club.

A few steps to the east take you to New East engine house. This 1894 engine house contained a small rotative engine, which was multi-purpose, in that it hoisted ore from New East Shaft, a short distance to the west, and also powered an auxiliary beam pump, which brought water up Magor Shaft from Deep Adit level. Much of the original boiler house remains, which is unusual on Cornish mines. In 1913 part of the building was converted for use as an electricity substation.

One of the most recently built extant buildings of the old Dolcoath Mine is the engine house on Williams Shaft. From New East it is necessary to walk southwards across the site and cross the small railway bridge. At the road, which runs around the northern flank of Carn Entral, turn right and walk up the slope to Williams Shaft. Despite its fairly recent construction the building is in ruins, the south-west wall having fallen down in the 1990s. The winding engine for which the building was constructed was unique and ahead of its time. To avoid 'angularity' of the rope on the drum a traversing system was adopted, whereby the carriage with the drum on it travelled 16 feet (5m) for the 1,000 yards of rope needed to hoist from the 550-fathom level. The drum was 10 feet (3m) diameter and measured 21 feet (6m) between its flanges. The winder was designed by William Morgan and built by Holman Brothers, of Camborne. Williams Shaft was sunk between 1895 and 1910 to a depth of just over 3,000 feet. On the deepest level, the 550-fathom level, were installed some of the most modern electric pumps available in the early years of the 20th century. Others were installed at the 220-fathom level. By the time the mine closed, in 1920,

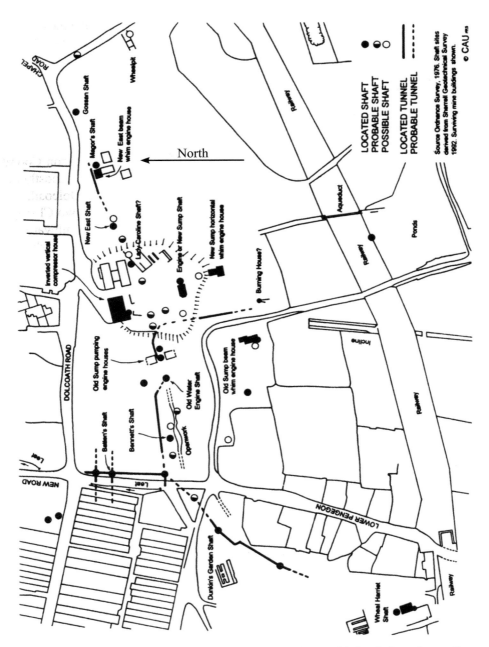

Figure 137. Map showing shallow tunnels, between 15 and 20 feet below the surface.

most of the ore from Dolcoath's deepest workings came up this shaft. It is a circular shaft, 17 feet 6 inches in diameter, and brick-lined from top to bottom. From the early 1950s water was pumped from the shaft to supply the government's secret establishment at Nancekuke on the former RAF Portreath airfield.

New Dolcoath at South Roskear.

This discrete three-acre site lies at the junction of North Roskear Road and South Roskear Terrace and includes a number of buildings, constructed over perhaps 200 years. Mining activities were being carried out in the area during the middle 1700s and continued until the 1880s. In 1871 a factory for making safety fuze was set up astride the north end of South Roskear Terrace, and this operated until 1924. The long two-storey building dates from this period, operated by Bennetts' Fuze Works, the other part of which is now incorporated in the Lidl supermarket. Lying adjacent to the boundary wall in South Roskear Terrace is an elegant 'plantation-style' bungalow, probably once occupied by an under-manager or supervisor. The building in the middle of the courtyard is the coal bunkers.

At the western end of the site is a complex of interlocking buildings which comprise a compressor house, winder house, boiler house and stack. At the north end of the boiler house, which contained six Lancashire boilers, is an air raid shelter. To the north-east of the boiler house lies the winder house, which, until recently held the remains of the Worsley Mesnes horizontal winding engine, installed in February-March 1924. Interestingly the loadings include blocks from Arthur Woolf's moorstone boiler, rebuilt at Entral in July 1771. The twin engine cylinders were removed (through the roof) by the Red Rose Steam Society, now based at the Astley Green Colliery Museum near Manchester, in the 1960s. The group was attempting to put together a collection of equipment built by Worsley Mesnes, and the cylinders were taken to Wigan Pier, where they were put in storage. Unfortunately, shortly after this they were stolen and never recovered. On the north-east side of the winder house is the ivy-covered compressor house. The equipment installed here was a Corliss stage compressor (a high-speed compressor with valves manufactured by the Corliss Company), built as a one-off by Holman Brothers and originally installed at Williams Shaft. This was probably the last big horizontal air compressor that the company built. Its cylinders measured 18 inches by 30 with a 42-inch stroke and had 18 and 28-inch stage cylinders with intercooler. The air valves were of a late Holman pattern. The bedplate was of the 'Mammoth' type with a flywheel that weighed over 12 tons. The compressor apparently remained in place, greased over, following the closure of New Dolcoath, but was gradually dismantled, along with other plant, after being acquired by South Crofty.

On the north side of the site are the paraphernalia of New Roskear Shaft: headframe, winder house and fan house; the remains of parts of the original headframe (brought

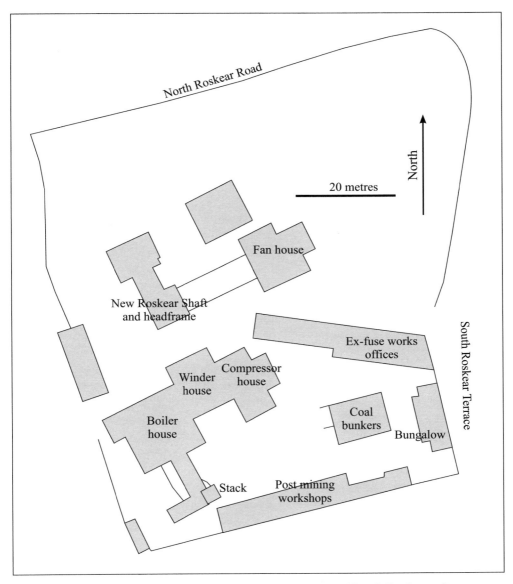

Figure 138. Principal features of the New Dolcoath/South Roskear site.

from Williams Shaft) can also be seen. The shaft, circular and brick-lined, is 17 feet 6 inches in diameter and 2,020 feet deep (to a 20-foot sump below the 2,000 foot level), commenced August 1923 and ultimate depth reached by April 29th 1926. The headframe arrived onsite in July 1924. The winder house contains two engines, the principal winder (the Mary Ann) which is built into the house, and the Pickrose, an auxiliary winder which is a separate, portable unit. Both winders are single drum and hydraulically operated, but neither now connects to the shaft. The air pipes from the fan house are covered by a large mound of earth and cannot be seen.

The New Roskear Shaft site is a marvellous mixture of structures from various periods, demonstrating continued use of the site for nearly 200 years, set within an urban landscape. The site contains a complete record of all of the activities of New Dolcoath Mine, and since 1830 the site has been home to at least 42 buildings, four mine shafts, three horse whim circles, three steel headframes and, presumably, several timber sheers. In addition, it has undergone major landscaping of the waste tips. The former presence of the remains of the Harrietts Shaft winding engine adds to the importance of the site, this type of machinery being very rare in Cornwall indeed.

There is also importance by association, with equipment having come from notable sites at Dolcoath: headframes, boilers and compressors and fragments of the famous moorstone boiler recycled for loadings. The 1920s was not a good time for Cornish mining: in 1919 nine mines had been operating, while in 1921 only Giew, previously part of St Ives Consols and not operating in 1919, remained as a producer. Finding mine buildings from this period when mines closed rather than opened may therefore be regarded as unusual.

Access to this site is no longer possible – except, apparently, by vandals. The old fuze factory building was recently gutted by a serious fire and small-scale damage to the other buildings is, sadly, a popular pastime.

BIBLIOGRAPHY

NEWSPAPERS & JOURNALS
Cornish Magazine
Cornishman
Cornish Post & Mining News
Cornish Telegraph
Gentleman's Magazine
History: Journal of the Historical Association
Journal of the Trevithick Society
Mining Magazine
Mining Journal
Mining & Smelting Magazine
Mining World
Philosophical Transactions of the Royal Society
Royal Cornwall Gazette
Sherborne Mercury
Transactions of the Institute of Engineers
Transactions of the Royal Cornwall Polytechnic Society
Transactions of the Royal Geological Society of Cornwall
Trevithick Society Newsletters
West Briton
Wheals Magazine

PUBLISHED BOOKS
D. B. Barton: The Cornish Beam Engine (1969)
D. B. Barton: A History of Tin Mining & Smelting in Cornwall (1967)
D. B. Barton: Copper Mining in Cornwall & Devon (1978)
D. B. Barton: Essays in Cornish Mining History vol.1 (1968)
D. B. Barton Essays in Cornish Mining History vol.2 (1971)
Peter Berg (Editor): R. R. Angerstein's Travels in England & Wales 1753-55 (1994)
Bibliotheca Cornubiensis (1874 & 1878)
William Borlase: Natural History of Cornwall (1970)
Allen Buckley (Editor): Hazards & Heroes in Cornish Mines (2007)
J. A. Buckley: A History of South Crofty Mine (1980)
J. A. Buckley: South Crofty Mine; A History (1997)
Allen Buckley: The Story of Mining in Cornwall (2007)
Allen Buckley: Princes of the Working Valley (2007)
Anthony Burton: Richard Trevithick: Giant of Steam (2000)
R. Burt (Editor): Cornish Mining (1969)
R. Burt (Editor): George Henwood Cornwall's Mines & Miners (1972)
R. Burt, P Waite & R Burnley Cornish Mines (1987)

Clive Carter: Holmans: Cornish Engineering 1801-1901 (2004)
Collectanea Cornubiensis (1890)
J. H. Collins: Observations on the West of England Mining Region (1912)
M. B. Donald: Elizabethan Copper (1994)
Bryan Earl: Cornish Explosives (2006)
Bryan Earl: Cornish Mining (1994)
R. J. Evans: The Victorian Age (1981)
Celia Fiennes: The Journeys of Celia Fiennes. Editor Christopher Morris. (1947)
H. S. A. Fox & O. J. Padel: The Cornish Lands of the Arundells of Lanherne 14th
to 16th Centuries (2000)
John Griffiths: The Third Man (1992)
John Harris: My Autobiography (1882)
T. R. Harris: Arthur Woolf: The Cornish Engineer. 1766-1837 (1966)
T. R. Harris: Dolcoath: Queen of Cornish Mines (1974)
Bridget Howard: Mr Lean & the Engine Reporters (2002)
F. Hitchens & S. Drew: The History of Cornwall (1824)
Dr A. K. Hamilton Jenkin: The Cornish Miner (1948)
Dr A. K. Hamilton Jenkin: News from Cornwall (1951)
Dr A. K. Hamilton Jenkin: Mines & Miners of Cornwall (16 volumes) (1961-1976)
Henry Kalmeter: The Kalmeter Journal. Justin Brooke (Editor) (2001)
Thomas Lean: On the Steam Engines of Cornwall (1839 & 1969)
E. C. Midwinter: Victorian Social Reform (1968)
T. A. Morrison: Cornwall's Central Mining District: Southern District (1983)
Cyril Noall: Cornish Mine Disasters (1989)
John Norden: Speculi Britanniae 'Historical Description of Cornwall' (1966)
Thomas Oliver: Autobiography of a Cornish Miner (1914)
O. J. Padel: Cornish Place-Name Elements (1985)
W. H. Pascoe: History of the Cornish Copper Company (1981)
Dr J. A. Paris: On Accidents Which Occur in the Mines of Cornwall (1817)
Dr J. A. Paris: A Guide to Mount's Bay & the Land's End (1816 & 1824)
William Pryce: Mineralogia Cornubiensis (1972)
Arthur Raistrick (Editor): The Hatchett Diary (1967)
Report on the Copper Trade (1798)
K. H. Rogers: The Newcomen Engine in the West of England (1976)
John Rowe: Cornwall in the Age of the Industrial Revolution (1993)
Thomas Spargo: The Mines of Cornwall: The Camborne Area (1865)
John Stengelhofen: Sketch of the Life of William West CE (1973)
Charles Thomas: Mrs Percival's Endowed School 1761-1876 (1982)
Herbert Thomas: Mining Interviews (1896)
Richard Thomas: Survey of the Mining District of Chacewater to Camborne (1819)
David Thomson: England in the 19th Century (1950)
A. C. Todd: The Search for Silver: Cornish Miners in Mexico 1824-1947 (1977)

Francis Trevithick: Life of Richard Trevithick (1872)
Richard Warner: A Tour through Cornwall in Autumn 1808 (1808)
J. Y. Watson: Compendium of British Mining (1843)
Anthony Wood: Nineteenth Century Britain 1815-1914 (1962)
Bennet Woodcroft: Alphabetical Index of Patentees of Inventions (1969)
R. N. Worth: Historical Notes on Progress of Mining Skill in Cornwall (1972)

Appendix 1 Dolcoath Copper Production (1799-1895)

Year	Value	Price per ton of Ore	Tons of Copper Ore
1799-1802	£7,267		
1803	£21,149		
1804	£150,000		27,591 tons (1799-1804)
1805	£114,121		
1806-10	£538,529 (5 years)		
1811	£64,626	£8.32	7,765
1812	£55,382	£6.60	8,389
1813	£62,055	£8.00	7,731
1814	£66,743	£8.86	8,275
1815	£66,394	£7.67	8,926
1816	£54,087	£6.07	9,838
1817	£48,548	£5.62	9,321
1818	£82,804	£7.38	11,215
1819	£67,755	£6.70	10,099
1820	£61,140	£5.95	10,268
1821	£55,863	£5.00	11,102
1822	£48,017	£5.13	9,471
1823	£39,851	£5.18	7,696
1824	£37,138	£4.95	7,504
1825	£43,093	£6.00	7,191
1826	£34,277	£4.66	7,975
1827	£47,923	£5.48	8,750
1828	£48,914	£5.71	8,563
1829	£68,437	£6.07	11,273
1830	£56,960	£5.65	10,079
1831	£56,680	£5.23	10.838
1832	£57,642	£6.26	9,194
1833	£51,747	£6.34	8,162
1834	£40,608	£5.86	7,046
1835	£33,831	£5.73	5,525
1836	£17,763	£5.27	3,373
1837	£14,098	£4.34	3,251
1838	£14,876	£4.89	3,043
1839	£17,039	£4.82	3,535
1840	£13,892	£3.82	3,638
1841	£20,055	£5.22	3,839
1842	£16,991	£4.69	3,620
1843	£18,721	£4.71	3,970
1844	£18,592	£4.82	3,860
1845	£16,997	£4.85	3,504
1846	£9,546	£4.43	2,156
1847	£9,408	£4.57	2,057
1848	£5,580	£4.46	1,254
1849	£5,197	£5.05	1,028
1850	£4,909	£4.40	1,115

1851	£3,626	£4.53	801
1852	£3,345	£4.02	832
1853	£4,920	£4.73	1,040
1854	£4,314	£4.35	992
1855	£2,634	£3.70	711
1856	£1,998	£3.24	617
1857	£2,430	£4.29	566
1858	£3,085	£5.20	593
1859	£3,532	£4.67	757
1860	£2,427	£3.41	712
1861	£1,589	£3.81	417
1862	£2,358	£4.64	508
1863	£3,029	£4.76	636
1864	£3,289	£5.30	621
1865	£3,510	£5.78	607
1866	£3,512	£5.10	688
1867	£1,068	£4.00	267
1868	£864	£5.65	153
1869	£649	£4.24	153
1870	£224	£3.93	57
1871	£326	£3.79	86
1872	£216	£4.70	46
1873	£78	£4.87	16
1874	£420	£5.60	75
1875			
1876	£163	£4.00	41
1877	£112	£3.73	30
1878	£27	£1.93	14
1879	£12	£3.00	4
1889	£10	£3.33	3

Appendix 2 Dolcoath Tin Production (1853-95)

Year	Value	Price per Ton	Tons of Black Tin Sold
1853	£22,680	£63	360
1854	£25,621	£69.40	364
1855	£23,170	£65.82	352
1856	£30,727	£73.68	417
1857	£42,880	£78.82	544
1858	£41,859	£65.82	636
1859	£53,506	£73.90	724
1860	£64,975	£80.71	805
1861	£63,862	£73.91	864
1862	£83,806	£67.35	1,246
1863	£69,742	£67.97	1,026
1864	£66,959	£65.00	1,030
1865	£53,238	£56.40	944
1866	£46,121	£50.18	919
1867	£46,170	£54.45	848
1868	£55,848	£56.76	984
1869	£59,694	£68.38	873
1870	£78,601	£75.94	1,035
1871	£95,373	£81.51	1,170
1872	£114,550	£89.14	1,285
1873	£82,501	£78.95	1,045
1874	£65,559	£58.48	1,121
1875	£65,347	£52.61	1,242
1876	£55,825	£44.20	1,263
1877	£59,180	£42.12	1,405
1878	£55,903	£36.32	1,539
1879	£71,216	£40.00	1,780
1880	£78,215	£51.22	1,527
	(209 tons from 1874 also sold for £15,487)		
1881	£102,039	£56.19	1,816
1882	£120,244	£60.85	1,976
1883	£101,707	£54.21	1,876
1884	£113,965	£47.03	2,423
1885	£124,998	£48.92	2,555
1886	£134,881	£56.60	2,383
1887	£152,241	£64.34	2,366
1888	£148,734	£66.43	2,239
1889	£114,029	£53.66	2,125
1890	£110,696	£54.69	2,024
1891	£114,761	£53.83	2,132
1892	£139,818	£55.15	2,535
1893	£124,841	£51.57	2,421
1894	£89,347	£42.03	2,126
1895	£68,389	£38.72	1,766
	(First six months of 1895)		

Appendix 3 Dolcoath Arsenic Production (1854-1907)

Year	Tonnage
1854	132.3 tons
1855	102
1867	49.9
1868	148.8
1869	43.3
1870	117.8
1871	59
1872	74
1873	309
1874	58.2
1875	102
1876	58.8
1877	38.5
1878	56.8
1879	73.4
1880	178
1881	35.8
1882	4.3
1886	94
1907	2

There were also some 640 tons of arsenical pyrites (or mundic) sold between 1880 and 1900.

Small quantities of cobalt, wolfram, bismuth, silver, lead, iron, zinc and other metallic minerals have also been found at Dolcoath over the centuries.

Appendix 4 Dolcoath Employment Figures (1780-1928)

1780	2,000	(according to Warner 1808)
1787	595	
1818	1,600	(Warner)
1836	590	
1841	732	(534 males & 198 females)
1842	200	(Watson)
1848	234	(Development & production miners – Tutworkers, Tributers & Stopers)
1849	292	ditto ditto
1850	259	ditto ditto
1851	208	ditto ditto
1852	207	ditto ditto
1853	256	ditto ditto
1854	211	ditto ditto
1855	234	ditto ditto
1856	273	ditto ditto
1857	?	
1858	291	ditto ditto
1859	359	ditto ditto
1860	378	ditto ditto
1861	410	ditto ditto
1862	452	ditto ditto
1863	470	ditto ditto
1863	920 total	(350 underground & 570 on surface – according to Capt.Charles Thomas)
1864	1,227 total	(492 on development & production)
1865	1,204 total	
1870	950 total	
1874	1,100 total	
1878	1,041 total	(405 underground & 636 surface)
1879	1,085 total	(432 underground & 653 surface)
1880	936 total	(478 underground & 458 surface)
1881	1,197 total	(560 underground & 637 surface)
1882	1,258 total	(618 underground & 640 surface)
1883	1,316 total	(613 underground & 703 surface)
1884	1,311 total	(626 underground & 685 surface)
1885	1,298 total	(598 underground & 700 surface)
1886	1,250 total	(496 underground & 754 surface)
1887	1,281 total	(586 underground & 695 surface)
1888	1,297 total	(610 underground & 687 surface)
1889	1,317 total	(605 underground & 712 surface)
1890	1,302 total	(604 underground & 698 surface)
1891	1,283 total	(624 underground & 659 surface)
1892	1,336 total	(591underground & 745 surface)
1893	1,356 total	(660 underground & 696 surface)
1894	1,309 total	(599 underground & 710 surface)
1895	1,168 total	(566 underground & 602 surface)
1896	1,307 total	(704 underground & 603 surface)
1897	1,366 total	(735 underground & 631 surface)

1898	1,204 total	(650 underground & 554 surface)
1899	1,338 total	(743 underground & 595 surface)
1900	1,379 total	(773 underground & 606 surface)
1901	1,309 total	(700 underground & 609 surface)
1902	1,267 total	(717 underground & 550 surface)
1903	1,178 total	(665 underground & 513 surface)
1904	1,119 total	(635 underground & 484 surface)
1905	1,101 total	(637 underground & 464 surface)
1906	1,142 total	(673 underground & 469 surface)
1907	1,225 total	(718 underground & 507 surface)
1908	1,128 total	(647 underground & 481 surface)
1909	1,142 total	(672 underground & 470 surface)
1910	1,064 total	(593 underground & 471 surface)
1911	1,023 total	(548 underground & 475 surface)
1912	1,050 total	(569 underground & 481 surface)
1913	1,091 total	(618 underground & 473 surface)
1914	959 total	(June)
1915	719 total	(December)
1916	699 total	(December)
1917	662 total	(December)
1918	640 total	(December)
1919	639 total	(December)
1920	500 total	(July)
1920	350 total	(November)
1926	75 total	(46 underground & 29 surface – February)
1928	153 total	(96 underground & 57 surface – April)

These figures have been collated from several different sources and some are open to question or contradict figures from other sources.

Appendix 5 Dolcoath Mine Ltd: Production & Income (1895-1920)

Year	Tonnage Crushed	Black Tin	Produce	Average Price	Tin Sales	Costs	Profit	Loss
1895	28,717	1,015	79.19lbs	£39	£39,769	£34,963	£3,230	
1896	63,727	2,039	71.96lbs	£36.5	£75,142	£69,757	£4,411	
1897	73,565	2,095	63.78lbs	£37.5	£79,397	£73,981	£5,565	
1898	78,697	2,302	65.58lbs	£43.5	£99,719	£75,882	£21,417	
1899	82,740	2,079	56.28lbs	£73	£151,875	£89,826	£53,524	
1900	88,356	2,004	50.78lbs	£82	£164,116	£99,764	£54,958	
1901	96,578	2,036	47.21lbs	£70.5	£143,808	£102,686	£33,176	
1902	100,450	1,829	40.88lbs	£72	£131,902	£97,984	£26,433	
1903	98,910	1,740	39.43lbs	£76.5	£133,458	£98,559	£28,118	
1904	100,549	1,705	37.98lbs	£76	£129,619	£103,858	£21,430	
1905	98,446	1,697	38.63lbs	£86.5	£146,982	£108,041	£34,726	
1906	100,179	1,814	40.56lbs	£109.5	£198,642	£111,909	£81,923	
1907	101,038	1,708	37.77lbs	£108	£184,643	£119,259	£58,176	
1908	98,718	1,783	40.45lbs	£79.5	£142,025	£124,306	£12,184	
1909	92,229	1,905	46.26lbs	£81	£154,276	£119,793	£27,549	
1910	91,938	1,731	42.21lbs	£93.5	£161,460	£115,612	£37,534	
1911	86,658	1,706	44.30lbs	£116.5	£198,696	£116,114	£71,951	
1912	109,197	1,665	34.41lbs	£130	£217,217	£125,322	£79,107	
1913	114,713	1,570	29.77lbs	£121.5	£185,637	£133,150	£42,193	
1914	105,292	1,439	30.80lbs	£88	£127,216	£118,822	£3,894	
1915	83,070	1,187	31.88lbs	£93	£110,908	£102,953	£646	
1916	79,347	1,076	30.36lbs	£104	£112,204	£102,003	£3,973	
1917	69,714	968	31.08lbs	£135.5	£130,696	£116,948	£10,412	
1918	61,499	827	30.21lbs	£188.5	£156,021	£134,446	£29,259	
1919	61,703	732	26.80lbs	£140.5	£102,059	£144,776		£37,573
1920	46,414	591	29.85lbs			£86,006		£11,276
Total	2,212,444	41,243			£3,477,487		£745,789	£48,849

Net Profit June 1895-June 1920 = £696,940

THE TREVITHICK SOCIETY

For Industrial Archaeology in Cornwall
Registered Charity No. 246586

The Trevithick Society can trace its history back via the Cornish Engines Preservation Society to 1935 and is therefore one of the oldest organisations in its field.

The Society's objectives are to educate the public in Cornish industry and technology, including its history around the world, by

- Encouraging and assisting in the preservation of buildings, machinery and sites connected with mining, engineering, china clay working and any other industry in Cornwall

- Collecting plant, machinery, records or other property connected with the above, encouraging their display and publishing any relevant matter

- Discussing with local government and other parties involved in the development and regeneration of existing and former industrial sites to ensure that heritage and preservation issues are given due consideration

Membership of the Society is open to all who support its objectives and share an interest in Cornwall's industrial and engineering history and heritage.

Members receive the award-winning Journal of the Trevithick Society, an annual series which has been running since 1973, and a quarterly Newsletter.

More information about the Society, its activities, collections and publications, can be found at www.trevithick-society.org.uk for membership details contact membership@trevithick-society.org.uk or write to PO Box 62, Camborne, Cornwall TR14 7ZN

Index

337
Californian, cost of 306
Californian, replacement of 419
Cornish 146, 151, 342
Cornish, being replaced 362
first steam engine ordered 155
new steam engine 287
pneumatic 293, 335, 340, 362, 364, 400
revolving 289
steam 158, 164, 165, 255, 262
steam, increase in number 258
total number 262
underground 289
water 158
Stannite 91
Stapleton, Thomas Henry
killed 285
St Aubyn, Sir John 36
St Cadix copper smelter 33
Stephens, Henry 383
Stevens, Roy 419
St Ives copper smelter 34
Stone, David 425
Stoneham, Allen 339, 342
death of 352
Stoneham, S. D. 328
Strauss, Arthur 282, 311, 328
Stray Park 1
Stray Park Engine Shaft 186, 257, 259
Stray Park Mine 19, 50, 205, 429
attempted sale of 285
connected with Dolcoath 185
for sale 276
purchase of machinery from 197
Stray Park section
bottom levels flooded 351
Stray Park Shaft 282, 288, 330, 337, 342,
343, 345, 350, 354, 357
new headgear 348
Strike, by tin dressers 199
Subsidiary shaft (in quotes) 372
Sumpmen 64
Swaine, Robert 35
Swaine, Sampson 34, 35, 38, 69
Talkarne, Justinian 4
Tamblyn, Captain Joseph 315, 327, 344

leaves Dolcoath 350
Tamping rod 140
Tangye 'Special' compressed air pump 253
Tantalite 274
Taylor, John 121
Teague, Captain William 198, 258
new patent ventilating apparatus 263
Tehidy mineral rights
sale of 356
Tehidy Minerals Ltd. 413
acquired by Baseresults 377
acquired by South Crofty Mine Ltd, 377
formation of 376
Telephone system, installation of 265
Tellam, Captain Matthew 8, 27
Tellam, Richard 6, 7
Temperatures in the mine 119
Tenby, John
injured 116
Terrill, Thomas
killed 86
Thomas, Captain Charles 120, 137, 153,
154, 164, 169, 178, 179, 184, 190
death 190
starts work at Dolcoath 115
Thomas, Captain J. 252
Thomas, Captain James 121, 122, 123, 130,
132, 134, 154
injured 116
Thomas, Captain Josiah 169, 193, 197, 249,
315, 329, 337, 339, 340, 342
appointed managing director of Dolcoath
Mine Ltd. 327
becomes manager 190
death of 346
given piece of silver plate 309
Thomas, Captain R. Arthur 315, 338, 343,
357, 374, 376, 390
appointed assistant manager of Dolcoath
Mine Ltd. 327
becomes manager of Dolcoath Mine Ltd.
346
becomes Chairman 384
retires 409
Thomas, Frederick William 327, 357
resigns 384

Williams, Captain John E. 266
Williams, George 256, 268, 286
  death of 294
Williams, Harvey & Co. 272, 286, 335,
    347, 359
Williams, James
  killed 189
Williams, J. C. MP 311
Williams, Kevin 425
Williams, Michael Henry 294, 309, 328,
    333
  appointed chairman of Dolcoath Mine
    Ltd. 327
Williams, Richard 85
Williams Shaft 302, 303, 304, 330, 333,
    337, 343, 346, 347, 349, 354, 358,
    360, 365, 377, 384
  accident at 366
  compressor 303
  cost of 362
  crosscut to intersect Main Lode 363
  crosscut to Roskear Mines started 381
  cutting ceremony 328
  dams installed 380
  decision to sink 327
  decline in hoisting 373
  increased hoisting at 367
  new air compressor 366
  new rock drill compressor for 365
  reaches 550 level 362
  removal of winding engine and compres-
    sor 394
  sinking resumed 357
  sinking suspended 340
  stone-breakers at 364
  winder stopped 367
  winding engine house 430
Williams, Sir Frederick M. 242, 246
  death of 252
Williams, Sir William
  death of 195
Williams, Walter
  injured 251
Williams, Williams & Grylls Bank 256
Willyams, Harvey & Co 258
Wise, John 66, 67

Woolf, Arthur 63, 65, 115
  as tutworker 79
Woolf, John 63
Woon Antron 3
Workers Union 376
Workforce
  children employed 171
  dressing floors 263
  numbers employed 139
  total 184, 197, 411
  underground 157, 158, 164, 167, 178,
    180, 188
World War I
  loss of men to armed forces 371, 372,
    374, 378
Worsley Mesnes 432
Worth, Thomas 34